THE BALTIC STORY

The Baltic in 1661, during the time of Sweden's domination of the region. Although the Gulf of Finland is unnamed, at its eastern end, the map already shows St Petersburg, which was not in fact founded for over another four decades.

THE BALTIC STORY

A THOUSAND-YEAR HISTORY OF ITS LANDS, SEA AND PEOPLES

CAROLINE BOGGIS-ROLFE

AMBERLEY

First published 2019

Amberley Publishing
The Hill, Stroud
Gloucestershire, GL5 4EP

www.amberley-books.com

British Library Cataloguing in Publication Data.
A catalogue record for this book is available from the British Library.

ISBN 978 1 4456 8850 3 (hardback)
ISBN 978 1 4456 8851 0 (ebook)

Map and table design by Thomas Bohm, User design.
Typesetting and Origination by Amberley Publishing.
Printed in the UK.

Contents

PART FIVE: MODERNITY, CHANGE AND REVOLUTION

Principal Family Trees

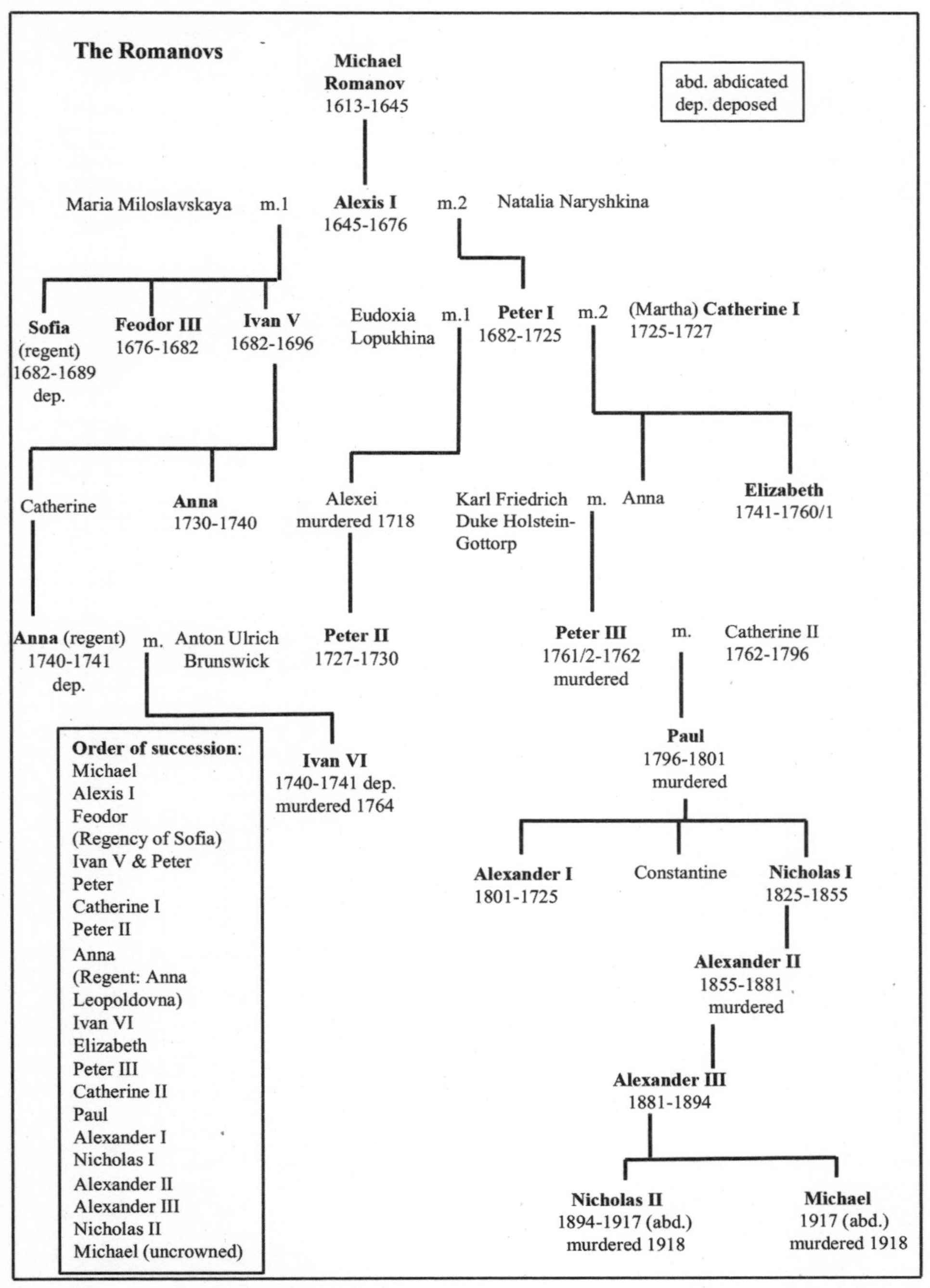

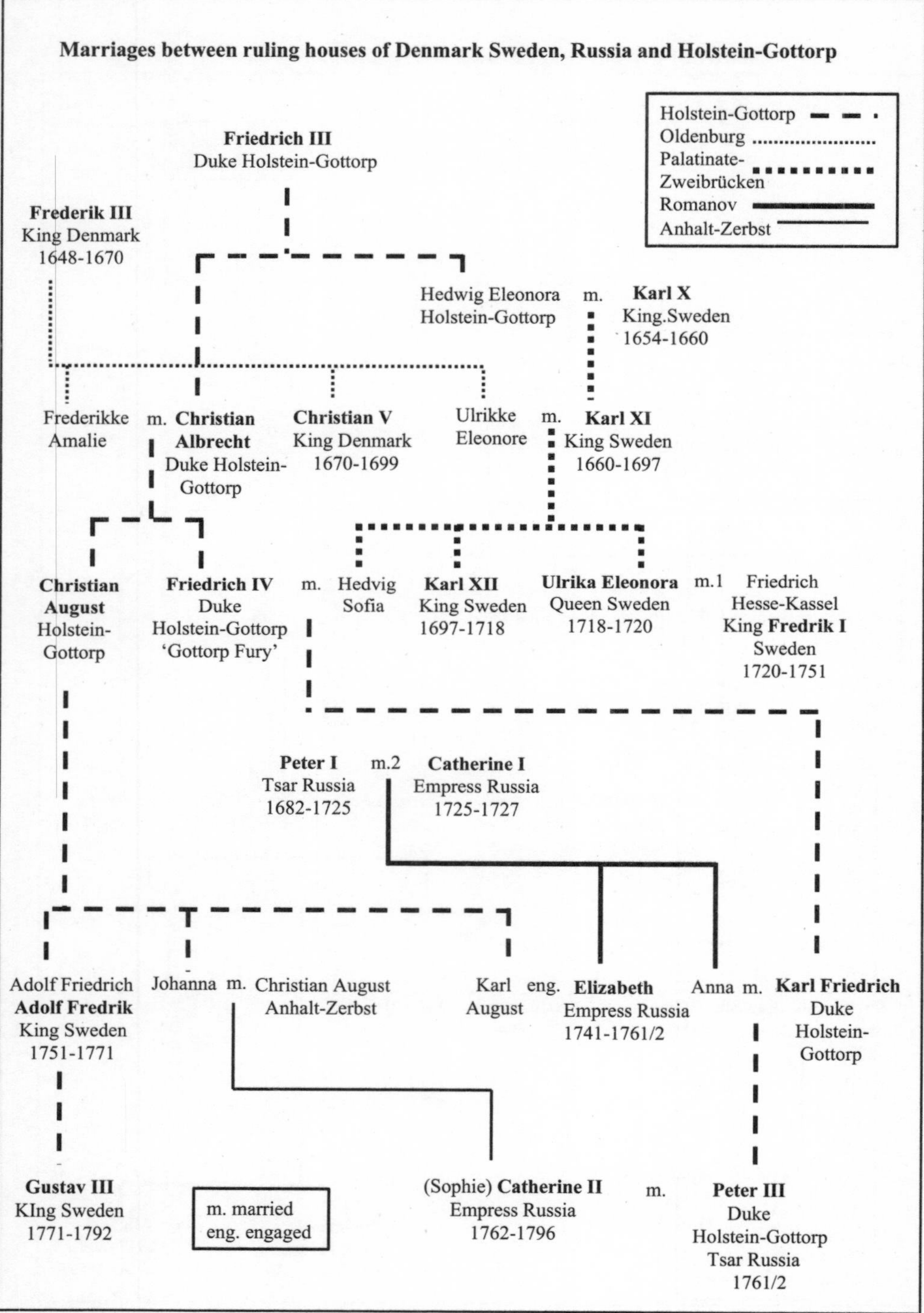
Marriages between ruling houses of Denmark Sweden, Russia and Holstein-Gottorp
Holstein-Gottorp
Oldenburg
Palatinate-Zweibrücken
Romanov
Anhalt-Zerbst
Friedrich III
Duke Holstein-Gottorp
Frederik III
King Denmark
1648-1670
Hedwig Eleonora
Holstein-Gottorp
m.
Karl X
King.Sweden
1654-1660
Frederikke
Amalie
m.
Christian
Albrecht
Duke Holstein-
Gottorp
Christian V
King Denmark
1670-1699
Ulrikke
Eleonore
m.
Karl XI
King Sweden
1660-1697
Christian
August
Holstein-
Gottorp
Friedrich IV
Duke
Holstein-Gottorp
'Gottorp Fury'
m.
Hedvig
Sofia
Karl XII
King Sweden
1697-1718
Ulrika Eleonora
Queen Sweden
1718-1720
m.1
Friedrich
Hesse-Kassel
King Fredrik I
Sweden
1720-1751
Peter I
Tsar Russia
1682-1725
m.2
Catherine I
Empress Russia
1725-1727
Adolf Friedrich
Adolf Fredrik
King Sweden
1751-1771
Johanna
m.
Christian August
Anhalt-Zerbst
Karl
August
eng.
Elizabeth
Empress Russia
1741-1761/2
Anna
m.
Karl Friedrich
Duke
Holstein-
Gottorp
Gustav III
KIng Sweden
1771-1792
m. married
eng. engaged
(Sophie) Catherine II
Empress Russia
1762-1796
m.
Peter III
Duke
Holstein-Gottorp
Tsar Russia
1761/2

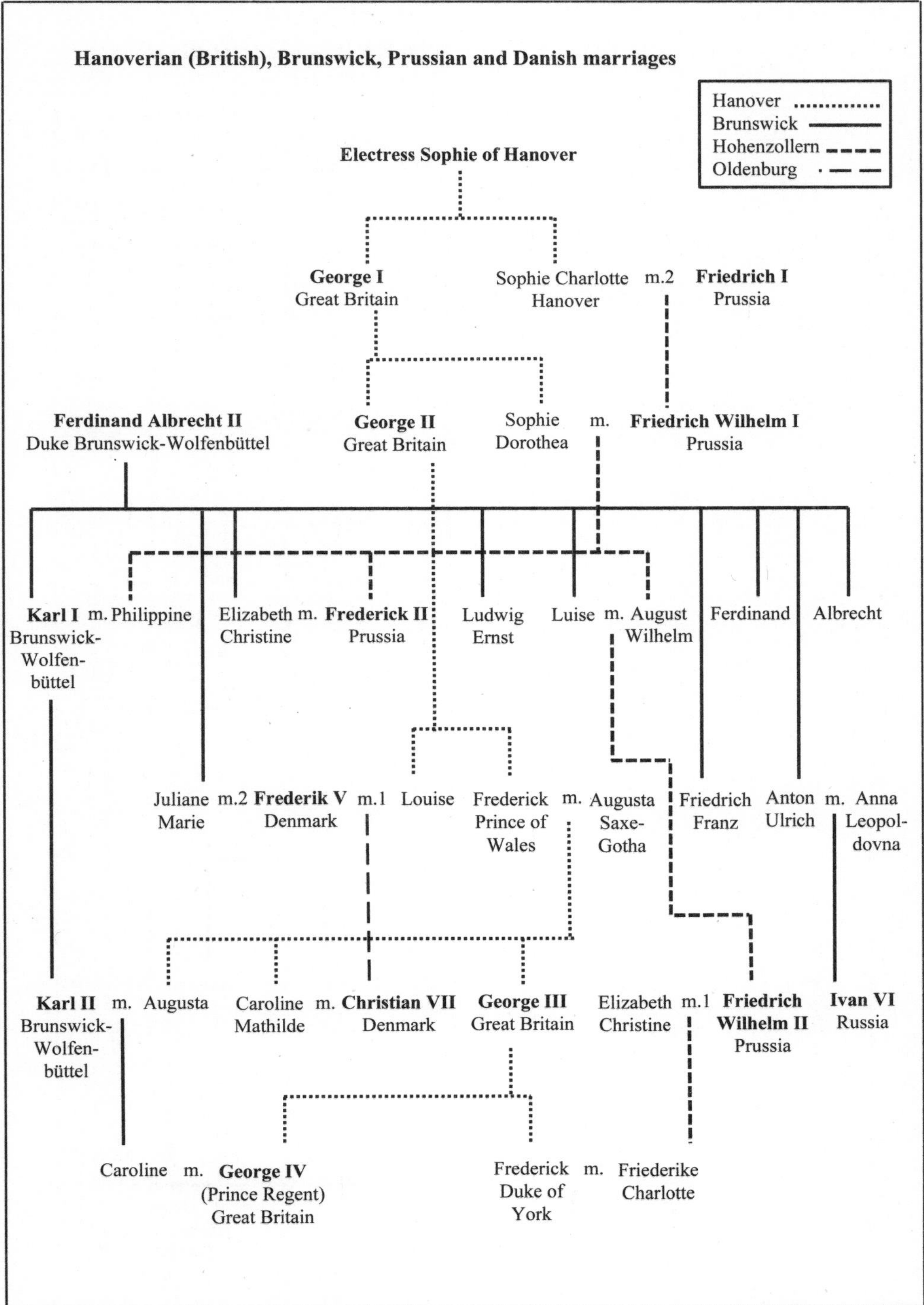
Hanoverian (British), Brunswick, Prussian and Danish marriages
Hanover
Brunswick
Hohenzollern
Oldenburg
Electress Sophie of Hanover
George I
Great Britain
Sophie Charlotte
Hanover
m.2
Friedrich I
Prussia
Ferdinand Albrecht II
Duke Brunswick-Wolfenbüttel
George II
Great Britain
Sophie
Dorothea
m.
Friedrich Wilhelm I
Prussia
Karl I
Brunswick-Wolfenbüttel
m.
Philippine
Elizabeth Christine
m.
Frederick II
Prussia
Ludwig Ernst
Luise
m.
August Wilhelm
Ferdinand
Albrecht
Juliane Marie
m.2
Frederik V
Denmark
m.1
Louise
Frederick
Prince of Wales
m.
Augusta
Saxe-Gotha
Friedrich Franz
Anton Ulrich
m.
Anna Leopoldovna
Karl II
Brunswick-Wolfenbüttel
m.
Augusta
Caroline Mathilde
m.
Christian VII
Denmark
George III
Great Britain
Elizabeth Christine
m.1
Friedrich Wilhelm II
Prussia
Ivan VI
Russia
Caroline
m.
George IV
(Prince Regent)
Great Britain
Frederick
Duke of York
m.
Friederike Charlotte

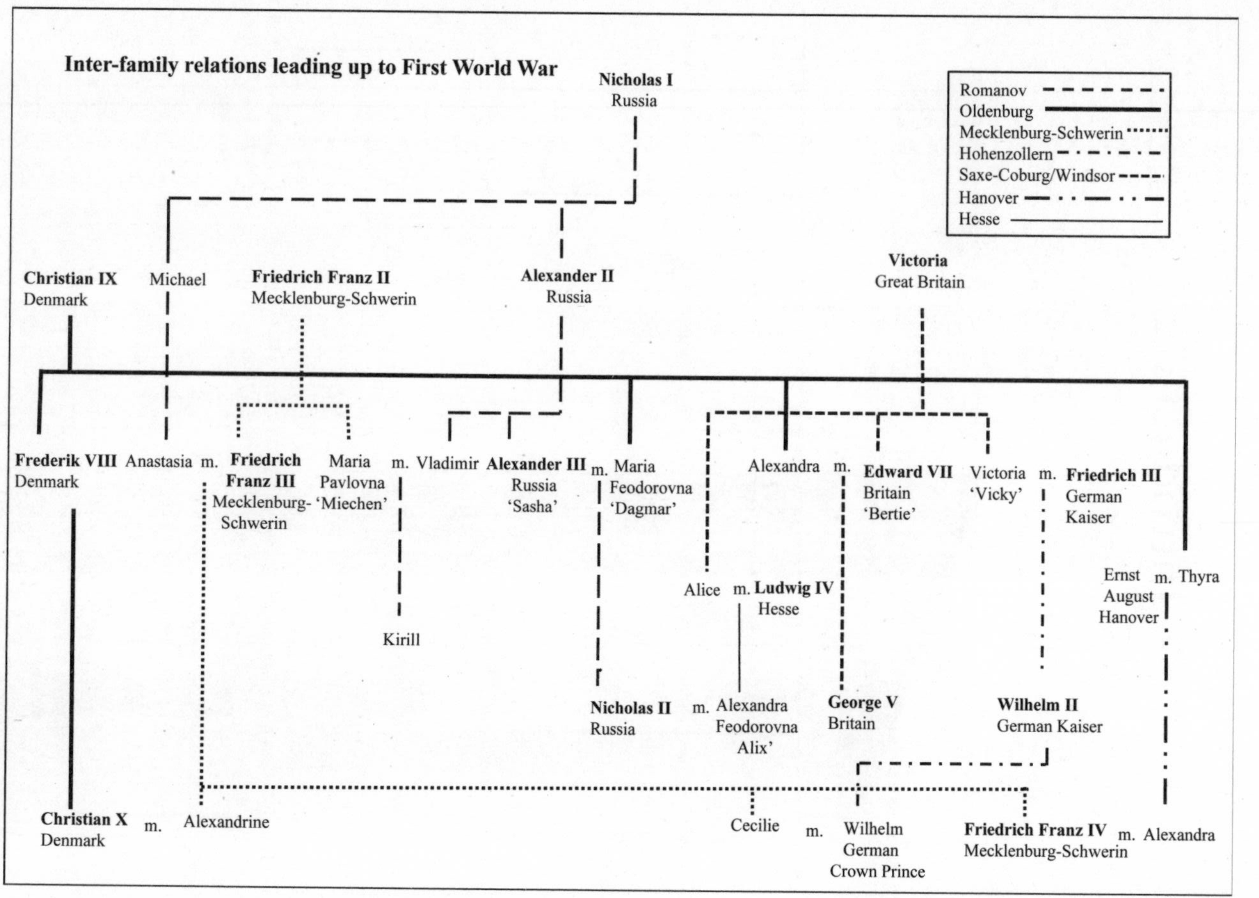
Inter-family relations leading up to First World War
Nicholas I Russia
Romanov
Oldenburg
Mecklenburg-Schwerin
Hohenzollern
Saxe-Coburg/Windsor
Hanover
Hesse
Christian IX Denmark
Michael
Friedrich Franz II Mecklenburg-Schwerin
Alexander II Russia
Victoria Great Britain
Frederik VIII Denmark
Anastasia m. Friedrich Franz III Mecklenburg-Schwerin
Maria Pavlovna 'Miechen' m. Vladimir
Alexander III Russia 'Sasha' m. Maria Feodorovna 'Dagmar'
Alexandra m. Edward VII Britain 'Bertie'
Victoria 'Vicky' m. Friedrich III German Kaiser
Ernst August Hanover m. Thyra
Kirill
Alice m. Ludwig IV Hesse
Nicholas II Russia m. Alexandra Feodorovna Alix'
George V Britain
Wilhelm II German Kaiser
Christian X Denmark m. Alexandrine
Cecilie m. Wilhelm German Crown Prince
Friedrich Franz IV Mecklenburg-Schwerin m. Alexandra

Introduction

'The Three Sisters', the typical fourteenth-century merchant houses in Tallinn's lower town.

My interest in the Baltic has developed over the many years that I have been visiting the region, but while I was lecturing on the subject, I discovered the shortage of mainstream studies of the area available to English speakers. I have therefore set out to produce something that fills that gap, giving an overview of its history through the lives of the people who shaped it. As the individual states around the Baltic have interlocking stories, I feel that to understand the narrative of one place it greatly helps to have a knowledge of the others. Loosely speaking the Hanseatic League was a leading presence by the fourteenth and fifteenth centuries, and Denmark by the fifteenth and sixteenth. Meanwhile, the vast, recently united Polish-Lithuanian Commonwealth had also risen to prominence, and it now held sway in the Baltic's more south-easterly parts. But during the early 1600s Sweden would start to overtake its rivals, and soon be the dominant power throughout the whole area, holding onto its position until challenged and ultimately defeated by Russia at the start of the eighteenth century. All this time, however, Prussia, too, had been growing in significance, so that by the mid-1700s it had in its turn become a key player in the affairs of the region, a role that it would maintain until the start of the Napoleonic Wars. Although it then suffered some crushing setbacks, it would eventually recover and become the major player in the newly formed German *Reich*, its king rising to be the first hereditary emperor or *kaiser*. Finally, during the course of the long and turbulent twentieth century, the other smaller states around the region would achieve their independence, at last separating themselves from the powers that had dominated them for hundreds of years. The Baltic was not just an area of local interest, as from early days its affairs had held commercial significance for places further afield, with the French, the Dutch, the British, and even to a certain extent the Austrian Habsburgs paying ever closer attention to events in this part of the world.

Today when cruising through the Baltic in a modern ship it can be hard to imagine the innumerable tumultuous events that have occurred in these waters over the centuries. Although during the summer months this sea is often deceptively calm, its surface literally smooth as glass, on other occasions it takes on a totally different character. From time to time the area is hit by such violent storms that in certain places waves can reach up to around 8 metres, with the odd individual one greatly exceeding even that. In addition, destructive storm surges can strike the shores, brought on by the combination of strong winds, shallow waters, and the changing sea levels – the latter caused by melting ice or rivers in flood. From earliest times the archives have recorded the many disasters occurring in this region, such as that of 1872 when the frequently battered German town of Warnemunde was so badly hit that many people were left homeless or dead. Most recently, in 2017 serious flooding struck all along the north German coast between Kiel and the Polish border, causing damage to Lübeck, Rostock, Wismar and many other places. Similarly,

St Petersburg, situated in the low-lying delta of the River Neva, has until recently faced repeated inundation beneath the surges that from time to time sweep up the Gulf of Finland, a situation now apparently resolved by the recently constructed flood barrier at Kronstadt. And for those living in the more northerly parts of the Baltic – in particular the furthest reaches of the Gulf of Bothnia just some 50 miles or so from the Arctic Circle – life is additionally complicated by the high latitudes with their long nights and freezing temperatures in winter, when the sea can, even in today's changing climate, be shrouded in a mantle of ice that cuts off most maritime communication. At such times in the past the only alternative for the local people was to make their way across the frozen water, a perilous route also used on occasion by invading armies.

Even while bearing all this in mind, for the summer tourist travelling in comfort today it is often difficult to identify with the experiences undergone by the intrepid pioneers, tradesmen and others of earlier times, people who would so often find themselves struggling against winds and waves and other equally unpredictable challenges. From the Vikings to the Hansa merchants, men would set out through the uncharted and often pirate-infested waters, the former probably seeking booty if not new lands, the latter in search of fish and other commodities. After them came the very possibly scared or sick sailors and soldiers, many of the latter no doubt at sea for the first time, who had to spend weeks in their tossing ships making their way towards the next bloody land or sea battle. And contemporary accounts also tell us of the apprehensive young brides, who all too often began their daunting exile battered for days by stormy conditions that left them in fear of their lives. A graveyard of ships attesting to these stories now lies on the seabed.

Although the Baltic is relatively small when viewed in world terms, it is nonetheless the home of a variety of peoples of different ethnic descent, speaking more or less ten major languages, not to mention several other dialects. Despite the attempts of the Soviet Union to wipe out or alter the local cultures in their Baltic states, these have been revitalised since their independence. Poland, with its constitutional government, now enjoys the freedom to revisit its past and express its individuality unhindered. And then, leaving aside the question of the northern Sami people, the Scandinavians, whose nations have for so long been brought together in various unions, still proclaim their differences in language and character. But despite this intentional separation in cultural terms, there has always been a connection between the regions, on the positive side represented by an exchange of goods, ideas, and peoples, on the negative by the multiple local conflicts and rivalries. It is this dichotomy that we shall now explore, examining the two sides of the Baltic, on one hand a crucible of different cultures, but on the other a circumscribed, close-knit community with the usual tensions and disputes that are found among families and near neighbours.

Dating from the time of the Vikings and on into the period of the Hanseatic League, trade was central to the area, and as the new independent states started to develop they protected their commercial interests by forming ever more complicated alliances. To cement these, the rulers began to draw up marriage contracts with their neighbours, but as the pool of eligible brides was so limited – in some cases made still more so by the religious dissensions after the Reformation – they had to turn repeatedly to the same few families.

As a result, relationships in the region became increasingly complex, the intermarriage causing new frictions, inbreeding, and even cases of mental and physical disability, including possibly porphyria, bi-polar disorders and autism, and most certainly haemophilia. But more seriously still, although the initial intent behind these unions was to ensure peace and prosperity, only too frequently they led to further warfare and general hardship. Brothers, cousins and various in-laws would repeatedly find themselves at war over some territorial claim, supported by the uncertain terms agreed in an earlier marriage contract.

When such conflicts broke out the women's problems would be further exacerbated. Many, having already been shipped abroad as young or very young girls to marry a possibly aged and maybe cruel stranger, were now confronted by the reality of their conflicting loyalties. Often commanded by a father or brother to spy on their new country, but already viewed with deep suspicion by their husbands' families, several would find themselves accused or condemned on all fronts, and the way they dealt with this dangerous conundrum would largely decide their ultimate success or failure.

Even when war did not play a part, certain foreign wives would be crushed by their experiences. While some would resolve their situation by retiring from court into virtual anonymity, a few others, desperate for affection, were drawn into scandalous relationships and would end their days in exile or confinement. But there were also those who made a name for themselves, bringing new ideas to their adopted country, advancing its cultural life, supporting or advising their husbands or sons, and acting as regents when the need arose. Some went even further, attaining full authority. Margrete (Margaret) I acted as the de facto ruler of Denmark, Norway and Sweden, and in 1397 changed the face of the Scandinavian region when she created the Kalmar Union that united the independent states under one monarch. Likewise, some four centuries later, Catherine the Great, after deposing her unpopular husband, went on to modernise and expand her vast empire, greatly raising Russia's renown abroad in the process.

To produce a book that links the various stories of the Baltic region, I have followed as far as possible a chronological sequence, rather than dividing it into geographical sections. So all discussion of Poland, Sweden, or elsewhere does not appear together, but follows on from the development of events elsewhere. By using this methodology, it is possible to show how intertwined the individual stories are.

Section 1, 'Beginnings', looks at the remarkable achievements of the Hanseatic League, who over nearly 400 years grew from a motley band of German traders into a far-reaching, prosperous association that was eventually able to influence, and at times dominate, the affairs of its contemporaries. And in the following chapter, concerning the rise of Poland, we see how Danzig (Gdańsk) was one of the important ports that came under the association's influence. The city remained a member from the days of the Teutonic Knights until the last Hansa meeting in the 1660s – the final *hansetag* taking place a century after Poland had become part of the vast Polish-Lithuanian Commonwealth.

Section 2, 'From the Middle Ages', goes on to look at the rise of the neighbouring states, who were equally determined to make their presence felt in the region. Initially, Denmark wielded most power, aided by its control of the waterways connecting the Baltic to the North Sea, primarily the Øresund ('the Sound'), essential for the free passage of commerce on which wealth was based. But following the break-up of its union with the other Scandinavian countries, gradually the new Swedish Vasa dynasty rose to power. Meanwhile, Russia remained on the margins, having little impact on the area until Ivan IV, 'the Terrible', chose in 1558 to invade the region today loosely referred to as the 'Baltic states', thus initiating the savage Livonian War. Later, Russia's domestic problems also spilled over to involve its neighbours. Poland was drawn into the vicious maelstrom that resulted from the mayhem that broke out a few years after Ivan's death, the 'Time of Troubles', which would end only with the establishment of the Romanov dynasty. By then the Poles had been expelled, but not before those who ranked highest in society, the *boyars*, had briefly offered the throne to the son of Poland's elected Vasa king – a member of the Swedish dynasty. And as for Sweden itself, although still underpopulated and relatively poor and backward, it had now begun its remarkable rise. In time its militarist Vasa and later Palatinate-Zweibrücken rulers, who were almost constantly at war with their Polish cousins or Danish neighbours, would make Sweden the principal power in the region.

Section 3, 'Absolutism and Autocracy', concentrates on the individuals who rose to pre-eminence during the early eighteenth century. In the long run, not all these autocrats were successful, but most left a lasting impact on their country, changing it forever. The imaginative but fearsome Peter of Russia, and the stubbornly courageous but unfortunate Karl XII of Sweden, both died prematurely, the former aged fifty-two, the latter just thirty-six. Karl was ultimately destroyed by his hubris and misplaced determination to avenge at all costs the insults of his neighbours, his dogged persistence ultimately leading to Sweden's ruin and the fall of its Baltic empire. Peter, meanwhile, having – it might be argued – brought his country 'in from the cold' and made it the greatest power in the region, did so at an enormous cost to most of his people. And although in Russia there would follow a time of uncertainty, with the succession then passing through a broken line that included two particularly underage tsars and a series of women rulers, Peter the Great's iron control would nonetheless be passed down to those that followed him. Abroad too, others began to adopt similar forms of autocratic rule, Denmark now embarking on its own roughly 200-year-long period of royal absolutism.

Section 4, 'Enlightenment', considers the later eighteenth century, a period marked by the 'enlightened despots', Catherine II of Russia and Frederick II of Prussia, rulers who held power well into their late sixties and early seventies. Although not without their critics, they were immensely hard-working and dedicated to the improvement and advancement of their countries, seeing themselves as 'servants' of the people. But both had the misfortune of living long enough to see the society that they had strived to create coming under the threat of the revolutionary changes that were emanating from France. By then, such problems were also infiltrating the affairs of other countries in the region, bringing terminal decline to Poland, a period of scandal and court rebellion to Denmark, and an age of murder and revolution to Sweden.

Section 5, 'Modernity, Change and Revolution', looks at the after-effects of the previous period, exploring how rulers sought to confront the problems that they had to face in a changing world. While some leaders gradually stumbled their way towards a more democratic system and were able to survive into the modern age, others attempted to put the clock back, introducing reactionary measures for which they and their dynasties would ultimately pay the price.

Finally, in the postscript, 'Into a New Era', the story is brought up to date with a brief look at the events of the twentieth century, outlining how, following the cataclysm of the First World War, society was changed for all time, and many of the old ruling houses ceased to exist. While in the Scandinavian countries the rulers managed to weather the storm by introducing reform and embracing increased democracy, elsewhere many of the old dynasties would be deposed, or – in the case of the Russians – virtually annihilated: those Romanovs who did not not flee abroad were rounded up and murdered by the Bolsheviks. And although, with the fall of the Russian empire, by the 1920s Finland and other new Baltic nations had gained their independence, before long they would become entangled in the murderous struggle for dominance between the two growing extremist regimes of the Nazis and Communists. As the Second World War began, the Baltic states in particular would become the site of some of Europe's most contested battlegrounds. Accordingly, once more they lost their autonomy, being first incorporated into the Third Reich, and then swallowed up by the Soviet Union. These regions – like the Warsaw Pact countries of Poland and the DDR (the eastern zone of a now divided Germany) – would remain in the Communist fold until they finally regained their full independence in the last decade of the century.

In the first chapters that focus on the early development of the Baltic area, there is often a lack of personal stories, but, wanting to give the account a more human face and to prevent it becoming a mere listing of historical points, I have here introduced some more marginal people and episodes. At the same time, certain other individuals I have chosen to omit altogether, my purpose being to simplify the overall picture and not weigh down the reader with too many new facts, names and places. These early years are of key importance to the understanding of how events ultimately progressed in the Baltic region, and how the situation has come to be as it is today.

In contrast, there is no shortage of significant figures of recent times, and here I have been able to include much more personal detail, thanks to the quantity of available material that exists – letters, published documents, portraits, and so forth. These private and public records are invaluable as, in my opinion, history is best understood by looking into the personalities of the people responsible for so many of the events. I have tried to give a balanced interpretation of the men and women here included, always seeking to understand better how their experiences often drove them to act the way they did. It becomes apparent when looking at their stories how, contrary to the often accepted image of their unfettered ambition and arrogance, many of those destined for power dreaded taking up their allotted role. Rather, aware of their unpreparedness and unsuitability, no small number felt themselves to be the victims of bitter misfortune.

With this history as a whole having been barely explored by English-speaking authors, some of the individuals may be little known to the average reader, although others have had innumerable studies written about them. Because this book covers a wide spectrum of time and place, I do not attempt to compete with the many in-depth monographs that exist of the more well-known people and events. However, although my studies are short, I have nonetheless strived to avoid the extremes of hagiography and vitriolic criticism. History's heroes and heroines often suffer in the same way as modern-day celebrities; once acclaimed for their achievements, they then become the targets of those who want to shoot them down. Similarly, when looking at so-called villains, occasionally some biographers are tempted to write out the negative elements that do not fit with their argument. But while all people are flawed, none are two-dimensional, and to understand them better we need to explore objectively the circumstances that they had to face. Whether they confronted their problems and difficult situations successfully or otherwise, they, like everyone else, deserve to be considered without bias.

In the mid-twentieth century, there was a move away from the study of famous historical figures and a greater concentration on more general social issues. At the same time, historians were sometimes criticised for paying too much attention to elite individuals or major events, and for not giving enough space to the world of the ordinary people. This argument is more than valid, but while recognising the role played by the poor of society, and acknowledging the hardship of their lives, for a study such as this the problem arises that little physical evidence remains to tell their story. As most were chiefly concerned in the struggle for their everyday survival, they left us with few, if any, artefacts or documents to detail their lives. While not denying the social injustice of the situation, we have to accept that it was the rich, the famous, and the powerful who moulded so much of history. Without them the big conflicts, rebellions and instances of persecution might well have not have taken place, but on the other hand the world would also not have seen so much of the art and architecture, science and industry, medicine, and urban and rural development that has embellished or improved our own lives. The beautiful buildings, paintings, clothes, carriages, as well as artificial lakes, canals and fortifications would not have come into existence without these people, and accordingly, we would have been the poorer for it.

Wanting to keep the text a reasonable length, I have restricted the number of battles mentioned. While many still litter these pages, here I have avoided in-depth descriptions and focused solely on the points of greater interest to the general reader. Similarly, I have limited myself to those places that best fit with the Baltic story I am trying to tell; for example, in the chapters on Poland, there is less reference to the capital Warsaw than there is to Gdańsk, and in the pages relating to Russia there is more description of St Petersburg than there is of Moscow.

Although seeking to weave the threads into a single narrative, I have also tried to make each chapter stand alone, allowing it to be read in isolation by someone with little time who maybe only wants to dip into the text, or concentrate on a particular period, person or place. This has meant that some repetition cannot be avoided, but I hope that where this occurs it only helps to re-enforce the information and to make even the lesser-known individuals and places become more recognisable. Added to that, it allows me to present certain events from an alternative standpoint, that is to say, to show how any action might be interpreted differently, for example a victory as a disaster, a brutal necessity as an atrocity, an act of heroism as proof of treachery.

A problem that I have had to overcome is the repetition of names. Dynasties intentionally repeated these to give weight to their claimed hereditary right, so for example, among the Poles there are frequent Zygmunts, Wladyslaws, and Stanislaws; the Brandenburg rulers favoured Friedrich, Wilhelm and Sophie; the Swedes, Gustav, Karl and Ulrika; the Romanovs, Peter, Anna, Catherine, Alexander or Alexandra; not forgetting the Danish kings who, for close on 500 years, were alternately Christian or Frederik. And names vary considerably in different languages, but after much consideration I have decided in the main to use the version used in the place of birth – an exception being in the case of those women who later became more famous as queens or empresses in their adoptive countries. This allows me to distinguish clearly between the many different people called Frederick, Catherine, Charles, etc., and I hope will enable the reader to identify them more easily. However, with certain particularly famous individuals, I have used the English name by which they are better known – Emperors Charles V and VI, Gustavus Adolphus, Queen Christina, Augustus 'the Strong', Frederick the Great, Maria Theresa, and all the popes.

One other exception concerns the Greeks and Russians. Apart from their names having been already transliterated, most are better known by their English versions, so for example, besides King George of the Hellenes, I speak of Paul rather than Pavel, Peter rather than Pyotr, Catherine rather than Ekaterina. In addition, as the later Russians (and British) frequently used nicknames among themselves, I have at times adopted these in order to differentiate them from their relatives. And, despite the male Russian rulers preferring to use the title 'Emperor' between the 1720s and the 1880s, in the main I continue to refer to them as tsars as this helps to distinguish them from their French and Habsburg contemporaries. For greater clarity, I have adopted the upper case for 'the (Holy Roman) Emperor' – the ruler of 'the Empire', and member of the 'Imperial' family – and also when speaking of either the later Austrian or Austrian-Hungarian Emperor, or Wilhelm II, popularly known as 'the (German) Kaiser'. Finally, for consistency, I have used the English version of all titles, for example, king, queen, prince and duke.

I have applied a similar methodology for modern place names, generally adopting the version a visitor would find on a regional map – exceptions being made with famous cities, such as Rome, Florence, Venice, Cologne, Vienna, St Petersburg, all the Baltic capitals, and the other Russian towns whose names have again been transliterated from the Cyrillic script. And to avoid confusion for English speakers, I refer to Zealand rather than Sjælland, to Schleswig-Holstein rather than Slesvig-Holsten, and use the English spelling for the houses of Hanover and Oldenburg, rather than Hannover and Oldenborg. Lastly, as over the centuries borders and ownership changed frequently, I have adopted the name that was in current use at the time, for example Reval for Tallinn, Danzig for Gdańsk.

Dates also present a problem. Although all Catholic countries adopted the calendar introduced by Pope Gregory XIII in 1587, Protestant Europe resisted the change for around a century or more. It was not until 1753 that they all finally abandoned the Julian calendar, with the exception of Russia, who held onto it until the Bolshevik revolution, the Orthodox Church alone still using it today. Therefore, I have tended to give just the months, except where the day is significant and still celebrated. However, even here we need to be cautious as during Karl XII's earlier campaigns, Sweden was adopting its own calendar, trying in an ultimately failed attempt to carry out the conversion in stages. While I have avoided using this Swedish system altogether, there might still be some confusion regarding the old Julian calendar and the new Gregorian one, and so I have either indicated the former by (OS) and the latter by (NS), or given the two dates together. Finally, to add to the complication, every century the difference between the two systems increased by a day, so for example, Karl XII was born on 17 June 1682 (27 June New Style), but when he was wounded on his birthday, 17 June 1709 – shortly before the all-important Battle of Poltava – in the new calendar the date had moved to 28 June.

Finally, in certain cases I have used the foreign version of a word as I believe it to be more accurate, for example *philosophes* for the Enlightenment thinkers (as only some were actual philosophers), *tsaritsa* for the wife of the tsar, rather than the English form 'tsarina'. Similarly, I use *tsesarevich* for the heir to the throne – the official title after 1797 – rather than the more usually found *tsarevich*, the earlier term for the son of the tsar that technically became defunct after Peter the Great had adopted the title 'Emperor' and made his sons Grand Dukes.

I am most grateful to the many biographies and other works of criticism I have used in this research. In this case they have been particularly invaluable as several original texts are written in the regional languages that regretfully I do not speak. However, to avoid an excessive number of footnotes, I have given references only when citing an original comment or statement. Nevertheless, I fully acknowledge my debt to all the authors listed in the bibliography, and apologise if any misrepresentation or interpretation of their work has slipped into my study. Any mistakes appearing in this book are entirely my own.

Acknowledgements

I would like to thank the people who directly or indirectly helped me produce this work, as without them it would probably never have come about. I am so grateful to those who have encouraged me over the years, among them Dr Felicity Baker who gave me unwavering support while I was studying for my PhD, my friends the Shiffners who personally contributed towards my research, Brian Elliot, and Sir Robert and Lady Corbett who kindly helped in the proofreading, and Mara Timon, who first introduced me to my wonderful agent, Thomas Cull. I also want to thank my publishers who took such care over the selection of images, and patiently put up with all my various requests and last-minute changes. And while I would like to acknowledge those people who attended my lectures over the years and first gave me the idea of writing this book, I particularly want to mention Dr Camilla Elphick who was responsible for getting me started. Finally, besides thanking my son Edward Boggis-Rolfe for his continuing support, I must also give special mention to my husband Nicholas, who has been unbelievably long-suffering throughout the whole process. Always uncomplaining about the many hours that I was buried away working on my text, he greatly helped me with his useful comments and suggestions. For this and his constant encouragement, I am immensely grateful.

PART 1

BEGINNINGS

1
The Rise and Fall of the Hanseatic League

A Hansa cog as depicted on a mediaeval seal of Stralsund.

The Vikings began trading in the Baltic in the eighth century, marking their presence with the runestones that still exist throughout the Scandinavian region today. But these memorial stones written in the runic languages are also to be found much further afield. Travelling in their longboats, by the eleventh century Vikings from the area of modern-day Norway had reached as far as Vinland on the shores of North America, while others primarily from

Denmark had settled in the British Isles, France and Spain, before eventually reaching North Africa and southern Italy. In contrast, the 'Swedish' Vikings made their way into the Baltic, from where they continued down the rivers into the hinterland of what is now Russia and Ukraine, before reaching the Black and Caspian Seas. Known as Varangians, some of these were referred to as the *Rus*, probably 'men that row', and this gave rise to the name for the whole region. In time they became rulers of the large Kievan Rus, and with many Varangians serving as imperial guards in the Byzantine court, by the start of the second millennium they had converted to Christianity.

Soon the Baltic island of Gotland became an important centre of Viking trade, the extent of which was further proved in 1999 with the discovery at Spilling Farm in the north-east of a large hoard of Viking silver that included a quantity of Islamic coins. Gotland would dominate trade in the region throughout the 1100s – benefiting further in 1237 by Henry III granting it exemption from the English custom dues – and its capital Visby would hold its pre-eminent position until it was challenged by the growing presence of the Hanseatic League.

In the year 800 Charlemagne was crowned the first Holy Roman Emperor, and nine years later he founded the city of Hamburg, which after some two centuries also began to trade with the Vikings. Then in 1189 a later emperor, Frederick I 'Barbarossa', granted a charter, making Hamburg an Imperial Free City. This exempted it from the many laws and restrictions impinging on all areas of life that, according to the customs of the times, were imposed on citizens by the nobility. Now answerable only to the emperor, the city merchants gained the right to trade freely in the North Sea, and with this Hamburg began to grow rapidly in importance.

Just thirty years before this, Barbarossa's cousin, Henry the Lion, Duke of both Bavaria and Saxony and son-in-law of Henry II of England, founded another new city, Lübeck, and this soon became important for its position at the crossroads between the Baltic and nearby Hamburg and the North Sea. Within seventy years, it, too, was an Imperial free city, and its wealth was rapidly growing, driven by its flourishing trade in Baltic herring. A staple of the diet at this time, the vast shoals continued to appear each year until the early fifteenth century. As their migration was seasonal and no fishing took place in the winter months, preservation was of key importance, and to this end salt was highly valued, referred to as 'white gold'. Therefore, following the discovery of salt mines at Lüneburg, around 30 miles south-east of Hamburg, a salt route was set up linking the two areas. Although still visible today, this was later replaced by the Stecknitz Canal, built at the end of the fourteenth century. A remarkable feat for the times, it incorporated seventeen locks, and was created by cutting through a roughly 7-mile-long watershed in order to link up with two rivers. Its value was soon proved, and by the early 1500s around 30,000 tons of salt were passing through it each year.[1]

Salted fish became an essential element of the exchange system used at the time, and in the early days it would be stored in the largest buildings of the town, usually the church. With this trade, Lübeck began to grow, and the wealth of the city manifested itself in the large buildings that were now starting to appear, vast constructions that, owing to the area's lack of a suitable stone, were created out of bricks made from the local clay, each brick carefully crafted to fit the often intricate design demanded by the architect. In 1173, Henry the Lion ordered the town council, the *Rat*, to construct a cathedral, the *Dom*, and by the time it was finally completed sixty years later, work was also underway on the town hall. Then, towards the end of the thirteenth century the merchant guilds displayed their increasing prosperity by building for themselves an even larger Gothic church dedicated to St Mary, the *Marienkircher.* Despite the near total destruction this suffered during a RAF air raid in March 1942, when extensive damage was also caused to the Dom and much of the rest of old Lübeck, it has now been carefully restored. And the red-brick Hospital of the Holy Spirit that dates from the same period is still today one of Europe's oldest and best-preserved establishments of its kind, it having been created for the care of the sick or needy – a role it still partly plays today. Moreover, around the time that these places were being constructed, Lübeck law began to be enforced, laying down the general building regulations that eventually spread to other towns and cities with whom the merchants traded. Houses now had to be of a limited width, gabled with designated areas for storage and accommodation and, to prevent the spread of fire, built of stone or brick, with easy access free of obstructions.

While in the English language the growing group of traders now forming around the Baltic and North Sea is called the Hanseatic League, in reality this was not an actual league, but more a loose association of merchants who in time all became members of separate guilds that dealt in a variety of commodities. This collaboration had no start or end date, and the number of places involved was never precise, as cities, towns and smaller trading posts would join and leave at different moments. But by the thirteenth century several were beginning to group together, among them Reval (Tallinn), Riga, and Rostock in the Baltic, and in the North Sea, Bremen – joined by the nearby Kiel – with the former group under the direction of Lübeck, the latter under that of Hamburg. Meanwhile, further inland, towns and cities on the great rivers were also now beginning to join, one of the earliest of these being Cologne, which had been independently trading with England from before the Norman Conquest. Over time subsequent English kings had increased this city's rights so that in 1157, two years before Lübeck was even founded, men from here had become the first official foreign traders in London. Later its privileges were increased by Richard the Lionheart, who on his return from the Third Crusade visited the city shortly after his release from his year-long imprisonment by the Duke of Austria. Then in 1266 Richard's nephew, Henry III, included Hamburg and Lübeck in the charter, and with this the three cities – now a corporation – started to set up new English storehouses. It was at this point that for the first time they became referred to as the German *Hanse* (later *Hansa*), a word possibly derived from a Norse one for a company, but the term was not used in the Baltic for another 100 years. From this period, the merchant's wealth continued to grow, over time becoming so immense that Edward III would use Cologne to finance his war debts by temporarily pawning his crown jewels to the city.

Apart from shared commerce, one of the purposes of the new association was to provide mutual protection. Trade was carried out in cog ships, similar to those used by the Vikings, although the larger Hansa ones were able to transport more cargo; they eventually grew to some 30 metres in length. The crew were subject to the captain and his on-board officers of the law, who for a variety of offences could impose serious penalties – even keel-hauling. In times of war, these cogs could be converted to carry a so-called castle from which archers were able to fire down on the enemy. Clinker-built out of Baltic oak, they were also flat-bottomed, which allowed the men to sail close into the shore, where they could find more shelter during storms, not to mention better protection against the ever-present threat of pirate attack. Moreover, to avoid wrecks and to help navigation in a period before proper maps, lighthouses were later built along the coastline. Finally, for added security, Hansa vessels travelled in flotillas, but the different towns and cities distinguished themselves by their pennants and sails displaying individual crests, all coloured white and red, with the exception of Riga with its white and black. Apart from the fact that the fish migration was seasonal, until the end of the fourteenth century the cogs with their square sails were unable to go into the wind, and so travel was dictated by the direction in which this was blowing. Furthermore, during the winter months, wishing to avoid unnecessary dangers, they remained in port, venturing out only when driven by the need for fish and beer, two commodities considered essential. These practices became official following the diet of 1391, which called for a cessation of all travel between St Martin's Day in early November and Candlemas in early February.

While the Hansa was gradually beginning to overtake the trade of the Vikings, in the late twelfth century another organisation also started to assert its presence in the Baltic region. The Teutonic Knights had arrived initially to mount a Northern Crusade against the local pagans who still dominated in the area. But, although primarily concerned with religious conversion, over time the Knights became equally – if not more – interested in territorial expansion, capturing (often with a remarkable display of brutality) large swathes of what is today Estonia, Latvia, Lithuania and northern Poland. Although in 1202 the pope's nephew, Bishop Albert of Riga, would found his own order of the Livonian Brothers of the Sword, just seventeen years later their unruliness forced him to seek help from Valdemar II of Denmark. But the king had his own ambitions and, after privately negotiating with the Knights, he then treacherously invaded Estonia, taking the area for himself. According to the local legend, during the battle for Tallinn the tide turned in favour of the Danes when their flag was seen descending from the sky, and after the victory Tallinn began to adopt the personal standard still used today that resembles the Danish *Dannebrog*. On Toompea Hill, Valdemar replaced the earlier castle, and ordered work to start nearby on the Cathedral of St Mary – Tallinn now taking its name from *Taani linn*, the Estonian for 'town of the Danes'.

In 1227 the Brotherhood of the Sword retook the town, holding it for eleven years, and it was during this time that the first German merchants arrived from Visby. But the brothers' success in the area did not last long. After their own defeat at the hands of the local Lithuanians and Semigallians in 1236, their independent order collapsed and, now called the Livonian Knights, they became just a branch of the larger Teutonic organisation. Two years after this, Tallinn was returned to the Danes and the town continued to grow, gaining rights to trade with Lübeck in 1248, before becoming a full member of the Hansa in 1284. During this medieval period, the nobility lived on the hill around Valdemar's castle, while the merchants settled in the separate lower town below Toompea's walls, where they began to build houses according to the rules laid down by Lübeck law. Today these typical buildings give the place its special historic character, earning it World Heritage status. And with the town's increasing contact with German speakers, it now started to be called Reval, a name that – derived from the former Estonian Rävala people – continued to be used until 1918, after which (with a brief interlude under German occupation in 1941–44) it reverted to the former Tallinn.

Meanwhile, after Bishop Albert had established his castle at Riga in 1201, the year before founding his separate order of Livonian Brothers, he began to expand the city's trade towards the Russian towns in the east, particularly Smolensk and Novgorod. Yet, German merchants from Bremen had already arrived in the region four decades earlier, their ship having been wrecked at the mouth of the Daugava (Düna) river in 1158. So in time, the bishop began to allow these men to be included in the local commerce, with the proviso that all their transactions were conducted through his city. This stipulation remained in force even after Riga joined the Hansa in 1282, the Knights still demanding all in-coming cargo to be unloaded, before being either sold locally, or reshipped on to other ports. As businesses grew, new guilds and various organisations began to form, among them the forerunners of the Brotherhood of the Blackheads. In the 1340s during the so-called St George's Night Uprising, an unsuccessful revolt by the pagan Estonian people against their foreign occupiers, these men came to the support of Reval's Christians. Originally a militia group, concerned with the defence of their towns, but later more involved with social matters, the brothers had probably taken their name from their Egyptian patron saint, St Maurice. All the members were foreign, unmarried merchants, who remained on average within the order for around five years, before they became eligible to join their town's Great Guild. Eventually the Blackheads formed a network throughout the region, and their later sixteenth-century

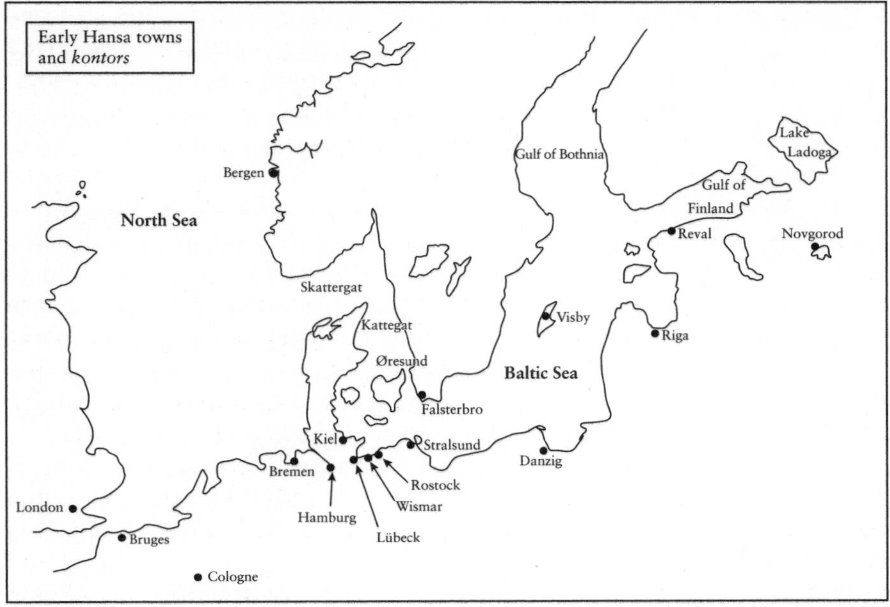

house in Tallinn still stands today, but the magnificent fourteenth-century building used by the brothers in Riga would be seriously damaged by the Germans in 1941. After the brotherhood had been disbanded on Hitler's orders, the members moved back to Germany, but finally in the 1960s they set up their present headquarters in Hamburg. Although Riga's destroyed House of the Blackheads was ultimately demolished by the Soviets, in the 1990s it was rebuilt and so has once again become one of the city's most important landmarks.

As early as the 1100s the Hansa, following the migration of the herring, had also created a minor presence on the northern shore of the Baltic across the water from Stralsund at Falsterbro – a peninsula in the region of Danish-owned Skåne (Scania), south of Malmö. This would mark a first challenge to the Danish hegemony in the area, one that by early the next century was turning into a real threat. By then Lübeck was starting to impose its will more forcefully on its Baltic neighbours, in 1247 sending pirates to attack Norwegian traders on their way to Visby, and later sacking Copenhagen and Stralsund. But in 1250, while the Norwegians were particularly vulnerable, suffering at the time from a famine, Lübeck made peace with the king, Haakon IV, an agreement that would lead to the Hansa's eventual commercial dominance in Bergen. The traders were also developing their business still further afield. In October 1297 Andrew de Murray and William Wallace, 'leaders of the army of the kingdom of Scotland', wrote in gratitude to their 'friends' in Lübeck and Hamburg, thanking them for their treatment of Scottish merchants, and promising the German traders open access to all Scotland's ports now freed 'from the power of the English'.[2]

Around a hundred years later in 1340, Valdemar IV Atterdag succeeded to the Danish throne and six years later, having inherited a bankrupt country, he decided to sell Reval back to the Knights for 4 tons of silver. Here, to increase their revenue, they now created an emporium similar to that found at Riga, and the city's wealth grew steadily through its commercial links with the increasing number of Hansa towns in the Baltic. Apart from benefiting from its trade in grain and timber, Reval gained from its position on the Amber Route that ran from the Baltic to Italy. Amber, produced over millions of years by the fossilisation of resin from the ancient forests, was found along the sea shores, from where fishermen scooped it up in large nets, giving it the popular name 'scoopstone'. Also dubbed 'northern gold', this was so highly prized that the local Knights strictly controlled its collection, imposing the death penalty on any offender caught working without licence.

Under the auspices of the Knights, Reval's commerce, like that of Riga, also stretched east to Novgorod, which, although formerly within the Kievan Rus, was now an independent republic. This city had long been trading with the Vikings and Visby when, in 1205, the Hansa arrived and began setting up their own 'eastern settlement' to deal in commodities such as furs, leather, wax, gold and silver. This trading post then developed into one of the four most important so-called *kontors* that traded as enclosed communities within towns and cities. The *kontor* in Novgorod, known as 'Peterhof', was large enough to include not just accommodation and storerooms but also a church, and even a gaol to punish its often undisciplined traders. These men were cut off from the outside by a surrounding fence that was guarded by watchmen and dogs, measures put in place to ensure the community's minimal contact with the local people, who were viewed as uncivilised and a threat to its security. Unlike Hansa merchants elsewhere, here the men stayed for periods of only around six months at a time, the summer traders interchanging with the winter ones. Moreover, at Novgorod strict rules were imposed on the local populace, preventing them (where possible) from trading with anyone not a member of the Hansa. Other foreign merchants were forbidden to learn Russian, and any local man caught trading at sea would be severely punished. In time, Kolin, the island in the middle of the Gulf of Finland – where years later Peter the Great would create his naval base of Kronstadt some 19 miles west of St Petersburg – was set up as an important transfer station for the city's trade. Twice a year all its imported and exported goods were shipped in riverboats to this spot, where the cargo was then handed over to seagoing Hansa ships in preparation for its transport on to the lucrative ports of the west.

However, the flexibility of the Hansa association allowed for a divergence in the customs found in the different trading areas. Another important *kontor* was opened in Bruges in the thirteenth century, but here the way of life was more sophisticated than that found in other places. The city was a key commercial centre for over 300 years, home to some fifteen different nationalities. The residents were better educated and more cosmopolitan, thanks in part to their attending the Champagne Fairs that since the Early Middle Ages had played such an essential role in the exchange of goods and ideas, with imports coming in from places as far afield as Tuscany. Moreover, as the Bruges regulations forbade new building to take place in the town centre, the various foreign traders were obliged to live in more mixed communities, and accordingly here the Hansa merchants, unlike those elsewhere, were not cut off from the rest of the population. As a result, they began to develop more cultured tastes, ideas and skills, many of which they would take back to their home towns after their period of service was over. In addition, when later the Italians from Lombardy brought banking to the city, the local Hansa merchants took up this system of payment, thereby breaking with the tradition of their colleagues in other towns, who continued to negotiate solely in cash or by the exchange of goods.

The stark differences among the various *kontors* is particularly clear when comparing the one at Bruges with that in Bergen on Norway's North Sea coast, where, by the time it finally officially opened in 1360, the merchants had excluded most of the foreign competition. In the 1240s men from Lübeck had first arrived and set up their business in the town, and although some other Hansa traders followed in their footsteps, for many years the Lübeckers remained predominant. Trading in a separate designated part of the town, they created their headquarters in the enclosed Bryggen area beside the harbour, today an important World Heritage Site that gives a vivid idea of the living conditions of the time. The complex itself was divided up into sections or 'gardens', each leading down through lawns to its own individual dock. Within the gardens there were rows of tenements, divided by long passages that led off at right-angles from the waterfront. These blocks comprised storerooms and offices with sleeping quarters above, some of which were heated, the remainder being used only during the summer. Contrary to the normal regulations stipulated by Lübeck law for the prevention of fire, here the buildings were made of wood, taken by the merchants from the local forests, and – as expected – these would periodically burn down. However, this was not the only problem that the *kontor* would face over the years. It would also be hit by the commercial rivalries between the Hansa towns, not to mention several pirate attacks, and repeated outbreaks of plague.

Although Bergen was one of the most important of the *kontors*, employing between 2,000 and 3,000 men, the behaviour of its merchants was boorish, rough and undisciplined. Here, where they remained in their separate community for ten years of service, they showed no respect for the local citizens, to such a degree that in 1361 the diet sitting in Stralsund felt the need to write and ask that they treat the Norwegian people better. As elsewhere, the merchants were ordered to remain celibate, restricted within the community's confines after dark, but again the correspondence from the diet raises questions as to how much this was adhered to, and how often relationships developed with the local women. But in this environment of tough, macho young men, unsurprisingly unruliness and disorder was rife, with fights frequently breaking out. Worse still, when, after seven years' apprenticeship employed in basic duties, a young man reached the time to become a 'journeyman', he was subjected to appalling initiation rites, or ordeals called *spelen*. These involved tortures such as whipping, burning, simulated suffocation and near drowning, trials not unknown to cause fatalities. Whether rich or poor, everyone was obliged to take part in these 'games' that were claimed to be valuable, not just for judging a candidate's suitability, but also for deterring the sons of prosperous and ambitious traders who might think that they could buy themselves into a position of influence in the company. During the 1540s, questions were still being asked at the diet about these games, to which it received the response that they were necessary for the maintenance of discipline. But in this period, cruel, brutal and coarse diversions such as these were widely popular, and when the Danish king Christian IV saw the games in 1599, he too was reported to have been greatly amused.

With the Hansa becoming a dominant presence in the Baltic, Visby was finally drawn into the association in 1359. As early as 1190, German merchants had begun to arrive on Gotland and by 1225 they had formed a settlement. Over time they erected many churches in the town, including a new cathedral that – unlike the brick ones in Lübeck and elsewhere – was built in the local white limestone. But the town's famed wealth, where rumours suggested that even the pigs 'ate out of silver troughs', made it the envy of others, causing civil war to break out between the townspeople and those living outside. Therefore, to defend itself, in the last years of the thirteenth century Visby began to create high encircling walls as protection from attack. Stretching for over 2 miles in length with more than fifty towers, these defences were almost unique in Scandinavia and, as most of them remain, Visby (another World Heritage Site) is still a remarkable example of a medieval walled town. With Gotland becoming militarised after 1939 and remaining at the forefront of Sweden's defence during the Cold War, Visby avoided the more negative influences of tourism and has kept much of its undiscovered charm. After 1989 the strong military presence was removed, but recently Russian activity has increased in the Baltic and during the Easter break of 2013 their fighter aircraft conducted an exercise over Swedish territory. Unable to respond, the government called on NATO for assistance, and with tensions increasing, in September 2016 military personnel returned to Gotland once more.

The Danish king Valdemar IV Atterdag became increasingly jealous of the Hansa, and so in 1361 he invaded Visby and killed around 1,800 people. According to legend, the king had gained access to the city by his seduction of a naive and unwitting local girl, and for her perceived act of treachery she was later buried alive in the so-called Virgin Tower. Meanwhile, having intentionally destroyed part of the fortifications to underline the city's vulnerability, Valdemar then demanded ransom from the remaining population. Ordered to fill three barrels with gold and silver by the end of the day, the citizens fulfilled his monstrous demands by emptying their coffers and stripping their churches. To add to the people's woes, soon after the Danes had left a fire broke out, wreaking further damage on the town, but Valdemar himself fared little better as his fleet was wrecked in a storm and much of his plundered treasure was lost at sea. While this outrage marks the beginning of an almost continuous 300-year period of Danish control, for the city it had an even more lasting significance. From this moment Visby began to lose the pre-eminent position that it had held in the region from the early days of the Vikings.

Following the plundering of Visby, Lübeck – joined by some of the other Hansa towns – declared war on Denmark, sending their fleet the next year to try and secure the free passage of the Øresund, 'the Sound', the strategic international waterway connecting the North Sea and the Baltic that today divides Denmark from Sweden. However, mistakes were made while besieging the fortress at Helsingborg, leading to the loss of twelve cogs. The admiral in charge at the time, the burgomaster, Johann Wittenborg, was subsequently made a scapegoat for the disaster, and following his public execution in Lübeck, he was then further disgraced by being buried in a criminal's grave. Despite the ruthlessness of his treatment, Wittenborg had been typical of many of the Hansa merchants of the time, his extensive trading throughout the Baltic and beyond having not just greatly increased his wealth, but also propelled him towards the highest position in his town.

The Battle of Helsingborg had come at a cost to the Danish king too, his son having died of wounds received during the fighting. But as if that was not enough, the situation now further deteriorated for Valdemar who, by ignoring the terms agreed in the truce, had reignited the fury of his neighbours. A diet was therefore called – for the first and only time at Cologne – attended by representatives from some seventy-seven Hansa towns. Here the delegates declared a second war on Denmark and, this time victorious, they sank the Danish fleet and captured Copenhagen. Finally, Valdemar sued for peace and the next year at Stralsund agreement was reached, allowing the Hansa to receive highly generous concessions that gave them control of trade in the Baltic.

Within the terms of the treaty they were granted two-thirds of the revenue of the Danish province of Skåne (Scania), special fishing rights, exemption from Denmark's tolls, and the temporary management of the Danish fortresses overlooking the Øresund. This Treaty of Stralsund of 1370 therefore marks the high point for the German Hansa – the name by which it had finally become widely known – and five years later its importance was further recognised by the Holy Roman Emperor, Karl IV of Luxembourg. Having previously shown little respect for the association, he now honoured Lübeck by visiting the city for ten days. But having reached its apogee, from this time onwards the Hansa would face the growing ambitions of the increasingly powerful rulers of the neighbouring countries.

Throughout the thirteenth and fourteenth centuries the Hansa had continued to grow, eventually gaining commercial rights in Antwerp and other places in the Low Countries. In the recently joined Baltic towns of Wismar and Danzig (Gdańsk), the increased trade had so greatly benefited the local economy that the citizens were now displaying their new wealth by building vast brick churches that emulated those found in Lübeck. However, everything was about to change, because in 1348 Europe was ravaged by the Black Death, when many places lost as much as two-thirds of their population. This would have a dramatic and lasting effect on the dynamic of much of the continent, and the political and social impact would be striking in many of the towns, as for example in Reval, where ties with the Hansa became stronger as a result of the Knights' need to find replacements for the large numbers of tradesmen lost during the epidemic. The horrors of the plague would long remain vivid in many people's minds, and more than a century later the travelling Pomeranian artist Bernt Notke would paint works such as his famous *Dance of Death* for the Hansa's church in Lübeck. On this long panel he interspersed images of emaciated corpses or skeletons between the various notable individuals, the emperor and empress, churchmen and merchants, illustrating to some degree the democratic nature of the disaster that had threatened, if not wiped out, even the highest in the land. This work of art (by then in replica form) was lost in the last war, but a smaller original version of the same, painted for Reval, is still on display in Tallinn's museum, today housed in St Nicolas – the thirteenth-century church of the German merchants from Gotland that was severely damaged in the same war. In addition, Notke's beautiful carved altar can be seen in Tallinn's Church of the Holy Spirit, while another earlier version is in the Århus (Aarhus) Cathedral on the Danish coast of Jutland. While Notke's carved crucifix – that fortunately survived the Allied bombing of the last war – hangs in Lübeck Cathedral, what many consider to be his finest masterpiece takes pride of place in Stockholm's Great Church, the Storkyrkan. This large wooden carving of St George and the dragon, the symbol of triumph over tyranny, commemorates the independence Sweden gained by its defeat of the Danish in 1471. The regent of the time, Sten Sture the Elder, who commissioned the work, most probably (without any display of false modesty) used his own face as a model for that of the saint.

In 1364, the Hansa supported Duke Albrecht of Mecklenburg when he invaded Sweden to take the crown from the joint rulers, his cousin Haakon VI (Norweigan: Håkon; Danish: Hakon; Swedish: Håkan) and his uncle Magnus IV. But Albrecht too was soon faced by a civil war, and although when it ended after eight years he remained the ruler for more than another decade, in time he lost all his support. Helped by the Danes, the Swedish rebels now defeated their king, holding him prisoner for the next six years. While the events of this time expose the complex relations between the Scandinavian countries, they also point to the continuing influence in the region of the Hansa, who now controlled Stockholm. Following Albrecht's release, the Hansa would put such pressure on the king to repay his indemnities that – unable to meet their demands – three years later he decided to renounce the throne and return to Mecklenburg. Here, after his death in 1412, he was buried beside the empty memorial tomb of his first wife at Doberan, around 9 miles from Rostock. (She was buried in Stockholm.) Doberan's large red-brick Gothic Cistercian abbey, the region's oldest monastery, was the traditional burial place for the Mecklenburg rulers and, despite the monks' departure during the Reformation and the abbey's conversion into a Lutheran minster, it continued to play the same special role for many years, with the odd family member choosing it for his interment even in the twentieth century. Despite suffering damage in the Thirty Years' War, and again during Napoleon's occupation, the building was spared in the fighting of 1939–45, and so it still possesses what is considered to be the greatest original medieval Cistercian interior in Europe. It contains early stained glass, finely carved pews and choir stalls, a fourteenth-century astronomical clock face, priceless altarpieces, and much else. And among all these treasures sit three remarkable painted, sculpted tombs: that of the thirteenth-century Margrethe Sambiria, the wife and regent of two of Denmark's first monarchs, and those of Sweden's unfortunate medieval king, Albrecht, and his queen, Richardis.

Meanwhile, the son of the deposed Magnus, who had replaced his father in 1362 as the Norwegian king, Haakon VI, had married Valdemar Atterdag's younger daughter, Margrete (Margaret). But her child, Olaf, born seven years later, was still only nine when Haakon died, just four years after his Danish father-in-law. As a result, Olaf was proclaimed King of Norway and Denmark, with Margrete acting as his regent. In 1387, Olaf also died unexpectedly at the age of only sixteen, giving rise to unfounded rumours, some asserting that he had been poisoned by his own mother. And, to add to the confusion, there was at the same time an equally unsubstantiated, but contradictory, suggestion that the boy had survived. This claim further threatened Margrete's position, a problem that was soon resolved by sending the pretender to the stake. However, although Norway now acknowledged Margrete as its queen, the Danes still refused to accept a female ruler, and so in Denmark she continued in her role as the regent, taking the title of 'all powerful lady and mistress'. Two years later Albrecht of Mecklenburg was deposed in Sweden, and while the country was looking for a new king, Margrete chose as her heir her young great-nephew Boguslaw of Pomerania, and he, having changed his name to Erik to please the Swedes, was now adopted as their monarch. But although this made Erik the official ruler of the three Scandinavian countries, his great-aunt continued to govern in all but name, and it was she who chose to cement the alliance by summoning representatives of the

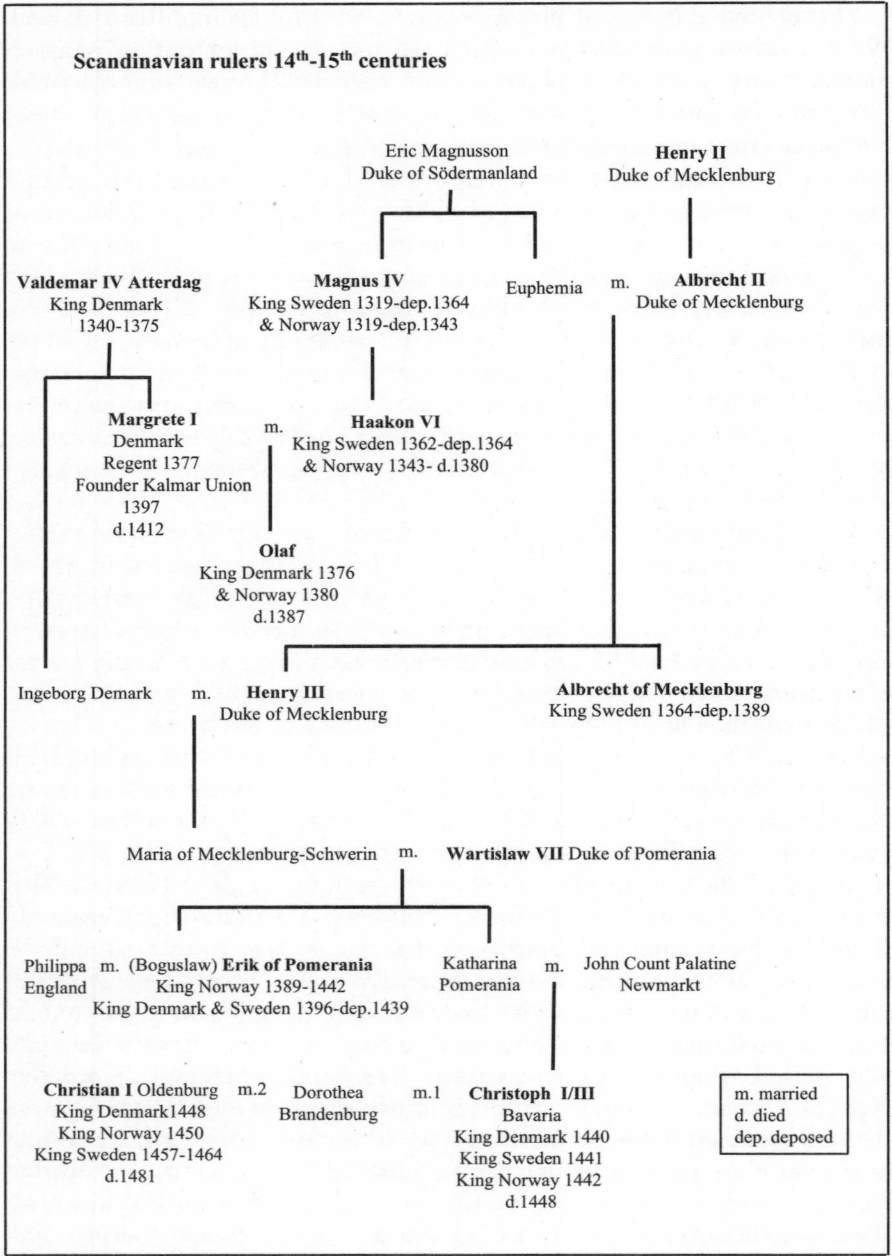

three countries to Kalmar, where they then officially agreed to bring the kingdoms together, united under one ruler. The resulting Kalmar Union of 1397 would last for more than 120 years, despite occasional interruption, such as during the period of Swedish independence that was celebrated by Notke's sculpture of St George in Stockholm.

Throughout this period piracy was rife, with towns like Rostock and Wismar acting as bases from which the men could set out to plunder passing ships or attack the local coastal towns. Margrete suffered from these assaults, but she received little help from the Hansa, some of whose members saw Denmark as a major rival. Some of the most savage and successful of these buccaneers were the Victual Brothers, who, having progressed from being suppliers of foodstuffs to full-blown pirates, now began to present a serious threat, attacking the island of Bornholm in 1391, sacking Bergen in 1393, and the next year occupying Gotland. Here they later set up their headquarters at Visby, keeping it for four years as their centre of activity. Eventually the Teutonic Knights – assisted by some of the Hansa – set out in eighty-four ships from Danzig and after laying siege to the town managed to drive the pirates out and take the place for themselves. But by the time the Knights finally sold Visby back to the Kalmar Union ten years later, they had wreaked still further damage, leaving much of it in ruins.

While at times the Hansa were content to see the pirates attacking their competitors, at others they were aware of the adverse effect of the Victual Brothers' activities on their own affairs. Therefore, in 1401 the Hamburg fleet set out to defeat them and, having arrested around seventy of their number, proceeded publicly to execute them and their larger-than-life leader, Klaus Störtebeker. This man, whose name was said to have come from his ability to drink 4 litres in one gulp, is still remembered in his home town of Wismar, and for some people he has become a folk hero – something that may explain how his skull came to be stolen briefly from the Hamburg museum. However, even after this defeat, the brothers were not finished, their piracy continuing to be a menacing presence until the 1440s.

Margrete died suddenly in 1412 while visiting Flensborg on the fiord that today marks the border between Denmark and Germany. A remarkable woman, she had been regent for thirty-six years, and de facto ruler of the Kalmar Union since 1397. Her bringing together of the three Scandinavian countries had been a politically astute move that had increased their standing and made them a force to be reckoned with in a period when the area was under considerable pressure from the Hansa. Abroad, although avoiding involvement in unnecessary wars, she had regained lands earlier lost, and at home had used her authority to maintain the peace and give the region a degree of stability that those coming after her would fail to match. Buried first in the abbey church at Sorø on Zealand, the next year her body was moved to Roskilde around 30 miles to the north-east, where it was then interred in a magnificent blue and white sarcophagus behind the high altar in the cathedral.

The year before Margrete died, Erik had begun to build himself a castle at Visby, and he now started work on a second one at Helsingør. This was situated at the narrowest point of the Øresund, guarding the important waterway that until the opening of the Kiel Canal in 1895 was the main access to the Baltic from the North Sea. Then in 1429, alongside his fortress, where the two shores are less than 3 miles apart, Erik set up a toll station to impose dues on all passing shipping.[3] These tariffs would prove a useful source of revenue for the king, but they immediately became a serious bone of contention with his neighbours, among them six of the Hansa towns – including Lübeck – that had already three years earlier declared war on the Kalmar Union. After attacking and plundering Bornholm, the Hansa suffered a naval defeat in the Sound, but then made two other assaults on Copenhagen. At the first of these, Erik was absent on one of his frequent trips abroad, but as usual he had left his wife Philippa, the daughter of Henry IV of England, standing in for him, and it would be she who encouraged the town to resist the bombardment until the Hansa were repelled – an act of bravery that earned her much respect. But, despite the continued seizure of Danish merchant vessels and Lübeck's later successful destruction of ships trapped in Copenhagen's harbour, Stralsund, finding itself threatened by the enemy, now decided with Rostock to sue for peace. Although these towns had dropped out of the war, others fought on, only agreeing to end the fighting in 1435. By that time, having made further significant gains, the Hansa could demand better terms, most importantly exemption from the hated Sound Dues charged on all other passing vessels.

Five years before the peace, Philippa, who had been loved not just by her husband but also the Danes and Swedes alike, died childless aged just thirty-five. She was buried at the Swedish Vadstena Abbey, where today she is honoured in the nineteenth-century stained-glass window erected above her grave. After her death, Erik became increasingly unpopular

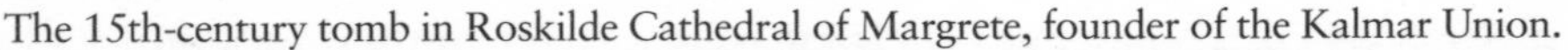

The 15th-century tomb in Roskilde Cathedral of Margrete, founder of the Kalmar Union.

even at home, and so nine years later he decided to move to Visby, where he remained for the next decade, residing in the castle that he had recently built, and – he too – lived off the profits of piracy. But finally, having been deposed and replaced by his nephew Christoph of Bavaria, he moved back to his Duchy of Pomerania, where ten years later, aged seventy-seven, he died and was buried in St Mary's Church in Rügenwalde (today Darlowo), approximately 100 miles west of Danzig. But by the time of Erik's death, Visby had lost its status in the Baltic and within around three decades of the king's departure it had ceased to be a member of the Hansa. As for the castle that Erik had built in the town, that would ultimately be destroyed by the Danes before their final surrender of the island to the Swedes in 1679.

By the mid-fourteenth century, the Hansa had begun to grow to such an extent, with numerous new cities, towns and settlements joining the association, that in 1347 the administration had been divided into thirds: the Westphalian-Prussian, Wendish-Saxon and Gotland-Livonian. To these a fourth Rhenish group would be added in 1554. While contemporary records suggest there by then some seventy towns included overall, today historians consider this to be merely the number that were actually run by the Hansa. In their view, such a figure does not include those other places with just a strong Hansa presence, and if we take these into account the total reaches around 180 all told. Meanwhile, apart from the four large *kontors* of Novgorod, Bruges, Bergen and London, there were other small trading houses in places as far afield as Lisbon and Seville, with Venice also having its 'German' storehouse in the Fondaco dei Tedeschi on the Grand Canal.

In Sweden, meanwhile, the Hansa played an important role in the export of its precious mining products from the Bergslag, a region lying primarily to the east of Stockholm. Here, merchants – chiefly from Lübeck – controlled the trade, using their own ships to export the goods and then import other much-needed items in their place. With the numbers of German traders in certain Swedish coastal towns constantly growing, by the mid-fifteenth century in Stockholm they made up possibly as much as 50 per cent of the population. On at least one occasion men from here were sent as spokesmen to one of the Hansa diets, the *hansetage*, which, attended by town and city representatives from all the regions, was now beginning to meet periodically, usually in the Wendish third and often at Lübeck. Still an Imperial city, Lübeck was held by the emperor to be one of his five main centres, on a par with Rome, Florence, Venice and Pisa. Having superseded Visby as the most important town in the Baltic, it now became widely recognised in 1418 as the 'Queen of the Hansa'. However, despite the Lübeck law, the Hansa still had no overall jurisdiction, and no way of punishing offenders other than imposing fines or ordering expulsion from the association. Various towns would at times find themselves excluded for crimes ranging from non-compliance with the wishes of the majority, to support of an enemy, or involvement in piracy: at one early point Bremen was barred for as long as fifty years.

However, over time many places had suffered outbreaks of violence and bloodshed, and Lübeck did not escape these problems unscathed. Internal unrest had always been feared, and by the end of the 1300s riots had erupted in the city. The situation was then exacerbated by new taxes being raised to solve the financial difficulties caused by the ongoing wars and continued pirate activity. To add to the uncertainty, when a town committee was created that insisted on more democratic elections for the council members, most of the old guard – including four previous mayors – vociferously announced their opposition to the changes and left the city. A new council was therefore formed, but this only complicated an already tense situation that had been made still more problematic by the two rival parties opting to take opposing sides in another dispute – one relating to the elected king of the Romans, the heir presumptive to the Holy Roman Emperor. With the new council supporting the earlier ousted King Wenceslaus (Wenzel), in 1410 the incumbent King Ruprecht (Rupert) issued a ban on Lübeck imposing restrictions on its commercial activities, thus seriously undermining its previously pre-eminent trading position. In fact, Ruprecht died shortly after, but it would take some six or seven years for things to return to the earlier status quo, and not before Lübeck had faced the very real risk of its own expulsion from the Hansa.

The fluidity of the association was particularly apparent in the inconsistency of the separate alliances formed at times between the towns. Pragmatism and greed often led to bizarre collaborations between enemies and equally active oppositions among former allies when their personal gain was seen to be at stake. Lübeck on more than one occasion joined in the assault on another town, and similarly, to further its own ambitions the Prussian third helped the Dutch gain access to the Baltic. This action had an especially negative effect on the trade of Lübeck, which up to this point had held a trump card – the city had control over the only alternative access to the North Sea, thanks to its position at the start of the overland porterage route that crossed the southern end of the Jutland peninsula. While Lübeck and Danzig, in particular, often fluctuated between mutual co-operation and rivalry depending on the current circumstances, towns would at times actually find themselves at war with each other. Therefore, Cologne – thinking of its own commercial interests – chose to back England during its war against Lübeck and Danzig, an action that led to the Rhenish city's expulsion from the Hansa for the duration of the fighting.

This conflict, which coincided with the long drawn-out English Civil War 'of the Roses', broke out after a considerable period of tension – again caused by arguments over trade. The situation had further escalated in 1468 when the Danish king commissioned some privateers from Danzig to capture English ships that were passing through the Øresund. In retaliation Edward IV closed the *kontor* in London and imprisoned its merchants, after which all-out hostilities began. Now a combined fleet from Danzig and Lübeck – and in lower numbers from Hamburg and Bremen – set about attacking some English coastal towns, in the process killing anyone who tried to resist. But in 1471 their loyalties changed, and they then helped the exiled Edward to return from Flanders and recapture his throne, with the result that when the war finally ended, at the Treaty of Utrecht the grateful king acknowledged his debt to the Hansa by granting new concessions. Accordingly, the merchants gained increased trading rights in England, receiving permission to set up new 'factories' around the country, not just in Bristol, but also in various places down the east coast, among them York, Boston and King's Lynn. Furthermore, Edward confirmed the merchants' ownership of the London *kontor* – now known as the Steelyard – whose traders were then made responsible for the upkeep of the red Baltic-brick Bishops Gate at the entrance to the city.

Since the time of its establishment, the London *kontor* had over the years suffered from attacks by the local mobs, some merchants even being slaughtered back at the time of the Peasants' Revolt of 1381. Therefore, for security, the men chose to live in a gated community, protected by a high surrounding wall with few windows. Within this enclosure close to the river, a short distance from London Bridge, there was a Great Hall, storehouses for the Rhenish wine that they were importing, kitchens, living accommodation and a garden with fruit trees and vines. Here, unlike in Bergen, the merchants, who came from a variety of Hansa towns, had good relations with the local dignitaries and citizens, becoming friends with men such as Sir Thomas More. They were now living like prosperous gentlemen, and Holbein's portrait painted in the 1530s of the young Steelyard merchant from Danzig shows how by this time the traders were enjoying the latest luxuries, such as fine clothes and well-stocked interiors. To demonstrate their sophistication and refinement they also commissioned other Holbein paintings to decorate their Great Hall, works much admired by those who saw them, but sadly lost in the Great Fire of 1666.

This love of display was also spreading back to the Hansa towns themselves, and representatives attending the *hansetage* would try to outdo their colleagues by the finery of their clothes and trappings. At the same time, the cultural life had developed as well, with artworks having now become much-desired objects. Among these were the Antwerp altarpiece that was donated to St Mary's Church in Lübeck, and Memling's triptych, today in the Gdańsk Narodowe museum, the latter less honestly acquired after it had been snatched while on its way to Italy. Printing was being introduced into the region, Lübeck publishing its first Bible in 1494, embellished with scores of beautiful original woodcuts. Cologne would remain a Catholic city, but after the Reformation most other towns converted to Lutheranism, so although the Lübeck Bible was written – like Cologne's two earlier editions – in the Middle Low German that was spoken by the traders, that language would soon begin to disappear when the Early New High German, used by Luther, became more popular with the spread of his reformed religion.

Gradually, the Hansa members found themselves coming under new competition from the United Provinces in the Low Countries. In the 1420s the herring again began to alter their migration, now moving into the North Sea. Here their arrival encouraged the development of the Dutch fishing business, a trade of considerable importance in this period when the Catholic Church imposed the eating of fish on Fridays and during Lent. In turn, this led to the growth of the Dutch shipping industry that over time would make its people the wealthiest and most powerful in Europe.

Meanwhile, the Hansa was still involved in foreign affairs, playing a key role in the events of the Kalmar Union following Christian II's accession. After being crowned in Norway and Denmark, the king went to Stockholm in 1520 for his third coronation. Having agreed an amnesty with his enemies, he invited them all to a banquet, whereupon the doors were shut, all were arrested and then soon after executed, an event still remembered as the Stockholm Bloodbath. But Gustav Vasa, the son of one of the murdered nobles, was not present at the slaughter, and having spent a year of exile in Lübeck, he returned to Sweden, where eventually, with Hansa support, he was able to capture Stockholm and take the throne. Acknowledging the important role Lübeck had played in these events, at his ceremony of affirmation the new ruler chose to honour the city's two representatives. While in the long term relations between the two parties would cool, by helping Gustav Vasa rise to power, the Hansa had ensured the final break-up of the Kalmar Union, and the beginning of Sweden's independence and gradual rise to power.

After that, the Hansa still continued to interfere in the business of others. Although helping the Danes to rid themselves of their now unpopular king and replace him with his uncle Frederik I, a decade later, after Frederik's death – in a complete and pragmatic reversal of policy – Lübeck decided to support the earlier ousted Christian II's attempt to retake his throne. Guided by its burgomaster, Jürgen Wullenwever, it backed the former king against his rival, Frederik's son, the later Christian III. With the mayor hoping this might enable the city to gain a share in Denmark's Sound Dues, in early 1534 he sent the army into Holstein, from where it went on to take Copenhagen the following June. But this aggressive policy, already opposed by other Hansa towns, succeeded in spurring Christian (III) into action and soon a savage civil war broke out. During this – 'the Counts' War' – some of Christian II's ragged peasant supporters would brutally take revenge on the nobility, attacking individuals and plundering or destroying their country manor houses. But by November of the same year Christian (III) had defeated Wullenwever's troops in Holstein, and was able to persuade Lübeck to agree temporarily to a peace. But within six months the war had restarted, and in June 1535 Lübeck's fleet was defeated in the waters off Bornholm, a disaster that soon led to the mayor's fall from power. The next year, two months after the hostilities had ended, Christian III entered Copenhagen and was officially acknowledged as Denmark's king.

After Jürgen Wullenwever had been appointed one of the city's burgomasters, he held the office for two years. But it had been a period of unrest, caused by the Reformation that had begun to take shape following Luther's first protest in 1517. Wullenwever, a supporter of Luther's religious thinking, had then decided, against the wishes of the Church, to bring the new faith to his city. This had just increased the enmity of his more ambitious colleagues, who were already bitterly opposed to his plans for the introduction of greater democracy in the administration. Moreover, to add to the mayor's problems, Lübeck, although one of the largest cities at the time with a population of around 25,000, was now beginning to lose its former status, a downturn that had been behind Wullenwever's ill-fated decision to become involved in the costly and disastrous Danish civil war. Now accepting his failure, Wullenwever resigned his position and left the city, and his council was deposed. With that, those who had formerly held office returned, and these more elitist members set out to increase once more the power of the local nobility, an action that in time would help undermine the Hansa and further hasten its decline. In the more immediate term, Wullenwever was arrested and accused of religious heresy, with the added charge of his having given support to the more radical Anabaptists. Despite his later repudiating the confession he had made under torture, in January 1536 he was executed and quartered in Wolfenbüttel on the orders of its Catholic duke.

By this time many more merchants had risen up the social scale, with some, now rich property owners, even accepted within the circles of the local nobility. Wishing to emphasise their new standing and outdo their rivals, they were constructing grand new houses, while the separate guilds were building halls where they could impress and entertain their visitors. Typical of such buildings is the red-brick gabled hall of the Seafarers, today probably Lübeck's most famous restaurant, which inside still has the long oak tables and benches where traders from the port would group together. Although visiting members from other towns were welcomed in these places, they would be expected to adhere to particular house rules inscribed on a clearly displayed blackboard that also recorded their offences. Despite the growing wealth and sophistication evident among those such as the aldermen, many of the ordinary traders still showed an unacceptable lack of refinement, as proved by the orders of the Danzig guild that specifically forbade the practices of making another drunk, passing on scandal, and – perhaps still most tellingly – throwing plates and dishes at other people.

Meanwhile, the Danes were now in debt, and so at this point they decided to pawn their island of Bornholm to Lübeck. Here the Hansa would remain for fifty years, rebuilding the Hammershus Castle during this time, but treating the locals so badly that they grew increasingly unpopular. And having become equally at odds with the people of Visby, in 1525 the men of Lübeck invaded the town, committing further acts of vandalism. With the exception of the cathedral, they destroyed all the many churches, leaving them in ruins as a lasting reminder of the bitter rivalries that so often divided the different communities of the Baltic in this period. However, while Visby now lost so much of its medieval heritage, still in the countryside of Gotland there remain around ninety other remarkable little churches dating from the twelfth to the fourteenth century, some displaying their original frescoed interiors that elsewhere were so often overpainted during the Reformation.

Lübeck was still continuing to develop, with large new buildings now appearing. Among these was the immense red-brick Holstentor Gate with its two massive round towers and pointed conical roofs, built as a main entrance into the old town through the medieval fortifications. Similarly, along the waterfront today there still exist the six spacious warehouses originally constructed at this time for the storage of salt. Nonetheless, Lübeck now had serious competition from Danzig, as these two cities, together with Rostock, had become rival boatbuilding centres, making large ships for foreign buyers like Henry VIII, who commissioned the 700-ton *Jesus* in 1544. After this there was the even larger 2–3,000-ton *Adler von Lübeck*, at the time one of the largest warships in existence. But elsewhere, things were already going badly. In Novgorod Lübeck's restrictions on free trade had made the merchants become extremely unpopular, a situation not helped by the religious difference between the Lutheran traders and the local Orthodox people. While tensions with the Knights and other naval conflicts at sea added to the Hansa's trading problems with the Russian cities, finally in 1494 Ivan III, Grand Prince of Moscow, closed the *kontor*, confiscated the stores, and imprisoned all the traders, thirty-six of whom subsequently died. Although later attempts were made to reopen this 'factory', the Hansa's influential presence in the area was over. And things in the Baltic region would become still more difficult under the Grand Prince's grandson, Ivan IV, 'the Fearsome' – or, as he is better known in English, 'the Terrible' – who, wanting to get access to the valuable trade, invaded his neighbouring country, starting the savage Livonian War that would continue for twenty-five years. Now besieged by the Russians, Reval sought help from the Swedes, and they, having arrived in the area in 1561, went on to conquer the whole of Estonia. Shortly after, the Livonian Knights were disbanded and their order came to an end.

After Denmark's new king, Christian III, entered into an alliance with Gustav Vasa of Sweden, Lübeck's influence also began to shrink, causing the Swedish king disparagingly to compare the Hansa to an old woman who was 'losing her teeth'. The traders' decline was further marked by the order given in 1559 to the Bergen *kontor* for a third of the merchants to be returned home to their German towns. The increasing power of the rulers of the neighbouring countries, and the growth of new markets in the

New World, India and the Far East, were now beginning to threaten the association's very survival.

At this point the merchants realised that they needed to establish a more unified and official system. Therefore, they now appointed a lawyer, Heinrich Sudermann, to oversee their affairs, but the measures came too late to stop the downturn. Bruges, already affected by events a century earlier during the Hundred Years' War, had begun to experience further change in the 1520s when the canal connecting the city to the North Sea had begun to silt up. Traders had then started to move to Antwerp, and with just a token number of merchants remaining, in 1593 the Bruges *kontor* finally closed. But that same year the Antwerp headquarters also shut down, less than thirty years after its completion. Although this was the largest of all secular Hansa buildings, it now lacked traders, these having fled less than two decades earlier when the Spanish sacked the city and massacred around 7,000 of the inhabitants. With their exodus from Antwerp, Hamburg, always more forward-looking than most of the other towns, grew in importance, now setting up a stock exchange and later a bank. Meanwhile, in England the merchants had lost their charter in 1552 and then, having antagonised the queen by their trade with Spain, were finally expelled by Elizabeth in 1597. The Steelyard was reopened by her successor, James I, but it never regained its former position, and the original building was eventually destroyed in the Great Fire of London.[4] In 1604 the Hansa's problems were further increased when the merchants' exemption from the Danish Sound Dues was rescinded, and they had to pay the same shipping tolls as others.

During the Thirty Years' War that began in 1618, the loss of life changed the face of much of central Europe, with a particularly serious effect on the area of Mecklenburg and Pomerania, where by the end of the fighting the population had fallen by around 50 per cent. During the war, despite the Imperial army occupying Wismar and Rostock and besieging Stralsund, the Hansa tried to remain neutral. It occasionally attempted to convene, but progressively fewer and fewer representatives attended the *hansetage*. In the late 1620s Lübeck, Bremen and Hamburg were acknowledged as the chief towns of the association, and when another diet was summoned in 1630, they alone attended. Most places were now beginning to resign their membership, hampered and impoverished by the war, and even Lübeck, unlike Hamburg, was finding it hard to adapt to the changing world. But although at the end of the Thirty Years' War many towns found themselves ruled by Sweden, the Hansa still managed to get itself included in the peace agreement. Finally, in 1669 a last effort was made to revitalise the association and an assembly met in Lübeck, this time with six representatives attending, but the delegates failed to reach any agreement, and the session ended with no conclusions of any kind. In effect, this marked the end of its affairs, although as the diet did not actually disband the Hansa, it just faded out of existence.

2
Poland's Rise to Power

Kazimierz III, 'the Great', the last of Poland's Piast kings.

The Baltic pagan cults would not be completely wiped out for several centuries, but around the beginning of the second millennium, Poland's leading family, the Piasts, decided to adopt Christianity. By doing this they were not just following the example of some of their neighbours, but also surely seeking to protect their dynasty against the territorial ambitions of the Holy Roman Empire. Thus, in 966 the whole court underwent conversion, the event taking place just a year after the marriage of Prince Mieszko to the Princess of Bohemia – a couple, according to some ancient texts, whose daughter would one day marry Sweyn Forkbeard, King of Denmark, and become the mother of Cnut (Canute), the later King of England. And as the Piasts were developing new towns, shortly after his wedding the prince founded Gdańsk in the recently conquered area of Pomerelia. With the dynasty continuing to flourish during Mieszko's reign, by the year 1000 his son was able to give the Holy Roman Emperor Otto III such an exceptionally lavish reception that his guest immediately declared him worthy to be called 'king'. Twenty-five years later, in the capital Gniezno, just shortly before his death Boleslaw I was finally crowned as the first King of Poland. But the situation for the Piasts would become seriously unsettled in the following century, civil war erupting between different contenders for the throne, and successive rulers losing parts of their territory – Gdańsk included. Moreover, titles became uncertain, some leaders known as 'kings', but others 'duke' or 'prince'.

When the later Duke Boleslaw III, 'the Wry-mouthed', died in 1138, the Piast rulers had again taken control of the whole of the region now designated as Poland, but following the duke's death the situation began to change once more. While the newly conquered area to the west of Pomerelia now achieved its independence, becoming the Duchy of Pomerania, there would be further disintegration of Boleslaw's former lands. In an attempt to stop sibling rivalry, he had stipulated in his will that his possessions should be shared out between his four sons – the Duchy of Masovia going to the second born. Rather than easing matters, this had only exacerbated the country's problems, and the situation would then be made still worse by further division of the land between later family members. As a result, over the next two centuries Poland would grow steadily weaker.

New difficulties then arose in 1226, when Boleslaw's grandson, Konrad I, the son of the Duke of Masovia, invited the Teutonic Knights to come and help him in his struggles against the pagans living on his borders, an invitation that would lead to long-lasting difficulties for his descendants. At the time of the Third Crusade in 1190, a religious military order of German knights had been founded, charged with the responsibility of caring for their fellow countrymen wounded during the ongoing Siege of Acre. Although originally seen as subordinate – if not inferior – by the Templars and the Hospitallers, eventually they had become an independent body, devoted to military action.

Konrad's request for the knights' help coincided with a Northern Crusade earlier declared by Pope Honorius III in 1217, a campaign that had as its objective the conversion of all the heathen peoples of the Baltic region. However, before accepting Konrad's invitation, the knights' leader, the fourth grand master, Herman von Salza, took the precaution of ensuring that he had the backing of both the Holy Roman Emperor, Frederick II, and the new pope, Gregory IX. Besides now receiving authorisation to hold the captured pagan lands in perpetuity (initially as a papal fiefdom), the knights were granted the region of Chelmo Land, an area south of Gdańsk, around 100 miles from the coast. Here they arrived soon after, and in 1233 they founded a fortress on the Vistula river at Thorn (Toruń), a town that just over thirty years later joined the Hansa, eventually becoming one of the most prosperous trading cities of the region – with much of its medieval centre left undamaged during the last war, it is today a World Heritage Site. However, within a few years the Knights had not just wiped out or assimilated the original Prussian tribes in the region, but had also become overlords of an extensive territory that stretched from Estonia to the borders of the Holy Roman Empire.

While he was at the helm, von Salza also greatly expanded the order's influence elsewhere, with the result that when he died in 1239 the Knights had footholds in countries as far afield as Greece and Spain. However, just over fifty years later, their order suffered a major setback when in 1291 Acre finally fell to the Muslims. After this defeat, having temporarily established themselves in Venice, the knights moved north to the Baltic area, and in 1309 they set up their base around 35 miles to the south-east of Gdańsk at Marienburg (today, Malbork). Here they set about enlarging their headquarters, turning it into a complex that eventually comprised two castles, an outer bailey and other further small buildings, so that by the time it was completed several years later it had become Europe's largest brick construction of its kind. This was used by the knights for their famously lavish entertainments and tournaments, and on occasion for the Hansa meetings, but following the order's defeat during the Thirteen Years' War, it was finally sold to the Polish king in 1457. It then remained a royal residence until the late eighteenth century. After Poland's Third Partition, the place was used by the Prussian military, a period when it would suffer from both vandalism and neglect. As a result, for a time Marienburg's very survival was in doubt, but shortly after the end of the Napoleonic Wars, in 1816 efforts were begun to save the building. This immense task continued on into the twentieth century, with further repairs being carried out after 1945 to put right the latest war damage. Today, besides being important as a prime example of medieval castle-building, it is valued for the restoration work's high level of historical accuracy, and since 1997 Malbork has held World Heritage status. Here stand four eighteenth-century statues of some of the most important Teutonic Knights, among them Herman von Salza, the grand master who first brought the order to the region.

After a turbulent period of upheaval and occupation under different masters, Pomerelia was finally brought back into the Piast's Kingdom of Poland. But when its earlier overlord, the Margrave of Brandenburg, threatened to retake the regional capital Gdańsk, Wladyslaw the Short (or Elbow-high), like his grandfather Konrad, appealed to the knights for their help, making a decision that he would soon come to rue. Shortly after their arrival in the town on 13 November 1308, the knights took the place over, slaughtering the Polish population during the conflict. The numbers killed in this massacre are unknown, the knights declaring some fifty or so to have died, the Poles several thousand. Whatever the truth, following this event – still remembered as the 'Gdańsk Slaughter' – the town was incorporated with the rest of Pomerelia into the surrounding lands of the Teutonic Order. However, now called by the German name of Danzig, it continued to grow, becoming through its increasing trade an ever wealthier city. Where a branch of the River Vistula enters the Baltic, the knights replaced the original wooden fort with one made of brick, and then, having created a lighthouse to help navigation, they began to charge a toll on passing ships. Having had trading ties with the Hansa for around 140 years, in 1361 Danzig finally became a full member of the association, and as its wealth grew, important new landmarks began to appear in the developing town. These included a first town hall on Long Market, the Gothic brick church of St Mary's – one of the largest buildings of its kind – and a vast fifteenth-century brick crane that replaced an earlier one destroyed by fire. At the time of its construction, this was the biggest crane in existence, capable with its treadwheel of lifting by manpower alone around 4 tons from the ships that would anchor with their cargoes in the river below.

Across the border from Pomerelia, at the beginning of the fourteenth century Poland's fortunes also began to improve, and in 1320 Wladyslaw the Short overcame opposition and was crowned Wladyslaw I, in what was the first coronation to take place in Kraków. Although plagued by warfare and attacks from Bohemia, the Burgundians and the Teutonic Knights, the king managed to reunite most of his country once more, a task made easier for him by the earlier death of two brothers whose lands he now inherited. After his own death in 1333, his son Kazimierz (Casimir) III, Poland's only home-grown 'Great' ruler, and the last of the Piast kings, continued the fight to reunify and expand his realm. Most of the Duchy of Masovia – an area that was eventually fully incorporated into the kingdom in the sixteenth century – now became his fiefdom and, although he had to renounce his right to Silesia, he succeeded in leaving a country that had doubled in size, with territory extending into the Ukraine and Moldavia.

Kazimierz III increased his authority at home by weakening the power of the nobility and giving his help and protection to other, lesser members of society. He also welcomed foreigners, offering special protection to the growing numbers of Jews fleeing from persecution elsewhere. Ever eager to embrace new ideas, he introduced a judicial system and legal code, built castles, cathedrals and towns and, in his pursuit of learning, founded a university at Kraków in 1364, one of the oldest in the world. Lying upstream on the River Vistula in so-called Little Poland, with even more ancient origins than Danzig, Kraków had become the capital after 1038, replacing Gniezno in Greater Poland to the west of the country. In later years much of Kraków would have to be rebuilt as a result of the repeated Mongol invasions it suffered throughout the thirteenth century – attacks that are still commemorated today with the hourly interrupted trumpet call from St Mary's Church, recalling the watchman killed at his post while warning of the enemy's arrival. But now, Kazimierz – whose focus was directed chiefly towards his new acquisitions taken in the east – set out to develop Kraków still further, expanding the city and founding on its outskirts a new walled town, which he named after himself, Kazimierz. And, like Danzig, Kraków had now become an important centre for trade, again helped by its membership of the Hansa.

Despite four marriages, two ending in divorce and the last very possibly bigamous, Kazimierz III 'the Great' failed to produce a legitimate son, and so on his death in 1370 his nephew, Louis I of Hungary, succeeded to the throne as King Ludwik. This was contrary to Kazimierz's wishes as laid down in his last will, where he appointed his grandson, the eighteen-year-old Duke of Pomerania, to be his heir. Louis, however, founded his claim on an agreement made some years before, when Kazimierz, although still hoping for a boy to add to his first two daughters, had designated him as his successor, should he ultimately fail to have a son. At the time, this arrangement had the advantage of ensuring Louis' support in the king's battles against the Teutonic Knights, but despite the threat from that quarter having now diminished, the younger man was not prepared to forget the earlier agreement.

When his uncle finally died, therefore, Louis moved quickly and, determined to pre-empt the succession of the Duke of Pomerania, marched straight to Kraków, where he then persuaded the nobles to give him the crown. However, although earning the title 'the Great' for his actions elsewhere, for the next twelve years he would rule Poland only in name, visiting the country just three times. Taken up with more pressing matters in the Balkans, Italy and elsewhere, he left the running of his kingdom to his strong-willed mother – Kazimierz's sister, Elizabeth of Poland. Arriving with her large Hungarian retinue, she was unpopular from the start, and so six years later, finally realising the danger she faced after 160 of her followers had been murdered, she fled back to Hungary. Living for the rest of her life in a monastery near Buda, she died just two years before her son, in 1380.

Like Kazimierz III before him, King Ludwik had no male heirs, but he had indicated that he wished to leave his thrones to at least one of his three daughters, and to that end had tried to ensure their futures by arranging their marriages while they were still infants. Although doubts remain among historians as to how exactly he wished his lands to be divided, with his oldest child having already predeceased him, on his death it would be the second, Mary, who was crowned, bizarrely, as 'King of Hungary' – a title chosen to appease the nobles who objected to a female ruler. However, her reign would not run smoothly, and she would soon be faced by rebellion, imprisonment, the loss of her throne, and even the murder of her mother. Although she eventually regained her crown, and ruled for a time with her husband, Sigismund of Luxembourg, just eight years later she died in childbirth.

At the time of Mary's coronation in Hungary, the question had arisen as to who should take the crown in Poland, the Poles opposing the idea of Sigismund being their king since they preferred a native-born ruler who would choose to reside permanently in the country. But two years after Mary had renounced her claim to the Polish throne, her younger sister Jadwiga (Hedwig) arrived in Kraków, and in October 1384 this approximately ten-year-old child was crowned (like her sister) as 'King of Poland'. But the nobles still wanted to exert their control and so they immediately locked her up in the city's castle in order to prevent her meeting the man to whom she had been betrothed since infancy, Wilhelm of Habsburg. He had already arrived in Kraków in search of his bride, but realising the hopelessness of his situation, he soon abandoned Poland and returned home. Jadwiga was said to be saddened when he left, but she accepted her loss and agreed to find a husband more acceptable to the Polish people.

Accordingly, two years later another marriage was arranged for her, one that cemented a new alliance. Her designated husband was the considerably older pagan Duke of Lithuania, Jogaila, the ruler of the large neighbouring country on Poland's eastern border. Its territory had grown to such an extent over the last two centuries that by this time it stretched from the Baltic to the Black Sea, an area that roughly corresponds today to Lithuania, Belarus, and much of western Russia and Ukraine. Shortly before his marriage, Jogaila converted to Christianity, taking the name of Wladyslaw II Jagiello, and with this the new Jagiellonian dynasty was founded. Although there was now a family union between the two countries of Lithuania and Poland, for nearly 200 years Wladyslaw's duchy and his wife's kingdom would remain separate, independent entities.

Despite the couple's age difference, the marriage was a success, and Jadwiga, who was an exceptional, well-educated young woman, speaking five languages, was personally involved in the running of her country, particularly devoting herself to spreading the Catholic faith among the pagans still living in Lithuania. Unlike her sister, who took a minor role in her kingdom, Jadwiga founded hospitals, churches, and a theological college, in addition to reviving the university at Kraków that had closed after Kazimierz III's death. Dying like her sister in childbirth when she was aged just twenty-five, she left no surviving children, but she was deeply missed by her husband and the Polish people at large. Remembered for her kindness and religious devotion, she was soon revered as a saint, although it was only in 1997 under the papacy of the Polish Pope John Paul II that she was canonised.

Meanwhile, the Teutonic Knights continued to be a significant presence in their regions to the north, controlling states that stretched from the land west of Danzig to Narva, today Estonia's fourth largest town that sits on its border with Russia. But in 1410, Wladyslaw Jagiello famously defeated the knights at Grunwald or Tannenberg, leaving the grand master and most of the order's leaders dead on the field. This key battle, one of the largest and most important of the period, would prove to be a turning point in the Knights' history, and from this time they began to lose their dominance in the area.

Wladyslaw Jagiello ruled well and was generally popular with all his people, but the situation in Poland became more complex after his death and the succession of his ten-year-old son born of his fourth marriage, who as Wladyslaw III would immediately face opposition from supporters of his half-sister's husband. In time these problems were resolved, but then six years later an event of still greater significance occurred, namely the death of his cousin, the Hungarian king. With the latter having left only an unborn child, Wladyslaw was offered this second crown, whereupon he left for his coronation, never again to return to Poland. Although now the two thrones were once more reunited, soon certain factions had developed in favour of the former Hungarian king's posthumous infant son, and before long a two-year civil war had broken out. But with Hungary facing other threats from the neighbouring Ottoman Empire, Wladyslaw then took his country to war against the sultan, personally leading his army to victory in 1442. After this peace was agreed, but when the pope later persuaded the king to renege on the terms of the treaty, Wladyslaw renewed the fighting and embarked on a crusade against the so-called 'infidel Turk'.[5] This culminated two years later at Varna on the Black Sea, where the twenty-year-old king vanished during the heat of the battle, most probably killed, very possibly decapitated by the sultan's elite guards, the Janissaries. But because his body and armour were never found, myths soon developed raising doubts about his death, with some people claiming he had fled to the Portuguese court and been granted lands in Madeira, others reporting a sighting of him on a pilgrimage to Jerusalem. The long-term result of the king's disappearance was the final separation of his two thrones, that of Hungary immediately going to the son the earlier king did not live to see, and that of Poland three years later to Wladyslaw's younger brother, Kazimierz IV.

In 1454, seven years after Kazimierz IV came to the throne, another thirteen-year-long war broke out against the Teutonic Knights, during which the latter, forced to flee from their large castle at Marienburg, set up a new stronghold at Königsberg (today Kaliningrad) on the shores of the Baltic. But when the conflict finally ended, the knights had to surrender still more, being forced to cede their areas in the west, including Pomerelia, which from this moment became fully incorporated into Poland as Royal or Polish Prussia. Danzig, in this period the kingdom's largest city with a population of roughly 30,000, particularly benefited from the ending of the knights' dominance, from now on receiving special new privileges that included the establishment of its own law.

Meanwhile, in the eastern part of their former territories, the knights were allowed to remain, although here, in what was now called Ducal Prussia, they became fiefs of the Polish king to whom they paid dues. In the 1520s, at the beginning of the Reformation, the knights converted to Lutheranism, and the state became secularised under its former grand master, Albrecht, the first Duke of Prussia. When his granddaughter Anna married the Elector of Brandenburg, the foundations were laid for the dynasty that would in time rule over both these separate regions. In 1657 Ducal Prussia would cease to be a fief of the Polish king, but the inherited situation created by the earlier union would continue to have an impact on the Brandenburg-Prussian rulers, whose lands remained physically divided by the Kingdom of Poland. Although the duchy would give its name to the dynasty's descendants, with the first monarchs taking the unusual title of Kings *in* Prussia, its detachment from the bulk of the Brandenburg estates would remain an issue that many years later would fuel Frederick the Great's ambitions for the First Partition of Poland.

With Kazimierz IV having eleven children who survived into adulthood, the Jagiellonians grew in importance, with members of the family – through marriage or birth – coming to rule around one third of Europe. Apart from their position in Poland and Lithuania, they sat in the courts of Bohemia, Hungary and Moravia. However, around 100 years later, the dynasty came to an end in Poland with its last king, Zygmunt (Sigismund) II Augustus. He was a grandson of Kazimierz IV, and the son of Zygmunt I 'the Old' and the notorious Bona Sforza, the daughter of the Duke of Milan. A strong woman who was one of Poland's two most famous queens, Bona was determined to guarantee the succession of her only surviving son, so in 1529, when he was just nine years old, she managed to manipulate his election and coronation. While this was done to ensure the child's future, carried out while his father was still alive and actively ruling the country, it would make Bona even more unpopular with the nobles.

Bona would eventually return to Italy after her husband's death, moving back to her childhood home in Bari, where shortly after, in 1557, she was poisoned by one of her retinue. In Poland she had been responsible for fostering the arts and developing its cultural life. For some time, the country had been going through its Golden Age, an intellectual and artistic flowering that preceded the Dutch Golden Age by almost a century. Throughout this period, famous names such as the Polish-born astronomer Copernicus from Thorn (Toruń) were working in the fields of the sciences, medicine, education and the arts, and under royal patronage, Danzig had also prospered, with foreign artisans and specialists coming to the city. Later Dutch architects would create for Zygmunt II at the entrance to Long Market a brick Flemish-style palace, 'the Green Gate', which took its name from the nearby lichen-covered bridge crossing the river. The king would never stay there, but today – fully restored after suffering serious damage in the last war – it is one of Gdańsk's architectural treasures.

However, even while the country was flourishing internally, the king's separately owned Lithuanian duchy remained under threat from its neighbour, Russia. In 1558, Tsar Ivan IV, 'the Terrible', invaded Livonia – an area lying just to the north of Lithuania – and this began the particularly vicious war that would last for a quarter of a century. Within three years of the outbreak, the Livonian branch of the Teutonic Knights was disbanded and the people of the region turned to their neighbour for help. While the greater part of southern Livonia became incorporated into Lithuania as a semi-autonomous duchy, and the new vassal Duchies of Courland and Semigallia were put under the protection of Poland, further to the north, Sweden took the remaining territory and made it part of Swedish Estonia. Finally, ten years after the war began, the Ukrainian region of Lithuania was incorporated into Crown Poland and, even more significantly, the kingdom and the duchy formalised at last the connection that up to now had been a purely family one. The next year, 1569, at Lublin the two states were officially brought together as the Polish-Lithuanian Commonwealth – one of the largest countries in Europe at the time.

Meanwhile, the Livonian War raged on, with both sides committing brutal acts of savagery that even included alleged instances of cannibalism. In this period other atrocities were also being committed as a result of the Reformation, and in France, where religious wars had broken out, in 1572 thousands of Huguenots were killed in the events known as the St Bartholomew's Day Massacre. As a result, many Protestants, seeking to escape the continuing persecution, now emigrated to the predominantly Lutheran and German-speaking Danzig, where all the churches had by this time converted to the Protestant faith. However – remarkably for the period – religious tolerance had been guaranteed only three years earlier in the Union of Lublin, so throughout the Commonwealth at large the free worship of a variety of faiths continued unmolested: the Polish peasantry and the king remained Catholic, the east was predominantly Orthodox, Ducal Prussia and Courland Lutheran, and Livonia a mixture of Lutheran and Calvinist. Furthermore, besides the scatterings of Anabaptists or Arians, there were also many Jews and a few Muslims.

The constitution brought in by the Union of Lublin in 1569 had also introduced certain other measures, one of the most significant being that from then on all future monarchs would be elected solely by the parliament, or *Sejm*. This body comprised the king, the Senate drawn from senior nobles and churchmen in the king's Council, and the Chamber of Deputies, a lower house with representatives from the lesser nobility – the *szlachta*. From this moment the king's authority was reduced, and new powers and privileges were granted to the nobles in the lower house, with the result that the period would become known as the time of the Golden Freedoms or Liberties. Thus, Poland was now the most democratic country in Europe, having a higher percentage of the population with the vote than anywhere else for years to come. But unimagined by the people of the time, this forward-looking change would open the way to a system that would ultimately help bring about the country's downfall. It increasingly gave the *szlachta* the power to undermine the king's authority, even to the point of their being able to block his most necessary reforms. With their growing ascendency and increasingly selfish ambitions, they would progressively bring about political stalemate, eventually rendering the country virtually ungovernable.

Following the Union of Lublin, Zygmunt II lived on for another four years. Earlier his much-loved second wife, Barbara Radziwill, had died, and although persuaded against his will to marry again in order to produce an heir, because of his dislike and distaste for his new queen, the Emperor Ferdinand I's daughter, Katarina, he refused to have any contact with her and, although there are suggestions of one miscarriage, the couple remained childless. Therefore, when the first Great Election took place following Zygmunt's death, the choice of candidates was wide open. Preferring a monarch without the support of any particular domestic faction, and also one able to call on foreign support for the country if needed, the *Sejm* now elected Henri, the third son of the Catholic dowager queen, Catherine de Medici. But within months of his arrival, his older brother Charles IX died and so, under cover of darkness, Henri slipped out of Poland to return home and take up his French throne. Crowned Henri III, he was killed sixteen years later, a victim of France's ongoing religious wars.

Henri's departure meant that the *Sejm* now had to elect another ruler, and this time they looked to Anna, the fifty-two-year-old sister of the former king, Zygmunt II. Having previously hoped she might become the wife and co-ruler of Henri, she now married instead a Hungarian, Stefan Batory (Hungarian: István Báthory), and together this couple would rule the Commonwealth for the next ten years. However, Danzig, often with ideas of its own, rejected Anna and Batory's election, preferring another candidate for the throne, the Emperor Maximilian II. Therefore, in punishment for its opposition, the new rulers transferred the city's valuable trade to the neighbouring town, Elbing (Elbląg), a move that threatened to be a commercial disaster for Danzig. As a result, it now felt forced to retaliate and, having melted down its gold and silver to pay for mercenaries, the city took the king on in battle. Soon defeated, and then subjected to five months under siege, Danzig finally surrendered and, having acknowledged the new rulers, was able to regain its trade and former rights and privileges.

Batory would build up a strong army, including among its ranks his famous 'winged hussars'. Wearing their characteristic dress, for some 200 years these elite horsemen would bring fear to the enemy by their rapid and deadly cavalry charges. Explanations for their unusual appearance vary, but whether to provide protection to the back of the men's necks, block out other sounds that might frighten the horses, or bring dread to the enemy, the tall wings they wore on their armour had the effect of causing the passing wind to create a sound that made their assaults still more terrifying to those under attack. With his improved army Batory continued his successful campaigning until the end of the Livonian War in 1583, by which time he had defeated the tsar and expelled him from the region. But three years later the king died, and with that his wife Anna decided to give up her throne, whereupon she promoted the cause of her nephew, Sigismund Vasa, the son of her sister, the Queen of Sweden, and grandson of the Swedish dynasty's founder, Gustav I.

PART 2

FROM THE MIDDLE AGES

3
Denmark's First Oldenburg Kings

Kronborg Castle from the water. (Courtesy of Guillaume Baviere under Creative Commons 2.0)

Having deposed Erik of Pomerania, by 1442 all the Scandinavian countries in the Kalmar Union had separately crowned in his place his nephew Christoph of Bavaria. By that time, having successfully put down a peasant uprising in Fyn (Funen) and Jutland, the new king had already penalised his Danish rebels and removed many of their former freedoms. This set up a system of serfdom that would persist in Denmark almost uninterrupted in one form or another until the end of the eighteenth century. Although Christoph had restored the peace, at the same time he had become more unpopular, a situation that only added to his other problems. He now found himself challenged not just by the Hansa, but also by the aristocracy, whose growing powers were threatening to undermine his own royal authority. Yet, before Christoph could confront these threats, in 1448, aged only thirty-two, he died suddenly without an heir.

Following the king's unexpected death, the Danes elected in his place one of his distant relations. Adding the proviso that he should marry Dorothea of Brandenburg, the widow of his predecessor, they offered the throne to Christian from the house of Oldenburg (Oldenborg). Close on two years later, Christian sailed to Bergen where, on being accepted as Norway's ruler, he signed a treaty that finally confirmed the end of the Norwegian hereditary monarchy. Although for a time Sweden continued to resist the king's election, in 1457 at last it came into line with its neighbours and the Kalmar Union was revived once more. For the Danes there was another, more long-term result of Christian I's accession. Even after the eventual collapse of the union the Oldenburgs retained their position in Denmark, becoming one of the longest-surviving dynasties in Europe. Despite the Danish monarchy remaining elective until the 1660s, for some 400 years the family was able to hold onto its power, regularly passing the crown to the ruler's closest male relative. Although, eventually, a junior branch descended from the Oldenburgs succeeded to the Danish throne, still today their descendents are found not just in the royal house of Denmark, but also in those of several other countries of Europe, including the United Kingdom.

Shortly before Christian I's accession two separate events occurred at Roskilde. In 1443, its great cathedral suffered serious damage in a fire, and King Christoph transferred the capital around 25 miles to the east, re-establishing it in Copenhagen – the city having grown in importance after Erik of Pomerania had moved to its castle just over twenty-five years earlier. These same events would be highly significant for the people of Roskilde, their town having been the Danish capital since the time of Harald Bluetooth, its last pagan Viking king. Today Roskilde's Viking Museum records its importance at that time, with its major exhibits being the five longboats that were recovered from the nearby fiord after they had been purposely sunk to form a blockade against enemy attack. At the end of the tenth century, after his conversion to Christianity, Harald Bluetooth had erected at this spot a simple wooden stave church, constructed in the current style with a palisade made from the split trunks of trees, and topped with a pitched roof. Over time, buildings like this one became more complicated and ornate in design. Although once common throughout the Scandinavian area, today the most remarkable are to be found in Norway, those in Denmark having since disappeared. Such is the case with Harald Bluetooth's church at Roskilde that was replaced in the eleventh century by a bigger one made of limestone. According to the most accepted legend, this was paid for with the money Harald Bluetooth's grandson Cnut (Canute) – the King of England – had given his sister as a penance for having murdered her husband in 1026. Later it too would be superseded, replaced by an even larger twelfth-century Romanesque-style cathedral that, taking a century to complete, was constructed out of bricks – a material newly introduced into the area. This building, which helped set the trend that became popular throughout the region, notably in the north German towns of Lübeck and elsewhere, would be the one damaged in the fire of 1443.

After this fire, while Roskilde's great cathedral was undergoing twenty years of restoration work, Christian and his wife Dorothea added a new chapel to the building, the Chapel of the Magi, designed to be the place for their future burial. Decorated with frescos, during the period of the Reformation the walls were whitewashed, but after the paintings' discovery in the nineteenth century they were restored and so are once more on view. On the granite pillar in the centre of the chapel a mark supposedly records the height of the king – so high as to appear an exaggeration – though it does suggest Christian was exceptionally tall, even theoretically surpassing Peter the Great, who had himself measured in the same place when visiting the city in 1716. Later some other tombs would be added here, in particular those of the king's grandson and great-grandson, Christian III and Frederik II. After them, Roskilde became the burial place of all the future Danish monarchs, and over the years several would add new chapels around the cathedral, each reflecting the architectural style of its time. As a result, this building that is now a UNESCO World Heritage Site, contains – in addition to its memorials to the early Viking kings – some thirty-nine royal tombs, with the earliest in the choir, the decorated blue and white Gothic sarcophagus topped with the effigy of Margrete, the Kalmar Union's founder.

Twelve years after Christian I's accession, the nobles of the Duchy of Schleswig and the County of Holstein also elected him to be their ruler, on the condition that the two regions would remain united for perpetuity, a stipulation that would lead to serious political problems some 400 years later. But in the immediate term the cost incurred by these elections placed the king in financial difficulties that were increased by the betrothal that same year of his daughter. Under continuing economic strain, in 1469 when, finally, the thirteen-year-old Margaret married the Scottish king James III, Christian had to guarantee her dowry by pawning the Shetland and Orkney Isles. Unfortunately for his country, the next year, still unable to raise the money, Christian was forced to surrender these to Scotland, thereby losing forever islands that had been Danish since the time of the Vikings.

However, not long after, in 1474, borrowing heavily from the Hansa merchants, Christian set out to visit the pope in Rome, staying on the way with his brother-in-law Ludovico Gonzaga of Mantua, the husband of Queen Dorothea's sister, Barbara. It was while he was there that Andrea Mantegna began work on the frescos that still decorate the Camera dei

Sposi in the ducal palace, and as a result the artist included the Danish king in the picture of *The Meeting Scene* that appears on the west wall of this room. Equally well received by Bartolomeo Colleoni at Malpaga near Bergamo, Christian was feted with days of celebrations that were again recorded in the frescos decorating the castle's great hall. But of still more significance for the king was the approval he now received from the pope for his two new projects. Sixtus IV granted him permission to found at Copenhagen a Catholic university, one of the oldest in the whole of Europe, and to create a new Danish order of chivalry that would be dedicated to the Mother of God. This, designed with a medallion showing the Virgin and Child, was to be worn on a chain fashioned out of linking elephants, an early symbol of chastity, loyalty and wisdom.

During his reign, Christian I faced serious challenges in his role as king of the separate countries of the Kalmar Union. In protest at his raising of taxes, in 1464 Sweden decided to break away, and it would actively oppose Christian until his final crushing defeat at the battle of Brunkeberg in 1471. This major Swedish victory – celebrated in the great statue of St George and the dragon in Stockholm's Storkyrkan – would bring the regent Sten Sture the Elder to power, a position that he then held almost uninterrupted for around three decades. The kings of Denmark had always wanted to keep the alliance together, but uncertainty about the union's future had now set in, and the tensions would continue to trouble Christian's two successors. Within a couple of years of his death his oldest son, Hans (John), was crowned in 1481 in Denmark and Norway, but Sweden still refused to co-operate, continuing to maintain its independence for the next sixteen years. Faced by these problems, Hans began to build up his navy, and, having gained a series of victories over the Swedes, he was eventually able to force them to acknowledge him as king. However, four years later Sten Sture regained his position, and the fighting then continued until the end of Hans' reign. Others, too, would suffer from these events, with Sweden's allies, the Hansa particularly, feeling a negative impact. By hitting the merchants' financial and commercial interests, the conflict further damaged the association's already declining fortunes.

When in 1513, to his followers' regret, Hans died in Ålborg (Aalborg) as a result of a riding accident, he was buried on the island of Fyn at Odense, where he and his wife were later interred in the town's cathedral. Here also on display is Claus Berg's remarkable carved altarpiece that was commissioned by the queen after her husband's death. Considered to be one of Denmark's greatest treasures, this work incorporates various religious scenes, beneath which the artist has included the royal couple, both kneeling alongside their son and his wife. It was this son, Christian II, who was now elected king of the Danes and Norwegians. But as the Swedes were still opposed to the union, the war with their neighbours continued, only ending seven years later after their defeat and Stockholm's surrender. Following his victory, Christian II was at last crowned in the Swedish capital, the occasion being celebrated with three days of feasting. On 7 November 1520, having promised an amnesty, he invited his opposition to a palace banquet where – possibly influenced by the devious Archbishop Trolle – without warning, he had his guests arrested. In the following days over eighty nobles were massacred, beheaded in the Stortorget, the square in the old centre of the town. After this atrocity, the so-called 'Stockholm Bloodbath', and other subsequent acts of butchery that killed hundreds more elsewhere around the country, the Kalmar Union was doomed. The Swedes refused to be ruled by 'Christian the Tyrant', and within three years Gustav Vasa had taken control and become the new king of his independent land. Norway remained loyal to Christian, but it now began to lose its autonomy. With the abolition of its state council, it became a mere territory of Denmark, a lesser status that it would hold for almost 300 years to come.

Earlier, shortly after his father's death, Christian II had approached the Emperor Maximilian I, proposing himself as a suitor for one of the emperor's granddaughters. Within weeks a marriage had been arranged with the younger of the two, Isabella (Elizabeth). Just a day after the twelve-year-old learnt of her betrothal, she was married by proxy in Brussels, her as yet unseen husband being absent at the time, celebrating his coronation in Copenhagen. The lavish ceremony was followed by the symbolic bedding of the young bride with the king's stand-in dressed in his full armour, after which there were further days of extravagant entertainments, including tournaments, balls and banquets. Still very young, Isabella did not leave for Denmark for another year, eventually arriving in her new country in July 1515 after an appalling journey by sea when her life was constantly in danger. Writing after her arrival to her aunt and former guardian, Margaret Duchess of Savoy, she described the 'distress' and 'great peril' she and others had suffered during the ten-day crossing. And sometime later, corresponding with her sister, she further spelled out the cruel reality of the lives of these young women, sent abroad as pawns in the diplomatic game:

> It is hard enough to marry a man whose face you have never seen, whom you do not know or love, and worse still to be required to leave home and kindred, and follow a stranger to the ends of the earth, without even being able to speak his language.[6]

However, when her elaborate official marriage and coronation took place on 12 August, despite her obvious exhaustion, she found herself more fortunate that some, since her husband was said to be young, charming and good-looking, later described by Albrecht Dürer as 'manly and handsome'. Contemporary accounts also speak of Isabella's beauty and sweetness, showing how she was loved by the Danes and all who met her. But, although Christian II was initially pleased with his young wife, he had some years earlier fallen in love with a young Dutch merchant's daughter called Dyveke Sigbritsdatter, whom he had met in the marketplace in Bergen. Enchanted by Dyveke, the king had later brought her and her scheming mother to court, and as their influence grew the queen became more and more sidelined. When news of Christian's behaviour reached the emperor, he was appalled and he wrote in fury to his grandson, the future Charles V. Condemning the Danish king's 'shameful life' with his concubine, he demanded that Charles should reprimand his brother-in-law for the suffering he was causing to his young wife. Christian, who was enraged by these attacks, continued to ignore Isabella and, rather than paying heed to the criticisms, he now closed the Øresund to ships coming from the Imperial Dutch provinces. However, in time his appreciation of Isabella grew, particularly after Dyveke died unexpectedly in 1517, her death rumoured by some to be the result of poison, an act of murder for which an ostensible culprit was found and subsequently executed. Nevertheless, despite her daughter's death, Dyveke's mother would remain for many years more a powerful presence and adviser at court, tolerated as usual by Isabella, but increasingly hated by others. At last she lost the king's favour and, according to some evidence, may eventually have been burned at the stake on a charge of witchcraft. Isabella had by then earned her husband's greater respect and was appointed regent whenever he was absent from Denmark, as on the occasion of his bloody coronation in Stockholm.

Christian was a complex character, loathed by some, but appreciated by others. An intelligent man, he had impressed many of the respected thinkers of the time such as Erasmus, whom he had met while in Brussels. Although modelling himself on other contemporary autocrats, he set out during his reign to introduce reforms to his country, earning the love of the ordinary people. He founded schools and hospitals, tried to improve the condition of the serfs, and imposed greater controls on piracy. But, already reviled by the Swedes for his earlier atrocities, his more liberal measures made him unpopular with the Danish nobles at home, and his tighter customs duties and increased Sound Dues angered the Hansa merchants and other foreign traders. The men of Lübeck particularly distrusted him for the way he had persuaded his brother-in-law, by now Emperor Charles V, to confirm Denmark's claim to their town, basing his argument on ancient rights that dated from the time of the Vikings. Lübeck therefore declared war against the king, and after rebellion had broken out in Jutland, the nobles announced their intention to depose Christian and replace him with his uncle, the Duke of Holstein and Schleswig, the later Frederik I. At this point, Christian, still loved by the ordinary people but threatened from all sides, decided to flee to the Netherlands, hoping to get help from the emperor. Therefore, on 14 April 1523, he left

Copenhagen with his wife and three surviving children. Taking with him his jewels and papers of state, he set off in a small fleet of some twenty ships, only again to be hit by ill luck when his fleet was caught in a storm.

Much of the king and queen's exile was spent travelling around Europe, seeking support for their cause in the hopes of returning to their kingdom in the future. Among other places, soon after their arrival in the Netherlands they visited England, meeting Henry VIII, his wife – Isabella's aunt – Queen Catherine of Aragon, and Cardinal Wolsey. But as time went by, the exiled king would anger his brother-in-law. Infuriated that Charles V would give him no assistance to regain his throne, Christian began attacking and plundering lands in the Low Countries. Isabella always remained loyal to her husband throughout their banishment, refusing to leave him, even when Frederik I offered her a pension and the possibility of returning to Denmark. Insisting that her place was by her husband's side, she declared she would continue to love and support him until the end of her life. Possibly as proof of this, and despite the horror of her Catholic relations at the development, during the period in which Christian leant towards the new religion she converted to Lutheranism. But some would still have doubts as to her true faith when aged twenty-four she died in Ghent in 1526, having been visited on her deathbed by both Catholic and Protestant priests. Finally, centuries later, her remains would be removed to Odense, where they then joined those of her husband.

In this uncertain period at the beginning of the Reformation, Christian II, like many others, wavered before finally deciding which religion to follow. Having studied the teachings of Martin Luther, for a while he favoured the Protestant faith, but then having heard that both Frederik and the Swedish king Gustav Vasa had allowed worship of the new religion in their countries, he reverted back to his earlier Catholicism. This suggests an element of pragmatism on his part, a change of heart that was possibly partly motivated by a desire to appease the pope and appeal to the discontented Danish Catholics, who might now be tempted to help him regain his throne. Still seeking to achieve this, in 1531 he persuaded the Dutch to provide him with the necessary ships and supplies for an invasion, and, although he then lost much of the new fleet in another storm, he succeeded in landing in Norway. But, although here acknowledged by the local people, before long he would be threatened by a combined Danish-Hansa fleet sent to oust him. Already suffering from diminishing reserves, and faced by opposition from those who remained loyal to Frederik, Christian was at last persuaded to surrender to his uncle. But on doing so, despite an earlier promise of safe passage, the deposed king was condemned to life imprisonment and taken to the fortress of Sønderborg. Here for the next fifteen years Christian would remain in the harshest of conditions until eventually he was moved on to better accommodation at Kalundborg Castle. After that, for the rest of his life, he would live in some comfort, even at times having enough freedom to take part in the hunt. A prisoner for a total of twenty-seven years, he would outlive two of his children and both the Danish kings who succeeded him.

While Christian II's only remaining son died the year after his capture, his two daughters survived him by two or three decades. The younger of these, Christine, only seventeen months old at the time of her parents' flight from Denmark, would one day make a stand to recover her father's lands. Widowed aged just thirteen on the death of her husband Francesco Sforza of Milan, she returned to the marriage market, being suggested for a time as the fourth wife of Henry VIII, a proposal that Christine later declared she would have only considered if she had possessed 'two heads'. However, with Henry choosing Anne of Cleves, this suggestion was dropped, and then – in a game of marital musical chairs – she married Anne's rejected fiancé, François, Duke of Lorraine. Again widowed in 1545, Christine refused all further suitors, but following her father's death fourteen years later, she began to assert her right to the Danish throne, styling herself Queen of Denmark, and drawing up schemes to overthrow the incumbent king.

While he was alive, Christian II continued to threaten the stability of the country, something that explains Frederik I's actions following his rival's capture. As so often, family loyalty counted for little when bigger issues were at stake. While, with some justification, Frederik has been accused of having gone back on his word to his nephew, in fact he died at Gottorp Castle just eighteen months later, and so he cannot be held responsible for the long-term fate of his prisoner. And regardless of this, Christian II and his immediate family would present a very real threat to Denmark's security for years to come – something made only too evident soon after Frederik I's death, when civil war broke out over the decision as to who should be his successor. The choice lay between the captive former king or Frederik I's own son, again called Christian, who on the conclusion of the 'Counts' War' became the new king Christian III. After this, all Denmark's future monarchs until the present queen Margrethe II would be called alternately Christian or Frederik. But there would also be another long-term result of Christian III's accession, one caused by his decision after his election to share his inherited family possessions of Schleswig and Holstein with his brothers. In time, the older of these would die without an heir, but his half-brother Adolf received the newly created dukedom of Holstein-Gottorp, the duchy that in future generations would come to play such an important role in Danish, Swedish and Russian history.

Having been influenced by his reformist tutors, and then much impressed on hearing Luther speak in 1521, the future Christian III had decided to break with the Catholic faith of his predecessors. However, following his father's death in 1533, the matter of his conversion became another cause for the civil war breaking out, and so it was only after two years of deep uncertainty and turmoil that he was eventually elected and the coronation took place. With that, Denmark became the first official Lutheran kingdom, and its king, now head of the Church, called for the Bible to be translated into Danish. Although he was sincerely devout, the king intentionally avoided the draconian and highly divisive measures that were the cause of so much violence and unrest abroad. His moderation helped ensure that the reformed religion was introduced peacefully into Denmark. And the break with Rome had further benefited the king. By his confiscation of the Church lands, he had greatly increased the Crown's coffers, adding to the wealth that he was steadily accumulating through his other measures. Being naturally abstemious and careful to avoid unnecessary involvement in war, by the end of his twenty-two-year-long reign, Christian had built up a vast fortune and was able to leave to his son a prosperous country that was enjoying a period of economic and cultural growth.

Despite Christian III's pursuit of peace, when his son Frederik II succeeded in 1559 he was soon faced with new conflicts. Rebellion had now broken out in the Dittsmarche, an area of Schleswig where the peasants had for a long time been threatening the local nobility with their claim to autonomy. While the new king was soon able to put down the uprising, by then Denmark, like most of the Baltic area, was becoming caught up in the war that had broken out following Tsar Ivan IV's invasion of Livonia the year before. Frederik, however, managed to avoid any greater involvement in this conflict by appointing his youngest brother Magnus to the bishopric in Estonia – a fiefdom of the tsar. But despite his aunt having been the first wife of Gustav Vasa, Frederik II proved less successful in his relations with Sweden, and within four years of coming to the throne, in 1563 the two countries were again engaged in conflict. This Northern Seven Years' War proved costly to both sides, and it also created tensions for the king nearer home. Frederik II had never been close to his mother, Dorothea, and he now discovered that she had been secretly trying to arrange the marriage of his brother Magnus to his cousin Sofia, sister of Sweden's new king, Erik XIV. Although in the event Dorothea's plan failed, the enraged Frederik still charged her with treachery. He then banished her for the rest of her life to the island castle of Sønderborg off Jutland, the former prison of Christian II that she and her husband had recently enlarged and renovated. This castle that they created in the Renaissance style no longer remains, having been later altered to the baroque by their descendant Frederik IV, but the new chapel that Dorothea commissioned shortly after her arrest is today the best preserved Lutheran sixteenth-century example of its kind, still having among other things its original font and impressive organ.

Just three and a half weeks after Frederik had come to the throne, the imprisoned former Danish king Christian II finally died, and it was at that point that his daughter Christine, Duchess of Lorraine, began her campaign to try and regain her family's regal position in Denmark. But although in 1561 she revived Christian III's earlier suggestions that Frederik might marry her daughter Renée, when the Northern War broke out two years later, she set her sights on another possible son-in-law, Erik XIV of Sweden. However, despite her offering to raise an army in his support, her proposal was rejected when he chose instead to marry his mistress, and, with Renée soon becoming the wife of Wilhelm of Bavaria, Christine finally gave up her ambitions for the Danish throne.

As Frederik II always wished to re-establish the Kalmar Union, the hard-fought war with his Swedish cousin continued, the situation becoming so difficult for the king in 1570 that for a time he threatened to abdicate. Nonetheless, before the year was over peace had been signed at Stettin, and with the ending of hostilities the Danish king finally accepted that the Kalmar Union was gone forever. But Denmark had now become the dominant country in the region, having since Christian III's accession built up the largest and most modern navy in Europe. And to cover the costs incurred by the war, Frederik boosted his revenue by increasing the Sound Dues, from this time on imposing charges according to the value of the individual cargoes being transported through the Øresund. With international trade having over the years greatly increased, the tolls now enabled him not just to return Denmark to its previously strong financial position, but also to embark on some major new building projects. Besides founding the new town of Fredriksstad in Norway, he ordered the reconstruction of Erik of Pomerania's Helsingør castle of Krogen, from this time renamed Kronborg. This impressive Renaissance-style building at the narrowest point of the Sound would later be made famous by Shakespeare's *Hamlet*, a play that in itself had been adapted from an ancient Danish legend first set down in the twelfth century.

Like Christian III before him, Frederik II wished to maintain the peace of his country, and so he forbade the bitter religious dispute that was disrupting so much of the rest of Europe. Probably dyslexic, he always had difficulty with reading, and he was also less intellectual than his father, but despite these things, he was not unintelligent. So, while his preferred pastimes were hunting and feasting, he also supported the arts and promoted the spread of learning. An elegant, good-looking man, he aimed to create a typical Renaissance court, modelled on those of the great monarchs of Europe. For this reason, in 1580 he reintroduced Christian I's chivalric order of the Mother of God – now renaming it after its symbolic elephant to appease Protestant feelings. This in turn would be reinstituted by his descendant Christian V, and the Order of the Elephant still continues to be the highest decoration in Denmark, awarded only to royalty and other heads of state, among them figures such as Winston

Churchill and presidents Dwight Eisenhower and Nelson Mandela. But Frederik himself would receive foreign honours, including the English Order of the Garter, given to him in 1552 when he became a suitor of the future Queen Elizabeth I. This was one of his many possible marriage alliances that came to nothing, other suggested brides including Eleonore, the daughter of Ferdinand I, the Holy Roman Emperor. This latter proposal might eventually have made Frederik eligible for the Imperial throne itself, and well into the 1580s many considered the king a viable candidate for the position. But Frederik, although apparently more enthusiastic about the lesser option of becoming King of the Romans, showed little interest either in the role of emperor, or in marriage to the Catholic Eleonore. Yet, despite his religious scruples, with the typical pragmatism of the times, Frederik, a true Protestant, did consider the newly widowed Catholic Mary, Queen of Scots, partly attracted to her as she was the rival of Elizabeth, who by now was being courted by his enemy and cousin, Erik XIV of Sweden. As William Herle, one of Elizabeth's advisers, would later describe him, Frederik could be remarkably 'changeable and heady, covetous and busy above measure'.[8] But although betrothal negotiations with Mary, Queen of Scots actually began in Paris, in 1565 they were dropped when she married her second husband, Lord Darnley.

This was not quite the end of Frederik's involvement with the Scottish queen. Within two years, not only had Mary given birth to her son James, but also her husband Darnley had been murdered. Having then married the Protestant earl, James Bothwell, Mary and her new husband were soon suspected of being responsible for Darnley's death. With her popularity now gone, Mary was arrested and soon forced to abdicate in favour of her son. Bothwell, however, had fled the country for Norway, apparently hoping that he might receive Frederik's help.

Having arrived in Bergen, he then had the misfortune to meet Anna Tronds – a woman thought to have been his first abandoned wife. As a result, he was now charged with desertion and subsequently imprisoned in the fortress. Later moved to Malmö, and finally transferred in 1573 to the even more grim Dragsholm Castle in Zealand (Sjaelland), he remained in chains until his death five years later, by which time he had completely lost his mind. Forgotten by the Danish king, whose interests had now moved elsewhere, Bothwell suffered treatment that was excessively brutal even by the standards of the time, for which Frederik II must be held responsible.

Meanwhile, the king remained highly eligible, but having long wanted to marry a lady-in-waiting, who was considered unsuitable, is was not until the 1570s that he agreed to consider an appropriate dynastic marriage for the good of the country. More potential wives were suggested, but Frederik declared that he would not accept anyone without having first seen her. Finally, in 1572 he met his fourteen-year-old first cousin,

Sophie of Mecklenburg-Güstrow from Wismar, who had been brought to Denmark in the retinue of the latest proposed bride. Contrary to what was expected, the latter was now rejected as Frederik immediately became enchanted by Sophie and declared his determination to marry her. Despite their twenty-four-year age difference, after a spectacular wedding in Copenhagen, followed by Sophie's coronation the next day, the marriage proved to be very happy. The king was a faithful husband and devoted father to his eight children. Although his youngest son, Hans, died shortly before his wedding to the daughter of Tsar Boris Godunov, all Frederik's four daughters would in time marry into the ruling houses of Europe.

The first agreement was drawn up between Frederik's second daughter, thirteen-year-old Anne, and James VI of Scotland, who at just ten months old had been taken from his mother, Mary, Queen of Scots, and brought up in the Protestant faith. But before the marriage could be celebrated, in 1588 at the age of fifty-three Frederik died, possibly from lung cancer, although popular rumours suggested his death was the result of his heavy drinking. He and (later) his adored wife would be the last Oldenburgs to be buried in the Chapel of the Magi at Roskilde. Nonetheless, the plans for the wedding went ahead and, after a proxy ceremony at her father's newly built Kronborg Castle, in August the following year the fourteen-year-old Anne set sail for her new country. But once again the voyage was beset by storms, and so after days at sea she had to take shelter in Oslo. The news of this mishap eventually reached James, who was waiting in Scotland, and on learning that Anne would not be making the journey until the following spring, he decided to set off and join her. This involved his crossing to south-west Norway, before embarking on a roughly 250-mile journey overland to Oslo, where another wedding took place. As the couple then spent the next few months in Denmark, visiting the bride's relations at Kronborg, and attending her older sister's wedding in Copenhagen, they did not arrive in Scotland until May 1590, just under a fortnight before Anne was crowned queen at Holyrood.

In 1603, the old English queen Elizabeth died, and with this her relative James VI of Scotland succeeded to his second throne as James I of England. But during his coronation at Westminster, Anne refused to take communion, an action that increased the doubts of those around her as to whether or not she had secret Catholic leanings, a matter of real concern at this time when religious tensions were growing in the country, and would soon make themselves manifest in the Gunpowder Plot. Although initially Anne had been enthusiastic about her engagement, and the king had been pleased when he had first met her, theirs had become a troubled marriage, causing them to spend much of their time apart. Although often dismissed as irrelevant by her critics, like her father Frederik II Anne played a significant role in supporting the arts. She commissioned new buildings such as the Queen's House at Greenwich, promoted an interest in the theatre, and even personally took part in the court plays and masques that she so much enjoyed. Seven years before she died she was devastated by the death of her oldest child, Henry, a victim of typhoid when he was eighteen years old. From then on her own health also declined, and in 1619, aged just forty-four, she died at Hampton Court. Even her husband was saddened by the news, but it was her son, later to be the unfortunate Charles I, who was with her in her last weeks.

While Anne was Queen of Scotland and England, her younger brother Christian IV was ruling in Denmark and Norway. He had been elected as heir to the throne when aged only three, and with his father's early death had succeeded shortly before his eleventh birthday, to be finally crowned in 1596 when he was nineteen. As a result of this early start, his reign would last fifty-nine years, becoming the longest in Danish history. And, despite both his messy private life with its domestic scandals, and his military lack of success, he remains one of the country's most popular kings.

The year after his coronation Christian married Anna Katharina of Brandenburg, who gave birth to seven children, of whom just three survived infancy. But these were not all the children Christian would have, producing altogether more than twenty as a result of his other relationships. However, showing possibly a degree of remorse or sympathy for his wife when she died in 1612, he ordered at her interment that she should be shown full respect, allowed even to take her jewels with her to the grave. Nonetheless, some four years later Christian married his mistress, Kirsten Munk, making her his morganatic wife in a non-church ceremony. Having lost at least two of her first babies, Kirsten went on to have ten or possibly more children, but the last of these the king would refuse to recognise, having by that time become aware that his wife had been unfaithful. With this discovery, Kirsten was disgraced and banished from the court, leaving behind her ambitious mother. The latter, concerned for her own position and that of her grandchildren, may well have been responsible for then finding a replacement for the king among her daughter's former ladies-in-waiting. The new favourite, Vibeke Kruse, would remain the king's mistress until the end of his life, during which time she gave him two further children. She too was a determined character who exerted her strong influence over Christian IV, stirring up tensions between members of his family, with the result that after he died Vibeke's step-children confiscated her estates and threatened her with a court action that she escaped only by her early death.

Like his brother-in-law, James I/VI, who had now set up the Virginia Company for the English colony at Jamestown, Christian IV soon had ambitions for foreign trading stations of his own. In 1602 he created the first of these in Iceland and later issued a charter for the Danish East India Company. Two years after that, in 1618 the company sent ships to India, where despite disasters and a heavy loss of life, in 1620 it opened a settlement at Tranquebar (Danish: Trankebar), today in the region of

Tamil Nadu in the far south. But this venture would be blighted by various problems, ones of location, climate, and competition from the Dutch and the English, so that by the time Christian died nearly three decades later the company was bankrupt. Although it closed soon after, it was later revived in the 1690s, becoming active again during most of the following century, until it was handed over to the British in the 1780s.

Besides these projects, Christian also had three failed expeditions that attempted to re-establish the colony that had been founded by the Vikings on Greenland, and another equally unsuccessful voyage in 1619 to try to find the Northwest Passage.

Despite being forward looking, Christian IV was a man of his times, enjoying rough entertainments such as the brutal games that took place at the Hansa *kontor* in Bergen. Even more difficult for us to understand today, like his brother-in-law James, Christian was obsessed by witchcraft. During this period, referred to as 'the burning times', people – on the whole women – accused of the offence would be summarily put to death in a variety of appalling ways that included drowning and burning at the stake. In line with the superstitions of the time, Christian's sister's failed sea voyage after her wedding was attributed to witchcraft, and Shakespeare would reflect the current concerns by introducing three witches into his play *Macbeth*. This irrational fear would continue on throughout the century, spreading to countries much further afield, including the colonies in the New World, where perceived 'outbreaks' would produce equally savage retribution, such as that which happened at Salem in the 1690s.

Meanwhile at home, tensions continued with Christian's neighbour Sweden, and in 1611 the Kalmar War broke out, but this – lasting just two years – brought no marked change in the situation for either country. However, the king's later decision of 1625 to become embroiled in the Thirty Years' War would prove considerably less anodyne. Although promised support by his nephew the new British king Charles I, Christian entered the war with insufficient forces. This decision had been driven by his wish to prevent Gustavus Adolphus of Sweden taking his place as the champion of the Protestant cause. Although initially successful, the next year at the Battle of Lutter the Danes were crushed by the emperor's army, and in the following months the Imperial troops proceeded to occupy and loot Jutland. More successfully, after agreeing a new alliance, Christian – helped by numbers of Scots – joined forces with the Swedes to raise the enemy's siege of Stralsund. Now Denmark chose to withdraw from the conflict, and for a time it avoided all further military involvement. However, as the years passed, Christian gradually grew more fearful of his Swedish neighbour's ever-increasing power, and with tensions coming to a head, by the end of 1643 the two countries were again militarily engaged, with Jutland soon falling into enemy hands once more. Before this so-called 'Torstenson War' was over, Christian's popularity would receive an unexpected boost after news was spread of his impressive display of courage. Having lost an eye and received more than a dozen other wounds during a naval battle, he had stayed at his post and continued to encourage his men until the fighting was over. But the next year, an exhausted Denmark was forced to make peace, and in the final agreement of 1645 it had to accept terms that were highly favourable to the Swedes. They now gained not just large areas of Danish territory, but also exemption from Denmark's Sound Dues.

Christian IV is most remembered for the new towns that he founded and the buildings that he created. He visited Norway at least some thirty times, for which he was much loved by the Norwegians, and after the wooden city of Oslo burned down in 1624, he rebuilt it on a site close by, renaming it Christiania – the name it would keep until the country had finally gained its independence in the early twentieth century. (Although Norway gained independence in 1905, the name of the capital was not changed until 1 January 1925.) Among Christian IV's projects in Copenhagen, he built a new castle (later demolished), Rosenborg (today the home of the crown jewels), the Old Stock Exchange, the Round Tower, Holmens Church, and the citadel and arsenal. He also contributed to the further embellishment of Roskilde Cathedral, donating – among other things – the pulpit, altarpiece, spires, and entrance. He rebuilt Kronborg at Helsingør after a fire had damaged it in 1629, and also altered Frederiksborg, his father's country castle where he had been born. After more than twenty years of work, Frederiksborg would become the largest Renaissance building of its kind in Scandinavia, but it again had to be largely rebuilt after another fire in 1859. Today, as the Museum of National History, it has among its exhibits some of Christian's personal possessions, not least of all his bed, which – as guides like to point out – although seemingly small for a man of his considerable height, in fact reflects the thinking of the times, a period when lying horizontal was believed to carry the risk of death.

A jovial, good-humoured, and straightforward man who enjoyed living life to the full, his pleasures included music, dancing and hunting. Like his brother-in-law James, he was a heavy drinker and when he visited England in 1606 the two men amazed people by the amount they could hold during festivities that left most of the guests unable to stand. However, his last years would be difficult, made worse by his military failures and Denmark's territorial losses. Moreover, despite having frequently raised the Sound Dues, his country was now seriously in debt, to the extent that even the royal crown had been pawned. And, as if this was not enough, his domestic life had grown still more complicated, troubled by the disputes between his various children from his different relationships. Then, just a year before the old king died, things were made still harder for him with the unexpected death in Saxony of his oldest son, another Christian. From this time his health began to decline and when aged seventy he died in February 1648 at Rosenborg, he was a broken man. He was later buried in the crypt of his new unfinished chapel in Roskilde Cathedral, alongside his first wife, who had died thirty-six years before him. But even here his plans did not go smoothly, as before its completion his monument was destroyed in a fire. The work on the wrought-iron gates had been done, but with Denmark now in financial difficulties, the rest of the chapel remained unfinished and would stay in that condition until the late nineteenth century. Then, at last, the interior was completed with the addition of several wall paintings, among them one showing the blinded, courageous king standing at his post in his naval battle with the Swedes.

Christian IV's son, who was now chosen to succeed him as Frederik III, was a very different character to his father, having a personality that was more withdrawn and self-controlled. The last of Denmark's elected kings, his accession came, not just as a result of his brother's unexpected and recent death, but also through his own calculated measures to overcome his opposition. Well educated and intelligent, as a young man Frederik had been awarded by his father the bishoprics of Bremen and Verden, but at the end of the Thirty Years' War he had been forced to hand these over to Queen Christina of Sweden. In recompense, Christian IV had given his son the duchies of Schleswig and Holstein, but here he fell out with the Danish commander and was soon at odds with the members of the council. With the death of his father, this became a more serious concern as the nobles now threatened to end his hopes of election to Denmark's throne. Therefore, seeking to win their approval, Frederik agreed to their stringent demands and promised new privileges that greatly reduced his own powers.

Before coming to the throne, in 1628 Frederik had married the sister of the future Elector of Hanover, Sophie Amalie of Braunschweig-Lüneburg, a strong, determined woman, who imposed her will on her husband and children.[9] Ignoring the financial difficulties that Frederik III now faced, on his accession she began to indulge her extravagant nature, introducing new French luxuries to the court and enjoying taking part in the many plays and masques. But jealous of the king's step-brothers and sisters, she became particularly vindictive towards the daughter of Christian IV's morganatic wife Kirsten. This young woman, the equally wilful Leonora Christina, had held much sway at court during the last years of her father's reign.

While Christian IV was alive Leonora Christina had been married at thirteen to the thirty-eight-year-old courtier Corfitz Ulfeldt, a devious, corrupt man who in time had made himself unpopular with the old king. And with Ulfeldt's loyalty then coming under suspicion, within three years of Frederik III's accession, Leonora and her husband had fled the country. Before long doubts regarding the latter's character were proved right when, having switched his allegiance to the Swedes, Ulfeldt then helped their king, Karl X, achieve his invasion of Denmark. In time, because of his repeated acts of treachery and changing of alliances, Ulfeldt became distrusted on all sides, and following his imprisonment in Sweden he was locked up with his wife in the Hammershus fortress on the Danish island of Bornholm. After having agreed to exchange their estates for freedom, the couple were released and Ulfeldt fled abroad, narrowly escaping the hangman and leaving his unfortunate wife to face her even worse future alone. Never again seeing her husband but staying loyal to his memory, she would be kept a prisoner in the dungeon of Copenhagen castle for nearly twenty-two years, living in appalling damp and rat-infested squalor. While the vindictive queen, Sophie Amalie, remained alive she resisted any suggestion of Leonora's release, and, although the next king would improve her conditions, he dared not free her until after his mother's death. But in the end Leonora Christina's triumph was greater than that of her unforgiving sister-in-law. By later writing an account of her years of imprisonment, she became a heroic figure, who was famed for her remarkable resilience. She is still admired by many Danish people today.

Frederik III and his wife Sophie Amalie would have eight children, of whom six would survive into adulthood. Many of these later made important dynastic marriages; the husbands of their four daughters included the Elector of Saxony, the Elector of the Palatine, the Duke of Holstein-Gottorp, and the King of Sweden. In addition, the wife chosen for their younger son George was Anne Stuart – great-granddaughter of her Danish namesake – who would later become the British and Irish Queen. Although Louis XIV had suggested George as a candidate for the Polish throne when it became vacant, the latter, a devout Lutheran, had refused the honour on grounds of his religion. However, his faith had made him highly suitable for the Catholic James II's younger Protestant daughter, who at the time was still just third in line to the English-Scottish throne. But, although the subsequent marriage was happy, there would be no surviving children from Anne's seventeen known pregnancies. Apart from multiple miscarriages and stillbirths, two of her infants were victims of smallpox, and her longest surviving child died of fever days after his eleventh birthday. So Anne would be succeeded by the Elector of Hanover, George I, her distant relative, who was also first cousin to her husband. The losses of her children were therefore not just a personal tragedy, but would also be the reason for the future British royal dynasty being Hanoverian, rather than Oldenburg.

Denmark had been spared the greater horrors of the Thirty Years' War, which came to an end the same year as Christian IV's death, but within a decade Frederik III was again in conflict with Sweden. Seeing his enemy embroiled in its war with Poland, in 1657 he decided to try and retake the lands that his father had lost twelve years previously. However, the Swedish king now extricated himself from his Polish campaign and mounted an invasion of Denmark, marching into Jutland and approaching Copenhagen via the islands, an audacious plan that was achieved by the king leading his men across the frozen sea lanes of the Little and Great Belts. Realising that he faced unequal odds, Frederik agreed to surrender to Karl X, and in the subsequent Treaty of Roskilde Denmark was forced to agree to the Swedish king's strict terms. The country now had to give up further large areas of its territory, above all the valuable, productive region of Skåne (Scania) – today the southern tip of Sweden. Among its other losses would be the island of Bornholm and a large central area of Norway around Trondheim, the latter (a Swedish possession for just two years) being of particular significance as it divided the rest of the country in two.

Nonetheless, Frederik wished to meet his former enemy and he invited Karl to visit him at Frederiksborg Castle, where the two men enjoyed three days of lavish entertainment, celebrating the treaty. But within four months of its signing, the Swedish king again attacked Denmark, excusing his actions by claiming that the Danes had not paid their war indemnities. However, Frederik, assuming control of the defence of his capital, immediately ordered all buildings outside the walls to be burned down, and the gates firmly closed, and then for twenty-two months the besieged city came under continued attack. But this was not Frederik's only concern. When another assault was started at Kronborg, he became afraid that he might lose control of the Øresund, and so he ordered the defenders in the last resort to destroy the castle rather than let it fall into Swedish hands. In the event, this command was never carried out as the Swedes managed to persuade the garrison to surrender and, having taken it over, their troops then occupied the country, while Karl's wife took up residence in Kronborg.

At this point the Dutch came to the rescue of the Danes and together their two fleets defeated the enemy in the Battle of the Sound of 1658. Karl X retaliated by attempting another all-out attack on Copenhagen, but this too ended in failure. Now things had begun to go against the Swedish king, with continued opposition from the Danes and the Dutch, and unrest in his recently conquered territories – the people of Bornholm actually killing the new Swedish governor. But for the Swedes, worse was to come as, in early 1660, after catching a chill, Karl X died unexpectedly. So within three months of his death the Treaty of Copenhagen was signed and Denmark was allowed to regain much of its previously lost territory. But while the borders became fixed more or less as they are today, at the time the Danes saw this agreement as unsatisfactory, Skåne (Scania) and its neighbouring areas being excluded from the deal. For Denmark this was a serious loss, finally taking away its total control of the strategic Øresund waterway.

Frederik drew one unexpected benefit from the siege of Copenhagen. During the assault, the king and queen had shown exceptional courage, inspiring the defenders to stand firm during the attack. Having declared that he would rather die like 'a bird in its nest' than surrender to the enemy, Frederik earned the admiration and love of the common people. Using his new-found popularity, he was then able to draw on their support to gain greater control over the all-powerful nobles, who were now forced by the lower Estates of the parliament to agree to a hereditary monarchy with absolute power. The council, or *Rigsråd*, was therefore abolished and five years later, in 1665, the king's divine right was officially enshrined for the first time in a European constitution. Frederik then marked the monarchy's new status by commissioning what he considered to be an appropriate new crown and throne, the latter modelled on that of King Solomon as described in the Bible. Created out of the tusks of narwhals – picturesquely described as 'unicorn horn' – and guarded by three life-sized silver lions ornamented with gold, this is today displayed in Rosenborg Castle in Copenhagen.

Seven years later however, one event would occur to tarnish the king's reputation with some abroad. Recalling the earlier assistance they had given Frederik against the Swedish onslaught, the Dutch appealed to him for help. The British Navy had blockaded the English Channel, preventing the returning Dutch East Indies trading fleet from reaching its home port. And with its having chosen an alternative route around the north of Scotland, it was then pursued by the enemy and obliged to seek temporary refuge in Bergen harbour. But Frederik, forgetting his debt to his former allies, treacherously agreed with the English to expel the Dutch from the port, hoping thereby to receive a share of the precious cargo carried in their merchant ships. However, during the battle that subsequently broke out, the Danish commander of the fort, unaware of Frederik's latest decision, fired on the British and forced them to retreat – an episode commemorated by their cannon ball still embedded in the wall of Bergen Cathedral.

Five years later in 1670, Frederik III died aged sixty in Copenhagen. Although forced by the nobles on his accession to sign a document greatly restricting his powers, through his careful administration, unostentatious manner, and above all courage in the face of danger, he had ultimately won the love of his people. And it was with their support that he had then been able to abolish the limitations originally placed on him and create the absolute monarchy that would survive in Denmark until 1848.

4
Sweden's Vasa Dynasty

Gustav I, 1497–1560, konung av Sverige, by David Frumerie after Jakob Binck (1666). (Courtesy of Nationalmuseum Stockholm)

Three years after the former Danish king of the Kalmar Union, Christian II, had massacred the Swedish nobles in the Stockholm Bloodbath, some 50 miles or so to the west of the capital at Strängnäs, the twenty-seven-year-old Gustav Eriksson was elected king of a now independent Sweden: acclaimed on 6 June 1523 – a date still celebrated as the National Day.[10] The day after this there was a mass of thanksgiving in the cathedral, and then on the 17th, helped by the Hansa of Lübeck, the new monarch finally entered Stockholm. Here after a second celebratory mass in the Storkyrkan, there were public celebrations throughout the city. Although Gustav delayed his coronation until early 1527, by these events he established the dynasty that would rule Sweden for the next 131 years.

Born into the nobility, Gustav I – or Gustav Vasa as he has been more recently labelled – like his father, had supported Sten Sture the Younger, a member of the influential family that for some fifty years had led the country's opposition to its foreign ruler. After being taken hostage in Denmark by Christian II during peace negotiations, Gustav had managed to escape abroad in 1519, fleeing to Lübeck, where he remained for eight months before finally returning home. But unlike others, he had not attended Christian II's coronation in Stockholm, making a decision that saved his life, since he was absent at the time of the subsequent massacre that killed his father, two uncles, a brother-in-law, and so many others. But while his grandmother, mother and three sisters remained imprisoned, he too was at risk, and so he spent the following months evading capture by travelling to and from Norway, a period in his life that has become part of Swedish legend. Stories of his near escapes, like those of so many national heroes, were later embroidered, but still today a famous 90-kilometre ski race involving thousands of competitors commemorates his flight to safety. Eventually, however, the Hansa of Lübeck became angered by Christian's raising of the Sound Dues – a measure that was contrary to an earlier agreement. So, already eager to limit the powers of the Kalmar Union, they decided in 1522 to come to Gustav's aid, twice providing him with a fleet to ensure his eventual victory over the Danes. But there would be one more long-lasting fallout of these events. From this moment, and for centuries to come, the lingering, bitter memories of Sweden's War of Liberation would feed into a savage Danish-Swedish rivalry which, sabotaging the two countries' relations, would repeatedly erupt into warfare.

Even though Gustav I represented a break from the harsh rule of the Danish king, he was himself a complex man with a fierce, unpredictable temper, and he held onto power by imposing his equivalently autocratic, at times brutal, authority. And he further strengthened his position and Sweden's independence by refusing to be cowed by the dictates of the pope. Initially disagreeing with the appointment of the pontiff's chosen archbishop, whom he saw as too pro-Danish, over time his differences with Rome increased and under his rule the country began to move towards the teachings of the Lutheran faith. As this break with the old religion was unpopular in certain quarters, a series of rebellions took place, but these were crushed without mercy by the king. And sensing that three of the Estates – the nobles, burgers and peasants – relied on him for the maintenance of order, Gustav manipulatively threatened them with his abdication, and thus succeeded in persuading them to lessen the powers and privileges of the clergy. Less devout than his successors, like his contemporary, Henry VIII, Gustav I largely embraced the Reformation for pragmatic reasons. Not only did it allow him to assert greater control over the state, but it also enabled him to buy the loyalty of his potentially unreliable nobles – winning their backing by granting them lands previously confiscated from the Church. But even though in 1541 he ordered the publication of a new Bible, giving the Swedes for the first time the whole text written in their own language, for some years to come the king continued to allow the question of individual religious adherence to remain fluid, and the establishment of the official Evangelical Lutheran Swedish Church did not take place until thirty-three years after his death.

Among the various brides now suggested for Gustav, his preferred choice was the Polish princess Jadwiga Jagiellon, but she rejected his proposal on religious grounds.[11] So on 24 September 1531, after lengthy negotiations, he married Katharina of Saxe-Lauenburg, who, in addition to her other influential relationships, was sister-in-law to the future Danish king, Christian III – family connections that Gustav hoped might bolster his position on the throne. But the wedding ceremony and subsequent coronation of Katharina would also be highly significant for another reason. Performed according to the new rites, with the king's very recently appointed Lutheran archbishop officiating, these ceremonies would mark the start of Sweden's progress towards becoming an official Protestant state. However, having given birth to a son, Erik, in 1533, just two years later, after what was reported to be a difficult marriage, Katharina died from an accident while she was again pregnant. Soon rumours were rife that the notoriously hot-headed king was responsible for his wife's death, stories spread by Gustav's enemies who claimed that he had hit her with a hammer or axe in a rage. Many incidences of his violent behaviour are documented, but physical evidence of this particular charge was found to be missing when her grave was later opened in the twentieth century. Whatever the truth, Gustav now selected as his next wife a Swedish nobleman's daughter, Margareta Leijonhufvud. During their reputedly happy marriage, she gave the king ten children, but her many pregnancies would in time undermine her health. So within eleven months of the birth of her last child, Karl, in August 1551, having contracted pneumonia, she died aged thirty-five.

As seven years before Margareta's death the king had managed to persuade the Council of State to grant hereditary rights to his dynasty, he now crafted an intentionally elaborate funeral, intended to emphasise the more elevated status of himself and his royal wife. With Margareta having died at Strängnäs, he initially considered its cathedral for her interment, but then chose the Storkykan in Stockholm, where sixteen years earlier her predecessor had been laid to rest in the choir. After Katharina's remains had been dressed in new robes, she was then moved to join Margareta in the sacristy, and here both women would stay for the next nine years. During this period, Gustav was planning his own royal burial site, having selected the cathedral in Uppsala, a place already revered for housing the relics of the twelfth-century Gothic king 'Erik the Saint'. Meanwhile, however, just a year after Margareta's death the fifty-six-year-old king married for a third time, on this occasion choosing for his wife Margareta's sixteen-year-old niece Katarina Stenbock. Katarina would remain childless during her eight years of marriage, but she would go on to act as a mediating influence during the troubled reigns of her stepsons. When, eventually, she died at the tremendous age of eighty-six, she was buried near her husband in the chapel at Uppsala.[12]

Apart from the repeated rebellions at home, Gustav I was little involved with troubles abroad, just experiencing towards the end of his reign minor skirmishes in a brief three-year conflict with the Russians in Ingria, a precursor to the later Livonian War. His only other engagement was during Denmark's civil war in the 1530s, when he specifically opposed Lübeck, which was now supporting the ousted Christian II. Although this city had earlier backed Gustav's own ambitions to the Swedish throne, by this time the good relations had broken down between the two parties, largely because the king had been angered by Lübeck's continued, and he thought exorbitant, demands for repayment of the debt he had incurred during the coup. However, now his chief concern was to introduce a more centralised government, a task in which he was helped by the nobles. But while the latter's power had been increased, the king had also reduced the size of their estates. This he had done in order to redistribute those same lands to the peasants, who – unlike the nobles – could then be taxed on their possessions. Through this and other practical policies, Gustav increased the Crown's revenue, so that by the end of his reign he was one of the richest monarchs in Europe, able to leave a country that was economically stronger and more united. Moreover, by having created a first, fledgling professional army to protect his own position, he had set Sweden on the path to a military greatness that over time would enable it to dominate the region for more than a century.

When after thirty-seven years on the throne Gustav I finally died in September 1560, once again the country faced instability. Anxious to prevent any unrest and ensure an uninterrupted succession, Gustav's son, Erik, began to prepare for the most impressive funeral ever yet seen in Sweden. Influenced by the teachings of his former humanist tutor, the new king copied the foreign rituals and displays adopted elsewhere. In a late echo of how the medieval world had imbued symbolism with spiritual significance, Erik now ordered a lifelike wax effigy of his fully dressed and crowned father to be placed on the top of his coffin. Although evidence is lacking to show that Sweden adhered to the earlier doctrine, that of 'the king's two bodies', the message Erik was seeking to convey was the same, namely that the diseased monarch remained spiritually present, and that royal power was unbroken.[13] But that was not all. In another symbolic move, Erik ordered that his mother's remains be reclothed again, this time adorned with a silver-gilt crown, sceptre and yet more elaborate robes – funerary rites that now fell to her stepson, Johan. Erik wished Katharina's particularly regal trappings to mark the superiority of her royal descent over that of the merely noble-born Margareta, who, although similarly re-dressed, was given somewhat lesser finery than that of her predecessor. Despite these preparations remaining unseen by the public, they transmitted the new king's subtle message to his half-brother, someone whose very presence could challenge his place on the throne – a threat that one day would become a reality. After the eight weeks of Gustav's official lying in state, an equally important display was laid on for the people at large. For two days the cortège bearing the three coffins, topped by their crowned effigies, slowly processed to Uppsala Cathedral, the recently appointed royal mausoleum. Here in the Lady Chapel behind the high altar Gustav I's body, dressed in his ornate robes, was finally interred beside the remains of his first two wives. The three wax effigies on top of their shared sarcophagus would remain in situ until they were replaced just over two decades later by the marble copies on view today. Since the opening of their tombs in 1945, visitors have also been able to see in the cathedral's museum the funerary crowns, sceptres and other regalia that had been purposely made to accompany them to the grave.

So with Gustav I Vasa having in 1544 taken the bold step and declared the monarchy to be hereditary, he was now succeeded by his twenty-six-year-old son, Erik XIV, who chose to number himself according to a mythical claim of thirteen previous rulers with the same name – the last being none other than Erik the Saint. An intelligent, well-educated and extremely talented man, with a good knowledge of languages, Erik – like his Danish cousin – was one of the various suitors of the Tudor Princess Elizabeth, but his proposal had been rejected on the orders of her sister, Queen Mary. However, nothing daunted, after the accession of both Elizabeth and himself to their separate thrones, Erik continued to press his suit. But eventually, as he began to accept the hopelessness of his case, he – again like Frederik II of Denmark – shifted his attention to Elizabeth's cousin, Mary, Queen of Scots. Like his other various proposals, this venture met with an equal lack of success.

During the Livonian War that had now broken out with Russia, unrest began to develop in the Danish-owned Duchy of Estonia, and the year after his accession Erik used the opportunity to send his troops to the region. Reval (Tallinn) now surrendered to the Swedes, beginning a period that would be remembered as 'the good old Swedish times'. However, this action would bring Erik into direct conflict with his recently crowned Danish cousin, and two years later they found themselves at war when their fleets engaged in action near the island of Bornholm. Erik also had other projects in mind and in his eagerness for new territory he soon began to set his sights on the Polish-owned part of Livonia, an ambition that caused him to be at odds, not just with Poland's King

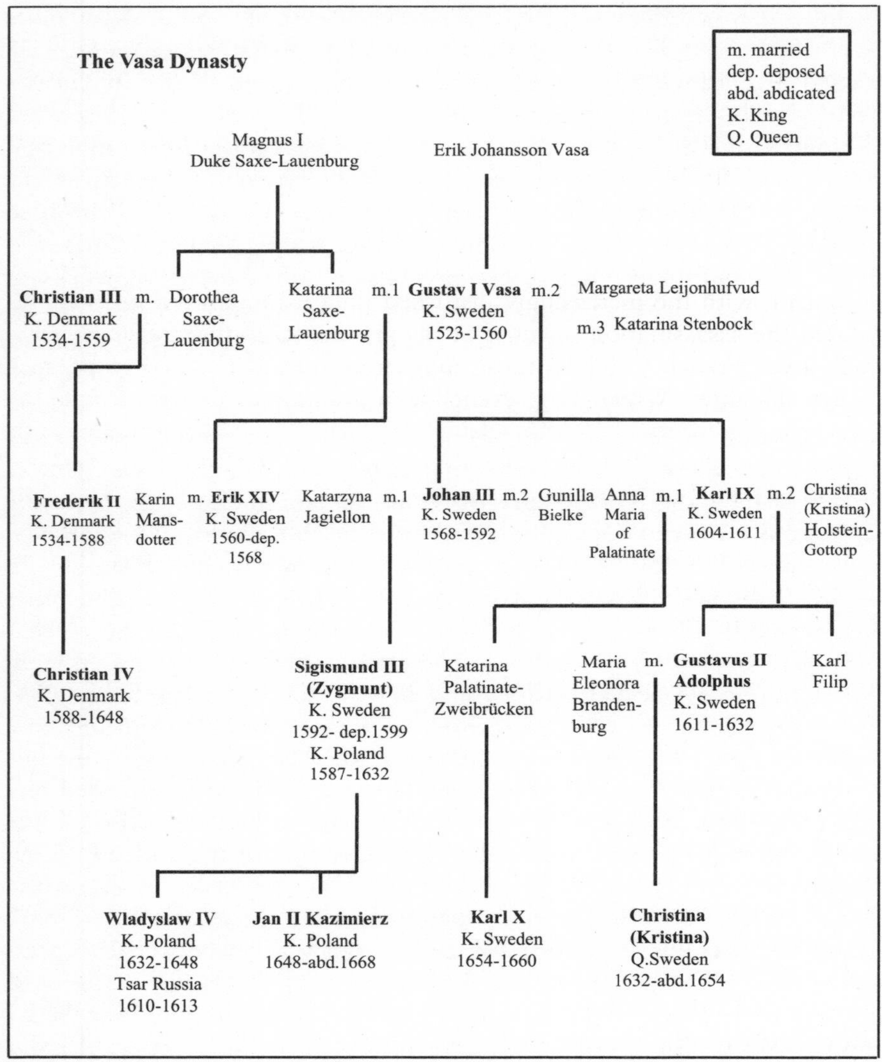

Zygmunt II, but also with his own brother Johan. The latter had by now married Zygmunt's sister, Katarzyna Jagiellon – ironically the half-sister of Jadwiga who had rejected Gustav I years before. Erik, a combative man with impractical ambitions, had from the time of his accession been showing signs of a mental disorder, a problem that would in time also affect his younger brother Magnus. In August 1563 the rivalry came to a head, when, suspected of treachery, Johan was arrested and imprisoned with his wife for the next four years.

Meanwhile, in the confused political game of the period, with the Livonian and Northern Seven Years' Wars both now in progress, Sweden found itself fighting on several fronts, at various times opposed by Denmark-Norway, Lübeck, the Polish-Lithuanian Commonwealth, and Russia. However, in 1567 – a year that Erik himself referred to as his *infelicissimus annus* – events still more damaging to his reputation began to take over. Tensions started to build up between the king and the famous Sture nobles and, now growing increasingly paranoid and fearful of opposition, Erik ordered several members of the family and their followers to be thrown into prison. Later in May, at a moment of serious mental imbalance during an argument, he stabbed Nils Sture, who was then killed outright by one of the guards. The situation began to escalate out of control, with the increasingly disturbed king losing all reason. Having ordered the assassination of most of his prisoners, he then turned on his much-loved French Calvinist tutor, murdering him as he tried to prevent further slaughter. While these events would continue to haunt Erik for some time, he eventually became calmer with the help of his attendants, in particular his mistress, a former servant girl, Karin Månsdotter.

At this point Erik decided to make Karin his morganatic wife, but then, to the horror of the nobility and his family, in July the next year he arranged another official marriage. This was followed the day after by her elaborate coronation, an occasion when their two, now legitimised, children were present. By this time the king's sanity was seriously deteriorating and although his brother had been released from his long imprisonment, there was further evidence of the king's weakening grasp on reality when, on meeting his freed sibling, Erik knelt before him in reverence, believing himself the prisoner and Johan the monarch. But worse was to come as Erik, by this time allied to Ivan IV 'the Terrible', then concurred with the latter's demand that Johan should divorce Katarzyna, to leave her free for the tsar – a suitor whom, as it happened, she had rejected years before. While Ivan's real purpose might in fact have been merely to use her as a hostage to put pressure on her brother the Polish king, unsurprisingly Johan, like his wife, was appalled by this proposal. Now seriously concerned about his brother's mental state, in 1568 he and other members of the nobility finally mounted a rebellion that ended with the capture of Stockholm.

Thereafter, Johan was declared the new king, while Erik – now pronounced unfit to rule – was kept prisoner for the next eight years in a variety of castles. Initially his wife was allowed to be with him, but after Karin had been delivered of two more children while in captivity, both of whom died in infancy, to prevent the birth of further potential heirs Erik was forcibly separated from his whole family. From this time on, he continued to endure his incarceration alone, suffering increasingly harsh conditions and, on occasion, even being subjected to the most savage treatment by his guards. He finally died in 1577. As verified by recent forensic research, the cause of death was arsenic poisoning, thus raising the probability that he was murdered according to the wishes of his brother. Support is given to this theory by the fact that Johan had earlier issued an order that, were an attempt made to release him, he should be killed rather than be allowed to escape.

By this time Karin's son had been sent abroad to escape the dangers that might face him from his uncle the new king, but his future would be little better than that of his father. Having been reduced to poverty and undergone a period as a prisoner of the tsar – the First False Dmitry – he finally died in Russia just short of his fortieth birthday. However, his sister, who remained in court circles, was luckier. Twice married to noblemen, she lived on into her late sixties. As for their mother, Karin, after her widowhood she was given an estate in Finland, where, having become popular with the local people, she eventually died and was buried in the cathedral in Åbo (Turku) in 1612.

Erik had reformed the army and greatly improved the navy, and so, within months of seizing the throne, Johan III was able to bring his war with Denmark to a close. Nonetheless, the Livonian War continued to grind on until 1583, when peace was finally achieved, mainly as a result of the military skills of the Polish king Stefan Batory. By joining forces with Batory's elite Polish troops, Johan had been able to share in the great victory over the Russians at Wenden in 1578, a battle that would be the forerunner of the series of successes that culminated three years later with the capture of Narva – a triumph that was then stained by the Swedes' brutal massacre of most of the citizens. After the war ended Ivan IV was forced to accept the treaty's harsh terms, but although these favoured his enemies, the relations between the Polish-Lithuanian Commonwealth and Sweden had also now come under strain. Batory felt that Johan had not acknowledged the important role that he had played in the tsar's defeat, and for a time the two kings' disagreements threatened to intensify to a dangerous level. However, eventually tempers cooled, the situation partly eased by the intervention of the men's wives, Anna and her sister Katarzyna. Katarzyna was particularly close to her husband Johan; after their initial incarceration in Åbo Castle she had chosen to share his further imprisonment at Gripsholm. It was here in 1566 that she had given birth to a son – christened Sigismund after his Polish grandfather. As Johan was much attached to his devout wife, he had then accepted her wishes that this child should be brought up in her own Catholic faith. Unwittingly, by this act of kindness Johan had prepared the ground for the many troubles that lay ahead. Sigismund's deep religious conviction would later be the cause not just of civil war at home, but also years of bitter conflict abroad.

Outside Stockholm Johan III bought for his beloved wife a palace called Torvesund, which was then renamed in her honour 'the Queen's Islet', Drottningholm. Although later rebuilt and for a time abandoned in the nineteenth and twentieth centuries, since its restoration this has become the chosen home of the present Swedish royal family, and today it is also one of the capital's primary tourist attractions. While Katarzyna was alive, Johan III continued to be much influenced by her, and as a result he treated the Catholics with tolerance, even – to the anxiety of the committed Protestants – introducing some changes to the Lutheran forms of worship. But twenty-one years after their marriage, in 1583 Katarzyna died, and eighteen months later Johan remarried. He now took as his new wife Gunilla Bielke, a devout Protestant noblewoman who not only encouraged the king's support of the new faith, but also brought up their one son as a Lutheran. However, despite Gunilla always being ready to interfere in Johan's affairs, as she was not of royal birth, she was treated with disdain by the rest of his family, something that particularly displeased her husband as his own mother, Margareta Leijonhufvud, had been of a similar background. Nonetheless, although still unpopular when the king died in 1592, Gunilla was allowed to continue living on comfortably, provided for by her husband's generous endowment and pension. And in time she too would be buried beside Johan and his first wife in the royal crypt at Uppsala.

Following Johan III's death, his older son by Katarzyna succeeded to the throne, having already been elected the Polish king Sigismund (Zygmunt) III in 1587. But the new king's strict adherence to the Catholic religion immediately raised tensions in the now officially Lutheran Sweden, where many feared his obvious ambition to restore the former faith. However, by agreeing to keep Catholics debarred from high office, the arguments over the Swedes' freedom of worship were eventually resolved. Nonetheless, Sigismund still faced other problems, first having to deal with the nobles' continuing demands for greater rights, and second confronting the political manoeuvring of his devout Protestant uncle, Karl – the regent during the long periods that the king was absent abroad. As Karl's nephew continued to rule from Poland, the situation grew increasingly tense until, five years after Sigismund's accession as the Swedish king, civil war broke out in the country. Determined to regain control, Sigismund marched into Sweden with his Polish troops, but after meeting the rebels in battle at Stångebro in Linköping in September 1598, his army was crushed and he himself was captured. Following his defeat, many of his followers were executed in the so-called Åbo and Linköping Bloodbaths, one of the victims being a royal relation, Johan Fleming, whom Karl had personally chosen for execution. This act of spite was in punishment for the determined opposition shown by Fleming's mother (the sister of the dowager queen Katarina Stenbock), who, unwavering in her support for the king, had courageously attempted to defend Åbo Castle when it was besieged by Karl's army – further evidence of the complicated family loyalties of this time. The next year Sigismund was finally deposed, and with his ten-year-old half-brother, Gunilla's son, having also renounced his claim, Karl became Sweden's acting ruler. At last, five years later he was officially acclaimed as Karl IX, choosing, like his brother Erik before him, to use a fictional number based on legendary records – in his case ones that linked him to the rebellious nobleman Karl Knutsson of the fifteenth century. From then on, during his seven-year-long reign, Karl IX would impose his efficient but brutal control. However, his seizure of the throne would have a more long-lasting significance, as the savage dispute that had now begun between the Vasas in Sweden and Poland would last until 1660, the year that the Polish king finally renounced his claim to the Swedish crown.

Previously, in 1589, after ten years of marriage, Karl's first wife, Anna Maria of the Palatinate, had died. By then she had given birth to six children, but as only one daughter had survived infancy, Karl soon decided to look for a new wife. He chose Christine, the daughter of the Duke of Holstein-Gottorp, a young woman who had in fact once been suggested as a bride for his ousted nephew, King Sigismund. After the early death of her first child, in 1594 Christine gave birth to a son, Gustav Adolf – the future internationally famous Gustavus Adolphus – who was then followed by a sister and brother.

In 1607, three years after her husband's acclamation, Karl and his wife were both finally crowned at Uppsala, the king having intentionally delayed his coronation in the aftermath of his coup in order to give his new position legality and make himself appear the rightful *elected* – rather than hereditary – king. During his reign, Christine (now known as Queen Kristina) would play a significant role at court. A strong, forceful woman, she would also act as regent whenever her husband was out of the country. Karl was constantly engaged in war with his neighbours, in Poland fighting against his nephew Sigismund, in Russia allying himself with the embattled tsar, and later engaging in a territorial dispute with the still-powerful Denmark. Although his army had now lapsed back to its former ill-trained self, Karl chose to come to the aid of Tsar Vasily, who was under threat from the latest pretender to the Russian throne, the Second False Dmitry. The next year, in June 1610, the Swedes and Russians were defeated by the Poles at Klushino, and within a month Vasily had been deposed. However, in 1611, after the Swedes had captured Novgorod, the inhabitants of the city suggested Karl's younger son, Karl Filip, to be their future tsar, a position already turned down by his older brother, Gustavus Adolphus. But Karl Filip never succeeded, partly because the situation had changed in the city, and also because his mother, in her unwillingness to be separated from her favourite child, had prevented his attendance when the election had taken place.

By the end of the same year, however, the status quo at home had also changed. Karl IX, having already been incapacitated by a stroke the year before, died in October, thus bringing to an end a reign that had been marred by plots and unrest. Although he had not wished to increase the *Riksdag*'s powers, he had granted it a greater role, thereby hoping to distance himself from policies that might make him unpopular.

Nonetheless, he had been disliked, if not hated, by large numbers of his people. Unloved by many of the nobility – being particularly loathed by those whose rebellious relations had suffered the king's violent butchery at Linköping – he had also been at odds with the Church, who suspected him of pro-Calvinist leanings.

In an effort to silence some of his opposition, Karl had therefore repeatedly (like his father) threatened to abdicate, knowing that this would leave his country in an even more unstable position. Although at times, when the policy had served him, he had earned the peasants' support by championing their cause, he had nonetheless been widely reviled for his mistaken foreign policies that had needlessly taken Sweden to war. With his stubbornness, intransigence, and violent Vasa temper, he had never won the affection of his people, and as a result there was little general regret at his death.

Now, in a break from the traditions of his father and brother Johan, and according to his personal wishes, he was buried at Strängnäs, in the cathedral where his father had first been acclaimed seventy-seven years earlier. With his heir, Gustavus Adolphus, still under age, for a time the young king's mother acted as regent, and even after he reached majority a few months later, she continued to advise him. It was on her insistence that a few years later he gave up the idea of marrying a nobleman's daughter, his much-loved Ebba Brahe, whom the dowager queen considered too low-born. Kristina would outlive three of her four children, but in 1625 she died aged fifty-two, and so she would never see the success and lasting fame that her son Gustavus Adolphus eventually achieved.

When the sixteen-year-old succeeded in 1611, he inherited his father's two ongoing conflicts, and his reign, like that of Karl IX, would be marked by almost constant fighting. Although Gustavus Adolphus' first 'Kalmar War' against the Danes was ultimately unsuccessful, it proved to be a useful learning experience for the young king, who, having invaded Skåne (Scania) without adequate preparation, was soon defeated. He was then forced to withdraw from the region, but not before he had nearly drowned after his horse had fallen through the ice during a cavalry charge over a frozen lake. Although this war was over within two years, it would be the first of the series of conflicts that would engage the two countries for most of the century.

The recently begun Ingrian War with Russia would last for another six years, ending finally with a peace that was highly favourable to Sweden. It now acquired Karelia and Ingria, including the strategic fortress of Nöteborg on Lake Ladoga that lies to the east of what is today St Petersburg – strategic gains for Sweden, but losses that were disastrous for Russia. Having renounced all claims to Estonia and Livonia, the tsar now found himself with a country that was cut off from the Baltic, and it was this situation that nearly a century later would drive the future Peter the Great's determination to declare war on Gustavus Adolphus' successor.

At this point the king's domestic life became more complicated. Having resigned himself to losing his adored Ebba Brahe as a bride, in 1617 Gustavus Adolphus visited Berlin incognito in order to meet Maria Eleonora, the daughter of the Elector of Brandenburg, who was a vassal of the Polish king. Despite initial opposition by her mother, the electress, who was against an alliance with Poland's enemy, Gustavus Adolphus used his charm to win her over and although Maria Eleonora's brother remained opposed, the marriage took place in Stockholm in November 1620.[a] However, the young queen was dismayed by the backwardness of her new country, and her blatant disdain for it did nothing to endear her to the Swedish people.

Already a mentally fragile woman, she would now suffer a series of far more bitter setbacks that would further undermine her state of mind. The year after her marriage, while Gustavus Adolphus was away campaigning near Riga, Maria Eleonora's first child was delivered stillborn. This loss was then followed by two others: first in 1624 a second daughter, who died within a few months of her birth, and then a son who was again delivered stillborn in May the following year.

Now, with his younger brother Karl Filip having been killed in battle, Gustavus Adolphus began to fear that the Swedish crown might revert to his ousted Catholic cousin and bitter rival, Sigismund III of Poland. To add to these concerns, the queen, although increasingly devoted to her husband, was beginning to display clearly unbalanced behaviour. She coped particularly badly with his absences, and her strange speech and writing even suggested that she might have suffered a stroke. Under these pressures, Gustavus Adolphus grew increasingly concerned and, although he had fathered a son, Gustav Gustavsson, by his Dutch mistress, he started to fear for the succession. But he continued to treat his wife with consideration, sometimes even taking her with him when he went abroad. It was most probably during one of these journeys that she conceived once more, finally giving birth in December 1626 to a healthy child. However, for whatever reason – the darkness of the room, the possibly unusual complications of the birth, or (as some suggest with doubtful evidence) the child's uncommon physical condition – those in attendance declared it to be a boy, only later to realise their mistake. While she herself would one day put this down to the fact of her having had a lot of hair and a lusty voice, the real cause may have been that she was born with the rare, but not serious, condition of a covering caul, or membrane. But now nervously wanting to correct the announcement, her aunt presented the naked child to Gustavus Adolphus, who was himself suffering from a fever at the time. He was said to have received the truth calmly, and his easy and immediate acceptance that the infant presented

a Maria Eleonora's mother, Electress Anna, was the daughter of Albrecht Friedrich, Duke of Prussia, and it was her marriage to Johann Sigismund of Brandenburg that first brought the two regions together. (*See* Chapter 11) to him was female undermines the often repeated suggestions that she was a hermaphrodite. In contrast to her husband, the queen, when she was eventually told of the mistake, became inconsolable. Nonetheless, the baby's baptism took place soon after and, like her older dead sister, she was christened Kristina Augusta (hereafter referred to as Christina). Her mother showed little love for her at this time, declaring her to be ugly, but Gustavus Adolphus became deeply attached to his daughter, joking about how she had tricked them all at her birth, and predicting that she would grow up to be clever.

Meanwhile, Gustavus Adolphus' campaigning had continued. Wanting to increase his country's security and to protect its trade, he had set out to conquer the lands surrounding the Baltic, his aim being to turn the sea into a virtual Swedish lake. In 1621, after a two-and-a-half-week-long siege, he took Riga, a city that at the time had a population twice the size of Stockholm. Two years later he also blockaded Danzig, forcing it to reject King Sigismund's demands for the citizens to provide him with a fleet with which he might regain his Swedish throne. After this, Gustavus Adolphus had further successes, in 1625 landing again at Riga and taking the Livonian town of Dorpat (Tartu), before capturing Courland the next year – victories that ensured his total control of the region around the Daugava (Düna)) River. Having achieved these objectives, he went back home on one of his frequent visits to attend to state business and see his wife, but by 1627 he had returned to the war and was once more besieging Danzig. But, while his early successes in the Baltic region had been helped by the neutrality of his brother-in-law, the Elector of Brandenburg – who at the time had allowed him access to Poland through his lands in Ducal Prussia – after a Swedish defeat the elector had reluctantly renounced his former neutrality and allied himself with Sigismund. The latter had at last received the *Sejm*'s permission to go to war, and the Polish army was now ready to engage in battle. Then in August the Swedes suffered a major setback, being forced to withdraw after Gustavus Adolphus was wounded at Dirschau (Tczew). His injuries on this occasion were so severe that for several weeks there were serious doubts that he would survive. And although three months later he had recovered sufficiently to be back in action, the Poles then roundly defeated the Swedish fleet that was blockading Danzig. The town, meanwhile, continued to hold out against the repeated assaults, also achieving – to Gustavus Adolphus' fury – its own small victory. Enraged, the king angrily questioned how 'a pacific, commercial rabble should beat a set of illustrious fellows, who made fighting their profession'.[14]

These battles, together with various storms, had caused Gustavus Adolphus to lose over a dozen of his ships, and so he now ordered several replacements to be built. His new flagship, named after the family dynasty, was launched in 1627, and on 10 August the following year, while the king was still in Poland, she set out on her maiden voyage. Local people and foreign dignitaries crowded around the Stockholm harbour to watch her set sail, but within minutes, caught by a crosswind, she began to keel over. Mistakenly designed with excess weight above the waterline, the ship's instability had been increased by two tiers of large cannons and much weighty oak ornamentation. With the top-heavy *Vasa* unable to right itself, water now began to rush in through the gun ports that had been left open ready for firing the celebratory salvoes.

Within minutes less than 400 feet from the shore the ship sank and around thirty of the crew were drowned. Gustavus Adolphus was shocked when he received the news, but no one was punished for the disaster, although the king immediately ordered alterations to be carried out on his other ships. Later efforts were made to recover the *Vasa*, now sunk into the mud of the harbour, but all attempts failed until it was finally achieved in 1961, since when the ship has become one of Stockholm's chief tourist attractions.

The struggle for control of Poland's Baltic region carried on with the last battle finally taking place in June 1629, one of the most fiercely fought engagements of the war that with typical understatement Gustavus Adolphus later described as his hottest 'bath'. The Battle of Trzciana, around 40 miles south-east of Danzig, would result in fewer losses to the Poles than to the Swedes, but in the truce that followed soon after, the king gained advantageous terms that gave him Elbing (Elbląg), and left him in control of the greater part of Livonia, where he held, among others, the important cities of Riga and for a time Memel (Klaipėda). Here, as at home, he then began to introduce reforms that included the opening of schools and the founding of a university at Dorpat, changes that would help bring a period of growth and prosperity to the area. But more significantly for Gustavus Adolphus, the truce allowed him at last to turn his attention towards the even larger conflict of the Thirty Years' War that was now at its height in central Europe.

The year before, the Emperor Ferdinand II had appointed Count Wallenstein Generalissimo of the Baltic and Open Seas, hoping that the count might be able to control the maritime trade of his rebellious Dutch subjects. Wallenstein had captured Jutland from the Danes and set up his headquarters in Wismar in Mecklenburg, a town that would now remain under Imperial control for three years. These events had caused Gustavus Adolphus to become gravely concerned for the security of Sweden, and so, free at last to redeploy his small army, he decided to invade Pomerania. This decision had the added advantage of allowing him to re-engage his many mercenaries, thus delaying the payment that they expected on their dismissal. But at this point the emperor made a costly mistake, replacing Wallenstein with Count Tilly, an action that caused the former's well-paid troops to desert the field. As a result, when the Swedish and Imperial armies met at Breitenfeld near Leipzig in September 1631, Gustavus Adolphus was able to achieve a resounding victory.

Although purporting to be fought in the name of religion, the fighting of the Thirty Years' War was in fact based on more pragmatic, political motivations, with allies of different creeds on occasion fighting together against a shared enemy, such as when Lutheran Sweden joined forces with Catholic France against the equally Catholic Habsburg Empire. Cardinal Richelieu went so far as to describe Gustavus Adolphus as 'the rising sun', who promised to wipe out Louis XIII's great rival. But the protagonists would continue to give loftier reasons to their actions and the Swedish king declared to the *Riksdag* that he was fighting for 'house and home [...] Fatherland and Faith'.[15] Thus, dubbed 'the Lion of the North', he became seen as the champion of the Protestant cause. After Breitenfeld, with his now vast army, comprising a majority of foreign mercenaries, Gustavus Adolphus continued his campaigning, heading further south into the empire. But having reached Bavaria, where he demanded ransom from Munich, his fortunes then began to change. Unable at Alte Veste to get past the now reinstated Wallenstein, for a period he rested in the nearby Nürnberg (Nuremberg), where he spent time drawing up plans to replace the Catholic Habsburg Empire with a new Protestant association that, despite denials, most believed he was hoping to lead.

However, now misfortune really began to set in for the Swedes, when on 6/16 November 1632 at Lützen, again near Leipzig, the king once more met Wallenstein in battle. As usual wearing light protective clothing – having, after his earlier injuries, found it difficult to wear full armour – during a cavalry charge Gustavus Adolphus became separated from his immediate followers and suffering from multiple wounds he fell to the ground, where he was killed by the enemy. Although, after a day of heavy fighting with high casualty numbers on both sides, the battle itself ended with the withdrawal of the Imperial troops, for the Swedes it was a hollow victory. Eventually, with their having discovered the dead king lying stripped and mutilated on the battlefield, his embalmed body was taken back to Sweden, where it was received by his grieving widow. Having become still more unbalanced, Maria Eleonora now refused to have her husband buried for more than a year, until, at last, she was persuaded to hand his remains over to the authorities and the funeral was finally able to take place in the Riddarholm Church in Stockholm in June 1634. Gustavus Adolphus' battledress, a thick buff coat that had been taken as booty back to the emperor, was eventually returned to Sweden in 1920, and today it is displayed in the Livrustkammaren, the Armoury Museum under the Royal Palace, here taking a central position beside the model of the king's horse that was later created using the animal's original hide.

Gustavus Adolphus' death was a major setback for the Protestant cause in Europe, whose fortunes now began to decline during the remaining sixteen years of the Thirty Years' War. Alongside his general reputation for military success, the king had become famous throughout Europe for the improvements he had made to his previously badly trained army, bringing in new tactics and better military discipline. For centuries to come he would be seen as an example to famous generals, and to mark his achievements, the year after his death the *Riksdag* granted him the posthumous title 'the Great'.[b] Immensely brave, he had always insisted on leading his men from the front, often putting himself in unnecessary danger and frequently being wounded as a result. But, while this had earned him the loyalty and devotion of his men, it had, with good reason, gravely concerned his ministers, who rightly feared that it could lead to his early death.

At the beginning of his military career, like most of his contemporaries, he had allowed his troops to sack and plunder their enemies' lands, with the result that after his early war with the Danes his reputation in Skåne would be damaged forever. However, although looting was rife in this period, to make it more acceptable Gustavus Adolphus had later begun to order inventories of seized goods to be drawn up, justifying their confiscation on the grounds of a need to provision his army. Believing that the war should pay for itself, he expected his troops to be maintained and provided for by the countries that they occupied. But understanding the negative impact on later remunerations of uncontrolled looting, he began to forbid its practice by his soldiers, replacing it with a more regulated sharing out of the spoils. In 1621, in order to ensure fairness and discipline in his ranks, he had first set out a code of behaviour for officers and men that, among other things, banned pillaging and rape. As a result, in his later campaigns his army's arrival in the already devastated regions was viewed with rather more relief than that of some others.[c]

In Sweden itself the king's death was seen as an even greater disaster than it was among his allies abroad. Here, helped by his able minister and close friend Axel Oxenstierna, Gustavus Adolphus had begun to move the country into the more modern age. Early in his reign in 1617, he had officially established the *Riksdag*, the parliamentary body that, comprising the four Estates of nobles, clergy, burgers and peasants, had first come noticeably to the fore at the time of his grandfather. He had modernised the navy, improved communications with new roads and canals, and also expanded industries, in the latter case demonstrating his very real interest by personally inspecting mining works taking place.

---

b Wilson shows that the king's modernisation of the army was in fact limited, and several of his reforms were abandoned after his early death at Lützen. In essence, the battle was inconclusive, yet Swedish propaganda presented it as a victory and so further promulgated Gustavus Adolphus' reputation as one of the greatest military leaders of all time. But, although the king was revered by many, Napoleon would later declare that his contemporaries, Tilly and Wallenstein, had been better generals. (See Peter H. Wilson, *Lützen*, p.106)

c Nonetheless, with his grandfather, Gustav I Vasa, having denuded his country of its religious books and works of art at the time of the Reformation, Gustavus Adolphus had no compunction in replenishing Sweden's cultural heritage by methodically stripping monasteries, churches and seats of learning of their priceless treasures.

In addition to building hospitals, he had raised the country's previously dire level of education with the establishment of schools, colleges and a university at Uppsala. Finally, he had promoted the country's commerce and financial growth by founding some seventeen new towns, among them, the war-damaged Göteborg (Gothenburg) that he had rebuilt after agreeing a peace with Denmark in 1613. Here, he had encouraged more Dutch and other foreign merchants to come and settle, thus ensuring the town could benefit from their various trades. And a few years later, when he had secured Sweden's access to the North Sea by buying the nearby Danish fortress at Elfsborg, he had given yet another boost to Göteborg's fortunes. While Gustavus Adolphus was not seen to be as democratic as his father, with many of his reforms and improvements being of no benefit to the peasant classes, nonetheless, throughout his reign even the poorest in the land continued to revere him, proud of their king whose famous military achievements were increasing their country's standing abroad.

Nevertheless, by dying at the age of only thirty-seven, Gustavus Adolphus had once more left the dynasty's survival in jeopardy. But having appreciated the potential danger to his country that his premature death in battle would present, he had previously voiced his concerns to Axel Oxenstierna. Anxious about leaving Sweden in the hands of his unpredictable wife and very young daughter, in 1627 he had persuaded the *Riksdag* to declare its allegiance to his only legitimate child, and before his last campaign had asked Oxenstierna to protect her position on the throne. Therefore, with seven-year-old Christina now acclaimed the new ruler (officially Sweden's 'king'), Oxenstierna established an official regency, one that soon excluded the unstable Maria Eleonora. Until this time Christina had lived mostly with her aunt away from her uncaring mother, but on the return of Gustavus Adolphus' body, his widow had changed character and became highly possessive of her daughter, seldom letting her out of her sight. She now enveloped the child in her grief, obliging her to share a bed over which she hung a golden casket containing the king's heart. During her extended period of exaggerated, maudlin mourning, while the dowager queen refused to allow her husband to be buried, she kept his coffin in her rooms, frequently opening it to see or touch the badly embalmed and now decaying body. Although eventually acceding to his delayed funeral, Maria Eleonora's mental state continued to become still more bizarre, so that two years later Oxenstierna decided to separate her more permanently from her daughter. Christina then moved back into the household of her father's half-sister, Katarina, Countess of Palatinate-Zweibrücken. Here the child would have a happier and more normal existence, playing with her cousins, and learning to speak fluent French, the family's chosen language that was now becoming more fashionable in many courts. Later she would have further contact with her mother, but by then Maria Eleonora was spending more time abroad in Denmark and Brandenburg, where she was received with growing exasperation by the Danish king, Christian IV, and her brother, the elector. Finally, to the relief of them both, she returned to Sweden where, having attended Christina's coronation, she died in 1655, the year after her daughter's abdication.

Having attended council meetings since the age of fourteen, four years later in 1644 Christina finally began to rule for herself. Intelligent and well educated, with a knowledge of several languages, she was keen to promote Stockholm as a new centre of learning. Seeing herself as Sweden's 'Pallas' – the goddess of wisdom – she wanted her capital to be recognised as the 'Athens of the North'. In her desire to further this aim, she studied the works of some of the greatest minds of the time, even inviting René Descartes to move to Stockholm to set up a scientific academy. Despite her never achieving her academy, Christina did eventually manage to persuade the unwilling Descartes to join her in October 1649. Every morning during this particularly cold winter she would get up at five o'clock to begin her studies, but her enthusiasm would prove detrimental to the health of her French guest. Having caught a chill in the poorly heated rooms of her palace, where protocol demanded he remain bareheaded throughout, he died of pneumonia less than four months after his arrival. But Christina was more successful when satisfying her passion to acquire precious works of art. In the last days of the Thirty Years' War, she ordered her troops to loot from Prague Castle as much as possible of the famous collection that had been accumulated by Emperor Rudolf II. Although this had already suffered serious plundering by Maximilian, Elector of Bavaria, at the beginning of the hostilities, enough remained in the fabulous treasury for her to seize some 40,000 precious items, including jewellery, various instruments, tons of silver and precious coins, the complete library, some 700 paintings, and the priceless Silver Bible of the Goths.

Christina reigned during a period of almost continuous fighting, during which time Sweden increasingly imposed its dominance over the Baltic. In the ten years after Gustavus Adolphus' death, the country had suffered a series of military setbacks, but in 1642 its fortunes began to improve when, at the site of Gustavus Adolphus' great victory at Breitenfeld, Field Marshal Torstenson defeated the Imperial army. Once more confident of their military strength, the next year the Swedes invaded Denmark-Norway and having occupied parts of each, forced Christian IV to abandon all his attempts at resistance. In the resulting peace of August 1645, the Danish king was obliged to accept the humiliating terms demanded by the Swedes, granting them exemption from the Sound Dues, and handing over parts of Norway and two important Baltic islands: Ösel off the west coast of Estonia, and even more significantly the strategically placed Gotland that had been a Danish possession for three centuries. But these would be only the first of Sweden's gains, as just three years later at the eventual conclusion of the Thirty Years' War, it would also receive western

Pomerania and Bremen-Verden. The Torstenson War effectively ended the Danish *dominium maris baltici* (though not forever, see page 119).

However, these protracted wars, on top of the modernising programme of Christina's father, put a strain on the state finances, to the extent that even back at the time of his funeral foreigners had been discouraged from attending in case they should witness the country's poverty. This problem was now further exacerbated by the queen's own extravagance, a trait in her character that would put her in financial difficulty throughout her life.

While growing up at her aunt's house, she had become close to her cousins, including Karl Gustav, and, just before he left on campaign in 1642, she had agreed to become engaged to him, even though privately she then expressed her distaste for all marriage. Previous suitors had been considered by her parents, but in time these schemes had come to nothing, and Christina would always harbour a desire to remain single, although she did form certain close, but undefined, friendships. One person for whom she showed particular affection was Ebba Sparre, whom she called 'Belle', and later in Rome she had a deep romantic attachment to Cardinal Decio Azzolino. Although these and other relationships were possibly platonic, the exact nature of them is unknown, but because of Christina's preference for wearing men's clothes, and her bizarre, if not manly, ways and appearance, questions have often been raised regarding her sexuality. Others, however, have argued that her maverick conduct and disregard for the accepted social norms suggest rather more an unusual behavioural condition, something possibly within the autistic spectrum. She later astounded the formal French with her eccentricities, swearing loudly and sitting with her legs over the arms of the chairs. Christina often lacked tact or diplomacy, and she held little regard for the manners of the period, and in the courtly environment with its stylised comportment and etiquette, her conduct fitted with neither female nor male typical behaviour. Proud and confident of her own abilities and regal importance, she did not hesitate to express her individuality, nor to question openly the ideas and beliefs that others took as a given.

In January 1649, Christina became particularly aware of her need to assure the succession. Her cousin Jan Kazimierz, son of Sigismund III, had just succeeded to the throne in Poland, and now married to his widowed sister-in-law, it was feasible that he might produce an heir. With Christina still single, it was once more a very real possibility that the Catholic Polish Vasas might in the future again lay claim to the Swedish crown. Therefore, still determined to remain unmarried, she decided to call the *Riksdag* and declare Karl Gustav to be her successor. This surprised the parliament, who, knowing she was engaged to her cousin, believed her doubts over the succession to be premature. However, when approached by a delegation sent to question her decision, she replied that it was 'impossible' for her to marry, refusing to give her reasons for this statement. At first the *Riksdag* refused to accept her decision, but by March they had changed their minds in the light of the rebellious movement now spreading through Europe that had manifested itself in Charles I's recent execution in London, the Fronde's rebellion against Louis XIV, and the breakout of disturbances in the various Spanish Habsburg possessions. And in Sweden there was equal unrest, with the demands of the nobility threatening to become out of hand. Because of a series of bad harvests and overall poor agricultural methods, food was now in short supply, a situation not helped by a general growing financial crisis. Despite these problems, however, in 1650 Christina finally began preparing for her excessively extravagant coronation, the cost of which was increased by the bejewelled robes and other elaborate trappings that she ordered to be brought from France. Adding still further to the expense, only five months before the event she declared that she wished it to take place in Stockholm, rather than the traditional Uppsala where preparations had already begun. With whispers suggesting that Christina did not plan to remain queen for long, in September she announced to the *Riksdag* that she wished Karl Gustav to be made her hereditary heir, an appointment that would guarantee his accession and not depend on any later election. Although this demand was first refused, in October just days before her coronation, she managed to manipulate the *Riksdag*'s agreement by promising the members concessions that in the event she would never fulfil. With this settled, on 20 October (OS) the glittering ceremony took place in Stockholm Cathedral, after which there followed an 1,800-gun salute, a vast banquet, and then days of further feasting and entertainment. Among the shows put on for the public's enjoyment there were even medieval-style jousts and combats between wild animals.

However, just six months later, Christina began to tell those close to her – including a horrified Karl Gustav – that she was planning to abdicate. For several more weeks, she said nothing to the council about her decision, and only eventually informed the members of it in August. As they immediately rejected the idea, the whole matter was then temporarily shelved. But Christina had frequently suffered from periods of ill health over the years, and she appeared at this time to experience some sort of physical collapse, very possibly brought on by the exhausting schedule she had been following since her youth. Therefore, on the advice of her French doctor, she began to drop her old way of life, becoming less absorbed in study and spending more time simply enjoying herself. This caused her reputation to suffer, and the official court historian Arnold Messenius and his son began to criticise her as a wildly extravagant woman, devoted solely to her own hedonistic pleasures. Moreover, they accused her of having reduced Crown property and impoverished the state by promoting nearly seventy new counts and barons, not to mention doubling the numbers of lesser nobles. Enraged by her two courtiers' disloyalty, she ordered the Messeniuses to be arrested and put to death, the older beheaded, while the younger was flogged and then broken on the wheel. And to add further to the tensions building up at this time, a plot was discovered, its purpose being to replace the queen with Karl Gustav. At first he had known nothing about the conspiracy but on later discovering it, had warned Christina before quickly distancing himself from the whole affair.

Meanwhile, since the spring of 1651 Christina had been receiving instruction from the Jesuits in the Catholic religion, having claimed that she had lost faith in the Lutheran teachings of her childhood. And although she never accepted certain aspects of Catholicism, the worship of relics and maybe even the fundamental dogmas, including the veneration of the sacraments, she now decided to prepare for her conversion to the Church of Rome. Later some Catholics would find her religious behaviour unconventional, frequently displaying a lack of sincerity and piety, but for the Protestants the conversion of the queen – the daughter of their great champion, Gustavus Adolphus – would be a far greater shock. Therefore, realising the reaction her apostasy would cause in Sweden, Christina continued for a time to keep her intentions to herself.

Having at last informed the *Riksdag* of her determination to give up the throne, in May 1654 the Estates accepted her decision, agreeing to her demands for financial maintenance and the retention of her title as 'queen'. The abdication then took place the following June in Uppsala, a moving ceremony for most present who witnessed the twenty-seven-year-old Christina gradually divesting herself of all her regalia of state. Within hours her cousin was crowned Karl X Gustav, and a few days later Christina finally left the country incognito. But before leaving she had arranged for much of her accumulated treasure – including some 427 paintings and seventy-one bronzes previously looted from Prague – to be shipped to her new home. While some of these artworks would later prove a useful source of funds to help cover her flamboyant lifestyle, others were left in her will to Cardinal Azzolino, eventually to be scattered when they were sold on to other collectors after his death.

Among her various stops on her journey south, Christina visited the Duke of Holstein-Gottorp, laying the foundations for a future marriage between his daughter and Sweden's new king, Karl X. Having eventually arrived in Brussels, on Christmas Eve in the Archduke's Palace she privately underwent her conversion, but anxious that it might cause the *Riksdag* to withdraw her Swedish pension, she continued to keep the information secret for nearly a year, not revealing the truth until she had reached the city of Innsbruck. A month after that, on 20 December 1655 (NS), she arrived in Rome, where she was then granted temporary accommodation in the Vatican by Pope Alexander VII. While she was staying with him, the pontiff personally conducted her confirmation, an honour that Christina marked by adding Alexandra to her name. Three days later she finally made her official entry into the city, riding into the Piazza del Popolo through Bernini's recently redesigned Flaminia gates, freshly inscribed in commemoration of her arrival. Her conversion had been such a coup for the Catholic Church in this uncertain time of the Counter-Reformation that the celebrations continued throughout the carnival period and for several months afterwards. She now took up residence in the first of her Roman homes, renting for the next six months the Palazzo Farnese that today houses the French Embassy. Although not treating the palace with the care she should have, even to the extent of turning a blind eye to her servants' pilfering of some of its treasures, Christina immediately fell in love with the city and over the years she would become a sponsor of its arts, befriending key figures like Bernini, Scarlatti and Corelli. Her exuberant lifestyle would often be limited by the ongoing question of funds, so at times the diminishing revenues from Sweden would have to be supplemented by loans from the pope, the French, and personal friends.

Christina's following years would be more uncertain. Having given up one crown, she later appeared to regret her decision, and began to seek others, for a time negotiating with Cardinal Mazarin in an unfulfilled attempt to become the new Queen of Naples. On the abdication of her cousin Jan Kazimierz, she would also consider the possibility of taking the throne of Poland. More poignantly still, when her cousin Karl X died in 1660, she revisited Sweden to present herself as heir to his five-year-old son. But by that time, in the eyes of the *Riksdag*, the Catholic Christina was no longer eligible, and in order to emphasise its opposition it demanded that once more she should officially renounce the throne. Six years later she again attempted to return to the country, but this time forbidden to visit Stockholm, she was finally forced to accept that she was no longer welcome in Sweden.

Her unpredictable and periodically cruel character would, on occasion, cause her popularity to be seriously damaged. Even in the Catholic courts, where she was welcomed as the new royal convert, she was sometimes looked on with abhorrence. During her second visit to France she became involved while staying at Fontainbleau in a disastrous domestic affair, when, believing her Italian Master of the Horse to be betraying her, she demanded that – without trial – he should be immediately put to death. Remaining resolute in her determination, and refusing all persuasion by her priest and others, she insisted that the barbaric murder should go ahead without delay while she remained unmoved in the next-door room. This unfeeling behaviour shocked Europe and, now condemned for her cold-hearted brutality, she was for a time widely unwelcome. Later still in Hamburg, in another example of her poor judgement, she laid on an extravagant party in celebration of the new pope's election, an action that gravely offended the Lutheran people of the city. This blunder not only made it necessary for her to flee her palace, but also had the far more disastrous result of causing an outbreak of violent rioting that ended with multiple injuries and several deaths.

Destined to rule since her birth, and acknowledged as monarch since her early childhood, Christina grew up convinced of her own inherited and inalienable royal status. While she, a lover of the arts, was eager to display her own abilities, some critics have dismissed her intellectual pursuits as having little depth, reflecting in her ever-changing pursuit of knowledge the restlessness she showed in every other aspect of her life. As she confessed herself, she hated to be contradicted, and she was often stubborn, even at times vicious. But she was prepared to speak out in favour of those who suffered persecution, and with her flexible approach to the current dictates of the Catholic Church, she not only rejected its stricter proscriptions placed on the theatre, actresses and even female dress, but also more significantly argued for the protection of the Jews living in Rome. Similarly, in her later life she was not afraid to criticise Louis XIV for his revocation of the Edict of Nantes and the resulting persecution of the Huguenots.

In 1689, twenty-nine years after her cousin Karl X, she died aged sixty-two in the Palazzo Riario, her last much-loved home on the Gianicolo hill in Rome. After her death, the pope ordered an official lying-in-state at which large crowds came to pay their respects, thus proving her popularity among many of the local people, who had appreciated her generosity and openness towards them. Her body was then taken to St Peter's where, in a particular mark of respect, it was laid in the crypt beside former popes. And finally thirteen years later, a monument in her memory was erected above in the nave of great basilica itself.

5

The Vasa Kings of the Polish-Lithuanian Commonwealth

Sigismund (Zygmunt) III, King of Poland, and the deposed King of Sweden, in about 1620. (Alte Pinakothek, Maxvorstadt, Germany)

Born while his parents were still prisoners of the Swedish king Eric XIV, Prince Sigismund had been taught to speak Polish fluently by his mother, a skill that made him popular when he was elected Zygmunt III, King of Poland, in 1587. But while the strong Catholic beliefs he had learnt as a child from his Jesuit instructors were fully acceptable in his new kingdom, the situation would be very different for him in Sweden, when five years later he succeeded his father, Johan III. Despite his promises to uphold the country's Lutheran faith, his devoutly Protestant subjects remained suspicious of his motives, convinced that their largely absentee king would force the country's eventual conversion to Catholicism. As a result, within a few years he was facing opposition from rebellious groups who were gathering around Johan's younger brother, and the situation finally came to a head in 1598 when the two men met in battle. The result was a disaster for Sigismund, who, following his defeat and capture, was forced to give up his Swedish crown to his uncle, who then replaced him as Karl IX. After that, the ousted Sigismund returned to his preferred Polish kingdom, but he would never come to terms with his loss. His constant ambition to regain his second throne would drive many of his future policies, and after his death the same bitter rivalries would persist between the Vasa cousins for decades to come. Before long, the two countries were again at war, with fighting breaking out in the much-disputed region of Livonia, an area that from this time would repeatedly find itself under changing ownership.

After his election as King of Poland and Duke of Lithuania, and while still King of Sweden, in the mid-1590s Sigismund (Zygmunt) decided to move his capital to a more central position, transferring it from the earlier Polish Kraków and Lithuanian Vilnius, to the Mazovian capital Warsaw. This had already grown in importance – since the sixteenth century its castle having been used as the royal residence, and the chosen place for many meetings of the *Sejm*. But Danzig with its population of around 80,000 was also booming, its prosperity driven by its thriving trade. The largest city on the Baltic and Poland's most important port, its elegantly dressed citizens lived in well-furnished houses that were filled with expensive luxuries. Here visitors were struck not just by the quantity of musical instruments and books, but also the numbers of printing presses that had been set up to meet the rising demand. In addition, by the start of the century, many impressive new buildings were under construction. Dutch architects were now designing in their mannerist style the Great Arsenal, and the new entrance to the Artus Court – the merchants' meeting place. And, at the same time, in front of the court on Long Market, the mayor had plans for a replacement of the old fountain, wanting to erect something more striking that would impress the foreigners coming to his city. After unforeseen delays, this artwork – dedicated to Neptune, the Roman god of the seas – would be finally completed in the 1630s. And at the far end of the same thoroughfare, the newly built Golden Gate marked the north-western entrance to the city and the start of what was now known as the Royal Way. Meanwhile there were other schemes to enhance the old town hall which, following a recent fire, had already been reconstructed in the Renaissance style, topped with a new spire, and crowned with a gilt statue of the earlier king, Zygmunt II. To embellish this building still further, in 1608 the ceiling of its summer chamber, the Red Room, was decorated by the resident Flemish painter's representation of Danzig's remarkable achievements, a symbolic portrayal of the city's 'Apotheosis'.

Meanwhile, however, Russia had descended into chaos, consumed by its Time of Troubles, when a series of pretenders came forward claiming to be the rightful heir to the throne, the long-dead Dmitry – son of Ivan IV – who had probably been murdered when he was eight. With the country riven by rebellion, Sigismund gave his support to the first pretender, seeing this as an opportunity to spread his religious faith and weaken his eastern neighbour. After fleeing to Poland, in 1604 this claimant – rumoured by some to be the Polish king Stefan Batory's illegitimate son – visited Sigismund's court, and it was here that he converted to Catholicism and became engaged to a young Polish woman, Maria Mniszech. The king personally attended their betrothal ceremony and a year later, having already provided him with a pension, offered the young man further assistance by privately funding his employment of Polish troops for a planned invasion of Russia. Although this military campaign soon proved successful, and in July the pretender was crowned tsar, only ten months later and just ten days after his official marriage, he – the so-called 'First False Dmitry' – was murdered in May 1606. So now the senior men in the land, the *boyars*, wanting to find a replacement, chose one of their own, electing Vasily Shuisky as their new tsar.

Although Polish and Lithuanian forces then gave their backing to a second pretender, it was not until Sweden agreed an alliance with Tsar Vasily three years later that Sigismund obtained the *Sejm*'s permission to declare war officially on Russia – a move that had the added advantage of distracting the attention of his own rebellious nobles at home. Having begun a two-year siege of the former Lithuanian town of Smolensk, in July 1610 Sigismund's army achieved a major victory at Klushino over a much larger number of Russians and their few, mainly mercenary, Swedish allies. This success then enabled the Poles to continue on to Moscow and capture the Kremlin. After their arrival in the city, the *boyars* deposed their puppet ruler, and Vasily Shuisky was forced into holy orders before being taken with his brothers to Poland. Here, after paying homage to the *Sejm*, he was imprisoned near Warsaw, remaining in captivity until his death two years later. Meanwhile in Moscow, with Sigismund's troops still occupying the city, the *boyars* made the probably pragmatic decision to elect as tsar the king's fifteen-year-old son, Prince Wladyslaw. But although agreeing to this, Wladyslaw would never be crowned, largely hindered by his father, who wanted to lay claim to the throne for himself.

This latter proposal the *boyars* refused to consider, and they also rejected Sigismund's next demand that he should rule as regent for his son. Now infuriated by their failure to recognise his authority, Sigismund punished those whom he held particularly responsible, among them the Patriarch Filaret. The latter was kept a prisoner in Poland for the next eight years, only returning to Russia after his son Michael had become the first Romanov tsar.

Having thrown away the goodwill that he had enjoyed on his arrival in Russia, Sigismund had grown deeply unpopular because of his demonstrably autocratic behaviour and strict adherence to his faith. His personal devotion and insistence on the Roman Catholic liturgy increasingly caused the Russian people to fear that they would be forced to give up their Orthodoxy. Similar issues had helped bring down the First False Dmitry, but Sigismund, a stubborn and bigoted man, failed to heed the warning signs, and repeatedly offended the people with his intolerance. By refusing to allow Wladyslaw to convert to the Orthodox religion, he had also weakened the prince's position, just as he had done earlier in Sweden with his refusal to permit his son's conversion to Lutheranism in exchange for the throne.

At last aware of the dangerous opposition they were facing, Sigismund and Wladyslaw left Russia and returned to Poland. Their troops, however, stayed on, besieged for nineteen months in the Kremlin until, forced by hunger to surrender, they were finally murdered while leaving the city. This episode marks the end of Poland's chances to hold power in the country, and just a year later with the election of Tsar Michael, the new Romanov dynasty was founded. However, Prince Wladyslaw continued to cling to his ambitions, and the eighteen-year-old would mount a failed attempt to take the Russian throne in 1616. Two years later, however, peace was finally agreed and in the treaty Tsar Michael conceded more territory to the Poles. With his handing over to the Commonwealth nearly 400,000 square miles, the country had now reached its maximum size, with an overall population of around eleven million people. But it was still vulnerable, threatened by both the Ottomans in the south and the Swedes in the north, and although the Commonwealth escaped the full ravages of the Thirty Years' War that was now raging on its western borders, throughout the 1620s it found itself under repeated assault from Sigismund's young cousin, the Swedish king Gustavus Adolphus. After invading Livonia and capturing Riga, Gustavus Adolphus had proceeded to strike further south, repeatedly attacking Danzig and the surrounding region. Eventually a truce was agreed and the Swedish king, satisfied with his extensive gains in Livonia, turned his attention to the bitter conflicts of the Thirty Years' War, where just five years later he would die in battle, only seven months after the death of his cousin Sigismund.

Exceptionally talented artistically, during the nearly forty-five years that he was on the Polish throne, Sigismund III would promote the arts, among other things, encouraging the development of drama. But during his reign he had often faced rebellion from his nobles, who objected to his attempts to restrict their powers. And as his unpopularity had grown at home, in 1620, while he was on his way to mass in Warsaw, he narrowly escaped an assassination attempt. The lone attacker, who had modelled himself on the Bourbon Henri IV's murderer, was then subjected to an equally brutal, prolonged and agonising execution as his French counterpart. But abroad too, Sigismund was viewed with suspicion, his willingness to change allegiances having earned him the distrust of his neighbours, the reason why he was so continuously threatened by the Ottomans, Russians and the Swedes. Still today, opinion is divided over this king, whose actions were driven for the greater part by his deep Catholic conviction, and by his desire to recover his Swedish crown or extend his territory elsewhere. While some critics praise him as the champion of the Counter-Reformation, others hold him largely responsible for Poland's later disastrous decline.

With his approaching death Sigismund tried to persuade the *Sejm* to elect his son as the next king, but this was rejected by the nobles. However, when the moment came in 1632, the prince, already popular with the *szlachta*, was duly appointed and crowned Wladyslaw IV Vasa. Despite the lull in fighting with the Swedes, within days of his coronation in Kraków he realised the need to go to war again against the Russians, they having now broken the terms of their previous peace agreement. Rejoining his troops after they had retaken Smolensk, he then led them for the next five bitter winter months, sharing the harsh living conditions with his men.

Although his army was greatly outnumbered, at last he succeeded in bringing the enemy to his knees, and with that in 1634 he was able to force the tsar to make peace. Poland now regained the territories it had lost during the fighting, and Russia was made to pay compensation towards the cost of the war, but in return Wladyslaw renounced at last his claim to the Russian throne. Yet, even now, things did not go entirely smoothly, as when the delegates came to Warsaw the next year, demanding to be given the original document that had proclaimed the king as tsar, despite much searching it could not be found. So, in recompense, the visitors were given the bodies of Vasily Shuisky and his brothers, and the deposed Russian ruler was finally accorded his proper place of burial in the Kremlin's Archangel Cathedral in Moscow.

A few months after the peace with Russia, Wladyslaw concluded another treaty with the Ottomans in the south, and then with the help of the French and English drew up a new agreement with the Swedes. But he soon angered the French by refusing their proposal for his marriage to Marie Louise Gonzaga, choosing instead Cecile Renata, the sister of the Habsburg Emperor Ferdinand II, an agreement that temporarily made the Duchy of Opole-Raciborz in Silesia part of Poland. Meanwhile, on the domestic front the situation was calm, with the king – unlike his father – not only displaying tolerance and allowing men to follow their consciences, but also retaining his popularity among the nobility. A very extravagant and enthusiastic collector who supported the arts, he spent much of his sixteen-year-long reign travelling abroad, and, as a result, he brought back to Poland many treasures and foreign fashions, among them a new taste for the opera. His court at Warsaw was modelled on those he had visited on his journeys around the continent, and in this way it contrasted sharply with that found in Moscow, leaving the question as to how he might have changed things in Russia had he indeed become tsar. In the event, over half a century would pass before Peter the Great would introduce the reforms and cultural changes that brought his country closer to those of western Europe.

When Wadyslaw's first wife died in March 1644, a proposal of marriage was sent to his relation Queen Christina. While this alliance promised to strengthen the claim of the Polish Vasas to the Swedish throne, the plan in fact came to nothing, hindered by Christina's refusal, and by the political manoeuvring of the French chief minister, Cardinal Mazarin. Wanting to create an alliance against France's long-time enemy the Habsburgs, Mazarin finally succeeded in bringing about Wladyslaw's betrothal to the earlier suggested candidate, French-born Marie Louise Gonzaga. In November 1645, a proxy ceremony therefore took place at Louis XIV's court, attended by the ten-year-old king himself. When the

An engraving dating from about 1640 of Wladyslaw IV, the elected but uncrowned Tsar of Russia, based on a portrait by Rubens. The king's fashionable European clothes, so remarkably different from those worn in the Romanov court, draw attention to the cultural gulf still dividing Europe and Russia at the time.

Polish train arrived to fetch the bride, even the French were astounded by its extravagance. Spectacular affairs, these Polish retinues always amazed the foreign courts that they visited, astonishing those that saw them with their multitude of richly dressed attendants, camels, exotic trappings, and general abundance of jewels. Now in a flamboyant display of largesse, the golden horseshoes were intentionally attached so loosely that they might fall off in the street and be gathered by the people of Paris. Such conspicuously excessive demonstrations of wealth, usually way beyond the financial means of the country, would continue in the years to come, regardless of the state of the national purse.

Finally, early the following year, Marie Louise arrived in Danzig, and although Wladyslaw was too unwell to receive her, in March the official wedding took place at Warsaw, with her coronation following soon after in Kraków. In deference to the Polish churchmen, who objected to a first-name use of Mary (that of the Holy Virgin), by now the new queen had become Ludwika Maria. But the Poles would continue to view her French ways with suspicion, and although she would advance the cultural and intellectual life of the country, they always remained highly critical of the tastes and fashions of the many foreigners who filled her court.

Her marriage to Wladyslaw did not last long. Just a year later the king was crushed by the sudden and unexpected death of his eight-year-old son, a boy who had shown much promise. Heartbroken, his father, whose health was already failing, was unable to attend the funeral, and then the following year he was further weighed down as tensions mounted in the east. These border regions were frequently subject to Cossack unrest and attacks by the Ottomans, not to mention the recurring raids of the Tatars, who were seeking to capture new victims to sell in their slave markets. But the king was now unable to deal with the latest threat, prevented from raising the necessary army by the *Sejm*'s refusal to back another war and provide the necessary finance. Suddenly in May 1648 on his way to Warsaw, aged just fifty-three, Wladyslaw IV Vasa died.

His brother, having been elected as the new king, Jan II Kazimierz, the following year married his widowed sister-in-law, Queen Ludwika, with whom as it happened he had already had an affair in 1640 while on his travels abroad. Two years before they had met, after an early successful military career fighting the Russians, Jan Kazimierz had set off for Spain, on the way stopping to inspect the port at Marseilles. This action had caused him to fall foul of the French authorities and, charged with spying, he was then imprisoned for two years on the orders of Louis XIII. After his eventual release, Jan Kazimierz decided to take holy orders, for a time joining the Jesuits before moving to Rome and becoming a cardinal. Having eventually resigned his position and returned to Poland, after his young nephew's death in 1647 he began to put himself forward as a viable successor to the throne.

His wife had had an equally complex past. The daughter of the Duke of Mantua and Catherine of Guise, she had originally planned to marry Gaston, Duke of Orléans, Louis XIII's brother. But this had angered the French king who, opposing the match, had then also imprisoned her for a time. But after her marriage to Jan Kazimierz, other still more bitter troubles would hit Ludwika Maria, not least of these being the deaths of her children, her one-year-old daughter having died shortly before her two-month-old younger brother.[16] Both parents were grief-stricken by this double tragedy, and after it they would remain childless for the rest of their lives. However, although the king and queen's relationship was often stormy, with violent arguments occasionally taking place in public, Ludwika Maria, the stronger partner, continued to give support to her husband throughout all the bad times ahead. During their difficult years while the Commonwealth struggled for survival, she would show her courage and maintain her determination to uphold the independence of her adopted country.

Jan Kazimierz had a less charismatic personality than his brother, and he soon found himself at increasing odds with his nobles, a situation not helped by his unpopular wife's efforts to limit their powers. To add to his problems, the unrest that had threatened the end of Wladyslaw's reign now became critical. The new king began to be faced by a series of rebellions and massacres in Lithuania, and by further Tatar and Cossack risings in southern Poland. Meanwhile, neighbouring countries Russia and Sweden, seeing the internal unrest in the Commonwealth, chose this moment to renew hostilities. In the north the Swedes, led by their king Karl X, again attacked Danzig, and then went on to occupy the whole of the north-west of the country. Following suit, the Russians took over most of the remaining Commonwealth territory in the south and the east, with the result that in 1655, at the height of this so-called 'Deluge', the royal couple found themselves forced to flee from Kraków and seek refuge in Silesia.

At last, four months after the death of their king Karl X, the Swedes agreed to make peace in 1660 at Oliwa near Danzig, and with this Jan II Kazimierz finally gave up the Polish Vasa claims to the Swedish throne. But although the Swedes withdrew without having gained any territory, they left Poland in ruins. While Danzig was one of just three cities to be spared, some 188 others were destroyed. Churches were pillaged and tons of loot shipped off to Sweden, where much of it still remains. Such plundering was a common practice of the Swedish rulers at this time, and although equal brutality was enacted on their departing army by the Poles, their – too often savage – behaviour left a lasting impression on the Polish people, creating a continuing bitterness towards the Swedes, and an intolerance of the Protestants in general. As for the looting, in 2011 when the Vistula's water level dropped during the summer drought, evidence of the Swedes' robbery was discovered lying on the riverbed.

However, in the east the war continued for another seven years under the second Romanov tsar, Alexis I, who wanted to regain the land that his father Michael had lost. When peace came in 1667, he achieved his aims and in the final agreement the Commonwealth had to surrender not just the area around Smolensk that it had so recently gained, but also Kiev and much of the region that makes up present-day Ukraine. At the same time, Jan II Kazimierz had to confirm the status quo in Livonia, acknowledging that this district, which had been under Swedish control for some years, was now a Swedish possession. These losses mark the beginning of the reduction of Polish territory that would culminate in the country's total disappearance from the map a century later.

Jan II Kazimierz's difficulties were compounded by the situation he faced with the *Sejm*. Whereas in 1569 the Union of Lublin had endeavoured to introduce a more democratic system allowing the king's authority to be controlled, now the advantage had begun to swing too far in favour of the nobility. The members in the lower house had increased their power to such an extent that every measure of the king could be blocked. From a minor incident when a deputy had walked out of the chamber, the situation had developed to one where any single person could annul the proceedings by the *liberum veto*. If an individual opposed a measure, all the matters leading up to it would be thrown out, and during the two centuries from the time of the Union until the First Partition of Poland, around a third of all the sittings failed to produce a result, with the situation becoming particularly bad during Jan Kazimierz's reign. Things were made worse by the fact that the lower house of the lesser nobility was dominated by men from the *szlachta*. This group professed an almost clan-like allegiance to each other, claiming descent from the ancient Sarmatians, a warlike tribe thought to have once lived in the area of the Black Sea. Unlike the nobility abroad, they based their status on a claim of ancient heritage, rather than on achievement, wealth, reward, or title. As a result, the *szlachta* embraced a spectrum of types, from landowners to the landless, from the very rich to the poor, the active to the idle, the educated to the illiterate. Instead, their sense of kinship was demonstrated by the way they dressed, and this over time became so eastern in appearance that occasionally when fighting the Ottomans they even needed to wear a distinguishing cockade in their hats. Proudly possessive of their identity, they opposed the king on anything they saw as an infringement of their ancient rights.

In addition, challenges came from the immensely rich magnates, in the main descended from Lithuanian landowners that at the time of the Union of Lublin had been exempted from the king's demands for the return of previously granted territory. As a result, many of the eastern estates were now so large that they included several farms, towns and one or two cities. In some cases, there were even private armies. Over the years, there had been a rapid increase in the size of these estates, and the magnates now sought to parade their wealth, wearing clothes covered with jewels and being accompanied by vast, equally sumptuously dressed retinues. Ambitious to maintain their position, if not increase their power, they confronted the king at will. Opposed to reform, they would not hesitate to take up arms against him when they considered their interests to be threatened, and following their victory over his troops in 1655, some had with impunity murdered his best soldiers. In the words of the later Jacques-Henri Bernardin de Saint-Pierre, there was nowhere with 'a more magnificent nobility, nor worse citizens'.[17]

Following his wife's death in 1667, the situation became unbearable for the king, and so the next year he abdicated, financially helped by those who hoped – ultimately without success – to replace him with his brother-in-law, Count Palatine Philip Wilhelm of Neuberg. Now Jan Kazimierz left Poland and, being like his brother a keen collector, he took with him many of the family treasures that had not been plundered during the Deluge. Having moved to France, he became an abbot and received seven monasteries from Louis XIV, profitable establishments that allowed him to live in considerable comfort. He then contracted a second morganatic marriage to a twice-widowed French adventuress in 1672, but just weeks later in December he died suddenly, apparently from the shock of hearing of another disastrous Ottoman defeat of the Poles. With Jan Kazimierz's abdication, the dynasty of the Polish Vasas ended, and the *Sejm* had to look for a new ruler at a time when the Commonwealth was in disarray. In reality the country had now begun its long decline that a hundred years after Jan II Kazimierz's death would result in its initial dismantling at the hands of its neighbours, a first disintegration of the state that would be followed two decades later by its total obliteration.

6

The Last Years of Sweden's Baltic Empire

Karl X Gustav, the first of the Swedish Palatinate-Zweibrücken rulers, in an engraving created about six decades after his death. (Peace Palace Library, The Hague)

Katarina, the daughter of Karl IX and his first wife, Anna Maria, had married Count Johann Casimir of Palatinate-Zweibrücken, and for a time she and her husband had lived in Alsace. But when the savagery of the Thirty Years' War had begun to threaten their safety, her half-brother Gustavus Adolphus had felt it expedient to move them and their two surviving older children further away from the centre of hostilities. He therefore instructed them to return to Sweden, where soon after, in November 1622 at Nyköping, Katarina gave birth to another child, Karl Gustav. An intelligent and sensible woman, Katarina was always close to her half-brother, and so when in 1631 he became concerned about his wife's state of mind, he chose his sister to act as guardian to his young daughter. Five years later after Gustavus Adolphus' death, this child, now Queen Christina, was moved more permanently into Katarina's care, and here, living with her young cousins, she became close to Karl Gustav, who was just four years older than her. Over time, he grew deeply attached to Christina so that by 1642 they had become engaged. She too had a genuine affection for her cousin, but having soon decided that she wanted to remain single, she had then set about persuading the – still unaware – *Riksdag* to accept Karl Gustav as her hereditary heir. Regardless of all this, Karl Gustav remained true to Christina, again proving his unwavering loyalty by warning her when he discovered the plot to depose her and put himself on the throne. Despite his unwillingness to replace his cousin, in June 1654 he was finally obliged to do so when Christina at last chose to abdicate at Uppsala.

His coronation the next day as Karl X Gustav marked the end of the direct line of the Vasa dynasty, and the beginning of Sweden's nearly seven decades of Palatinate-Zweibrücken rule. Just over four months later (as Christina had arranged) the new king married a member of the Holstein-Gottorps, but he decided on this occasion to follow his own preferences by choosing the prettier, younger daughter, Hedwig Eleonora, leaving his intended bride-to-be compensated with a marriage to her sister's earlier rejected fiancé. Just over a year after the wedding and coronation of 'Queen Hedvig' in Stockholm, the couple's only child, a son, was born and christened like his father, Karl.

Karl X Gustav had during his early adulthood gained valuable military experience in the wars that were at that time consuming Europe. Having learnt from Field Marshal Torstenson much of the craft that would be so useful to him in the future, by the end of the Thirty Years' War he had become commander of the Swedish troops in Germany. A well-educated man, he had also developed his diplomatic skills by acting as Queen Christina's representative at the Nürnberg (Nuremberg) Congress that followed the end of hostilities. But on the domestic front, the new king would soon face the financial and social problems that had developed during his predecessor's reign. Christina's personal extravagance and profligate dispensing of a quarter of the crown lands to the non-tax-paying nobility had left the exchequer greatly depleted. With her having considerably increased their number, the nobles now owned 72 per cent of the country, where they were in the process of building enormous palaces. Their lifestyle had further divorced them from the rest of the populace, with the result that greater dissent had begun to build up in society at large. Karl X, a believer in a strong, authoritarian monarchy, opposed the growth of an oligarchy, and so he soon instructed the nobles to return some of their property. This measure – later also taken up by his son – would by the end of the century reduce the nobles' possession of land to around a third of the overall national total. The king then redistributed these estates in smaller parcels to his army conscripts as recognition for their services, the recipients being tax-payers whose contributions would help increase the state's revenue. This was applauded by the majority of people. But Karl also succeeded in appeasing the nobles by his modesty and politeness and, whether or not they opposed him, he treated them all with equal fairness, avoiding any display of favouritism.

A year after Karl X's accession, the *Riksdag* approved his demand to renew hostilities with the Polish-Lithuanian Commonwealth, a conflict that became most commonly known as the Second or Little Northern War. Twenty years earlier in 1635, to ease tensions with King Wladyslaw IV, Queen Christina had renewed the truce with Poland, at the same time returning some cities in Prussia and Livonia south of the Daugava, the river flowing east–west into the Baltic at Riga.[18] These possessions Karl now wanted to regain, but he was also concerned about the intentions of Tsar Alexis, whose probable impending attack on the Commonwealth would threaten Swedish interests in the rest of Livonia. He was right to be fearful of the tsar's intentions, as the following year the Russians overran southern Finland, Ingria, Estonia, and Livonia, where for two months they besieged Riga, one of Sweden's largest cities. But Karl had two further reasons for wanting to attack Poland: first to renew the age-old Vasa family feud that had divided the two nations for nearly half a century, and second to support the Protestants who were living in the country.

The Swedish army invaded the Commonwealth in July 1655, deploying over 7,000 men to Livonia, and sending nearly 14,000 more into Poland through Brandenburg. Karl then arrived from Pomerania with 12,700 additional troops, and soon, with the Swedes in the north and west, and a simultaneous Russian invasion in the east, nearly all the country was occupied in 'the Deluge'. But this was not the limit of Polish king Jan II Kazimierz's problems. The Commonwealth was also threatened by internal unrest, with opposition being shown not just by the Cossacks in the south, but also by the Lithuanian magnate, Grand Hetman Janusz Radziwill – he now agreeing a separate peace with Karl and being proclaimed the new Duke of Lithuania. The situation had become so grave for Jan Kazimierz that a month later on arriving in Warsaw, Karl found that the king had already abandoned his capital and gone to Kraków. However, within a week of arriving there, Jan Kazimierz, having realised that he was still vulnerable, had fled with his wife to Silesia, leaving the city just the day before Karl arrived in the area. Despite the recent improvements made to Kraków's defences, largely funded by the sale of the queen's jewels, eighteen days after coming under siege, on 5 October (OS) it was forced to surrender. But this would be just one of the many places to fall into Swedish hands, and by the end of the year only Danzig, Lwów (Lviv) and Zamość remained in Commonwealth possession.

Karl's troops, swelled by large numbers of mercenaries, now proceeded to plunder and destroy whatever they could lay their hands on, their behaviour very possibly further motivated by their lack of pay. With the impoverished Poles unable to render the expected contributions, the army now wreaked vengeance on the people, destroying their towns and stripping the Catholic churches of their treasures. Ironically, these actions blighted the lives of those very Protestants whom Karl had promised to help, because they now found themselves objects of hatred in what had previously been a country renowned for its tolerance. Although the Swedes were not alone in their uncivilised behaviour, with the Russians and Cossacks committing similar outrages, despite Karl's attempt to exert some control over his men – even executing a few of the worst offenders – the troops' actions gave the lie to their reputed better discipline. While precious loot was also shipped out of the country to fill the royal collection, towns were vandalised and destroyed, and many local people raped and murdered. These atrocities led to further reprisals, with brutal acts of savagery carried out on both sides. As a result of the general mayhem witnessed during the occupation, by the time the war was over a lasting hatred of Sweden was entrenched in the minds of the Polish people.

The violence of Karl's marauding troops had revived the patriotism of the Poles, and at the end of the year Jan Kazimierz decided to leave his refuge in Oberglogau in Silesia – today the Polish town of Głogówek, just a few miles from the Czech border – and having returned to his country with the emperor's military backing, in June he was able to retake Warsaw. However, as the Swedes had conquered the Polish fiefdoms on the Baltic seaboard, namely the duchies of Prussia and Courland, the Duke of Prussia (the Great Elector of Brandenburg) now signed a treaty with Karl that confirmed his change of status to that of a Swedish vassal. With this agreement in place, the Great Elector then joined the king in his fight against the Poles, an action for which the people of his duchy would later suffer savage retribution by the Polish Tatars. In July 1656 the combined armies were able to retake Warsaw after a bitterly fought three-day battle, throughout which the Swedish queen, Hedvig Eleonora, remained in the city. After the fighting was over, the victorious Swedish king – considered by many today to be the worst royal plunderer of the period – stripped

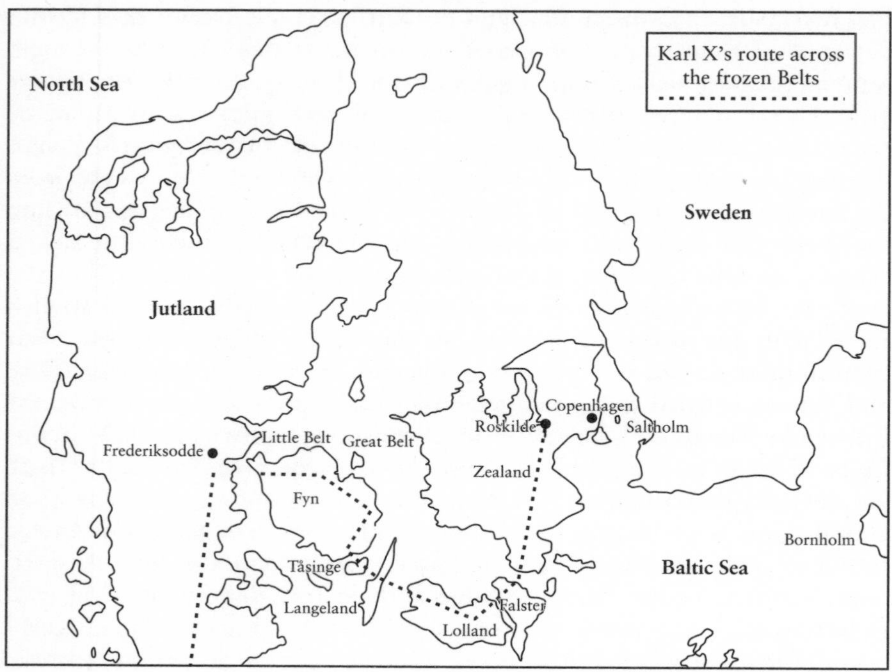

the capital and its palaces of its treasures, sending back to Sweden loads of paintings, statues, porcelain, precious documents and much more. According to contemporary witnesses, in the search for loot, his troops destroyed everything, even razing the royal gateway.

However, by this time the Swedes were facing growing opposition, and Karl X's position was becoming weaker everywhere. That same month, Danzig, under Swedish blockade since the start of the invasion, was saved by the arrival of a Dutch fleet that accompanied by nine Danish ships was able to bring some 1,400 men to defend the city. And with the Russians under Tsar Alexis still ravaging Sweden's Baltic possessions in Livonia, Ingria and Karelia, in November the Great Elector, encouraged by these Swedish reverses, demanded that in exchange for his continued support he should be accorded sovereignty and the ending of his status as Karl's vassal. Meanwhile, the Danes saw their own opportunity to recover their losses from the earlier Torstenson War and, seizing his chance, in June 1657 their new king, Frederik III, invaded Bremen and mainland Sweden. Karl, now concerned for his territories at home, therefore decided to abandon his campaigning in Poland, and immediately hurried back to his country's defence.

Having marched through the Baltic states of Mecklenburg, Pomerania, Holstein and Schleswig – and also relieved Bremen – Karl pursued the fleeing Danes north up the Jutland peninsula to Fredriksodde (Fredericia). Here he stopped, and having engaged the Danish fleet protecting the town, mounted a siege on the newly strengthened fortification where the enemy had taken shelter. Two months later the fortress fell, and with Karl having defeated the Danish navy, he was now ready to embark on one of the most famous episodes of his life. Although his fleet was sitting out the winter at Wismar, making a naval assault on his main objective of Copenhagen impossible, in December an exceptionally heavy freeze set in, giving him the idea for a daring new plan to lead his army to the Danish capital over the frozen sea. At the end of January 1658 the advance began, crossing the nearly 900-yard-wide waterway of the Little Belt to the island of Fyn (Funen). Despite on the way losing some of his men and horses when the ice broke beneath them, here the king was able to defeat a small Danish force. With this success behind him, six days later Karl turned his mind to the still more daring venture of how to cross the 10-mile-wide Great Belt, and, having listened to advice, he chose to take a more indirect route via the smaller islands and the intervening waterways that separated them. But by now the weather had turned milder and, having set off to Langeland via Tåsinge, the horses and men soon found themselves splashing their way through some 2 feet of water as the ice began to melt under their combined weight. Later, those taking part in this remarkable feat described their terrifying ordeal as they tramped along for miles in the darkness, expecting the ice to give way at any moment, and for them to be plunged into the freezing water below, a fate that met several of their colleagues. Having reached Langeland, the army continued, making further transits over the sea to Lolland and Falster, before eventually arriving at Zealand eight days after departure from Jutland. The size of the army involved in this campaign is uncertain, at the start (according to the inconsistent figures recorded) varying between 9,000 and 12,000 men. Most probably around 5,000 eventually reached their destination, their numbers reduced not just through losses, but also by those left en route to defend the islands that they had captured on the way.

Having been taken by surprise, the Danes were now forced to surrender, and at the end of February 1658 at Roskilde a new peace treaty was drawn up, one that obliged Denmark to cede the island of Bornholm and the territory it had taken in the south of the Swedish mainland. Sweden also insisted on being given the area around Trondheim in Norway, a particularly stringent demand as this cut the northern region of the country off from that of the south. But by July Karl X was annoyed that the terms of the recent treaty had not yet been met by the Danes. They had been encouraged to procrastinate by the Dutch, the latter always keen to prevent excessive power going to any one nation who might then interrupt their trade in the region. Therefore, Karl decided to mount another attack on Copenhagen, first taking control of both shores of the Øresund by capturing the strategic Kronborg fortress at Helsingør, around 30 miles to the north of the city. Here Queen Hedvig Eleonora took up residence, amusing herself over the next few weeks with hunting, entertaining foreign dignitaries, and visiting the neighbouring Fredriksborg. But that was not all that she gained from her visit as, after her departure, again many items were found to have been pilfered. Among the things taken at this time were certain precious relics from Roskilde, most notably the golden gown – still today in Uppsala Cathedral's museum – reputed to have once belonged to Margrete, the founder of the Kalmar Union.

Meanwhile, for Karl the more immediate purpose behind the capture of Kronborg had been to set up a naval blockade that could cut off supplies to the Danish capital that was now placed under siege. However, at this point the Dutch again intervened, sending forty-five ships to aid the Danes, and thereby ensuring their victory in the ensuing Battle of the Sound of October 1658. This allowed the allies to reopen the straits and bring some much-needed supplies to the beleaguered Copenhagen. Nevertheless, Karl did not give up in his attempt to take the city and, on the departure of the Dutch, re-established the blockade, which he then kept in place for the next four months. Eventually, in February he launched a final assault, but resilient to the last, the defenders held out, widening the ice-free moats surrounding the fortress, and thereby inflicting serious losses on the Swedes when they attempted to bridge the gap. At last, accepting his failure, Karl gave the order for his men to withdraw, and Copenhagen was spared.

By this time the Swedish king's other enemies were also rallying against him. Having mounted attacks on his possessions south of the Baltic, the Great Elector, the emperor and the Poles began to drive his troops from the Jutland peninsula, ultimately forcing the Swedes in May to evacuate the now largely destroyed Fredriksodde. And there would be yet more setbacks at the end of the year, when the 6,000-strong force defending the islands of Fyn and Langeland was defeated by the Danes, and numbers of Karl's best men were taken prisoner.

In Norway, too, Karl faced opposition, above all from the people living in the recently occupied area of Trondelag, who particularly disliked the taxes and involuntary recruitment being imposed on them. With the tensions rising, the garrison at Trondheim was forced to surrender and leave the country, although it was allowed to do so with full honours. Faced by these challenges, Karl finally accepted that he must begin peace negotiations, but he wanted first to strengthen his hand by extending his Norwegian territory elsewhere. This time he concentrated chiefly on the area of Halden, around 75 miles to the south of Christiania (Oslo) – a place where just under sixty years later his famous grandson, Karl XII, would meet his death. But as the fortress of Fredriksten managed to withstand his repeated attacks, the king at last accepted that he must summon the *Riksdag* to Göteborg (Gothenburg) and begin the delayed peace talks.

However, two months before any agreement was reached, in February 1660 Karl died unexpectedly, aged just thirty-seven. A chill that he had caught while inspecting works in the city turned into pneumonia, and this, having been wrongly diagnosed and treated, resulted in sepsis. Nonetheless, peace was agreed in a series of treaties: first, at Oliwa in Royal Prussia on 3 May (NS) Livonia was officially acknowledged as a Swedish possession, and Jan Kazimierz of Poland finally renounced his dynasty's claims to the Swedish throne; second, a month later at Copenhagen, Bornholm was given to Denmark and the borders dividing the two Scandinavian countries fixed to all intents and purposes along the lines that we see today. And finally, the following year at Cardis near Dorpat (Tartu) on 1 July 1661 (NS), Russia had to surrender its recently captured gains in Karelia, Ingria, Estonia and Livonia.

Karl X Gustav was an exceptional soldier, as well as a person of talent and charm. Although small, thickset and physically unprepossessing, the emperor's ambassador, Count Montecuccoli, would picturesquely describe him as a very easy-going, popular man, whose heavy drinking had 'endeared' him to his people. However, one instance when Karl's diplomacy failed him was during his dealings with the Poles, and by his sacking of their country he damaged relations between Sweden and the Commonwealth for years to come. Like so many of his predecessors, Karl was guilty of plundering his conquered territories, following the current and accepted practice of seizing war booty to fill the royal coffers. But this he carried to even greater excess, giving a bad example to his men, whom he then failed to control when they went beyond the limits of behaviour earlier set down by Gustavus Adolphus. The latter, like Karl X, had not been above looting himself, but he had dictated that while the common soldier's reward was to be taken from the 'contributions' of the local people, pillage and violence would be severely punished. But for Gustavus Adolphus, campaigning in the richer German states, this policy was easier to uphold than it was for Karl fighting in the much more impoverished Polish countryside, where most of the action took place during his six years on the throne. And while this does not excuse Karl, it partly explains what happened on his watch. Receiving little local remuneration, and vastly outnumbered by the often unruly mercenary troops fighting by their side, the men soon forgot their vaunted Swedish discipline. And as things spiralled out of control, it was instead their greed and savagery that became the talk of Europe. However, at home Karl X was admired for his military courage and achievements, and during his short reign he took steps to place his country's administration on a surer footing. Although he had the temperament to achieve much, his programme was cut short by his early death, and it would be some years before Sweden would be in the hands of a wise ruler, able to take on the domestic reforms that he had initiated.

In his will, Karl X had named his wife, Hedvig Eleonora, as leader of the regency for his four-year-old son, who was now the new king Karl XI. The day after her husband's death, the queen summoned the council to assert her position and, although initially opposed, three months later she finally received its approval. Although still only twenty-four when she was widowed, she decided against remarriage, refusing an offer from the Stuart king, Charles II, and choosing instead to dedicate her life to her much-loved son. A devout woman, for the next twelve years she took care of his moral and religious instruction and, having concerns about his delicate health, she also concentrated on his physical development. However, although an intelligent woman with a lifelong interest in collecting books, she failed to provide a sound education for Karl XI, who was possibly dyslexic. As a result, although he became a good soldier and keen huntsman, he grew up to be ill-informed and virtually illiterate, things that in later life would cause him to be shy and diffident in public.

Hedvig Eleonora, one of sixteen children, had grown up at her father's cultured court at Gottorp, surrounded by artists and thinkers of the period. The great-niece of the Danish king Christian IV and his sister, Anne, Queen of England and Scotland, and a granddaughter of the Elector of Saxony, she was connected to many of the ruling houses of Europe. Her interest in the arts, which had developed during her childhood, would in time enrich the cultural heritage of Sweden. On Karl X's death she commissioned in his memory the large silver chandelier that still hangs in the Riddarholm Church, and the following year bought the palace at Drottningholm that had been sold eleven years earlier to her husband's brother-in-law, the immensely rich statesman Magnus de la Gardie. This building burnt down shortly afterwards and so she commissioned Nicodemus Tessin the Elder to design another on the same site. When he died nineteen years later the architect had finished the staircase, the Ehrenstrahl Drawing Room (or Large Audience Room), and the Queen's State Bedroom, but the work was still not quite finished. After it had been completed by his son, Tessin the Younger, Hedvig Eleonora moved into the less formal south wing, and from that period the palace became her main summer residence. In addition to this, being a serious collector she soon set about enlarging the national collection that had been considerably denuded by Queen Christina's removal of treasures at the time of her abdication. Hedvig Eleonora personally paid for many items in the royal treasury and, having a keen interest in Eastern artefacts, she also invested in Sweden's growing trade with China.

During the Long Regency of her son, there was a return to the extravagance that had marred Queen Christina's reign, and corruption became endemic. The country stagnated, and Karl X's military reforms were discontinued, hastening the decline of the army and the navy. Karl XI finally reached his majority in 1672, but he still relied on his mother's opinion, and continued to follow the advice of Magnus de la Gardie, the Regency Council's most influential member. The son of Jacob de la Gardie and Ebbe Brahe – the woman whom Gustavus Adolphus had wished to marry – Magnus de la Gardie had been for a time a favourite of Queen Christina, and later had served as a general under Karl X. But his reliance on French subsidies as an answer to the Swedish financial problems meant that by 1672 the country was virtually in Louis XIV's pay. Having that year drawn up an agreement at Stockholm to keep an army in Sweden's dominions on the southern shores of the Baltic, a force that was always ready to come to the service of the French king, during the Franco-Dutch war the Swedes found themselves called on to invade Brandenburg from the neighbouring Swedish Pomerania. As a result of this the Great Elector, Friedrich Wilhelm, mounted his own surprise attack on the Swedish troops at Fehrbellin on 28 June 1675 (NS), and the victory he then achieved with his smaller army greatly undermined Sweden's earlier reputation as a military power.

Now aware of the country's obvious weakness, in September the Danes joined in the fighting, allying themselves with Brandenburg-Prussia and others to mount an assault on Bremen-Verden, which had been in personal union with Sweden since the end of the Thirty Years' War. Having already invaded Pomerania, and engaged in skirmishes and battles along the Norwegian-Swedish border, Denmark's main objective was to regain the lands recently lost in the south of the Swedish mainland. So in June 1676, after winning a naval battle near the island of Öland, the Danish and Dutch fleets seized Helsingborg lying just across the water from Kronborg on the east coast of the Øresund. They then went on to take possession of the whole of Skåne (Scania) with the exception of Malmö. As a result of these disasters, de la Gardie lost favour, and the newly crowned Karl XI started to be more influenced by Johan Gyllenstierna, who at the end of the hostilities three years later became governor of these reclaimed regions. Although here he would impose a harsh, if not brutal, regime on its people, this same man would be responsible for inspiring the young king with new peace-loving ideas. From this time, Karl set out to avoid further warfare, an ambition that would be combined with his determination to halt the ever-growing power of the corrupt magnates. These two policies would gradually enable him to rebuild his country and repair Sweden's fragile economic and political status.

In 1675, the same month as the defeat at Fehrbellin, in order to improve international relations, a diplomatic marriage had been arranged for Karl with Ulrikke Eleonore, daughter of Frederik III of Denmark, but within three months her brother Christian V had made his declaration of war on Sweden. The next year in October Karl personally led his troops back to Skåne, where in December at Lund his smaller army defeated the Danes. This, although a particularly savage battle that left many dead, made Karl XI's name, and his reputation was then further burnished when in July the next year he won a second victory at Landskrona and forced the Danish king to retreat. However, as the war continued, the Swedes in turn would suffer their own setbacks, their serious naval defeats leaving Denmark in total control of the Baltic, and so by 1679 both countries were ready to agree a peace. In the subsequent treaties Louis XIV acted as arbiter, but although he ensured that officially Sweden regained its lost territories, he privately agreed to Brandenburg receiving some small parts of its German possessions, and as a result of this act of deceit, Karl XI developed a lasting hatred and distrust of the French.

When, with the outbreak of this 'Scanian War', the Danish princess Ulrikke had been given the option of breaking off her engagement to Karl XI, she had refused, even turning down proposals from the Prince of Orange and the future Holy Roman Emperor, Leopold I. Instead, she had been kind to the Swedish prisoners, and had avoided taking part in any celebrations following their defeats. So finally, with the ending of hostilities, in May 1680, five years after her engagement, the marriage was celebrated in a ceremony that was made intentionally low-key so that king would not have to invite the hated French ambassador. By this time Ulrikke (now Queen Ulrika) had replaced all her Danish entourage with Swedish courtiers, and in a further popular measure, the next year she named her first child Hedvig Sofia after her mother-in-law. Although the young queen then continued to give birth every year until 1686, only the oldest of her five boys, Karl, would survive infancy. Nevertheless, in 1688 a second daughter (Ulrika Eleonora) was born, and she, like both her older siblings, would live into adulthood and eventually play a leading role in future events.

By the time of Queen Ulrika's marriage, the financial situation in Sweden had become so grave as a result of the expenses incurred by the recently concluded Scanian War that Karl XI persuaded the *Riksdag* at last to ratify the reduction system that his father had previously favoured, thereby enabling the Crown to recover all its former lands and entitlements. This act caused many nobles to lose vast fortunes, none more so that de la Gardie, who had to give up his several large estates, retaining just one mansion where he lived on until his death. The young queen became concerned when some people were left seriously impoverished by these measures, and she therefore chose to finance them personally from her private funds, still remembering them on her deathbed when she made a last, personal request, asking the king to help them through their difficulties.

Despite her being Danish, Ulrika Eleonora's gentle character and charitable works, made her extremely popular with the Swedish people, but her relations with Hedvig Eleonora would always be strained. Karl XI remained devoted to his mother, giving her precedence over his wife, whom he never referred to as 'the Queen' until after her death, and for a time this caused Ulrika such distress that she chose to take up residence at Uppsala. While some of her mother-in-law's antagonism may have been caused by straightforward jealousy, it was also fuelled by the enmity she shared with all her family towards the Danish people. The dowager queen would never forgive them for having besieged her father just before his death at Tönning in 1659, nor for forcing her brother Duke Christian Albrecht of Holstein-Gottorp into exile. While Denmark's relations were often fraught with the neighbouring duchy, the situation had been made still worse when in 1675 Christian V ousted the duke – his own brother-in-law – from his homelands. And in 1689, Ulrika's loyalties were further

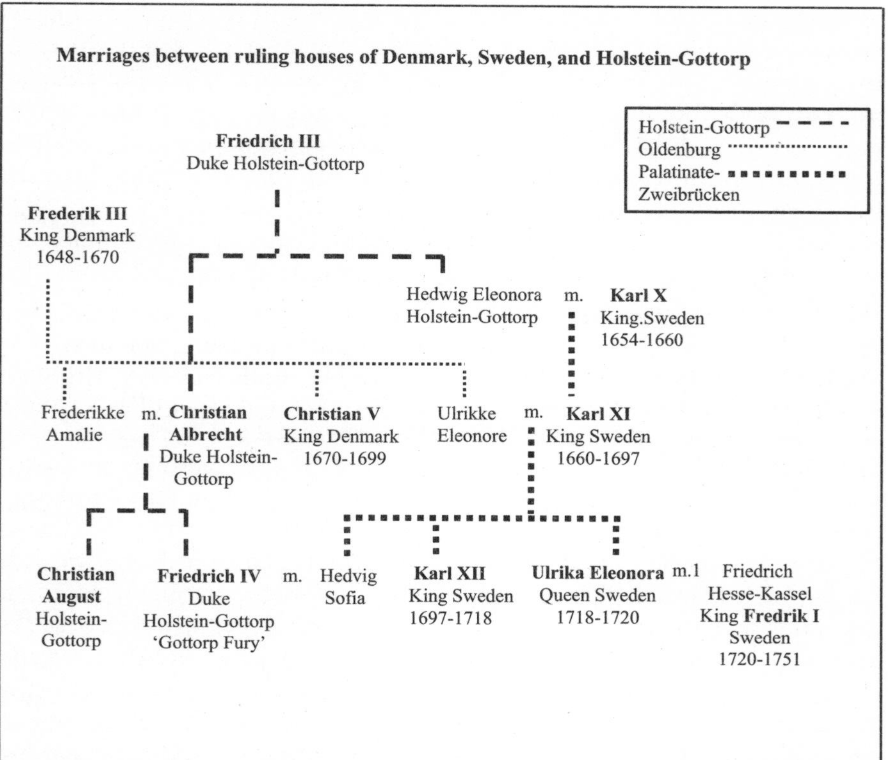

tested when her husband once more opposed her brother by supporting the duke's efforts to wrest his possessions back from the Danish king.

However, over time Karl XI's respect for his wife had grown, and in 1690 he named her regent for their son in the event of his own death while the boy was still underage. The king had now become aware of his wife's qualities, and the difficult path she had had to tread during a period when Denmark and Sweden were so often at odds with each other. But her health was declining, undermined by her seven pregnancies in less than eight years, and in July 1693 she died aged thirty-six. Having been largely ignored by her husband during her marriage, he now stayed with her throughout her final illness and was heartbroken by her death. Although from this time he grew closer to his children, at the end of his own life four years later he would declare that from the day she had died, he had ceased to be happy.

During the final twenty years of his reign, when Karl XI maintained the peace and established a financially sound state, he also improved Sweden's defences by founding a new naval base on the Baltic at Karlskrona. And although he was always dubious about the loyalty of the conquered people of Skåne, who were barred from joining their local regiments, they too were part of his now well-trained army of some

90,000 men. A profoundly devout Lutheran, he imposed a strict religious adherence on his people, and by his example he also instilled in them his own hard-working mentality. As a result, at the meeting of the *Riksdag* in 1680, he had been acknowledged as independent of his council, free to make decisions by himself. However, as the senior nobles still remained too assertive, thirteen years later the Estates had further strengthened the king's authority, issuing the Declaration of Sovereignty. This act made Karl an absolute ruler, but with his premature death aged forty-one from stomach cancer in April 1697, these total powers passed to a minor, his fourteen-year-old son, Karl XII.

Now the dowager queen, Hedvig Eleonora, found herself once again acting as regent; but within days Karl XII showed his maturity, calmly saving her and his sisters when a fire broke out in the old Tre Konor Castle in Stockholm. While he also succeeded in rescuing the body of his father, who was still lying in state, the greater part of the palace was destroyed, taking with it much of the recently accumulated royal treasures, and most of Hedvig Eleonora's precious collection of books. Later those responsible for the outbreak of the fire were punished, first ordered to run the gauntlet, and then sent to endure years of forced labour. A little over ten weeks after this disaster, Karl celebrated his fifteenth birthday and then, within seven months of his accession – despite the opposition of the clergy – the *Riksdag* abolished the regency, declaring him fit to rule. In December, even before the mourning had ended for his father, Karl XII received the homage of his nobles in the square outside the Riddarholm Church, and the next day, still dressed in black except for his purple robe of office, he was anointed in the Storkyrkan in a service of consecration. Not wanting a traditional coronation as he wished to assert his inherited right to rule as Sweden's absolute monarch, Karl placed the crown on his own head, and from this time onwards he would continue to listen attentively to the advice of others, but all final decisions would be his alone.

PART 3

ABSOLUTISM AND AUTOCRACY

7

Denmark's First Absolute Rulers

The Chapel of the Order of the Elephant at Frederiksborg Castle, where new members' coats of arms continue to be added to the walls in the upper gallery.

When Frederik III died in February 1670, his twenty-three-year-old son Christian V succeeded as the first of Denmark's absolute, hereditary kings. In a sumptuous ceremony made still more spectacular by the addition of impressive new regalia, Christian was anointed at Fredriksborg Castle the following June. To emphasise his newly acquired inalienable status, seated on the elaborate throne created by Frederik, Christian placed on his own head the magnificent crown that had also been commissioned by his father; no longer worn by the Danish monarchs at coronations, this still plays a symbolic role at the funeral of the sovereign, last appearing on the coffin of Frederik IX when he died in 1972. Together with the other royal jewels, today this crown is on display in the royal treasury housed in Rosenborg Castle. Like Frederik III before him, Christian V was immediately aware of the potential dangers to his position that the over-powerful Danish aristocracy posed, and so he now chose to appoint either nobles from his duchy of Holstein, or commoners who might later be promoted to his newly created ranks of count or baron.

Hoping to raise the standing of his country still further, the year after his accession Christian V set out to expand Denmark's colonial territories abroad, claiming the Caribbean island of St Thomas, where he renamed the capital Amalienborg in honour of his wife Charlotte Amalie. While at this time such overseas possessions were seen to represent the wealth and importance of European countries, the reality was that from this moment Denmark, like the others, began to be involved in the slave trade. Soon discovering the need for men and women able to work in the harsh tropical conditions of the plantations, ships began to transport thousands of Africans from Denmark's recently acquired trading posts on the Gold Coast. Four years after acquiring St Thomas, the country also took the island of St John, with St Croix, bought from the French, later becoming the third of Denmark's West Indian possessions in 1733.

These were brutal times everywhere and so although in 1683 Christian V gave Denmark a new more moderate legal code that softened the penalties imposed on offenders, punishments were still severe; no longer executed, thieves were now flogged, and instead of being burned at the stake, witches were pilloried. In certain regions of the country, serfdom still bound many peasants to the land, putting them under the control of the local landlords. Christian's son Frederik IV would abolish this system in 1702, but it reappeared again later in an even harsher form, not finally dying out until as late as the 1780s. Meanwhile, slavery continued in the Caribbean colonies until 1848, after which the islands remained in Danish possession until 1917, when they were finally sold to the USA for twenty-five million dollars, thereafter becoming the American Virgin Isles.

Christian V's thinking had been formulated by his experiences as a young man when he had visited the French court while travelling around Europe. Here he had witnessed the divine right of kings and, impressed by what he had seen, on his accession had become determined to model himself on the majestic Louis XIV. For much the same reason, he would reintroduce Frederik II's Order of the Elephant, establishing its official chapel in Frederiksborg Castle, where today scores of heraldic shields decorate its walls. However, even after his accession, Christian always remained under the influence of his formidable mother, Sophie Amalie, and it was on her instigation that in 1667 he had married Charlotte Amalie of Hesse-Kassel. While his bride would never be on good terms with her mother-in-law, she would also face continuous opposition from the Church, who denied her a coronation on account of her Calvinist religion. As Charlotte Amalie was devoted to her faith, she refused ever to convert to Denmark's official Lutheranism, but her determined display of piety did not mean that she lacked tolerance. She was deeply opposed to the dowager queen's unforgiving stance regarding her husband's aunt – the unfortunate Leonora Christina, who was still incarcerated in her dungeon (see page 74) – and similarly she would later help a twice-divorced noblewoman, Marie Grubbe, who, charged with adultery, had escaped execution but then been reduced to a state of poverty.

The king, who declared hunting, warfare, maritime affairs and courtship as his preferred pleasures, always showed respect for his better educated and more intelligent wife, according her the recognition due to her position as queen. But although in time the couple would produce eight children, five years after his marriage Christian met the daughter of his doctor, a young woman called Sophie Amalie Moth, with whom he then began an affair. Following the fashion of Versailles, and to the great displeasure of his wife, he now made Sophie a countess, and introduced her to court as his official mistress. As the first woman to hold this title in Denmark, she would go on to give Christian six more children.

Again influenced by his mother, in 1675 Christian V decided to draw up a marriage contract between his youngest sister Ulrikke Eleonore, and the new Swedish king Karl XI. Although the ambitious dowager queen Sophie Amalie had already succeeded in finding distinguished husbands for her three older daughters, marrying them off in turn to the Elector of Saxony, the Duke of Holstein-Gottorp and the Elector of the Palatine, she was now eager to cap these achievements by making Ulrikke Queen of Sweden. But while this alliance was intended to improve relations between the two countries, within days of the betrothal being announced, political tensions came to a head, and with Christian then declaring war on his neighbour, the marriage negotiations were for the moment put on hold.

By this time France had created an alliance with the young Swedish king Karl XI, forcing the latter to invade Brandenburg, where he was then defeated in battle. This event proved to Christian that the Swedish army was no longer the powerful force that it once had been, and encouraged by this, he decided to make the most of his opportunity and invade Skåne, the province that had been lost during his father's reign. Personally leading his army into battle, he achieved his aim, managing to retake all the region with the exception of Malmö. But, although over the next two years the Danish fleet would achieve other significant victories at sea, as time went by Christian's troops on land were less successful and so, with the war now proving highly costly to both parties, peace was eventually agreed. The treaty left the previous situation little changed, the disputed territories being returned to their pre-war status, to Christian's bitter regret, Skåne remaining in Swedish hands. According to some, in his disappointment he now ordered the eastern-facing windows of Kronborg Castle to be blocked up so he might not have to look on Denmark's lost possessions across the Øresund.

However, with the peace agreed, the marriage negotiations between Ulrikke Eleonore and the Swedish king could be renewed, and the simple ceremony was finally able to take place in May 1680. On leaving her country, Ulrikke showed that she fully appreciated the importance of her role, describing herself as a 'pawn of peace', and declaring to her brother that she prayed that God would give her the grace 'to fulfil such a glorious commitment'.[19] Although she would be treated coolly by her mother-in-law, she would soon be loved by the people of her new country.

All this time back in Denmark Christian V was beginning to make changes to his capital. Now using Swedish prisoners of war who had been captured during his father's time, he created the Nyhavn, a new harbour area where goods could be brought right into the recently developed part of the city. However, because of the limited space, over time this became unable to cope with the increasingly large ships, and as a result its busy maritime trade started to decline. While during the nineteenth century hotels and other such buildings among the warehouses began to provide accommodation for various guests, including famous names like Hans Christian Andersen, by the time of the First World War the whole area had become insalubrious and unsafe. A renowned red-light district, it was avoided by the majority of people until an urban redevelopment programme in the 1970s cleaned it up and made it the colourful and lively spot it is today.

At the north-western end of the Nyhavn, Christian created a new square, the largest in the city, the New Royal Market or Kongens Nytorv that had been modelled on the Place des Vosges in Paris. Here two years before his death he would give his mistress Sophie Moth one of the large houses that ringed the area, and this building is today the French Embassy. And in the square's central garden, in 1688 Christian erected a statue of himself created by the French sculptor Abraham-César Lamoureux. This, again following the tastes of Versailles, depicted him as a Roman emperor, mounted on his horse and surrounded by classical figures representing courage, strength, honour and wisdom. But in time, this – the oldest such statue in Scandinavia – began to collapse under its own weight, and so finally in the 1940s a decision was made to recast it. With the replica back in place, the square is still a focal centre in the city, each year becoming a favourite gathering point for the students newly graduated from the nearby university.

Just a year after Christian's statue had been put in place, the former dowager queen's residence in Copenhagen, the Sophie Amalienborg Palace, was burned to the ground. Four years after his mother's death, the king had begun to use this palace for his own entertainment, but in the middle of a performance of the opera, put on during a week of

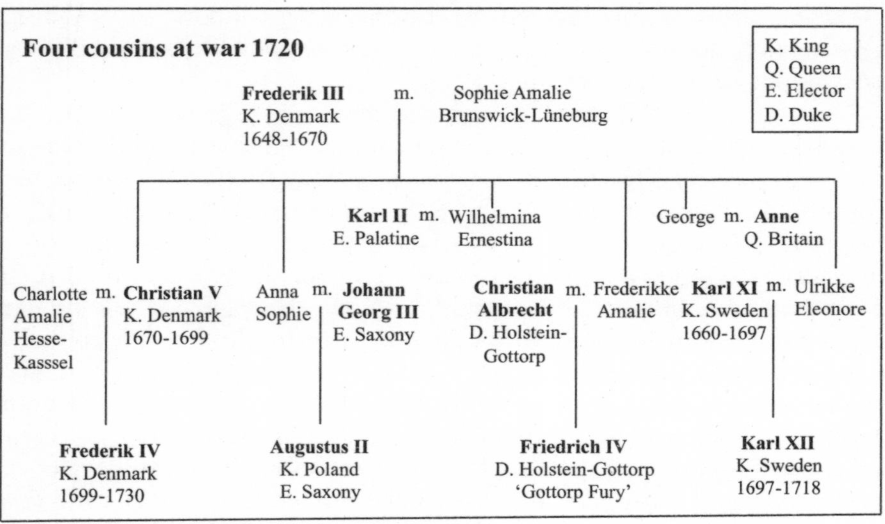

celebrations for his birthday, the fire took hold, eventually causing the deaths of some 180 people. While, in the long run this disaster would give space to the development of the area that now constitutes the royal palace, in the immediate term it would mark the beginning of a sequence of tragedies to hit the royal family. In June 1695 Christian's third son, again called Christian, died having caught smallpox while on his way to Italy, and then four years later the king himself had an accident while out hunting, suffering injuries that eventually led to his death. Following that, his mistress retired from Copenhagen to the estate he had given her around 25 miles south of the capital, and his widow, Charlotte Amalie, moved into the same square where Sophie had previously lived. Here fifteen years later she died in Charlottenborg, her baroque palace on the corner of the Nyhavn that is today the Royal Danish Academy of Fine Arts. After her death Charlotte Amalie would be buried at Roskilde Cathedral, placed beside her husband in the chancel, where their magnificent, ornate baroque marble tombs would in time be joined by those of their son Frederik IV and his wife.

Christian V's untimely death in August 1699 brought to the throne his twenty-seven-year-old son, Frederik IV, one of the group of young bravado rulers who now came to power. These men, who included Peter of Russia, Karl XII of Sweden, Augustus of Saxony (the new King of Poland), and Friedrich IV, Duke of Holstein-Gottorp, would subsequently disrupt the peace of the continent, and bring two decades of turmoil to the region. As a further complication, all bar the tsar were first cousins, a situation that had been brought about by Sophie Amalie's earlier ambitions to arrange important dynastic marriages. Now, with a tragic disregard for family loyalties, these men would find themselves taking opposing sides in the coming Great Northern War.

While his father was still on the throne, in 1695 Frederik was given little choice but to marry Luise of Mecklenburg-Güstrow, a match considered suitable as she was descended not just from Frederik II of Denmark, but also Friedrich III of Holstein-Gottorp – and thus she was also the niece of the dowager Swedish queen Hedvig Eleonora. But she had grown up in a strictly religious household, living at the family castle of Güstrow near Rostock, and with her quiet, withdrawn personality, she would never be popular at court. Although producing five children, she soon had to suffer the king's infidelities, and within four years of her marriage, Frederik, following the example set by his father, had begun a relationship with his sister's lady-in-waiting, Helene von Vieregg. Having acknowledged her as his mistress in 1701, two years later he went further and married Helene without bothering to divorce his wife. This bigamous marriage was, however, accepted by the Church authorities, who chose to explain their decision by finding a biblical precedent for it. But within two years Helene had died in childbirth, and Frederik had already found a new favourite from among her ladies-in-waiting. Yet on this occasion the Church refused to give their permission to his marriage, obliging the king to keep her merely as his mistress until 1712, by which time his affections had moved on. He had now fallen for Anna Sophie Reventlow, a young woman whom he had seen at a ball. However, as his intention to make her his new mistress was opposed by the girl's own mother, he overcame the impasse by abducting Anna Sophie to Skanderborg in Jutland, where he then took part in a second bigamous marriage ceremony. However, as Anna Sophie still remained unrecognised at court, and was pointedly ignored by her step-children, she continued to live in her own house in Copenhagen until finally in 1721 Queen Luise died. Then after just twenty days of mourning, Anna Sophie's official wedding took place, followed soon after by her coronation. The nobility was appalled, considering the new queen to be sociably unsuitable, and so when – like the offspring of Frederik's other mistresses – none of her six children survived, many held it as proof that God had disapproved of the king's illicit relationships.

For twenty years during Frederik IV's reign, the Great Northern War would predominate over affairs in the Baltic region. His father, just the year before his death, had joined an alliance with Augustus of Poland and Peter of Russia against their common foe, the Swedish king. Meanwhile, however, Karl XII was in league with his cousin and brother-in-law the Duke of Holstein-Gottorp, ruler of the duchy whose lands lay on Denmark's southern border. Then, in March 1700, just months after his accession, Frederik IV decided to send his troops into this disputed region and mount an attack on the Swedish garrison in the fortress at Tönning, thus beginning what would become a five-month-long siege. Immediately

Karl retaliated by successfully invading Zealand and marching on Copenhagen, where – in the absence of her son – the dowager queen Charlotte Amalie had taken his place, encouraging the city's defenders to stand firm against the Swedish assault.

Having soon realised the danger facing his capital, without further delay Frederik hurried back from Holstein and before long had agreed to make peace with Karl. By the terms of this agreement, in addition to acknowledging Holstein-Gottorp's sovereignty, Frederik was obliged to pay compensation to the duke. But more importantly still, Denmark withdrew from the wider-ranging war that had now broken out, and with that the Swedish king turned his attention to the more serious challenges that were facing him elsewhere.

No longer involved in the conflict that was now raging among his neighbours, Frederik began from this time to focus his attention on other matters. He reformed his army, and, having paid heed to the opinions and complaints of his people, ended the system of serfdom on the island of Zealand. Although not well educated, Frederik had travelled abroad as a young man and become particularly influenced by Italian culture. So on his return, with his father's permission, he had begun to build near Copenhagen a small palace called Frederiksberg – this not to be confused with the similarly named Frederiksborg some 25 miles to the north of the city. Later Frederiksberg would be extended into a large baroque building that replaced Rosenborg as the favourite summer residence, and it was here that Frederik would receive Tsar Peter I during his travels around Europe in 1716. Today it is home to the Royal Danish Military Academy.

Eight years earlier, leaving his wife in Denmark as acting regent, Frederik had returned to Italy, accompanied by around seventy followers. After stopping for a time in Florence – where he had used the opportunity to visit a nun who had been one of his former lovers – he had then moved on to Venice, where for the next nine weeks he enjoyed the regatta and the various operas and plays that were put on for his pleasure. His stay in the city was deemed a success, despite the exceptional cold of the winter in early 1709, during which the ice covering the lagoon was so thick that it became possible to cross over it to the mainland.

In the Ukraine these same bitter winter conditions were now assaulting the exhausted Swedish army, deeply ensnared in its Russian campaign. But at the same time there was also another natural phenomenon that was now starting to cause panic across Europe. The plague had recently begun to spread through the continent, apparently moving north along the trade routes from Constantinople (Istanbul).[20] In the vast areas recently devastated by war, many people were already close to starving, and this left them with little resistance when the infection began to hit. As a result, in certain places the effects of the disease would be catastrophic, wiping out as many as two-thirds or even three-quarters of the population. When the epidemic reached the Baltic, Danzig tried to conceal the news in order to protect its trade, but this just helped spread the sickness further. And the problem was made still worse by numbers of deserting Swedish soldiers struggling back home from Russia. To confront these challenges, for a time the Danes set up a quarantine control on the island of Saltholm in the Sound, but although this possibly helped delay the arrival of the disease, in November 1710 the first cases appeared just north of Helsingør. Soon breaking out in other places as well, it eventually reached Copenhagen the following June, where it remained for the next five months. Although this would be the last instance of the plague in the region, during this outbreak unknown numbers would die in the city, with the reported figures varying between 12,000 and 23,000 from what was an overall population of around only 70,000. However, Jutland, helped by Denmark's island topography, was spared, and by 1714 the danger was over for the whole country.

The year 1709 had also brought good news to Frederik as he learnt that at last during the summer his cousin Karl XII had been soundly defeated by the Russians at Poltava in the Ukraine. The tables were now completely turned, and Frederik therefore saw his opportunity to rejoin his former allies and re-engage in the war. And with the remaining Swedish army now facing unequal odds, opposed at different moments by Russians, Poles, Saxons, Prussians and Hanoverians, in 1712 the Danish were able to occupy the Swedish-owned Bremen-Verden, holding it for three years until they sold it to the Hanoverian elector, the recently crowned English king, George I. The year after, Frederik was able to drive another of his cousins, the new duke, Karl Friedrich, out of Holstein-Gottorp, and two years later Denmark also took control of Stralsund and the surrounding Pomerania. But finally after the Swedish king had been killed on campaign in Norway, in 1720 Frederik made peace with Sweden, signing a treaty at Frederiksborg, where Denmark exchanged Wismar and the other Pomeranian possessions for control of Schleswig-Holstein.

With the war at last over, Frederik could now return to his other projects, among them the sponsoring of the Bergen-Greenland Company that aimed to recolonise Greenland. The first Norse settlements had disappeared from the region in the early seventh century, and Christian IV's later expeditions had not only failed to discover what had happened to the original settlers, but also to re-establish a new community in the area. So now attempting to rectify the situation, three little ships set sail from Bergen, carrying on board a missionary family and a few other aspiring colonists. But having reached their destination, they too failed to find any surviving settlers and, as they began to suffer from scurvy, many of them chose to abandon the scheme and return home. Although Frederik promoted a further colonising effort, this again would be blighted by disease, and after some of the community started to mutiny the king decided to abandon the whole idea. But with some missionaries still staying on, Denmark's claim to the region was upheld, so that today Greenland, despite having home rule, remains part of the Danish kingdom.

At home too, the king continued to work hard, setting out to reduce the country's debt, regulate the tax system, control corruption, register landownership, build new schools, and found Copenhagen's Royal Theatre. He also started work on a new castle to replace the one formerly belonging to his grandmother that had earlier been destroyed by fire. And then for his personal use, around 25 miles from the city on his hunting estate he built a new baroque country residence. This was completed in 1726 and, to commemorate the ending of the Great Northern War, it was named Fredensborg – the 'Peace Castle'. While Frederik would not have long to enjoy this new palace, it was much loved by later generations, and still today remains the country home of the royal family. Despite these extravagances, however, by now the king had become more religious, having turned to the Protestant Pietist movement, a strict branch of the Lutheran teaching. He therefore started to forbid all entertainments such as masques, plays and general feasting taking place on Sundays, and even fined or pilloried those who did not attend the day's religious service. But soon he was faced by more serious concerns. First, just two years before his death, in October 1728 Copenhagen suffered a major fire that having lasted for three days eventually left nearly half of the old city destroyed. Second, Frederik had by now contracted tuberculosis and was gravely ill. In October 1730, while he was on his way back to Copenhagen, he collapsed and died.

Frederik IV's deeply religious son, Christian VI, although well educated, was a shy and retiring man who having followed his mother's example was also a Pietist. He never gained the affection of his people, his popularity not helped by the fact that having a poor grasp of Danish, he mainly spoke German – the language of his childhood tutors. While his father had been given little option in the matter of his marriage, Christian had been allowed to select his own wife, choosing the equally devout Sophie Magdalene, a lady-in-waiting to the wife of Augustus II, King of Poland. Although she was considered by the nobles to be of inferior birth, the couple were well suited and happy together, and after her husband's accession in 1730, they shut themselves away and were seldom seen in public. Despite their court being one of the most sumptuous of the time, it was now known for its piety, puritanism, tedium and retrograde customs and ideas. Plays continued to be banned and theatres closed, while banquets and feasts were abandoned. Moreover, as the straight-laced Christian VI had been appalled by his father's earlier lifestyle, above all by his scandalous and bigamous relationships, after coming to the throne he disobeyed Frederik IV's last wishes to care for his stepmother. Anna Sophie was immediately banished from court to her childhood home, Clausholm Castle, where she remained for the last thirteen years of her life. Moreover, Christian VI purposely bought a new chapel at Roskilde, designed so that after her death she might be buried as far away as possible from the tombs of her dead husband and the other members of his family in the high chancel.

Still more significant, in a particularly retrogressive measure, just three years after his accession, worried about the negative fallout of his father's policy, Christian VI reversed his measures to free the serfs. With their newly won freedom, numbers of people had migrated to the cities, a movement that had not just created a shortage of manpower for the country's defence, but also undermined the Danish economy. To redress these problems and ensure the peasants' constant readiness to serve their local lord in both war and peace, the new king therefore reintroduced the ban on their free movement, and thus he again condemned the poorest in society to their former life of hardship and forced servitude.

In contrast, concerned for the educational development of his country, Christian VI rebuilt and enlarged the university that had been destroyed in the Copenhagen fire of 1728, and – despite his own poor knowledge of the language – promoted the general use of Danish. Wanting to increase the royal family's personal standing, he also took on projects such as the building of Hirscholm (now demolished), and the rebuilding of Christiansborg – the unstable former castle in Copenhagen that was now replaced with a large, impressive baroque palace. To pay for these extravagant schemes Christian reverted to that old practice of raising the Sound Dues. Finally, in a further move to maintain his country's peace, he agreed with George II in 1743 to the marriage of the Danish crown prince Frederik, and the English king's youngest surviving daughter, Louisa. While for Christian this was a dynastically suitable match that united the two Protestant kingdoms, it also had an additional advantage in that the bride-to-be was well connected to other influential ruling houses. Chief among these were the Hohenzollerns of Prussia, from whom Louisa's cousins, Frederick II and his sister Luise Ulrike, had been chosen as her godparents.

Christian was less successful when it came to Sweden, where he had hoped to make himself or one of his children heir to the childless king, Fredrik I – a plan that was ultimately thwarted when the crown passed instead to the husband of the same Luise Ulrike. Christian VI had long suffered from ill health, and so just three years after his son's marriage, the day before he celebrated his own silver wedding anniversary, he died at his new Hirscholm castle, aged just forty-six.

After his death in August 1746 Christian VI was succeeded by his oldest son, Frederik V, who by this time was married to the popular and approachable Louisa, now 'Queen Louise'. Despite Frederik's strict religious upbringing, he had grown into a wild youth, already on the downhill path to a life of uncontrolled hedonism. His heavy drinking and unsuitable liaisons had been behind his parents' decision to marry him while still only twenty, hoping to curb their son's undisciplined and promiscuous behaviour. However, rather than diminishing, Frederik's debauchery now increased, and despite loving his wife, he spent much of his time either with his one long-term mistress – by whom he had five children – or partaking in orgies with prostitutes. Meanwhile the queen, who contrived to ignore these affairs, became increasingly popular with the Danish people, particularly pleasing them by learning their language. Unlike her parents-in-law and the rest of the court, who continued to use German, she spoke Danish, personally using it when bringing up her family. From 1745 she gave birth to a child every year, but the oldest of the four to survive, Sophie Magdalene, was still only five at the time of her mother's death. Nonetheless, by that time this child was already promised in marriage to the future Swedish king, despite the strong protest of Louise, who suspected – rightly – that her daughter would eventually face antagonism from her future mother-in-law, the difficult Luise Ulrike.

During her five years as Danish queen, Louise encouraged a cultural revival, among other things promoting music and the theatre. The king also supported this movement, inaugurating three years after her death the Royal Danish Academy of Portraiture, Sculpture, and Architecture – today collectively known as the Fine Arts. But this was just part of Frederik V's lasting legacy in Copenhagen. Previously in 1748, two years after coming to the throne he had ordered the building of a new area, the Frederiksstaden, commissioned to celebrate the 300th anniversary of the Oldenburgs ascending to the Danish throne. Such development of the city had been considered since the time of Christian IV at the start of the seventeenth century, but it was now that this major new building programme took off. Copenhagen was growing, largely as a result of the wealth accumulated through the trade in sugar, and this commodity, brought to Denmark from its colonies in the West Indies, gave rise to associated industries such as rope making, boatbuilding and even the expansion of the navy. Warehouses and shipyards grew up not just in the Danish capital, but also in some other provincial ports. Much of this building boom was sponsored by the merchants, some of whom were also involved in the slave trade itself, and certain of these traders paraded their financial success by bringing back to Denmark black slaves to act as pages. They were seen as a sort of status symbol, and the fashion would be similarly practised in many of the courts and aristocratic houses of Europe. The king also became a beneficiary of the colonial trade, when, having bought the Caribbean islands for himself in 1754, he set up a turtle pond at Christiansted on Saint Croix – its animals, after they had been eaten, providing shells that could then be turned into luxury objects.

Within the Fredriksstaden development a new area called the Amalienborg was also created, named after the two castles that had previously been on the site, the first destroyed by fire, the second begun by

Frederik IV but now demolished to give space to the king's new project. Here four identical noblemen's houses were built in the rococo style around a square, in the centre of which work soon started on erecting a bronze equestrian statue of Frederik V. This took fourteen years to complete, designed by the Frenchman Jacques Saly, and it is estimated to have cost more than all the four surrounding palaces together. By the time of the statue's official unveiling in 1771, the king was dead, but as one of Copenhagen's most important works of art, is still stands in the Amalienborg, which for more than 200 years has been used as the royal palace. In addition to this, work started around the same time on the nearby Frederiks Kirke, now known as the Marble Church. However, for reasons of cost, the construction was stopped by the acting head of state, Struensee, in the 1770s, after which the building was left abandoned and decaying. Work was finally restarted in 1874 and the church was completed in limestone twenty years later, topped by a dome that is the largest in Scandinavia.

Shortly after Frederik's anniversary celebrations, in December 1751 tragedy struck when Louise died suddenly, with her sixth child now delivered stillborn. Although greatly mourned by king and country, to the shock of the Danish people, within seven months Frederik remarried, encouraged by his ministers, who hoped thereby to restrain him from his most serious excesses. His new wife was Juliane Marie, one of the Brunswick-Wolfenbüttels whose many well-placed relations included her sister, Frederick II of Prussia's unfortunate wife, and her nephew, the even more unfortunate deposed and still imprisoned Ivan VI of Russia. Furthermore, one of her mother's sisters had been married to the Emperor Charles VI, and another to Alexei, Peter the Great's son who had died a prisoner in St Petersburg's infamous fortress. With a less appealing personality than her predecessor, Juliane Marie was in the difficult position of trying to take Louise's place, something she never fully succeeded in doing, failing to gain the affection of the king or the court with her stiff formality and rigid adherence to protocol. But in October 1753 she gave birth to a son, again called Frederik, and in time he would assume a significant role following the dramatic events that later hit the royal family.

Three years after this latest birth, the disastrous Seven Years' War broke out, but with the Danish government determinedly avoiding any involvement in the conflict, the country was able to benefit commercially and economically. However, the king, still following his profligate and dissolute lifestyle, was by now not just an alcoholic, but also in chronically poor health. As a result, he had handed over the management of the country to his counsellors, and was playing only a minimal role in the affairs of state. But he still remained popular among the Danes, and so when in 1766 his extravagant lifestyle finally caught up with him and he died aged forty-two, he was mourned by his people.

8

The Early Romanovs to the Founding of St Petersburg

Peter the Great's fortress, the first stone building of St Petersburg, with the European-style Cathedral of Sts Peter and Paul that was still not completed at the time of the tsar's death.

At the beginning of the seventeenth century, Russia had gone through a period of serious unrest, with rebellion, foreign invasion, war, and political murder. In 1584, on the death of Ivan IV, 'the Terrible', his adviser, the *boyar* Boris Godunov, had acted as regent to Ivan's heir, his delicate son Feodor I. A brother-in-law of Feodor, Godunov was in a strong position to replace the sickly young tsar when he died less than fourteen years later, the regent's ambitions being helped by the earlier unexplained death of Feodor's younger half-brother, eight-year-old Dmitry. While this may well have been an accident, some rumours suggested that the boy had been murdered on Godunov's orders, a version of events that is central to the play by Pushkin that became the basis for Mussorgsky's later opera. But in 1605, just seven years after coming to the throne, Godunov himself died and, although his son succeeded as Feodor II, the situation soon descended into mayhem. During this period, known as the 'Time of Troubles', the turmoil was made worse by the arrival of a series of pretenders claiming to be Ivan IV's dead child, and in the chaos that then ensued, two months after Feodor II's accession, he was murdered by followers of the so-called First False Dmitry. This man was acclaimed tsar, but within a year of his coronation, he too was assassinated. This did not prevent the arrival of another impostor, the Second False Dmitry, who subsequently married Marina Mniszech, the Polish widow of his predecessor. Bizarrely, if not pragmatically, she declared him to be her former husband, hoping by this to strengthen his claim and ensure her own position. Ultimately no more fortunate than the first pretender, he too would be killed while he was drunk, murdered by a disgruntled Tatar. Eventually, Marina was captured, and just five months after the execution of her three-year-old son, she died a prisoner of the new tsar, Michael Romanov. (The details of the 'execution' of a three-year-old boggle the mind.)

Although for some time Poles, Cossacks and disenchanted Russians supported these False Dmitrys, shortly after the death of the first pretender, the *boyars* again appointed one of their own as Tsar Vasily IV Shuisky. A devious character whose loyalties switched as he felt expedient, he had for a time upheld the claims of the First False Dmitry, even though in 1591, on Godunov's orders, he had personally identified the body of the dead child. But, in an equally unprincipled turnaround, he had then retracted his earlier support of the impostor in order to advance his own position. After four years on the throne, all his ambitions came to an end. In 1610 the Poles invaded Russia and occupied the Kremlin, whereupon Vasily was deposed and taken to Poland, where two years later he died still in captivity. With the Russians once more needing to find a tsar, in the wake of the Poles' military success at Klushino and their occupation of the capital, the Polish king's fifteen-year-old son Prince Wladyslaw was elected to be the new ruler. However, as this decision was not popular with the people of Moscow – who feared, among other things, their forced conversion to Catholicism – in time the prince and his father had to leave the city, and Wladyslaw was never crowned. For two more years the remaining Poles held out under siege in the Kremlin, but most would be murdered following their eventual surrender. During this period, known in Poland as the *Dmitriades*, more pretenders continued to come forward, and then to add to Russia's problems, the country was soon again at war with the Polish-Lithuanian Commonwealth.

It was against this background of chaos that in 1613 the Zemsky Sobor, or Assembly of the Land, a body comprised of representatives of the *boyars*, men of the church and local officials, merchants and landowners, decided it was necessary to start afresh, find if possible another ruling dynasty. They looked to the family of the Romanovs, whose head was by now Feodor, the nephew of Anastasia Romanova, the first and favourite wife of Ivan IV. But following Ivan's death, Boris Godunov had forced the Romanov family into exile, and its leader Feodor to take holy orders, thus disqualifying him from becoming tsar. Later the Second False Dmitry would further promote this man, making him the Patriarch Filaret. However, after falling foul of the Polish king Sigismund III – whose authority in Moscow he had questioned – Filaret had been taken captive. So it was while he was still imprisoned in Poland that the search began for a new tsar and the assembly chose to elect his sixteen-year-old son Michael. But no one knew where the boy was hiding. With the Poles still at large, he and his mother were sheltering in a monastery around 250 miles from Moscow. A month later, in March, having found them at Kostroma, the large delegation offered Michael the throne. This he refused, he and his mother being only too aware of the inherent risks of the position. She insisted that her young son, raised in a monastery, was unqualified to take on the dangerous responsibilities that would fall to him. However, at last, after considerable prayers and pleading by the delegates, who begged him to save their country, Michael agreed to accept the crown. The events of this period became famous in the legend of Ivan Susanin, which is central to another opera – that of Glinka, later renamed *A Life for the Tsar.* Here the plot tells of the heroic action of a Russian patriot who is ordered by the Poles to guide them to the tsar's hiding place. Leading them deep into the forest, where they become lost, Susanin saves the boy, but pays for the deception with his own life. Later, in recognition of his self-sacrifice, Susanin's family was rewarded by the Romanovs, and the story became part of Russian mythology. But there is a further strange and poignant irony to these events, in that the Romanov dynasty began at Michael's refuge, the Ipatiev Monastery, a place that had the same name as the house at Ekaterinburg where, just over 300 years later in 1918, the dynasty came to an end with the murder of its final crowned head, Tsar Nicholas II.

Lacking the necessary experience to rule, the young tsar was initially guided by his mother and her family, but in 1619 his father returned from his six years of Polish captivity. Having then taken charge, Patriarch Filaret would continue to direct affairs until his death in 1633.

During his son's reign war broke out again with the Polish-Lithuanian Commonwealth, and when eventually peace was agreed in 1634, Russia surrendered new areas to its neighbour. However, in return Wladyslaw IV – who had now succeeded his father as King of Poland – finally agreed to renounce his claim to the Russian throne, and with that a line was at last drawn under the uncertainties of the Time of Troubles.

When Michael died in 1645, he was succeeded by his sixteen-year-old son Alexis, a deeply pious man who, although remembered as the 'Gentle Tsar', would again take Russia to war, and in doing so further expand the country's borders. His portraits depict him in the iconic style of the period, representing him as a quasi-divine figure, to be revered with almost religious adoration by his people. It is when comparing this traditional image with that of Alexis' contemporary kings, the British Charles II and the Polish Wladyslaw IV, that the chasm between the cultures of seventeenth-century Russia and the rest of Europe becomes apparent. Pictures of the tsar in this period act as a reminder of how great the reforms brought in by his son, Peter, half a century later, would be.

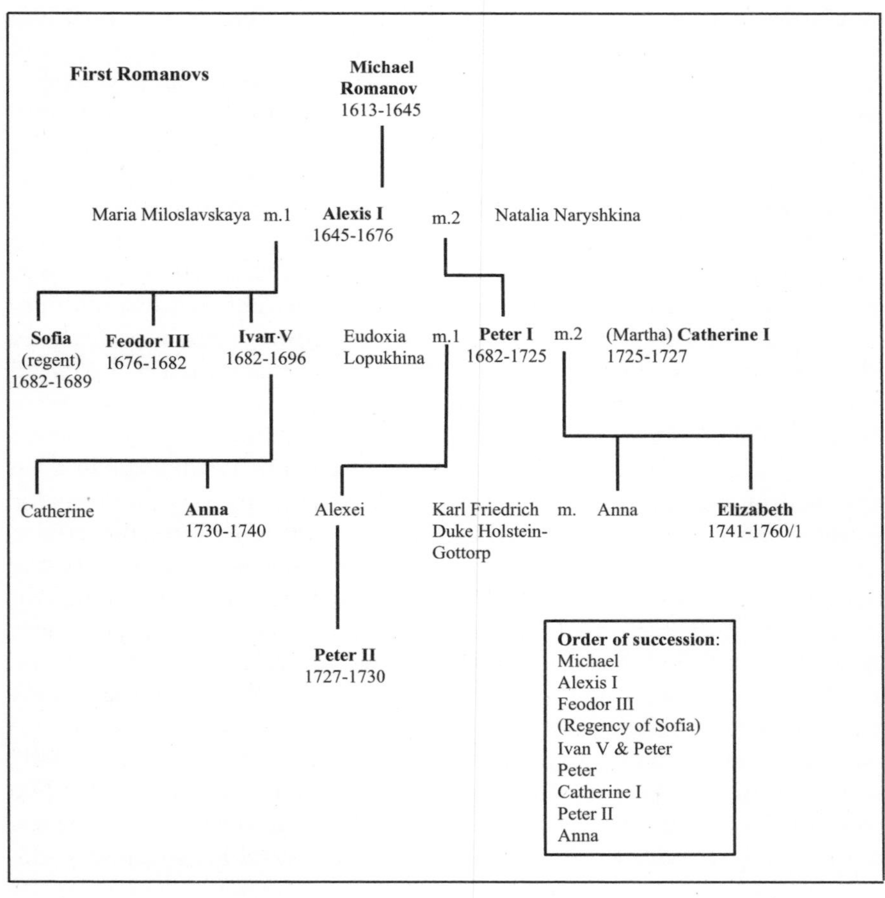

Alexis, like his predecessors, chose his first wife in a bride show, a sort of beauty parade of young women from whom the ruler made his choice. Many applicants would gather for this, but their initial numbers were reduced in the preliminary selections that were made by scheming members of the court, men who sought to promote only those candidates who might further their personal ambitions. The practice of the bride show was one of the customs that had entered Russia from the Byzantine court following Ivan III's marriage to his second wife, Sofia (known by the Greeks as Zoë). She had been the niece of the last East Roman Emperor, Constantine XI, who had disappeared during the Fall of Constantinople in 1453. After the Islamic Ottomans had conquered the city, Russia began to see itself as the guardian of the Orthodox faith, and Moscow as the new Third Rome. From that time its rulers had begun to adopt the Byzantine double-headed eagle as the symbol of their temporal and spiritual power. Taking the name tsar, a title derived from the Roman *caesar*, the Russian heads of state now began to follow the example of the earlier Byzantine rulers – the *basileis* – who had accorded to their position a dual quality that comprised an equal spiritual and secular authority. With the Slavonic Church's translation of the Greek texts, this concept of the ruler's double secular and spiritual role became embedded within the newly defined tsardom. But other practical changes were also introduced to Russia at this time. Once more following the traditions of Constantinople, Ivan III introduced a Great Code that among its reforms included certain Byzantine restrictions and impositions, such as the seclusion of women, the male-dominated rights of inheritance, and the more brutal punishment of offenders.

The questionable internal politics of the court became evident following Alexis's first bride show, when his choice was dismissed by his chief advisers making highly spurious claims as to the candidate's unsuitability due to poor health. One story suggests that she was made to faint by having her hair too tightly braided. Whatever the truth, she was banished from court and summarily replaced by Maria Miloslavskaya. This young girl, who was very pious and traditional, followed the practice now accepted for high-born women and was never seen in public. She remained hidden away in the Kremlin, and when she had to leave the palace in her carriage, she did so screened from view, behind curtains. The rest of the time she lived in her special quarters of the Terem Palace, accompanied by the tsar's sisters, aunts, and female cousins, all forbidden to marry as no Russian would be worthy of them, and all foreign royalty were held to be infidels. Religion was always an issue for the Romanovs, and the proposed marriage of Michael's daughter to the son of the Danish king, Christian IV, had earlier failed to come about for the very reason that the bridegroom had refused to change his faith – the shock he caused by his refusal having reputedly hastened the tsar's death soon after. While the less conventional Tsar Peter arranged the marriage of his son, Alexei, to a bride who remained Lutheran, later there would be a return to the stricter religious practices of before, and women marrying the Russian heir to the throne would all be expected to adopt the Orthodox faith.

In 1669, after twenty-one years of marriage and thirteen children, Maria died. Shortly afterwards the tsar met and fell in love with nineteen-year-old Natalia Naryshkina, who was living in the house of his close friend and chief adviser, Artamon Matveev. Matveev, an intelligent and sophisticated man, was married to a Scottish woman, Mary Hamilton, and Western culture, including music and art, was enjoyed in the household. Natalia, a ward of Matveev, grew up embracing these more foreign and progressive ideas, later sometimes shocking the Muscovites by actually being seen when out in her carriage in the city. Although she was from a comparatively poor family, Alexis now wanted to marry her, but – according to Pierre Nicolas Chantreau's account, written about a century later – Matveev feared that accusations of favouritism would be made against him. To prevent these, in September 1670 another bride show with fifty or more candidates was arranged in the Kremlin. Unknown to the young women and the court, the result was a foregone conclusion and Alexis selected Natalia, presenting her with a crown of roses to symbolise his choice. Five months later the marriage took place, and in May 1672 a healthy child, Peter, was born. He was followed by two sisters, of whom only the elder survived to adulthood, the other dying shortly after her third birthday.

The situation now looked promising, but in 1676, when Peter was three, everything changed. His forty-six-year-old father, who had been previously in good health, caught a chill, developed further complications, and died unexpectedly. The security of the dynasty now lay in the hands of three young boys. Despite the multiple births of Alexis' first wife, all Maria's five sons had not been strong, so now just two of these remained. A few months later, shortly after his fifteenth birthday, the physically disabled older boy was carried to his coronation and crowned as the third Tsar Feodor.[21] An intelligent young man who would introduce some more progressive reforms, he would treat his half-brother Peter well during his six years on the throne. However, his first wife died in childbirth, her son living on for just a few days, and although Feodor then remarried, he too would die soon after. This left the Romanov succession in a particularly precarious position, and the country now faced serious problems as Feodor's younger brother, fifteen-year-old Ivan, suffered both physically and mentally. So the *boyars*, remembering the disasters of the Time of Troubles, decided that it would be better to elect as tsar Ivan's half-brother, nine-year-old Peter, a solution that unsurprisingly appalled Ivan's Miloslavsky relations.

In the 1580s, Ivan IV had created regiments of musketeers called the Streltsy, whose purpose was the defence of the city in time of attack. As the main military force in this period, before the creation of regular armies, it comprised an unruly and unpredictable gathering of men, who were easily incited to violence. Evidence suggests that the infuriated Miloslavsky now spread rumours suggesting that Natalia, ambitious for her son Peter, had killed Ivan, and maybe even Feodor too. Enraged by these stories, the Streltsy stormed to the Kremlin, determined to wreak their vengeance on Natalia and her family. But rising to the occasion, she appeared at the top of the palace's ceremonial Red Staircase and presented Ivan and Peter to the mass below, showing them both to be still alive and well. With her former guardian, Matveev, having then further defused the situation, Natalia prepared to leave. But at that very moment an officer's criticism of the men's behaviour reignited their anger and, in fury, they turned on the speaker and murdered him. That done, the mob charged up the stairs, seized Matveev, threw him over the balcony and hacked him to pieces.

After this, havoc continued for three days, with Peter and his family forced into hiding while other atrocities continued to take place across the city. As the Streltsy particularly sought revenge against anybody thought to be connected with the Naryshkins, the violence continued, showing no sign of abating, until finally Natalia's brother Ivan was persuaded to give himself up to the rioters. He was then dragged away and brutally put to death. The child Peter witnessed the horror of these days, and the memory of it resulted in a lifelong hatred of Moscow, a bitter dislike that would later reinforce his determination to move the capital to his beloved new city, St Petersburg.

The murder of Ivan Naryshkin helped to sate the bloodlust of the rebels, and now the situation began to calm down. But a decision was needed as to how the country should be ruled, and so a compromise was found. From this time on the two boys would be joint tsars, with the senior, the older Ivan, and the junior, the younger Peter. To make this possible, a regent would also be appointed, none other than Ivan's older sister Sofia, even though it was probably she who had been instrumental in spreading the rumours that had earlier incited the Streltsy to rebellion. An intelligent young woman, she carried out her responsibilities well. To help direct affairs, she ordered a redesigning of the silver throne, constructing a double seat where the two tsars could sit side by side. And at the back, a small window was created through which she could listen to the proceedings and whisper instructions to her two brothers – a literal embodiment of the power behind the throne. Today this, alongside the tsars' other regalia, is on display in the Kremlin.

Unlike most women of her time, Sofia was well educated and had even sat in on her brother Feodor's meetings. But she was also unusual in that she apparently took at least one lover, Vasily Galitzine, another of the Russians of the period who was already influenced by Western culture. A good linguist, a lover of fine things, he was a sophisticated, cultivated man who during the seven years of the regency helped Sofia run the country efficiently. However, Galitzine, a courtier not a soldier, was obliged against his will to lead two campaigns against the Tatars in the south, both of which ended in failure. Although at first he and Sofia tried to contain the bad news, the truth leaked out and he was then disgraced and sent into exile, remaining for the rest of his life far away from the more sophisticated world that he had previously enjoyed.

But the disgrace also impinged on Sofia, and she too was now in jeopardy, her position not helped by both her brothers having reached adulthood. Ivan had married early on in the regency, producing the first of his five daughters in 1689, while in January of the same year Peter's mother had arranged her sixteen-year-old son's engagement to a pious, traditional young girl from the nobility. A few months after his wedding, Peter's supporters – warned this time by the Streltsy – began to fear that Sofia was about to try and secure her future by mounting a coup against him. Therefore, in the middle of the night they hurriedly awoke him, telling him that his life was in danger and that he must seek shelter at the holy site of the monastery of the Trinity St Sergius, some 45 miles from Moscow. Bundled off while still in his nightclothes, Peter was deeply shaken by this event and coming on top of the traumas of his childhood, the experience may have contributed to his developing epileptic symptoms from which he would suffer for the rest of his life. As for Sofia's feared coup, that never materialised, but her days in power were over and she was now deposed and sent to live in a convent, although as yet she did not have to take religious orders.

Peter was still not ready to take a significant role in the running of his country, leaving it instead to his mother, Natalia, who now took control of affairs. Just over a year after his marriage, his wife, Eudoxia Lopukhina, gave birth to her first child, Alexei – the only one of her three children to survive infancy. However, as it was soon clear that she and her husband were totally incompatible, before long the marriage was deemed a failure. Increasingly ignoring Eudoxia, Peter began to spend more and more time in the so-called German Quarter. Despite its name, this area of Moscow, recently relocated by his father to outside the city, was occupied not just by Germans, but also by a variety of other non-Russian nationalities. At the time of Ivan IV, many Protestants from the German states had begun to settle in the country, and Peter's father, shocked by the execution of Charles I in England, had offered refuge to the cavalier émigrés – regardless of whether they were Anglican or Catholic. In her turn, Sofia had provided a safe haven to the persecuted Huguenots fleeing France after Louis XIV's revocation of the Edict of Nantes. In addition to these various refugees, Russia had also opened its doors to traders, merchants and various experts, all useful providers of the much-needed foreign products and skills that the country lacked. So by the time Peter visited the German Quarter, it had become a mixed community of roughly 3,000 inhabitants whose way of life was very different from that found in the rest of Moscow. The residents had brick houses, where the interiors contained the latest comforts in furniture, stoves and ornaments; they wore Western-style clothes, enjoyed music, plays, and other entertainments, and had social gatherings where men and women mixed freely together. Peter visited this area frequently, intrigued by the novelty of the things he heard and saw, and here he first started to adopt European dress and to learn new languages: Dutch, a certain amount of German and some Latin. He also began to form new friendships among the foreigners, becoming particularly attached to the old Scottish Catholic and Jacobite supporter General Patrick Gordon and the Swiss-born Franz Lefort, an intelligent and cultured individual who would become one of Peter's closest companions. Both he and Peter were very heavy drinkers, even by the standards of Russia, which had been renowned since the times of the earliest foreign travellers for its high level of drunkenness. Probably at Lefort's house, Peter met Anna Mons, the pretty daughter of a Dutch or German wine merchant, who had possibly been Lefort's mistress. Having taken her for himself, Peter then gave her a house in the German Quarter, and she would remain close to him for twelve years until she was finally disgraced on grounds of her suspected infidelity. Then, after her release from temporary arrest, she married the Prussian ambassador, but died just three years after the wedding.

With his newly made male friends, both foreigners and Russians, Peter formed a sort of club. Although its name appears translated in a variety of ways, such as the Jolly Company, the All Mad, All Jesting, All Drunken Society, and the Drunken Synod, its objectives were clear. The members, generally decidedly the worse-for-wear for drink, behaved in a particularly boorish manner, going around the city disturbing or abusing residents, vandalising properties, and parodying authority. Over time within the large group there were, among others, a Mock King of Poland, a Mock Patriarch (later replaced by the Mock Pope), and even a Mock Tsar, a role taken by Peter's childhood companion Feodor Romodanovsky. While such behaviour was not uncommon in other ruling families of the time – with the young Karl XII of Sweden and his wild cousin the Duke of Holstein-Gottorp particularly coming to mind – what strikes us about Peter's behaviour is the fact that it occurred not just during his youth, but throughout his life. Well into his middle age he was still enjoying practical jokes, buffoonery and pranks of highly questionable taste, such as staged marriages of the very young and the very old, the disabled, or those considered comically unusual – stutterers, dwarfs and the like. This is one area where the paradox of Peter's character is highlighted. He was a man of immense contradictions, capable of acts of genuine kindness and generosity, as well as unspeakable brutality; at times he showed a readiness to forgive the faults of his friends, and at others a hard-hearted vindictiveness against those who had angered him. When visiting England in 1698, he impressed the people he met with his sophisticated appreciation of beauty and learning, but then shocked his hosts with his drunken destructiveness, carried to an extreme at Sayes Court, the house that he borrowed from the diarist Sir John Evelyn at Deptford. He left the place in such a wrecked condition, with windows broken, carpets and pictures damaged, and furniture very probably burnt as firewood, that the English government was faced with a repair bill estimated at the immensely large sum for the time of £350.[d] After the departure of the group, Evelyn's servant succinctly described the Russian visitors as 'right nasty'.

Peter had grown up outside Moscow where, with other young boys living or working on his father's estate, he had amused himself by creating a toy army out of real men. At times, as the mock battles became increasingly realistic, the war games had resulted in casualties, even the odd fatality. To help her half-brother in these activities, Sofia had provided him with cannons that actually fired, but in an age when rulers were expected to lead their troops to war in person, such dangerous play-acting was viewed as a necessary, if not an enjoyable, part of a young man's training. Toy armies were not unusual, and for many years young rulers and their heirs engaged in similar activities: Karl XII of Sweden was among those who first honed their military skills in a similar way. Peter's toy army gave him an early introduction to the intricacies of warfare, and over time it grew to several thousand men, becoming the foundation of his later famous Guards regiments, one of which, the Preobrazhensky, took its name from the very estate where these games had begun.

It was also during this period that Peter made a significant discovery. One day he came across a small, rotting sailing boat different from any that he had previously seen. This was able to sail into the wind, unlike those craft traditionally found in Russia, where they were designed merely to travel along the country's rivers. The origins of this particular boat have become lost in mythology, with claims even suggesting it was a gift from the English queen, Elizabeth, to Ivan IV. The truth would appear to be more prosaic. It was probably the work of a Dutchman who either built it in Russia or later brought it to the country. Wherever it came from, Peter was fascinated and immediately began sailing it on the river in Moscow, later taking it up to Lake Pleshcheyevo around 85 miles to the north-east of the capital. Here he was then able to become more adventurous, and with the assistance of other Dutchmen, some from Zaandam in Holland, he now began to create a small toy fleet of around twelve ships, including one or two large enough to carry thirty cannons. Just as his toy army had developed his military interests and skills, his small fleet taught him the first rudiments of shipbuilding and introduced him to the naval tactics that he practised in mock battles on the lake. His passion for boats was now fully awakened, and he continued to visit the boatyard at Lake Pleshcheyevo for some years until he was prevented by other duties. And Peter always treasured that first discovered little boat which, as the inspiration for the creation of his later fleets, became dubbed the *Grandfather of the Navy*. Throughout his reign this would continue to take pride of place at all future important ceremonies, and today it remains a prime exhibit in the Naval Museum in St Petersburg.

With his new interest in boats, in 1693, and again the following year, Peter decided to travel on further north to visit Archangel on the White Sea,

---

d According to some estimates, this could have represented anything between roughly £250,000 and £350,000.

just south of the Arctic Circle. Although his father Alexis had made some small efforts to open up shipping on the Caspian, at this time Archangel remained Russia's only port. Despite being ice-bound throughout the winter, during the summer months it was a hive of activity with an influx of foreign ships, arriving particularly from the trading countries of England and the Netherlands. These, which came primarily in search of the commodities that were so necessary for their naval industries – timber, pitch, tar, and hemp – also took back home fur and caviar, luxuries that were exchanged for the new European products which were becoming more fashionable among the Russians. To Peter, this was a new world of fascinating discoveries, and here at Archangel he worked physically on the building of his first seagoing ship the *St Paul*, and – despite his mother's earlier pleas – also went out to sea for the first time. Natalia's fears were nearly realised when his ship was wrecked during a storm, but even this did not deter him from his love of boats, and she never heard of the disaster, having already died in the intervening winter between Peter's two visits.

With his mother's death, Peter now began to take a more serious interest in the running of his country. After what he had seen at Archangel, he realised Russia's need for a warm-water port. The Caspian remained vulnerable to the Tatars, Cossacks and Persians, but he saw the potential of Azov in the south. If he could capture the fortress from the Ottomans, he might eventually be able to gain access to the Black Sea, and thereby to the European markets lying beyond. However, his first attempt to take the fortress failed, not helped by the complicated logistics involved in getting to the region. To arrive at their destination, the Russians had sailed down the Volga as far as Tsaritsyn – today Volgograd, but better known by many as Stalingrad. They then had to drag their ships across land to reach the River Don, before sailing downstream to make their abortive attack on the fort. After this failure, Peter decided on a new plan and he set up a boatbuilding yard further north up the Don at Voronezh. Here, during the following winter he ordered the building of a small fleet of various craft, including two warships and twenty-three galleys. In these, when spring came, the Russians were able finally to sail back south and take the Azov fortress. With the Ottoman forces overthrown, Peter then began plans to create a boatyard and naval base further along the coast at Taganrog – a scheme that was completed two years later. However, around this time he heard news that five months before his half-brother Ivan had died, and as a result he was now the sole Tsar of Russia.

Soon after these events, Peter decided to embark on a major expedition outside the country, the first such trip by a Russian tsar. He had two goals. First, in light of the ongoing Ottoman threat, he sought to form an alliance with the Austrian Habsburgs, and second, he wanted to learn as much as possible from the countries of the west. For the same reason, he decided that several of the young men accompanying him should remain abroad, not returning until they had acquired the skills that Russia needed – a proposal that left most of the chosen candidates far from enthusiastic.

Overall the expedition, known as Peter's Grand Embassy, comprised around 250 people, with Lefort acting as one of the ambassadors, and Peter travelling supposedly incognito, under the name of Peter Mikhailov. This was a popular practice among royalty and heads of state as it allowed them to avoid much of the protocol that diplomacy demanded. But in Peter's case the subterfuge would soon make things more complicated.

Having left Moscow, in March 1697 the tsar crossed into the Swedish territory of Livonia, arriving eventually at Riga in the embassy's vanguard. Initially the governor of the town was unaware that Peter was present and, although later he recognised him, he remained uncertain as to how he should entertain his undeclared visitor. As a result, he did not offer the entertainment that Peter, perhaps unfairly, still expected. Furthermore, suffering from a recent famine, Riga was in no condition to provide for the large influx of unexpected visitors, who would remain in the town for several days. But worse was to follow. A disagreement broke out when a guard challenged the unrecognised tsar, who was closely inspecting their defences. Having been so recently at war with Russia, the Swedes understandably viewed with suspicion his intense interest in their battlements, but Peter was enraged and finally left the town offended by what he viewed as the people's lack of hospitality. Still harbouring a grudge, thirteen years later during the Great Northern War, he wreaked his revenge on the town.

On hearing that Poland had just elected its new king, and the threatened dispute between the French and Saxon candidates had now been resolved, Peter crossed the border into the neighbouring Duchy of Courland and Semigallia, the semi-autonomous Polish fiefdom. Here no expense was spared on his entertainment by the local duke, who made such a favourable impression on the tsar that more than a decade later he chose the duke's son to marry his niece, Anna. And Peter was similarly well received at Königsberg, where he remained for the next seven weeks visiting Friedrich, Elector of Brandenburg – soon to be promoted the first King in Prussia. But Friedrich's wife, Sophie Charlotte, was not present, and so later in August she and her mother, Sophie, Electress of Hanover, arranged their own meeting at Koppenbrigge (Coppenbrügge) near Hameln (Hamelin). Knowing Peter to be shy, they limited the party to a few family members, made up of the older woman's son, Georg Ludwig (the future British King George I), and his children – the future George II and Sophie Dorothea, later queen in Prussia. Peter was at first overawed by the two cultured, highly intelligent, and redoubtable aristocratic women, who were so unlike those that he had previously met in Russia. However, after he had relaxed and become very talkative, the visit proved to be a great success. Much enjoying his company, the women even stayed on until four in the morning, dancing 'in the Muscovite fashion'. Later recounting the events in a letter to her niece, the older electress described Peter as an extraordinary, 'naturally gifted' man with a 'just' repartee, and a 'great vivacity of mind'. And, although lacking in social graces, he had – despite expectations – remained completely sober throughout the evening, an abstemiousness that, according to Sophie, his suite 'made up for' after the royal party had left.[22]

Eventually in mid-August, five months after leaving Russia, Peter arrived in Amsterdam, where he ordered his companions to follow his example and get down to learning new skills and techniques. When looking for work for himself in the boatyards of Zaandam across the water from the main city, he met by chance one of the Dutchmen who had previously been involved with the building of his small fleet on Lake Pleshcheyevo. Thanks to this encounter, he now found nearby accommodation for himself in a little two-roomed wooden hut. Despite his exceptional height – at 6 foot 6 or 7, remarkable for the period – Peter never minded staying in small, possibly rather uncomfortable places, preferring in fact, even in his palaces, to live in moderately sized rooms that were simply furnished. However, to his disappointment, almost immediately he began to attract unwanted attention. Numbers of curious people started to flock to this unfashionable area, anxious to get sight of the visiting tsar, fabled for his wealth and exoticism. Contrary to what they expected, they found a young man dressed in everyday workman's clothes and engaged in manual labour. His appearance, no doubt extraordinary to the people who saw him at the time, was in stark contrast to the stiff and formal image we find portrayed in the portraits of his father, and this difference markedly underlines what an incredible revolution Peter was now setting in motion. But plagued by gaping crowds, he felt unable to continue where he was and so, just eight days after his arrival, he accepted an offer from the VOC, the Dutch East India Company, to move to their boatyards in the city of Amsterdam itself. After his initial welcome, accompanied by fireworks and a mock naval battle that particularly delighted him, he was then able to settle down to working undisturbed, actively taking part in the making of a new frigate.

Aside from his naval interests, Peter used his stay in the Netherlands to learn about as many other things as possible. Besides visiting asylums and orphanages, printing presses, botanical gardens and much else, he attended lectures at Leiden University. He watched operations and post-mortems, the latter being at the time open to members of the public who wanted to increase their knowledge (or goggle at the dead). Peter was never squeamish, always brutally critical of those who were, and he now began to take a further interest in the current fashion for cabinets of curiosities. These showcases usually contained a wide variety of exhibits, some of artistic, historic or genuine academic merit, others of a more questionable taste that tapped into the pseudo-scientific thinking of the time. Not alone in his interest, with men like Gustavus Adolphus and Augustus the Strong of Saxony among the collectors, Peter was now intrigued and, having acquired his first exhibits, sent them back to Russia, where they would become the foundation of his later Kunstkamera. Eventually he would open this museum to the public, persuading people to visit with the offer of a free glass of vodka, a custom that is still maintained in the tourist shops of St Petersburg today.

While in the Netherlands, Peter met the Stadtholder William of Orange, who ten years before had also become William III of Great Britain, and he, having invited the tsar to visit his new country, then sent a ship to fetch him. Throughout the twenty-four-hour crossing of the Channel, Peter remained on deck, determined as usual not to miss out on any part of the experience. Shortly after his arrival, he would be painted by Sir Godfrey Kneller, the Lübeck-born artist who, on moving to England just over twenty years earlier, had become the fashionable portraitist. He represented Peter in the style popular in European court circles at the time, showing the tsar dressed in armour against a background where a fleet lies at anchor. This picture, totally unlike the earlier stylised images of his predecessors, again defines Peter's break with the past. Said to be a good likeness, it obviously pleased the tsar, and although he gave the portrait to King William, he frequently had the image reproduced in prints and on medals.

In England Peter again took the opportunity to learn as much as possible. He visited Parliament, the Royal Observatory, the Royal Society, and the Mint, which at the time was in the Tower of London. Outside the city he went, among other places, to Windsor, Oxford and Portsmouth. He watched a review of the fleet off Spithead and, while living in the house of the unfortunate John Evelyn, spent much of his time visiting the boatyards on the Thames at Deptford. At last, after three months in the country, he finally left England and from there he made his way to Dresden. The Elector of Saxony, Augustus the Strong, who had recently been elected King of Poland, was absent when Peter arrived, but the tsar was able to inspect, among other things, his particularly famous cabinet of curiosities. Peter then continued on to Vienna, where he hoped to draw up an alliance against the Ottomans with the ageing Holy Roman Emperor, Ferdinand II, but before any agreement was reached he received news of another Streltsy rebellion in Russia. Therefore, although he had wanted to go on to Venice, he now realised that he needed to return home. However, when he reached Poland, he heard that the uprising had been crushed, and so was able to delay his journey for a time, enjoying a few days with Augustus, whom he had earlier failed to meet in Saxony. These similarly aged men who were equally heavy drinkers and practical jokers soon found that they shared much else besides, including their interest in the sciences, arts and architecture. Unsurprisingly, therefore, the two men got on well, and they soon agreed to form an alliance that would unite them against their common neighbour and rival, Sweden.

Despite the latest Streltsy rebellion being over, when Peter finally reached home he was determined to impose his authority by instilling fear in his people. He demanded that all those thought to be implicated in the uprising should be put to death. Showing medieval brutality, he ordered various forms of execution to be carried out on some 2,000 people, around 1,200 dying in Moscow on one day alone, a massacre in which Peter was said to have taken part, performing some of the killings himself. Although he never balked from doing things that he ordered others to do, his probable personal involvement in this slaughter demonstrates once again the paradox that underpins his character. His actions manifest the striking contrast between the two sides of his personality: the enlightened ruler, who had so recently delighted the people of Europe; and the brutal despot, who was still attached to the savage ways of old Russia. As the news spread abroad, his former hosts were appalled.

On returning to Russia, Peter began the first of his reforms, among them famously ordering the *boyars* to shorten their robes, something which the men perceived to be almost an act of sacrilege. Like beards, which were also banned, the traditional mode of dress did not just mark the wearer's aristocratic standing, but more significantly symbolised his personal relationship to the biblical patriarchs. Beards would later be allowed for the clergy and peasants, but others who still did not conform to the ruling were then taxed instead. Besides wanting to bring his country into the modern age, Peter was now seeking to create a more egalitarian society, one where status depended on service rather than on birth. Three years before his death, in 1722 he would set out his intentions in more detail by introducing his Table of Ranks. Although the length of service he demanded would later be reduced to twenty-five years under Empress Anna, and still more under Catherine II, this Table, which precisely defined the link between title or privilege and service, would remain in force until the end of the dynasty. Furthermore, while bringing similar reforms into the Orthodox Church, after the death of the patriarch, Adrian, he chose not to appoint a successor. From then on the position would be left vacant until the twentieth century. Nonetheless, in 1721 he created his new Holy Synod with a president, vice-president and eight other members, a body that – subject to the tsar's will – was responsible for all Church matters other than religious doctrine.

Another significant change was introduced on 1 January 1700 (OS), when Peter finally dropped the country's old calendar, which was still based on the date of the supposed year of the creation: it had now reached 7206. But while this was obviously wildly inaccurate, even Europe's Julian calendar, originally devised by Julius Caesar, was imperfect, and so in 1587 Pope Gregory XIII, wanting to formalise the dating of Easter, had ordered the introduction of a more precise system. This had been immediately taken up by the Catholic countries but, with the Reformation in full flood, Protestant states had at first refused to follow suit. However, with the discrepancy between the two calendars increasing by a day each century, gradually these countries had begun to accept that they needed to change, and by 1700 most of Europe had come – or were coming – into line. Britain, one of the last to do so, resisted until 1752, and even then riots broke out with people protesting at what they saw as the loss of eight days of their life, if not their wages. However, out of step with the rest of Europe, Peter chose to adopt the earlier, now widely rejected, older system. The reasons for this are unclear, a possible explanation being that already in places around the country the Julian calendar had begun to be adopted, or alternatively that he felt the imposition of a nominally papal calendar on the Orthodox believers would be a step too far. The rivalry between the two great Christian confessions remained intense. Whatever the cause for the tsar's decision, the Julian calendar remained in force in Russia until the Soviet revolution, and it continues to be used today by the Orthodox Church.

On his return to Russia from his Grand Embassy, other changes took place in Peter's private life. First, believing his sister Sofia to have been behind the most recent Streltsy rising, he forced her at last to take the veil. At the same time, he decided to divorce his wife, and she too was sent to a convent. In 1699 Peter faced tragedies that hit him personally when two of his closest companions died: Lefort, and the old Scot, General Gordon. He was heartbroken by these two deaths and was with Gordon right to the end. However, both companions were soon replaced by another favourite, Alexander Menshikov, who was typical of the new men that he was now promoting. Although Menshikov's true origins are unknown, his enemies later suggesting him to be the son of a pie seller, his father had very probably been Tsar Alexis' Lithuanian stable boy. While he was living on the Preobrazhenskoe estate, he had become a member of Peter's toy army, and later had worked alongside the tsar in the boatyards in Amsterdam. Although he remained virtually illiterate all his life, he was immensely ambitious and in time became the richest and most powerful man in the land apart from the tsar. He was appointed to senior positions, given multiple honours and awards, and ultimately ennobled as Prince Menshikov. However, extremely corrupt, he frequently incurred the tsar's wrath and faced the risk of disgrace, but by appealing to Peter's sense of humour he always managed to be forgiven, retaining his position as his favourite until the end of the reign.

Through Menshikov Peter now met a young woman, Martha Skavronskaya, thought to be the daughter of a Livonian army quartermaster, Johann Rabe. According to Eugeni V. Ansisimov, most historians now believe 'she was born on April 5, 1684, in Livland'.[23] As Livland or Livonia was at the time under Swedish rule, this would explain not just why she was fluent in the language, but also why Peter frequently referred to her as having Swedish roots. Much of her early life is uncertain, but, as Ansisimov again explains, having probably been orphaned while she was still very young she was then moved into the care of a German pastor living in the area. Here she remained as his domestic servant until she may very briefly have become the wife of a Swedish soldier, probably a trumpeter. Soon after, when the war broke out and the Russians captured and sacked Marienburg, she was taken as part of their booty. From this time on she was handed around until she was given to the elderly commander, Field Marshal Sheremetev, staying with him for around six months as his laundress and possible concubine. Then, having been passed on to Menshikov, in 1703 he introduced her to Peter, who, having employed her as a servant, a year later took her to replace his now disgraced mistress Anna Mons. At this point Martha began to learn Russian and, after her conversion to Orthodoxy, she adopted her new name, Catherine Alekseyevna.

Having gained strength though her past experiences, Catherine's good humour and straightforward pragmatism would help her bear with equanimity the many discomforts and disappointments she would suffer because of Peter's frenetic and unpredictable lifestyle. He would be constantly on the move, driven by an extraordinary energy and curiosity, and throughout their life together he would be frequently unfaithful, at times suffering from the inevitable diseases resulting from his sexual escapades. But Catherine accepted all his failings with tolerance and understanding. Furthermore, she managed to cope with his tempers and repeated bouts of ill health, proving to be the only person able to calm him when he was experiencing one of his fits. She cheerfully acknowledged her simple beginnings and probably remained always more or less illiterate, but throughout the next two decades she would be Peter's loving and much-loved companion.

Catherine had been captured by the Russians during the Great Northern War, which was only finally brought to an end two decades later. Three years after Karl XI's death in Sweden in 1697, the country's neighbours saw their chance to attack his young son and regain the territory that they had lost in the previous century. Sweden's ally France would soon be caught up in another dispute involving the powers of western Europe where, following the death of the childless Carlos II of Spain, the claims of rival French and Habsburg pretenders had begun to harden, eventually causing the War of the Spanish Succession to break out in 1701. This French engagement helped Peter and his allies, and with his earlier objective of creating an anti-Ottoman alliance with the emperor now abandoned, he set out to agree a truce with the sultan so that within a few weeks of the start of hostilities he was able turn his attention to the area of the Baltic. By that time, ignoring their family loyalties, Karl XII's two cousins Frederik IV of Denmark and Augustus II of Poland had joined in the fight against him. These men underestimated their enemy, and within six weeks Karl II had succeeded in defeating the Danes. This success was followed by another unexpected Swedish victory against the Russians at the Estonian fortress of Narva, where Peter's troops had been besieging the Swedish garrison. In spite of the winter weather, Karl was able to make a lightning attack, ending with a rout of the tsar's inexperienced army, a shocking defeat that left the Swedish king the hero of the hour, and Peter reviled and ridiculed. Having left the town the night before the battle, Peter was widely charged with cowardice, an accusation still being levelled at him in 1895 by R. Nisbet Bain, who, describing him as 'drunk with brandy and mad with fear', claimed that he had sought to find a false excuse for his departure.[24] He was still new to campaigning, and Peter's actions – like those of the later Frederick the Great at his first battle – might have been partly caused by a lack of experience. Whether or not this was the case, modern research has been kinder in its interpretation of the events, suggesting that while the immediate Swedish attack was unexpected, Peter had set off to rally reinforcements and discuss the developing military situation with his ally Augustus. Whatever the truth, his courage would never again come into question, and within a short period he would redeem his reputation. He recaptured Narva in 1704, just two years after taking the Swedish Oreshek (Nöteborg) Fortress at the entrance to the River Neva on Lake Ladoga – a strategically placed fort, which, renamed Schlüsselburg from the German word for key, would in time become a notorious prison, its most famous captive being Tsar Ivan VI.

Karl XII followed up his victory at Narva by further defeats of the Saxon and Polish armies, and after his successful campaigning across Poland he managed at last to force Augustus II to abdicate and to replace him with the young Pole, Stanislaw Leszczyński. But having through his excessive hubris and his dogged determination to defeat Peter made the disastrous decision to invade Russia, eventually in 1709 Karl found himself at Poltava in the Ukraine. Here, met by Peter with his greatly improved army, he suffered a major defeat, and, finding himself totally crushed, he then fled into the Ottoman Empire, where he remained for the next five years as the guest of the sultan. For Peter, the Battle of Poltava was a major triumph that marked the end of Swedish dominance in the Baltic and the beginning of Russia's hegemony. He was the new hero of Europe, now unofficially dubbed 'the Great'.

Peter's joy was further increased in the days after the battle, when he heard that Catherine had given birth to a daughter, Elizabeth. This child and her older sister Anna would be the only two of the couple's twelve children to survive to adulthood, and both would have an impact on future events, Elizabeth in time becoming the Russian empress, and Anna the mother of Peter III, the unfortunate husband of Catherine the Great.

Meanwhile, however, the war continued, and for the tsar not always with the same success. Just two years after Poltava, Peter suffered defeat at the hands of the Ottomans, when the sultan, persuaded by his guest Karl XII, sent his army to challenge him in Moldavia (today Romania). However, to the chagrin of the Swedish king, following the Russian surrender at the resulting battle on the River Pruth, the tsar gained more generous peace terms than might otherwise have been expected. Although Peter had to return Azov to the Ottomans and at the same time destroy certain fortresses, including his naval base at Taganrog – thus ending for ever his hope of reaching the Black Sea – he was permitted to retreat with his army moderately intact. This allowed him to return to the fight and continue his country's rise to power, and later in the century the Ottomans would pay dearly for this lost opportunity to crush their

Russian neighbours. Evidence suggests that the generosity of the peace agreement was largely due to Catherine, who, present at the negotiations, was able to persuade the grand vizier to moderate his terms, possibly bribing him with her jewellery, if not (as her enemies suggested) by taking the relationship to a more intimate level. Regardless of the truth, the man would later suffer for his act of leniency by being sent into exile.

Whenever she could, Catherine accompanied Peter on his campaigns, showing her stamina and good nature in the most uncomfortable and dangerous of situations. Even before leaving for the Pruth campaign, Peter had recognised these qualities and decided to honour her by publicly marrying her. Shortly after his return, the religious ceremony took place in the chapel of Menshikov's palace, followed by a private banquet for a select number of the tsar's chosen friends and companions. In choosing to make a low-born foreigner his bride, yet again Peter was breaking with the accepted traditions of previous Russian rulers. Although possibly married secretly some years before in 1707, Catherine was now formally the tsar's wife, and their children were officially legitimised. And as a still further acknowledgement of the courage she had shown during the dangerous Pruth campaign, three years later in 1714 Peter created the Order of St Catherine in her honour.

With the defeat of Karl XII, Stanislaw I abdicated as King of Poland and Augustus retook his throne. Meanwhile, other players also joined or rejoined the war, among them the Prussian king Friedrich I and Frederik IV of Denmark. Meanwhile, Russia continued to gain territory around the Baltic. In 1710, Riga was the first city to fall, the tsar personally making it pay dearly for its earlier treatment of him, and then Reval (Tallinn) and all of Estonia were captured soon after. In addition to these successes, in 1714, just off the Hanko (Swedish: Hangö) Peninsula in the Gulf of Finland, Peter won his most resounding naval battle, his galleys having proved to be more practical and manoeuvrable than the Swedish ships in the gulf's shallow, sheltered waters. The Russians, who call this the Battle of Gangut, still honour the victory today, always having one vessel named after it in their navy. At the end of the fighting, nine captured Swedish ships were towed with their flagship into St Petersburg, the celebrations being led by Peter's first little boat, the *Grandfather of the Navy*. But while the tsar himself appeared as a Rear Admiral, he never wishing to take a rank above that which he considered he deserved, to the surprise of the Swedish captives it was the 'Mock Tsar' who presided over the proceedings – another inappropriate example of how Peter had never lost his childish sense of humour.

At last in 1721 the war came to an end. With Karl XII's death three years earlier, and his people crushed by the conflict, in the final peace talks Sweden had to give up many of its former possessions, thereafter ceasing to be a principal player in the region and no longer the dominant power that it had been before. Benefiting the most from its collapse, Russia took all its south-eastern Baltic lands that had stretched from the Finnish

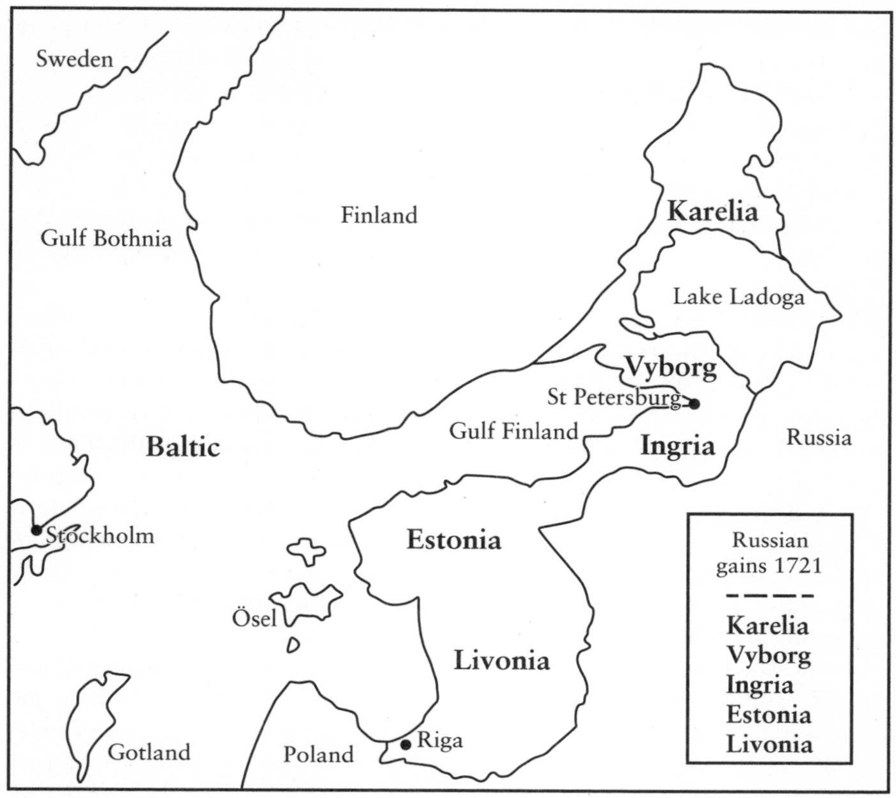

border right round to Riga. But of still more personal importance to Peter, the future of his new capital, St Petersburg, was at last secure.

With his winning position thus confirmed, Peter was now not just officially recognised as 'the Great', but also began to be called 'Emperor', a more European-sounding title that until the last two Slavophile tsars all the Romanov rulers would prefer to use. However, Peter's renown did not come just from his military success, but also from the multiple innovations and reforms that he had brought to his vast country. As he had soon found an absence of maps, something without which it was impossible to govern efficiently, he had ordered the printing of a new atlas by the famous cartographers in the Netherlands, makers of the majority of the world's maps during the seventeenth century. But wanting more for Russia, Peter then brought into the country printing presses such as those he had seen while he was in Holland. These would produce a wide range of manuals to instruct the Russians on a variety of subjects, from construction work to etiquette or manners, a task made easier for the printers by the tsar's introduction of a simplified new alphabet. In addition, he set up various industries, such as paper mills and ironworks, and improved transport and communication by building new canals. Wanting to prevent fraud, he also modernised the coinage system, applying what he had learnt on his visit to the Mint in London. And, finally, again learning from his experience abroad, he created orders with medals and titles such as 'Prince' and 'Count', a move that enabled him to reward people at minimal expense. His new Order of St Andrew, worn with the blue sash that appears in so many portraits, would become one of the most important honours in Russia. But of all his achievements, the one that is probably most widely remembered today is his creation of St Petersburg.

Peter's choice of site for his new city was extraordinary. Apart from the fact that it lay far north where the winters were long and severe, it was situated in the delta of the River Neva, a place extremely vulnerable to flooding. Within three years of its foundation, St Petersburg found itself more than 8 feet under water, and over the years to come inundation would remain a constant risk, only finally resolved with President Putin's order for the completion of a dam across the gulf by Kronstadt in 2011. The climate in this region is also very unhealthy – damp and cold in winter, mosquito-prone in summer – and throughout the nineteenth century illness would plague several empresses and their children, forcing them to recuperate in the south or abroad. In addition, there was a lack of stone for building, and with the ground being either swampy or poor, it was difficult to grow the crops necessary for the provision of the city. But, above all, when Peter announced his decision, the area was hard to defend. The country was already at war, and for several years the Swedes remained an ever-present threat in the region. At any moment they could have mounted an attack and destroyed Peter's ambitious works, thus bringing his dreams to a premature end. When on 16 May 1703 (OS), according to the traditional story, he cut a turf on the small Hare Island in the river delta, the Swedes had been expelled from their settlement close by only a few days before.

However, as Peter was now determined to go ahead, he chose the place where Menshikov had previously erected a little wooden fort during his campaign against the enemy. Here, according to the myth, on the feast day of St Peter and St Paul, while an eagle flew overhead, the tsar declared he would build his new city, St Petersburg. The imagination and single-mindedness behind this project was remarkable, and, even more remarkably, within just a few years it had been largely achieved. On the island itself Peter ordered the erection of a new fort, a building that would in time become the first stone construction in the city. Although not completed within his lifetime, in the centre of this he commissioned his Swiss-Italian architect, Domenico Trezzini, to design him a new cathedral, named in honour of the two saints. This would be totally unlike anything seen before in Russia. The dark, heavy Slavonic style, with its ornate onion domes, was now gone, replaced by a light, European-looking building, topped with a delicate golden spire. Still today – with the exception of a radio mast – the Sts Peter and Paul Cathedral remains the highest point in St Petersburg.

Peter personally supervised all the work, rowing across to the fort each day to inspect progress. Initially, during the summer months he lived in a little wooden cabin that, built in just a matter of days, comprised three small main rooms. Having in 1711 moved this building to a new site on the other side of the river, two years before his death the tsar ordered it to be protected from the weather with an outer shell. While this covering would later be replaced, the cabin inside has always been carefully preserved, and it remains much as it was in those pioneering days shortly after the city's birth. Working with incredible speed, before the end of the year Peter was able to welcome to St Petersburg the first trading vessel, the merchants having been encouraged to come to his city by his offers of a financial reward. With his long-held ambition to establish an important trading port and naval yard now taking shape, the following year he also created the first arsenal, one that would eventually be replaced on similar lines in the nineteenth century. So, although St Petersburg would usually freeze up in the winter, now at last Russia had a maritime base that could be active for a greater part of the year. Famously labelled by Count Algarotti as 'Russia's window on the West', the new city had in fact created an opening for both Russians and Europeans, clearing the way for a more expansive two-way traffic of new trade and ideas.

Work soon began on other buildings too, and although by the time of Peter's death much of St Petersburg was still made of wood, the first stone palaces had begun to appear in the city. To help his programme along, he forbade stone construction elsewhere in the country and ordered all visitors to bring with them supplies of the much-needed materials. Controlling every stage of St Petersburg's development, he imposed precise building regulations, giving the place a uniformity of height and design that is still a characteristic today. Visualising a city linked by water on the lines of Amsterdam or Venice, he also opposed the construction of bridges over the Neva, thereby making the people dependent on boats until the river eventually froze over in the winter.[25]

In 1708 Peter invited his sister Natalia and other members of the court to St Petersburg, an invitation that was in effect an order. Although a keen follower of European taste, enjoying its fashion and entertainment, Natalia – like many others – was unenthusiastic about leaving the more traditional Moscow. Most of the nobles dreaded the discomfort and expense that the move entailed, and grumbled about the excessive cost of constructing their palaces to Peter's strict specifications. They hated the harsh climate, long winters, and inconvenience of living on a building site. But, nonetheless, their numbers now began to grow and four years later Peter declared St Petersburg to be his new capital. Enchanted by his so-called 'paradise', he displayed little concern for the serious cost its creation entailed, not just financially, but also in human lives. From accidents and disease, thousands of people, maybe as many as 30,000, died in its making, giving St Petersburg another more dubious title, 'the city built on bones'.

Initially Peter directed his chosen architect Trezzini to design him a wooden 'Winter Palace', but this was later replaced by another built in stone. Here he installed the famous Amber Room that in 1716 he acquired in exchange for some exceptionally tall soldiers suitable for the Prussian king's 'army of giants'. Friedrich I, on becoming King in Prussia in 1700, had wished to create a royal court on the lines of Versailles and, wildly extravagant, he had commissioned the making of the Amber Room. But his bluff, down-to-earth son Friedrich Wilhelm I, a dedicated soldier, was passionate about creating a disciplined army, one that he felt would be even more impressive with the addition of some particularly tall soldiers. So when Peter admired the Amber Room on a visit to Friedrich Wilhelm, the king was happy with the exchange of gifts. Later, under Empress Elizabeth, this room would be moved to her new palace outside St Petersburg, remaining there until the Second World War, when it disappeared, very possibly eventually ending up in Poland. Still today people come forward claiming to have discovered where it may be hidden, but in the meantime the Russians, with German financial backing, have created a replica that now takes its place in the Catherine Palace at Tsarskoye Selo.

In addition to his Winter Palace, Peter ordered Trezzini to design the city Summer Palace, a building that has recently undergone important restoration work. Standing beside the Fontanka River, close to where it runs into the Neva, this backs onto the Summer Gardens, a park Peter created specifically for the people's enjoyment. One of the earliest of such public spaces, this is still popular with St Petersburg residents, who during the summer months enjoy the shady avenues decorated with statues and fountains. As for the Summer Palace itself, it was designed to be small, its lower rooms plainly furnished in the Dutch style that the tsar had come so much to admire during his Grand Embassy, but the upper rooms for his wife were decorated to suit her more extravagant taste. Here the couple enjoyed their quiet evenings on their own or with a few friends, but when Peter wanted to entertain in a more lavish manner, he used Menshikov's larger palace across the water. This was the biggest such building in the city at the time, containing a ballroom and several reception rooms, and it too was decorated in the Dutch style that the tsar favoured. In addition to his Dutch paintings, furniture, and porcelain stoves, Menshikov had the walls extensively covered with the costly Delft tiles that were now so popular.

This was not all that Menshikov possessed, having used his immense wealth to create his sumptuous Oranienbaum palace on the southern shore of the Gulf of Finland, only some 7 or 8 miles west of the tsar's summer residence of Peterhof. This latter building Peter constructed on a ridge lying approximately 100 yards from the shore, but connected to the sea by a channel, something that enabled Peter when sailing the roughly 15 miles from St Petersburg to arrive directly at the foot of the terrace in front of the building. Although Peterhof was later altered and enlarged by the tsar's daughter Elizabeth, it still contains the more modest private rooms that her father preferred. These, like the rest of the palace, have undergone remarkable restoration work over the last sixty years, a long-drawn-out project that has repaired the appalling damage caused during the war. Reputedly this devastation was perpetrated by both the German occupiers and Stalin, the latter said to have bombed it to prevent Hitler holding a party in the palace. But whoever was responsible, the photographs displayed in its passages vividly demonstrate the mindless destruction that it suffered during the 1940s.

With its inspiration having come from Louis XIV's palace, Peterhof soon became dubbed the 'Russian Versailles', and here in the grounds the tsar then built other small buildings and pavilions, his particular favourite being Monplaisir at the water's edge. In addition, he designed wooded walks that were decorated like the Summer Gardens in the city with many statues and fountains. The largest of these is the Grand Cascade and the Samson Fountain that was erected just below the palace terrace to celebrate the great victory at Poltava, won on the Orthodox feast day of St Samson. Still able to shoot a jet 66 feet into the air, this uses a supply of water brought by natural feed from a reservoir several miles away – a design superior to that used by the French king, who had to depend on a complicated system of pumps. Yet, even here in this sophisticated setting, Peter could not resist his love of practical jokes, concealing sprays ready to squirt water on his unwary visitors, a prank still enjoyed by children visiting the park today.

The idea for this latest palace came during Peter's visit to the French court in 1717. By that time, having wanted to mount an all-out assault on Sweden, he had taken steps to build up an alliance with Karl XII's other enemies, reinforcing his position by promoting the marriage of his niece Catherine Ivanovna (his brother Ivan's daughter) to the Duke of Mecklenburg-Schwerin. After bringing his troops down the coast to Rostock, Peter then visited Frederik IV in Copenhagen, where he was given a spectacular welcome. But the camaraderie was not to last, and in time the coalition Peter had hoped to form would collapse as concerns grew regarding his true ambitions. Despite the eventual removal of the majority of his men from the region, many of the area's rulers began to fear for their own territories, leaving only the Prussian king still prepared to give the tsar his backing and agree to their meeting. This was a time when other alliances were also changing, with the French, in particular, now considering a closer relationship with Britain, the former having abandoned their earlier support of Sweden. Furthermore, despite Karl XII having at last returned home from his Ottoman exile, Swedish fortunes were clearly in decline, and although the Great Northern War still raged on, the odds were now moving in Russia's favour. Therefore, with the situation having improved, Peter decided not to return home immediately but rather to carry on travelling west. After a period spent in Amsterdam, he made his first visit to France, finally arriving in the capital in May. Here, having received a triumphal welcome, he was offered accommodation in the Louvre, but – with his usual preference for simpler surroundings – turned down this option and chose when not out in the Grand Trianon at Versailles to take up residence in the less imposing Hôtel Lesdiguières. Peter soon delighted his hosts, even though he astounded the French courtiers with his disregard for their rigid etiquette, in particular when picking up and kissing the seven-year-old king, Louis XV. During his time in France, he set out – as always – to learn as much as he could, exploring new ideas, and visiting places such as the Academy of Sciences, the Gobelin factory, and the National Mint. Before his departure there was again an exchange of extravagant gifts, and the visit was generally deemed to have been a success.

But while Peter's visit had displayed the more positive side of his character, his treatment of his son, Alexei, was of a totally different order. The sole surviving child of the tsar's first marriage, over time he became increasingly estranged from his father. Of a more conservative, religious, and less energetic nature, and furthermore not drawn to the army and military service, the young man had little in common with his father. Opposed to many of his changes, Alexei attracted the support of those with more reactionary ideas, thus causing his father to suspect him of plotting against him. Peter having already made his son abjure his right to the throne, the tsar's violent rages then began to make Alexei fear for his life. And among other things, Peter, with some justification but also a certain amount of hypocrisy, condemned his son for his bad treatment of his wife, Charlotte of Wolfenbuttel, whom he had married in 1711. This young woman, who was the first German bride of a Romanov, produced two children for her husband: Natalia, who died at fourteen, and Peter, who would eventually become Tsar Peter II. But shortly after her son's birth, Charlotte died and soon Alexei decided he needed to escape Russia and his terrifyingly unpredictable father. With his mistress, Afrosinia, he fled to Vienna to seek the protection of the Emperor Charles VI, brother-in-law of the ill-treated Charlotte – a lack of sensitivity typical of the time. However, Charles, fearing Peter's wrath, sent Alexei on to Naples, a city that had just come under Imperial rule, and it was here that the tsar's henchman, Peter Tolstoy, finally caught up with him. He deceived the young man into thinking that it was safe to return to Russia, but once back in St Petersburg, Alexei was arrested and, after being interrogated by his father at Peterhof, was imprisoned in the Peter and Paul Fortress. Not helped by his former mistress, who now betrayed him by stating that he had plotted against the tsar, Alexei was subsequently charged with treachery, then tortured, and finally condemned to death. While doubts still exist about what happened next, the fact remains that he died soon after. Although some were convinced that this had occurred as a result of his brutal treatment, others believed the questionable account of a Guards officer, Alexander Rumiantsev, who claimed that he personally had strangled him on the tsar's orders – the murder performed while Peter and Catherine were close by. Whatever the truth, Peter the Great was certainly responsible for his son's death.

In the meantime, Catherine had continued to have further children. Just over two weeks after the arrival of Alexei's son, she too had given birth to a boy, again called Peter. Both the parents had been overjoyed, with the tsar proclaiming the infant to be his heir. To the parents' despair, as had happened so often before, the child died in 1719 when he was around three and a half. Nonetheless, Peter still believed that there would be more sons, and three years later he confirmed his authority to choose his heir with the 'Charter on the Succession to the Throne', a decree that ended the automatic right of the first-born male. As a result of this, however, when Peter himself eventually died, the stability that he had strived to ensure for his country would once more be threatened.

Having captured Estonia from the Swedes, Peter now began to build up the port at Reval, visiting the area frequently and also buying a small four-roomed cottage where he and Catherine could stay. Renovated in 2004, today this little house, now a museum, gives a good insight into the simple tastes and preferences of Russia's autocratic ruler. But Peter then decided to build Catherine the baroque Kadriorg Palace nearby, designed by an Italian architect, Nicola Michetti. This was completed only after the tsar's death, and with Peter gone, the palace was visited only occasionally for the next century – the cottage meanwhile abandoned. Finally, the Kadriorg was restored by Catherine the Great's grandson, Nicholas I, who visited the area at a time when it became fashionable as a summer retreat. Here the court and aristocracy came to enjoy the fresh air and to bathe in the sea, and Reval remained an important resort until rail travel opened up new, more distant areas such as the Crimea.

In 1722, going to war for the last time, Peter set off with Catherine down to the Caspian Sea, where he took Derbent from the Persians. Although a difficult campaign, made still worse by the extreme heat, Catherine bore it all with her usual good humour, even to the point of shaving her head like her husband to make life more comfortable. Peter, however, became unwell and was forced to return home, so his army continued on without him. It succeeded in taking Baku the next year, but this would be only a temporary gain, as Russia was soon obliged to hand it back. Nonetheless, during the campaign Catherine had yet again proved herself, and her relationship with Peter was now so strong that in 1724 he declared that he wished to honour her further, taking the remarkable decision to crown her empress in her own right. Although disliking finery and unnecessary or frivolous extravagance, Peter spared no expense for her coronation in Moscow, ordering a lavish red gown and cloak for Catherine, even exchanging his own usual (and preferred) worn-out everyday clothes for an elaborate court dress. The ceremony took place in the traditional setting of the Cathedral of the Assumption in the Kremlin.

Shortly afterwards, Catherine nearly lost everything that she had gained. For some time there had been rumours that she was too much linked to her chamberlain William Mons, coincidently the brother of Peter's first mistress, Anna. He and another sister had grown close to Catherine, and although evidence neither proves nor disproves that he had an affair with the empress, as her favourite he had undoubtedly used his position to further his own interests. Although most people knew him to be extremely corrupt, a failing that the tsar particularly abhorred, Peter took longer to pick up on the gossip. When he did, he was furious, raging at Catherine and for a time refusing to speak to her. While William's sister escaped with a whipping, the chamberlain himself was arrested, interrogated by Peter Tolstoy, and subsequently executed. In a final grotesque touch, his head was then preserved and added to Peter's cabinet of curiosities in the Kunstkamera, where it joined the other 'freaks' in the tsar's collection. Some versions of this story suggest that Peter made Catherine watch the execution, others that she was presented with the severed head. But whatever happened, Peter made certain that she suffered cruelly for her behaviour. To reduce the suspicion of any true affection felt by her for the young man, on the day of his death she again managed to play her part cannily, appearing cheerful and unconcerned. And using her undoubted skills, over the next few weeks she gradually managed to win back Peter's forgiveness, although – according to the latest research – he most probably destroyed his earlier will appointing her as his heir.

By now Peter's health had become chronically bad. After a frenetic life of work, travelling, heavy drinking, feasting, playing and fighting, although only aged fifty-two he was suffering from several complaints, including most seriously of all bladder and prostate complications. Throughout his period on the throne he had seldom stopped, constantly driven by his immense energy and his desire to take on new projects. Always seeing his role as one of service to the state, he was forever at the front of any action required, even in his last months. Thus, when in November 1724 a boat carrying soldiers capsized at the mouth of the river, he plunged into the freezing waters to help rescue the drowning men. While this event has again passed into Russian mythology, at the time it served to undermine still further Peter's already declining health.

By the end of January of the next year, the tsar was obviously dying. He fought desperately against his protracted death, even reverting to some of the superstitions of former times, releasing prisoners and pardoning others, following a long-held belief that this might save his soul. According to witnesses, despite his often almost sacrilegious behaviour, he remained a believer, and he repeatedly appealed to God and the Church. Nonetheless, he would not designate his successor, and his courtiers, still in awe of their despotic ruler, dared not anger him further, fearing he might make an unexpected recovery. His earlier diktat that he alone could elect who should follow him now became a matter of key importance. Those with him in his last days gave varying accounts of this time, some reporting that he called for his daughter Anna, possibly with the intention of leaving her the crown. Another apocryphal story reports that he asked for writing materials and scrawled, 'Leave all to….', before the pen dropped from his grasp. A more prosaic account suggests that he just dismissed the question with an impatient wave of his hand and the muttered word 'later'. Regardless of what in fact happened, after several days of agony, Peter died on 28 January 1725 (OS), leaving the matter unresolved, and the country once more in danger of unrest.

After forty days of lying in state in his Winter Palace, his body was then taken in procession to its funeral in the unfinished Peter and Paul Cathedral, where it was laid to rest; this would start a tradition followed by all later Romanov rulers, except two – his grandson Peter II, buried in Moscow, and the murdered Ivan VI, in an unmarked grave. The country that had for so long lived under his dominating presence was now aware of the void that his death had brought. As the historian Mikhail Pogdin summarised more than a century later, his influence would be profound and long lasting:

> We wake up. What day is it? 1 January 1841 – Peter the Great ordered that years be counted from the birth of Christ and months of the year from January. It's time to get dressed – our clothing is sewn in the fashion given by Peter the First, a uniform by his pattern. The cloth is woven at a factory that he established, the wool is shorn from sheep he introduced in Russia. A book catches your eye – Peter the Great put the script into use and himself cut out the letters. You start reading – this is the language that under Peter was made into a bookish and literary one, forcing out the previous church idiom. Newspapers are delivered – Peter the Great launched them. You need to purchase various things – all of them, from the silk neckerchief to the sole of the boot, will remind you of Peter the Great. … At dinner, from the salted herring to the potatoes that he ordered down to the wine that he introduced, all the dishes remind you of Peter the Great. After dinner you go out for a visit – this is Peter the Great's assemblies, public social functions. You meet ladies there who were permitted into men's company at the demand of Peter the Great.[26]

Menshikov realised the threat to both the country and himself caused by Peter's reluctance to make a definitive decision as to who should follow him. Among possible claimants were his two direct descendants: Anna, his daughter by Catherine, and grandson Peter Alexeievich, son of the dead Alexei.[27] Anna, by now engaged to the Duke of Holstein-Gottorp – the nephew of Peter's former enemy, Karl XII, and heir presumptive to the Swedish throne – was soon ruled out. But the child Peter, although only nine years old, was supported by some members of the reactionary old aristocracy, who hoped to regain the standing they had previously held before the arrival of Peter's new men and new ideas. However, Menshikov, helped by Peter Tolstoy, immediately called the Guards and with their very visible backing was able to secure the crown for his long-time friend, the tsar's widow Catherine. Thus, within three hours of her husband's death, the very possibly still illiterate former Livonian servant girl became acknowledged as Russia's first empress, Catherine I. She now rewarded Tolstoy by promoting him a count and happily left the affairs of state to others, in particular Menshikov, her ever-loyal supporter. Finally released from her subservient role as wife to the unpredictable, autocratic Peter, she began a period of self-centred pleasure-seeking, surrounded by her favourites, possible lovers, and friends. Having enlarged the Winter Palace, she entertained lavishly, enjoying the questionable diversions that Peter had introduced her to, such as drinking competitions, performing dwarfs and other such antics. But the empress did not long survive her husband, dying while still in her forties little more than two years after him.

Once again the country was at risk of upheaval, but soon, with the approval of the nobles and Menshikov, the young Peter Alexeievich received the crown denied to him earlier. Menshikov, foreseeing Catherine's approaching death, had already taken steps to try and ensure his position by arranging Peter's engagement to his own daughter. Before long all his ambitious plans had failed. Not just unpopular with those he had earlier befriended for his latest change of allegiance, Menshikov now found himself equally hated by the tsar, who on his accession banished his grandfather's favourite to Siberia. Finally disgraced and stripped of all his power, Menshikov would remain in exile with his family for the rest of his life. Similarly, Count Tolstoy also paid a price for the role he had played in returning Peter II's father from Naples to meet his death. Exiled from court like Menshikov, Tolstoy died two years later by the White Sea. These changes would present the illustrious Dolgoruky family with a chance to further their own ambitions, and they quickly brought the still juvenile Peter II under their influence

One of the Dolgorukys, Prince Ivan, who was just seven years older than the young tsar, became his favourite, encouraging him to follow his own hedonistic and degenerate lifestyle. Spending much of their time hunting in the forests around Moscow, they thought only of their own amusement, and under the Dolgorukys' malign influence the tsar's behaviour rapidly deteriorated. So despite his reputed good looks, he was soon said to have a character in which there was 'nothing attractive nor agreeable'.[28] His short reign would be one of idleness and self-gratification, and whether or not he would have changed as he matured, we have no way of telling. To the end the Dolgorukys pursued their ambitions, finally arranging Peter's betrothal to their daughter Catherine, Ivan's younger sister. But their schemes would be thwarted when the tsar contracted smallpox and shortly after, early in the morning of 19 January 1730 (OS), the very day of his proposed wedding. Like his sister before him, he died aged just fourteen.

During his brief period on the throne, the tsar had brought his grandmother, Peter the Great's first rejected wife, Eudoxia, back to court. She had had a more eventful life than perhaps might have been expected when she was first sent to the convent at Suzdal. Having later taken a lover – who was eventually executed – for a time after Peter I's death she had even been hailed as sovereign by the men of the Church, who hated the dead tsar's reforms. After having been temporarily imprisoned at Schlüsselburg by Catherine I, she was finally able to end her days in some comfort at her grandson's court. This was now back in Moscow, the capital once again on his orders, Peter II having always hated St Petersburg. For that reason, when he died in the Kremlin, he was buried in the Cathedral of the Archangel alongside his earlier Romanov ancestors and their predecessors – a further contradiction of the wishes of his grandfather, who had intended all his descendants to be buried with him in the Peter and Paul Fortress in his new city.

Now the glory days of St Petersburg seemed to be over. No longer the capital, it was abandoned by the nobility and the unfinished city faced the risk of becoming forgotten and left to decay. Peter the Great had more than once expressed his fears for the survival of many of his revolutionary ideas and reforms, and the future of these, too, now seemed to be in doubt. The direct male line of the Romanovs had come to an end, and once more the country was threatened with upheaval and a return to the troubles that had so often marked the previous century. Searching for a resolution to these problems, the Supreme Privy Council therefore chose to appoint as empress Peter the Great's impoverished niece Anna Ivanovna, the daughter of the unfortunate, mentally disabled Ivan V.

With Anna's accession, the Romanov dynasty was able to survive, passing through the female line. As empress she became the second of a series of women who would rule the country for around two-thirds of the eighteenth century. Preferring St Petersburg to Moscow, in 1731 Anna moved the capital back to the new city, and here it would remain until 1918. And in addition to the new Winter Palace that was now built alongside the old one, there would be more developments and projects during Anna's reign, among them the completed Kunstkamera that housed her uncle's much-loved collection of oddities. Thus St Petersburg was not forgotten, but continued to grow into one of the world's most beautiful capitals, a lasting memorial to its exceptional and highly complex founder, Peter the Great.

9

Karl XII of Sweden: Triumph to Disaster

The statue in Stockholm of Karl XII pointing towards Russia. The four mortars surrounding the plinth were captured in 1701 at Dünamunde, while the king was at the height of his military fame.

As his father had wanted to give him the education that he had never had himself, from an early age Karl XII was well taught, in time becoming widely read, a very able mathematician, and a good linguist. Apart from a little Greek, he was fluent in four other languages: Swedish, German, Latin, and even French, but the last he usually refused to speak, showing an aversion to French culture that he had possibly inherited from his father. In addition, while still a child Karl had become an excellent rider and keen huntsman, killing his first wolf when he was only seven years old, and a bear when he was just twelve. Having later made these chases still more dangerous by pitting himself against the animals with only wooden weapons, he had then taken on other equally daring challenges, stunts such as swimming across freezing rivers, or careering down steep slopes on sledges. After his mother's early death, when he was still only eleven years old, he had begun to spend more time with his father, and had often accompanied the king on troop inspections. Having already begun his military training as a young boy, during these visits Karl was able to gain further experience, occasionally even receiving minor injuries when taking part in the army's high-risk exercises and war games. And as these official tours also allowed him to learn about the laws and running of the country, he became better prepared for the administrative role that he would soon have to take on.

After fifteen-year-old Karl XII became king in 1697, marriage plans soon began to be considered for himself and his older sister, Hedvig Sofia: he to marry the Danish king's daughter, she the same king's younger son. However, these proposals came to nothing, partly because Karl's grandmother had another plan for her favourite granddaughter, choosing instead the girl's cousin, Friedrich IV, Duke of Holstein-Gottorp. Accordingly, despite Hedvig Sofia's strong and well-founded reservations about her intended husband, this engagement went ahead. But the dowager queen's plans for her grandson to marry the duke's sister came to nothing, and, despite the diplomatic efforts of several other contenders, Karl would remain unmarried all his life. With the exception of his sisters and his grandmother, to whom he was greatly attached, he showed no interest in women as a whole, something that has raised questions regarding his sexuality. Whatever the truth, by the age of eighteen he had already become dedicated to the military life, later announcing that he believed a soldier to be happier without a wife – a view to be subsequently reiterated by that other great general (and womaniser), Maurice de Saxe.

Just a year after Karl's accession, the twenty-six-year-old Friedrich of Holstein-Gottorp was given a lavish welcome when arriving in Stockholm for his wedding with Hedvig Sofia. Having become the duke only three years earlier, Friedrich was one of the five young men who came to prominence in this decade; besides Karl the others were Frederik IV of Denmark (1699), Augustus II of Poland (1697), and Tsar Peter, the sole ruler of Russia after 1696. All less than thirty years old, these men through their bravado and youthful ambitions would soon plunge Europe into war. However, for now Sweden was enjoying its last years of peace, and during this time Karl and the duke became close companions, indulging in heavy drinking and engaging in various wild pranks and acts of vandalism, riotous behaviour that soon earned the duke the sobriquet the 'Gottorp Fury'. Eventually this period, dubbed the 'Holstein Frenzy', came to an end, when Karl, apparently shamed by his grandmother's obvious disapproval, finally settled down. Having now virtually given up drink forever, he began to commit himself full time to his responsibilities, rising early every morning to begin work on state affairs.

After their wedding, Friedrich and Hedvig Sofia moved to Gottorp, where she was soon unhappy living with her wild and debauched husband.

The following year, fearing the growing tensions developing across the border in Denmark, they both returned to Stockholm, taking up residence in Hedvig's childhood home of Karlberg. It was here that after the early death of her mother, she and her siblings had grown up under the care of their grandmother. This palace, formerly one of the many possessions of the exceptionally wealthy Magnus de la Gardie, is today altered and enlarged, housing a military academy, but in the garden a gravestone still marks the place where Karl's much-loved dog was buried.

In this period, court life was an extravagant round of masked balls, plays and entertainments, during which, despite the anxieties of his advisers, the young king dissipated much of the wealth accumulated by his parsimonious father. Taking part in the dancing and festivities that regularly took place, Karl also erected a new theatre and brought performers from abroad. However, things then began to change, and by the time Hedvig Sofia gave birth to a son in April 1700, the Great Northern War had broken out just a few weeks earlier.[e] By then, Karl XII, faced with the reality of war, had abandoned the hedonistic lifestyle he had been following and, dedicating himself to his military career, had begun to take up the Spartan existence of an ascetic. Renouncing all the luxuries and comforts that most of his contemporaries enjoyed, he dispensed with the fashionable wig of the period to wear his own hair cut short, and for the rest of his life he would dress in the plain, unadorned blue and yellow uniform of the Swedish soldier.

The Great Northern War would engage the countries round the Baltic for the next two decades, changing forever the balance of power in Europe. Within a year of Karl XII's accession, his neighbours had begun to create alliances with the purpose of regaining the possessions that they had lost during the seventeenth century's repeated conflicts. Mistakenly believing the eighteen-year-old Karl to be a soft target, they began to gather, ready to attack Sweden on three fronts. In February the Saxon army of his cousin Augustus invaded Swedish-owned Livonia and although failing to take Riga, in March he captured the nearby Dünamünde fortress. This was followed two weeks later by a second attack led by another of Karl's cousins, Frederik IV of Denmark, who chose this moment to begin besieging the Swedish contingent garrisoned in Tönning in the Duchy of Holstein-Gottorp. Karl immediately resolved to retaliate, and leaving Stockholm in April – never again to see the capital, his sister Hedvig Sofia, nor his grandmother (the reappointed regent) – he set off to Karlskrona to inspect his fleet. By July this was ready to join the Anglo-Dutch force that, having come to his aid, was now anchored north of Helsingør. Having already gathered 12,000 troops in preparation for a land assault on Copenhagen, on 24 July/4 August the force began its transit of the Øresund, passing the Swedish island of Hven

e Two years later this child would become the new Duke of Holstein-Gottorp when his father was killed in battle.

(Ven), where Karl joined it the next day. Five hours later after a stormy crossing the king and his men arrived around 25 miles north of the Danish capital. On landing, without hesitation the impatient young king plunged into the water, leading his army from the front, in the manner for which he would become famous in the years ahead. With the help of the combined fleets, he was then able to begin to threaten Copenhagen, but before any action began Frederik IV abandoned his siege in Holstein and agreed to start peace talks at Travendal (Traventhal). Within just six weeks, Karl XII's prompt response had forced Denmark to withdraw from the war.

Meanwhile in July, Augustus had led his Saxon troops in a second attempt to take Riga, only finally conceding defeat in September before sending his army into their winter quarters south of the city. But at this point the Russians began to represent a more immediate danger to Karl, as they were no longer embroiled in fighting the Ottomans. While this had previously made Tsar Peter unwilling to declare war on Sweden, having now agreed a peace with the sultan, he was ready to take a more active role alongside his allies. By October his troops were threatening Swedish territory, and having invaded Ingria they had begun to besiege Narva, a strategic fortress in Swedish Estonia.

Accordingly, Karl immediately set his mind to dealing with these new threats. For five days after setting sail from Karlskrona, his fleet battled through a severe storm that caused men and horses to suffer alike, but finally on 25 September/6 October his army arrived at Pernau (Pärnu) in the Bay of Riga. But having received news that the immediate threat presented by Augustus had passed, after allowing his force to recover from the effects of their voyage, Karl decided to turn his attention instead to the defence of his fortress in the north. With winter fast approaching, the army set off along the wet, muddy tracks to Reval (Tallinn), from where they then continued on to Wesenberg (Rakvere), around 70 miles west of his objective. Here the king planned to await reinforcements, but soon anxious for his besieged garrison, he decided to delay no longer. After a further week of travelling through difficult terrain and a countryside that had been laid barren by the Russians, at last – to the enemy's surprise – his exhausted and half-starving men and horses reached Narva on 19/30 November. Estimates suggest that while the Swedish army numbered around 9,000, the Russians probably had a force of between 35,000 and 40,000. Moreover, they were well dug in, strung out in two lines of entrenchments, arching around the fortress to the river that enclosed it on its remaining side. With their position apparently secure, the Russian leaders did not expect the small Swedish army to attack, presuming that it too would rather dig in and create another tier to the siege. But to their further surprise, at two in the afternoon Karl ordered the assault to begin. By this time the conditions had deteriorated even further, with a snowstorm now in full force, but the weather only played into the hands of the Swedes, blinding the opposition to their advance. As they then broke through the centre of the enemy lines, pouring over the defences and slaughtering everyone in their path, the Russian soldiers fled in panic towards the river. Many were drowned, some were swept away on their horses when attempting to wade their way across, others were thrown into the water when the bridge collapsed under their combined weight. Because the majority of the Russian army had lacked sufficient training, the main fighting was over within three hours and although for a time Peter's Guards regiments continued to hold out, before the night was over they too had agreed to surrender. While the officers were taken prisoner, the men were allowed to lay down their arms and retreat back to Russia, their numbers too excessive for Karl to hold them all captive.

The king had personally engaged in the thick of the fighting, twice losing his horse during the battle, and he was now revered for his courage and leadership. Fought against enormous odds, the victory, with its comparatively few Swedish casualties, would become the talk of Europe. While among his men this success began to earn him a reputation for invincibility, in Karl himself it created a disdain for the Russian troops, a lasting underestimation of their potential that in the long run would bring about his downfall. However, he now faced a more immediate problem. In the aftermath of the battle his exhausted soldiers had taken over the abandoned enemy tents, using them as welcome overnight shelters, not realising that many Russians had been suffering from disease. Over the next days and weeks this would spread through the Swedish camp, with many falling sick and others dying. The king himself was spared, but in future he would not make the same mistake, choosing when necessary to sleep in the open, regardless of the weather.

As soon as his army had recovered and the winter season had passed, Karl began preparations to take on his next enemy, Augustus. In July he arrived at Dünamünde where he proceeded to carry out a successful crossing of the Düna (Daugava), using boats and rafts to ferry his men over the river. Drawing on the experience gained at Narva, he also ordered damp straw to be lit on the leading craft, using the favourable wind to blow smoke into the eyes of his enemy. Having achieved the crossing, he then defeated the Saxon army that Augustus had brought to the region – the recently elected king still lacking the *Sejm*'s permission to use Polish troops – and with their retreat the way became open for Karl to move on into the Duchy of Courland.

By December 1701 Augustus was becoming increasingly concerned, and so he now attempted to persuade the nobles in Warsaw to back his cause and allow him to employ Polish troops in his fight against the Swedes. Having failed in this, the next year he adopted another plan, sending his former mistress Maria Aurora von Königsmarck to try and persuade Karl XII to agree to his generous offers of peace. She was a particular favourite of the Polish king and the mother of one of his few acknowledged bastards, Maurice de Saxe, and despite being nearly forty, was still famed for her beauty and captivating charm. Nonetheless, Karl refused to meet her; she even failed to gain his attention when she accosted him, kneeling before him in the road. Turning his back on her, he quickly rode off, and later would indicate his disgust for all such women by rounding up the female followers of his soldiers, submitting them to a sermon on piety, and then expelling them from the camp. Augustus did not give up and continued to make peaceful overtures, but – against the advice of his ministers – Karl turned them down. Despising his cousin for his treachery and louche lifestyle, the king was determined to carry on his pursuit until he had removed Augustus from power. So, now intending to persuade the Poles to depose their king, Karl entered Warsaw, but before any agreement was reached, Augustus, contrary to the terms agreed at his election, re-entered Poland at the head of his Saxon army. When the two cousins then met at Kliszów, the Swedish king achieved yet another remarkable victory against a larger force. This time his achievement did not come without personal cost, his brother-in-law, the 'Gottorp Fury', being among the 300 or so killed on the Swedish side. Nonetheless, this latest military success enabled Karl to march on and then take Kraków.

Continuing to distrust Augustus, in 1704 Karl finally convinced the Polish *Sejm* to dethrone their king and replace him with one of their own nobles, Stanislaw Leszczyński. Despite opposition from other rival members of the nobility, many of whom purposely boycotted the election, the following year the young man was crowned in Warsaw as Stanislaw I. But Augustus, aided by the Russians, still refused to concede defeat, and so for another two years the fighting continued, with Karl zigzagging back and forth across Poland, capturing towns and winning further battles. At last, having decided to invade Saxony, in September 1706 he arrived at Altranstädt near Leipzig. Many, including the wife and mother of the elector, fled in fear of their lives, but most returned when things became more settled. By the end of the month Karl was already drawing up a treaty for Augustus to sign, one in which he officially renounced his Polish throne and recognised the new king.

This treaty would also include a further stipulation. Karl insisted that Johann Patkul, an ambitious Livonian nobleman who had sought to gain his country's independence from Sweden, should be handed over. Having previously been declared a traitor by the king's father, Patkul had for a time fled abroad, only returning to Swedish territory after Karl XI's death, when he hoped to be pardoned by the new ruler. As this request had been refused, Patkul had then offered his services to Augustus, acting for a time as envoy to Tsar Peter. Under the terms of the treaty, Augustus was now obliged to give him up, and the Livonian was immediately condemned to death for his treason. Despite pleas for clemency from Karl's younger sister, the king remained resolute, determined not just to take revenge on the man who had dared oppose the Swedish crown, but also to impart a strong message to those tempted to follow his lead. On his orders, therefore, Patkul was brutally executed. After he had been broken on the wheel, his quartered body was put on public display, only eventually removed six years later by the reinstated King Augustus. While Karl was now feared by the people, he was also widely condemned abroad, with even the tsar – who was not above such behaviour himself – adding his voice to the general outcry. Although the Swedish king expected discipline from his troops, regulating their plundering of the battlefield according to the laws of the time, nonetheless, under his command they often acted with immense savagery, and he himself occasionally displayed an utterly ruthless streak. In some instances, Karl was generous to his captives, as when he provided food to the surrendering, but starving, survivors of the siege at Thorn, but at other times he was unconditionally cold-blooded, showing little concern for those he had conquered. He was not above calling for cruel reprisals and massacres of whole communities who had carried out attacks on his men.

In the days before the treaty was finally agreed, Augustus was still dealing with the other side. Even while the peace process was in progress, he was secretly approaching the Russians, who in turn were kept ignorant of his negotiations with Karl. But becoming aware of the dangerous game he was playing, when Peter's general Menshikov arrived with his army at Kalisz, Augustus made a last-minute attempt to stop the fighting by informing the Swedish commander of the peace that was about to be signed. Having no other verification of this, and suspicious of the notoriously untrustworthy Saxon, the general refused to believe the information. Instead, under pressure from his Polish allies, he decided – against his better judgement – to engage the enemy, and so, just days after agreement had been reached, on 18/29 October 1706 the battle began. As the small Swedish force was greatly outnumbered, a situation made worse by most of the Poles soon fleeing the field, within three hours Menshikov had achieved a resounding victory that resulted in the capture of nearly 3,000 Swedes and Poles and the death of something like 2,000. Nonetheless, while news of this disaster greatly angered Karl, who again accused his cousin of deviousness, by the end of November Augustus' abdication had become public knowledge, and soon after the two cousins met at Altranstädt. With the treaty now signed, Karl decided to remain in the town for much of the next year, overseeing the rest and replenishment of his troops, and taking the opportunity to visit the nearby battlefield where his predecessor the great Gustavus Adolphus had been killed.

By this time events had taken a new turn in the rest of Europe, as a result of the death in 1700 of the disabled King Carlos II of Spain. While Carlos had continued to survive longer than expected, always without an heir, rival pretenders in France and Austria had been waiting impatiently in the wings for the moment when they might lay claim to his throne. By 1701 the dispute had escalated, finally causing the thirteen-year-long War of the Spanish Succession to break out. In this uncertain period, the allied nations became concerned that events in eastern Europe might further complicate their own situation, and accordingly foreign dignitaries now began to queue up to meet the famous young Swedish king residing in Saxony. One of the most important of these was John Churchill, later Duke of Marlborough, who in April 1707 came as Queen

Anne's representative to visit Karl in his simple quarters. Churchill, like Augustus, wore the flamboyant clothes and full wig of the typical courtier, and he conducted himself according to the stylised etiquette of the period, marking a sharp contrast with the Swedish king's laconic, direct manner, and unconventional appearance. According to the British envoy George Stepney, Karl's uniform was always dirty, his cropped hair unkempt, and his table manners uncivilised. But for Churchill, of more importance was the fact that during the meeting, having probably caught sight of the king's maps, he became convinced that Karl's objective was now to march into Russia, with Moscow as his probable goal.

During the intervening years, while Karl had become so absorbed by affairs with his cousin in Poland, he had failed to register to what extent Peter had been improving the performance of his army. Having had the first of their successes in Livonia at the end of 1701, only four years after their defeat at Narva the Russians had returned and captured the town. Furthermore, in the autumn of 1702 the tsar had managed to take the Swedish fortress of Nöteborg (Schlüsselburg) close to where the River Neva enters Lake Ladoga, just upstream from where he would soon start to construct his new city of St Petersburg. Despite these gains, Karl still believed the Russians were foes of no account, whose conquest he could postpone until he had dealt with his troublesome Saxon relation. So it was not until the end of August 1707 that he finally began to move, setting off with his newly re-equipped and impressively well-turned-out army of some 44,000 men. Then, apparently on a whim, just five days after setting out from Altranstädt, he briefly left his troops to make a private call on his relatives in Dresden, receiving a warm welcome from Augustus and his mother – behaviour that was again not untypical in this period of complicated dynastic alliances. While warfare was seen almost as a chivalric exercise for gentlemen, rulers were often able to separate their personal relationships from the political or national. In the same way, many of the mercenary soldiers and famous generals of the age would switch sides with an impunity that can often appear strange to most modern eyes.

After his short visit to Dresden, Karl continued his progress east, travelling through the difficult terrain of Poland and Lithuania that had been intentionally laid waste by the Russians, a march made still more treacherous by the many large rivers that the army had to cross, and the increasing hostility of the local peasantry. Having chosen to skirt the waiting enemy encamped in the region of Warsaw, he had selected the considerably more challenging northern route through the virtually impenetrable marshy area of Masovia. At last, after some minor engagements with the Russians, he arrived in the spring of 1708 at the Lithuanian town of Grodno (today in Belarus). Here Peter, unwilling to engage, quietly withdrew his men without a fight, still uncertain of the king's plans for attack, and fearing in particular for the safety of his fledgling city of St Petersburg to the north. To hamper the enemy's advance, the tsar therefore continued to lay waste the surrounding countryside, again razing towns, poisoning wells, and destroying everything that could provision the invading army. The Swedes nevertheless pressed on east through the freezing weather and barren country, stopping briefly at Smorgoni before being driven forward again in the quest for supplies. Finally, they stopped at Radoshkoviche less than 25 miles north-west of Minsk. Here Karl allowed his men to rest for three months. They endeavoured to survive by seeking out the buried stores that the peasants had attempted to conceal under the snow. With his men by this time suffering from hunger and disease, Karl sent instructions to General Lewenhaupt in Livonia, ordering him to bring supplies. But with delays in the delivery of the message, and logistical problems over the collection of the requested items, several weeks passed before the relief force was eventually able to set out from Riga to reach their suffering comrades.

In June, when the condition of the roads had improved, having left some of his troops to support his protégé, King Stanislaw, Karl set off with his remaining army, still heading towards the east. But by July the Russians under the command of Menshikov, Sheremetev and Repnin had blocked his path, having taken up a position at Holowczyn, to the west of Mogilev. The Russian defence stretched along one shore of a small tributary of the Drut, leaving undefended a central marshy area that separated their two flanks. It was here that Karl now chose to attack, leading his men over the river, through water so deep that it reached high up the soldiers' chests, forcing them to carry their weapons above their heads. After the Swedes had at last successfully broken the defensive line, the Russians opted for a retreat. While this gave Karl the victory, one he later declared to have been his 'favourite battle', it would be his last real success, and he had now become aware of how much Peter had improved his army. However, when in the aftermath of his defeat, Peter proposed to discuss peace terms, with his usual stubbornness Karl turned down the offer, announcing with bravado that he would not parley until he had arrived in Moscow – a decision that he would later have much reason to regret.

And now Karl's luck began to turn. Having marched on to Mogilev, for a month the king waited, expecting the arrival at any time of Lewenhaupt with his 12,500-strong army. In August, losing patience, he decided to set off again after the Russians. Although wishing to engage in battle, he was unable to force the enemy to confront him, and instead was constantly harried by the small-scale attacks or ambushes of Peter's Cossack soldiers. Nonetheless, he continued to pursue his enemy towards Smolensk, until finally in September, within reach of the town and just 150 miles from Moscow itself, he abandoned his original plan. Confronted by Peter's recently constructed line of defence stretching for hundreds of miles from Pskov to Briansk that lay directly in his path, and concerned about the near-starving condition of his troops, he decided that Moscow would have to wait until the next year. Therefore, having sent instructions to Lewenhaupt to follow him, he turned south towards the province of Severia and the richer pastures of the Ukraine that lay beyond.

Meanwhile, following the king's orders, Lewenhaupt had at last set off to join him, but on 28 September (OS), when he arrived with his vast train at Lesnaya (today in Belarus), he found the Russians waiting for him, and he was forced to engage with them in battle. Although there was no outright victory for either side, in the hours that followed discipline broke down in the Swedish camp and, in the subsequent confusion and disarray, the general saw no option other than to make a hasty retreat, having first destroyed his supplies in order to prevent them falling into the enemy's hands. Using the unhitched wagon horses to speed the journey of the infantry, the ragged army made better progress and, despite suffering other lesser attacks, reached Karl's camp on 12 October (OS). Here, however, the remaining 6,000 exhausted and battered soldiers only served to increase the logistical problems the king was already facing.

Karl XII had been encouraged to move into the Ukraine by the Cossack Hetman, Ivan Mazepa, with whom he had been in touch for some time, conducting their negotiations in Latin, the diplomatic language. Mazepa – whose colourful life was later elaborated in the poems of Byron and Pushkin, and Tchaikovsky's eponymous opera – had been born in the region of Kiev, an area that at the time was part of the Polish-Lithuanian Commonwealth. Having been educated in Warsaw, and served for a time at the Polish court, he had returned to his place of birth, where he had become the Hetman of the Left Bank Cossacks. These controlled the autonomous region on the east bank of the River Dnieper, a semi-independent area that after Poland's 'Deluge' had become a protectorate of Russia. But now Mazepa had finally decided to join Karl, deserting Peter, who – he believed – had failed to ensure the independence of his people. Mazepa assured the king of the support of some 3,000 of his men, with the possibility of still more Cossacks joining from the Zaporizhian Host, and he also promised that he would be able to provide supplies for the Swedish army. But within a month, in November Peter wreaked vengeance on Mazepa's people for their leader's act of treachery, ordering hundreds to be executed. He also demanded the destruction of their stronghold at Baturin, an act of savagery during which thousands more were slaughtered before, in a final refinement of cruelty, they were thrown into the Dnieper to transmit the news of the tsar's terrifying vengeance to others downstream.

Peter's actions had caused Karl to lose Mazepa's valuable provisions, and soon other problems would also bedevil the Swedes. By the end of the year the most severe winter on record had begun to set in, and things reached a nadir on 5 January (NS). Exceptionally low temperatures now hit the whole of Europe, freezing up the Øresund, icing over the port in Marseilles, and killing domestic and wild animals wherever they sheltered. As these appalling conditions persisted for the next three months, frostbite took its toll on the Swedish army, with thousands of the men losing limbs or dying from the cold. But as ever Karl shared in the hardships of his soldiers, and earned their loyalty by eating their simple food, sleeping on the bare ground, and suffering his repeated injuries without complaint.

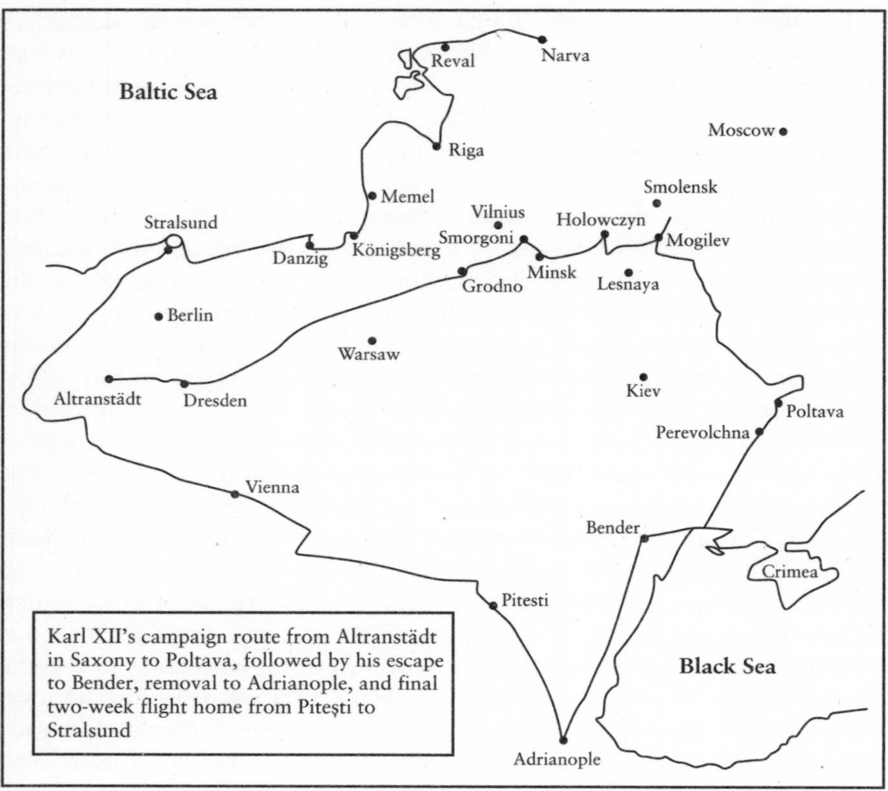

Karl XII's campaign route from Altranstädt in Saxony to Poltava, followed by his escape to Bender, removal to Adrianople, and final two-week flight home from Piteşti to Stralsund

Revered for his bravery, and always appearing fearless in the face of danger, he was strengthened by his own deep religious faith, convinced that God would protect him until the allotted time for his death.

Having arrived in the Ukraine, throughout the winter the Swedes repeatedly tried to drive the Russians from the region, while all the time they pressed on south seeking better supplies for the men and more fodder for the horses. Finally, in May 1709 Karl's greatly depleted army, which had been still further reduced by the plague, arrived at the Russian-held fortress of Poltava, a little over 200 miles to the south-east of Kiev, and here the king began to mount a siege. As the days went by, more Russian forces started to arrive in support of their beleaguered garrison, and minor skirmishes took place, during which on 17 June (OS) – his twenty-seventh birthday – Karl was wounded in the foot. Soon complications set in and he became seriously ill, only just recovering when ten days later on 27 June/8 July the situation escalated and early in the morning the full-scale battle began. The king, now anxious about the deteriorating condition of his army, had decided he could wait no longer and had called for the attack to start, hoping to take the enemy by surprise – a plan that soon failed because of his senior commanding officer's inadequate preparations, which had resulted in delays to the start of the fighting. Because of his injury, Karl had to watch the events unfold while lying on a litter, having delegated the leadership to Field Marshal Rehnskiöld and his subordinate General Lewenhaupt. To add to the Swedes' disadvantage, they were outnumbered by more than two to one, seriously under-equipped, and with a dire shortage of ammunition, something that may partly explain Karl's decision to keep his four artillery guns in reserve. Besides these problems, things were made still worse by the two commanders' personality differences, which only added to the misunderstandings and eventual breakdown in communications. In time discipline began to disintegrate and as the situation deteriorated the soldiers started to flee, whereupon Karl finally ordered the retreat. He personally came under attack, but his elite bodyguard remained with him, many being killed as they tried to protect him. Eventually, his litter was destroyed, leaving him without transport, and so he struggled with his heavily bleeding foot onto a nearby riderless horse, only for that immediately to be dismembered under him. Needing a replacement, he abruptly commanded one of his badly wounded soldiers to give up his mount, something for which the man was later ennobled, having – contrary to the account given by Voltaire – eventually, and miraculously, been saved by the actions of his own brothers, who had gone back in search of him.

Having withdrawn from the scene, Karl was at last persuaded to flee for his life, and so he and Mazepa with around 1,600 of his loyal Cossacks were ferried over the River Dnieper, taking with them a certain quantity of gold and treasure. But owing to the insufficient number of boats available, the majority of the surviving army was left behind, placed under the command of Lewenhaupt, who was now instructed to march to the Crimea so that he might later link up with his king. But the next day some 8,000–9,000 Russians caught up with the retreating ranks at Perevolochna, and although they were superior in number, the roughly 14,000 Swedes were so exhausted and demoralised that the general decided to avoid further bloodshed by surrendering his entire army. When later hearing the news, Karl was furious about Lewenhaupt's capitulation without a fight, but by then the captive Swedes were already being marched back to Russia. Those Cossacks who, unlike some of their number, had not deserted Karl in the battle, were even more unfortunate, being instantly slaughtered. However, while many of the 23,000 Swedes taken prisoner – both during and after the battle – would later put down roots in Russia, some eventually made their way home. Among these was Field Marshal Rehnskiöld, who, having been captured in the heat of the fighting, was eventually allowed to return to Sweden in 1718. No efforts were made ensure the release of the unfortunate Lewenhaupt, who died an exile in Moscow ten years after the disastrous defeat.

The victory reversed the political situation in Europe, with Karl now the fallen hero. In contrast Peter was the new champion of the hour, acclaimed as 'the Great' by the Russians and many others – with the exception of the Ukrainians, who still today regard the Swedes' defeat as marking the end of their hopes of independence for centuries to come. Ten days after their escape over the Dnieper, the Swedish king and the remnants of his army crossed the River Bug and found asylum in the Ottoman Empire, where they eventually settled at Bender (today in Moldova). Here just two months later Mazepa died, but Karl had already suffered a more grievous loss as shortly after arriving in the town in July the news had been broken to him that his much-loved older sister Hedvig Sofia had succumbed to smallpox the previous December. The tragedy totally overwhelmed the king, causing him on this rare occasion to give way to utter despair.

Karl XII was now the guest of Sultan Ahmed III, who afforded him the hospitality due to a visiting head of state, and placed him under the protection of his special Janissary guards. In time, with the arrival of more Swedish troops, the king's makeshift place of settlement turned into a proper encampment, from where he continued his long-distance running of his country's affairs. Already respected as the enemy of the Russians (the Ottomans' age-old foe), Karl was even more revered by his hosts for his heroic prowess and disciplined lifestyle. Nevertheless, before long he became exceedingly demanding, and on discovering the corruption of the grand vizier, who was plotting his downfall with the Russian ambassador, Peter Tolstoy, in 1711 Karl persuaded the sultan to punish both men – dismissing the first, and imprisoning the second, who was then confined for close on four years in Constantinople's Seven Towers (the Yedikule). With such treatment of an envoy being a virtual declaration of war, Ahmed now sent his new grand vizier, Baltacı Mehmet Pasha, into Moldavia with his large army to begin the Pruth Campaign against Russia. This conflict finally ended with the defeat of Peter the Great at the four-day Battle of Stănileşti (today in Romania), a victory witnessed by Karl, who, although not permitted to take part in the fighting, had ridden over to watch the events. Angered by the generous peace terms then granted to the Russians, his later bitter complaints to the sultan would be the cause of the grand vizier's disgrace.

This was not the only disagreement that the king would have with his hosts. As he grew increasingly troublesome, they became eager to get rid of him, and two years later, after days of rumour regarding plans to remove him and return him to Sweden, one Sunday morning in February a bizarre event occurred. While the king was at prayer, numbers of irate Tatars and Turks attacked his headquarters at Bender. Terrified, many of his men fled, but for the next eight hours Karl and his two to three dozen remaining supporters continued to hold out. While the exact figures are unknown, this small band of men reputedly resisted the onslaught of hundreds – some claim even several thousands – of assailants. Eventually, however, the house was set on fire, forcing Karl and his handful of companions to leave. While they were charging from the burning building, the king tripped on his spurs and fell to the ground. Having been immediately arrested, he was then taken to Timurtasch near Adrianople (Edirne), where he remained a captive. Remembered as the 'Kalabalik' after the Turkish word for a tumult, this episode soon became news around Europe, and exaggerated reports of what had occurred increased in certain quarters the heroic image of Sweden's young king.

Although Karl's hosts were becoming increasingly tired of their vexatious and costly guest, on hearing of the victory by Sweden's Baltic troops at Gadebusch near Lübeck in December 1712, the sultan decided to release the king, sending apologies to him for the treatment that he had received. Although now moved to nearby Demotika, Karl had gone into a decline, and for many months he refused to leave his room, only eventually doing so after receiving news of growing unrest at home. Once more galvanised, he started to make plans for his return to Sweden. Finally, in October 1714, five years after his arrival in the Ottoman Empire, he received an elaborate send-off. Having made his way to Piteşti in Wallachia (today Romania), near the border with the Habsburg Empire, he was joined by Swedish troops recently arrived from Bender. But wishing to avoid capture by his enemies, he soon decided that it would be wiser to continue his journey accompanied by just two of his followers – men who were especially chosen for their riding skills. According to the popular story, the next month the three slipped over the border and began their mad dash north, passing through Hungary, Austria and the German states. Travelling incognito as Peter Frisk, Karl added to his disguise by wearing for the first time in years a wig that today, with his mud-caked uniform, is exhibited in the Armoury Museum in Stockholm. Seldom stopping and having barely rested, in just sixteen days – spent mostly in the saddle – he covered over 1,400 miles.

However, this version of events is now questioned. Cecilia Nordenkull has found proof that Karl personally spread the account of his heroic ride north, a story that not only added to his reputation, but, more significantly, concealed the visit he secretly made to the French court. Having left the Ottoman lands earlier than widely claimed, he had travelled via the Hapsburg Empire and his territory of Deux Ponts [Pfalz-Zweibrücken] to Versailles. On meeting Louis XIV, he had then agreed to give his support to James Francis Edward Stuart, the Old Pretender, who was planning a second invasion of Scotland. Although it was only two months since Queen Anne's death and George I's succession as the British king, Karl had long had concerns regarding the Hanoverian's ambitions to seize Sweden's German territories. So, with Louis' offer of financial backing, Karl now promised logistical support to the Jacobite invasion – an arrangement that following the old king's death the next year would in fact come to nothing, not helped by the deterioration of French-Swedish relations under the Regent.[29] After this French detour, on 11 November (OS) Karl finally arrived with just one of his two companions at the well-defended Baltic fortress of Stralsund in Swedish Pomerania. Here he remained for the next year, hoping once more to pick up the fight before returning, again the hero, to his country.

After the disaster at Poltava, not only had Augustus II regained his throne in Poland, but the Russians had continued to extend their control over Sweden's Baltic regions, helped by Karl's former defeated enemies who had returned to the war. Furthermore, the allies had been joined by the Prussian king and the Elector of Hanover (the later George I). Nevertheless, during Karl's exile, his generals had rustled up enough men to continue the fight in the north, with Magnus Stenbock taking Rostock in 1711, and then Gadebusch in December the next year. But five months later, with his troops now starving, Stenbock had been forced to surrender at Tönning, and by the end of the year the enemy had occupied Pomerania and taken Stettin, leaving just the south Baltic ports of Wismar and Stralsund in Swedish hands. But in July 1715, eight months after Karl's arrival at Stralsund, the situation became still more serious when some 40,000 combined enemy troops approached the town and began to put it under siege.

By December the attackers were beginning to penetrate the defences, and so shortly before the place finally surrendered, Karl was persuaded to leave. With three others he slipped away in a small boat that, accompanied by two other craft, made its way out to sea through a channel that had been purposely cut through the fast-forming ice surrounding the town. After twelve hours the three boats were still only level with the island of Hiddensee, lying close to the northern coast of the island of Rugen that was now under Danish occupation. They struggled on, until finally, having reached the stormy open sea, they met up with a Swedish ship. Three days later, early in the morning this landed the men on Sweden's southern tip at Trelleborg, and Karl was back on the Swedish mainland after an absence of fifteen years. Having lingered in Stralsund for so long, he was too late to see his grandmother once more, who less than three weeks before had died aged seventy-nine.

Throughout her grandson's absence Hedvig Eleonora had continued to act as regent until two years before her death handing the responsibility over to her granddaughter, Ulrika Eleonora. Although often dismissed as an insignificant woman with little political understanding, recent research has been more generous, acknowledging Hedvig's valuable contribution to Sweden's artistic heritage. Apart from her personal investment in works of art, she had promoted important architectural projects, such as ordering the reconstruction of Drottningholm, and buying the palace of Magnus de la Gardie near Stockholm – later renamed Ulriksdal after a grandson who died in infancy. But the way Hedvig Eleonora played her role as regent also needs to be re-examined; she deserves some credit for avoiding the pitfalls that would too often cause women in her position to be accused of political meddling. Even though she was lucky in that her two countries – that of her birth, Holstein-Gottorp, and her new home Sweden – were always allies, her position was soon complicated by the early death of her husband Karl X. Having unexpectedly lost his protection only six years after arriving in Sweden, against the wishes of the council, she had then found herself acting as the leading member of her son's regency. During this time, she seldom attended the meetings, giving the impression that she was more absorbed with domestic issues, her lapdogs and the playing of cards. But, as her extensive correspondence shows, she was in fact interested in national and foreign affairs, and her stepping back from the everyday workings of the council may well have been partly motivated by a wish to escape the accusation of over-interference in the matters of state.

Over her family Hedvig Eleonora always exerted her control, directly influencing the lives of her son and grandchildren, at times with little regard for their feelings. She pushed her favourite granddaughter into a marriage that she did not want, and treated her Danish daughter-in-law, Ulrika (Ulrikke), particularly unkindly. Whether or not in the latter case her behaviour could be partly explained by the bitter political differences between Denmark and her beloved Holstein-Gottorp, it was nonetheless inexcusable. But Hedvig Eleonora's forceful personality had no doubt been partly moulded by the fact that from the age of eighteen until her death, she would hold the senior female position at court. The former Queen Christina's unstable mother died five months after Hedvig Eleonora's marriage, and the gentle and retiring Ulrika never presented any opposition. Moreover, after the latter's death, Karl XI remained a widower and his son never married, leaving the old dowager queen's position still unchallenged.

On his arrival in Sweden, Karl was unwilling to visit Stockholm, wanting to wait until his situation had improved. He therefore set about rebuilding his army so that he might recover his lost territories, believing that any peace agreements should not be conducted until he was in a position of strength. He therefore ordered a fierce recruitment drive, forcing any vaguely eligible male into service, but this would denude the countryside of men able to work the fields. The brutality of the system, and the increased taxes he demanded, would add to the misery of his people and stoke up a growing disenchantment against him. Karl was helped in his work by Baron Görtz from Holstein-Gottorp, a man with extravagant tastes, who on becoming the second most powerful person in the country would be dubbed the king's 'Grand Vizier'. After meeting Karl for the first time at Stralsund, Görtz had gained the king's full confidence, and having taken control of diplomatic and financial affairs he would until the end of the reign continue to strive to save Sweden from collapse. Although he wished to form alliances, he was often hampered by the deviousness of foreign powers, but after Wismar – the last of Sweden's possessions south of the Baltic – had fallen to the enemy in April 1716, he was able to start peace negotiations with Peter the Great. But Karl refused to consider the offered terms, being still determined to fight on until he had regained his lost territories. His intransigence would force Görtz to find new ways to raise the necessary finance, and having first introduced tokens and paper money, the minister then went further and devalued the currency. Already seen as an outsider, Görtz now became still more unpopular and from this time he was viewed with even more suspicion by many Swedes, among them the supporters of the king's younger sister, Ulrika Eleonora, and her husband, Friedrich of Hesse-Kassel.

Within a month of his return, Karl XII was already preparing for another attack on Copenhagen, and although this was aborted when the weather changed, in March he proceeded to lead his men against Christiania (Oslo), where he attempted to capture the Arkhus Fortress. However, when the Danish troops returned from the siege of Stralsund and began to threaten his army from the rear, Karl gave up the attempt, and led his men back down the fiord to Frederikshald (Halden). Here too his assault failed after the local people intentionally set fire to the town, and following another defeat of his fleet, the king decided to abandon the whole campaign. Still loath to go to Stockholm, he settled in Lund where he would remain for the next eighteen months, during which time he briefly visited his sister Ulrika Eleonora.

Having spent a last few days with Ulrika, her husband, and his nephew the young Duke of Holstein-Gottorp, Karl began to mount another campaign against the Danes. Having sent General Armfeldt to take Trondheim on the west coast of Norway, in late 1718 the king embarked on a new assault of Frederikshald, setting up another siege of the Fredriksten fortress. According to reports, on 30 November (OS) while he was leaning over the parapet to inspect the works, the three men near him became concerned, and on approaching they discovered that he had been shot by a sniper and had died instantly. Fearful now of the effect on the soldiers' morale, his companions covered his body, and in a bizarre twist, placed a wig on his head to disguise his identity further, before taking him back to their headquarters.

Following his sudden death his army withdrew from the region. Another disaster struck further north when the following January the separate Swedish force under Carl Gustaf Armfeldt became caught in a violent storm during its retreat from Norway, leaving some 8,000 men dead, killed by the cold and the brutal guerrilla attacks of the local people. Finally, in February, there would be one more victim of the previous regime. The day after the king's death, the hated Görtz, returning from the latest peace talks with Peter the Great, was arrested by Karl's brother-in-law, Friedrich of Hesse-Kassel. Given a summary trial, the recently appointed *generalissimo* was executed three months later.

After embalming, Karl XII's body was returned to his childhood home of Karlberg in Stockholm, remaining there until the following February, when the thirty-six-year-old king was finally buried in the Riddarholm church beside the tombs of his predecessors. Within days of his killing the first rumours had begun to be spread and as is the way with such events, conspiracy theories soon started to grow; a pretender even appeared on the scene later on. The instant and unexpected nature of Karl's death had caused people to raise doubts, with many questioning who might have fired the fatal shot. Having brought his country to its knees, there were those who were relieved that their years of fighting and bitter hardship were over, and this gave rise to suggestions that he might have been killed by a disgruntled Swede wishing to bring an end to the war. But within weeks there were also other more sinister whispers, ones hinting that Ulrika Eleonora and her husband, Friedrich, had been implicated in his death, an event from which they had both ultimately benefited. But this was just the start, as over the years still more people came under suspicion and various theories regarding what had happened continued to multiply. As the essential questions remained unanswered, in an effort to clarify the situation, repeated exhumations were carried out, seeking to determine the direction and make-up of the fatal shot. But as the findings of these investigations were always inconclusive, the matter continued to be unresolved, remaining a subject of debate even until today. Cecilia Nordenkull presents new evidence in her recently published book where she asserts that Karl was in fact assassinated by his brother-in-law, the later Fredrik I.

While initially the Swedish people showed little sadness over the loss of their king, others abroad expressed their regret, none more so than Karl's main rival Peter the Great, who mourned his death, describing him as the 'perfect hero'. As the years went by, opinions would vary in Sweden, with some condemning the king's rashness, others extolling his courage in the face of adversity. Finally, however, in 1868, a century and a half after his death, during a period of increased patriotism and anti-Russian feeling, across the water from the palace the people of Stockholm erected a modest statue to their former king. Dressed in his usual uniform, he stands pointing out towards Russia. Around the base there are four mortars, ones captured by Karl in 1701 after his defeat of Augustus at Dünamünde, taken during the period of his greatest success following his resounding defeat of his three chief enemies. If Karl XII had chosen to make peace at that time, his military reputation would have been left undimmed and his country would have probably retained its position as an important power for some years to come, a leader among the Baltic countries. But confident of his role as an absolute king, and ambitious and obdurate, he refused to be swayed by any advice that he did not want to hear, and despite the increasing odds against him, he remained determined to wreak his full vengeance on those who had earlier threatened him. His resolution, as declared early on in his reign to the Senate, 'never to begin an unrighteous war' nor 'to finish a righteous war' without having first 'utterly crushed' his enemies, became the guiding principle throughout his period on the throne.[30] A complex character, combining greatness and foolhardiness, his tragedy was to leave the prosperous Sweden that he had inherited a broken country, a kingdom that would take years to recover at home, and would never again regain its former remarkable international standing.

10

Russia's Years of Transition

Engraving of Anna, Duchess of Courland, after she had become Empress of Russia. (National Library of Austria)

Anna Ivanovna was born on 28 January 1693 (OS), the fourth of five daughters of the mentally and physically disabled Tsar Ivan – Peter the Great's half-brother. When her father died four years later, she and her two surviving sisters, Catherine and Praskovia, moved with their mother to Izmailovo, one of her grandfather's estates near Moscow. Anna lived happily here until she was fifteen, and she later showed her love for the place when, like her uncle with his Preobrazinsky Guards, she named her new regiment after this childhood home. In 1708 on Peter the Great's orders the family joined the rest of the court and moved to St Petersburg.

Two years later the tsar wanted to arrange the engagement of one of his nieces to the Duke of Courland and Semigallia, the grandson of the Great Elector of Brandenburg. The duchy, created in 1561 from the territories of the old Livonian Order of Knights, had been briefly divided, Courland separated from its neighbour Semigallia, but in 1617 the two duchies had reunited when they became a fiefdom of Poland. During the mid-seventeenth century the region had grown in importance, even joining the race in the land grab abroad, possessing, for a time, settlements on the River Gambia in Africa, and a colony on the island of Tobago. In 1698, just a year after Tsar Peter's successful visit with his Grand Embassy to Courland's capital at Mitau (today Jelgava in Latvia), the fourth duke died, leaving a five-year-old son, Friedrich Wilhelm. But in 1701 at the beginning of the Great Northern War the Swedes occupied his country, and so the young duke and his mother fled the duchy and took shelter with her half-brother, the newly crowned Prussian king Friedrich I. Here they remained for the next eight years, until at last, after the tsar's defeat of the Swedes, Friedrich Wilhelm was able to return home. It was at this point, while the Russians were the dominant presence in the area, that Peter drew up his plans for the duke's marriage to one of his nieces. But as their strong-willed mother did not yet want to lose her favourite child, Catherine, she persuaded her brother-in-law to choose her younger daughter, seventeen-year-old Anna Ivanovna, with whom she had always been on less good terms. As a result, Anna became the first daughter of a tsar to be married to a foreigner. This was a remarkable break with Russian tradition, although it would soon be capped by Peter's own official marriage to his former, humbly born, Livonian mistress, Catherine.

On 31 October 1710 (OS) Anna's wedding took place in Prince Menshikov's still unfinished palace in St Petersburg. The event was then marked by days of heavy drinking and various boisterous diversions that appealed to the tsar's tasteless sense of humour. As a highlight of these amusements, two dwarfs, having appeared out of large pies, were then made to take part in a mock marriage ceremony, attended by seventy or more others, purposely brought from all over the empire for the occasion. The Russians roared with laughter at their antics, and Anna no doubt enjoyed the show, as years later when she was empress she arranged similar types of entertainment. On one particularly infamous occasion she ordered the marriage of an elderly courtier, and then forced him and his equally ancient wife to spend their 'wedding night' in an ice palace purposely constructed for the event.

Following her own wedding, Anna's pleasure was short-lived. Soon after leaving the city, on the journey home her new husband caught a chill and died unexpectedly, his death reportedly hastened by his overeating and drinking during the recent celebrations. So with the duchy now passing to Friedrich Wilhelm's uncle, Ferdinand Kettler, Anna returned to St Petersburg. But after Karl XII's earlier victory at Dünamünde in 1701, when the young duke had first been forced to abandon his home, Ferdinand had also fled, taking refuge in Danzig, where he would remain for the rest of his life, refusing to return to Courland. This now gave Peter an opportunity to ensure that Russian influence in the region did not wane, and for that purpose he ordered Anna to go back to the duchy and take up the role of regent. Here, without any friends, she soon felt ostracised and alone, but before long her loneliness would be the least of her challenges, her desperate appeals to her uncle for help with her severe financial problems receiving no response from St Petersburg.

In 1725, the year of Peter the Great's death, Maurice de Saxe – the illegitimate son of Augustus II of Poland and his mistress Aurora von Königsmarck – was persuaded to stand for election as the next duke. He was duly elected by the council the following year. However, the tsar's widow, the new Russian empress Catherine I, had by that time become concerned about her loss of influence in Courland, and so she actively opposed him, even sending Menshikov with troops to bring about his overthrow.[31] As a result, although Anna had hoped that she might become the wife of this famed philanderer, in 1727 de Saxe decided to give up his duchy and leave the country. As the field was therefore now open to other contenders, Menshikov hoped that he might be able to claim the dukedom for himself, but before long his plans were thwarted, possibly prevented by the machinations of the Russian representative Peter Bestuzhev-Ryumin. Although Anna was still the regent, Bestuzhev had now become her adviser and first lover, a position he would hold onto until he was eventually ousted by a rival. Having unwisely – as it happened – introduced Anna to the brother of one of his other mistresses, Bestuzhev was in time superseded, replaced by the new favourite, Ernst Johan Biren (Bühren). Biren came from a Courland family that over the last two generations had risen in society from their moderately humble beginnings. Becoming in time immensely powerful, he would remain Anna's constant companion for the rest of her life and, having even possibly fathered a child by her, he was at her bedside when she died many years later.

In 1730 Anna's life underwent a dramatic change. Following the sudden death of the fourteen-year-old tsar, Peter II, the Supreme Privy Council chose to elect her as the new Russian empress, believing that as an impoverished widow she might be easily manipulated. To that end, while she was still in Courland, the council directed her to sign a contract, not just agreeing to more limited powers, but also accepting that any failure on her part to adhere to their eight 'Conditions' would result in her removal. However, while the council members had hoped by this to gain greater authority, they had in reality just created a new crisis. Some of the other nobles, objecting to their secretive and underhand actions, decided to give Anna their backing, and with their support she felt confident enough to tear up in public the earlier document. Having by this reclaimed her autocratic rights, only a month after arriving in the country, she was crowned as Russia's absolute ruler.

Earlier in 1713, Tsar Peter had formed another alliance with the autocratic Duke of Mecklenburg, Karl Leopold. After giving the duke support against his troublesome nobles, Peter had then agreed to help him regain his lands lost to Sweden during the war. To cement this agreement, on 8 April 1716 in Danzig, the twice-divorced duke married Anna's older sister, Catherine Ivanovna. Although she was a plump, merry woman who was more easy-going than Anna and more popular with most people, Catherine's marriage to the uncouth, unkind and actively cruel duke proved to be so unhappy that she longed to return home. Having given birth to a daughter called Elizabeth Catherine in Rostock on 7 December 1718 (OS), four years later she was able at last to leave Mecklenburg with her child. Although her purpose was now to see her sick mother, who died the following year, Catherine Ivanovna would remain in Russia, never to return to the duchy or see her husband again.

Three years after her sister's accession, in 1733 things began to change for Catherine Ivanovna's child. Empress Anna, still an unmarried widow, chose Elizabeth Catherine to be her heir. Having moved into the Winter Palace in St Petersburg, a month before her mother's death Elizabeth Catherine finally renounced her Lutheran faith, converted to Orthodoxy and, taking the name of her aunt, became known as Anna Leopoldovna. That same year her chosen husband, nineteen-year-old Anton Ulrich of Brunswick-Lüneburg, arrived in Russia. Although a member of a dynastically important family who had connections to many of the ruling houses of Europe, he was a mild-mannered young man who disappointed everyone at the Russian court, including the empress and his naturally reserved and unsociable fiancée. Anna Leopoldovna was particularly cold towards him, showing no affection for her future husband. During the six years of their long betrothal she may very possibly have engaged in a love affair with a courtier. With suspicions growing, the man was summarily dismissed, and he would remain banned from the court until eventually invited back by Anna Leopoldovna after her aunt's death.

On coming to the Russian throne in 1730, Anna quickly decided to remove those who had initially tried to limit her powers. Having exiled her opposition, she also sent Peter II's favourites, the Dolgorukys, to Siberia, where on her orders the females were later incarcerated in convents and the males executed. Always anxious for her safety – and eager to listen to gossip – Empress Anna would come to rely on the findings of her investigative Chief of Political Police, whose evidence for the most part was gathered by devious methods that included bribery, snooping and interrogation under torture. On her accession, she had formed for her own protection the Izmailovsky Guards, and she filled this regiment with foreigners whose loyalty she felt she could better trust. As all these things were not enough to make her feel secure in Moscow, where Peter II had re-established the court, she decided to order a new Winter Palace to be built in St Petersburg. When she finally moved to this in January 1732, the city once more became the capital, remaining as such until the end of the Romanov dynasty.

At the time of her accession, Anna's favourite Biren and his loyal, long-suffering wife had also come to Russia and after the coronation Biren was made Count of the Holy Roman Empire, at the same time changing his name and adopting the more important sounding 'von Biron' [*sic*], thereby falsely claiming relationship to a French noble house. Immediately, he took control of the affairs of state, brutally enforcing his authority, and condemning to exile or death thousands of people opposed to the new regime. In this way he maintained the peace, but as his inexorable rise continued, his cruelty, corruption, extravagance and ostentatious wealth earned him many enemies. Meanwhile, after Anna had left for Russia, her husband's uncle Ferdinand had been recognised as Courland's new duke, and even though he still refused to leave Danzig, he held onto his title until his death seven years later. But as he had died without an heir, leaving the dukedom vacant, Anna then took it upon herself to bribe the duchy's neighbours and nobility to appoint her chosen candidate, and with that her beloved Biron became the new Duke of Courland.

During her reign of ten years, while Anna left the detailed running of her country to her ministers, she chose to occupy her time playing with her dwarfs and pursuing her favourite pastimes, in particular shooting. A crack shot, she spent weeks during the summer months at Peterhof killing – sometimes from the windows of the palace itself – the large numbers of birds and animals that were especially laid on for her sport. A tall, plain woman with manly features, she was stout and extremely strong, but despite her apparent robustness, unexpectedly her health started rapidly to decline. Having developed chronic kidney failure, she died at the age of only forty-seven on 17 October 1740 (OS). However, as just two months earlier her niece Anna Leopoldovna had given birth to a son – named Ivan after his great-grandfather – the mortally ill empress had then pronounced this child to be her heir. As a result, in the last weeks of the empress's life, the country once more faced the threat of unrest. Biron used the uncertainty to encourage senior members of the court to designate him as the future regent. Although he was finally able to persuade Anna to confirm this appointment, within three weeks of her death (as she had feared) his position came under attack. Even before her funeral, Biron was arrested by his enemies, and in June 1741 sent into exile, first in Siberia and then, after a pardon from the Empress Elizabeth, at Yaroslavl on the Volga. Courland now had to find a replacement for him in the duchy, and the choice fell on another member of the Brunswick-Lüneburg-Bevern family: Ludwig Ernst – uncharitably nicknamed 'Fat Louis' by his brother-in-law Frederick the Great. But he too was deposed within a year and a half, and the management of the country then passed into the hands of a council.

Meanwhile in Russia, Anna Leopoldovna was declared the new regent for her baby son, Ivan VI. Although she had been supported by Field Marshal Münnich during the overthrow of Biron, before long she demoted him as well, choosing instead to raise her husband Anton Ulrich to military commander. At the same time, she selected Andrei Osterman as her political adviser, but this and her other appointments of foreigners only served to make her unpopular with the Russians. The accession of the two-month-old Ivan VI was marked in October by an official visit from the Shah of Persia, who brought the child extravagant gifts, including quantities of jewels and numbers of elephants and camels, a display of wealth that amazed the people of St Petersburg.

Anna Leopoldovna was unprepared for her role and, naturally lazy, she was up to the difficult task of running the country. Besides lacking charisma, her character did not inspire the respect, admiration or awe of her people. Accustomed to being dazzled by their rulers, the Russians did not understand this woman, who dressed plainly, seldom smiled and chose to live away from the public view. She preferred the company of her two favourites, her possible former lover Count Lynar, and her equally close female friend Julia von Mengden. After fifteen months of her regency, some of her supporters, suspecting the ambitions of her chief minister Osterman, persuaded her to consider assuming power for herself. While this plan intended that she should become empress on her twenty-third birthday, twelve days before it actually took place, on 6 December 1741 (OS) Peter the Great's daughter, Elizabeth, mounted a coup and stormed the palace. Anna Leopoldovna surrendered without resistance, and accompanied by her husband, young son and recently born daughter, she left the palace for the last time. Ivan VI's reign was over.

Although Elizabeth had initially intended to return the family to Brunswick, as she grew more concerned about possible foreign support for the exiles she became increasingly undecided about what to do with her captives. As a result of her indecision, the family meandered around the empire, being moved from one place to another, until, after a journey of many months, they eventually arrived at the Dünamünde fortress near Riga. Here they would settle for a year, during which time Anna Leopoldovna produced two more children. The family members were then transferred to Ranenburg in Voronezh province, where they would spend their last seven months all together. Finally, one night an officer came to their rooms and removed the four-year-old Ivan, who was taken all alone towards an intended destination far north at Solovki, a fortress out in the middle of the White Sea. Shortly after losing her child, to Anna Leopoldovna's further grief she was also separated from her close friend Julia, and now the remaining members of the family were uprooted yet again, unwittingly taken along the same route as that of Ivan. But the journey proved difficult and when the moment came to sail to Solovki, the weather made the crossing impossible. So having halted at Kholmogory near Archangel, they were once more imprisoned, unaware all the time that Ivan was in a cell nearby. It was here that two years later Anna, still ignorant of her son's fate, died following the birth of her fifth child. Her body was then taken back to St Petersburg, where Elizabeth ordered that she should be buried at the Alexander Nevsky Monastery, her tomb inscribed simply with the words 'Princess Anna of Brunswick-Lüneburg'.

Anna's four youngest children remained in prison with their father until he died, and then finally, after an incarceration of thirty-four years, the new Russian empress, Catherine II, agreed to their release. Offered a home by their aunt Queen Juliane Marie, the widow of Frederik V, they were taken to Jutland in Denmark. Here the siblings remained, still cut off from society. Suffering from poor health, they soon began to die. Unvisited by their aunt, and by now unaccustomed to life outside their prison walls, they were unhappy in their new environment, so that when Anna Leopoldovna's oldest and last surviving child found herself on her own, she begged to be allowed to return to the place of her long captivity in Russia. Her request was not granted and aged sixty-five she died alone in Denmark in 1807. She was buried beside her three exiled siblings in the crypt of Horsens Abbey Church in Jutland, where a simple memorial in the chapel above acts as a poignant reminder of the tragically wasted lives of this family, who through no fault of their own became victims of the dynastic ambitions of others.

Meanwhile, Ivan VI had been given a new name by his guards, now cynically called Grigory in imitation of the earlier pretender during the Time of Troubles, the First False Dmitry. Permanently cut off from his family and deprived of company and education, the originally healthy, active child became over time broken in body and mind. With the growing Russo-Prussian tensions that would soon manifest themselves in the Seven Years' War, the empress Elizabeth apparently became disturbed by a possible attempt from abroad to release her prisoner. Fearing that Ivan threatened her own position, she wanted him moved to somewhere more secure, and so in January 1756 his separation from his family became complete.

Elizabeth ordered him to be secretly transferred from the prison he had shared (unknowingly) with his family to Schlüsselburg on Lake Ladoga. But before this was carried out, curious to see him, she had him brought briefly to St Petersburg, where he was found to be still lucid and aware of who he was. Yet even this discovery did not soften the empress's resolve, and he was then taken on to continue his isolation in his new prison, where he would remain for the rest of his life until his death in 1764. The incarceration was still not enough for Elizabeth, who proceeded to have all records of him and his mother destroyed in an attempt to wipe his name from history.

The future Empress Elizabeth was born on 18 December 1709 (OS), shortly after Tsar Peter's resounding victory at Poltava that had marked the beginning of Russia's rise to dominance. During most of her childhood her parents were away on campaign, and so she grew up mainly under the care of her father's sister, Natalia, or in the household of Peter's favourite, Menshikov. Here, in addition to the companionship of Menshikov's two daughters, she had the company of her own sisters, Anna, who was just a year older, and Natalia, born in 1718, who would die as a six-year-old just a month after their father in 1725. In his letters written while on campaign, Peter showed his love and concern for his children, and he began sending personal notes to them when they were still only three or four. Whether or not he and Catherine had a secret wedding in 1707, the two oldest sisters would be formally legitimised when their parents officially married on 9 February 1712 (OS), the ceremony being followed by a private banquet at which the two little girls were allowed to appear.

Elizabeth became a good dancer and – despite her somewhat limited education – an able linguist, speaking, among other things, fluent French, the language that during her reign would replace the German previously spoken at court. A pretty fair-haired child, loved by her father, Elizabeth grew up to be a beauty, even though in June 1717 she caught smallpox. Luckily she was left unscarred, a matter of essential importance for young women destined for the marriage market, and soon this was something that Peter had in mind. When the tsar visited France that year, confident of his newly acquired status, he suggested one of his daughters, most probably Elizabeth, might marry the young Louis XV, a suggestion that left Versailles less than enthusiastic. For the French court, where even Louis XIV's legitimised children born to noblewomen were treated with disrespect by the rest of the Bourbon family, a future queen with such questionable origins – a servant girl's daughter apparently born out of wedlock – was a matter of deep concern. As a result, the question was shelved, with excuses being found in the fact that the king was still so young, but then in September 1721, following the conclusion of the Great Northern War, Peter again raised the idea of a French marriage. Just over two months before Elizabeth's twelfth birthday, she was officially declared to be of marriageable age, and the Regent of France, Philippe, the Duke of Orléans, now saw new possibilities in forging an alliance. His son, the Duke of Chartres, might by marrying Elizabeth be better able to promote his election to the Polish throne. But this scheme – like others – came to nothing, complicated by diplomatic disagreements and practical difficulties, and the matter was finally forgotten soon after the tsar died four years later. By that time the Duke of Chartres had been happily married for two years to a princess of Baden-Baden, and six months after Peter's death, Louis XV married the daughter of the former Polish king Stanislaw I Leszczyński.

However, Peter's widow, Catherine I, was soon making new plans for Elizabeth. With her older sister Anna already married to the Duke of

Holstein-Gottorp (nephew of the tsar's former enemy, Karl XII), in 1727 the empress arranged Elizabeth's betrothal to the duke's cousin, Karl August. But before the summer was over, the intended bridegroom had caught smallpox and died, just two weeks after the death of the empress Catherine herself. The loss of her fiancé left Elizabeth heartbroken, but it also instilled in her an affection for the Holstein-Gottorp family that would influence her later decisions.

During the reign of Peter II, Elizabeth had enjoyed a period in the spotlight. She had become very close to her nephew, and despite his age, rumours had circulated that their relationship went further. Some, seeing her as having too much influence, even feared that she was leading her precocious relation astray. But for her this was a period of unmitigated enjoyment, a libertine world where she, the senior female in the land, could amuse herself riding, attending parties and balls, and over time even finding new male companions and lovers.

In 1728 Elizabeth was greatly saddened to hear of the death in Kiel of her sister Anna, who had died within two weeks of the birth of her son Karl Peter. Anna's had been an unhappy marriage, far from home and with a husband who was frequently boorish, drunken and unfaithful, and so she had asked to be buried back in St Petersburg near her parents, a funeral at which Elizabeth, for whatever reason, was not present. Possibly too occupied with her diversions, she also did not attend the funeral two years later of her nephew, Peter II, and so when the question of the succession was raised, she was absent. As a result, Anna Ivanovna was chosen as the new empress by the Supreme Privy Council, the members preferring the child of Ivan V with her 'pure' imperial Russian blood to Elizabeth, the daughter of the Livonian peasant woman.

With Anna Ivanovna's accession, Elizabeth found herself sidelined, no longer the senior woman in the land and unpopular with the new empress, who viewed her much younger and more beautiful relation with suspicion and jealousy. Anna now imposed stricter spending limits on Elizabeth, and although she considered further marriages for her, these came to nothing on account of the empress's fear of any foreign interference that might threaten her own position on the throne. While she continued to watch her cousin closely, for Elizabeth – who preferred dancing and riding to playing cards or being entertained by the empress's dwarfs – life at court became increasingly dull.

After Empress Anna's death, Elizabeth again found herself in a tenuous position, and tensions grew as she was viewed with increasing suspicion by Anna Leopoldovna. As the latter became more unpopular, Elizabeth began to consider the regent's overthrow, but, despite the fact that even abroad rumours were heard that a coup was brewing, Anna Leopoldovna failed to realise its seriousness. Instead, just two days before it took place, she exacerbated the danger by publicly accusing Elizabeth of plotting, and then, having made the charge, failed to take further action. This episode would finally persuade Elizabeth that she had to act quickly before the situation grew yet more dangerous. In the year leading up to the coup, Elizabeth's cause had received backing from France and Sweden, both countries opposed to the Austro-Russian alliance that had formed under Catherine I in 1726. And as Sweden wished to reverse its losses suffered in the Great Northern War, above all to regain its Baltic lands, the Swedish envoy had approached Elizabeth with two proposals: first he offered to mount an attack on Russia that would help bring about Anna Leopoldovna's fall, and second to give Elizabeth generous financial backing should she then attempt to take the throne. In return – this plan stipulated – she would return to Sweden its lost territories. In the end, Elizabeth hesitated before signing her agreement and so, having lost patience, at the end of July 1741 the Swedes went ahead with their declaration of war against Russia, a decision that ultimately for them was a disaster, resulting in a serious defeat. But Elizabeth had now decided to proceed alone.

When Anna Leopoldovna confronted her with her suspicions, Elizabeth denied everything, and with both women reduced to tears, the regent was sufficiently reassured not to take any further measures. But as this had seriously frightened Elizabeth, early on the morning of 25 November 1741 (OS), she left her palace near the Field of Mars, and putting on a cavalry breastplate went to the barracks of the Preobrazhensky Guards. Then, accompanied by just some 300 or so loyal followers, she continued directly to the Winter Palace, where her supporters picked her up and physically carried her into the building. The infant tsar and his family were arrested and taken to Elizabeth's own palace, from where they would later set out on their journey into exile. The next day, on entering the Winter Palace, Elizabeth took the oath and was acknowledged as the new empress. After this, in tune with her accession manifesto that had promised her deliverance of Russia from a 'degrading foreign oppression', she replaced her predecessor's foreign advisers with Russians.[32] Three months later, at her coronation in the Cathedral of the Dormition in Moscow, she put the crown on her own head and became Russia's new autocratic ruler.

As empress, Elizabeth continued to enjoy the theatre and masquerades, and during her reign she introduced public concerts to St Petersburg. She loved music, particularly that coming from Italy, and she appreciated the new taste for opera. But she also took an interest in foreign affairs, and when two years later in 1743 the war with Sweden came to an end, in the concluding treaty at Åbo (Turku) she succeeded in adding yet more territory in southern Finland to her empire. In addition, at the peace talks she was able to persuade the Swedes to agree to another of her demands, that her nephew, Karl Peter of Holstein-Gottorp, renounce his right to the Swedish throne. The boy's claim was now bequeathed to his cousin, the man in whose household he had lived since the death of both his parents, Adolf Friedrich, the uncle of Princess Sophie Friederike of Anhalt-Zerbst, the future Catherine the Great. Elizabeth's purpose behind this manoeuvring was to leave her nephew free to come to Russia, where, after his conversion to Orthodoxy, he officially became her heir as the Grand Duke Peter. Then, in a final move to ensure the future of the dynasty, Elizabeth summoned to her court Peter's second cousin, Sophie. She – after her own conversion – was married to Peter in 1745, becoming known as the Grand Duchess Catherine, a title she would hold for the next sixteen-and-a-half years. As Elizabeth had never forgotten her one-time fiancé, her first meeting with Sophie would have a certain touching poignancy, showing evidence of the empress's more emotional side. When seeing the girl's mother, she broke down, struck by the older woman's similarity to her brother, the man whom Elizabeth had at one time expected to marry. Of more lasting significance, by choosing her successors from amongst this family, she raised to pre-eminence the Holstein-Gottorps, making them the forebears of all the future Romanov rulers.

Over time, as Elizabeth became increasingly reluctant to concern herself with the affairs of state, she took the easier option of reverting to measures introduced by her energetic father. Her policies followed these exactly, and where changes had been brought in by his successors, she now reversed them, bringing back among other things the Senate to replace the newly founded Cabinet of Ministers. Although she lacked her father's energy in this area, in other ways she was very similar to him, not just constantly on the move, but also an enthusiastic builder. Like Peter, she indulged her passion for construction projects, ones in her case that were particularly extravagant, such as the alteration and extension of Peterhof, the rebuilding of the Winter Palace, the founding of the Smolny Convent and, in distant Kiev, the creation of the Maryinski Palace and St Andrew's Church. She was profoundly religious, often visiting holy sites, or funding convents. Her Orthodoxy had little rrom for tolerance towards other faiths: Jews were deported, mosques demolished and other sects persecuted.

Elizabeth was recklessly extravagant when it came to her building schemes, employing her favourite architect, the Italian Francesco Bartolomeo Rastrelli, to undertake increasingly lavish projects, all designed in the flamboyant baroque style he had brought to Russia. One of the biggest of these was the Great Palace at Tsarskoe Selo, since 1910 named – in memory of Elizabeth's mother – the Catherine Palace. Here, following the empress's orders, Rastrelli had demolished and replaced Catherine's small summer residence, creating in its place a vast blue and white building, covered with quantities of gold leaf, constructed around an inner courtyard whose sides stretched to over 350 yards in length. This took eleven years to complete, and when the empress's visitors saw it for the first time, they were amazed by its lavish golden interiors, which comprised a grand staircase, the *enfilade* of interconnecting rooms, and the spectacular ballroom. Here by day 300 mirrors reflected the light from the opposite windows, while at night the scene was lit by 1,200 flickering candles. Although this building

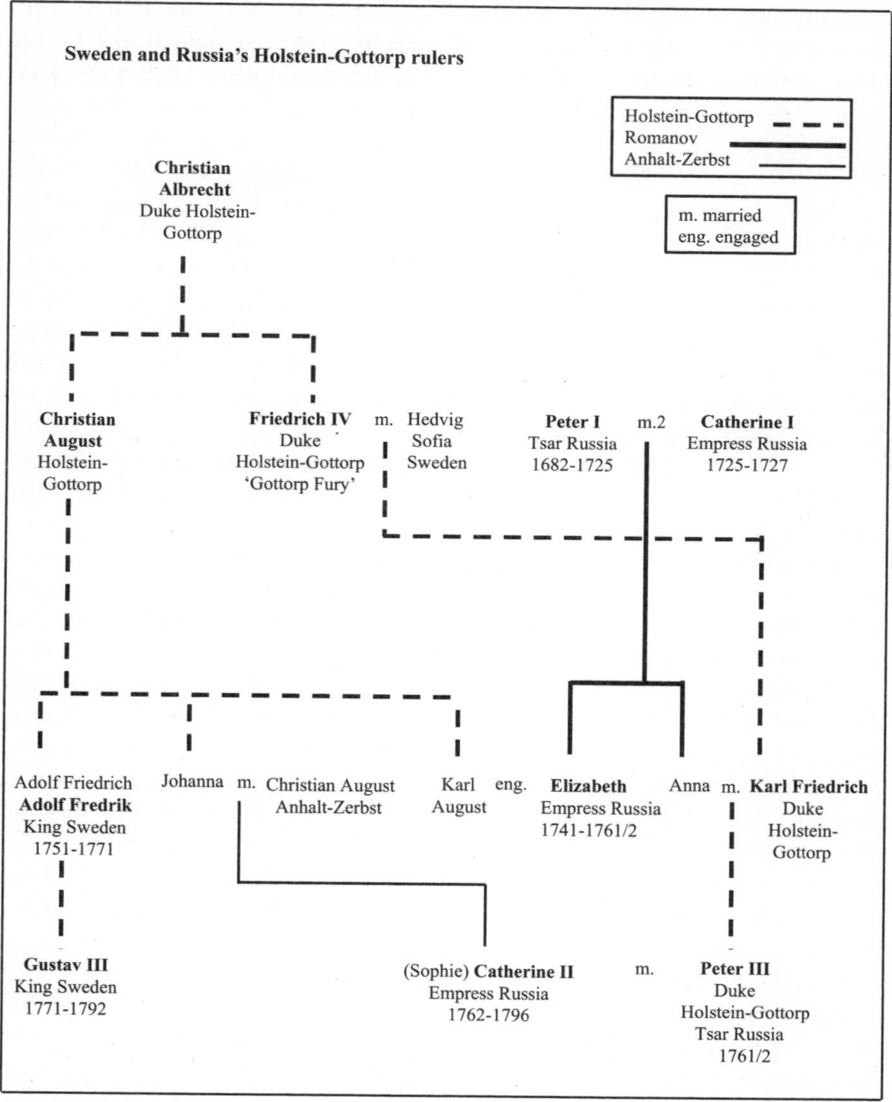

was finished in Elizabeth's lifetime, Rastrelli was still working on her equally breathtaking Winter Palace in St Petersburg when she died. But although that was completed soon after, the architect then found himself no longer in favour, as Catherine II would consider his style too ornate. Therefore, having left Russia, he moved to Courland, where he then resumed his work on the unfinished palaces he was building for the rehabilitated Biron, who had just recently been reinstated in his duchy by the new empress.

Elizabeth's early favourite was Alexei Shubin, who was then replaced by a Ukrainian singer, Alexei Razumovsky, whom she had met in 1731. Having become Elizabeth's chamberlain, rumours claimed that he married the empress secretly in 1742, after which, according to further gossip, they may have had children. Although none of this can be verified, later a claimant came forward, and Catherine II, who was often threatened by pretenders, would be sufficiently concerned to order the girl's arrest and imprisonment in the Peter and Paul Fortress where she died. However, whatever the facts of this later case, while Razumovsky was close to Elizabeth, he did not embroil himself in state affairs, and when in 1749 he was replaced by a new favourite, Ivan Shuvalov, he retired gracefully to the Anichkov Palace that the empress had given him on one of the city's main thoroughfares – known after 1781 as the Nevsky Prospekt. Shuvalov, eighteen years younger than Elizabeth, would remain at her side until her death, occupying the role that he later confessed to Voltaire had been 'above [his] ambition' and contrary to the simple life that he preferred.[33] Not corrupt, as were so many other favourites of the time, he was also an intelligent man who supported the arts and artists, and for the rest of Elizabeth's reign he would play a significant role helping the empress in her day-to-day duties.

Elizabeth had come to the throne just two years after her virtual contemporary Maria Theresa succeeded her father in Austria, and they were soon on friendly terms, corresponding with each other. Therefore, when the Habsburg empress was once more under attack from Prussia in 1756, she received aid from Elizabeth, who, like Maria Theresa, had now come to loathe Frederick II. By this action, for the next four years, Russia became embroiled in the Seven Years' War, during the hostilities winning two major victories over the Prussians, besides annexing the eastern duchy, taking Königsberg and briefly (with the Austrians) occupying Berlin. After years of bitter conflict, the situation was now grave for the Prussians, and with their capital once again under threat, in 1761 the country faced imminent defeat. However, at this crucial moment Elizabeth died, and with her heir Peter III having called for an immediate halt to the fighting, Russia dropped out of the war.

Since the late 1750s Elizabeth's health had been failing, worn out by the hedonistic life she had led. As time passed, she had begun to withdraw from public view, unwilling because of her vanity to show her ageing face. She refused to see visitors and eventually on Christmas Day 1761 (OS), accompanied only by her favourite, Shuvalov, she died at the Catherine Palace, aged fifty-two.

Elizabeth was a lazy, vain, unpredictable woman whose main objective had been to live a life dedicated to pleasure. She could be mean over small things, and yet wildly profligate when it suited her, spending to excess on her appearance or on her magnificent palaces. Her vanity and extravagance was such that she was said to change her clothes four or five times a day, and she reputedly never wore her dresses more than once. In 1751 4,000 of these were lost in a fire, and yet when she died ten years later she left another 15,000, of which many had never been worn at all. Catherine II described the difficulty of life in Elizabeth's court, and the uncertainty she and others were subject to through the wilfulness and changing moods of the empress. Among her more petty and inconsiderate moves was her ban on anyone wearing the same thing twice, indelibly marking the women's dresses to prevent any repetitions, and thus causing extra, and needless, expense to the members of her court. At other times she ordered everyone to appear in transvestite clothes, which, according to Catherine, made them look ridiculous, but showed the fine-figured empress off to her best. A remarkable beauty in her youth, Elizabeth hated becoming older and loathed being outshone in any way, so that when iat one time she lost her own hair, she forced the women to shave theirs and like her take to wearing a wig.

As all the eighteenth-century Russian empresses came to power indirectly, either through a coup, or with the help of the Guards or courtiers – ambitious to advance their own position – with the possible exception of Catherine I, most would face serious personal danger and possible overthrow. Not just extremely superstitious, but also seriously frightened of death, Elizabeth was above all terrified of assassination. As a result, fearing to sleep in the same place for any length of time, she would keep moving from one residence to another. And, with a real dread of the dark, she would stay up for most of the night, not going to bed until six o'clock in the morning. While memories of her night-time overthrow of her predecessor had no doubt added to these fears, her anxieties were not without reason, since in the very year of her coronation a plot to kill her had been uncovered.

Like her father, Elizabeth was happy in any company and, until they had been dismissed by Empress Anna, she had enjoyed the companionship of her Livonian relations, brought to St Petersburg by her mother, Catherine I. Unlike the nobles, who disdained their simple origins, Elizabeth did not look down on her humbly born relatives. It was this ability to mix with people from less exalted backgrounds that had stood her in good stead at the time of her coup, when only fifty-four of her supporters belonged to the nobility. She was particularly popular with the lower ranks, and had – in accordance with Orthodox custom – become godmother to many of their children, just as her father had done before her. One of Peter's godchildren had been his black slave Gannibal, who had later risen to prominence as a general, before becoming in Elizabeth's reign superintendent of Reval, residing in a palace that still stands just below Parliament Square on Tallinn's Toompea Hill. Following the teaching of the Orthodox Church, a godchild's relations were granted a greater degree of familiarity, something that often surprised foreigners at the Russian court, who were struck by the notable lack of formality in such cases. Although she was popular among ordinary people, some of the nobles considered that Elizabeth displayed a lack of dignity, a trait inherited, they believed, from her peasant-born mother.

There were other characteristics that the empress had apparently acquired from her father. Like him, she could be erratic in her behaviour, moving from one extreme to the other. While occasionally she would explode in a furious rage, acting in a cruel way that suggested an inability to relate to a person's feelings, another time she could appear kind, generous and considerate. This inconsistency in her nature becomes graphically apparent when looking at her treatment of the wretched Ivan VI. At her coup, after picking up the sleeping child and comforting him, murmuring that he was 'blameless' over the events that were unfolding, she handed him back to the care of his parents. But later, when he was still only four years old, she ordered his separation from the family, condemned him to solitary confinement, and even prevented him from seeing a doctor when he was seriously ill with measles and smallpox. Although opposed to the death penalty and, unusually for her time, a ruler whose reign saw no executions, her treatment of Ivan would become little more than a protracted death sentence.

Despite Elizabeth's uncertain rise to power, she maintained the stability of her country and apart from the war with Sweden that was soon over by 1743, it was not until 1756 and the outbreak of the Seven Years' War that Russia became tied up in another conflict. For fourteen years, during which time much of Europe was engaged in fighting, Russia remained at peace. Although she could be idle, taking an age to add her signature to documents, on the plus side Elizabeth never acted impetuously or hastily. Moreover, she took an interest in foreign affairs, created the first Russian university in Moscow, reformed the Academy of Science, and with the help of Shuvalov founded the Academy of Fine Arts. She improved education for everyone other than the serfs, and during her reign trade and industry grew, particularly iron production.

While Elizabeth's extravagant architectural fantasies were solely vanity projects, exorbitantly expensive for her country and of no benefit to the majority of her people, in the long term they have enriched Russia's artistic heritage. While Elizabeth was creating these outstanding buildings, the country and all strata of society remained stuck in a way of life that was still well behind that of Europe with its greater everyday comforts, not to mention sophistication and culture. Visitors remarked on the poor condition of the roads, the shabbiness and dampness of many of the houses and even palaces, and the unkempt state of the retinues of the nobles. With a shortage of furniture, scratched and damaged tables and chairs would be moved with Elizabeth as she changed her place of residence. Similarly, there remained a boorishness in the behaviour of many of the sumptuously dressed nobles, who prided themselves on their superficial adoption of Western ways. Elizabeth's reign, therefore, stands as a period of transition between Peter the Great's revolution of the backward-looking, medieval, Russia, and the forward-looking country with its more enlightened ideals that would come to the fore within a few years under Catherine the Great.

PART 4
ENLIGHTENMENT

11

The Early Hohenzollerns to Frederick the Great

Eighteenth-century engraving of a contemporary portrait of the Great Elector of Brandenburg from Anselmus van Hulle's *Les hommes illustres qui ont vécu dans le XVII siècle* (1717).

Although by the time of Frederick the Great Brandenburg-Prussia was viewed as one of Europe's major powers, it had grown to pre-eminence only some hundred years earlier. Since the fifteenth century, the history of the Hohenzollern dynasty had been decided by the complicated series of political treaties and marriage alliances that had brought various scattered regions into its possession. In 1411 Sigismund of Luxembourg, Prince-elector of Brandenburg, the brother-in-law of Jadwiga 'King of Poland', had been elected King of the Romans and four years later, grateful to Friedrich Hohenzollern for the support he had given him during the election, he officially granted him the margraviate of Brandenburg. After that Sigismund's own status would continue to rise, culminating in his becoming the Holy Roman Emperor in 1433, but his gift to Friedrich would have a more long-term significance, marking the end of the Luxembourgs' rule of the electorate, and the beginning of the Hohenzollerns' rise to power in the region.

On their receiving Brandenburg in 1415, the Hohenzollerns would also become entitled to be among the select number of electors, men who had the responsibility of choosing the emperor. There were initially only seven electorates, although by the eighteenth century the number had increased to nine, with a tenth, Hesse-Kassel, being added just three years before the Holy Roman Empire was abolished in 1806. Brandenburg had been one of the first to receive this honour, its early Ascanian rulers being involved in the election of 1257. Later, their successors, the Wittelsbachs, were present when the electoral college was formally established by decree in 1356. This, the so-called 'Golden Bull', officially gave the margrave the title of 'Elector', thereby granting him the honorary hereditary right that would subsequently be passed down, first to the dynasty of the Luxembourgs, and eventually to the Hohenzollens.

Nearly a century after Friedrich became margrave, in 1510 his great-grandson, Albrecht of Brandenburg-Ansbach, was appointed Grand Master of the Teutonic Knights. Since its defeat by Kazimierz IV in the mid-fifteenth century, this order's headquarters had been at Königsberg in Ducal Prussia, where the knights served as vassals of the Polish king. But as that same Kazimierz had been Albrecht's maternal grandfather, the Grand Master now came in line for further promotion. In 1525, having converted to Lutheranism and secularised the former religious order, he paid homage to his uncle, Zygmunt I 'the Old', who then acknowledged Albrecht as duke of the former Teutonic lands. Although it was now the first official Lutheran state, the duchy remained a fiefdom of Poland. Here Duke Albrecht would continue to rule until 1568, but after his death his lands passed to his fourteen-year-old mentally disabled son, Albrecht Friedrich. While ruling only in name, the new duke would live on for another fifty years, by which time he had been predeceased by his two sons. As a result, the duchy passed to his son-in-law and distant cousin Johann Sigismund from the main house of Brandenburg. This transfer of power followed an arrangement made nearly five decades earlier by two brothers-in-law, Johann Sigismund's great-grandfather, Elector Joachim II Hector, and Zygmunt II Augustus of Poland. Their agreement had specified that if the duchy's male line should die out, the elector's descendants would succeed in their place.

So, despite Johann Sigismund having been left largely disabled by a serious stroke in 1617, the next year Brandenburg and the separate Duchy of Prussia – lying some 500 miles to the east – became united under one ruler. In 1619 Johann Sigismund died. A year earlier the Thirty Years' War had broken out over religious differences between the Catholic emperor and some of the fragmented Protestant states within his empire. This long conflict – unjustifiably claimed to have been fought on religious grounds – became ever more complex as the separate parties changed sides repeatedly, pragmatically forming and reforming alliances to suit their own ends. The price paid by the Hohenzollerns would be particularly high, as Brandenburg, situated at the heart of the fighting, was constantly ravaged, its towns and countryside destroyed, and its people subjected to a slaughter that would eventually leave the population virtually halved. When Georg Wilhelm succeeded as the new ruler, these would be some of the serious challenges he would face. But before long another problem also arose. Eleven months after his succession, against his wishes, his sister Maria Eleonora married the Swedish king Gustavus Adolphus, who was the enemy of the elector's Polish overlord in Ducal Prussia. To resolve this tricky situation, Georg Wilhelm sought to pacify the two opposing sides, but by 1626 his brother-in-law had invaded the duchy, blocking his access to the sea. In an attempt to avoid involvement in the major conflict being fought out in the west, Georg Wilhelm had previously declared his neutrality, but the year after Gustavus Adolphus' invasion of Ducal Prussia, he finally decided – despite his Calvinist faith – to give his backing to the Catholic emperor, thereby allowing the Imperial troops to cross through Brandenburg. However, when in 1631 these lands were invaded by Gustavus Adolphus, once again Georg Wilhelm felt it expedient to change his allegiances. After he had signed two treaties with his brother-in-law, the Swedes occupied the region and took command of his military. This arrangement did not bring a stop to the fighting in the electorate, and the subsequent battles between the Swedes and the Imperial armies would result in the repeated plundering of Brandenburg, and the prolonged suffering of its people. However, far to the east Ducal Prussia had remained outside the conflict of the Thirty Years' War, and so it was to here that Georg Wilhelm finally retired in 1637, dying three years later in Königsberg.

Now Georg Wilhelm's son, Friedrich Wilhelm, became the new elector in Brandenburg and duke in Prussia. While in essence his father had been an ineffectual ruler, Friedrich Wilhelm would prove to be quite the opposite, in time becoming known as the Great Elector. Succeeding in the last years of the Thirty Years' War, he set out to redeem the broken

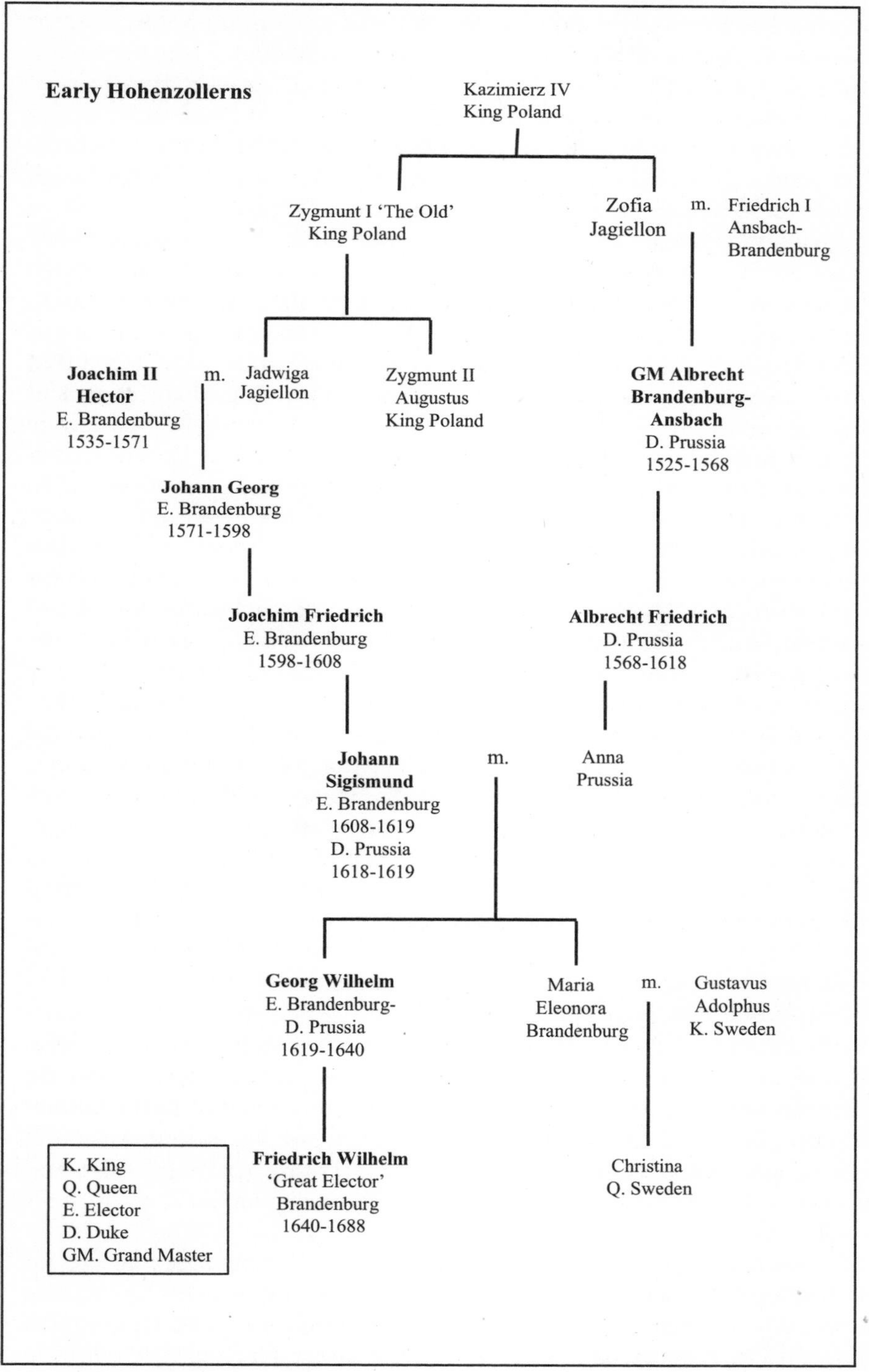
Early Hohenzollerns
Kazimierz IV
King Poland
Zygmunt I 'The Old'
King Poland
Zofia
Jagiellon
m.
Friedrich I
Ansbach-
Brandenburg
Joachim II
Hector
E. Brandenburg
1535-1571
m.
Jadwiga
Jagiellon
Zygmunt II
Augustus
King Poland
GM Albrecht
Brandenburg-
Ansbach
D. Prussia
1525-1568
Johann Georg
E. Brandenburg
1571-1598
Joachim Friedrich
E. Brandenburg
1598-1608
Albrecht Friedrich
D. Prussia
1568-1618
Johann
Sigismund
E. Brandenburg
1608-1619
D. Prussia
1618-1619
m.
Anna
Prussia
Georg Wilhelm
E. Brandenburg-
D. Prussia
1619-1640
Maria
Eleonora
Brandenburg
m.
Gustavus
Adolphus
K. Sweden
Friedrich Wilhelm
'Great Elector'
Brandenburg
1640-1688
Christina
Q. Sweden
K. King
Q. Queen
E. Elector
D. Duke
GM. Grand Master

situation of his country. Having chosen to remain initially in Königsberg, he agreed to an armistice with Sweden, and managed to escape involvement in the main area of conflict until peace negotiations were eventually begun. When at last the Thirty Years' War ended with the Peace of Westphalia in 1648, the Swedes agreed to a division of the Duchy of Pomerania, ceding the eastern part to Brandenburg, while holding the western as Swedish Pomerania. Though as this gave Friedrich Wilhelm less than he had hoped for, it would remain an area of dispute for years to come.

Just seven years after the peace, Brandenburg-Prussia would suffer again during the Northern War, when Friedrich Wilhelm turned down the unfavourable terms for an alliance with his uncle the Swedish king, Karl X. But with Karl then invading Ducal Prussia, by the beginning of 1656 Friedrich Wilhelm had to agree to make peace and concede that his duchy was now a vassal state of Sweden. This obliged the elector to provide forces to assist Karl in his campaign against the Poles. But despite the two armies' great victory at Warsaw soon after, because the Polish king Jan Kazimierz was greatly angered by the deviousness of Friedrich Wilhelm, he now sent his general into Ducal Prussia, where the troops then wreaked havoc on the local people. Karl X himself was by this time facing greater opposition, and so at this point he offered the elector freedom from his former Swedish vassalage. Nonetheless, by the end of the year, seeing the Swedish king tied up with affairs in Denmark, the ever pragmatic, if not duplicitous, Friedrich Wilhelm, had switched sides again, now joining forces with the Polish king. In return, Jan Kasimierz granted him full sovereignty over his duchy, thus ending at last the region's long period as a Polish vassal. Having been a fiefdom since the defeat of the Teutonic Knights in 1466, the Duchy of Prussia had finally gained its recognition as a hereditary, sovereign state.

Fifteen years later, war broke out between the French and Dutch and their various allies, and once again Friedrich Wilhelm found himself threatened by the Swedes, who under pressure from France in December 1674 invaded Brandenburg from Swedish Pomerania. On hearing the unexpected news, the elector left his Imperial allies fighting the French in the Alsace region, and after wintering in Bavaria made a rapid march north, covering roughly 150 miles in only two weeks. In June he was able to take on the unsuspecting Swedes, meeting them at Fehrbellin, around 40 miles to the north-west of Berlin. By the end of the day, Friedrich Wilhelm had succeeded in routing the army of the young Karl XI, achieving a victory that, besides earning him his title as the Great Elector, would destroy Sweden's long-held reputation for invincibility.

Meanwhile in Berlin, since the Peace of Westphalia, Friedrich Wilhelm had begun to carry out work on Joachim II's old renaissance palace on the banks of the River Spree. Having been built on the site of an earlier castle, this had been the dynasty's permanent residence in the mid-1500s, but in 1576 the city had suffered from an outbreak of the plague that had killed roughly half those living in the region. This disaster had then brought about a shortage of labour and, as food production began to fall, famine had taken hold. But this was not the end of Berlin's problems as another estimated third of the population would later die during the Thirty Years' War, when the city suffered still further destruction. So now Friedrich Wilhelm set to work on restoring the place, making it the centre of a growing area that combined several small villages. This he then connected to the surrounding countryside by a network of roads, among them the Unter den Linden. Potsdam was also an important centre, and here, having created his hunting lodge in 1660, Friedrich Wilhelm began converting the old medieval castle, turning it into the chief residence for himself and his court. Like all his other works, with the exception of the lakeside Caputh Palace – built for his wife in 1662 – this was seriously damaged in the last war.

Now large numbers of Protestants fleeing France started to arrive in Brandenburg and as a result Potsdam began to increase rapidly in size. In 1685 Louis XIV revoked the Edict of Nantes, thus ending seventy-seven years of religious tolerance in his country. In response, Friedrich Wilhelm immediately issued his own Edict of Potsdam, a decree that offered asylum to any who were fleeing persecution. But the elector then went further, and he now sent ships to Amsterdam to fetch the refugees who were sheltering there. On the migrants' arrival in the electorate, he granted them freedom to choose where they would like to settle, allowing them to go wherever they found it 'most convenient to practise their professions and trades'.[34] In addition, the newcomers were not only granted a period of exemption from taxes and duties, but also provided with the equipment they needed to establish their homes and businesses. Some estimated 20,000 Huguenots arrived at this time, and others would follow well into the next reign, with the result that the French language would continue to be spoken widely throughout the country until the time of Napoleon. However, although Friedrich Wilhelm was and is rightly revered for his generosity towards the refugees, his measures were not without pragmatism. The immigrants brought wealth to Brandenburg-Prussia, and helped to repopulate the country's under-inhabited regions, particularly those that had suffered so greatly in the recent wars. This was not all that the elector achieved. Besides improving his army, upgrading the communications and developing the country's trade and industries, Friedrich Wilhelm had extended his territories and brought his country to greater prominence.

When the Great Elector died in 1688, he was succeeded by his third son, Elector Friedrich III, who thirteen years later in 1701 was upgraded to king by Emperor Leopold I. This promotion was received in exchange for his support of the Habsburgs against the French, Friedrich having promised an additional 8,000 soldiers for the Imperial army. As his court in Brandenburg lay within the empire, where with the exception of Bohemia no kingdoms could exist, he now became Friedrich I, King *in* Prussia, adopting the unusual title in an effort to appease the Polish *Sejm*, who opposed his new position. His coronation in his eastern duchy was an intentionally spectacular and lavish affair, preceded by the arrival of 1,800 carriages bringing the members of the court from Berlin to Königsberg. But his promotion to monarch was not unique, as over the years other electors would acquire similar positions: Frederick V of the Palatine briefly becoming King of Bohemia in 1619; Augustus II of Saxony, King of Poland in 1697; and Georg Ludwig of Hanover, George I of Great Britain and Ireland in 1714.

Before his coronation, in 1691 Friedrich founded on the previous site next to Cölln his new city of Berlin, which in 1710 he then made his capital. Eye-wateringly extravagant, the king had ambitions to create a court comparable to Versailles, and among his expensive projects was his baroque City Palace, still under construction when he moved to it in 1701. In addition, after he became king, a country palace to the north-west of the city was enlarged and further embellished with extensive formal gardens. This building had been commissioned by the queen, Sophie Charlotte, on the estate her husband had given her five years earlier. Originally called Leitzenburg or Lützenburg, following her sudden death in 1705, it would be renamed Charlottenburg in her memory. And here Friedrich then ordered further expensive and elaborate changes, such as the addition of an orangery and central dome, things designed to make the place still more impressive. The second of the king's three wives, Sophie Charlotte was the daughter of Sophie, the Electress of Hanover, who – as granddaughter of James I – would have become the British queen had she not died less than two months before Queen Anne. Nonetheless, with the latter remaining childless, in 1714 the British throne passed to the Hanoverian line, and the brother of the Prussian queen, Sophie Charlotte, succeeded as George I.

Having been for a time considered as a possible bride for the Grand Dauphin, and then also suggested as the wife of his father, the widowed Louis XIV, just before her sixteenth birthday Sophie Charlotte had finally married the widowed elector Friedrich in 1684. Despite his taking an official mistress, for him a pre-requisite for any monarch modelling himself on the French king, he adored his young wife. Like so many of her family, she was very musical, besides being a good linguist and highly intelligent. But, having grown up in the cultured Hanover court, she found life in Berlin dull and unsophisticated and, while he was alive, she would find herself at odds with her father-in-law, the abstemious Great Elector. And, despite sharing her husband's love of spending on cultural projects, she was intellectually superior to him, so she preferred to live by herself in her country palace – dubbed by her 'Lustenburg', her place of pleasure. Here she rarely invited Friedrich to visit her, choosing instead to devote much of her time to studying the works of the great thinkers, including her mother's favourite court philosopher, Leibnitz. With an equally enquiring and open mind to that of the old electress, she accompanied her on the visit to see Tsar Peter while he was on his way to Amsterdam in 1698, a meeting where the approachable and unceremonious mother and daughter had put the gauche young tsar at his ease.

Lacking many of the qualities of his father, Friedrich I did not involve himself with the day-to-day running of his country, and his grandson, the later Friedrich (hereafter Frederick II), would cuttingly describe him as 'great in small matters and small in great matters'.[35] Nonetheless, the king introduced Enlightenment culture and thinking, creating not just new Academies for the Arts and Sciences – the latter under the Presidency of Leibnitz who had encouraged its foundation – but also a university at Halle. At the same time, he carried on with his father's other practical measures, continuing the improvement of roads, canals and the country's agriculture. And, moreover, by his coronation he had raised the status of Brandenburg-Prussia, lifting it above many of the other innumerable German states, and earning it the respect of the various royal courts abroad.

Friedrich I's profligacy was, however, excessive, particularly apparent in 1701 when he commissioned the Amber Room for his wife's expanding Lietzenburg. But as this – now called Charlottenburg – took some ten years to complete, the room was finally placed instead in a smaller area of the main palace in Berlin, a change of plan that made it necessary for some of the amber panels to be put into store. Meanwhile, the king continued to add further embellishment to this building, and so the City Palace was still unfinished when he died in 1713, leaving his son, Friedrich Wilhelm I, to oversee its hurried completion. Soon discovering the enormous debts his father had left him, and having little appreciation for his parent's extravagant taste, the new king immediately set about repairing the state coffers. Three years after coming to the throne, in an overgenerous display of largesse, he cemented an alliance with Tsar Peter by giving him the Amber Room, receiving eventually in exchange some minor gifts, most particularly fifty-five tall soldiers for his army. Now the priceless treasure was transferred in eighteen crates to Memel, and then shipped on via Riga to St Petersburg, where it was eventually reassembled. First placed in Peter's Winter Palace, it was finally moved by the Empress Elizabeth to her new summer residence at Tsarskoe Selo. Here, where her architect Rastrelli adapted it to the larger room by incorporating the stored panels and some further additions, it would remain in its original form until its disappearance in the 1940s.

Friedrich Wilhelm I was totally different from his parents, Friedrich and Sophie Charlotte. Having rejected a coronation, he then continued to pursue his particularly frugal lifestyle. Dubbed the 'Soldier King', he had an overriding passion for the army, and above all for outstandingly tall men. Some of these were around 7 foot, an exceptional height at the time, but while they were impressive to look at, not all of them possessed qualities other than that of their size. Whatever their military abilities, and with some these were few, even before his succession the king had begun to create his regiment of 'Potsdam Giants'. Nicknamed by the locals as 'Long Guys', these were acquired by any means possible: payment, exchange and even abduction.

Wanting to build up his army further, but opposed by Berliners who did not wish him to create garrisons in their city, Friedrich Wilhelm brought battalions to Potsdam, where he then pulled down the old buildings and constructed new houses in which the owners could accommodate some of his soldiers. Also in the town, he later created a Dutch Quarter that he hoped would encourage new migration from the Netherlands, and although this did not prove particularly successful with few Dutchmen coming, years later his son Frederick the Great would enlarge Potsdam further, adding his own French and Italian quarters.

An unceremonious, no-nonsense man, Friedrich William purposely sought to avoid extravagance, making a rare exception in 1720 when he had the summer dining room at the Caputh Palace embellished with the roughly 7,500 Dutch faience tiles that still decorate this former hunting lodge today. This was a fashion now sweeping Europe, popular at courts stretching from the palaces of St Petersburg to Hampton Court in London, the French Château de Beauregard on the Loire to the palace of Nymphenburg near Munich. But the king's usual abstemiousness did nothing to endear him to his wife – and cousin – Sophie Dorothea (the daughter of the later king George I), who despite her husband's devotion, did not reciprocate his feelings. Having like her mother-in-law grown up in the more cultured court of Hanover, she bitterly disliked the plain life she was now subjected to in Brandenburg. Furthermore, she had little respect for her husband, to the extent that she particularly asked not to be buried with him on her death. Nonetheless, she would produce fourteen children, beginning with two sons – both called Friedrich – who died as infants, and a daughter (Friederike) Wilhelmine, who was followed two-and-a-half years later in 1712 by the future Frederick II. These early children would always remain particularly close, although they were later joined by ten more siblings, of whom four brothers and three sisters would survive into adulthood.

Despite Friedrich Wilhelm's love for his 'little Fritz', his oldest son grew up in a troubled home. The king increasingly gave vent to bouts of violent rage, causing his wife to fear for the well-being of her children, who often suffered severe beatings during his explosive outbursts. Some people have questioned whether Friedrich Wilhelm suffered from porphyria, a disease that has been put forward as a possible cause of the 'madness' of his later relative, George III, and taking this theory further, they have also suggested it may have been inherited from their common ancestor, Mary,

Queen of Scots. The medical findings are still uncertain. The children would grow up chiefly in the gloomy Wusterhausen castle that, although loved by the king, was for them a detested place. They lived in Spartan conditions, having only few staff, and with all the family except the queen eating off pewter or wood as the king had sold off most of Friedrich I's gold and silver. Preferring these unpretentious surroundings, here the king would hold his *Tabakscollegium*, gatherings of his male companions, who sat around smoking pipes and discussing political affairs.

When the crown prince was thirteen, he was commissioned into the Potsdam Guards, three years later being made a lieutenant-colonel. And in that same year of 1728, Frederick was taken by his father on a trip to visit Augustus II 'the Strong', Elector of Saxony and the restored King of Poland. Although Augustus' court was so notoriously degenerate that Friedrich Wilhelm had refused to take his wife with him, his young son was delighted by what he saw. After the drabness of life back in Brandenburg, he was entranced by the beauty of the court they now visited in Dresden, and it was here that Frederick may have had his first liaison with a young Polish woman, Anna Karolina Orzelska. He later had a similar sort of relationship with a young harpsichord player, but this ended with his father furiously reprimanding him and the poor young woman being whipped and then imprisoned.

Besides disapproving of these relationships, the king attacked his son for other perceived failings, such as his long hair and lack of washing. In fact, Frederick would never be very clean, and later as an old king, would wear stained or tatty clothes, often covered with dog hairs. In addition, Friedrich Wilhelm accused his son of effeminacy, condemning his lack of 'manly inclinations', a charge that included Frederick's intense dislike of hunting. Viewing killing for pleasure as 'odious', after his accession the latter would never again visit his father's newly built hunting lodge at Potsdam. And despite being a keen, but untalented, artist himself, Friedrich Wilhelm also disapproved of his son's love of music and poetry, and preference for French, a language he personally detested.

Frederick, who was a good linguist, would later write his name as 'Frédéric', and always try to avoid using German, which he, like Voltaire, considered to be ugly – an attitude that may have helped delay the flowering of German literature. However, despite his father's disapproval, in 1730 the English envoy, Sir Charles Hotham, gave a complimentary description of Frederick, writing: 'There is something charming and engaging in the Prince and one day he'll be somebody. One hears nothing but good of him.'[36]

In time, with relations between father and son fast deteriorating, Frederick became depressed, and began to consider escape, an act considered as treachery for the heir to the throne. Nonetheless, together with two Keith brothers and an officer called Hans Herman von Katte, he then made plans to flee to England. In the event only the Keith brothers

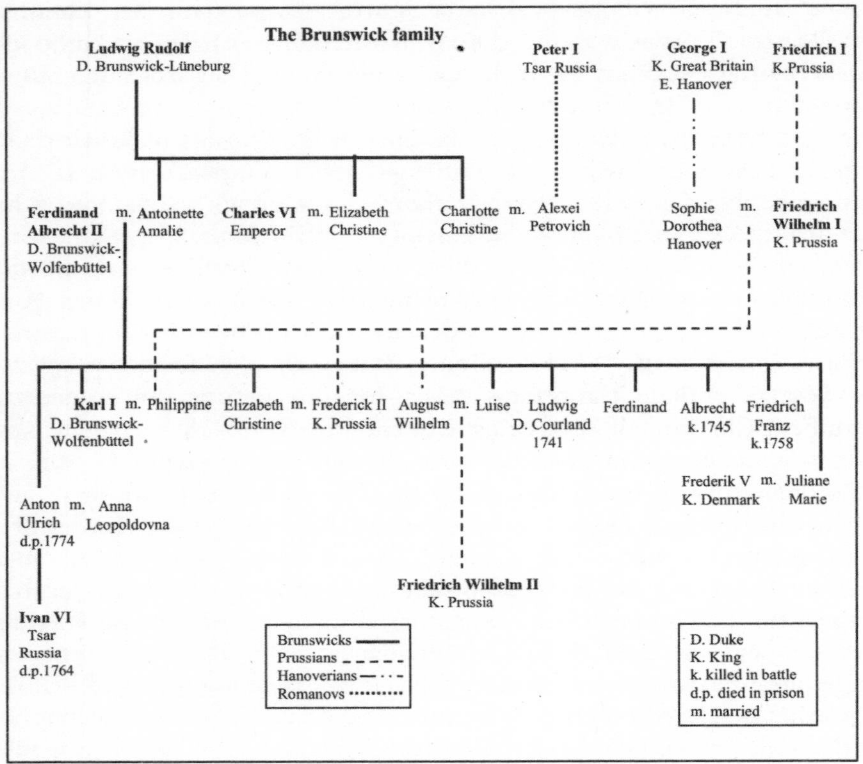

succeeded in getting across the Channel, while von Katte and Frederick were arrested, interrogated and found guilty. With both then locked up in the castle at Küstrin on Oder, the king gave orders that von Katte should be put to death, and Frederick, forced to watch, fainted as the execution of his friend took place.

While Frederick remained in disgrace, his older sister Wilhelmine was whipped by her father for her knowledge of the plot. However, gradually the crown prince's relations with Friedrich Wilhelm began to improve, and in time he would swear his obedience to the king. Frederick himself commented in later years that perhaps his earlier behaviour had been lacking in moderation, and his dubious choice of friends before his arrest does show a marked lack of judgement. Even Wilhelmine had apparently not approved of one of the Keith brothers. Hans von Katte's behaviour had also often been questionable, at times bragging about his close relationship with the crown prince. What its nature was, we do not know, but Frederick's feelings would never again be so openly and passionately displayed.

With the situation at home more or less restored to normal, Sophie Dorothea became determined to try and arrange marriages for her two oldest children. Her plan was for a double alliance with their cousins, the Prince of Wales and his younger sister Amelia. Initially, Frederick was enthusiastic about the idea, but as the negotiations began to falter, once more he became depressed, again considering escape and even mentioning suicide. Sophie Dorothea continued to pin her hopes on these English marriages, but she was despised by her brother, George II, and his impossible demands forced her eventually to accept the failure of the scheme and turn elsewhere. Now, to Frederick's fury, Wilhelmine was engaged to the Margrave of Bayreuth, who, in her brother's opinion, was an 'idiot', sure to make his sister's life unhappy. But with this settled, new matches were suggested for Frederick too, among them – his preferred choice – Elizabeth of Mecklenburg (the later Anna Leopoldovna). However, eventually the person chosen for him was the well-connected Elizabeth Christine of Brunswick-Wolfenbüttel-Bevern, a pretty but shy young woman, whom Frederick then dismissively described as 'stupid, silly and silent'.[37] Apart from her many distinguished relations in the European courts, her sister and brother would marry two of Frederick's own siblings.

Even Elizabeth Christine's important connections did nothing towards improving relations with her intended family. She was unpopular with her new mother and sisters-in-law, who sarcastically criticised her manners and appearance and even declared uncharitably that she smelt. Worse still, immediately after her wedding in June 1733, her husband wrote to his sister Wilhelmine: 'God be praised it is over.'[38]

Opposed to the marriage from the start, he had no intention of making it work, summing up their relationship by saying: 'There can be neither love nor friendship between us.'[39] In the early years, when he was sometimes joined by his wife, Frederick lived on an estate called Rheinsberg, given to him by his father some 60 miles north-west of Berlin. During this time, known as the *Remusberg* period, he was visited by the Italian polymath Count Algarotti, and by Karl Philipp Bach, the second of Johann Sebastian's five sons. Inheriting the Hanoverian talent, Frederick, like his siblings, was extremely musical, composing many flute sonatas, concertos and symphonies that are still performed today.

In addition, he now began writing books, and in August 1736 he wrote for the first time to Voltaire, starting a correspondence that would last (with some interruption) until the latter's death. He finally met the *philosophe* four years later at Kleve (Cleves), and after this the Frenchman became a visitor to Rheinsberg. Unlike his Calvinist forebears, and in particular his Pietist father, Frederick had by now turned his back on established religious teaching, and so while Voltaire advised him on his writing, the two men also debated Enlightenment philosophical topics, such as the question of free will and the meaning of tolerance. Following these discussions Voltaire, who believed that society was happiest when governed by an enlightened despot, became confident that when the time came Frederick, the 'Solomon of the North', would be a benevolent and wise king.

In this period after his marriage Frederick had his first experience of life on the battlefield. In 1734 his father took him to see the front during the War of the Polish Succession that had broken out the year before over the question of who should replace the now dead Augustus II of Poland. Here the twenty-two-year-old met Prince Eugene, the famous general commanding the Imperial army and, after their long talk together, the old prince told Friedrich Wilhelm that he felt sure his son would one day become a great military leader.

In May 1740, Friedrich Wilhelm I died and was buried in the Garrison Church in Potsdam. Having during his twenty-three-year-long reign recovered the country's finances, he left the kingdom in an economically strong position. He had also founded schools and hospitals, brought in reforms, and, by his creation of a civil service, generally developed the governance of the country. In addition, he had encouraged more French Huguenot migrants to come to his kingdom to help repopulate the eastern Prussian duchy that had suffered serious losses in the plague outbreak of 1709. And although he had largely avoided becoming involved in war, with his much-improved the army he had occupied the Swedish Baltic town of Stettin (Szczecin) in a peace-keeping role in 1713, two years before he finally joined the coalition opposing Karl XII. As a result, after Karl died, Brandenburg gained the southern portion of Swedish Pomerania, where just a few years later the future Catherine the Great would be born while her father was in service to the Prussian king.

Despite their past differences, by the time Friedrich Wilhelm died, relations had improved between him and Frederick, and on his deathbed he declared that he died in peace, confident that he left his country in the hands of his 'worthy son and successor', words that left Frederick deeply moved.[40] The new king, now Frederick II, respected much of what his father had achieved, and would claim that he had never stopped venerating him. Although disbanding the 'Potsdam Giants', he soon formed some of his own new regiments, and it was by building onto the well-trained army that his father had left him that he was later able to fulfil his ambitions and achieve his resounding military successes.

Frederick II, like his father, chose to have no coronation, and he now moved to his grandparents' Charlottenburg palace, which had been abandoned by Friedrich Wilhelm. But as he needed to enlarge this building to make it his main Berlin residence, Frederick constructed a new wing containing elegant interiors that were decorated in the latest rococo style. His wife, who seldom came here, remained mostly in her apartments in the nearby City Palace, or at the alternative Monbijou – this eventually demolished after suffering major damage in the last war. But Schönhausen, which still stands, was Elizabeth's favourite summer residence. Frederick never came to it. Here she was visited by the British envoy, Sir Charles

Hanbury Williams. An intelligent and cultured man who hated Berlin and found it very dull, he was highly critical of the king, and many of his attacks on him would be vitriolic. He loathed Frederick and described him to Henry Fox as 'the compleatest [*sic*] Tyrant that God ever sent for a scourge to an offending people'.[41] Although later he would moderate somewhat his opinion, he now felt sorry for Elizabeth and blamed Frederick's 'unnatural tastes' for his not wanting to live with her.[42]

After his succession, Frederick founded a new Academy of Sciences and, on Voltaire's advice, appointed the French *philosophe* Maupertuis as president, at the same time making another Frenchman, the Marquis d'Argens, Director of Philosophy. In addition, he commissioned the building of a new Berlin opera house, bringing – with some persuasion – the famous dancer Barbara Campanini from Venice to perform. Again there is some suggestion, rumours possibly promoted by Frederick himself, that she might have become his mistress, although she left Berlin some years later with Francesco Algarotti.

In 1740 Europe was rocked by two further deaths following that of Friedrich Wilhelm. In Russia, the Empress Anna died, leaving her throne to her infant great nephew, Ivan VI, and, shortly after, the Holy Roman Emperor Charles VI died from eating some poisonous mushrooms. Voltaire succinctly summed up the seriousness of this disaster with the comment: 'That plate of toadstools changed the destiny of Europe.'[43] Previously, Charles had persuaded the European countries to give approval to his daughter's accession – as opposed to that of her female cousins – in an agreement known as the Pragmatic Sanction, and so the Habsburg dynasty was now in the hands of twenty-three-year-old Maria Theresa. Despite her being eventually crowned queen of the Habsburg kingdoms of Hungary and Bohemia, before long the major powers had gone back on their earlier promises. Within weeks of the emperor's death, to the shock of Voltaire and others, Frederick – the supposedly enlightened, peaceful ruler that they had believed in – mounted a pre-emptive attack on Maria Theresa by invading her lands in Silesia. With the First Silesian War having broken out, soon after Europe became embroiled in the larger conflict known as the War of the Austrian Succession. With the electors having refused to appoint a female head of the empire, two years later they eventually elected Maria Theresa's cousin by marriage, Karl Albrecht of Bavaria. This marked the beginning of the only (very brief) period after 1438 when a Habsburg did not rule the empire, and the Austrian and Austro-Hungarian empires that succeeded it.

Silesia was a region that was rich in mining and industry, and Frederick explained his action by pointing to an ancient Brandenburg claim to the area. However, still very inexperienced in warfare, during his first battle against the Austrians at Mollwitz, thinking he was facing defeat, he fled the field. While his army went on to save the day, later Frederick would explain his actions by making reference to his youth and inexperience, suggesting that Mollwitz had been his 'school'. His next victory at Chotusitz was also won by the military discipline of his men. He was then able to proceed to Breslau (Wrocław), where in 1742 he received the homage of the people. With this a peace was drawn up and Maria Theresa surrendered Silesia to the king. Although she had now lost most of the region forever, she would never stop trying to regain it.

Being still at this time on good terms with Empress Elizabeth, who had now seized the throne of Russia, Frederick was keen to strengthen their alliance by helping her find a bride for her heir, Grand Duke Peter. But even Frederick was not enthusiastic about the empress's suggestion that this should be his sister Luise Ulrike. Believing she might face a precarious future at the Russian court, he left Luise Ulrike free to marry the future Swedish king, while he looked around for another suitable candidate to take her place. After he had recommended Sophie of Anhalt-Zerbst, the empress wanted to inspect the young girl, and so in January 1744 she set off for Russia, where eighteen years later she would mount a coup and become the Empress Catherine II. Frederick, who had met Sophie before, was now eager to see her for one more time, and so on her journey east he invited her to Berlin. Here their meeting went well, she impressing him, and he treating her with the kindness and cordiality that was too often absent in his dealings with women.

A few months later, and just two years after the Peace of Breslau, war broke out again over the territory that Austria wanted to take back from Prussia, and now for the first time, in 1745, Frederick made his name at Hohenfriedberg in Silesia. This was followed soon after by another victory at Soor (today in the Czech Republic), a battle that was harder fought, and one where his brother-in-law Ferdinand would particularly distinguish himself – fighting as it happened against his own older brother, 'Fat Louis', who was engaged in the Austrian army. While this gives another example of the way in which family loyalties were so often stretched or simply ignored, in this instance Frederick II's lack of feeling was remarkable even by the standards of the times: on hearing that yet another of his wife's brothers, twenty-year-old Albrecht, had been killed, he dismissively declared that the young man's death was 'not much loss', and instead of showing sympathy for his wife, demonstrated a far greater concern for his missing dog. Even the forgiving Elizabeth Christine, who was used to her husband's bad manners, declared that on this occasion his behaviour had been 'too cruel'.[44]

Within three months of these victories the Second Silesian War was over, the last battle having been won by Frederick's general, the Prince of Anhalt-Dessau, nicknamed 'the Old Dessauer', the man who invented the goose-step. While once again Maria Theresa had to acknowledge the loss of Silesia, she now received in return Frederick's recognition of her husband as the new emperor, elected to replace his unfortunate predecessor who had just died after only three years on the throne. As Franz I, the new emperor had to renounce his title as Duke of Lorraine, and so his duchy was handed on to Stanislaw Leszczyński, the former King of Poland, who some ten years earlier had lost his throne for the second time. This was a redistribution of territories that was typical in the period, and one that displayed the little consideration that rulers of the age gave to the wishes of the local people. Through her husband's new appointment, Maria Theresa now became empress by default, even though Frederick always pointedly continued to refer to her merely as the Queen of Hungary.

Although the War of the Austrian Succession did not officially end until the Treaty of Aix-la-Chapelle in 1748, with the acquisition of Silesia the king had increased Prussia's prosperity and population, and he now began to be acclaimed as Frederick the Great. While on his triumphant return to Berlin the people more affectionately began to dub him 'Old Fritz', he – flushed with his own success – started to call himself King *of* Prussia, rejecting the earlier less impressive title assumed by his grandfather.

Hating the main palace in Berlin, which he used only for particular occasions like the carnival or winter receptions, he now began work on changing Potsdam's City Palace. In time this became one of the Hohenzollerns' official winter residences and, although damaged in the last war and demolished in 1959, in 2013 it was externally reconstructed around a modern interior. However, a year after starting work on the City Palace, Frederick began planning for a new summer palace that he would call Sans Souci – a home 'without cares'. Having personally produced the first sketches, in March 1745 he laid the foundation stone for this elegant rococo-style one-storey building. Sitting on a ridge, it is fronted by a series of French doors that open out onto the first of a flight of descending terraces, each planted with vines, and interspersed with orange trees and statues. When Frederick moved into this palace two years later, he was delighted, and it became his pride and joy. Here he would receive his male friends, entertaining them with one of his seventy or eighty compositions for the flute, an instrument that he would continue to play for many years until regretfully he had to give it up having lost too many teeth. Later he would add other buildings and pavilions to the park surrounding Sans Souci, but it was not until the 1760s, when he was in his fifties, that women were invited here, and even then his wife never came.

One person who now became a permanent member of the court was Voltaire, who finally accepted the king's invitation in 1750, following the death of his much-loved mistress, Emilie du Châtelet. Part of Frederick's purpose in inviting such people was to create an environment that could compare with Versailles, and, by attracting to it some of the best minds of the time he wished to make Potsdam renowned as a centre of Enlightenment. But Voltaire saw further advantage to the visit. For him it was also an opportunity at last to ingratiate himself with Louis XV, for whom he had agreed to act as a sort of spy, sending back to France information regarding the situation at the Prussian court. Initially the visit was a success, and the two men spent much time in discussion, but in the rarified atmosphere of Sans Souci rivalries and jealousies began to develop, and over time Voltaire started to feel undervalued. He was deeply hurt when told of a comment regarding himself made by the king, who had declared 'when the orange is squeezed you throw it away.' Equally, Frederick was offended by Voltaire publishing a satirical demolition of the writings of his chosen President of the Academy, Maupertuis.[45] Finally, things came to a head when Voltaire, ever eager to make a profit, became involved in a questionable, if not illegal, financial speculation with a moneylender over some diamonds that proved to be fake. Furious, Frederick described this as an affair involving 'a cheat and a crook', and as a result Voltaire decided the time had come for him to leave.[46] But his disgrace was not over as at Frankfurt he was arrested with his niece Madame Denis. Accused of stealing the king's manuscript, his bags were searched. After five weeks he was finally exonerated and released, but the relationship between Frederick and Voltaire had unsurprisingly cooled, and they would cease to write to each other for some years to come.

However, Voltaire was not finished with the whole affair, and his experiences at the Prussian court would colour his later texts. In his most famous *conte*, *Candide*, he introduces the *Bulgars* to mock aspects of the Prussian court, depicting the rigid discipline enforced by the whipping of offenders, made to run the gauntlet between their comrades. And while in the story an innuendo is also introduced by his choice of name for the soldiers, in his *Mémoires* Voltaire goes further, implying a relationship between Frederick and some of the soldiers who are invited to his rooms each morning. Much of this later text has to be read with an open mind, not just because Voltaire was furious and hurt at the time of writing, but also as the episodes described may be merely instances of his often unguarded wit. Voltaire, whose own sexuality has been much questioned, consistently condemned the man-made rules of morality that were dictated by a dogmatic authority, and so his sardonic mockery of the king's court can be read as a satirical criticism of the paradoxes underlying human society and all human behaviour. Whatever the exact nature of their relationship, these two opinionated men were probably bound to fall out when together for such a long and concentrated period. But eventually their correspondence would be renewed, and, despite its content, Frederick loved *Candide*, describing it as the only text that you could 'read and re-read'.[47]

By now, Frederick had reached the high point of his reign and in the 1750s he began to encroach on neighbouring Poland, raiding the country across the border for men and foodstuffs for his army. But other consequential events now began to take shape, as significant changes started to alter the political situation of Europe as a whole: new alliances formed, with Prussia, England and Hanover aligning themselves against France, Austria, Russia and Sweden. As a result, five years after Adolf Friedrich of Holstein-Gottorp became the Swedish king in 1751, Frederick found himself facing his brother-in-law and his allies on the battlefield. This, the Seven Years' War, a terrible conflict that Winston Churchill labelled the first 'world war', broke out following Frederick's decision to make another pre-emptive strike, invading neutral Saxony purportedly to strengthen Prussia's defences against the threat posed by the coalition forces gathering against him. Whatever his true intent, Leipzig and Dresden now came under attack, and Frederick had set in motion the war that would spread to countries and colonies far overseas, leaving most of the combatants financially ruined. But, although reviled by his enemies, initially Frederick was popular among his allies, and after a particularly hard-fought battle at Prague, he became so feted in England that pubswere named after him – some still existing today, despite the disappearance of many during the First World War.

This conflict proved much harder for Frederick than the previous Silesian War, and in 1757 he suffered his first major defeat at Kolin around 35 miles east of Prague. Thrilled, Maria Theresa created an order of merit, and the anniversary of the battle would become a day of celebration for the Austrians. Frederick, not for the first time, suffered depression and, particularly after the death of his mother, began carrying a little box of pills and talking of suicide. This caused his sister Wilhelmine to become so worried that she wrote to Voltaire asking for his help. As a result, the two men's correspondence was renewed. But the year continued badly for Frederick, with the Russians invading his eastern duchy, and Berlin coming under threat from the Austrians and Hungarians. However, with France now in decline and the Austrian army under poor leadership, Frederick then won two of his greatest victories. At the first of these in November at Rossbach in Saxony, he defeated a much larger French and Austrian army within an hour and a half, leaving the enemy with around 10,000 casualties to the Prussians 500–600. And immediately after, Frederick embarked on what would prove to be a still more impressive undertaking. Having led his men on a forced march of close on 200 miles, a month later he was able to crush an Austrian army twice the size of his own at Leuthen (today in Poland), a victory that Napoleon later declared had made Frederick one of the world's greatest military leaders of all time. This battle would eventually become still more legendary with stories of how the night before the action started, the exhausted king – like Henry V before Agincourt – had addressed his men, not denying the unequal odds facing them, but encouraging them to fight for the sake of Prussia's glory. And then, when night fell after the fighting was over, another poignant episode occurred, as across the snow-covered field that was scattered with wounded men more and more voices gradually began to sing, 'Now thank we all our God.'

However, the year after his two great victories, Frederick would face a new disaster when a tragedy hit the family, one that had particular personal implications for the king. Earlier, while blaming his younger brother August Wilhelm for certain military failures, he had threatened him with court martial, and his bullying had become so intense that his other brother Heinrich had fallen out with him as well. The situation was then made far worse when, shortly after August Wilhelm had left the army, in June 1758 he died suddenly, aged only thirty-five. His death had most probably been caused by a stroke or brain tumour, but with rumours suggesting it to have been the result of a broken heart, Frederick was overcome with bitter remorse. With his expected successor dead, and his own marriage still childless, his nephew, August Wilhelm's thirteen-year-old son, now became the new heir – he later succeeding as Friedrich Wilhelm II.

Frederick's next disaster occurred just two months later when his army was involved in a major battle at Zorndorf. Catherine the Great would later say that although the battle was declared won by the Russians, in truth 'both sides were beaten', a reality that was again mocked in *Candide* where Voltaire describes each of the armies singing the victory hymn the *Te Deum* while surrounded by the mutilated bodies of their fallen comrades.[48] And Zorndorf was not the end of Frederick's calamities as two months later, on the same day that his great friend James Keith and his wife's youngest brother were both killed during the Prussian defeat at Hochkirch, his beloved sister Wilhelmine also died, leaving Frederick utterly bereft. He now wrote again to Voltaire, telling him that he had lost all who were dear to him.

He became still more depressed the next year after his third big defeat at Künersdorf, when he lost two-thirds of his army and was forced to flee from the Cossacks. Although he was soon back achieving some minor victories, any chance of ultimate success was now fast disappearing. In October 1760 the enemy had briefly occupied Berlin and despite the comparatively better behaviour of the Russians, the Austrians had proceeded to create havoc, taking revenge on the people and leaving Charlottenburg and much else in ruins. Then Frederick's position became still more vulnerable when a little over a year later, not only were the Russians back again threatening the city, but also Britain decided to stop providing him with subsidies. But in early January 1762, he heard to his utter relief that his hated enemy Empress Elizabeth had died, information he greeted with undisguised delight, declaring triumphantly, '*Morta la Bestia*' (the beast is dead).[49] Soon after he received still more astounding news. As the new tsar Peter III had always greatly revered the king, on his succession he had declared an end to the war, offering at the same time to return to Prussia all the lands that Russia had taken. This unexpected turn of fate Frederick would label as 'the Miracle of Brandenburg'. It not only saved him and his dynasty from disaster, but also allowed him to continue the fight against his other enemies. As a result, in the final peace of 1763 he was able to achieve better terms, retaining Silesia and gaining possession of Pomerania.

Despite some notable victories during the war, Prussia had also suffered major losses and Frederick's army was now only around 60,000 strong. As the king was exhausted by the long conflict, he crept back to Berlin, returning to the city with none of the triumph that had marked the end of the Silesian Wars. While the people remarked on how much he had aged during the past seven years, he too was aware of how he had changed, writing to his brother Heinrich: 'I am very old dear brother, useless to the world and a burden to myself.'[50] However, he now began to spend more time in female company, enjoying mixing with intelligent women, and even occasionally seeing his wife, whom he ungraciously described as being 'fatter'. But his main interest was to rebuild his country, establishing new industries such as the porcelain factory in Berlin, reforming the tax system, and modernising the bureaucracy. Having invited the Frenchman Helvetius to Prussia to help him, he then also set about improving the country's dire finances by devaluing the currency, a measure that was not in fact popular with the people. However, he brought in other changes which were to their immediate benefit, among them the ending of torture and the censorship of the press.

Seeing himself as the 'servant of the state', Frederick strove tirelessly for the good of his country, getting up early each morning to begin work. And for the same reason he supported any group having the potential to be of service. Therefore, he allowed the first synagogue to open in Potsdam, and granted the Marquis d'Argens' request that his friend Moses Mendelssohn might be given the status of a 'protected Jew' – a limited concession in a period when anti-Jewish feeling was rife in much of Europe. Mendelssohn, the grandfather of the later composer Felix, was one of the key thinkers of the time, a central figure in the development of the Jewish Enlightenment, and regardless of how much the king's actions were driven by pure pragmatism, he considered Frederick the 'wisest sovereign' who deserved to be commended for his 'sensible freedom of thought'.[51]

Among Frederick's other projects he began to make further developments to his growing capital. He introduced a new French theatre and commissioned a palace for his brother Heinrich, one that today houses the Humboldt University. Frederick's most flamboyant construction was the New Palace out at Potsdam, built to send the message that Prussia had not been crushed during the Seven Years' War. This large building was surmounted by a cupola on the top of which was placed a statue of the Three Graces, rumoured to be modelled on the three women the king most disliked: Louis XV's mistress, Madame de Pompadour – who had called his court 'unnatural' – Empress Elizabeth, the 'Messalina of the North', and Maria Theresa. While, in fact, Frederick had some respect for the Habsburg empress, describing her achievements as 'those of a great man', she herself was never able to forgive him for his destruction of her country, and always referred to him as the 'evil man' in Sans Souci.[52]

Frederick's moderate admiration for Maria Theresa was not matched by his feelings for her husband. When Franz I died in 1765, the king commented that he would be 'soon forgotten by everyone but his widow'.[53] Now she became co-ruler with their oldest son, Emperor Joseph II, and he, being a follower of the current Enlightenment thinking, was – despite his mother's opposition – eager to meet the Prussian king. At last, four years later the two met in Silesia, and during their time together they began to discuss Frederick's proposal for the partitioning of Poland, a scheme that besides benefiting Prussia, also promised to appease Russia and Austria's acquisitive ambitions by compensating them with other lands. While the men justified themselves with lofty or practical reasons for their intended actions, Maria Theresa was opposed to the idea overall, but she soon found herself outnumbered. As a result, in 1772 the First Partition took place with the three powers annexing the regions on their borders. Although Danzig was exempted from Prussia's seizure, Frederick at last received the Polish lands that had for centuries divided Brandenburg from its distant possessions in the east. However, he refused to visit the duchy – now referred to as East Prussia – having been greatly angered by its acknowledgement of the hated Empress Elizabeth at the time of the earlier Russian invasion during the Seven Years' War.

For the remaining years of Frederick's life, he continued to work for the good of his country, draining land for agriculture and building canals to help communications. In 1778 he had to go into battle for the last time, when the War of the Bavarian Succession broke out. This was a short-lived, minor conflict, but it became significant for promoting the consumption of potatoes in Prussia. The starving troops now began to eat the vegetables lying in the fields that they had previously rejected on grounds of the plant's similarity to deadly nightshade – a widespread fear of this nutritious crop, and one that in France Marie Antoinette had tried to overcome in the public mind by actually wearing the flowers. With potatoes now growing more popular in Prussia, the conflict became known locally as the Potato War.

After this, Frederick would go out of his way to avoid Prussia's involvement in further conflict, but the world was now changing. In 1776 the American colonies made their declaration of independence, and nine years later Frederick was visited by Lafayette, the French general who had taken part in the American Revolutionary War of Independence. Then just a few months before the king's death, he received another visitor, Count Mirabeau, the moderate French revolutionary who on his return to France would publish a sarcastic account of the Prussian court. Frederick was now fading fast, suffering from a variety of ailments, including asthma, dropsy and severe headaches, where the pain was so bad that he described it as 'a pitiless torturer that smothers you without finishing you off'.[54] Known as an irritable 'old bear' by his servants, he had no desire to live on, although he continued to face his troubles with stoicism. His faithful wife, who had never ceased to love him, offered to visit him, but she was refused, and she never saw him again. But she remained loyal to his memory, praising his qualities until her death some ten years later.

Despite his increasing pain and suffering, Frederick continued working on until just two days before he died. As the end approached, his last requests would be much in character, asking to hear a passage from Voltaire, and instructing his servant to cover his shivering dog who was cold. In the early morning of 17 August 1786, Frederick died in the arms of his orderly at his beloved Sans Souci. And it was here in the grounds of this, his favourite palace, that he asked to be buried in a simple grave alongside those of his adored dogs. However, as these wishes were seen as unfitting for a dead king, they were ignored by his nephew – now Friedrich Wilhelm II – who ordered him to be interred in the Garrison Church beside his father. Here his tomb would later be visited first by Tsar Alexander I, and then by Napoleon, who, having just captured Berlin, said to his followers, 'Hats off gentlemen – if he were still alive we should not be here,' adding, 'it was not the army that defended Prussia for seven years [...] it was Frederick the Great.'[55] But that was not the end of the story, as in 1945, with the approach of the Soviet army, his body and that of his father were temporarily moved for safety to a salt mine. Soon they were taken on again by the Americans to Marburg in Hesse, where they were placed in the town's famous old church built by the Teutonic Knights, the Elizabethkirche. With the situation having changed by 1952, the remains were then transferred to the Hohenzollern castle, around an hour to the south of Stuttgart. In the meantime, the Garrison Church at Potsdam had suffered serious war damage and so eventually in 1968 it was demolished. As a result, when – after Germany's reunification – Friedrich Wilhelm was interred for the final time in 1991 at Potsdam, his reburial took place in the Friedenskirche. But other arrangements would be made for his son who, in accordance with his wishes, was at last laid to rest beside his dogs in the gardens of his much-loved Sans Souci. Here today, people come to remember him, some leaving on his tombstone a potato that acts as a suitably plain and practical symbol of remembrance, one showing their respect for an honoured but unostentatious leader, who was not afraid to share the hardships of his men.

While Frederick had many natural talents, being exceptionally musical, artistic, intelligent and hard-working, he remains a controversial figure. There is strange duality to his life: while theoretically a believer in the Enlightenment ideals of peace and justice, in practice he was prepared to go to war on a spurious claim. And although in line with the thinking of the *philosophes* – he promoted the theories of tolerance and understanding – he himself was often uncompromising and highly critical. While not deserving to be charged with hypocrisy, this apparent paradox may be partly linked to certain private insecurities dating from his youth, and these could have influenced his complicated relations with family, friends and contemporaries, and explain why he turned his affections more and more towards his faithful dogs. A common thread of nastiness and bullying appears to run through members of his family, including his cousins the Hanoverians, who are well known for their bad relations, particularly between father and son. And just as his uncle George II had been on poor terms with his own sister, Sophie Dorothea, Frederick would often be at odds with his siblings, notably with Prince Heinrich and, still more particularly, with Princess Amalie, who actively loathed him. While the archives are littered with his caustic, if not downright cruel, remarks, the same could be said for many of his brothers and sisters, in particular Luise Ulrike, who soured the atmosphere at the Swedish court. Although difficult childhoods may partly explain this behaviour, it does not excuse it, and Frederick's treatment of his wife and brother August Wilhelm was quite unacceptable.

The king was clearly a complex, sensitive and often troubled individual, there being much evidence of his bouts of depression, his suggestions of suicide, and what Wilhelmine described as his tendency to suffer 'black moods'.[56] But on the positive side, although often sarcastic and autocratic, he had genuine affection for certain individuals, treating those such as his nephew Heinrich and his friend James Keith with generosity. Both these and many others would predecease him, and in later life he would face loneliness. He confronted his pain and suffering with resignation, finally writing to his sister Philippine just days before his death that it was the role of the old 'to make way for the young'.[57]

Despite the strains and complexities in his private life, Frederick's relations with his soldiers were exemplary. He was an exceptional military leader, not just for his famous victories, but also for the way he achieved them by inspiring the love and loyalty of those who followed him. Although just 5 feet 5 inches tall and slightly built, he earned the confidence and trust of his men through his courage, stamina and willingness to share their dangers and discomforts. But Frederick's memory has suffered over time, and only now is his reputation being reassessed. In 1851 a statue was erected to him on the Unter den Linden, and during the period of the Second *Reich* he was still revered as Prussia's great military leader. With the fall of the empire and the abdication of the Kaiser in 1918, the country's militaristic past became condemned. Having continued building on the achievements of his able ancestors, Frederick became responsible for the further rise of his country, but his successes achieved on the battlefield would present a base on which the two kaisers Wilhelm I and II would found their military state. Frederick II was not accountable for his descendants' grandiose ambitions, nor is he to blame for the horrors of the Nazi regime, just as it was not his fault that Hitler chose to honour him and have his portrait hanging in his bunker. Selective interpretations of events and people can become useful tools in the hands of those who want to present an alternative personal agenda, backed by an apparent but false attribution to someone famous. Voltaire's reputation suffered in the same way when the French antisemites of the 1940s unwarrantedly claimed him as their hero. While Germany was coming to terms with its recent past, the Hohenzollerns were an embarrassment. Attempts were made to obliterate any reference to the Prussian past, as made evident by the demolition of the ruined city palaces in Berlin and Potsdam. With over half a century having passed, things are now changing and so these places have been rebuilt, but tensions still remain, and for that reason when Frederick was finally brought back to Potsdam in 1991, to avoid a demonstration of anti-Prussian opposition his reburial was carried out with only family members present. The private, unpretentious king might well have preferred the quiet simplicity of that occasion.

12

Catherine the Great: German Princess to Empress of Russia

An allegorical cartoon representing the First Partition of Poland, showing Catherine II, Frederick II and Emperor Joseph II dividing up the map, while Stanislaw II resignedly points to his remaining territory.

After the Swedish town of Stettin in Pomerania (Szczecin) had become a Prussian possession in 1720, Prince Christian August of Anhalt-Zerbst was appointed the governor of the garrison. Nine years later, while he was still in service to Friedrich Wilhelm I, on 21 April/2 May 1729 his first child was born. Known in the family as 'Fidgen', but later famous as Catherine the Great, she was initially baptised as Sophie Friederike Auguste. While – at least in her view – her parents had been disappointed at having a daughter, she was followed by four younger siblings, but only one of these would survive into adulthood.

Although her father's principality of Anhalt-Zerbst was one of the minor German states among the 300 or so in existence at this time, Catherine's background was more eminent than is sometimes suggested. Her mother, Johanna Elizabeth, a member of the illustrious Holstein-Gottorp family descended from the Danish kings, had several important family connections. Her oldest brother had been briefly engaged to the future Russian empress Elizabeth, and her cousin Duke Karl Friedrich had married Elizabeth's sister, Anna Petrovna. And, with the duke being the grandson of the former Swedish king, Anna's only child, Karl Peter Ulrich, was in line to succeed Sweden's now childless rulers. Having grown up against this background, Johanna would soon dislike living in her husband's rather lacklustre and insignificant court, and for that reason she spent much of her time taking her daughter on trips to her richer and more distinguished relations and acquaintances elsewhere. On one such visit when she was ten, the little girl would meet for the first time her recently orphaned eleven-year-old second cousin Karl Peter, who was living at Eutin in the house of another of Johanna's brothers, Adolf Friedrich.

In the 1740s, dramatic changes caused the family's status to rise still higher. After the unmarried Elizabeth had seized the Russian throne from the baby Ivan VI, she chose her young Holstein-Gottorp nephew to be her successor. Although Karl Peter had just been elected crown prince by the *Riksdag*, Sweden had suffered a disastrous defeat in its recent Hats War against Russia, and so during the peace talks at Åbo (Turku) in August 1743, it had to accept Elizabeth's alternative wishes. As a result, Karl Peter was instructed against his will to renounce his rights to the Swedish throne and the Estates were persuaded to agree to the empress's proposal that Adolf Friedrich should replace him. Thus it would be Sophie's uncle and his wife – Frederick II of Prussia's sister – who became Sweden's crowned heads a few years later.

Then, following an invitation from the empress, in early in 1744 the fourteen-year-old Sophie set off to Russia so that she might be inspected as a potential bride for her cousin, who was now the Grand Duke Peter. Although Elizabeth included Sophie's mother in the visit, she excluded her father, a move that was not unknown in such early marriage negotiations, but one that reflected, nonetheless, the empress's open disregard for his status. Three years later at the time of his death Elizabeth again showed her disdain for Christian August's inferior social standing by reprimanding his daughter for showing inappropriately excessive grief for someone who 'was not a king'.[58] Sophie/Catherine had not seen her father since leaving Berlin, when they had had a poignant parting and he had made his final request that she should stay true to her Lutheran faith. Unable in the event to do so, obliged by the Russian court to convert to Orthodoxy before her marriage, she had, however, attempted to explain her actions by reasoning that the two confessions had much in common – an argument also used a century and a half later to persuade the devout Alexandra of Hesse to accept the proposal of the future Nicholas II.

With Frederick II of Prussia having initially suggested Sophie as a bride for the empress's nephew, he was now keen to see her before she left for Russia – a meeting that Catherine confessed she had initially viewed with some nervousness. However, despite Frederick's well-known misogyny, he treated her well and was impressed by the young girl seated beside him at the dinner he had laid on for the occasion. His approval shows how even at this early age Catherine possessed that skill for winning people over with the charm and intelligence for which she would become renowned in later years. Her mother, by contrast, was a foolish and at times sulky or bad-tempered woman, whose relations with her daughter were often tense. But proud of her own growing influence, Johanna promised Frederick that she would report back to him from Russia, a diplomatic task for which she would prove totally unsuitable. When her intriguing caused her position at Elizabeth's court to become untenable, the empress made her feelings clear to both parties, dismissing Johanna and then using her as messenger to the Prussian king, who was now instructed to recall his envoy from Russia. While this would be the start of the bad relations between the two rulers, Frederick got his revenge on Johanna a few years later by invading Anhalt-Zerbst and adding it to Prussia's possessions, leaving the widow with no option other than to end her days in exile in Paris.

After an uncomfortable journey to the Russian border at Riga, Sophie then began to experience how her life would now change. She was transferred to a large sleigh pulled by ten horses and wrapped in furs was swept under cavalry escort first to St Petersburg and then on to Moscow, where she finally met the empress on 29 January 1744 (OS). After she had received Elizabeth's approval, preparations went ahead for her conversion, and she immediately dedicated herself to studying both the Orthodox teachings and the Russian language. On these things she worked so hard, even getting up in the cold hours of the early morning to continue her studies, that she caught a chill and became seriously ill with pleurisy. Johanna, at last showing some concern for her daughter, suggested that she should see a Lutheran pastor, but not for the first time Sophie displayed more wisdom than her mother, diplomatically calling for her Orthodox instructor. Her later memoirs claim that while these things would serve to increase her mother's growing unpopularity, her own actions had greatly pleased the devout Elizabeth. And later she further impressed the court when, during her long conversion ceremony, she showed how much Russian she had learnt in the four months since her arrival. Over time she would become fully fluent and, although always retaining a German accent, in later years she would produce more of her official documents in Russian than in French, the fashionable court language that she had learnt as a child. The day after her conversion, when Sophie finally became *Ekaterina Alexeyevna*, adopting the name of the Empress's mother, Catherine I, she was at last officially betrothed.

During the fourteen months of her engagement, Catherine began to feel lonely and ignored. At first she had got on well with the equally young Peter, but gradually during this period the differences in their characters became more apparent, and she increasingly began to find him childish. She saw little of her future husband, who spent most of his time playing with his toy soldiers or enjoying war games with his small army of other boys. She therefore now concentrated on learning to ride well and reading the works of the French *philosophes*. But then things deteriorated further, as in the autumn of 1744, Peter, whom originally she had thought to be quite good looking, contracted smallpox. Still only recovering when Catherine next saw him, he now appeared to her to have become 'hideous'.

Despite these tensions and Catherine's own growing reservations, in August 1745 the marriage went ahead in the Church of Kazan in St Petersburg, after which there followed ten days of celebrations. But from the start Peter showed no interest in his wife, not even visiting her on the first night when, according to Catherine, he 'paid absolutely no attention' to her, and instead was 'constantly playing soldier with his valets, drilling them in his room, or changing uniforms twenty times a-day'.[59] And she recounts that as the years passed Peter's behaviour became more and more bizarre, once even court-martialling a rat that ate some of his military pieces, another time spying on the empress through a hole made in the door of her apartments, and frequently bringing so many dogs into their bedroom that the place grew unbearable with their noise and smell. Moreover, Catherine claimed that Peter, a drinker since his youth, became increasingly alcoholic, and had on one occasion actually assaulted her. Her later lover Stanislaw Poniatowski confirms this assessment, declaring that Peter 'was not stupid, but mad, and as he liked to drink, he upset thereby the little brain he had'.[60] But we have to read Catherine's memoirs with caution, as she would repeatedly edit them over the years, redefining her story for posterity.

After seven years of marriage there were still no children, and Elizabeth now became deeply concerned, her sole objective in bringing the couple together having been to ensure the succession. But while the still immature and inexperienced Peter freely declared his love for other women, he continued to show no interest in his wife. Catherine, who by this time was feeling utterly rejected, was then introduced to a young courtier, Sergei Saltykov, a roué who, although married, freely enjoyed the libertine pleasures offered by the court. Seeing the innocent young duchess as a challenge, with the apparent knowledge, if not collusion, of the empress's women, he purposely set out to try and seduce her. Although initially on her guard, before long Catherine fell in love with him, and eventually she gave way and their affair began. Finally, after suffering two miscarriages, in 1754 she gave birth to a son, Paul. Elizabeth was delighted and immediately swept the boy away, determined to take charge of his upbringing, while the young mother, all alone, forgotten and unattended, was left probably suffering from post-natal depression. But more seriously still, not just unable to see Paul throughout his first month, later she would also be given only rare access to him, with the result that she would never develop a close or good relationship with her child.

Equally significantly, the question remains as to the boy's legitimacy. Although recognised by the empress as the heir presumptive, Grand Duke Paul, in her memoirs Catherine implies that he was the son of Saltykov. Her reasons for suggesting this are not clear, and we have to ask whether she believed it to be true, or whether it was a later attempt by her to strengthen her position on the throne. At the time of the coup in 1762 there were some, like Catherine's later foreign minister Nikita Panin, who favoured the idea of Peter being replaced by Paul, with Catherine acting as her child's regent. While she was empress several rebellions threatened to depose her, and it is possible that, wishing to prevent any greater claim being made by her son, she chose to suggest his illegitimacy. While some historians find his likeness to his Peter too strong for this to be true, others are of the opposite opinion. But whatever the truth, when the later Romanovs discovered the memoirs they were appalled. Fearing that these would undermine their own right to the throne, they locked them away from view and they were not published until the twentieth century.

Even before Paul's birth, Catherine, although still in love with Saltykov, had become aware that he was losing interest. When this situation was confirmed by accounts of his frequent sexual peccadillos in Sweden and Saxony, she felt abandoned and let down, but became determined to learn from the experience. However, she would not be friendless for long, as the year after Paul's birth, Sir Charles Hanbury Williams, the former envoy to Berlin, arrived as London's new ambassador to St Petersburg. Besides being a politician and diplomat, he was a novelist and writer of satirical verses, ones that had earned him the praise of his contemporaries, including Horace Walpole, who described Hanbury Williams as the greatest poet of his age. On meeting the lonely Catherine, this sophisticated man had been immediately impressed by her intelligence and charm, and from that moment he had become her mentor and companion. But, more significantly, the diplomat had brought with him a secretary, the twenty-three-year-old Polish nobleman Stanislaw Poniatowski, who, although two years younger than Catherine, was well travelled and educated, having spent time in the intellectual world of the salons of Paris. Soon enjoying each other's company, by the end of the year the young couple's friendship had turned into a passionate affair.

On 29 August 1756 (NS) Frederick II invaded Saxony, and the Seven Years' War began. Stanislaw, who was in the service of the Saxon elector, now found himself on the opposing side to his English employer, and so he had to return to Poland. Here he remained, while Catherine, desperate at losing him, appealed for help from Elizabeth's chief minister, Alexei Bestuzhev-Ryumin – the son of Empress Anna's earlier favourite. He had initially been appalled to learn of the affair, but had in time come to support the couple in their relationship. Eventually, at the end of the year Bestuzhev was able to arrange for Stanislaw's return as the Saxon ambassador, and with that the affair began once more. Almost exactly a year later, on 9 December 1757 (OS), Catherine gave birth to a daughter, Anna, who survived just fifteen months. But the affair was no longer secret, and although Peter – who now had his own mistress – was relaxed about his wife's relationship with her lover, by August 1758 things had become so dangerous for Poniatowski that he had to leave Russia once more. While he believed that this latest separation from Catherine would be only temporary, his departure in fact marked the end of the affair and he would not return to St Petersburg until after her death, nearly four decades later.

The situation had been made particularly difficult as Catherine was having her personal problems with the empress, her own position now being in jeopardy. For two months, she and Bestuzhev had been under constant questioning, as Elizabeth had got wind of a planned coup to overthrow her chosen heir, Peter. Bestuzhev, who had always loathed Frederick II, had originally been opposed to Catherine's marriage, fearing that she would belong to a pro-Prussian party. But over the years he had come to respect the young grand duchess and he now felt that she would be more suitable than her husband to succeed the ageing and obviously failing Elizabeth. But his plotting proved too much for the empress, who banished her minister from court to his estate outside Moscow, and here he would remain until the end of her reign. As for Catherine, she saved herself only by going down on her knees and begging to be sent home, an action that finally earned her the empress's pardon. This suggests a change of heart on the part of Elizabeth, who may now have started to have doubts about the suitability of Peter, a theory supported by her alleged comment to a maid that she considered her nephew 'a monster'.[61]

After his departure, Stanislaw continued to correspond regularly with Catherine, refusing to accept that their relationship had ended. But just a year later she had met Grigory Orlov, one of five brothers. Soon falling for this dashing Guards officer who had been wounded in the terrible battle of Zorndorf, within around two years Catherine had embarked on another genuine love affair, one that lasted for over eleven years. Her minister Panin later remarked that he believed she would have married this man if it had been acceptable to the Russian people to be ruled by a 'Madame Orlova'. Nonetheless, Stanislaw continued to write her passionate letters, causing deep embarrassment to Catherine, who was once again pregnant.[62] While the Pole still wanted to return to Russia, she pleaded with him not to do so, insisting that such an action would put her position in danger.

During the last years of her reign, Elizabeth's favourite architect Rastrelli was creating the Winter Palace that still stands today, and again Catherine's memoirs give a good insight into this period, describing the discomfort that the court had to tolerate while the work was going on. The building was still not quite finished when at the end of 1761 on Christmas Day, 25 December (OS), Elizabeth died. Taking care to conceal her pregnancy, Catherine visited her throughout her last weeks and after her death paid due respects to the dead empress. However, her husband, now Peter III, immediately began to commit a series of foolish or grave blunders. Even at Elizabeth's funeral he acted disrespectfully, intentionally upsetting the dignity of the procession by repeatedly changing his pace, at times walking quickly, at others slowly. He had never learnt to speak good Russian and, having always shown his preference for his old Lutheran faith, he now offended the Orthodox Church with new reforms, even indicating that he wished 'to change the religion of the country'. Summing up the situation for Poniatowski, Catherine declared that Peter had now 'lost the small share of sense which naturally belonged to him' and that he had 'openly offended all parties'.[63] During his brief reign Peter did introduce some more liberal and popular measures, among them the abolition of the Secret Chancellery (or secret police) and the exemption during peacetime of the nobles from compulsory military service. He also brought in new measures to improve the status of some of the peasants and serfs, and had he remained longer on the throne, his policies might have produced several long-term beneficial results. After his death the British envoy Robert Keith – although remarking on his bizarre behaviour – would describe him as having 'many excellent qualities' and having never done 'a violent or cruel action in the course of his short reign'.[64] But his mistakes would soon make him unpopular in several quarters. Elizabeth and Frederick II had come to detest each other, but Peter III greatly admired the Prussian king, and so on declaring an immediate halt to the war, offered to return to him all the lands that over the years Russia had fought so hard to gain. While this spared Frederick at the moment of his probable total defeat, it was not enough for Peter, who then ordered his troops to abandon their uniforms and adopt those of their hated former enemies. Catherine claimed he even planned to dismiss the Guards in order to 'replace them by his Holstein troops, who were to be stationed in the city'.[65] Finally, Peter pushed the army's patience too far by declaring that his war-weary soldiers should now go and fight in Schleswig for the return of his Holstein-Gottorp lands that the Danes had taken years earlier at the end of the Great Northern War.

Peter also stirred up antagonism on the domestic front. By announcing that he wished to marry his mistress, Elizabeth Vorontsova, he indicated that he wanted to divorce Catherine and very possibly banish her to a convent. After he had intentionally insulted his wife publicly one evening, her followers started to tell her that she should consider mounting a coup to overthrow him, and it was from this time that she began to take the idea seriously. She had the backing of the Guards, particularly Grigory Orlov, his brothers, and thirty or forty other officers, plus in time nearly ten thousand men. And among the various members of the court who supported her was Catherine Dashkova, a highly intelligent woman who later became Director of the Imperial Academy of Arts and Sciences, President of the Russian Academy, and an honorary member of the Royal Swedish Academy of Sciences. She would be present at key moments in the coup ahead, although – to Catherine's annoyance – would afterwards exaggerate the importance of the role that she had played. Nevertheless, with her being the sister of Peter's mistress, Dashkova's endorsement underlines the complexity of the tensions that now divided the different factions surrounding the imperial couple.

For the moment, however, nothing could be done as Catherine was still in the middle of her pregnancy, but eventually Orlov's child was born on 11 April 1762 (OS). Baptised Alexei Bobrinski, he was then placed into foster care, and nineteen years later Catherine acknowledged him as her child. His many descendants are still alive today. In the meantime, the conspirators had continued with their plans for the coup, and finally two months after the birth things came to a head. A rumour was spread that Catherine had been taken into custody, and following the arrest of one of the plotters, the Guards decided they could no longer delay. At this time, Catherine was staying out at Peterhof, in Peter the Great's favourite little waterside palace of Monplaisir. Here she was woken at 6 a.m. on 28 June (OS) by Orlov's younger brother Alexei, who told her she must hurry at once to St Petersburg. She was then bundled into her carriage, and with her hairdresser even attending to her on the journey, eventually arrived in the capital, where, having met some of the Guards regiments, she went to the Church of Kazan to give thanks. She continued on to the Winter Palace, where, once oaths had been taken recognising her as Russia's new ruler, she appeared with her son Paul on the balcony and was hailed by the vast crowds who had now gathered below. After that, she and her companion Dashkova borrowed uniforms from the Guardsmen, and together they then rode out of the city in front of some 14,000 soldiers. Having rested briefly in a monastery near Peterhof, early on the 30th Catherine returned to the city to receive another triumphal welcome, during which the troops removed their hated Prussian uniforms and trampled them underfoot. Eventually, having celebrated the Mass, she went to bed in the Winter Palace, but even then was woken at 2 a.m. to pacify her drunken troops, who feared that she was about to be abducted by the Prussians.

Catherine later used these events to create an iconic image of herself, one that would mark the start of her reign. Like Elizabeth I in England, she knew the significance that such portraits could have in asserting her power and claim to the throne. In Vigilius Eriksen's painting of 1762, Catherine endeavoured to invest herself with an almost androgynous quality that would assert her authority. Here she intentionally understated her femininity by presenting herself in male dress, as the commander of her men, who was leading her country into a victorious future.[66]

This portrait by the Danish artist, which shows her seated on her grey horse called Brilliant, dressed in the uniform of Peter the Great's favourite Preobrazhensky Guards, she later hung in the throne room at Peterhof, where it still remains today. As a non-blood relation of the Romanovs, she was determined to assert her legitimacy by presenting herself as the saviour who had rescued the country from her dangerously unpredictable husband. Further to justify her own actions, she later emphasised his unsuitability by purposely exaggerating his failings:

> The death of the Empress Elizabeth plunged all Russians into deep mourning, especially all good patriots, because they saw in her successor a ruler of violent character and narrow intellect, who hated and despised the Russians, did not know his country, was incompetent to do hard work, avaricious and wasteful, and gave himself up wholly to his desires and to those who slavishly flattered him.[67]

Meanwhile, Peter was staying at Oranienbaum, the vast palace that Peter the Great's favourite Prince Menshikov had built for himself on the Gulf of Finland. Now he decided he wanted to see his wife so that she could celebrate his name day, a particularly important occasion for Russians. So he went to Peterhof, but, not finding her, he then took a galley across to Kronstadt, the naval fortress lying out in the middle of the gulf. However, here the admiral that Catherine had already put in charge refused to receive him, and utterly crushed Peter returned to Oranienbaum. Having – according to his wife – renounced the empire 'in full liberty, surrounded by fifteen hundred Holstein troops', he was then taken by Alexei Orlov back to Peterhof.[68] After he had written a letter to Catherine to apologise for his treatment of her, he signed his abdication, asking only in return that he might be allowed to go abroad with his mistress. Frederick II, who had so much to thank Peter for, remarked, with his usual caustic wit, that he had given up his throne 'like a child being sent to bed'.[69]

Peter's request was not granted, however, and he was now taken to the palace of Ropsha, while apartments were prepared for him at Schlüsselburg on Lake Ladoga. Here just a few days later he died in mysterious circumstances, probably killed in a drunken brawl. Grigory Orlov was not present at the time, but his brother Alexei was, and he now wrote a letter of apology to Catherine, saying that he could not explain or find excuse for what had happened. This letter, which remained among

Catherine's papers until her death, goes a long way towards exonerating her of the murder. She was certainly responsible for her part in the coup, and whether she had fully considered or not how her deposed husband would have to be dealt with afterwards, she does not appear to have ordered his death. Although Frederick II did not believe her personally responsible, she would be charged with Peter's murder by many people in the years to come.

The tsar's body was now taken to the Alexander Nevsky Monastery, where it lay in state before burial. Witnesses later reported seeing marks on the neck and face, but as Catherine was determined to defuse any rumours that might arise, she had immediately ordered a postmortem to take place. This declared that Peter had died of hemorrhoidal colic, piles, findings that were instantly mocked throughout Europe. Having been invited to tutor Grand Duke Paul, Jean le Rond d'Alembert laughingly wrote to Voltaire attributing his refusal to accept the invitation to the fact that he suffered from piles. Similarly, Frederick II, remarking on the alleged cause of death, declared sarcastically, 'we know how dangerous that illness is in Russia.'[70]

As soon as her husband's funeral was over, Catherine began to make plans for her coronation. Peter had displeased the people by not arranging one for himself, thus imitating his hero Frederick, but he had not realised the importance given to this ceremony in Russia, and this was a mistake that Catherine was determined to avoid. Therefore, just three months after taking the throne, on 22 September (OS) she was crowned in the traditional place for such events: the Cathedral of the Assumption (Dormition) in Moscow. Not wanting to spare any expense on this highly symbolic occasion, she commissioned a new crown shaped in the style of the Orthodox mitres, and further stressed her recently acquired authority by wearing a robe embroidered with the imperial double-headed eagle. This was covered with the cloak of her predecessor, Catherine I – another foreign-born widow, who like her had succeeded to her husband's throne. Later she repeatedly had herself painted, dressed in her coronation robes and adorned with the imperial regalia, again using official portraiture to spread the message that she was now the newly anointed and crowned head of state.

Following her coronation, Catherine embarked on a project determining how she intended to govern her country. Drawing on her reading of the *philosophes*, she began work on her *nakaz*, or Great Instruction. Pursuing the Enlightenment thinking of men like Montesquieu and Beccaria, she endeavoured to set out her plans for a Russian form of constitution, modelled on these thinkers' progressive ideas. Her proposals included various reforms, such as recognising the equality of all men, renouncing torture, and limiting the use of the death sentence. These suggestions she presented for approval to the Legislative Commission, her advisory parliamentary body that was made up of delegates chosen from different rungs of society. The Commission saw it as a continuation of the revolution begun by Peter I, and declared that in recognition of her work Catherine should like him receive the title of 'Great'. The delegates also dubbed her the 'Mother of the nation', and from this period Catherine began to adopt this alternative, more feminine, persona, intentionally creating an image of herself as the traditional Russian matriarch or *babushka*, caring for her people.[71] For this reason, Catherine chose at times to be painted in national dress, in 1769 giving a copy of one such portrait to the visiting doctor Sir Thomas Dimsdale. In the event, after long debates, none of her measures proposed in the *nakaz* would be passed by the Legislative Commission, and for this reason Catherine has been accused by some people of engaging in nothing more than a public relations exercise. However, in truth, she laboured immensely hard for two years on this project, getting up early every morning to start work, and long after it had been abandoned she would continue to explore other similar reforms. In 1787 on her trip to the Crimea she was still studying the possibilities of comparable programmes.

Catherine soon discovered the difficulty of putting theory into practice. Ever since the empress Elizabeth had seized the throne from the infant Ivan VI, the deposed tsar had been held in captivity, and his existence had continued to represent a threat to the succeeding rulers. Each in turn would be curious to see him and so, just as Elizabeth had him brought to St Petersburg for inspection in 1756, Peter III had gone to visit him in March 1762. After several hours of talking with him, he had become convinced of Ivan's sanity, and had then indicated that he intended to release him. But nothing was done over the next four months, and Ivan was still a prisoner when Peter died.

In the early days after her coup, Catherine was under pressure from repeated plots, and anonymous letters began to appear focusing on Ivan, some of which even suggested that she might marry the young man herself. Worried by these threats, within weeks of her husband's overthrow, she too decided to visit the prisoner. Later she wrote that – unlike Peter – she had found Ivan broken in mind and body, and so had considered moving him to somewhere more suitable, 'commensurate with his nature and upbringing', presumably a monastery.[72] Whether Catherine did genuinely find him mentally damaged, or whether she was merely seeking to represent him as unsuitable to replace her, we cannot tell, but again his release did not happen, and he remained incarcerated in his harsh conditions for a further two years until events took another turn.

On her coming to the throne, Catherine had ratified the order issued by Elizabeth that on pain of death should Ivan be allowed to escape, and so when in July 1764 an attempt was made to release him, his guards obeyed the imperial instructions to the letter, and Ivan was murdered. Although his body was then buried at Schlüsselburg, a recent discovery made in 2008 suggests that he was later taken to Kholmogory in the region of Archangel. This claim has been supported by careful forensic work carried out on the coffin and its contents that were found close to the altar in the city's Church of the Assumption. The assertion that these are the remains of Ivan VI is further endorsed by the argument that for several years after his death his father and siblings were still imprisoned in this area, and therefore his body may well have been returned to the family as was the normal practice.

The facts leading up to his murder must be examined. While his death might indeed have been caused purely by the ill-fated attempt to release him, other evidence suggests that it could have been a political assassination. On hearing the news, Catherine's minister Panin expressed relief that through 'God's miraculous providence' the problem was over.[73] The unsuccessful rescuer Mirovich was never tortured after his arrest, his relations were never called at the trial, and at his eventual execution he was seen to be relaxed as if expecting a pardon. Catherine always sought to be humane, and many of her actions do show that she wished to avoid unnecessary brutality or suffering, but here the suspicion remains that someone in authority might have condoned, if not ordered, this killing for political expediency.

Over the last 150 years Russians had seen how uncertainty could threaten rebellion and bloodshed, and all the empresses came to the throne following a military intervention or political coup. The sense of insecurity created by this had encouraged Anna to set up her Chancellery of Secret Investigations, while Elizabeth's fears had caused her to be constantly on the move. And Catherine's position was even more precarious than that of her two predecessors as, unlike them, she was not a Romanov by birth. Assassination was a real danger for these women, as it was for the tsars and their families who followed them. However, Catherine's policies were not driven just by personal concerns, but also by her ambitions for Russia. Of all the empresses, she was the most dedicated, working to the end of her life to improve the condition of her adopted country. So while Ivan's death might indeed have been an accident caused by unfortunate circumstances and overzealous guards, it could equally have been the result of a cold-eyed decision by one of her ministers.

Catherine at this time was still dedicated to her Enlightenment ideals, so her personal involvement would seem to be unlikely, but she might have been prepared to turn a blind eye to the actions of others.[74] Those in power have always had to make difficult life and death choices when deciding whether or not to go to war, and for the authorities the sacrifice of one individual could have been a price worth paying for the stability not just of the empress, but also of her country. A self-confessed ambitious woman, who sincerely believed that she might be of service to Russia, Catherine saw herself as the perfect typical eighteenth-century enlightened despotic ruler that the country needed. By August of 1762, because she had survived politically the death of her husband, her position had become stronger, and this earlier apparently 'fortunate' event may have encouraged someone at court to believe that the murder of the remaining tsar would further remove any dangerous insurrection, perhaps by a pretender. This would certainly not excuse whoever was responsible, but in the light of the times, it might explain it. However, while we can never claim to know the truth of these events, Catherine would be soon be blamed at home and abroad for Ivan's death, and the murder of a second tsar so early in her reign would have a long-lasting negative impact on her public image.

However, Catherine was more successful when it came to the matter of the election of a king of Poland. With Augustus III's death in October 1763, a new candidate had to be found for this elective monarchy. With Russia's ever-growing influence in the country, Catherine was in a good position to impose her will and bring about the coronation of her choice, namely that of her former lover Stanislaw Poniatowski, who now became Stanislaw II Augustus. But although he would remain true to Catherine for decades to come, he did not prove to be quite as manipulable as she had hoped. While both adhered to Enlightenment ideas, she did not approve of liberal reforms being introduced into Poland, where she felt they might undermine Russia's interests. As a result, over the years the two rulers' relationship would become increasingly difficult, and their ambitions would collide in a way that would lead to Poland's eventual destruction.

On the home front, Catherine soon began a programme of modernisation. She built embankments along the River Neva in an attempt to control the flooding that remained a constant threat to St Petersburg, and she founded new hospitals, orphanages, schools and academies. These included two institutes, one for the education of young women of non-noble background, another for daughters of the nobility, the famous Smolny Institute that was first set up in the baroque convent that Rastrelli had built for Elizabeth in St Petersburg. Later, after Catherine's death, the students would move to a new classical building next door, and this would eventually become Lenin's headquarters during the Bolshevik revolution. Catherine also commissioned other building projects of her own, such as the rococo-style Chinese Pavilion at Oranienbaum – built for her by Antonio Rinaldi as a private summer residence or *dacha* – and the Small Hermitage next to the Winter Palace in St Petersburg. Having bought 200 to 300 paintings from a Berlin dealer in 1764, this building, constructed by Yuri Felten to house her growing collection of works of art, would become a favourite place for her to entertain her closest friends.

Catherine then decided that she wanted to see more of her empire for herself. So on 29 May 1767 (OS) she wrote to Voltaire that she was in Asia, having arrived at Kazan on the Volga. Here, although delighted by the city, she was struck by the twenty very different ethnic groups with their diverse customs that she soon encountered. She now told Voltaire that her task was to find a 'suit' that fitted all her people, a comment that shows just how aware she had become of the difficulties that she faced as ruler of such a vast and disparate country.[75]

In October 1768 the English doctor Sir Thomas Dimsdale arrived in St Petersburg in response to Catherine's invitation to come and inoculate her family. Since her childhood, she had greatly feared smallpox, and in the eighteenth century it was a deadly disease, killing around 400,000 people each year in Europe, and leaving many others blind or badly pockmarked. One such person scarred by the disease was Lady Mary Wortley-Montagu, who accompanied her husband the English ambassador to Constantinople in 1718. Here she saw Circassian women intentionally infecting their daughters with a small dose of the smallpox bacillus to immunise them so that they might retain their beauty and enter the sultan's harem. Struck by this, Lady Mary decided to take the risk and inoculate her small son, an operation that proved successful. On her return to England in 1721, the idea was gradually taken up by society women, including Caroline, Princess of Wales. As a result, in 1724 George I wrote to his daughter Sophie Dorothea, Queen in Prussia, encouraging her to support the practice – the very year that the queen's son, the future Frederick II, contracted the disease. When Voltaire visited England in 1726, he was highly impressed by the courage of these people, and used this as a metaphor for English free thinking. This subject becomes part of his criticism of France in his *Lettres Philosophiques* (published in England as *English Letters*), where he contrasts the country's openness to new ideas with the rigid social and religious dogmatism found in his homeland. Catholic countries resisted inoculation on the grounds that it was contrary to the will of God, but the same year that Catherine brought it to Russia, Maria Theresa introduced it in Vienna, following a terrible period when the epidemic swept through the court, killing her daughter-in-law and daughter, both named Josepha. It also nearly took the life of the Habsburg Empress and another daughter, Elizabeth, but the latter was left so badly scarred that she was now deemed unmarriageable. Likewise, after smallpox killed Louis XV in 1774 – a death described by Catherine as 'shameful' in the circumstances – his heir, Louis XVI, finally inoculated his family. By that time, courts all over Europe had taken up the idea, but the process was not without risk. Around 2 per cent of those treated may have died as a result of inoculation, George III's two youngest sons among them.[76] Fnally a safer vaccine based on cowpox was tried in the 1760s and eventually made popular by Edward Jenner three decades later.

Despite the dangers, and the suspicion of many Russians for the practice, Catherine now ordered Dimsdale to inoculate herself and Paul. But first she ensured the safety of the doctor and his son who was assisting him by providing the means for their quick escape from the country if she should become ill or die. This shows not just her concern for them, but her doubts as to its safety and the courage she needed to attempt the process. However, things went according to plan and with that other members of the court followed Catherine's example, after which she set up inoculation centres for the public in St Petersburg. As for Dimsdale, he and his son were rewarded with titles, both made Barons of the Empire, and before they left the country Catherine gave them several extravagant gifts in gratitude for their services.

Meanwhile, tensions were growing in Poland against the heavy presence of the Russians and in 1766 the situation exploded into outright rebellion following the formation of the Bar Confederation – a historic form of association designed for legal protest. Eventually, two years later, the civil war was brought to an end and the Russian troops pursued the remaining rebels over the border, but their trespassing on Ottoman lands resulted in the sultan declaring war. During the conflict, the Russians proved the stronger and in 1770 Catherine's navy won a resounding victory at Çesme near the island of Chios. This was the most serious defeat of the so-called 'Turks' in almost exactly 200 years, the first such naval victory since the battle of Lepanto in 1571. But to achieve this success in the Mediterranean, the admiral, Alexei Orlov, had been forced to make a long diversion. With Russia still having no southern ports, the fleet had had to sail via the Baltic, North Sea and Atlantic, and the battle therefore illustrates clearly the reason why, since the time of Peter the Great, Russia had wanted to have access to the all-important Black Sea.

Having rewarded Alexei with the title of Count Chemensky, Catherine commemorated the battle further by erecting in the gardens of the Great Palace at Tsarskoe Selo a rostral column – imitating an idea from classical times when, marking a great naval victory, such columns would have been decorated with the prows of the captured ships.[77] In St Petersburg the same design would be taken up again in 1810 when two large red columns with beacons on top were constructed across the water from the Winter Palace. And while Alexei Orlov was being recognised for his achievement, his brother Grigory was also having his own measure of success, managing in 1771 to restore order to Moscow. Following an outbreak of the plague, rioting had broken out in the city, during which the people had set upon the archbishop and beaten him to death. Catherine was appalled by these events and again wrote to Voltaire, decrying how little in reality the eighteenth century had 'to boast about'.[78] She was now beginning to lose some of the optimism and confidence of her youth, fully realising the difficulties of educating her country and bringing it into a more enlightened age.

During the 1760s Catherine had given Grigory Orlov the country estate of Gatchina, where Rinaldi had built him a magnificent palace, and now along the embankment in St Petersburg the empress also presented him with Rinaldi's impressive Marble Palace – still unfinished at the time of the count's death. But despite his success in Moscow, he was falling out of favour, and as a result of his infidelity Catherine decided to bring their long love affair to an end. He tried to win her back by giving her the magnificent 'Orlov diamond' that – later placed in the imperial sceptre – is on display in the Kremlin. This did not change her mind, and after accepting that he had lost her, he married another woman, but died soon after in 1783, suffering from dementia, probably brought on by syphilis. Catherine, still fond of him, was greatly saddened when she heard the news.

Elsewhere, concern was increasing that the empress was becoming too successful in her war against the Ottomans, the Habsburgs in particular growing fearful that she would expand into the lands on their borders. Frederick II of Prussia therefore came up with an idea that might satisfy the Viennese court and further his own ambitions. His younger brother, Prince Heinrich, a childhood friend of Catherine, now visited St Petersburg and laid out a scheme that would entail the annexation and redistribution of parts of Poland by the three powers. While Catherine would give up her claims in the south to Austria, she would be compensated with new territories in the area of Smolensk. Frederick would gain the region of Poland that separated his eastern Prussian lands from Brandenburg. Despite criticism from the other countries of Europe, the scheme went ahead in 1772 with the tacit agreement of Poland's powerless king, Stanislaw II.

These were not Catherine's only territorial gains. Already in 1764 she had received the Polish border lands of the Cossack Hetmanate, and now ten years later with her first Ottoman war ending in victory, the Crimean Khanate, a former protectorate of the Ottoman Empire, came under her protection. Moreover, in the area lying between these two regions, she destroyed the Sich or stronghold of the Zaporizhian Cossacks, whose lands she then proceeded to confiscate. This action was in answer to the most serious rebellion of her reign.

The previous year Pugachev, a Cossack from the Urals, having claimed to be her dead husband, had begun to attract a large following. Although nothing like the former tsar, for over a year and a half the pretender convinced enough supporters to threaten Moscow, sack Kazan, and attack towns and villages throughout the southern part of the country. Finally, he was captured and put to death, although, to the disappointment of the crowd who wished for a more gory scene, Catherine, in an act of mercy, ordered his decapitation before the quartering of his body – a public execution in stark contrast to the brutal, prolonged punishment meted out in Paris eighteen years earlier to Damiens, the failed assassin of Louis XV.

While this uprising was the most dangerous challenge of Catherine's reign, she was threatened overall by around twenty rebellions and the claims of some twenty-six pretenders, including the one purporting to be Empress Elizabeth's daughter, Princess Tarakanova.

With the departure of Orlov from her life, Catherine briefly had a relationship with a young officer, but this did not last long as he was not happy with his position at court, and she soon found him boring. But then in 1774 she began an affair with Grigory Potemkin, thought to be the most significant man in her life, whom she had first seen several years before when during the coup he had bounded forward to offer her his sword knot. Over ten years younger than Catherine, Potemkin was amusing, intelligent, and considerably more of an intellectual than either Orlov or her husband Peter had been. At last having found someone with whom she was so compatible, she may even have secretly married him. Over time they would give each other spectacular gifts, among them her presents of the 700-piece Sèvres dinner service, and the Anichkov Palace on the Nevsky Prospekt that had formerly belonged to Empress Elizabeth's favourite. In exchange, among other things, he gave her the fabulous golden Peacock Clock that was made by the Englishman James Cox, now on show in the Winter Palace Museum. With its complicated automatons still in working order, this remains a prime exhibit in the Pavilion Hall of the Small Hermitage.

These two strong and determined characters were unable to maintain the relationship for long and tensions began to develop between them. Within two years, Potemkin, frustrated by the limitations of court life and his secondary role to Catherine, decided to return to the south, where he then concentrated on their 'Greek project' to recreate the empire of the earlier Byzantines. But the affair would never fully die and, despite their taking other lovers, their mutual affection lasted until his death. Catherine is famous for her affairs, but Potemkin was no different. He had several mistresses, including some who were his nieces, a relationship at the time seen as less shocking than it is today: Catherine's uncle had proposed to her when she was still young, Voltaire's niece Madame Denis was his long-time lover, and the Habsburg women (with papal dispensation) frequently were married to their much older uncles. But now Potemkin and Catherine's relationship would become similar to an open marriage, he taking up his position at her side and in her bed whenever he returned to St Petersburg. Always supportive and loyal to her, he continued to play a key role in her life, even to the point of personally choosing most of her future favourites.

It was at this point that Catherine began the series of love affairs that has tarnished her reputation. Wanting to defame her, her enemies soon promulgated salacious gossip, which was then repeated by later generations who enjoyed the titillation of spreading these malicious stories. Because Catherine's lovers were all young while she grew older, the gap in their ages grew more significant, and this added extra fuel to the scurrilous myths. But in each of these affairs, the empress, who always professed that she needed to be loved, was looking for a close companion with whom she might share her few private moments away from the pressures of her position. Using a modern term, she was a 'serial monogamist', and she did not have – as is often suggested – a stable of young lovers in the fashion of her contemporary Louis XV. And there were many others who could be similarly mentioned, including Frederik V of Denmark, Augustus II of Poland, Fredrik I of Sweden, and Friedrich Wilhelm III of Prussia. Even King Stanislaw, despite his sincere love for Catherine, would father several illegitimate children. Catherine, however, moved on to a new favourite when the previous one had left and, again contrary to popular opinion, several of her relationships came to an end when the favourite let her down. Of her seven known lovers during the final years of her reign, two were unfaithful – although she still gave one a generous wedding present – two plotted against her beloved Potemkin, one outlived her, and her supreme favourite died of diphtheria in 1784. This last was Alexander Lanskoy, the perfect courtier who was with her for four years, and whose death left her so utterly grief-struck that Potemkin had to return to St Petersburg to comfort her when members of the court became worried over her state of mind. Much of the criticism of Catherine's private life no doubt comes from the fact that she was a woman, and a successful one at that. The Empresses Anna and Elizabeth, with similarly questionable lifestyles, come in for far less general criticism on this score, while her contemporary male rulers receive little public comment on their dalliances, their promiscuity being seen as more or less understandable, if not acceptable. The moral climate of the times was different, but although it was a period that accepted official royal mistresses, Catherine as a female ruler was expected to conform to a different standard, following perhaps the example of the devoutly Catholic and chaste Maria Theresa. This judgemental imbalance carried on into the next century when some of Catherine's male heirs would – with a certain amount of hypocrisy – be shocked by the liberal morals of her libertine, and typically eighteenth-century, court. As a result, they would attempt to whitewash over this aspect of her reign.

Catherine still much admired the works of the French *philosophes*, paying for Denis Diderot's library in advance when he needed money for his daughter's dowry, and buying Voltaire's library when he died in 1778. For years she had corresponded with this latter – most famous – writer, claiming that it was he who had first taught her to think. But the two would never meet, as, having become concerned that the journey and harsh Russian climate would be too much for the old man, she had earlier begged her other correspondent and long-time confidant in Paris, Baron Grimm, to prevent him from visiting her. Nonetheless, in 1773, Diderot came to St Petersburg, remaining for around five months, during which time Catherine enjoyed daily talks with him, even though, by the end of his visit, both had realised the differences in their positions.

While he supported more philosophic and idealistic ideas, Catherine was faced with the reality of her everyday situation, and writing to him she remarked that while she admired his 'brilliant mind', he had just 'to work on paper', whereas she had 'to work on skin' – a comment that once again shows how she was only too aware of the chasm that separated theory from practice.[79]

In 1776 tragedy struck in the imperial family, when Paul's young wife, Grand Duchess Natalia, formerly Wilhelmine of Hesse-Darmstadt, died just three years after her marriage while giving birth to a stillborn child. Her suffering was appalling, lasting around a week, during which time Catherine was mostly at her bedside. Paul was overcome by her death, until his mother, for better or worse, thought it prudent to inform him that his dead wife had been unfaithful. But now having gone to Berlin to recover from his loss, Paul met the young woman who had been proposed as his bride in 1773. At the time she had been rejected as too young, but now aged sixteen, Sophie Dorothee of Württemberg was seen by Paul to be ideal, and by the end of the same year she had converted to Orthodoxy, taking the name Maria Feodorovna. After their marriage, she would continue to adore Paul and would give him ten children, thus becoming the first of several Romanov wives to have a large family. To celebrate the arrival of their first child, Catherine gave them the Palace of Pavlovsk, which Maria, renowned for her good taste, then decorated in the latest classical style.

Alexander, the oldest of their children, was born the year after the marriage, and sixteen months later he was followed by Constantine. There were then six sisters, a son, Nicholas – born four months before Catherine's death – and finally Michael. However, Catherine was chiefly interested in the two eldest boys, and she now swept them off to bring them up herself, in much the same way as Elizabeth had done when Paul was born. Wishing to educate her grandsons in the principles of the Enlightenment, over the years she would dream up schemes for their futures. While she may well have hoped to make Alexander her immediate heir, thus bypassing his father Paul, her ambitions for Constantine were to install him as ruler of the new Greek empire she hoped to create on territory recaptured from the Ottomans.

Meanwhile, Catherine spent much of her summers out at Tsarskoe Selo in the vast baroque Grand Palace, today better known as the Catherine Palace after Elizabeth's mother. While she preferred this to Oranienbaum and Peterhof, where she had spent much of her unhappy engagement and early years of marriage, she found its ostentatious taste excessive, if not vulgar, describing it as being like whipped cream. Rather than the gold interiors, she preferred the classical style that was also favoured by her daughter-in-law, and for that reason she commissioned her Scottish architect Charles Cameron to design some new rooms. To these he later added a bathhouse and gallery, while in the park surrounding the palace the Hanoverian father and son John and Joseph Bush laid out an English-style gardens, where in her later years the empress would enjoy walking with her much-loved dogs.

All the time Catherine continued to add to her works of art. In 1779 she bought the outstanding collection that had been put together by Robert Walpole, the man generally considered to be the first British prime minister. Unlike so many of his contemporaries, Walpole had survived the South Sea Bubble crisis when many people were financially ruined, and he was able to hand on to his descendants a collection that included some major works of art by Rembrandt and other masters. However, the family had now run up such serious debts that his grandson decided to sell the collection for the colossal sum of £40,555, a figure (equating to around three million today) which was so enormous that questions were asked in the House of Commons as to whether the sale should go ahead. Having now acquired these artworks, Catherine needed to enlarge her palace buildings and Yuri Felten was called in again to create a new extension – today called the Old or Great Hermitage. At the same time, the empress decided to demolish the adjacent, already decaying Winter Palace of Peter the Great, and on the (still visible) foundations of this old building, Giacomo Quarenghi then created a new Palladian court theatre. Having been first invited to the country in 1779 and become a popular architect with the Russians, the Italian would never return home, eventually dying in St Petersburg in 1817.

Catherine also invited the French sculptor Etienne Maurice Falconet to create a statue of her predecessor Peter the Great. Falconet, a difficult man, took years to complete this work, adding to the problems by demanding that a huge boulder be dragged and floated several miles from the Finnish swamps to act as a plinth. Thanks to the labours of around 1,000 people, after some eighteen months it eventually arrived in the city, where it was then greatly reduced in size. Finally, after sixteen years, aided by an assistant, Falconet finished the statue and it was erected in the capital. This, later known as the *Bronze Horseman* after Pushkin's famous poem, presents Peter in an almost classical pose, dressed like a Roman general riding out to defeat his enemies. But although this sculpture was officially erected in memory of the tsar, it also served another purpose. Just as Catherine had done with portraits over the years, with this monument she was subtly delivering a clear message. On the plinth she had engraved in Latin and Russian 'from Peter the First to Catherine the Second', thus linking herself to her famous predecessor and the Romanov dynasty, and asserting her rightful heritage to the throne as the second of Russia's great rulers.

In 1783 Potemkin advised Catherine that, as the situation had now altered in the south, the status of the Crimean lands, still a Russian protectorate, should be changed. Therefore, following his advice, Catherine annexed the whole area, and it was fully incorporated into her empire as the Taurida region, returning to its name from classical times. Potemkin, its Governor General, would later become Prince of Taurida, Serenissimus and the Prince of Princes, titles that were added to his earlier one of Prince of the Holy Roman Empire, which Emperor Joseph II – on Catherine's persuasion – had given him in 1776. But more significantly, with this annexation Russia at last attained its own southern warm water ports. Now, as Peter the Great had always wanted, but failed to achieve, Catherine had gained direct access to the Mediterranean and beyond, and her country at last could establish a Black Sea fleet.

Four years later, the empress decided she should visit her new regions, so choosing to leave in January when travelling was easier across the snow-covered ground, she set off in a convoy of a 124 sleighs until she arrived at the Dnieper River, where she transferred to a fleet of galleys and other craft. Along some of its length, this river formed the border with Poland, and it was here that she met her former lover, Stanislaw II Augustus Poniatowski. After the meeting, which was a mixed success, Catherine then moved south to join Emperor Joseph II, and together they travelled on to inspect the work done by Potemkin, who, to mark their arrival, had arranged a spectacular reception with fireworks and other celebrations. His enemies quickly spread rumours that much of his development of the region was false and that the villages through which Catherine and the emperor passed were mere façades to impress them, stories that had appeared in St Petersburg even before Catherine's departure. But she, Joseph and the Prince de Ligne who accompanied them, were all impressed by what they saw, and the so-called Potemkin Villages, a byword for fakery, appear to be largely another creation of malicious scandalmongering. While no doubt considerable work remained to be done, and Potemkin very probably beautified what was unfinished, much had been achieved and the trip was generally hailed as a success by those who took part in it.[80]

However, Catherines's triumphal journey reignited tensions with the Ottoman Empire, and in 1787 the sultan, fearing that she was becoming too powerful in the region, declared war. Again, this, her second 'Turkish' war, would end five years later in victory for the Russians. The empire now acquired yet more territory in the Yedisan region between the Dniester and Dnieper rivers (today the border area between Moldavia and Ukraine). Just a year after the fighting began, a successful Russian siege took place at Ochakov, an event that gave its name to a crisis that broke out in England, where questions were raised in Parliament regarding Catherine's territorial ambitions. While the British feared that Russia's growing power in the south might impact negatively on their interests in India, the upshot of the crisis was that scurrilous cartoons now began to appear in the British press, some going so far as to take a swipe at Catherine's personal life. The lewd and libellous innuendos these contained were comparable to those suffered by Marie Antoinette at this time, and they would create lasting damage to Catherine's memory. Many of the salacious stories that are still repeated date from this period.

In 1791, three years after the events of Ochakov, Potemkin, who had been present at the siege and the battle that ended it, returned to St Petersburg for the last time. During his four months in the city he spent a fortune laying on entertainments, including a magnificent party with some 3,000 guests at the Taurida Palace that Catherine had earlier given him. While this was held in her honour, she had already instructed him that the time had come for him to return to his duties, and so at the end of the evening the couple sadly parted. Still deeply attached to him, in her letter soon after to Grimm, she declared that he had been 'handsome', 'gay', 'brilliant' and 'more witty than ever'.[81] Potemkin left St Petersburg in October and returned south, but while travelling from Jassy he collapsed with a fever beside the road and died aged just fifty-two. His body was then taken on to Kerson, the town that he had created, and here it was eventually buried in the newly built Church of St Catherine. The empress was heartbroken and later bought his Taurida Palace, but after her death, Paul, who hated his mother and her favourites, handed it over to the Imperial Guard. In 1905 the building became the seat of the Duma, and following the 1917 revolution it was used first by the Provisional Government and then by the Bolsheviks.

By this time, however, Catherine had other concerns on her mind. Earlier in 1789 two events had taken place that marked the beginning of a new age and a more insecure future for hereditary monarchs. On 30 April George Washington became the first president of the newly declared United States, and on 14 July the Bastille was stormed in Paris. The following year Catherine's former protégé Alexander Radischev returned to Russia with the new revolutionary ideas he had now picked up in France. He published a book entitled *From St Petersburg to Moscow*, in which he criticised the situation in Catherine's empire. Horrified, she arrested and later exiled the author, and then, going against all her former principles, brought in censorship of the press, imposing a ban that included the *philosophes' Encyclopédie,* which had questioned the fundamental ideas of society. And in September 1791, her shock was further increased when Louis XVI reluctantly agreed to a constitution in France.

However, that was not all. While Catherine had been engaged fighting the Ottomans in the south, her first cousin Gustav III of Sweden had used the moment to declare his own war against Russia. When this second conflict began in 1788 at Hogland off the coast of Reval (Tallinn), the Russians under their commander, the Scottish admiral Samuel Greig, succeeded in preventing a Swedish invasion. Greig had come to Russia in 1764, brought in like several foreigners to help improve the navy, and he had taken part in the earlier great victory at Çesme. But just days after the Battle of Hogland, Greig died in Reval of a fever, and Catherine ordered that he should be honoured with a state funeral. And after this had taken place in St Mary's Lutheran Cathedral on Toompea Hill, she then commissioned Querenghi to create the impressive marble tomb that, now topped with its Scottish saltire, continues to predominate in the north aisle.

Over time Swedish fortunes improved and after their resounding victory in the Second Svensksund Battle in July 1790, both Catherine and Gustav agreed a peace. But within two years the Swedish king had been assassinated and with the revolutionary mood mounting throughout Europe, just a year after his death Louis XVI was sent to the guillotine, followed a few months later by his wife, Marie Antoinette. Catherine was appalled by these events and having finally lost faith in the teachings of the *philosophes*, she now questioned the Enlightenment thinking that she had so long admired.

As the rise of Jacobinism had increased Catherine's fear of rebellion breaking out in Poland, she now joined forces with the new Prussian king, Friedrich Wilhelm II, and together the two leaders then carried out Poland's Second Partition, each seizing more territory on their borders. But the revolts did not stop, and so two years later in 1795, once more joined by Austria, they completed the country's destruction in the Third Partition, removing all the remaining lands. This was one of Catherine's more questionable moves, but even though the ambitious greed of the rulers of the three powers was condemned by the rest of Europe, the political difficulties of the times led to no action being taken to save Poland from extinction. Yet, the empress's motives have to be considered in the context of the period. Apart from her desire to protect her country from the revolutionary unrest on her borders, she, like most of her contemporaries, saw territorial expansion as commendable. She approached all affairs of state with a cool-headed pragmatism and emotional detachment, and in this particular case, had placed Russia above any private feelings she might earlier have had for the Polish king. Having obliterated his county, she left Stanislaw II Augustus Poniatowski with no option other than to abdicate.

With the new lands Catherine had acquired from Poland, she found herself with a greatly increased population, many of whom were Jewish. Large numbers of these were artisans who were considerably more skilled than the native-born Russians, and Catherine feared that this influx would lead to unrest in the towns where the local residents might find themselves displaced by the incomers. Therefore, having over the years gained vast new unpopulated territories that needed settlers, she came up with an idea that would resolve both her problems. She now created an extensive enclosed area for the Jews, where they could work without presenting unwanted competition, and also build up the population. This was not anything but a practical measure, and even those who have sought to defame her have not charged her with anti-Jewishness. But the same cannot be said for her descendants, and – to use the later term – subsequent tsars were openly antisemitic, among them Nicholas I who, having enlarged the area, tightened restrictions and named it the Pale.

In the last years of her life, Catherine commissioned two final artistic projects: first, the beautiful Raffael Loggias in the Hermitage that were copied from the famous frescoed rooms in the Vatican, and second, the New Palace at Tsarskoe Selo (later known as the Alexander Palace) that was created as a present for the empress's grandson following his marriage in 1793. And that same year, despite her rejecting the title, Catherine was officially acclaimed 'the Great'.

Yet, in spite of the general esteem in which she was now held, three years later the empress would be put through a humiliating experience when the new seventeen-year-old Swedish king came to St Petersburg. Although the reason for his visit was his official engagement to Catherine's oldest granddaughter, Alexandra, when the time came for the ceremony he failed to turn up. On hearing that his bride would not be changing from Orthodoxy to his own faith, Gustav IV Adolf, a devout Lutheran, had refused to attend. As a result, she was left heartbroken and the marriage never took place. By the next year the young king had already found himself another wife. For Alexandra worse was to come. Five years later, by then married to Joseph II's nephew, she would die aged just seventeen in childbirth.

The young Swedish king's disrespectful treatment of the ageing empress was an immense shock to Catherine, and many blamed Gustav's behaviour for her now declining health. Two months later, at the age of sixty-seven, she suffered a massive stroke, from which she never recovered consciousness. During the next thirty-six hours that she lay in a coma her son Paul proceeded to rifle through her papers, and evidence suggests that he may have discovered a will that bypassed him from the succession – the empress having bequeathed the throne directly to her adored grandson Alexander. Such an action would have been in accordance with the declaration first made by Peter the Great in 1722 that all the future Russian rulers would be free to choose their heir. Yet, if this were the case, on finding the document, Paul most probably destroyed it. And over the next few days he continued taking steps to disobey his mother's wishes and dishonour her memory. However, ultimately it would be Catherine who was proved right, her reservations appearing to have been well founded. Paul would be no more able than his father to maintain his position, and within just five years he too had been murdered by his disgruntled courtiers.

One of the charges laid against Catherine is that she failed to abolish serfdom. When writing her Great Instruction, she had questioned the morality of this system, but had been persuaded that its abolition was impossible. In the first year of her reign she had tried to introduce an alternative method of agreed payment to those working in the mining and industrial sectors, but this had resulted in strikes, which had to be put down with force. She still wanted to root out abusive behaviour by owners and, with some foresight, she wrote: 'If we do not agree to reduce cruelty and moderate a situation intolerable for human beings, then they themselves will take things in hand.'[82] But she soon realised that her position on the throne was dependent on the support of those who were the serfs' owners, and knowing that she could not afford to lose these people's backing, she continued to reward her favourites generously with the gift of 'souls', thereby increasing the numbers affected. While land was not at a premium in Russia, the wealth of an estate lay in the number of its workers, and so over the years she granted thousands of new serfs to members of the nobility. Already unable to see how Russia could function any other way, Catherine finally abandoned her earlier intentions to improve the people's lot after the Pugachev rebellion. As it had seriously shaken her, once the rising had been put down, she imposed a new form of local government that could wield stricter control over the peasants, and from then until the end of her reign any further moderating of the serfdom system was abandoned. We also have to remember that serfdom remained in the Austrians' empire until 1783, in Denmark until 1788, and only finally ended in all Prussia in 1810. After that slavery continued to exist in the colonies and elsewhere, until 1865 in the United States, 1885 in Brazil, and even today it still persists in some parts of the world. That does not mean that the faults of one person or country justify those of another, but Catherine does deserve to be viewed by the standards of her times, and in the light of the particular problems that she faced. She and her four successors saw the inherent difficulties of abolishing the system, as became only too apparent when Alexander II, 'the Liberator', finally brought it to an end in 1861. After repeated attempts on his life, the tsar was assassinated twenty years later, the victim of the social unrest that had continued to grow in the cities, which was exacerbated by the migration of impoverished and out-of-work peasants seeking employment.

Catherine has also been charged with hypocrisy, many people accusing her of proposing unfulfilled policies purely for her self-promotion. However, the extent to which she worked, getting up at five or six every morning, lighting her own fire, and starting the day before she could be distracted by others, attests to her determination to take an active part in the governing of her country. Unlike Catherine I, Anna and Elizabeth before her, she was not content to leave the rule of her empire to others, delegating her duties in order to have greater time to spend on her own amusements and pleasures. Some of her policies, in particular those directed towards Poland, are unacceptable today, but the depth of her love for Russia and her desire to make it a great and stable county cannot be doubted. She set out to continue the revolution begun by Peter the Great, and in doing so she moved the country further into the modern world, introducing new ideas in science and medicine, updating the navy, improving communications, and promoting education and the arts.

In 1795, having fled the revolution, Marie Antoinette's French portrait painter, Vigée Le Brun, arrived in Russia, where she painted several members of the court. Although Catherine was not one of them, Le Brun would meet her and record her personal impression of the empress. She described her as being stout and smaller than expected – less than 5 feet 3 inches tall – but with a great presence and considerable charm. The Frenchwoman also remarked on her approachability and easy manner, characteristics that had impressed so many other people before her. While Catherine was not without her flaws, she had given Russia a greater stability than it had known for years, and by bringing it closer to the rest of Europe, had increased the respect with which it was viewed from abroad. These qualites Le Brun recognised, and in her memoirs she listed the many benefits the empress had brought to her country, and this contemporary assessment of Catherine's achievements therefore makes a fitting epitaph for this remarkable woman:

> The Russian people lived very happily under the rule of Catherine; by great and lowly have I heard the name of her blessed to whom the nation owed so much glory and so much well-being. I do not speak of the conquests by which the national vanity was so prodigiously flattered, but of the real, lasting good that this Empress did her people. During the space of the thirty-four years she reigned, her beneficent genius fathered or furthered all that was useful, all that was grand.[83]

13
Poland's Last Years of Decline

Augustus II of Poland by H. Rodakowski. (Courtesy of Lviv National Art Gallery)

Following the abdication of Jan II Kasimierz Vasa, in 1668 the *Sejm* elected a surprise new king, Michal Korybut Wiśniowiecki, who had shown so little interest in the affair that he had to be rooted out of a Warsaw brothel before being taken to the election field for his proclamation. A magnate's son and a member of a distinguished Polish family related to the fifteenth-century Władysław II Jagiełło, he had been chosen by the nobles as they believed him unlikely to impinge upon their liberties. Although supported by his wife's brother, Emperor Leopold I, Michal soon found out just how difficult his country was to rule. Civil war now broke out, and his problems were then increased with Ottoman troops once more invading the Commonwealth. After a twenty-six-day siege they took the border fortress of Kamianets-Podilskyi (today in Ukraine), and then captured more territory, where they forced the king to pay dues to the sultan. And, although in 1673 Michal's general, Jan Sobieski, defeated the enemy at Kothyn, reversing most of the former losses, the king did not live to see the recovery. The night before the battle, he died of food poisoning, giving Sobieski's enemies reason to claim that the general had personally ordered his murder in order to better his chances to gain the throne for himself. While there is minimal evidence to verify these charges, whatever the truth, after his great victory Sobieski was elected by the *Sejm* to be the next King of Poland.

Jan III Sobieski, who was also the son of a magnate, had spent some of his time abroad and was a good linguist, speaking several languages including Turkish and Tatar. In 1665 he married a twenty-four-year-old French widow, Marie Casimire, who as a child had come to Poland in the train of the former queen, Ludwika Maria. The king adored his little wife, who was nicknamed 'Marysienka' because of her small size, and the couple would write to each other almost every day while they were apart, a correspondence that gives us a good insight into the events of the time. But, although initially, unlike Michal, Jan Sobieski supported his country's pro-French faction rather than that aligned to the Habsburgs, he gradually grew disillusioned with the policies of Louis XIV, and so began to ally himself more to the emperor's cause. As a result, in 1683 he became the champion of Christendom when his personal interaction saved Vienna from falling to the 'Turks' – the last occasion that the emperor's capital would ever be threatened by the Ottomans. Sobieski arrived in the last stages of the battle when, after two months under siege, the city was on the point of collapse, and by his defeat of the sultan's army he would ensure the future dominance of the Christian faith in Europe.

Following this victory, the king continued to battle against the retreating enemy, but his later campaigns met with less success. In addition, like his predecessors, he found himself increasingly hamstrung by the nobility who, wishing to maintain – if not strengthen – their privileges, endeavoured to prevent him from carrying out the reforms that he sought. Nonetheless, he encouraged the arts and created new buildings, and during his reign the Royal Chapel in Danzig was finally completed. But when he died in 1696, his standing was not enough to guarantee the election of his son, one of the ten candidates put forward as contenders for the throne.

Eventually there were two favourites in the competition to replace Sobieski: the Prince de Conti and Frederick Augustus I, who three years earlier had succeeded his dead brother as Elector of Saxony. It was this man who now managed to persuade the *Sejm* to elect him as Poland's new king. To help his cause, the Saxon had initially used bribes, financed by his plundering of private and public resources, among them Lauenburg, which he sold to Hanover. But the bribes had not been enough, and with the voting soon becoming split, the elector had then brought further pressure to bear on the Poles by marching his troops into the country. Even so doubts remained, and up to the last moment before his coronation at Kraków on 15 September 1697, Frederick Augustus had been uncertain whether he would get possession of the traditional crown needed for the ceremony. To prevent a further hitch, therefore, he had ordered a new one to be made, but this would prove an unnecessary precaution as just the night before the event two of his supporters managed to burrow through the walls of the castle and take the official regalia. So the replacement was unused, and today it is back in Dresden where it was made. While all this had been going on, Frederick Augustus' chief rival, accompanied by five French warships, had arrived in Danzig, but after hearing news of the coronation the Prince de Conti finally conceded defeat and returned to France, leaving the Saxon unopposed on his throne. These events took much of Europe by surprise, and Louis XIV's sister-in-law, the sharp-tongued Liselotte, writing in disgust to her aunt, Electress Sophie of Hanover, condemned the Poles, declaring them 'a treacherous and greedy people' who were 'even worse than the English'.[84]

Although being little over 5 foot 9, the new king, now called Augustus II, would be known by later generations as 'the Strong'. A sturdy, immensely powerful man, he was a heavy drinker, practical joker, and extremely extravagant. Always ambitious and eager to promote himself in any way, among his later aspirations would be a desire to see his Wettin dynasty replacing that of the Habsburgs, with either himself or his son succeeding as the emperor. In his youth he had enjoyed military action, declaring in his memoirs that his sole aim had been 'to win glory as a warrior', but in later years he would appear more rarely on the battlefield.[85] However, when he did, he would arrive in full finery, with decorations, court dress and even large feathers in his hat, creating a sharp contrast with his more practically turned-out contemporaries: Tsar Peter of Russia and Karl XII of Sweden. Despite the huge debts caused by his lavish lifestyle, to impress others he continued to spend exorbitantly, carrying his excess to new heights in 1719 when celebrating his son's wedding with the Emperor Joseph I's daughter. To honour this occasion, he built a particularly large new opera house in Dresden, and then laid on a month of spectacular entertainments, with sumptuous banquets, balls and festivals. He also enjoyed less attractive pursuits, such as the tossing and baiting of animals, or public spectacles like the contest he laid on in 1695 between wild boar, dogs and various rare beasts, including lions and tigers. His hunt was enlivened by the addition of large numbers of game purposely provided for the sport, in one instance, according to Sir Charles Hanbury Williams, the bag including forty-two bison and twenty-five elk. But such behaviour just helped to increase the king's standing among other foreign royalty, and as his prestige grew, many eminent marriage contracts were arranged for his grandchildren. However, while in the words of one of his earliest biographers, Baron Pöllnitz, Augustus' court was 'the most brilliant in Europe', the louche behaviour of king and courtiers also shocked the more puritanical heads of state, such as the Prussian king, Friedrich Wilhelm I.[86]

Eventually, Augustus acknowledged some of his children from the probable eight to ten born as a result of his multiple affairs with lovers or official mistresses, but his risqué reputation was such that exaggerated rumours spead throughout Europe, later encouraged largely by Frederick the Great's sister, Wilhelmine. She made the wildly extravagant claim that he had fathered 365 or more bastards, but, as Tom Sharp has pointed out, this was probably no more than a reference to the eighteenth-century German figure of speech for a large number. Casual over questions of religion, to please the Poles at the time of his election Augustus had converted to Catholicism, but renowned for his tendency to dissimulate, his apostasy appeared to many to have been little more than a pragmatic sham. Having never displayed a sincere adherence to any faith, he now showed a marked disrespect for his new church's teachings. Nonetheless, his conversion would horrify Protestant Europe, the Saxons in particular being appalled as they considered themselves to be the upholders of the Reformation. Similarly, the queen, Christiane Eberhardine, a very devout woman, was so shocked that she refused to attend his coronation, and she would never agree to go to Poland.

Augustus had initially been delighted by his wife, greatly admiring her looks, but later, when she was described uncharitably by the English diplomat George Stepney as having not much 'beauty or wit', she had become sidelined by her husband.[87] While Augustus would advise his son that it was better to contract a dynastic marriage without love, in 1705 the poor, ignored queen would write to her father that she was 'the most miserable wretch on earth'.[88] When eventually in 1733 Augustus died, largely as the result of alcohol poisoning, he sadly summed up his controversial past with the words, 'My whole life has been one uninterrupted sin. God have mercy on me.'[89]

The court in which Augustus had grown up had been equally disreputable. His older brother, the later Elector Johann Georg IV, after his official wedding to the widowed Margravine of Brandenburg-Ansbach, had probably entered into a bigamous marriage with the daughter of his father's mistress – a relationship that was quite possibly, knowingly or unknowingly, incestuous. The 'bride' was the ambitious Magdalena Sybilla, 'Billa', whose growing hold on the young elector would over time enable her to exert ever-increasing power. Having her eye on becoming the official reigning consort, she also received titles, lands, and priceless jewels. But while her relatives were given other notable positions, her rival, the rejected electress, found herself facing not just ever-increasing threats of divorce, but also physical – possibly intentionally murderous – attacks by her hot-tempered husband.[90] Less than three years after Johann Georg's succession, Billa died, to be followed shortly after by the twenty-five-year-old elector himself. While both were said to be the victims of smallpox, it was a period of rumoured or at times real poisonings, causing some historians to have doubts regarding the actual causes of death. Having no clear evidence or answers, this question remains open, but although the contemporary gossip did not accuse Augustus of foul play, he would, nonetheless, benefit from this turn of events. He believed himself to be more suited than his brother to the role of elector, and immediately began clearing the court of the last vestiges of Billa's influence. Her family lost their positions, and her mother – charged with dubious crimes including witchcraft – was incarcerated, tortured, and not released from her harsh confinement for another three years.

This display of ruthlessness, typical of many rulers of the period, would mark Augustus's dealings from time to time. When a certain situation apparently called for a tough response, he would accept with unemotional equanimity the suffering and perhaps death of the particular individual involved. While such would undoubtedly be the case with the Livonian Johann Patkul, some like Oscar Browning would suggest Augustus even considered a hunting 'accident' for his cousin Karl XII.

Yet, despite his obvious flaws, Augustus was in the main a good-natured man who deserves to be given some recognition. A lover of the arts and a passionate collector, he patronised painters and architects and promoted the transformation of his Saxon capital Dresden into one of the most beautiful cultural centres, famous in its time as the 'Florence on the Elbe'. In addition, he created other magnificent country palaces and baroque castles, accumulated astounding collections of paintings and jewels, and – with the help of his virtual prisoner, the bogus alchemist Böttger – introduced to Saxony a first porcelain factory at Meissen; its products were able to compete for quality with those imported from China, and Saxony's priceless discovery would soon become known as 'white gold'. With this innovation, Augustus initiated a fashion that spread quickly over the whole continent, boosting demand and later spawning similar manufacture at Nymphenburg, Derby, Sèvres, Berlin and elsewhere. Furthermore, in 1713, the king bought a new palace in

Warsaw, which he and his son would then alter and enlarge. Although other significant changes were made to this building in the nineteenth century, it was finally destroyed by the departing Germans in 1944. The present financial situation in Poland has temporarily put the plans for its reconstruction on hold, but the nearby Saxon Garden that Augustus opened in 1727 as one of the first such public spaces still exists as a park for the people of Warsaw. And finally, among the lasting traditions the king handed down was the Order of the White Eagle that he founded in 1705. Now re-established after various intervals when it was no longer awarded, this continues today to be given to Poles and certain foreigners of distinction.

A year after Augustus' coronation, Tsar Peter, on his way home from his Grand Embassy to Europe, visited the king for three days in August at Rawa-Ruska – today just inside the Ukrainian border. Having got on well together, the two men then agreed they would form an alliance against their common Swedish neighbour, their intention being to regain some of their countries' former territories. This was equally the objective of one of Augustus' cousins, Frederik IV of Denmark, who now began to make similar preparations, and by early 1700 the two kings had started to pursue their own personal ends, both eager to attack their other cousin, Karl XII. Making no actual declaration of war, early in the year Augustus mounted the first surprise assault, sending several hundred Saxons to try and capture the Swedish fortress in Livonia at Riga, but this ultimately came to nothing after the soldiers were debilitatd by frostbite. As a second endeavour was no more successful, in March the Saxons abandoned their efforts and moved a short way downstream to the mouth of the Düna (Daugava), where they were eventually able to take the smaller Dünamünde fort. Although they then returned to renew their attack on Riga, after hearing of the events in Denmark, finally in August they lifted the siege.

Earlier in March, while Peter remained engaged with the Ottomans, the Danish king had made his own surprise attack against the Swedes in Holstein. Karl had immediately responded and by August he had defeated Frederik, forcing him – just the day before the tsar finally officially joined the war – to withdraw from the hostilities. Following this first success, the eighteen-year-old Swedish king then moved on to crush the tsar's larger army at Narva in November, before moving south the following July to face the Saxons who were still in the region of Riga. Although Augustus had hoped to take part in this battle, he had recently been injured in a riding accident and was unable to do so. However, despite the *Sejm* still refusing him permission to engage Commonwealth troops, he now had a larger army, his Saxons having been joined by German mercenaries and some of Peter's Russians. But, having negotiated a skilful crossing of the river by Dünamünde, Karl defeated his enemy, and with that he marched into the neighbouring Courland. While here, furious at his cousin's treachery, he would make his first demand to the Poles that they should depose their king, but before any agreement was reached, in early 1702 Karl had moved on again, now having entered Poland itself. Feeling threatened by his arrival, the *Sejm* at last gave Augustus permission to keep Saxon soldiers in the country, and to employ Commonwealth troops in his army. This, however, would be of little help to the king when in the following July the two cousins had their only meeting in battle at Kliszów. The Poles soon abandoned the field and Karl won yet another great victory, forcing Augustus to retreat. With that, for the next four years the Swedish king would continue his successful campaigning across the country.

While Karl was a stubborn man, driven by his determination to punish each of his declared enemies, Augustus was equally inflexible. Therefore, in 1704 he refused the Swede's demand for him to abdicate in Poland, and with that the country was plunged into civil war. But after the Swedish invasion of his Saxon electorate two years later, Augustus finally acknowledged in a secret agreement that he had lost his Polish throne. When the news of this became public, there was amazement, and some would ridicule him for surrendering too lightly. Others were more shocked by his acceptance of certain terms of the agreement – in particular the surrender of Patkul, who having (mistakenly) ensured the king of the support waiting for him in Swedish Livonia, had also been instrumental in setting up his negotiations with Tsar Peter. But once the Saxon had agreed to hand the rebel over, there was little he could do to save him from Karl's savage revenge. While, years later, after regaining his throne, Augustus would arrange for the recovery of the executed victim's remains, for the time being all his influence had gone, and in Poland the Swedish king had already promoted his successor.

Under pressure from the Swedes, the *Sejm* had finally concurred with Karl's choice, at last agreeing to elect the Polish nobleman Stanislaw Leszczyński, who the following year in 1705 was crowned Stanislaw I, the ceremony taking place in the less historic setting of Warsaw rather than Kraków. However, Leszczyński did not keep his new position for long, soon being deprived of the active support of his Swedish champion. Having renewed his campaign against the Russians, in 1709 Karl suffered his major defeat at Poltava in the Ukraine, and was forced to flee to the protection of the sultan. With the political situation now reversed, Leszczyński decided to give up his crown, but, on visiting Karl in the Ottoman Empire, was temporarily dissuaded from doing so. However, Augustus had other plans, and, having marched to meet Peter at Thorn (Toruń), a little over 100 miles south of Danzig, he drew up a new treaty. Then, with the tsar's help, the deposed Augustus was finally able to recover his throne, and Leszczyński abdicated. Having started his exile on Swedish soil, in 1714 the ousted king chose to settle on Karl's privately inherited lands at Zweibrücken in the Rhineland. Here, two years later, a Saxon officer would try to assassinate him, but he would be saved by

A fifteenth-century depiction of Lübeck from the Nuremberg Chronicle.

Riga's House of Blackheads as it is today, after its reconstruction in the 1990s. [Courtesy of Diliff under Creative Commons]

Visby in an image created for the nineteenth-century 'Voyages de la Commission scientifique du Nord', showing the city walls, white limestone cathedral, and some of the churches probably ruined by the men of Lübeck.

Above: The effigies of Sweden's deposed king, Albrecht of Mecklenburg, and his wife, on their tombs in Doberan Abbey near Rostock.

Left: A mocking portrait of Lübeck's mayor Jürgen Wullenwever, painted in 1537, two years after his death. The inscription describes him as a seditionist and champion of conspirators, who deserved his (savage) execution. [St Ann's Museum, Lübeck]

Above: Christian II, King of Denmark, with his wife Isabella, sister of Emperor Charles V, as portrayed in the Helsingør altarpiece painted in about 1514. [National Museum of Denmark]

Below left: Frederik II of Denmark – creator of Kronborg, the 'Elsinore Castle' made famous by Hamlet. [Rijksmuseum]

Below right: Christian IV, Denmark's longest serving monarch, painted by Karel van Mander. [National Museum of Sweden]

Above left: Gustavus Adolphus, King of Sweden, by Jacob Hoefnagel. [Royal Armoury, Sweden]

Above right: Gustavus Adolphus' unstable wife, Maria Eleonora, mother of Queen Christina. [National Museum of Sweden]

Left: Queen Christina of Sweden painted by David Beck in 1650, a few years before her abdication. [National Museum of Sweden]

Above: View of Long Market, Danzig (Gdańsk) looking towards the town hall where Zygmunt II's statue tops the spire.

Right: The Apotheosis of Gdańsk on the ceiling of the Red Room in the city's town hall.

Engraving of Marie Louise Gonzaga's proxy wedding to King Wladyslaw IV of Poland, at which the Polish cortege so amazed the people of Paris in 1645. [Metropolitan Museum of Art]

Above: Drottningholm Palace, which was rebuilt by Nicodemus Tessin 'the Elder' in the 1660s for the dowager Queen Hedvig Eleonora.

Left: The 'Sunny Side' of the Nyhavn in Copenhagen, now a popular tourist destination.

Below left: Frederik V's statue, erected in the Amalienborg, that probably cost more to create than the four surrounding palaces together.

Right: Tsar Alexis, whose iconic portrait epitomises the style of ancient Russia before his son Peter the Great introduced his reforms. [National Museum of Sweden]

Below left: An engraving of Peter I, based on the picture painted in England by Sir Godfrey Kneller that was then given to King William. It marked a break with traditional Russian portraiture and, considered a good likeness, would frequently be copied. [*Rambaud's Russia*, 1898]

Below right: Empress Elizabeth of Russia, painted *circa* 1743–49 by Georg Christoph Grooth. [Metropolitan Museum of Art]

Above left: The largest palace in St Petersburg during Peter I's reign, belonging to his rich and powerful favourite, Alexander Menshikov.

Left: Peterhov's Great Cascade with the Samson Fountain that commemorated the victory at Poltava.

Below: The favourite summer palace built by Rastrelli for Count Biron at Rundāle, (today in Latvia). Although smaller than his main palace nearby at Jelgava, it gives an indication of the wealth and power of Empress Anna's favourite. Despite his disgrace after her death, he eventually returned to Rundāle in the 1760s and then visited it frequently until he died in 1772. After the Third Partition of Poland, Catherine the Great gave the palace to the Zubovs, and it ultimately became the possession of her last favourite, Platon Zubov.

Schlüsselburg Fortress in Lake Ladoga, where Ivan VI was ultimately held prisoner until his death. [Artem]

The ornate Baroque Catherine Palace, designed for Empress Elizabeth by Rastrelli, seen from the gardens.

The Winter Palace in St Petersburg, seen from the Neva, with Catherine the Great's Small Hermitage on the left, between the main building and the Old Hermitage.

Above: The palace of Sans Souci, seen from below the vine-covered terraces.

Left: Frederick II, 'the Great'. [Rijksmuseum]

Below left: The simple grave of Frederick II in the gardens of Sans Souci, where visitors still leave potatoes as a mark of respect.

Above left: The later Peter III and Catherine II in 1756, while they were the Grand Duke and Grand Duchess of Russia. [National Museum of Sweden]

Above right: Vigilius Eriksen's portrait in the throne room at Peterhof that shows Catherine II at the time of the 1762 coup when she came to power. [National Museum of Denmark]

Below: A map demonstrating the three partitions of Poland. [Halibutt under Creative Commons 3.0]

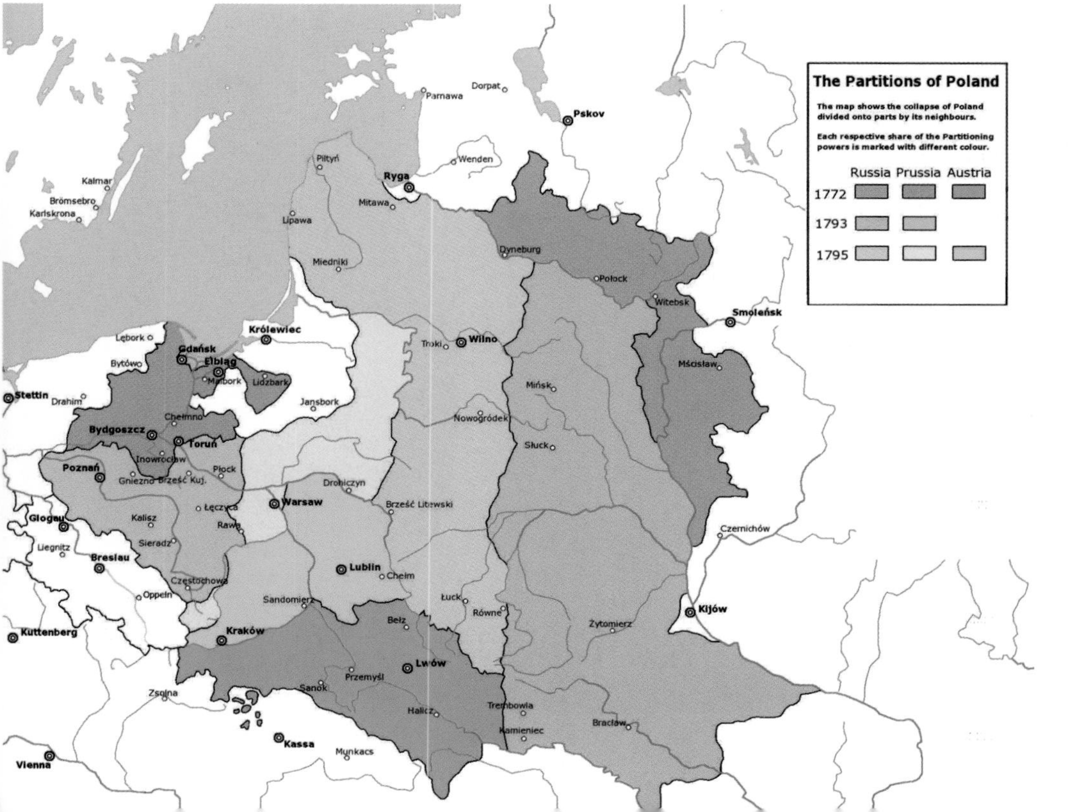

Left: Catherine II's former lover Stanislaw II Augustus Poniatowski, the King of Poland.

Below left: Caroline Mathilde, the disgraced Queen of Denmark, painted by Carl Gustav Pilo. [National Museum of Sweden/Anna Danielsson]

Below right: The doctor Johann Struensee, the queen's lover, who gained supreme power in Denmark, but was eventually executed for treason. [National Museum of Sweden/Bodil Beckman]

Above left: Alexander I, the tsar who five years after Tilsit would face Napoleon's ill-fated invasion of Russia. [Rijksmuseum]

Above right: The statue of Luise of Prussia and her younger sister (on the right) that was made at the time of their joint engagements around 1793. [Staatliche Museen zu Berlin/Friedrichswerdersche Kirche, photograph by Til Niermann]

Below: After the Treaties at Tilsit in 1807 Prussia had to cede the territories marked with a blue line, retaining only those in pink. After 1815, some areas were regained (green) or given as compensation for the kingdom's losses (yellow). The other coloured parts were later acquisitions.

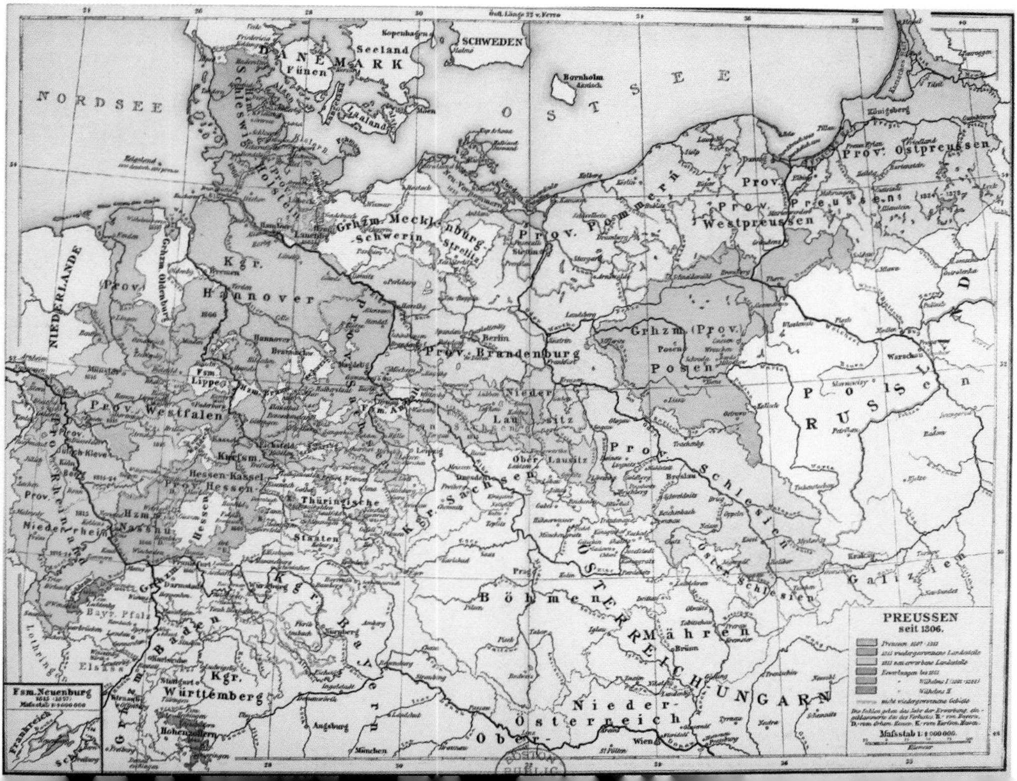

Above left: Nicholas I, painted towards the end of his reign when his pressures were mounting, his problems eventually culminating in 1853 with the outbreak of the disastrous Crimean War. [*Electic Magazine*, 1850s]

Above right: Alexander II, 'the Liberator', who, twenty years after ending serfdom in Russia, would die following a seventh attempt on his life. [National Archives of Canada]

Below: The Church of the Saviour on the Spilled Blood that was built over the spot on the canal embankment where Alexander II was fatally wounded by a bomb in 1881.

Above left: Alexander III, the Slavophile tsar, who wished to return his country to its old Russian ways. [Rijksmuseum]

Above right: Empress Maria (on the right) with her favourite sister Queen Alexandra in 1903. [Library of Congress]

Below left: Alexandra ('Alix'), the adored, but extremely shy, wife of Nicholas II. Already feeling the pressure of her role as empress, her deep concerns for her chronically sick son would then put her under further intense strain. [Library of Congress]

Below right: This disrespectful cartoon of Rasputin suggests his closeness to the Russian imperial couple, but other images would be still more slanderous.

Above: A painting of the new Swedish dynasty, the Bernadottes, showing Karl IV Johan, and his successors – the future Oscar I and his son, Karl XV (on the king's immediate right), and Oscar II (on the extreme left of the painting) next to Queen Desideria. [National Museum of Sweden]

Below left: The strong-willed Maria Pavlovna, 'Miechen', the wife of Grand Duke Vladimir, whose court rivalled that of the imperial couple, and whose son Kirill in 1924 offended the Empress Maria Feodorovna by pronouncing himself the new Russian tsar. [Library of Congress]

Below right: The fairy-tale Schwerin Castle, built in the mid-1800s, that displayed the wealth and importance of the Mecklenburg-Schwerin family at the time.

his diplomat Stanislaw Poniatowski, a veteran from Poltava.[f] Then in 1720 Leszczyński moved again, this time going to Wissenbourg in Alsace, and here he remained for five years, until at last French nobles came looking for a suitable wife for the fifteen-year-old Louis XV. Wanting to find a young woman with little if any political influence, they had decided on Leszczyński's impoverished, and probably tractable, daughter Maria. Rather than growing up in the courtly environment of wealth and political intrigue, she had shared the uncertainties and hardships of her father's exile, even, on one bizarre occasion, having been nearly abandoned in her cot in the stable, forgotten by everyone during a hurried escape. With her now becoming the most senior woman in France, her father was found more suitable accommodation in the Loire's large royal *château* at Chambord.

Meanwhile, Augustus, as the re-established King of Poland, had rejoined the fighting, remaining involved in the hostilities until the end of the Great Northern War and the final defeat of Sweden. But by the time of the peace, the king was facing increased opposition from the *Sejm*. Having attempted unsuccessfully to return as Poland's absolute ruler, he had sought to enforce his authority by again bringing his troops into the country from Saxony. However, as this was contrary to his coronation pledge, tensions grew that again raised the spectre of widespread rebellion. In his preferred Saxony, where, according to Pöllnitz he was adored, his rule was absolute, but in Poland, he had only 'the vain Pageantry of Royalty'.[91] With his power more limited than that any other sovereign, Augustus now appealed to his ally for support and, responding to his request, in 1717 Peter brought his troops into the country and stationed them in Warsaw. This enabled the tsar to assert his authority over the *Sejm*, leaving the nobles unable to speak and enact their *liberum veto* that over the years had so often brought stalemate to most of the proceedings. Their tacit compliance in this so-called 'Silent *Sejm*' demonstrated the extent to which the Polish king and his parliament had now lost their power. Besides showing how much the tables had turned since Peter's first meeting with the king, it marks the beginning of the Russian hegemony that in time would come to exert full authority over the Commonwealth's affairs.

Finally, in early 1733 Augustus became so seriously ill that on arriving in Warsaw he needed assistance to leave his carriage, but then while struggling into the palace he 'unfortunately struck the toe of his distempered foot such a blow' that it began to bleed, after which he passed out, and did not come round for several hours.[92] This caused the infection to spread and after a fever had taken hold, the sixty-two-year-old king died early on the morning of 1 February. Following his death Stanislaw Leszczyński returned to Poland in disguise, once more

---

f He should not be confused with his son of the same name, the later lover of Catherine the Great and future King of Poland.

intent on regaining his throne, but, although he was acknowledged in Warsaw, the Russian troops then brought pressure on the *szlachta* and persuaded the nobles to proclaim the dead Saxon king's only legitimate son as Augustus III. Now Leszczyński, who had lost the loyalty of men such as his former supporter Poniatowski, fled to Danzig, where he awaited the arrival of his allies the French. But with their fleet soon being recalled, the Russians would be the first to reach the area, and in February 1734 they began their eight-month-long siege of the city. And although, at last, in May five more French ships arrived with back-up, their small force was defeated by the Russians and the War of the Polish Succession now began in earnest. In June Danzig fell, the day after Stanislaw Leszczyński, again in disguise, had fled the country to Könisberg in Ducal Prussia. By that time Augustus III had been crowned, the coronation having taken place in Kraków in January 1734, and so finally, exactly two years later, Leszczyński officially abdicated for the second time.

When the peace was eventually ratified nearly three years later in November 1738, Augustus III was at last publicly acknowledged as the new monarch. But Stanislaw Leszczyński was also allowed to retain the honorary title of king, and he was further compensated with an alternative position as a ruler. He was now given a lifetime holding of the recently acquired French possession of Lorraine, a duchy that was granted to him on the proviso that the region would be returned to France on his death. With some relief, Stanislaw Leszczyński left the Château of Chambord, a castle that during his eight years as resident he had found to be damp in winter and plagued by mosquitoes in summer. He moved to his new court at Lunéville near his capital, Nancy. A follower of the Enlightenment, he would be regularly visited by Voltaire and his mistress Madame du Châtelet, and here he became a patron of learning and the arts, among other things setting up an academy for the free education of young men from Poland. He also encouraged new urban planning, one of his most exceptional works being the development of Nancy's spectacular central square that is now named in his honour. With its surrounding eighteenth-century buildings and central nineteenth-century bronze statue of the king, this is today a UNESCO World Heritage Site.

A popular and kind ruler who would even send his blessing to his later successor Stanislaw II Poniatowski, his reign in the duchy would last for nearly thirty years. Although when he finally died in 1766 he had reached the impressively advanced age of eighty-eight, his death would be caused by a tragic accident. Having fallen asleep close to the fire, his clothes had caught alight, leaving him with such serious burns that he was unable to survive for more than a few days. Initially he was buried in Nancy, but after the French Revolution his remains were taken back to Kraków, where his tomb would then join those of the many other Polish monarchs in Wawel Cathedral.

The new King of Poland, Augustus III, had been brought up a Lutheran by his mother in Saxony, but to help ensure his succession and to further his marriage chances with the emperor's daughter, while he was on his European travels, in Bologna in 1712 he had converted to Catholicism, keeping the matter secret until after the death of his Protestant grandmother five years later. In 1719 he had finally married Maria Josepha, the oldest child of Emperor Joseph I, a young woman who had been expected to succeed her uncle Emperor Charles VI until – six years before her marriage – he had persuaded Europe to accept his own daughter Maria Theresa instead. Despite the uncharitable remark of the often acerbic English diplomat Hanbury Williams, who later described Maria Josepha as 'ugly beyond painting and malicious beyond expression', the marriage was happy and the queen, a devoted mother, would produce sixteen children, many of whom married into the senior royal houses of Europe.[93] Among these, one would become the wife of the French Dauphin and the mother of Louis XVI, Louis XVIII and Charles X.

Maria Josepha was devoutly Catholic, but nonetheless, she encouraged religious tolerance. She enjoyed spending time in Poland and would set out to learn its language. In contrast, her husband during the three decades he was on the throne stayed in his kingdom for only around three years in total, usually just visiting when his security was threatened in Dresden. This would be particularly the case in the last years of his reign, when most of Europe became tied up in the horrors of the Seven Years' War. Although Poland, protected by Empress Elizabeth, would be largely able to escape involvement in the conflict, Augustus' separate electorate was not so lucky. The fighting had started in 1756 when Frederick II, without warning, had invaded Saxony. After that he had set himself up in the country, using it as a source of manpower and also as a base from where he could finance his war by flooding neighbouring Poland with his debased coinage. In time, the Austrians would oust the Prussians, but Frederick would return in 1760 and try and retake the capital. Although he was unsuccessful, Dresden was left seriously damaged, adding to the grim toll of destruction, loss of life, and financial ruin suffered by the electorate during these years.

Augustus III was an idle, seriously overweight man, who spent most his time enjoying hunting and other similar diversions. Preferring life in Saxony, he took little interest in Polish affairs. But as he was happy to leave the running of his kingdom to the *szlachta*, many of the nobles were content with his lack of interference. Others became dissatisfied with their sovereign and began to consider mounting a coup to replace him. Although the proposed conspiracy came to nothing, when the king died in 1763 the *Sejm* turned their back on the Wettin dynasty of Saxon rulers. Having rejected the candidature of Augustus III's son, the *szlachta* elected instead the young Stanislaw Poniatowski, the son of that diplomat and politician of the same name who had once saved and supported Leszczyński.

Poniatowski was a member of the Polish nobility, with connections through marriage to the powerful so-called *Familia* of the Czartoryskis. His earlier affair with the Grand Duchess Catherine, which had begun while he was serving under the British ambassador in St Petersburg, had been a key turning point in his life. Although the relationship had come to an end when he had been forced to leave the Russian capital, he would remain devoted to Catherine for years to come and the affair would prove to have changed his future forever.

With the succession of Peter III in 1761, Russia had withdrawn from the war. But while the conflict still ground on elsewhere, Augustus III had fled his electorate to Warsaw. Finally, when peace came, he decided to return to Saxony, only then to die shortly after his arrival back in Dresden. By this time the new Russian tsar had been dead for more than a year, his six-month-long reign having come to an untimely end when his wife Catherine had seized his throne. As she was now empress, on Augustus' death she decided to promote the election of her former lover to the Polish crown, hoping thereby to maintain the influence that Russia had been exerting on the country over the past decades. By offering financial sweeteners and threatening military intervention, Catherine persuaded the *szlachta* to elect her candidate, and with that Poniatowski was crowned at Warsaw, taking the names of his predecessors as Stanislaw II Augustus. Some of the nobility opposed his election on the grounds of his apparent closeness to Russia, and the more conservative were also shocked by his appearance at the coronation. Expecting their monarch to appear dressed in the traditional Polish style, they disapproved of his breeches and long hair, fashions that were more typical of western European courts.

During the early period of Stanislaw II's reign, what he called his 'years of hope', he began programmes of reform. Following his Enlightenment principles, he initiated various cultural changes, including the promotion of learning and the introduction of new music and art. At the same time, in Warsaw he brought in urban lighting, improved the streets and commissioned the construction of buildings in the latest classical style, with the result that his capital would become known as 'the Paris of the East'. Nevertheless, like his predecessors, he was confronted with the difficult task of appeasing a fractious nobility, who constantly prioritised their private interests over those of the country as a whole. Several objected to his reforms, and later he was even opposed by some of his relations in the *Familia*, who preferred to advance and protect their personal positions. And while Russia remained a dominating presence, threatening war or invasion if ever it believed its influence to be at risk, some of the wealthy magnates began to form confederations. These traditional, historic Polish forms of protest against the government were then manipulated by the Russians in order to increase the king's difficulties and make him more dependent on his 'protectress' the empress. Faced with these challenges, Stanislaw Poniatowski wavered, often uncertain which side to favour, and his indecision only added to his unpopularity. He was accused by both parties, blamed by some for being too much in Catherine II's camp, and by others for not supporting the Russians enough.

Continuing to believe that Catherine still cared for him, Stanislaw did not appreciate that her overriding objective was now to further Russia's prospects. Driven by her ambitions for the country, she – like Frederick II of Prussia – wanted to keep Poland in a weakened state to prevent it becoming a threat to her empire. So she upheld the *liberum veto*, not just to keep the *Sejm* unworkable, but also to block the king's reforms. She feared that these might undermine Russia's internal security, and even perhaps tempt some of her own people to migrate. And Stanislaw II's problems were increased by the smallness of the Polish army, it still being restricted in size by the terms of the agreement first drawn up with Tsar Peter in 1717. As a result, when his neighbours began to encroach on his lands and the discord started to develop into civil war, Stanislaw did not have the necessary forces to resist his opposition. Disheartened by the difficulties facing him, and disappointed by his failures, he told the British envoy James Harris that he would have already thrown his crown of thorns to the devils had he not been ashamed 'to abandon his post'.[94]

These problems became fully evident when in 1768 a group of nobles became so angered by the Russian intervention that they came together at Bar to form a new confederation. The movement spread with outbreaks of rebellion erupting throughout the country, and the resulting civil war continued for the next four years. At first the king supported the rebel faction, but then realising that the situation was threatening to undermne the stability of the whole country, he changed his mind and began to go against it. Initially the rebels gained the backing of certain foreign powers, and in 1770, from their headquarters in the Hungarian kingdom, they announced the dethronement of the king. Going further, the following year on the evening of 3 November a small group attacked the king's carriage while he was driving through Warsaw. Four of his escort were killed and Stanislaw was wounded before being captured and spirited out of the city. But the plot had been badly planned, and those accompanying him soon became lost in the countryside. As a result by the next morning Stanislaw had been rescued and was back in Warsaw, where he was welcomed enthusiastically by the people. In Poland the event revived support for the king, and abroad the news horrified the foreign powers, who now withdrew their backing of the opposition. But the War of the Bar Confederation would produce two further results. First, in the south-east Catherine's soldiers pursued the remaining rebels into the Ottoman Empire, leading to the outbreak of another Russian-Turkish war, and, second, it gave the Commonwealth's neighbours an excuse to carry out their first dismantlement of Stanislaw's country. Even before the fighting was over, Austria and Prussia had begun to seize Polish territory on their borders and, being soon joined by Russia, the three powers began to plan the First Partition of Poland.

Having long had his eyes on the Baltic area of Polish Royal Prussia, the region that since the fifteenth century had separated his eastern duchy from his Brandenburg lands, Frederick II now saw his chance to take possession of the intervening territory. However, he realised that he must first find a resolution that would satisfy both Catherine and the Austrians. Wanting to separate the Habsburgs from a potential alliance with the French, Frederick set out to persuade the Russians to cede their newly captured Moravia to the rulers in Vienna, tempting Catherine by way of compensation with the promise of lands on Russia's Polish border. The Prussian king believed that this would satisfy all parties. Although the Austrians had feared Russian expansion into their neighbouring Ottoman region, and Frederick's compromise would be to their advantage, Maria Theresa initially balked at the idea, but sharing the rule of her country with her son, Joseph II, she eventually submitted to pressure from him and her forceful minister, Kaunitz. As a result, the First Partition went ahead in 1772, causing Frederick to mock Maria Theresa with the words, 'She wept and she took.'[95] He then went on to question sarcastically how she, a pious woman, had squared her action with her confessor. The partition would in fact always be something that troubled her, and she wrote to Joseph on 20 January 1772 regarding their newly promised acquisitions: 'I shall always regard our possession as having been bought too dearly, since they were purchased at the expense of the honour, of the reputation of the Monarchy, of our good faith and virtue.'[96] And again she later declared, 'I am haunted by it now. It weighs sharply on my heart and tortures my brain and embitters my days.'[97] The rest of Europe was shocked by the event, but they were still recovering from the ravages of the Seven Years' War and, fearing to bring on a repeat of that conflict, did nothing to help the Poles. Having forced Stanislaw to concede to their terms, the three powers left him with just the central part of his country, which comprised around two-thirds of its former territory and half its population. Although he had been unable to resist the aggressive actions of his neighbours, the threat of invasion having presented him with no option of refusal, he was condemned by many Poles for his apathetic acceptance of this virtual theft of their lands.

The First Partition added further to Poland's problems in more ways than one. While the country was greatly impoverished by its loss of some of its most valuable territory – including the greater part of its important trading areas along the Baltic shore – Prussia now also imposed on the Poles some particularly severe new customs regulations. Stanislaw received no better treatment from the Russians who, despite still representing themselves as Poland's protectors, actively opposed any of his reforms that they felt threatened their own position. Still powerless in the face of this, the year after the Partition he saw all too clearly the reality of his position. Catherine's ambassador in Warsaw, Stackelberg, reported to the king that she had announced that if he continued to resist her, she would have him deposed and his advisers executed. Finally recognising the true state of her feelings for him, Stanislaw wrote, 'This last blow, I confess, has pierced my heart because it attacks my dignity and most of all because it comes straight from her whom my heart has never wronged.'[98]

More than a decade later, on 6 May 1787 Stanislaw travelled to Kaniów on the Dnieper River to meet Catherine on her way south to visit the new territories that she had recently annexed in the Crimea. Here on her galley, the two rulers met for the first time in around thirty years, a meeting which she later described as being rather embarrassing. She also added that both had found each other greatly changed, and although some witnesses said the lunch was 'very merry', others reported that the atmosphere seemed tense.[99] After they had spent around half an hour in private, Stanislaw emerged apparently saddened, and later he would be disappointed by the empress's refusal to attend the ball that he had arranged for her that night. However, he had used the occasion to put forward his plans for an alliance, one by which he promised Commonwealth troops to assist Russia in its wars against the Ottomans, for which he would receive in exchange some new possessions in Moldavia and on the Black Sea. Before they parted, Catherine complimented him, declaring that she liked his idea and thought it good, and Stanislaw's correspondence shows that he remained positive about the results of their meeting. He was particularly encouraged on learning that she had later been discussing Poland's affairs with the Emperor Joseph II, and that she had also remarked that 'the King of Poland must be made happy, he deserves it.'[100] But while these things helped him retain his trust in Catherine for a little longer, in the event his plans were never fulfilled. Moreover, he would eventually be let down by the Habsburgs as well, despite the promised support of Joseph II, who at this point had declared that Poland would lose no further territory. But for the time being, Stanislaw retained enough mistaken confidence to write to Stanislaw Badeni that now 'nobody will take even a scrap of land from us.'[101]

The following year in 1788, the Great *Sejm* opened, a parliamentary session that would last for four years, a period during which a group of magnates openly opposed the king and his government. Calling themselves the Patriots, and wearing traditional Polish dress, they declaimed their opposition to Russian dominance and demanded that Poland should be given greater autonomy. Gaining support from the Prussians, who now feared the influence of a Russian-Austrian alliance, these Patriots were able to achieve a withdrawal of Catherine's troops. But they also wanted to make the country better able to stand up to the growing Prussian and Russian forces, and so they overturned the limits that had been earlier placed on the size of the Polish army – paying for these increases by ordering taxes to be levied for the first time on the *szlachta* and the Church. Although Stanislaw had originally opposed the Patriots, he now began to support them, approving these and their other reforms. Then, by choosing a moment when several of the more conservative members were not present, the parliamentary deputies managed to pass a new constitution on 3 May 1791. When word of this spread to the streets of Warsaw, a *Te Deum* was sung in the church and the burgers carried the king in triumph through the city. This constitution, preceded only by that of America, was also hailed by liberals and freethinkers throughout many countries of Europe, and the period would later be referred to as Poland's First Republic. While the reactionary members of the *szlachta* were strongly opposed to any potential loss of their liberties, Catherine had also been shocked by the events happening in France, and she was now becoming deeply concerned about the potential rise of Jacobinism on her borders.

Following the fall of the Bastille and the Declaration of the Rights of Man in 1789, a mood of republicanism had begun to spread throughout Poland, and this increased the opposition of those who already objected to the recent reforms. Fearing, among other things, a loss of their country's autonomy as a result of the constitution, in 1792 some Lithuanians approached Catherine in St Petersburg and having received her assurance of protection, in April they announced a confederation at Targowica – a town on the Russian-Commonwealth border. Claiming to be the legal government, this confederation then annulled the constitution and demanded the abdication of the king. With that, assisted by Catherine's troops, the rebels marched into the Commonwealth, and war broke out. Although the Polish army had been allowed to grow by the Great *Sejm*, it still remained considerably smaller than that of the Russians, but nonetheless, the loyal Poles won some early victories – their successes backed by Stanislaw who hoped that they would ultimately bolster his position at the negotiating table. In a further, later bid to save his country, he also promised Catherine he would appoint her grandson Constantine as heir to his throne. But she refused to consider his terms, and so, finally, wanting to avoid more serious unrest, Stanislaw decided to follow the wishes of his cabinet; having changed his allegiances, he agreed at last to join the Targowica Confederation, and with his acknowledgement of Russia's authority, the war came to an end.

At this moment the new Prussian king, Friedrich Wilhelm II, saw his own chance for further expansion, and he now broke his previous alliance with the Poles to make a separate agreement with Catherine. This resulted in the Second Partition of Poland of 1793, a further dismemberment of the country by the two powers that left it with only around 83,000 square miles and a mere four million people. Most of Poland's historical lands were now lost and the important city of Danzig – exempted from the First Partition – finally became a Prussian possession. Adding to Stanislaw's humiliation, Catherine insisted that the new Partition should be ratified by the *Sejm*, this taking place in the Lithuanian city of Grodno, rather than in Warsaw, the centre for rebellious Poles. After being subjected to Russian bullying, including at times physical abuse and outright threats, the deputies eventually did as they were asked and accepted the official annulment of the constitution. With Russians now the dominating presence throughout the country, numbers of Poles resigned their positions, and many people went abroad. Finally, having lost all faith in Catherine, Stanislaw recognised how little he meant to her, he at last understanding that her primary loyalties were to Russia alone.

After the Second Partition the remaining area of Poland found itself still more economically and commercially weakened. Although it remained technically independent, in effect Russians held positions of authority, their position secured by their troops stationed in the towns. But not all opposition had been quashed, and Andrzej Tadeusz Kosciuszko, one of Poland's national heroes, would lead a rebellion that broke out in Kraków in March 1794. During the Kosciuszko Uprising that would last for nearly eight months, the newly created Polish army, comprising both regular soldiers and peasants armed with scythes, defeated the Russians and took back Kraków and Warsaw. While this was not supported by everyone, the king personally contributed to the cause, and for a time the insurrection succeeded. But Stanislaw's potential defender, Emperor Joseph, had died, as had his successor, his brother Leopold. With their nephew Franz II now on the throne, the Austrians again joined forces with the Russians and the Prussians to defeat the Poles, and in November they retook Warsaw. The following January, Catherine again forced Stanislaw to leave the capital for Grodno, and here he remained a prisoner in the castle for the next two years.

With that, the three powers drew up the Third Partition, dividing the remaining Polish territory between them, the largest portion going to Russia, Warsaw to Prussia, and Kraków, now a Free City, put under the protection of the emperor. A month after the agreement was signed, on 25 November 1795, Stanislaw II Augustus finally abdicated, and the powers, not satisfied with anything less than Poland's obliteration, then proceeded to remove it from all documents. The country was literally wiped off the map.

Almost exactly a year after Stanislaw's abdication, Catherine died, and just a few months later her son Paul, invited the deposed king to settle in St Petersburg. Stanislaw had originally wished to go abroad, possibly taking up his exile in Italy, but he had found himself financially unable to do so. Therefore, having sold his own lands in Poland, he accepted the tsar's invitation, and on arriving in St Petersburg was provided with accommodation in the Marble Palace, the magnificent building that years before Catherine had given to her lover, Count Orlov – the man who had replaced Stanislaw first in her favours. Whether or not this was an intentional insult on the behalf of the tsar is unknown, as are his reasons for inviting Stanislaw to Russia in the first place. A complex, often irrational man, Paul may have wished even after her death to offend his hated mother, or publicly criticise her past policies and behaviour. Others, however, suggest that he simply wanted to increase his own standing as the host to a banished king. Whatever the truth, Stanislaw regretfully left Grodno on 17 February 1797 and arrived in St Petersburg just under a month later. Over the following year, he was given full honours, and he was frequently visited and entertained by members of the Russian imperial family, and the many Poles living in the capital. He finally died of a stroke on 12 February 1798 (NS). Having ordered a state funeral, the tsar personally led the mourning. Stanislaw was eventually laid to rest in St Catherine's Catholic Church on the Nevsky Prospekt in St Petersburg. Here he would remain until 1938.

Stanislaw II Augustus has become a controversial figure. Over the years many have blamed him for the loss of his country, but responsibility for Poland's demise cannot be laid just at his door. His misfortune was to be king when the country's position was already virtually untenable. Since the Union of Lublin in 1569 the monarch had steadily lost power, increasingly hampered by the selfish ambitions of the *szlachta*, who wished to uphold their rights through the *liberum veto*, and by the magnates whose concerns were centred on the maintenance of their vast estates and immense wealth. Further to that, by the time Stanislaw II came to the throne, Poland was seriously threatened by its neighbours, led in particular by two of the most determined and ambitious rulers of any period: Frederick II of Prussia, and Catherine II of Russia. Undoubtedly, Catherine treated her former lover shabbily, but she too was attempting to rule a potentially unstable country. Her own position was tenuous, she having no imperial blood and being dependent on the loyalty of the Guards who had helped her come to the throne in the most dubious of circumstances. And, although unfairly and inaccurately represented as a highly promiscuous woman with quantities of male lovers at any one moment, in truth by the 1760s she had begun a new long-term monogamous affair with Grigory Orlov, and so Stanislaw's continued professed adoration for her would have been embarrassing at this time. But although Stanislaw would also enjoy several other relationships over the years, his liaisons were mere dalliances and his love for Catherine remained constant, to a certain extent surviving even her later ill treatment of him. He never married, and he broke down on hearing of her death.[g] For several years he dreamed of her as his wife, and imagined that they might rule together, he as King of Poland and she as Empress of Russia. But, after her coronation, Catherine's primary objective became the good of her empire, and like the Prussian king, she feared a strong Poland on her borders. In her determination to prevent such a situation developing, she was not prepared to be influenced by past feelings for its king. The description that Stanislaw had given of himself to Catherine years before could also be true of her: 'Born with a vast and ardent ambition, ideas of reform, of glory and of being useful to my country have become as it were the canvas on which I apply all my affairs and my whole life.'[102] Although at times she was no doubt pragmatic and hard-hearted, the success of her policies was proved by the fact that she was the last ruler in Russia to leave the empire in a relatively strong or stable position when she died. The difficulty of running her vast country became only too obvious with her successors, who would suffer from repeated disasters, including invasion, military defeat, plots, rebellion, revolution and three further assassinations of the ruler, not to mention the eventual abolition of the dynasty.

As Poland's neighbours grew in power, they represented the Commonwealth as a lost cause and a failed state, where the people needed saving from themselves. Justifying their actions by claiming that they were giving protection to the country's religious minorities and preventing its descent into total anarchy, they completed their final Partition with the minimum of opposition from the rest of Europe. The latter, shocked by the events of France, now ignored the country's plight and accepted the obliteration of Poland as the inevitable result of *real politique*. From the start Stanislaw had found himself in a weak position, a mere puppet of Russia, but he remained throughout determined to do his best for his country, modernising it and bringing in the necessary reforms wherever possible. Kind to his servants who loved him, and immensely hard-working, in his last desperate attempt to save his country he was prepared even to humiliate himself. If he had come to the throne in other circumstances, he would have been remembered with affection by his people, but instead for many years he would be forgotten, if not reviled. When in the 1930s the Soviet government advised the Poles of their intentions to demolish the church in Leningrad – formerly St Petersburg – where he was buried, the body was unceremoniously removed and transported to the king's place of birth, Wolczyn, in present-day Belarus. Here his coffin, enclosed in the church walls, would remain in its undistinguished surroundings,

g There were some unconfirmed rumours after his death – probably spread by his mistress herself – that she, Elżbieta Szydłowska, had been his morganatic wife.

suffering from the wear and tear of time, and then ultimately undergoing still greater violence at the hands of the Red Army during the Second World War.

So by the time plans were made in the late 1980s to move Stanislaw back to Poland, what remained of him had been largely scattered. But even now, while some wished him to be buried beside the earlier kings in Wawel Cathedral in Kraków, others continued to oppose such a move, still holding the king as personally responsible for Poland's earlier annihilation. Thus, because of the dissension over how he should be remembered, an awkwardness and uncertainty arose as to where he should be buried, and it was not until 1995 that his battered remains were finally laid to rest in the Cathedral Basilica of St John in Warsaw.

14

Denmark: Success, Scandal and Survival

Christian VII of Denmark by Alexander Roslin. (Courtesy of National Museum, Denmark)

Despite Frederik V's lack of involvement in the running of his country, thanks to the services of his able ministers, he had left Denmark in a stable and prosperous condition, and so when Christian VII, his only surviving son by his marriage to Queen Louise, succeeded just days before his seventeenth birthday, the situation still looked promising. Although the new king was not lacking in intelligence or charm, he was however a delicate man, who had already begun to show signs of a mental instability, a condition that had possibly been worsened by the excessively strict and, at times, brutal upbringing.[h] The harsh and unkind treatment of his first instructors had caused him to develop deep anxieties, and, despite the efforts of his more understanding later Swiss tutor, Élie Reverdil – brought in to teach him French – his early insecurities had continued to develop over the years.

Nonetheless, by the time of Frederik V's death his marriage had already been arranged with his first cousin, the Hanoverian princess Caroline Matilda, granddaughter of George II and sister of the new king, George III. Born in 1751, just three and a half months after her father's death, she was the last of nine siblings, but had been chosen as Christian's wife instead of her sickly older sister Louisa, who died four years after Caroline Matilda's betrothal took place in 1764.

Although her oldest brother had growing concerns about the evident dangers and diplomatic complexities his young, impressionable sister might face, following Frederik V's death the marriage was brought forward. On 1 October 1766, just nine months after Christian's accession, a proxy ceremony took place in London, during which another of Caroline Matilda's brothers, Edward, Duke of York, stood in for the absent bridegroom. Witnesses recorded that during the ceremony, the fifteen-year-old bride appeared pale and tearful, clearly depressed at leaving home and uneasy about what lay ahead of her. Nonetheless, the very next day she set off for her new country and, after a rough crossing to Rotterdam, around three weeks later arrived in the border town of Altona near Hamburg. Here all her ties to her previous home were cut, and Danish attendants replaced those who had accompanied her from England. Now surrounded by strangers, she found herself facing an unknown future in an alien world. Her contemporary, Elizabeth Carter, pessimistically summed up the challenges that confronted the young woman at this time:

> It is worse than dying: for die she must to all she has ever seen or known; but then it is only dying out of one bad world into another just like it, and where she is to have cares and fears, and dangers and sorrows, that will all yet be new to her.[103]

---

h Among other possible reasons for his mental state, some people have questioned whether he had inherited porphyria from his Hanoverian mother. See Johan Schioldann, 'Struensée's memoir of the King'.

Having at last met her future husband in Roskilde, a month later on 8 November at the Christiansborg Palace in Copenhagen, she and Christian took part in another marriage that was then followed by the usual extended weeks of celebrations. The Danes, who had greatly loved their earlier English queen, Louise, enthusiastically welcomed her niece, who, intelligent, musical and well educated, charmed many at court with her attractive personality and swift mastery of Danish – one of the four languages she soon spoke fluently.

However, the informality of the young queen – from this time called by the Danish name Caroline Mathilde – displeased her husband's stepmother, the strict Juliane Marie. Although already connected by her nephew's marriage to Caroline Mathilde's oldest sister, Augusta, the dowager treated the latest arrival with cold formality. So, before long, she turned for companionship to her chief lady-in-waiting, Louise von Plessen, and gradually, against the advice of her more cautious oldest brother, George, came to depend on this older woman, seeing her as a mother figure in whom she could confide.

Von Plessen was a determined, moralistic individual who despised the degeneracy of many of those living at court, and so she set out to protect her mistress from their libertine ways. Moreover, wanting to increase Caroline Mathilde's hold over the king and encourage his greater interest in her, von Plessen persuaded her to ignore her husband's advances, but this, rather than improving the couple's relationship, just succeeded in exacerbating their problems. Christian now gave Caroline Mathilde scarce attention, declaring that it was 'not fashionable' for a husband to love his wife, and as a result, she, feeling increasingly rejected, became more temperamental. Eventually, Reverdil was able to remind the king of his dynastic duty to father an heir, and so in January 1768 the queen gave birth to a son, Crown Prince Frederik.

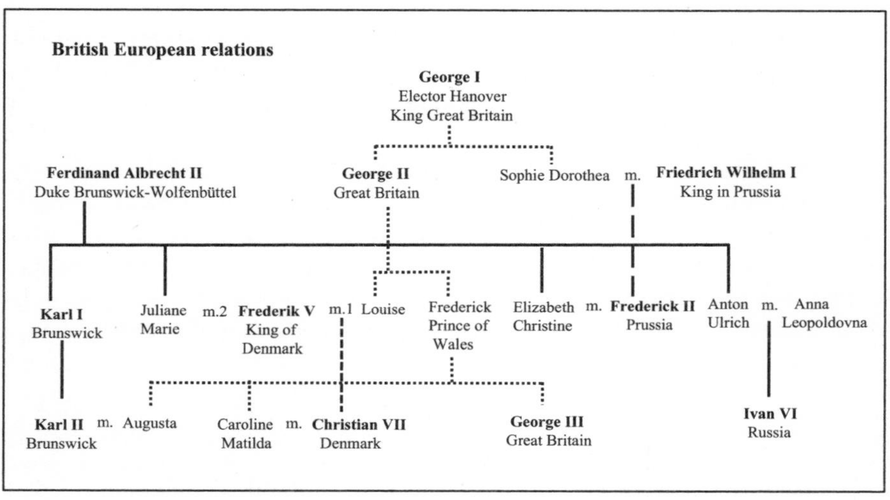

Christian, who had long shown violent tendencies and a preference for sadomasochistic practices, had now begun to spend an even greater amount of time out in the city with his louche companions, drinking to excess, committing acts of vandalism, and visiting the brothels. Going further, he had then taken a mistress, a courtesan dubbed dismissively as Støvlet-Cathrine (Boots Catherine), a name given to her either because of her small feet, or more probably in reference to her mother's role as a bootmaker. Although she was viewed by the nobles as highly unsuitable, the king had given her the title of baroness and brought her to court, and here she remained until shortly before the queen gave birth. However, wishing to avoid a scandal, Christian's ministers at last succeeded in encouraging him to banish the young woman, after which she was imprisoned in Hamburg and then Holstein, before being finally released with a pension in 1770.

The birth of the heir came as a relief to most of the court, even though for the dowager queen, Juliane Marie, it dashed any hopes for the succession of her son, who was now distinguished from his newborn nephew as *Hereditary* Prince Frederik. But while Caroline Mathilde found great happiness in her child, within weeks her chief companion, Louise von Plessen, was summarily sent away from court in punishment for her earlier role in damaging the royal couple's relationship. Unable even to see the queen before leaving, she eventually settled outside Denmark at her property in Celle in the Hanoverian electorate. At the time, von Plessen's dismissal caused much distress to Caroline Mathilde, who had no success in getting the king to reverse his decision, but later, in an ironic twist of fate, after the queen's own disgrace, it would prove to be a source of comfort.

In May 1768, Christian set off with fifty-five companions on what would become an exorbitantly expensive eight-month European tour, travelling through Germany and the Low Countries to England, before returning via Paris to Copenhagen. Because of the king's capricious state of mind, the plans for this trip remained uncertain to the end, and even when they arrived in Holstein, their destination was undecided. According to Bernstorff, the nephew of the Minister of Affairs, 'nothing was assured until the king was seated in his carriage.'[104]

Such behaviour was now typical of Christian's declining mental health, and it was fast becoming apparent that he needed a personal physician to accompany him on his journey. So while the party was in Altona, a young doctor, Johann Struensee, the son of a renowned Prussian Pietist theologian and pastor, was introduced to the king by Enevold Brandt. Brandt, a close friend of Struensee, had earlier been part of the king's circle of wild young companions. And the doctor was also brought to Christian's notice by another acquaintance, the lawyer Count Schack Karl Rantzau-Ascheberg. A devious, ambitious man who had previously been dismissed from the army, Rantzau-Ascheberg saw this introduction as a chance to rehabilitate himself at court. Struensee was now appointed the king's temporary physician, and he remained beside Christian throughout the rest of his tour.

The doctor's caring and attentive approach had a calming effect on his patient, and so by the time the travellers returned to Copenhagen in January 1769, he had made himself indispensable, regarded by Christian as his closest companion and friend.

For the two months he was in England, the king was frequently on the move, making whistle-stop tours to a variety of places, including Manchester, York, and the university towns of Oxford and Cambridge, where he and Struensee would both receive honorary doctorates. Besides the balls and many other entertainments laid on for his amusement, while in London Christian continued to follow his usual, more dissolute pattern of behaviour. He frequented the city's insalubrious nightspots, brought common prostitutes back to St James', and during his visit caused considerable damage to his apartments in the palace. So, while the public at large were charmed by the angelically fair, small and delicate-looking young king, who physically resembled his British relations, his visit was less popular with George III. Not just concerned about the high cost of entertaining his visitors, he had also now become anxious about his sister, having heard stories of his brother-in-law's cruelty to Caroline Mathilde. As a result, George viewed the whole thing as 'very disagreeable', and when eventually the time came, he greeted the Danes' departure with more than a little relief, a feeling expressed in a note to Lord Weymouth dated 8 June 1768.

After leaving England, Christian then moved on with his entourage to Paris, where he remained for a similar length of time, again pursuing a hectic programme that included visits to the theatre, the Sorbonne and the French academies. Recently, Voltaire, shocked by the Catholic Church's persecution of the Protestant Pierre-Paul Sirven, had come to the man's defence, mounting a campaign with the financial support of rulers such as Frederick II of Prussia, Catherine II of Russia, and also Christian. As a result, the Danish king now wished to meet him, but with Voltaire living down in Ferney near the Swiss border, the introduction proved to be impossible. Nonetheless, the Danish emissary arranged a gathering of some twenty or so other famous French Enlightenment thinkers, among them Jean le Rond d'Alembert. While d'Alembert used the occasion to praise the king for his support of the new ideas and scientific discoveries, more tellingly, after the event was over, he wrote to Frederick the Great, giving a further insight into the Danish king's mental and physical state at this time:

> The king of Denmark, whom we have had here for six weeks, left eight days ago, worn out, bored, harassed by celebrations which have exhausted him, dinners where he neither ate nor conversed, and balls where he danced yawning and grimacing. I do not doubt at all that

> when he gets back to Copenhagen he will not issue an edict outlawing balls and dinners for ever.[105]

By the time Christian returned to Denmark, Struensee's position was confirmed and he had been appointed the king's permanent personal physician. Despite having earlier pleaded with her husband to be included on the visit to her homeland, Caroline Mathilde had been excluded on the European tour, and so it was only now that she met Struensee for the first time. Having heard reports of his licentious behaviour, she was initially suspicious of him, wary that he might exert the same negative influence on her husband as had his former favourites. However, when she became seriously ill – suffering apparently from depression, if not, as some suggested, from a sexually transmitted disease caught from Christian – she was instructed to see the doctor. Struensee treated her with sensitivity and paid her the attention she lacked from others, and so little by little her feelings began to change. The doctor encouraged her to take up new activities, riding and even walking – an unheard-of, if not shocking, activity for society women of the period. And finding that they had a common interest in the ideas of the Enlightenment, gradually the couple began to spend more and more time together, until Caroline Mathilde became infatuated with this intelligent and experienced man who was thirteen years older than herself. By the end of February 1770 their friendship had developed into a love affair, and even though Struensee would continue to be unfaithful to the queen, she would remain besotted with him until his death.

As Struensee was still close to Christian, now the relationship between Caroline Mathilde and her husband also improved, leading to the bizarre situation whereby they began to live in a sort of threesome. At the same time as the king's mental instability increased, the doctor, having encouraged Caroline Mathilde to take a greater role in state affairs, started to put himself in the position of her adviser. While his detractors would argue that from the very start his objective had been to attain supreme power, it is hard to believe that even an ambitious man could have envisaged the meteoric rise that he now went on to achieve over the next two years. Although wanting to support his mistress, and no doubt keen to lead Denmark down a more progressive path, at this time he would have been fully aware that his position was dependent on the unreliable approval of Denmark's absolute ruler. Struensee only came to assume full authority as Christian's condition further deteriorated, and the king started to place more and more trust in him. But as the doctor and Caroline Mathilde grew more confident, he began to treat the monarch with less deference, and she started to show a streak of stubbornness that manifested itself in an unwillingness to listen to advice. Her letters to her brother in England became less frequent, and those she wrote displayed a marked change of tone, suggesting she intended to demonstrate to George III that she now had a mind of her own, and was no longer prepared to be Britain's diplomatic pawn.

Shortly after the affair began, Struensee had made himself yet more indispensable to Caroline Mathilde by successfully inoculating the young crown prince during a smallpox epidemic. From that time his influence over the queen steadily increased, he now encouraging her to bring up her child following the freer, but at times more austere, methods suggested by Rousseau in his fashionable text *Emile*. The radical practices that this book recommended broke with the traditional ideas of child-rearing, and Caroline Mathilde's adoption of the Frenchman's ideas shocked many at court. The couple's enemies would later suggest that by following Rousseau's theories they had damaged the boy, leaving him with many of the character flaws of his father. Basing their charges on spurious claims of Prince Frederik's unconventional behaviour, some people hinted at the child's mental deficiencies, maintaining a rumour that would last until the very moment he eventually took power several years later. Up to that time the critics of Caroline Mathilde and Struensee would hold them responsible for Frederik's 'condition', even though he had been removed from his mother's care when he was still only four years old. In reality, the lack of maternal affection and the perfunctory and disparaging treatment he received after the crisis would have had far greater potential to damage his development than anything he had experienced before.

Struensee became Christian's official adviser in May 1770, and by December he had risen still higher to privy counsellor, *Maître des requêtes*, after which he was able to dismiss all the members of the council and take full responsibility in the king's name. From this time, over the next sixteen months while he was in office, a period known as the 'Time of Struensee', he continued to work feverishly, seldom resting, and introducing in the last ten months alone 1,069 new orders. These introduced measures that promoted the ideas of the Enlightenment, including the end of torture, the reduction of the use of the death penalty, and various practical steps for the improvement of the people's daily way of life. In addition, he criminalised bribery, tried to reduce corruption, and brought in freedom of the press, the last spurring Voltaire to write his *Epître au roi de Danemark* in the king's honour. Besides these things, Struensee attempted to reduce costs and improve the state finances by cutting the size of the army, and halting expensive projects and public works – among them the construction of the building later known as the Marble Church. While these savings led to increased unemployment and growing discontent among the people, some other reforms were equally unpopular with the nobility, in particular the measure that had allowed any creditor to arrest his debtor. This had caused several aristocrats to lose their palaces in Copenhagen. Now all these people, as well as the more conservative religious members of society – who condemned Struensee's deist (if not atheist) ideas – joined the doctor's growing number of enemies.

Rather than showing discretion, the queen and her lover continued with their incautious behaviour regardless. On 7 July 1771 Caroline Mathilde gave birth at Hirscholm to a daughter, Louise Auguste, who was soon rumoured to be the doctor's child and dubbed *la petite Struensee*. Ignoring the gossip, at her christening later that month Struensee was appointed a count, the highest honour in the land. And, in addition, just a week after the birth Christian had made him the Privy Cabinet Minister, an appointment that enabled him to act in the king's name and produce his own laws. As this, therefore, dispensed with the need for royal approval or even signature, the doctor had finally gained absolute power. Although by this time concerns were growing in the English court at the reports coming from Denmark, Caroline Mathilde – now a stout, determined woman – bluntly ignored the advice offered by her brother, George III. Similarly, she was cold and offhand when she finally agreed to meet her mother at Lüneburg near Hanover. Although Augusta, Princess of Wales, wished to talk to her daughter privately, Caroline Mathilde claimed to have lost much of her English, and insisted on speaking in German so that the ever-present Struensee might follow the conversation. Therefore, discouraged at not having achieved anything, Augusta returned home, and the two women would never meet again.

Meanwhile, as Christian disliked etiquette and royal duties, to the added displeasure of the dowager queen, Juliane Marie, the royal couple and the doctor seldom attended official functions, choosing instead to spend their time enjoying their own private, lavish entertainments. Their personal extravagance, which was in direct contradiction to the measures they had passed for limiting public expenditure, only served to increase further their unpopularity. And, with a lack of sensitivity, Struensee, by now a fat, prosperous-looking man, dressed in the finest of clothes, incautiously vaunted his new wealth by travelling around the city in his golden carriage.

For the Danes at large, there was yet another cause for their growing dislike. Because Struensee and Caroline Mathilde had sought to conceal the true state of the king's mind, the people were unaware of Christian's mental condition. While condemning Struensee's lack of respect, they believed that he and the queen were keeping the monarch a virtual prisoner. As public antipathy grew for the doctor's high-handedness, self-promotion, and obvious ambition, critical cartoons and leaflets began to appear around the city. Benefiting from the press freedom Struensee had recently brought in, these soon became highly scurrilous attacks on him and Caroline Mathilde. But within the royal family itself, opposition was also taking shape, directed by Juliane Marie, who was one of the pair's bitterest enemies. Not only was she revolted by the couple's suspected affair, but, a stickler for etiquette and protocol, she hated the informality that they had introduced into royal circles. On occasion, Caroline Mathilde further shocked the court by choosing to wear men's clothes, and like Catherine the Great at the time of her coup, she even had herself painted in male uniform, thereby possibly suggesting that she too was eligible to rule in place of her unfit husband.

Evidence from mid-1771 suggests that Struensee was beginning to crumble under the mountain of work and other pressures that were now piling on him. In an attempt to limit criticism, he reintroduced censorship of the press, excusing his action by claiming that the country had proved unworthy of its freedom. But his unpopularity continued to grow, stoked by the crude tracts and pasquinades that still appeared. At the same time, there began to be public demonstrations, protests and even threats of mutiny within the army. As a result, Struensee started to swing between periods of energy and apathy, at times acting as an autocrat, at others displaying his terror of assassination. Accordingly, during their last summer together Caroline Mathilde and Struensee spent much of their time away from view at her favourite residence, Hirscholm, and they only appeared in public when protected by armed escorts. Copenhagen was in growing turmoil, but despite being aware of the dangers facing them, at court the couple still failed to moderate their behaviour. The British ambassador, Robert Murray Keith, whom they declined to meet privately, tried repeatedly to pass on the words of warning being sent by George III to his sister. Similarly, even Brandt, the king's chamberlain, who had himself at times failed to show Christian the deference owed to him, attempted to alert the couple to the growing dangers.[106]

At court a plot to unseat Struensee had now begun to take shape, one led by the dowager queen and backed by Rantzau-Ascheberg, the very man who had first played his part in introducing the doctor to the king. An unprincipled individual, he had become Struensee's enemy after he had been overlooked as head of the foreign office. And Caroline Mathilde would be equally betrayed by her maids, with one – embittered by her earlier dismissal as lady-in-waiting – providing salacious intimate evidence of the ongoing affair. In January 1772 things came to a head when the king and queen and Struensee returned to Copenhagen. Having attended a masked ball in the Christiansborg Palace and retired to their separate rooms, Struensee, Caroline Mathilde and the unfortunate Brandt were all arrested. With her four-year-old son now taken from her care, the queen was sent with her baby daughter to the Kronborg Castle at Helsingør, where for the next three months she would be confined to the governor's rooms.

Worse was to come for the two men, who, accused of *lès-majesté*, were removed to the citadel and imprisoned in chains in the fortress. Brandt had physically assaulted the mentally unbalanced Christian during one serious altercation, and for this he was condemned for the treasonable act of laying his hands 'on the sacred person of his Majesty'.[107] Meanwhile, Struensee faced further accusations, most notably that of having an adulterous relationship with the queen. Although he initially denied this charge, under pressure he finally admitted his guilt, whereupon, confronted with the evidence, Caroline Mathilde, who believed he had been tortured, reaffirmed his statement. By doing so, she hoped she might save her lover, but on realising her mistake, she soon changed her mind and declared her innocence. Meanwhile, the authorities wanted to undermine all Struensee's policies, and so they now ordered the Lutheran preacher Dr Münter to speak to the prisoner. At last, after many repeated visits, Münter succeeded in persuading Struensee to recant his radical religious views, which had been so contentious to the established Church. While possibly still hoping that this might save his life, Struensee's change of heart came when in fact his fate was most clearly sealed, and so his precise reasons for reaffirming the official Christian beliefs of his childhood are unclear. Whether or not his confession was totally sincere, for the new administration, directed by Juliane Marie, it helped to demolish everything that he and his fellow Enlightenment thinkers had stood for.

Although at first Struensee may have hoped the king might pardon him, over time he, like Caroline Mathilde, came to realise that Christian was now in the hands of their enemies and there would be no clemency. Accordingly, in April he and Brandt were taken to the eastern gates of the city, and there, before vast crowds, they had their right hands cut off, were beheaded, and finally drawn and quartered. After this brutal act of butchery, their remains were transported through the centre of Copenhagen to the west gates, and there their body parts were laid out on wheels for display, their heads and hands mounted on poles. While some reports suggested that Juliane Marie watched the execution from the tower at Christiansborg, her detractors went further and claimed that after the event she always preferred to stay in the small rooms of the palace, so that she might still get sight of the remains of her former enemies. A foreign visitor to Copenhagen, Archdeacon Coxe, reported seeing these grisly exhibits still on view some two years later.

While Struensee was undoubtedly capable and initially, at least, motivated by reforming ideals, his behaviour was also arrogant and dismissive towards the Danes, whose language he did not speak. Furthermore, behind his self-promotion and self-enrichment there lurks a suspicion of corruption. As a result, many historians question all his motives, suggesting that his affair with the queen was none other than an act of seduction by an older man of a young and vulnerable woman in order to attain power. While Caroline Mathilde's passionate affection for him is usually accepted as a given, his feelings have been more questioned.[i] His critics would soon claim that he had shown no true

---

i Prince Karl of Hesse, Christian's brother-in-law – who was no supporter of the doctor – claimed in his memoirs that Struensee treated the queen in such a high-handed, critical, if not controlling, manner that she appeared to be 'always ill at ease' when he was present. (See William Henry Wilkins, *A Queen of Tears: Caroline Matilda, Queen of Denmark and Norway*, loc.2696.)

affection for the queen, nor expressed any sorrow that he had been the cause of her shame. This accusation was in spite of the fact that in his final memoir he had confessed to feeling guilty of a crime that he could not, and would not, justify or excuse, and which had left him 'with nothing but remorse and regrets over the whole past'.[108] During their affair, blinded by their power, the couple had undoubtedly lost much of their reason and all of their moderation. Struensee had become proud and greedy, and Caroline Mathilde obstinate and unwilling to listen to any advice. As she had grown more obsessed by her lover, her manners had deteriorated and she had ceased to treat others with the consideration that had initially charmed so many people. But both she and Struensee were products of their age, a period when there was a clash between lax morals, free thinking, rigid etiquette, and the accepted religious principles. Like many of his contemporaries, Struensee supported the current libertinage, a movement whose loose attitudes to moral behaviour were symbolic of the contemporary questioning of the man-made dogmas of society. The Enlightenment came in for a period of bitter criticism in the nineteenth century when, traumatised by the brutality of the Terror, critics unequivocally blamed outright the eighteenth-century *philosophes* for the French Revolution. Elements of this all-embracing, uncritical condemnation of the Age of Reason in many ways mirror how Caroline Mathilde and Struensee were viewed by their detractors. So although some apologists for the queen later attempted to whitewash her story, reiterating the unsubstantiated claims that on her deathbed she insisted the affair had never taken place, when the scandal broke she was unfairly accused of any crime that could be attributed to her. Known to be an adoring mother who sincerely believed in the benefits of a Rousseauesque upbringing predicated on fresh air, simple living, and necessary chastisement, she was charged with cruelty by members of the court, who still adhered to the earlier ideas of how to raise young kings and princes. They favoured the more typical system of deference, formality and forced learning that often would produce a spoiled, self-absorbed ruler such as Louis XV.

Similarly, descriptions of Struensee concentrating on his faults have often disregarded his achievements and, however we choose to interpret his behaviour, his departure would be a bitterly felt loss to the king. In time the poor, mentally fragile Christian would make a little sketch of his two former friends, Struensee and Brandt, writing on his drawing, 'I wish I could have saved them both.' And with a further indication of how he had been manipulated, the king made the additional comment that responsibility for their deaths lay with Juliane Marie and her eighteen-year-old son. After the coup, although remaining nominally as Denmark's absolute king, Christian VII was held by the court to be too ill to rule, and so the same Juliane Marie took over control of the government, while her son, Hereditary Prince Frederik, was acknowledged as the acting regent.

On 2 April 1772 Caroline Mathilde was officially divorced and her name removed from public prayers, although bizarrely at the same time, to minimise the scandal, her daughter was declared legitimate. For a time, plans were afoot to banish the disgraced queen for the rest of her life to the small Danish town of Ålborg (Aalborg) in Jutland, but the British envoy, whom she had earlier chosen to ignore, Robert Murray Keith, now came to her aid. Although the deteriorating situation threatened to escalate into open conflict between Britain and Denmark, eventually, thanks to Keith's diplomacy, Juliane Marie's government conceded that Caroline Mathilde, the sister of a reigning king, should be allowed to leave the country and live abroad. Therefore, on 27 May, having at last come to accept the evidence of his sister's guilt, George III sent three British ships to fetch her from Kronborg and take her into exile. Although she was now rescued, Caroline Mathilde's departure was not without a cost, she being at this point forcibly separated from her remaining child, Louise Auguste. She would never see either of her children again.

Following a brief stay near Lüneburg, Caroline Mathilde finally settled at Celle, around 20 miles from Hanover. Her brother had intentionally chosen this town, hoping that by keeping her in his electorate and well away from his kingdom, he might prevent any further problems arising from the scandal. And apart from the fact that his wife, Queen Charlotte, bitterly disapproved of his sister's behaviour, fearing that it set a poor example for her young family, George III was now embroiled in new problems with his North American colonies. With war threatening, the king wished at all costs to prevent any other diplomatic confrontations breaking out.

After being comfortably ensconced in the refurbished palace at Celle, the disgraced queen was rejoined by her former lady-in-waiting Louise von Plessen, and frequently visited by her sister Augusta, the duchess of the neighbouring Brunswick. Fourteen years older than Caroline Mathilde, Augusta was still very English in her ways and only too happy to escape from her duchy, where she was not particularly popular. And Caroline Mathilde's arrival was greeted with enthusiasm by the people of Celle, where, having recovered her previous good manners, she soon became popular for her charity work, kindness and easy approachability. But she never gave up her hope that one day she might return to Denmark and be reunited with her children. While in exile, opponents of the country's new regime began to approach her, proposing a coup to reinstate her as regent for her son. With Struensee now gone, and the new Danish government becoming increasingly unpopular, support had begun to grow for the banished queen. So, encouraged by a young English go-between, Nathaniel Wraxall, who visited her three times in Celle, Caroline Mathilde began to consider joining the conspirators, on the condition that she received the backing of her brother. However, the embryonic plans received only partial support from George III, who was still concerned to avoid involvement in any additional international conflict. Then, before things could develop further, in May 1775 Caroline

Mathilde died, aged only twenty-three, probably of scarlet fever, maybe typhus, and, in the opinion of some, possibly porphyria. According to the British envoy in Copenhagen, Christian VII on hearing of his wife's death appeared shocked, and in contrast, in the brief period before the information was made official, Juliane Marie showed scant concern, even attending a ball that same night, and later ordering the minimum amount of court mourning to be observed. Although Caroline Mathilde had wanted to be buried in England, the war in America broke out soon after she died and this made her wishes impractical. As a result, she was finally interred in Celle at the Stadtkirche St Marien, alongside her great-grandmother, another equally disgraced royal 'adulteress', Sophie Dorothea, the divorced wife of George I.[109]

Juliane Marie, who now ruled in the place of her son, Hereditary Prince Frederik, was helped by her minster Ove Höegh-Guldberg. Together they overturned most of Struensee's reforms and took the country back to its more conservative past, their agenda including a restoration of the nobles' rights and, significantly, the outlawing of foreigners from public office. To support this more xenophobic policy, the use of German for military command was now replaced by Danish, a measure that Juliane Marie introduced despite the fact that she had been brought up in a German court and never fully mastered the Danish language herself. But she was determined to avoid the mistakes that had brought about Struensee's fall, and it was this concern that led her to try and satisfy the rising middle classes, who had so often been disregarded in the doctor's programme of reform. Fully aware of the tenuous nature of her position, she found a way to give legitimacy to her seizure of power. Every 17 January, the anniversary of the coup, she persuaded Christian VII to publish a letter thanking the government for his earlier 'deliverance'.

Under the new regime Denmark continued to avoid involvement in conflict, and while other countries – Britain in particular – became involved in the American Revolutionary War of Independence, it was able to expand its free trade and enjoy a period of exceptional commercial success. Among other things, it increased manufacture and founded the porcelain factory that is famous today as the Royal Copenhagen. Meanwhile, although Frederick the Great was cruel in his treatment of his wife – Juliane Marie's sister – Denmark's dowager queen always supported Prussia and was on good terms with its king. And until they both died in 1796, she frequently corresponded with Catherine the Great, with the result that in 1780 the two women came to an agreement regarding the family of Ivan VI. Having offered refuge to her two nieces and two nephews, the siblings of the previously murdered tsar, the ever-dutiful Juliane Marie now gave them accommodation, establishing them far away from court at Horsens in East Jutland. This again suggests her lack of warmth and approachability, traits in her character that may have exacerbated her already difficult relations with Caroline Mathilde's son and daughter. Equally, she would impose a strict and pious regime on the children of her predecessor, Queen Louise, although in this case there would be more affection between her and her stepdaughter Sophie Magdalene.

When Caroline Mathilde's son, Crown Prince Frederik, reached fourteen he was due to be confirmed, a church sacrament that would acknowledge his maturity and thereby qualify him to attend the Privy Councils. Juliane Marie wished to delay this event in order to retain her control over the government, but in 1784 she could no longer postpone it. When the confirmation took place, Crown Prince Frederik impressed the foreign representatives with his responses, proving himself – contrary to the popular rumour – to be clear-minded, unlike his father. But more was to come as during the following council meeting, the prince interrupted the proceedings and placed in the unwitting Christian VII's hands a document for signature. This dismissed the standing government and authorised the crown prince to become a co-signatory with the king. By the time the *hereditary* prince registered what was happening, there was little he could do, and his last-minute attempt to take control of the – by now totally confused – Christian ended in an undignified scuffle between him and his nephew. The latter physically held onto his father, and thereby was able to maintain his authority and become the new official regent. This coup took Juliane Marie by surprise, but despite her fury and the advice of Gustav III of Sweden that she should attempt to regain her power, she accepted the absolutism of the monarch and, having conceded her defeat, retired with her son to Fredensborg.

Juliane Marie has received a bad press for her role in the earlier coup against Caroline Mathilde and Struensee, and some of her actions may have been partly driven by her ambition and desire to place her own child on the throne. However, her decision to remove the crown prince from his unsuitable 'immoral' mother was probably understandable in the climate of the times, and some credit must be accorded to her for the way she eventually accepted her overthrow. By her submission and withdrawal from involvement in government, she avoided more serious civil unrest breaking out. Strictly brought up, she had never been able to condone the degenerate ways of her husband and the moral laxity of the Danish court, nor the questionable relationship of Caroline Mathilde and Struensee. Wanting to present the royal family as an example of moral probity, her desire was to remove the stain left by its previous behaviour. The fear of scandal may also explain her wish to bring up *la petite Struensee* as the king's legitimate daughter, so that perhaps for Juliane Marie the removal of Caroline Mathilde's children was not so much an act of spite, but rather one of practical, political expediency.

Still only aged sixteen, the new regent, Crown Prince Frederik, was guided by his Foreign Minister, Andreas Peter Bernstorff, and during these early years he introduced some of his more liberal measures. In 1785 Frederik wished to marry one of his British cousins, but George III now refused to allow any of his own daughters to become further connected to the Danes, who had treated their aunt so cruelly. So by default in 1790 Frederik married another cousin, Marie Sophie Friederike of Hesse-Kassel, granddaughter of Frederik V and great-granddaughter of George II. Having grown up in Denmark, she was popular with the Danes, but her relationship was more strained with her sister-in-law Louise Auguste, who had become particularly close to her brother during their childhood years of separation from their mother. However, Marie Sophie would become politically well-informed, able to advise her husband and to act for him when he was abroad, and even though the king had a mistress and four illegitimate offspring, her relationship with Frederik remained good. Of the eight children born of their marriage, six would die as infants, leaving only two surviving daughters.

While Frederik was still regent, in 1794 a fire destroyed the Christiansborg castle, making it necessary for him to move with his family to the Amalienborg, where they then took over one of the noblemen's palaces. With this, and another of the buildings being given to Juliane Marie and her son, the square now became the royal city residence that it is today. The following year, Copenhagen itself suffered another devastating fire, which for some time left many thousands homeless, but the disaster ultimately led to a major new rebuilding programme. During this time, Christiansborg would be one of the places reconstructed, but some ninety years later it again suffered the same fate, and was finally replaced in the early twentieth century by the present building that today serves as the seat of Parliament, the office of the Prime Minister, and the High Court.

After his more cautious Foreign Minister Bernstorff died in 1797, Frederik began to assert his absolute rule, famously rejecting all unwanted advice with the reply, 'only we know.' Previously under Juliane Marie, in 1780 Denmark had joined a coalition with Russia and Sweden in an attempt to defend Baltic shipping from the British, and now twenty years later in 1800 Frederik became part of another League of Armed Neutrality with Russia, Sweden and Prussia. This alliance, led by the new tsar Paul, sought to resist the blockade of the Baltic that Britain had imposed to prevent any trade with revolutionary France. On 2 April 1801, fearing that Denmark would break the embargo, Britain mounted its pre-emptive attack on the Danish fleet at Copenhagen. Frederik watched the hard-fought battle from the citadel, until Nelson ultimately saved the day for the Royal Navy by turning his blind eye at the order to retreat.

However, Napoleon, who had crowned himself emperor in 1804, was still on the rise, and he now forced Denmark and others to close their ports to the British. After the latter had unsuccessfully attempted to bribe Frederik to reverse this order, in August 1807, while the king was away from his city, the Royal Navy mounted another attack. This second Battle of Copenhagen was disastrous for the Danes, as not only was their fleet either destroyed or captured, but also the capital itself would suffer a heavy bombardment that ultimately left it in ruins. So two months later, Frederik, who had now further increased his control of affairs by suspending the Council of State, officially declared war on the British, initiating the so-called 'Gunboat War' that would drag on until 1814.[110]

By now Christian VII's mental condition had gravely deteriorated, and in March 1808 he died in Schleswig and was buried in the cathedral at Roskilde. With his death, at last the crown prince became Frederik VI, but because of the war, his anointment at Frederiksborg did not take place until 31 July 1815. But in the meantime, Frederik had other ambitions. Wanting to create a new Scandinavian union, he believed himself – as a descendent of Gustav Vasa – to be the right person to become Sweden's elected monarch when the ageing, childless Karl XIII died. So, after declaring war on his near neighbour, he set out to promote himself as the future Nordic king of the combined countries by sending balloons bearing his message across to the southern territories of Skåne (Scania). However, only a year after this lesser conflict had ended, in 1810 the Swedish *Riksdag* chose an alternative crown prince, electing Frederik's distant Oldenburg relation, Christian August of Augustenburg – the brother-in-law of *la petite Struensee*. To the surprise of all, within weeks this man had collapsed and was dead, to be replaced by the French marshal Jean Bernadotte.

While the Napoleonic Wars continued, Frederik VI remained loyal to the French emperor, even after the *Grande Armée*'s disastrous retreat from Russia in 1812. At that point, some, including the king's cousin Christian Frederik, suggested that Denmark should change its allegiances, but Frederik stayed true to his ally, possibly largely because he feared a French attack on the shipping lanes that were so necessary for the provision of Norway. Soon worse would come. After Napoleon's defeat at the Battle of Leipzig in 1813, Sweden invaded Frederik's duchy of Holstein, beating the Danes in what would be the last battle ever fought between the two countries. While this marked the end of centuries of warfare, the following January Denmark was forced at the Treaty of Kiel to surrender Norway, ceding it to Sweden after 430 years of possession. In return, Frederik received Swedish Pomerania, which he soon exchanged with Prussia for Lauenburg – a territory that had previously belonged to Hanover. Denmark still held onto Iceland and Greenland, but for many Danes these latest concessions did not compensate for the loss of Norway and, as a result, still today there are those who blame the king for diminishing his country's international status. They hold him responsible for having started Denmark's decline through his unwavering, but unfortunate, support of Napoleon.

In Norway too, things did not go smoothly at first. While the previous year Frederik VI had sent his cousin to act as his representative in the region after the Treaty of Kiel, this same man, Christian Frederik, was chosen as leader of a nationalist group who opposed the country's new union with Sweden. While Frederik VI may have secretly supported these rebels, sending supplies of grain to the starving Norwegians and thereby increasing the popularity of the Danes, he could not act openly for fear of Swedish retaliation. Then, only a month after the signing at Kiel, in February 1814 Christian Frederik summoned an assembly of twenty-one leading Norwegians to Eidsvoll, around 45 miles from Christiania (Oslo), and here he was elected Regent of Norway. Now, having the approval of the Norwegian Constitutional Assembly, he was eligible to stand for election to the throne, and on 17 May the constitution was signed and he was finally confirmed as King Christian Frederik – a date still celebrated in Norway as a national holiday. But his position was immediately questioned by the other powers, who demanded that he abide by the terms of the earlier treaty. The new king refused to take any action without the approval of the Norwegian parliament, and so in July the Swedes invaded under the command of their recently elected crown prince, Jean Bernadotte. Within just two months, the Norwegians were defeated and the war was over, and in the subsequent peace talks Christian Frederik was instructed to abdicate. To this he agreed, possibly hoping by doing so to ensure his or his son's later accession to the Swedish throne. If this was his aim, ultimately he was no more successful than Frederik VI, Jean Bernadotte succeeding when the old king Karl XIII died in 1818. However, having achieved one victory during the fighting, Christian Frederik was able to add a proviso to his abdication: namely that Sweden should accept the new Norwegian constitution. So, while it continued for the next ninety-one years to be in union with the Swedish monarchy, after more than four centuries Norway ceased to be a mere province of one of its larger neighbours.

Frederik VI had been surprised and shocked when the throne had been offered to Bernadotte rather than to himself, but the French marshal was believed to hold more moderate ideas than the autocratic king. Now, with the semi-autonomous Norway under the Swedish crown, things started to become even harder. With the war having caused the Danes to lose their agricultural markets and much of their maritime business, the country had entered a period of financial downturn. In time, this situation led to a series of bankruptcies that, having hit the state and individual traders alike, would eventually leave Denmark seriously in debt. In 1817 things became still worse when a crisis started to develop in the sugar trade, the problems caused not just by inadequate production and outdated refineries, but also by the competition now coming from sugar beet.

During his time in power, Frederik had introduced a number of reforms, among them improvements in education and prison conditions, and the granting of minority rights to the Jews. In addition, back in 1788 he had ended serfdom, and fourteen years later banned the slave trade. And, even though in his old age he had become more conservative and autocratic, by the end of his reign most of his people were enjoying a period of peace. However, things were different in Schleswig and Holstein where trouble was now brewing. Despite the Romanovs having ceded the remaining parts of these duchies over half a century before, the standard of living in the region was lower than it was in the rest of the country.[111] As a result, open unrest had now begun to take shape, the opposition being encouraged by the news of the 1830 revolution in France. Therefore, four years later, Frederik decided to slacken his autocratic hold and to grant the duchies a degree of constitutional reform.

Finally, after fifty-five years in total as ruler, first as regent and later as king, in 1839 Frederik VI died, leaving just two surviving legitimate daughters. According to the Danish constitution, these women were ineligible to succeed their father, and so the crown now passed to Frederik VI's cousin, the former Norwegian king Christian Frederik. Although some rumours suggested this man to be the illegitimate child of a member of the court, as the son of the Hereditary Prince Frederik, and grandson of Juliane Marie and Frederik V, he was now recognized as Denmark's rightful ruler, Christian VIII.

Christian had divorced his first wife on the grounds of her adultery, but not before the marriage had produced a boy who, aged still only one, had then been permanently separated from his mother. Two years after becoming viceroy in Norway, Christian had taken as his second wife Caroline Amalie, the daughter of Louise Auguste, *la petite Struensee*, an arrangement that finally united the two branches of Frederik V's family that had been for so long at odds. In the event, the couple remained childless – despite Christian fathering ten illegitimate offspring through his continuing extramarital affairs – but the marriage was happy, the king and queen both enjoying their individual interests, he pursuing his scientific studies, and she composing and playing music when not involved in her charitable work. And despite Caroline Amalie having no children, Struensee's probable line did not die out. After Louise Auguste's death aged seventy-one in 1843, her son's granddaughter would become the last German empress, the ancestor of Queen Sofia of Spain and her brother King Constantine of the Hellenes.

Having grown up in a cultured court, Christian VIII initially appeared more enlightened than his predecessor, and with his charm and good looks he was liked by the Danish people. But his popularity evaporated over the years as he became more reactionary and conservative than had been originally expected. Although, like Frederik VI, he now began to consider the ending of slave labour in the colonies, his cautious approach meant that he had only just started to put the measures into force when he died, and full abolition would not be enacted until the following year. But nearer home, his predecessor's offer of limited autonomy to the provinces, had now begun to open the way to opposition movements in his more impoverished duchies of Schleswig and Holstein, particularly in the latter where the majority was German-speaking. While the situation became increasingly tense, Christian appeared indecisive, giving no direction until just two years before his death, when he came out in support of the Danes, who wished to retain Schleswig in South Jutland. But as the duchies had long been united, the ethnic Germans wanted independence for the two regions together, and, to make things still more complicated for the king, there were differences of opinion even within his own family. His brothers-in-law supported the pro-German nationalists, and even his wife, Caroline Amalie, had similar leanings, something that ultimately caused her own popularity to wane.

In addition to these concerns, Christian had also come to realise the problems that faced the succession, his son by his first marriage, Frederik, showing little likelihood of ever producing a legitimate heir. Therefore, in 1846 the king introduced a change to Denmark's hereditary laws, and the following year, having gained foreign approval, appointed his niece's husband to become Frederik's successor; this would be made official five years later. While Christian planned to go further and also introduce a Danish constitution, in this he would be thwarted when in January 1848, he died unexpectedly from blood poisoning, his last words being, 'I didn't make it.'

With Christian VIII's death, once again the country was faced with the prospect of an unsuitable monarch. During his youth in Geneva, the young Frederik had become involved in various scandals and, to the added distaste of the more conservative Danes, had picked up foreign republican ideas. Then his marriage when aged twenty to Frederik VI's second surviving daughter, Vilhelmine, had become so troubled that it had ended in a bitter divorce in 1837.

Following the break-up, Frederik was banished to Jutland, and there he met his future mistress, Louise Rasmussen. But four years later he married again, this time his wife being Caroline Charlotte of Mecklenburg-Strelitz, the great-niece of George III's wife, Queen Charlotte, and niece of Prussia's much-loved Queen Luise. But she was no happier than her predecessor and, while visiting her family in Mecklenburg three years after her wedding, she refused to return to Denmark, so again Frederik's marriage ended in divorce.

Two years after succeeding as Frederik VII, to the horror of the nobility, in August 1850 he decided to marry for a third time, now choosing his commoner mistress, Louise. As a former ballet dancer who ran a hat and dress-making shop, she was considered unsuitable to be his official consort, and so she became his morganatic wife, receiving the title Countess of Danner. Although she continued to be treated with contempt by the upper classes of society, she would act as the king's adviser, and also prove able to temper the behaviour of her quick-tempered and profligate husband. And later, when pressures caused him to become mentally and physically ill, she would continue to encourage and support him.

On his coming to the throne, Frederik VII had been immediately faced with the growing problems in Schleswig and Holstein, where the demands for independence were becoming ever louder. To add to the already unstable situation, since Christian VIII's decree of 1846, the hereditary laws in Denmark and the duchies differed, raising the question as to who should eventually succeed the king in the two regions. Inspired by the latest revolutionary events in Paris the previous month, in March 1848 deputies from the duchies visited the king in Copenhagen, demanding his recognition of an independent, united Schleswig-Holstein. While Frederik conceded these rights to the more German-populated Holstein, he denied that he had the power to grant the same to the predominantly Danish-speaking Schleswig. As a result, rebellion broke out, led by the king's nephew, Christian August II, Duke of Augustenburg – the son of *la petite Struensee* – and with the rebels taking possession of Kiel and briefly occupying Flensborg (Flensburg), by early April the First Schleswig War had begun. While this was going on, Frederik, having listened to the demands of his own Danish radicals, signed a new constitution for Denmark, and the following year a two-chamber parliament was established that finally ended nearly 200 years of royal absolutism. This made the king popular with the Danes, and after his death the people of Copenhagen would erect a statue in his honour outside the Christiansborg Palace.

While details of the king's private life and relationships are uncertain, similar doubts remain as to whether or not he had any offspring. Although, usually represented as unable to have children, recently some people have come forward with different theories. According to one, in 1843 his earlier mistress Else (Marie) Pedersen gave birth to his son, Frederik Poulsen. To support this argument, letters have now been found written by the king expressing his love for the child, and revealing how he wished to provide for him. Recently, yet another claim has been made that in 1851 his third wife, Louise, gave birth to a daughter who was later brought up in Wales as Elizabeth Wynn. However, with such children – born illegitimate or to a morganatic marriage – excluded from the throne, whatever the truth of these cases, they and any other similar offspring would never have been in a position to alter the succession.

When at last the First Schleswig War ended in 1852, the London Protocol drawn up in May confirmed Denmark's new status – from this time a federation, personally united through the monarch with the independent duchies of Schleswig and Holstein. However, the problems had only been postponed, complicated by the fact that since Christian VIII's edict, a difference remained within the laws of the separate areas. While the duchies retained their adherence to Salic law, Denmark now accepted a semi-Salic system that allowed descent to pass through, or even to, a female born into the Oldenburg family. So, as might have been expected,

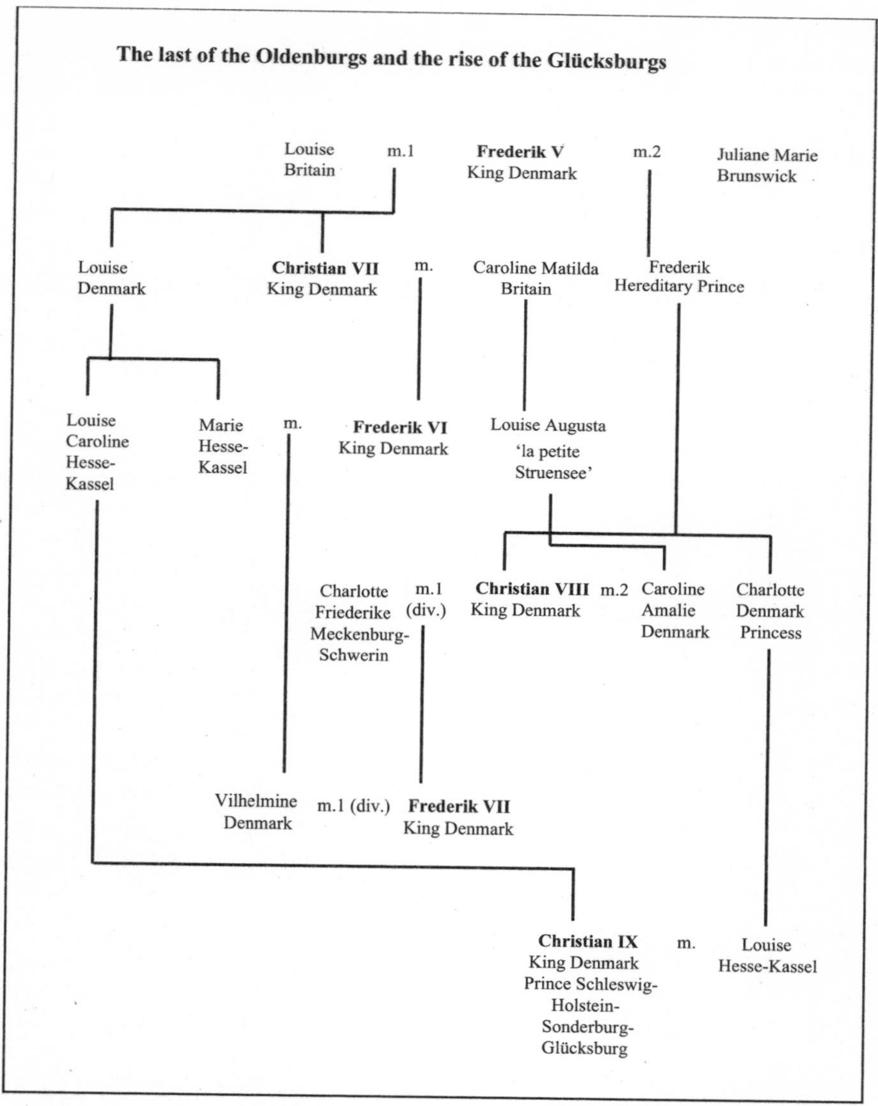

when finally Frederik VII died in November 1863 – ending the direct line of the Oldenburgs – tensions soon resurfaced and the situation rapidly escalated, coming to a head with the Second Schleswig War that broke out in February the following year. By then however a new Danish king had been proclaimed. Despite various candidates having come forward, asserting their alternative rights to the throne, the earlier chosen member of the junior family branch of the Schleswig-Holstein-Sonderburg-Glucksburgs succeeded as Christian IX, thereby initiating after more than 400 years a new Danish dynasty.

15

Sweden: A Century of Revolution

King Gustav III of Sweden [on the the left] with his brothers, Prince Fredrik Adolf [standing], and Prince Karl (later King Karl XIII), by Alexander Roslin (1771). (Courtesy National Museum of Fine Arts, Sweden)

After his defeat at Poltava and five years of exile in the Ottoman Empire, Karl XII of Sweden had returned north to renew his campaigning against his various Baltic neighbours. Four years later in 1718, his early death from a sniper's shot while on campaign in Norway had left the succession in doubt. The unmarried king had already been predeceased by his favourite sister, Hedvig Sofia, the widow of the Duke of Holstein-Gottorp, the so-called 'Gottorp Fury', who had been killed in battle during the first years of the Great Northern War. But while at the time of her brother's death Hedvig's eighteen-year-old son, Karl Friedrich, was the strongest claimant to the throne, his aunt, Ulrika Eleonora, had other plans. Asserting her own rights as Karl's XII's younger sister, she was able to convince the parliament that she would be a more suitable ruler than her spoilt and degenerate young nephew, and at last, on her agreeing to renounce the absolute power first assumed by her father, the *Riksdag* elected her to be queen. Having three years earlier married Friedrich of Hesse-Kassel, she wished her much-loved husband to share her rule, visualising that they might reign together in the manner of Britain's joint monarchs William and Mary. The parliament rejected this idea, but then put forward an alternative option, namely that Friedrich should assume the throne in his wife's stead. At last, the queen agreed to this proposal, and just fourteen months after her accession, in February 1720, Ulrika Eleonora abdicated in her husband's favour. This, she later described as the greatest sacrifice of her life. Friedrich was now the sole ruler, Fredrik I.

While the absolute monarch Karl XII had remained on the throne, Sweden had been unable to withdraw from the ongoing war. Stubborn to the end, the king had carried on his fight against his enemies, not just disregarding the ever-growing odds stacked against him, but also ignoring the steady ruination of his country. Although initially viewed by the Swedes as one of their greatest generals and national heroes, after the disaster at Poltava and the later continuing costly sieges and battles, opposition to Karl had grown to such a degree that for many his death had come as a relief. As over the following weeks people began to speculate over who might have been responsible for his death, gradually both Danes and Swedes came under suspicion, with some rumours even suggesting the new king to have been the guilty party. Reinforcing this charge, Cecilia Nordenkull-Jorgensen has found evidence of a German conspiracy and cover-up. She declares that the former Friedrich of Hesse, backed by outside powers – among them the British king – had contrived to assassinate Karl in order to secure the position of his wife, who had been acknowledged as queen in a coup the previous month.[j] In 1721, it would be Fredrik who signed with Peter the Great at Nystad in Finland a peace agreement that ended at last the Great Northern War. The prolonged conflict had been disastrous for Sweden, the country now financially ruined with a destroyed agriculture, broken industry, and a shortage of men of working age. Of even more long-term significance, the final treaty had forced the king to

j Fredrik intentionally denigrated the reputation of Karl, who Nordenkull-Jorgensen describes as 'one of Europe's most talented and visionary monarchs'. Although Karl's famous contemporary Emanuel Swedenborg greatly revered him, as Nordenkull-Jorgensen shows, in later centuries Swedenborg's remarks were falsely interpreted and Fredrik's faults ascribed to his predecessor. See Cecilia Nordenkulls, *Karl XII: Kungamord*, p.13.

hand over large areas of territory: Bremen-Verden in the west going to Hanover; Swedish Pomerania to Prussia; and Livonia, Estonia, Ingria, and part of Karelia and southern Finland to Russia – losses that proved Sweden's days as a great northern power were now over forever. With the signing of the peace treaty, Russia had finally become the dominant presence in the Baltic region.

Holstein-Gottorp had also suffered in the war, punished as its dukes had sided with Sweden. After Karl XII's fortunes had begun to decline, a more confident Denmark had returned to the conflict, and in 1713 it had occupied the whole duchy. At the end of the war all Schleswig was surrendered, and the young Duke of Holstein-Gottorp's rights as a vassal of the Danish king were removed. But he was more fortunate in Holstein, where, still a fief of the emperor, after the Danes had withdrawn, he finally recovered his lands. However, three years later when Duke Karl Friedrich failed to take the Swedish throne, he decided to move to Russia. Here he became betrothed to Anna Petrovna, and shortly after the death of her father, Peter the Great, in 1725 the couple were married. Three years later, back in their Kiel castle in Holstein, Anna died a few days after giving birth to a son, Karl Peter Ulrich. Orphaned when he was eleven, this child then inherited the remnants of his father's duchies and, more importantly, his claim to the Swedish throne. This, however, he would never inherit as by the time that Fredrik I died, the political manoeuvring of others had already pushed him towards a different future in Russia.

Now, with the new constitution and ending of the absolute monarchy, Sweden entered a period dubbed the 'Age of Liberty'. Having attained new freedoms, the nobles began to increase their power, and although Fredrik I had initially attempted to play a key role in government, before long he found himself sidelined. Naturally indolent, he was then content to leave affairs to his ministers, allowing them to use a stamp to ratify the documents in place of his written signature. Besides amusing himself hunting, he spent much of his time with prostitutes until 1731, when he met the sixteen-year-old Hedvig Taube and became determined to make her his full-time mistress. Dismayed at the prospect of this relationship with the fifty-five-year-old king, she bemoaned the 'loss of virtue' now forced on her by her family in the hopes of settling their serious debts. Nevertheless, under pressure she accepted an appointment as the queen's lady-in-waiting, and three years later, after the birth of her son, became the first official mistress of a Swedish king. The devout Ulrika Eleonora was gravely offended and upset by this latest turn of events, and for two weeks after Hedvig's first court appearance in her new role, she refused to leave her room. But Hedvig herself was never happy with her position, and although she gave her support to the arts and had some political influence on the king, she chose to live discreetly out of sight. Nonetheless, questions began to be raised in the *Riksdag* regarding the king's adultery, a blatant breaking of his coronation oath always to love and respect the queen. For a time, some considered that she might replace her husband on the throne, but her health was now clearly deteriorating. Already seriously hurt by her husband's infidelity, her situation had been made still harder by the fact that she had remained childless, while his mistress had provided the king with two surviving illegitimate sons. But just three years after the queen's death from smallpox in 1741, Hedvig, still deploring the 'immoral' way of life that had been forced on her, died shortly after giving birth to a second daughter. To public disgust, for a time the king returned to common prostitutes. Eventually he found a new mistress, Catarina Ebba Horn, who would remain as his favourite for the next three years.

For the first two decades following the death of Karl XII, the government was led by the Chancery President, Count Arvid Horn, the head of the 'Caps', a party whose popular name came from their rivals, the more traditional faction of the gentry, the 'Hats'. During the twenty years of peace when Horn was in power, Sweden began to recover from the ravages that it had suffered during the Great Northern War, and in this period the Swedish East India Company was formed under royal charter in the west coast city of Göteborg (Gothenburg) on the Kattegat. Now embarking on voyages that lasted between eighteen months and two years, traders began to import valuable, much-sought-after commodities from the east, notably tea, spices, silk and Chinese porcelain. With this growing commerce Göteborg increased in importance, its prosperity further promoted by the foreigners who had now taken up residence in the city. After the Dutch came the Scots, in the main Jacobite supporters who were seeking a place of safety in exile, and for a time some of these had considered mounting a Swedish invasion to oust their hated Hanoverian king. However, such plans had been dropped after the arrest in London of the pro-Stuart diplomat, Carl Gyllenborg in 1717, and Karl XII's death the next year.

Nevertheless, Scotsmen had continued to come to Göteborg, among them Colin Campbell, who had initially fled abroad to escape his debts after the South Sea Bubble disaster. For a time, he had remained in Ostend trying to set up a trading company in the Low Countries, but eventually had arrived in Göteborg in 1731. Here, having changed his citizenship, he was able to become a co-founder of the new Swedish East India Company and then take part in its maiden voyage, acting for the occasion as Sweden's first envoy to the emperor of China. But while this trip was highly successful and profitable, the journey was dangerous and not all the expeditions of the company's ships would end so well. In 1745, the large returning *Eastindiaman* – named after the city – ran aground and sank just outside the entrance to the harbour. Although the *Göteborg* was lost in the disaster, there were no casualties and around a third of its precious cargo was eventually salvaged, some of which is now in the city museum, situated in the company's former headquarters. Between 2005 and 2007, a full-sized replica of this ship completed a two-year commemorative voyage to China and it is today berthed downstream on the right bank of the river. Meanwhile, Campbell had become a member of the Swedish nobility, his coat of arms appearing on the Chinese porcelain that is also displayed alongside his portrait in the museum. As one of the East India Company's main shareholders, he amassed a vast fortune. A decade before his death in 1757, he used some of his great wealth to help another Stuart cause. Some of the Jacobites living in Göteborg hoped to mount a rescue attempt for the Young Pretender, sending a trading boat to save him after his disastrous defeat at Culloden in 1746. While his supporters intended to bring him back to Sweden to renew his campaign, the scheme ultimately failed and Bonnie Prince Charlie made his own escape to France before ending his days as an exile in Rome.

Even though, during the two decades of peace following the Great Northern War, Sweden had begun to recover, the 'Hats' still despaired of the country's lost international standing. Eventually, in 1738 they overthrew the 'Caps' and regained power under their leader, that same Carl Gyllenborg – formerly arrested in London – who was now the new Chancery President. Ambitious to recover their lost territories, two years later in 1740 the Hats saw an opportunity to achieve their ambitions when, within months of each other, three rulers died: Friedrich Wilhelm I of Prussia; Anna, Empress of Russia; and Charles VI, the Holy Roman Emperor. Immediately the new Prussian king Frederick II declared war on the emperor's daughter, Maria Theresa, and with Europe now engaged in the War of the Austrian Succession, in August 1741 the Swedes used the moment to mount their own separate attack on the Russians. But this 'Hats War' would again prove disastrous for Sweden, with much of its Finnish territory coming under enemy occupation in the so-called Lesser Wrath. As a result, at the peace signed at Åbo (Turku) in 1743, the country was forced to accept two demands issued by the new Russian empress, Elizabeth: first, Sweden would give up yet more territory in Finland; and second, it would accept her choice of heir to the Swedish crown, this being a matter of pressing importance, as the widowed Fredrik I was in his sixties and still without legitimate children. Although Karl Peter Ulrich of Holstein-Gottorp was the nearest in line to follow him, Elizabeth had already chosen the boy to become her own successor as the Grand Duke Peter. For that reason, she now instructed the Swedes to replace the young duke with his cousin, and so it was he, Adolf Friedrich of Holstein-Gottorp, who was then appointed the Swedish heir to the throne.

The year after this treaty at Åbo, the new Swedish crown prince married the pretty, talented and musical Luise Ulrike, one of the younger sisters of Frederick II of Prussia, and goddaughter of the former Swedish queen after whom she had been named. However, even her brother – himself not the easiest of men – had initially questioned this marriage, describing Luise Ulrike as having 'a haughty and domineering nature'.[112] Having considered that his sister Amalie would make a better wife for the future king, Frederick now predicted that Luise Ulrike would not be content to be part of a monarchy whose authority was so limited. He was right. She would eventually become unpopular with the Swedes and, as her brother had again suggested, would dominate her mild-mannered husband. And she would be equally difficult with her children, showing particularly scant affection for the two eldest, whose wives she then included in her bullying. However, initially Sweden greeted its new Crown Princess (now Lovisa Ulrika) with enthusiasm, the people hoping that at last – after half a century of waiting – an heir might be born to the royal family. Their wish would be fulfilled two years later when following one stillbirth, in January 1746 she produced a son, the future Crown Prince Gustav.

Like her brother the Prussian king, Lovisa Ulrika was a patron of the arts. Having been given Dottningholm Palace outside Stockholm as a wedding present, she then redecorated the interior in the more sophisticated French rococo style. And later in the grounds, in 1753 her husband gave her the surprise birthday present of an elegant wooden Chinese pavilion. She was delighted, *Chinoiserie* being now in vogue, popular in many courts at the time, including at Potsdam where her

The strong-willed Luise Ulrike of Prussia, painted by Antoine Pesne in 1744, at the time of her marriage, six years before she became Queen Lovisa Ulrika of Sweden.

brother Frederick II built his own Chinese House shortly afterwards. However, in Sweden the woodwork of this structure soon began to suffer from the weather conditions, and so in the 1760s it was replaced with the more robust stone-built Chinese Pavilion, which Lovisa Ulrika then filled with some of the imported Eastern silks and artefacts that were now arriving at Göteborg. Around the same time that this was being built, the original Drottningholm theatre burnt down during a performance, so Lovisa Ulrika commissioned another larger one seating 400 people to replace it. This is an exceptional example of its period, and today, like the rest of the park, it is a UNESCO World Heritage Site. Still containing some of the original stage machinery, the theatre continues to be used for special events and opera performances during the summer season.

In this period, when lighting and heat was provided by open flames, fire was always a hazard, and so similar reconstruction work had been needed back in the city itself, where in 1697, just days after Karl XI's death, the old Royal Palace of the Tre Kronor had also burnt down. The young king Karl XII had immediately ordered Nicodemus Tessin the Younger – the son of the designer of the palace at Drottningholm – to draw up plans for a new baroque building, but following the disaster of the Battle of Poltava, work had been halted. Only after the end of the Great Northern War had the *Riksdag* granted funds for this to recommence, and so it was not until 1754, three years after Fredrik I died, that the royal family was able to move back into the Stockholm palace.

With Fredrik I's death, Lovisa Ulrika's husband had become the new king, Adolf Fredrik I, thus establishing the Holstein-Gottorp dynasty that would rule the country for nearly seven decades. Two years after the king's accession, Sweden, the last of the European powers – with the exclusion of Russia – finally adopted the Gregorian calendar. This was also a time of progress in other fields, with the proponents of the Swedish Enlightenment now spreading new ideas. Among the various thinkers was the scientist Carl Linnaeus, whose taxonomy, or classification of all living organisms, is still in use for the binomial naming of plants. Included among the other key figures in this period were Anders Celsius, who in 1742 would produce his temperature scale, and the later naturalist Anders Sparrman, a disciple of Linnaeus, who in 1772–76 travelled with James Cook on his second voyage to Antarctica. Abroad others were similarly involved in the search for answers, and so in 1736 the Frenchman Pierre Louis Maupertuis came to Sweden seeking to prove mathematically the shape of the globe. Choosing the high latitudes of Lapland for his required measurements, he set up his base at the head of the Gulf of Bothnia in Tornio, using the church steeple as a high point from which to take his readings. For a year he was subjected to the discomforts of the harsh northern climate, only then to suffer shipwreck before he eventually succeeded in arriving home.

Just as Frederick II had warned, the queen was now becoming unhappy with her country's constitutional rule. Finding herself in dispute with the Estates, Lovisa Ulrika wanted to dissolve the parliament and reinstate the absolute monarchy that had been enjoyed by Karl XI and Karl XII. After some aborted attempts at achieving this, in 1756, just five years after her husband's accession, she mounted a coup, supported by her noble followers within her 'royal court party'. To help finance her cause, she had pawned her jewels in Berlin, among them forty-four diamonds from the crown that had been made for her at the time of the coronation. When her actions were reported to the government by her lady-in-waiting, the ministers demanded to see the missing gems, and she only just managed to get them back in time. But the plot had now been discovered, and while some of the arrested conspirators were whipped, exiled or imprisoned, eight of the nobles were publicly executed outside the palace. There was then some suggestion that the queen should be divorced but this never came to anything and Lovisa Ulrika herself was not punished. Nevertheless, to her bitter humiliation, she was forced, grudgingly, to apologise to the *Riksdag*, something, as she later complained to her brother, she considered to be much 'beneath her'.

Frederick II was now occupied with other affairs. In August, wishing to pre-empt the actions of his enemies, he invaded Saxony, thus triggering the Seven Years' War. During this conflict across five continents the brother and sister found themselves on different sides, with the Swedes encouraged by the French to join the allies opposing Prussia. But although this, their 'Pomeranian War', would again be costly for the country, Sweden was only partially involved in the main event, and its engagement in just five small, unsuccessful campaigns would later prompt Frederick to question sarcastically whether the two countries had in fact ever been at war. But Lovisa Ulrika was able to play her part in the final peace negotiations, where she helped ensure that Sweden managed to keep its possessions on the Baltic's southern shores.

Four years later Crown Prince Gustav finally married the Danish princess who had been his proposed bride since she was just four years old. The *Riksdag* had promoted the alliance many years before in an attempt to improve the frequently difficult relations between the two countries. Although the bride's mother, the popular Danish queen Louise, first wife of Frederik V, had always been against the match, apprehensive about the malign influence of Lovisa Ulrika, having died soon after her daughter's betrothal she had been unable to prevent it. As she had feared, the young woman, now Crown Princess Sofia Magdalena, was soon unhappy in her new country, where her shyness was interpreted by many as coldness. Having been brought up by her strict and puritanical stepmother, Queen Juliane Marie, she was poorly prepared for the disreputable Swedish court with its free and easy morals. Moreover, her sophisticated, free-thinking husband, who had little interest in women in general, hated the Danes and showed her scant consideration. With the exception of her father-in-law the king, the princess received little kindness from her new family, and so she moved to her own palace outside Stockholm. But in 1771 Adolf Fredrik died, collapsing at dinner before dying in the arms of his close friend Fredrik Axel von Fersen, his death caused probably by a heart attack brought on by overeating – his vast final meal reputedly comprised several courses and fourteen helpings of his favourite pudding.

Although ineffective as a ruler, Adolf Fredrik was remembered by those who knew him as gentle and good-natured, a man who was friendly to everyone, including his servants. Nonetheless, his reign had not been easy, his problems exacerbated by the increasingly bitter divisions between the Hats and Caps. With the increase of financial crises and bankruptcies in this period, the nobility had grown steadily more autocratic. So for a time in 1768 the king, possibly guided by his son, had even threatened to abdicate, refusing to sign documents as a way of protesting at the nobles' high-handedness.

When his father died, Gustav was in France, where he was visiting the court and meeting many of the Enlightenment thinkers in Paris. Always writing and speaking better French than Swedish, he impressed the *philosophes*, showing his understanding and appreciation of their ideas, ones that would soon come to influence his policies as king. Tellingly, on hearing the news from Sweden, one of his first concerns was for his mother's safety, and, realising how little she was loved, he immediately ordered that she should be given protection. She had now lost much of her former status, and, to her great disatisfaction, from this time onwards would find herself in the unenviable role of the dowager queen. With plans for the coronation soon going ahead after her son's return to the country, the ceremony finally took place at Stockholm in May the following year. Wanting to mark the lavish occasion, the new king, now Gustav III, ordered Carl Pilo to record the event in a large painting, but this work – today in Stockholm's National Museum – would never be completed, being left still unfinished after Gustav's unexpected and untimely death.

By this time, it was obvious that the Age of Liberty was clearly failing, the nobles' excessive power and greater freedoms making government unworkable. Moreover, because Frederick II had persuaded his sister to support the policies of Catherine II, Russia now wielded too much influence on Swedish affairs. Wishing to increase his royal authority and resolve his problems, just two days after his coronation, Gustav began to prepare for a coup. First he sent Count Toll south to Skåne (Scania) to bribe the Kristianstad garrison to revolt, and second he instructed the Finnish Baron Sprengtporten to go and make the Sveaborg fortress at the entrance to Helsingfors (Helsinki) harbour ready to come to his assistance. However, earlier than planned, news of the king's plot leaked out, and so back in the capital Gustav quickly gathered his supporters. Now distinguishing themselves in their 'revolutionary suits', complete with a rapier and a white cloth worn like an armband, the king and his men marched to the Privy Council and arrested the members. Three days later, on 19 August, having appeared before the *Riksdag* and declared a new constitution, he was hailed by the general public, who were happy to see an end to the power of the nobility. Subsequently, the court musician Carl Michael Bellman would compose an anthem in praise of Gustav's achievement, and the king would mark the occasion by having himself repeatedly painted in his 'revolutionary' clothes. Having attained greater authority, Gustav now set out to introduce his new Enlightenment measures, including an end of torture, the improvement of health care, moves against corruption, the increase of trade, and the modernisation of Sweden's agricultural methods. But while the king was an autocrat, intent on modelling himself on the typical eighteenth-century enlightened despot who used his wise authority for the good of his people, he did not always blindly support a monarchist cause, and in 1777 he would give his backing to the supporters of the new American republic.

Meanwhile, the king's marriage was still unconsummated, and so seeing the need for an heir, Gustav encouraged the betrothal of his younger brother Karl to their pretty fifteen-year-old cousin Hedwig (now Hedvig) Elizabeth Charlotte of Holstein-Gottorp, who in July 1774 was officially welcomed to Stockholm. After the marriage, she would go on to have more than one pregnancy, but her only living child died just six days after birth – a tragedy that in years to come would leave the succession in doubt. Unlike her sister-in-law, Queen Sofia Magdalena, Karl's wife was vivacious and sociable and, before long, she was a central figure at court. While her husband continued to enjoy his mistresses, gossip suggested she too had her own affairs, causing her critical mother-in-law dismissively to label her as 'flirtatious'. Lovisa Ulrika, who favoured her third son and one daughter, was always remarkably unkind to the rest of the family, being particularly cruel towards Gustav's wife. On their first meeting, she had described her as 'stupid looking', before maliciously adding that she might therefore be more suitable for her brother-in-law, the younger Karl.

However, now, worse was to come. When, after twelve years of marriage, in 1778 the queen finally gave birth to a son, Gustav Adolf, instead of celebrating, her mother-in-law began repeating the scurrilous, highly suggestive rumours that were soon circulating in the court. These questioned the child's conception, suggesting that the Finnish nobleman Adolf Monk had played a significant role. Putting aside the earlier rumours that the king and queen had engaged in extramarital affairs, now some gossips claimed that Sofia Magdalena had been divorced and married to Monk so that he might father her child. Well into the 1780s, Gustav's opposition would continue to repeat such stories, over the years the versions becoming ever more titillating as they were stoked by the spread of obscene cartoons and pamphlets. Sofia Magdalena was, understandably, horrified by the highly salacious rumours, and she now refused to speak to Lovisa Ulrika ever again. The king, too, was furious and, having ordered his mother to apologise publicly, he then cut off all ties with her, only finally visiting her on her deathbed four years later through the persuasion of his sister-in-law, Hedvig.

During her last days, Lovisa Ulrika had the company of her daughter and godchild, Adolf Badin, a boy probably born into slavery in Africa or the colonies. Similar to the situation with Peter the Great and his black godson, Gannibal, Badin had been given to Lovisa Ulrika when he was a child, and she had then decided to raise him within the family as a sort of 'experiment'. He grew up with the queen's children and became virtually a member of the royal household, eventually in later life becoming Lovisa Ulrika's butler. She trusted him implicitly, even to the extent that shortly before her death she gave him the key to her personal papers. These documents he later handed over to her youngest two children with whom he was very close, and it was this closeness that in time gave rise to a rumour suggesting that Lovisa Ulrika's daughter, Sofia Albertina, had had an affair with him. While the princess never married, later becoming Princess-Abbess of Quedlinburg Abbey, further gossip suggested that she had given birth to a child, who, according to some, had been fathered by Badin. There is again no evidence to prove or disprove this, but the fact that the query exists points to the paradox that lies at the heart of the Age of Reason.

Despite the royal family and other educated members of the court espousing the Enlightenment's principles, in 1784 Sweden bought from France St Barthelemy an island with a very small population and no water supply of its own. Here the numbers of inhabitants increased rapidly, and before long the Caribbean outpost became a slave colony offering a free port to traders from other countries. Such overseas possessions were seen as an essential element of a modern flourishing European state, and to confirm its importance, two years after acquiring the island, the Swedish West India Company was founded, the king being its largest shareholder. In 1788 Anders Sparrman, who had become an abolitionist after the shocking things he had seen while travelling with James Cook, visited Gustav, and the king assured him that Sweden was not involved in the slave trade and never would be. This ignored the fact that while no vessel carrying the human cargo was sailing under the Swedish flag, the country was indirectly involved in the trade and, therefore, benefiting from its profits. In his support of this double standard Gustav was not alone, the actions of other significant followers of the Enlightenment displaying the same contradiction: Voltaire's early investments included the profits raised by imports brought to France in ships involved in the triangular trade, and Thomas Jefferson would continue to own slaves until the end of his days. Recently in Sweden there has been much academic soul-searching, but while researchers acknowledge the country's role in the commerce, still today the majority of Swedish people are ignorant of – or even deny – any involvement in the practice.

In 1783 Gustav III, who had met his first cousin, Catherine II, some years before, arranged a second meeting with the empress. This took place in Fredrickshamm in Finland, which Catherine considered a 'most wretched country', the weather being so bad that she jokingly challenged anyone to complain about living in 'the surroundings of Petersburg'.[113] The two rulers then exchanged valuable gifts, but while Gustav endeavoured to emphasise their family bonds, Catherine would later remark that she found the king unreliable and naive. After this visit, Gustav set off on another trip south, travelling incognito as Count of Haga. Eventually, he joined up with the Emperor Joseph II, and also visited Pope Pius VI in Rome, where the pontiff personally showed him around the Vatican museum. During the several months he spent in the city, Gustav began to acquire the many antique treasures that he would later leave to Sweden in his will – they forming the basis of what would become one of the world's first public museums.

After Rome, the king moved on to Paris and Versailles, accompanied by Count Hans Axel von Fersen, the son of his father's former friend and statesman. Fersen had already met Marie Antoinette ten years before, but they now renewed their acquaintance, and very probably became lovers. Finally, the king returned to Sweden, and, inspired by the French example, fulfilled Queen Christina's earlier ambition, establishing a Swedish Academy to join the academies he had already founded for music and fine arts.

Despite his progressive policies and achievements, Gustav III had begun to be unpopular with the poorer people at large. While during the 1780s Sweden was suffering from famine, the elite were still displaying their ever-increasing wealth and luxurious lifestyles, with the result that the general public had now grown angry and restless. At the same time, the king's problems with the *Riksdag* had continued, not helped by the support given to his opposition by Russia. Gustav therefore needed a way to deal with both problems, and falling back on an age-old means of diverting attention from domestic difficulties, he decided to declare war on his interfering neighbour. With his cousin Catherine once again embroiled with the Ottomans, Gustav felt it to be an opportune moment to make his move, but according to the terms of the constitution, he was unable to start any hostilities without the backing of the *Riksdag*. Looking for a pretext to satisfy the Estates, he therefore commissioned the opera house to supply his soldiers with some Cossack costumes, in which they then mounted a bogus raid on a Swedish outpost near the Russian border at Puumala in Finland. Now having the excuse of an 'unprovoked attack', Gustav was able to obtain the *Riksdag*'s permission for him to declare war.

Initially the king planned an assault on St Petersburg, one to be led by his brother Karl, but this strategy failed, and Gustav was then faced by further problems in the west. Denmark, honouring an earlier agreement with the Russians, had declared its own war on Sweden and had begun to threaten Göteborg. This minor conflict, known as the Lingonberry War after the fruit eaten by the hungry soldiers, was soon over, with the British and Prussians negotiating a peace. But before the fighting had concluded, a plot had been discovered to overthrow the king in Finland. At Anjala, a group of dissatisfied Finnish officers had attempted to correspond with Catherine in Russia, promising her their support if in return she would guarantee the independence of their country. Having other preoccupations, the empress took little notice of their proposals, and before things could go further, the officers had been arrested and one conspirator put to death. This mutiny had the opposite effect to that which the rebels had wanted, as their perceived treachery now increased support for the king. Accordingly, in 1789 the three lower Estates of the *Riksdag* passed the Act of Union and Security, granting Gustav a new constitution that made him virtually an absolute ruler. As this took away many of the nobles' old privileges, it was not popular with some at court, and several of the women demonstrated their protest by not attending the official functions. Among them was Gustav's sister Sofia Albertina, and also his sister-in-law Hedvig, who, having become interested in political affairs, was now even considering an attempt to depose the king. But while she intended to replace him with her husband, Karl refused to take up her plan and in time Gustav was able to quash the opposition. Meanwhile, the new constitution had given him the freedom to renew his war against the Russians, and after some setbacks and defeats, in 1790 his navy finally won a resounding victory at the Second Battle of Svensksund. The captured colours were taken back in triumph to Stockholm, and later Gustav commissioned an obelisk to be erected in the city's centre as a mark of recognition for his people's support during the conflict. Both countries now decided to sue for peace, Sweden being weary of fighting, and Catherine still involved in her war with the Ottomans.

For the remaining two years of his life, Gustav continued to promote the arts, supporting the works of writers, poets, philosophers and musicians. Among others, he invited the German composer Kraus to Sweden, and here he became famous as 'the Swedish Mozart'. Besides creating and performing in his own plays, the king built theatres – among them a new Opera House – and founded the Royal Opera and Ballet. After his visit to France, he also decided to build a palace on the lines of Versailles, one that was to be worthy of his 'Paris of the North'. This would be at Haga, just over a mile from central Stockholm, where he had already created a beautiful park with a variety of smaller buildings. Chief among these was the rococo and neoclassical Pavilion that, under the close supervision of the king, had been constructed following the French taste. Its cool, elegant salon remains a prime example of the so-called Gustavian style that now had become fashionable for all aspects of interior design. The king liked to stay here frequently, but his larger project for the main palace would never be completed, all building work halted at the foundation stage following the king's death.

By now Europe was moving into a period of turmoil. In 1789 the Bastille had fallen, and the same year the women of Paris had marched to Versailles. After many hours under siege, when their very lives were in jeopardy, the royal family had been forced to return to the capital, leaving the great palace for the last time. While they were living as virtual captives in the Tuilleries, Marie Antoinette's former favourite Axel von Fersen became determined to organise their escape. So hiring a large berline coach, in June 1791 he managed to smuggle the family out of the city. Thinking they were now safe, he left them to continue, but around 40 miles from the border with the Austrian Netherlands, at Varennes Louis XVI was recognised. The family were then forced to return to Paris, where the silence that greeted them marked the symbolic moment when power passed from the French monarchy to the people. Unable to help them any further, and with his own life in danger, Fersen regretfully fled the country, travelling eventually to Vienna where he tried to encourage the French queen's brother Emperor Leopold to declare war on France. For political reasons, Leopold turned down any participation by Swedish troops, and the situation became one of stalemate. So in disguise Fersen returned to Paris, where again meeting the royal couple in December he proposed a new escape attempt, but this was rejected by the cautious and unwilling king. With that Fersen returned to Sweden, unable to save Marie Antoinette or her husband before they both went to the guillotine in 1793. But by then other dramatic events had occurred in Stockholm.

In March 1792 Gustav III left Haga to attend a masked ball at his newly completed Opera House in the city – a building demolished a century later to allow for the construction of the present one. On his arrival, the king first went to dine with some of his closest friends in an upper room from where he was able to watch the events taking place below. Then, although receiving a letter warning him of the plot to assassinate him that night, he went downstairs to join the other guests, and here he was soon surrounded by five conspirators, all like him dressed in cloaks and masks. One of these men, twenty-nine-year-old Captain Jacob Anckarström, stepped forward and, having greeted the king, shot him in the back. Although still alive, Gustav slumped to the floor and his attacker was immediately seized.

The plotters were a group of eight noblemen angered by the king's autocratic removal of their rights. One of the group had had last-minute doubts about their actions, it being he who had attempted to warn the king, but all were now arrested and imprisoned.[114] Although mortally wounded, Gustav lived on for thirteen days. Despite his request that Anckarström should be reprieved, his brother Karl ordered that the murderer should be severely punished according to the brutal practices still current throughout Europe at this time. Therefore, following three days in irons, in front of large crowds the prisoner was given a public flogging, his hand was cut off, and then after his beheading his body was quartered. By the time of his execution, Gustav III was already dead, succumbing on 29 March to gangrene and blood poisoning. In spite of the difficulties of their marriage, the queen was deeply shocked by what had happened, and in the days after the attack she visited her husband, until she and the other women were forbidden by him from entering his now stinking sickroom.

While Gustav's revolution of 1789 was primarily responsible for this disaster, the king's actions during his reign had in fact prevented Sweden from suffering the same fate as Poland, where a self-centred and idle aristocracy had weakened the state to the point where it became unable to avoid its total annihilation at the hands of others. Although strengthening his own power with the new constitution, Gustav had at the same time loosened the stranglehold of the nobility and accelerated the process of democracy. The Swedish people now came to admire him for his courage and progressive ideas, and, realising what they had lost, they mourned the death of their young king who had promised so much. Abroad too, the news of his murder was met with horror, and later playwrights would take up the story. Giuseppe Verdi, for one, would return to it when composing his *Un ballo in maschera*, although the libretto then had to be altered to satisfy the Italian censors, who had become particularly sensitive in the aftermath of the failed attempt on Napoleon III's life in 1858.

Following the king's early death, his fourteen-year-old son became Gustav IV Adolf, and soon after his mother retired from court. Although deeply attached to her son, now with considerable relief Sofia Magdalena withdrew from public life. The conspirators had wanted her to become the regent, but with her departure, the role was given instead to the young king's uncle, Karl, Duke of Södermanland. However, in 1796, at the age of seventeen, Gustav IV Adolf began to rule for himself, and soon his strong views and principles would become all too apparent, most notably when he visited St Petersburg in September and failed to turn up for his official betrothal to Catherine the Great's granddaughter, Grand Duchess Alexandra. On having heard that his bride would not be converting to Lutheranism, the young king had left the imperial party waiting for over four hours – a shocking show of disrespect to the ageing Russian empress, who died less than two months later. And again, the next year, Gustav Adolf's lack of finer feelings was displayed when he chose a fiancée who was related to the rejected Alexandra – the sister-in-law of her brother.

Nevertheless, when the bride Friederike Dorothea of Baden arrived in Sweden, Sofia Magdalena gave her a warm welcome, a reception that totally contrasted with the one she had personally received on first arriving in the country many years before.

Meanwhile in Russia, five years after the death of Catherine the Great, Paul proved to be the unpopular and unsuccessful ruler his mother had feared. During a coup to depose him, he was strangled by a group of his nobles, leaving his oldest son to succeed as Alexander I. Although the new tsar was married to Gustav IV's sister-in-law, before long family relations had once again failed to prevent new tensions developing. Having originally opposed Napoleon, after his defeat at Austerlitz and Friedland, in 1807 Alexander decided to make peace with his former enemy. But Gustav IV, who had been violently shaken by his father's murder and the events of the French Revolution, remained adamantly opposed to everything to do with France, and he now joined the Third Coalition. This put the two brothers-in-law at odds, and the next year the tsar invaded Finland and occupied the country, an action that would have disastrous results for the Swedish king, who was already unpopular for his reactionary ideas. Having now lost all patience with him, in March the following year, seven army officers entered his rooms and arrested him. While the event was similar to that which had brought about Tsar Paul's downfall, in this case the victim was not killed and Gustav Adolf was taken instead about 45 miles out of the city to be imprisoned at Gripsholm Castle. Here, he finally abdicated two weeks later, hoping by doing so to enable his son to retain the throne. In this he was disappointed, the *Riksdag* banning from the succession the crown prince as well. After that, Gustav Adolf was allowed to be visited by his family, but, to his mother's distress, she was prevented from seeing him, and they would never meet again. Having later moved abroad and divorced his wife, the deposed king settled in a small hotel at St Gallen in Switzerland, and it was here that he finally died alone in 1837.

For the Swedes the recent war had been a disaster, and even before the fighting had ended, in very same month as Gustav IV Adolf's abdication, a diet at Porvoo had proclaimed a new Grand Duchy of Finland. With Tsar Alexander the grand duke, Finland and Russia were now in a personal union that would last until the end of the Romanov dynasty. Meanwhile, in Sweden the ousted king had been replaced by Gustav III's younger brother, and on his accession as Karl XIII, a new constitution had been introduced and the autocracy of the monarchy had finally come to an end. But with the sixty-year-old king already displaying the first signs of senility, and – more importantly – having no children, the succession was still a matter of concern. Therefore, the Danish viceroy of Norway, Christian August of Augustenburg, was quickly appointed as the new heir to the throne.[115] Renamed Crown Prince Karl August, the next year he received a warm welcome from the Swedes, but within weeks of his arrival, he died when falling off his horse after apparently suffering a stroke. There was a general outpouring of grief at his death, but as earlier some supporters of Gustav IV's son had opposed his election, soon there began to be whispers of foul play. Responsibility for the crown prince's unexpected death was levelled at members of the so-called Gustavian Party, among them Marie Antoinette's former friend and champion Axel von Fersen, who was now falsely accused of having poisoned the dead man. With a remarkable lack of tact or common sense, Fersen appeared at the funeral dressed in his finery and arriving in his ostentatious carriage. This behaviour further enraged the crowds, who, already in a state of high emotion, fell on him while he was passing through the square by the Riddarhuset, the House of the Nobility. Having dragged him from his carriage, they proceeded to lynch him, murdering him while the soldiers on duty stood by and did nothing to save him. Eventually exonerated of all responsibility for Karl August's death, Fersen would be given a burial with full honours, his memorial still standing in the gardens of his former palace outside Stockholm.

With Karl August's death, the country was in need of a new heir to the throne, and so the decision was now taken to elect Jean-Baptiste Bernadotte, Napoleon's former marshal who had become popular with the Swedes for his earlier humane treatment of their prisoners of war. And as the king was largely unfit to rule by this time, Bernadotte was soon taking control of his affairs. He and his wife, the former Désirée Clary – an earlier fiancée of the youthful Napoleon – were viewed as upstarts by members of the court, but three years before her death, in 1810 the dowager queen Sofia Magdalena met them and treated them with a courtesy they had not received from others.

By 1813, Bernadotte had other preoccupations, as he now had to lead the Swedish army to war for the last time against its old foes, first Denmark and then Norway. When peace came two years later, Sweden finally turned its back on its militaristic past, from this time onwards adopting the policy of neutrality that it still holds today. But the treaty with the Danes had done more, taking away the latter's long-held possession of Norway, and uniting the country with Sweden in a personal union that would last until 1905. As a result, while for the next four years Karl XIII, the last of the Holstein-Gottorp dynasty, was also King of Norway, on his death in 1818 both his titles passed to Bernadotte, who, as Karl XIV Johan of Sweden and Karl III Johan of Norway, founded with his wife, Queen Desideria, the House of Bernadotte that still sits on the Swedish throne today.

PART 5

MODERNITY, CHANGE AND REVOLUTION

16

The Nineteenth-century Romanov Rulers

Paul I wearing the Order of St John as a Grand Master. (Courtesy of Rijksmuseum)

Paul, aged fifty-two at the time of Catherine the Great's death, was the only one of her three children held to be legitimate, although questions would always remain as to whether Peter III or the courtier Sergei Saltykov had been his true father. Having been removed from his mother at birth and then brought up for the next seven years by Empress Elizabeth, his relationship with Catherine had never been close, and over time he had grown to hate her. While in her case the feeling was reciprocated, she had also come to doubt his suitability to rule after her, fearing, among other things, he would turn Russia 'into a province dependent on the will of Prussia'.[116] For that reason, according to the evidence, she may have written a will excluding him from the succession, favouring instead her much-loved oldest grandchild, Alexander. However, following the empress's stroke on the morning of 6 November 1796 (OS), Paul was called to the Winter Palace, and while she lingered in a coma, he spent several hours searching through her papers. Besides very possibly discovering and destroying her will excluding him from the succession, he also most probably came across the letter written by Alexei Orlov to his mother thirty-four years earlier, explaining the circumstances relating to the murder of his father, Peter III. While this document exonerated Catherine from responsibility for the crime, it also undermined the evidence published by the subsequent postmortem explaining the death as due to natural causes. Instead, it clearly laid out the unfortunate, probably accidental, events that had taken place at Ropsha, and the part played at that time by the Guards officers in charge of the deposed tsar. Now knowing the truth, the new emperor was determined to get his revenge. After his father's body had been exhumed from its resting place in the Alexander Nevsky Monastery, Paul ordered it to lie in state beside his dead mother. Both his parents were then taken in full pomp to the Peter and Paul Cathedral, where they were buried like joint monarchs, side by side. And in one further act of spite, as he particularly wished to make Orlov pay for his guilt, during the funeral procession Paul ordered him to carry Peter's crown, thus obliging the count to honour posthumously the man whose murder he had earlier brought about.

On the day of his coronation, in an act that further reflected his resentment towards his mother, Paul revoked Peter the Great's earlier decree, and despite Russian empresses having ruled for around two-thirds of the eighteenth century, he returned to a hereditary system that privileged the right of the oldest surviving male, introducing a new semi-Salic law that made it virtually impossible for any woman ever again to succeed to the throne. Only in the highly improbable case of all males of Romanov descent dying out would a female become eligible to succeed, a constitutional change that just over a century later would have a disastrous effect on the events leading to the fall of the dynasty. After the birth of four daughters, in 1904 the desperate imperial couple finally produced the chronically sick *tsesarevich*, and the mother's concerns for her much-adored invalid son would negatively influence the decisions taken by her and her husband. This, Paul's final act of malicious defiance against Catherine, flew in the face of the evidence, whereby – with the exception of Peter the Great – throughout the century the women had in the main proved more successful as rulers than the men. Putting aside the fate of the baby Ivan VI, and the early death of fourteen-year-old Peter II, neither of the other two males of the period, Peter III and later his son Paul, fully appreciated the complexities of their position. As a result, within a brief period of coming to power, both had become unpopular and had lost not just their thrones, but also their lives.

In 1776, three years after marrying Wilhelmine Luise of Hesse-Darmstadt – thereafter known as Natalia Alexeievna – Paul became widowed when his wife died following a long and agonising delivery of a stillborn child. However, soon after he met the sixteen-year-old great-niece of Frederick II, Sophie Dorothee of Württemberg, who at the time was betrothed to Paul's former brother-in-law, Ludwig. In the typically pragmatic way of the period, after the latter had been financially rewarded to end his engagement, Sophie converted to Orthodoxy and by the end of the year was married to Paul, becoming the Grand Duchess Maria Feodorovna.[117] Catherine II was originally among those in favour of this match, attracted to the well-educated young girl who like her had been born in Stettin. But in time, during the further twenty years of the old empress's reign, the two women's relationship would deteriorate as a result of Maria's undying loyalty to Paul. He was devoted to her, and from their first meeting she had also adored him, continuing in the years ahead to love him despite the tensions caused by his later erratic behaviour and unspecified liaisons with other women. But Maria was the more intelligent and when, five years after their wedding, they went as the 'Count and Countess of the North' on a tour of Europe, it would be she who impressed the people they met. A tall, attractive, cultured, and artistic young woman who was also a good linguist, she made her mark at the courts of Versailles and Vienna, and was generally admired while staying in Venice for the carnival.

Maria delighted in the style and formal etiquette of the Russian imperial court, and, although always careful about her spending, she would sponsor the arts and other charitable works. Having excellent taste, in time she enjoyed making changes to their two palaces: Gatchina, the former country home of Catherine's early lover, Grigory Orlov; and Pavlovsk. On this estate, initially given to the couple by the empress to mark their son Alexander's birth, they replaced the first residences with a new neoclassical building, designed by Catherine's Scottish architect Charles Cameron. He was also made responsible for the surrounding landscaped park and gardens where, besides damming the river to make a lake, he created the pavilions and other small structures that had now become so popular on aristocratic and royal estates throughout Europe. However, before long, considering his schemes too modest, Paul and his wife grew to be so much at odds with the architect that they replaced him with his assistant, Vicenzo Brenna. More attentive to their wishes, Brenna set about replicating the Greek, Roman, French and other styles that the couple had come to appreciate while on their travels. They were soon happy with their new palace, filling it with artefacts collected or imported from abroad. After Catherine's death, wanting to create an imperial residence that better reflected Paul's new status, they instructed Brenna to add on two extra wings so as to make the place more impressive. Much of this palace would be seriously damaged in the fire that broke out two years after Paul's death, but, repaired by his widow, it would survive until the German army's mindless destruction in the 1940s made new restoration work necessary, a massive task that has now been completed. Although Paul had preferred Gatchina, Maria would always remain attached to Pavlovsk, choosing it as her home throughout her twenty-seven-year-long widowhood.

Although not unintelligent, Paul was a small, plain and unprepossessing man. Stubborn, inflexible, and hating contradiction, he resisted advice and stuck rigidly to his reactionary principles, some of which were driven by his opposition to the policies or actions of his mother. Accordingly, after his accession he offered asylum to the deposed Polish king, Stanislaw II and, more paradoxically, also pardoned men such as Alexander Radischev, whose strong radical ideas had earlier so offended Catherine. Like his wife, Paul despised the behaviour of his mother's libertine court, and loathing those whom she had favoured, he spitefully turned Potemkin's Taurida Palace into a barracks, thereafter the men's horses being stabled in the magnificent ballroom. But worse still, in an uncalled-for and disproportionate act of vengeance, wanting to abolish all trace of Potemkin's grave, he demanded the body be disinterred and its remains scattered – orders that in the event were never carried out.

Like his putative father, Paul was passionate about the military, taking immense pleasure in watching his soldiers carry out their daily parades, where his eagle eye was ready to punish excessively any minor lapse in the performance of their drill. On one occasion, his unbalanced reaction to a lack of precision resulted in the offenders being commanded to leave for Siberia without delay, an order halted on the very day they had set off on their long march. Opposed to all the practical changes brought in by Potemkin, Paul reintroduced the uncomfortable Prussian-style uniforms that had been so loved by his father, but bitterly disliked by the men. While, within weeks of his accession, people began to remark on how much things were now being 'turned upside down', Paul continued with his often petty regulations and directives that ranged from restricting certain forms of private entertainment or imposing rules of appropriate society dress, to the banning of imported foreign books or the teaching of new ideas. But although shocked by the ways of his mother's court, nonetheless Paul rewarded his own chosen favourites so generously that over his short time in power he granted them more serfs than Catherine had done throughout her entire reign.

Being naturally devout, Paul disliked the new anti-religious stance of republican France, and having been horrified, as were many other leaders of the time, by the extreme Jacobin actions during the later years of the revolution, he was initially against everything that came from that post-monarchist country. A supporter of the counter-revolution, in 1798 he offered Louis XVIII asylum in Courland, the duchy finally annexed by Russia some three years earlier. Although Louis, the younger brother of the guillotined Louis XVI, had – since the death in prison in 1795 of his young nephew 'Louis XVII' – been acclaimed king by his followers, he was still in need of foreign sanctuary. Earlier, in 1791, at the time of the French king and queen's attempted escape and subsequent capture at Varennes, he (again with the help of Count Fersen) had fled to Brussels before spending the next few years in constant movement around Europe in search of refuge. For a time as the guest of Duke Karl Wilhelm Ferdinand, he had settled in a small two-roomed flat at Blankenburg in the Harz mountains of Brunswick.

A cultured and enlightened ruler, Duke Karl Wilhelm Ferdinand of Brunswick-Wolfenbüttel modelled himself on his famous uncle, Frederick II. Married to his second cousin Augusta, the sister of George III and the luckless Danish queen Caroline Mathilde, he was closely connected to many of the ruling houses of Europe. However, domestically, the duke considered himself most unfortunate, with three of his four sons – very possibly through inbreeding – having a varying degree of mental and physical disabilities. Furthermore, the wildly inappropriate behaviour of his two surviving daughters would eventually see their lives end in scandal; the older, in time separated from her husband, would eventually die in Russia while giving birth to an illegitimate child, and the younger – the notorious Caroline, who was married to her cousin, the British Prince Regent – would later have the intimate details of her salacious affairs picked over in the divorce courts. Karl himself, no doubt reflecting on his own experiences, lamented the fate of those in high positions who were forced into unhappy dynastic marriages, which so often brought further disaster, including the birth of descendants who, in his words, were 'mostly cripples in mind and body'.[118] Hedvig Elizabeth Charlotte, the wife of the Swedish king Karl XIII, although complimentary about the duke, was unsparing in her criticism of the other members of the family. Her description of the different individuals painted them as either boring, strange, or else as showing signs of 'peculiarity', 'imbecility' and even immorality.

In 1792 Duke Karl had given his name to the so-called 'Brunswick Manifesto' that had promised support for the French king against the threatening anarchy. While this had only succeeded in further inflaming the situation in France, and hastening Louis XVI's death, the duke then continued to try and help the Bourbons. For two years he gave asylum to Louis XVIII, until forced by the French in 1798 to rescind his invitation.

It was against this background that Louis now accepted the tsar's offer of a subsidy and took up residence in Courland's capital, Mitau (Jelgava). Here, around 35 miles from Riga, for the only time during his exile the French king would live in style, occupying the baroque palace that had been built by Rastrelli for Empress Anna's former favourite Biron, Duke of Courland. Already accompanied by an entourage of over eighty people, Louis was then allowed to have the protection of some hundred of his royal bodyguard. Soon several more émigrés settled in the town, making the king's expatriate court a centre for French culture. In Louis' own view, it now represented France, the country as it were embodied in his own person, and here he would be visited by various dignitaries, among them Paul's son, the Grand Duke Constantine. In time he was also joined by Marie Antoinette's only surviving child, Marie Thérèse, known as Madame Royale, who, after her release from incarceration at the Temple in Paris in 1795, had spent the subsequent period sheltering with her Austrian relations in Vienna. She finally arrived at Mitau in June of 1799, just days before she was married in the palace chapel to Louis' nephew, her cousin the Duke of Angoulème. Although he then offered his services to the Russian emperor, two years later Paul changed his political allegiances, and so, with little warning, he expelled the whole family. As a result the French king moved on to Warsaw, which had become a Prussian garrison town after the Third Partition of Poland, and here in their rather simpler accommodation he and his followers remained for the next three years as guests of the new Prussian king, Friedrich Wilhelm III.

The cause of Paul's change of heart regarding his French visitor lay in the events of some years earlier. Wanting to increase his chances of gaining a base in the Mediterranean, he had responded positively when asked to help those Knights of Malta – Poles and French émigrés – living in the Russian lands acquired since the partitioning of Poland. In 1797, having officially become their protector, he granted them new priories in Russia. But the next year the French occupied Malta, causing the Catholic Knights to surrender and finally leave their island, and therefore many of these now also moved to St Petersburg. With that, Paul, although an Orthodox himself, was elected Grand Master of the now relocated order. Being proud of this role, besides having himself painted in his official robes he incorporated the Maltese cross into his coat of arms, and publicly displayed it in a variety of places such as Pavlovsk, where he had the Knights' Room suitably redecorated for his ceremonial gatherings. But more significantly, because of his recent appointment, he strongly objected when two years later the British captured Malta from the French. In a complete *volte face*, he switched his support to Napoleon, and in 1801 joined Denmark, Sweden and Prussia in a League of Armed Neutrality – an alliance intended to prevent the British setting up a blockade of the Baltic to hinder French trade. Fearing that France might receive help from the Danes, in April of the same year the British mounted their first successful naval attack on the Danish capital, after which they set their sights on St Petersburg. However, not long after they abandoned their advance, having received news at Reval (Tallinn) of Paul's unexpected death, and within a few months Britain and Russia were at peace.

In 1783 Catherine had ratified a treaty with Georgia, offering the country her protection, and, although this backing had ceased to be forthcoming, the Russians had maintained their interest in the area. So, when in 1800 unrest broke out following the death of the country's king, Paul decided the time had come to intervene; he declared that the Georgian monarchy should be abolished and the former kingdom incorporated into the Russian Empire. While this objective was realised in the reign of his son Alexander, another of Paul's ambitious schemes would not be achieved because of his premature death. Despite a dire shortage of maps, to the concern of many the tsar had planned with the French to mount a joint invasion of British India. Twenty thousand Don Cossacks were therefore sent on their way in January, but within weeks when they were close to the Aral Sea news reached them that Paul had died, and with that the Russian campaign was aborted.

In the final years of his reign, Paul would increasingly act on a whim, and some of his decisions were so poorly reasoned that even his son Constantine was quoted as saying that the emperor had declared 'war on common sense'.[119] The tsar's maverick nature was particularly evident in his relationship with his nobles, where his violent likes and dislikes were so marked and unpredictable that he became intensely unpopular. His increasingly bizarre behaviour, changing moods, volatile outbursts of rage and paranoia caused those close to him to question his sanity, and some began to develop plans to bring about his abdication. Looking to the earlier events in Britain, where for a time the incapacitated George III had already been temporarily replaced by his son, some of the conspirators decided to approach Alexander, suggesting that he might be able to act as regent for his unbalanced father. But while Alexander listened to the proposal, he remained indecisive and no further action was taken.

In the last decade of the eighteenth century the position of rulers had become notoriously precarious, with not just the overthrow and execution of the French king and queen, but also the murder of the tsar's cousin Gustav III of Sweden. With assassination now an altogether too real possibility, Paul's fears for his own safety began to take hold. The year after his accession, feeling at risk in the Winter Palace and wanting a more secure residence, he had demolished the decaying Summer Palace of Empress Elizabeth and commissioned in its place a new fortified and moated building: the Castle of St Michael. This was completed four years later, and Paul then erected in the courtyard outside the entrance the equestrian sculpture earlier created by Rastrelli of Peter the Great.

The fact that Catherine II had never liked this piece no doubt made it still more attractive to her son, who now used it to score further points over his hated mother. While she, when commissioning the famous work by Falconet, had underlined her rightful place within the ruling dynasty with her inscription, 'From Peter I to Catherine II', Paul would go further. Parodying her words, he emphasised his actual and personal bloodline to the Romanovs by writing on the plinth beneath Rastrelli's statue, 'From Great-Grandson to Great-Grandfather'.

Paul's fears of assassination were not unfounded, and both he and his wife soon began to suspect that a plot was in the making, very possibly backed by their son. Then, just over a month after they and all their immediate family had moved into the new castle, during the night of 12 March (OS) eighteen officers, including Catherine's last favourite, Platon Zubov, broke into Paul's rooms, their intention being to force him to abdicate. Terrified, he tried to escape, screening himself behind a curtain, but he was soon dragged out and in the scuffle that ensued was beaten, strangled and suffocated, thus becoming the third of the Romanov tsars to be murdered. Zubov's brother, another of the plotters, then went to Alexander to inform him of the news. After being first approached, Alexander had remained aware of the conspiracy, but he had not intended that Paul should die. Acknowledging the erratic nature of his father's behaviour, he had accepted that he might need to be deposed, but – perhaps naively – had believed in the possibility of a bloodless transition of power. For years to come he would reproach himself for Paul's murder, and for a time his mother, Maria Feodorovna, refused to speak to him, believing him largely responsible for what had happened. Nonetheless, an official pronouncement soon declared that Paul had died of apoplexy, and, following the assassination, the family returned to the Winter Palace, abandoning within weeks of its completion the large, forbidding castle that from this time would never again be an imperial residence. Still only forty-two when she was widowed, initially the strong-willed and grief-stricken Maria Feodorovna considered succeeding her husband on the throne, just as her mother-in-law had done when she superseded her child Paul, but the situation was now different. Being already an adult, Alexander's position was stronger than that of his young father in 1762, and so Maria was persuaded to step aside. Nonetheless, she would succeed in creating a fresh role for herself, not just remaining a dominant presence at court but also inaugurating a new Romanov custom that lasted until the end of the dynasty. From this moment, every dowager empress would take precedence over her daughter-in-law and successor, the wife of the new ruling tsar.

With Paul's death, as Catherine the Great had wanted, her twenty-three-year-old grandson became Alexander I. In 1792, despite her concerns for their extreme youth, Catherine had arranged Alexander's marriage to the fourteen-year-old niece of his father's first wife; she, Luise of Baden, would become, after her Orthodox conversion, the Grand Duchess Elizabeth Alexeievna. The shy Alexander, who was only a year older than his bride, was unfriendly to her at first, but in time the pair became closer. Meanwhile, Catherine welcomed Elizabeth warmly and, delighted with her 'dearest children', the next year she gave them the New Palace, an elegant yellow and white neoclassical building designed by Giacomo Querenghi at Tsarskoe Selo. Although the couple moved into it within days of its completion in June 1796, with Alexander preferring the neighbouring Great (Catherine) Palace abandoned by his father, he seldom visited it after his accession. But – now known as the Alexander Palace – in time it would become a favourite residence for several future Romanovs, and eventually the principal home for the dynasty's last ruler, Tsar Nicholas II, and his unfortunate family.

Even though the people welcomed Alexander's accession, believing it promised a relaxation of some of his father's more draconian measures, Paul's questionable death had, nonetheless, produced a degree of uncertainty. And to add to the general sense of unease, Alexander, besides suffering remorse over the murder, was already a complex character. As noted by Elizabeth Alexeievna even before their marriage, in his eagerness to please he often appeared indecisive or even insincere.

This was just one of the problems that faced the young bride. Although she loved her husband and was popular with Catherine, she soon became the subject of malicious court gossip. When she later produced two daughters – both of whom died as infants – her critics started to spread rumours regarding the father of the elder girl, using the baby's darker colouring to suggest that she was the illegitimate child of Alexander's Polish friend Adam Czartoryski. But while such stories of Elizabeth's possible infidelity were merely rumoured, Alexander would soon be openly enjoying several affairs of his own, including one begun in 1799 with a long-term mistress who not only gave him four or five children, but would actually accompany him to Vienna at the time of the Congress in 1815. On what was most probably a more platonic level, Alexander was also particularly attracted to the beautiful and extremely popular Luise, the wife of the Prussian king Friedrich Wilhelm III. After a first visit to Memel in East Prussia in 1802, the tsar had become friends with the royal couple, staying with them again a few years later in Berlin.

Although wanting to maintain peace in order to concentrate on the reform of his country, after the war resumed between France and Britain, Alexander began increasingly to fear Napoleon, seeing him as an ambitious man who could not be trusted to honour the terms of his earlier agreements. But still unsure of his nearer neighbour Austria, and not realising the extent of the domestic and financial problems it now faced, Alexander was at first hesitant to form a close alliance with the Habsburg Emperor. However, after the shocking execution of the Bourbon Duke d'Enghien in 1804, and Napoleon's self-coronation at the end of the same year, in 1805 the tsar was finally persuaded to join the Third Coalition against the French.[k] As a result, in December he found himself leading a combined Russian-Austrian army into battle at Austerlitz near Brno (today in the Czech Republic). After nine hours of heavy fighting, this 'Battle of the Three Emperors' ended with the crushing and chaotic defeat of the allies. Following this, in July the next year Napoleon created the Confederation of the Rhine from the lands he had taken from the empire, leaving Franz II with little option other than to abdicate his Imperial crown. This brought to an end, after some 800 years, the major European power – first conceived by Charlemagne back in 800 AD – that had come to be known as the Holy Roman Empire. However, in compensation, Franz now took on a new title, becoming Emperor of Austria.

Until this point the Prussian king had sought to maintain neutrality, but after Austerlitz he finally agreed to join the allies in opposing Napoleon. However, this would lead to his own bitter defeat in the double conflict of Jena-Auerstädt (Auerstedt), a humiliating disaster that forced him to flee with his family to the far reaches of his kingdom.[120] Having arrived in his eastern capital, Königsberg (Kaliningrad), Friedrich Wilhelm then moved on some further 130 miles or so to the north-east, settling for the next three years as a virtual exile at Memel (Klaipėda), where he would devote his time mainly to introducing new reforms and restructuring his army. But the French emperor had further ambitions and, a month after the besieged Danzig fell to his Marshal Lefebvre, in June 1807 he personally led his men into battle against the Russians at Friedland (Pravdinsk), a little over 30 miles south-east of Königsberg. Here he achieved a major victory, which was followed by a disastrous retreat by the Russians, many of whom were drowned while trying to escape across the nearby river. The tsar himself was not present at this latest catastrophe, but on hearing the news he decided the time had come to make peace.

Therefore, in early July Alexander joined Napoleon near Tilsit in East Prussia (today in Sovetsk, Kaliningrad Oblast). Here at the French headquarters, following their first showy meeting on a raft in the centre of the Niemen River, the two men spent several days agreeing the final terms of the treaty, before exchanging gifts and decorations – Napoleon receiving the Order of St Andrew, Alexander the Légion d'honneur. Friedrich Wilhelm, who had been largely ignored in the negotiations, now suffered further humiliation, finding himself forced to pay heavy indemnities and accept the surrender of almost half his territory. With her husband crushed, the Prussian queen agreed to meet Napoleon, but despite her desperate pleas for him to show moderation, the French emperor remained intransigent. Abroad, many were shocked by Alexander's betrayal of Friedrich Wilhelm, and mocking cartoons began to appear reviling the tsar for the way he had abandoned his former friend.

---

k Kidnapped on the orders of Napoleon while he was in Baden, the duke was accused of conspiracy and then summarily shot. The foreign courts were horrified at the news.

By his coming to an agreement with Napoleon, Alexander was now in opposition to the British, and after their second attack on Copenhagen, he officially declared war against them. In the event, Britain were barely engaged in any later action, other than providing some support to the Swedes, who now faced open attack from their eastern neighbour. Responding to Napoleon's inducements to share in the dividing up of Europe, Alexander had agreed at Tilsit to invade Sweden's Finnish lands, and by the next year his troops had occupied the whole southern region of Finland. Moreover, in March 1809 the Russians carried out two successful invasions of the Swedish mainland by marching over the frozen Gulf of Bothnia, first taking a route via the Åland islands towards Stockholm, and later another to Ulea further north. By that time, Sweden's defeat was becoming inevitable, and the same month, even before the fighting had ended, a diet was summoned at Porvoo to decide Finland's future. Here, in the cathedral of this attractive little town some 30 miles north-east of Helsingfors (Helsinki), the new autonomous Grand Duchy of Finland was established, and the Romanov tsar officially recognised as its hereditary grand duke. Later, in 1812 Alexander decided to move the duchy's capital nearer to St Petersburg, choosing the more conveniently placed, and now renamed, Helsinki. Finally, after a devastating fire in 1827 had destroyed some three-quarters of Turku, which had briefly been the capital, the remaining government buildings were relocated to their new site. As the century progressed, Helsinki thus began to grow in importance, its rising status being marked by the arrival of new classical-style buildings similar to those found in St Petersburg, and by the two imposing Lutheran and Orthodox cathedrals that still dominate the skyline above the port.

Alexander's alliance with the French did not last long, the treaty having never been popular with many Russians, in particular the dowager Empress Maria Feodorovna, who was always bitterly opposed to Napoleon. So when in 1809 rumours reached the tsar that the emperor, now in the throes of his divorce, intended to marry his favourite sister, Catherine, hurried arrangements were immediately made to find an alternative husband. Her cousin, Georg of Oldenburg, was chosen instead. When his duchy was annexed by Napoleon two years later, relations between the emperors became still more strained.

While Alexander had his doubts as to the trustworthiness of Napoleon, the French emperor had his own misgivings regarding the tsar. Having heard hints of a possible Russian attack on France, in 1812 he made the decision to invade Russia with his *Grande Armée*, a vast force of over 600,000 men, many of whom were drawn from the countries and states already conquered by Napoleon. Having crossed the border on 24 June (NS), in September, having already lost large numbers of men – many through typhus and other sicknesses – the French army met the Russians at Borodino, a village lying some 70 miles from Moscow. The resulting conflict, described by Napoleon as his 'most terrible' battle, resulted in appalling casualties for both sides and no conclusive outcome: although the French were nominally the victors, the Russians were not totally crushed. Field Marshal Kutuzov now withdrew, choosing to retreat to the east of Moscow, where his troops were then able to avoid further engagement. This encouraged Napoleon – against the advice of most of his generals – to continue on, penetrating deeper into the country, until a week later he arrived in Moscow, to find much of the place had been deserted. With the army greatly reduced in size by the multiple difficulties it had already encountered, it now faced further problems as fires began to break out around the city, possibly – as argued by Leo Tolstoy and others – caused accidentally by the soldiers' open fires, or, alternatively (if not additionally) started on the orders of the mayor in an effort to hinder the invaders and speed their departure. With much of the place still constructed out of wood, the situation was then made worse by the shortage of still-intact fire hoses, many of these having apparently been sabotaged by the fleeing citizens – an action that reinforces the argument that the Russians had intentionally sought to destroy anything of service to the enemy. Whatever the initial causes of the fires that were now breaking out, a persistent wind was blowing and this soon further whipped up the conflagration, making it virtually unstoppable. The blaze raged on for over three days, in the time probably destroying some three-quarters of the city's buildings. And although at last the flames were extinguished, by then the struggle to find food and fodder had grown still worse. Nonetheless, as the warm weather continued, Napoleon lingered, waiting for Russia's agreement to an armistice. This, however, was rejected outright, and finally, on receiving news of further problems developing at home, five weeks after his arrival in the city he gave the order to retreat. But within days the winter had set in, and over the next two months, thousands more of his men and horses would die on the terrible journey back, killed by the cold, hunger, rampant disease, and suicide, not forgetting the guerrilla attacks that the Russians made on the exhausted retreating army. When eventually he arrived at Vilnius, Napoleon handed over his command so that he might hurry back and deal with matters in France, but as a recent discovery of a mass grave has verified, the sick would continue to die in their thousands, and by the time the army eventually reached Poland, it had probably little more than 20,000 men in its ranks.

Alexander's reputation, damaged after his earlier failures, was now redeemed, and he soon became revered as the saviour of the Russian people. Pursuing his enemy, he continued to lead his army across Europe, chasing Napoleon to France, and eventually reaching the outskirts of the capital. His arrival in the city was met with enthusiasm, and the tall, good-looking young man became the hero of the hour. Having grown considerably more religious, at the Treaty of Paris he sought to ensure peace by uniting the powers in a Holy Alliance, all the while confident like them that Napoleon would continue to live out his days in exile on Elba. Although the former French emperor had now abdicated, he was still ambitious, and so, after escaping the island, he landed on France's mainland near Cannes. From here he proceeded to march north, gathering ever-increasing numbers of supporters to his side. For the next famous 'hundred days' Europe watched with bated breath until eventually Napoleon was defeated in his last battle at Waterloo in June 1815. This time his enemies would be more careful to prevent his return, choosing to send him to the more distant Atlantic island of St Helena, where six years later he died on 5 May 1821.

Since September 1814 Napoleon's former enemies had been gathering at Vienna to decide the future of the continent. Hoping to maintain the peace, this Congress set out to realign the balance of power by reshaping the borders and countries of Europe. Among other things, it created from most of Napoleon's recently formed Duchy of Warsaw a new nominally independent state, the 'Congress Kingdom' of Poland, which was to be in personal union with Russia under the rule of the tsar.

In Paris Alexander had played a key role in the events, but after that time he had gradually become more reclusive, reducing his involvement in political and international affairs, and appearing to be more absorbed by mysticism and spirituality. Nevertheless, back in St Petersburg his victory over the French continued to be celebrated. Previously in 1801 Paul had commissioned the building of the new Kazan Cathedral that, modelled on St Peter's Basilica in Rome, had been completed after his death. This, following Paul's instructions, had become the home of the priceless icon of Our Lady of Kazan that is still much venerated by Russian believers today. Considered to have miraculous qualities, since the time of Peter the Great's father the icon had been held as the protectress of the Romanovs. When the captured French standards were also housed in the building after Napoleon's retreat in 1812, the cathedral gained further importance as the chief site chosen to mark the French defeat. Here Russia's saviour, Field Marshal Kutuzov, would be buried, and honoured by the monument that stands in the square outside. Elsewhere too, around the city other structures now celebrated Russia's salvation and ultimate triumph, among them Querenghi's wooden arch designed specifically to welcome back the victorious soldiers. This, the Narva Gate, after its reconstruction in brick and copper, was officially reopened in 1834, the same year that an immensely tall, red-granite victory column was erected in the square outside the Winter Palace. This was topped with an angel whose face was said to be modelled on that of the emperor abd on the plinth below the inscription read, 'To Alexander I from a Grateful Russia'.

Despite his earlier liberal ideas and promises of reform, Alexander had with time become more conservative and autocratic. Now appearing less often in public, he also told those around him how he wished he might rid himself of the responsibility of ruling. Then in 1824 a series of events occurred to deepen his growing depression. In early November St Petersburg suffered one of its most disastrous floods with the water rising to more than 13 feet, leaving 569 people dead, and thousands sick or injured. This came at the end of a year that had also brought personal tragedy to the tsar. While getting over a serious illness in the early summer, in June he had heard to his utter despair that his beloved and sole surviving illegitimate daughter had just died. However, his wife was then so understanding and supportive that the couple grew to be closer once again. But like most nineteenth-century empresses, Elizabeth Alexeievna was not strong, and her health had been further undermined by the unhealthy climate of St Petersburg. Alexander therefore decided to take her south to Taganrog on the Sea of Azov so that she might escape the approaching harsh winter months of the north. Having arrived in the town they then stayed together in the governor's small house, until Alexander decided he would go and inspect some of the military units stationed in the Crimea. While his visits were popular with the men, his long, exhausting trip to some possibly disease-infected areas would later prove to have been ill-conceived. When returning from Balaklava he caught a chill, and with complications soon developing, by the time he got back to Taganrog his condition was starting to be serious. Soon his illness had become life-threatening, with intermittent bouts of severe headaches, outbreaks of high fever, and even the loss of consciousness. Within days, to the distress of all those around him, the forty-seven-year-old emperor was dead. Elizabeth Alexeievna remained by her husband's bier for much of the following weeks, but already gravely ill and further worn out by her recent loss, she too would die soon after, while on the journey home to St Petersburg.

Although the tsar's body was now embalmed, the local practitioner in Taganrog had been so inexpert that when it eventually arrived back in the capital, Alexander's own mother, Maria Feodorovna, declared her son to be 'greatly changed'. This soon added to the conspiracy theories that now began to develop following Alexander's unexpected death. Claims were made that the body returned for burial was not that of the tsar, and other rumours suggested that he had finally achieved his ambition to abdicate. Certain people declared that he had become a holy man, and over a decade later when a wandering monk appeared in the capital some believed him to be the former tsar. Even Nicholas I would choose to see this man, although – for whatever reason – he did not then think it worth mentioning in his memoirs.

Back in 1825 confusion now developed over the actual succession. The news of Alexander's death had already taken time to arrive in St Petersburg, and further delays had been incurred as the message had to be passed on to his oldest brother Constantine in Poland. When eventually a reply arrived back in the city it brought astonishing news. Divorced and with no legitimate sons, Constantine had previously agreed with Alexander to renounce his right to the throne. Although he had been obliged to do so after taking a second, morganatic wife, a Polish noble woman without royal or imperial blood, he actually wanted to remain in Poland, and, moreover, was glad – as he later indicated – to avoid what he saw as the possibility of suffering the same fate as his father. However, the earlier agreement with his older sibling had been kept secret, not fully divulged even to the very man on whom it all most impinged, Alexander and Constantine's younger brother, Nicholas.

Born in 1779, Constantine had grown up physically to resemble his father, Paul, who, apparently preferring him to his elder brother, had even gone so far as to pronounce him to be the *tsesarevich*, his successor. However, after Alexander's accession and the defeat of Napoleon, Constantine took on the unofficial role of acting viceroy in the Kingdom of Poland, where, despite his sympathies for the Polish people, his strict, autocratic, and often cruel regime, designed to uphold the interests of the Russian empire, soon made him unpopular. He had been no more successful in his home life, his first marriage to Juliana of Saxe-Coburg-Saalfeld, later Anna Feodorovna – a match arranged by Catherine when she was fourteen and he just seventeen – had finally ended after nearly two decades. Juliana, sister of Leopold (later the first King of the Belgians, and uncle of both Queen Victoria and Prince Albert), had fled her marriage after just three years, and despite a later half-hearted attempt at reconciliation, she was finally sent home because of her inappropriate behaviour. So in 1814, Constantine had asked permission from his older brother for an annulment, and in May 1820, two months after obtaining it, he was remarried. While this marriage – childless like his first – excluded him and any potential heirs from the succession, it proved to be happier than the first.

Constantine had ambitions for Poland and so continued to sue for peace with Napoleon even after 1812. He also trusted the Polish army to the extent that, following his younger brother's accession, he would annoy Nicholas I by refusing to believe that Poles had been involved in the Decembrist Revolt at the beginning of his reign. Nonetheless in 1830 Constantine would find himself in danger when an attempt was made to assassinate him in his palace in Warsaw. Although he managed to escape disguised as a woman, the November Rising then broke out, a struggle for Polish independence that was supported even by Constantine's personal Guards. The following year, Nicholas succeeded in crushing this rebellion before taking away the Kingdom of Poland's independence and incorporating it into the Russian Empire, but by that time Constantine had died of cholera at Vitebsk (today in Belarus). He therefore did not live to see the rebellion's defeat, and the subsequent large emigration of Poles, many of whom went to France from where they would give their support to the later Polish uprisings of the 1840s.

Nicholas, the second youngest of Paul and Maria Feodorovna's ten children, was born after a run of six daughters on 25 June (OS) 1796, five months before his grandmother's death. At the time Catherine was impressed by her healthy new grandson, and writing with strange premonition to her long-time correspondent in Paris, Baron Grimm, she predicted that he was 'destined, thanks to his unusual strength, to reign, even though he does have two older brothers'.[121] Still an infant when the empress died, Nicholas would be brought up solely by his parents, following a more conservative education than that of his older brothers. His father had treated the child with obvious affection, but the boy was still only five at the time of Paul's murder, and although later attached to his severe mother, Nicholas had been frightened of her while he was young. Under her direction his upbringing was strict by design, made still more so by his disciplinarian tutor who regularly beat him. Whereas Catherine had endeavoured to encourage Alexander and Constantine with the Enlightenment ideas that for the greater part of her reign she had embraced, Nicholas was encouraged to adhere to more uncompromising views. And even though his mother had tried to discourage his interest in the military, he would become much inspired by the struggles against Napoleon during Russia's 'Patriotic War'. Finally allowed by his brother Alexander to join the army in 1814, Nicholas was delighted by his experiences with the troops in Paris. But like his father and grandfather, over time he grew to be a stickler for rigid discipline and precise drill, something that would eventually make him unpopular with the Guards.

When he returned from Paris with his younger brother Michael, he stayed for a time in Berlin, and here he first met Charlotte, the oldest surviving daughter of Friedrich Wilhelm III and his wife Luise. On a second visit the next year the couple became engaged, and in 1817, having arrived in Russia with her brother Wilhelm (later to be Kaiser Wilhelm I), Charlotte converted to Orthodoxy and became known as Alexandra Feodorovna. Finally, on 1 July (OS), the wedding took place in the Great Church of the Winter Palace. The marriage proved to be highly successful, with Nicholas describing their life together in the Anichkov Palace as 'paradise'. To add to the couple's happiness, just a year after the wedding, while visiting Moscow, Alexandra gave birth to her first child, the future Alexander II, and then, over the next fourteen years, in addition to one stillborn daughter, she had six further children, four of whom would live into their sixties. As a result of this, the imperial couple would eventually have more than thirty grandchildren, and there would be a rapid increase in the numbers of grand dukes and duchesses.[1]

However, Nicholas and Alexandra's peaceful private life was not destined to last. According to her memoirs, two years after their marriage one evening at a private dinner Alexander I declared that he hoped one day to be able to abdicate, in which case he intended to appoint Nicholas as his heir. The couple were appalled at this announcement, but

1 To the great displeasure of future members of the family, in 1886 Alexander III would try to reduce the expenses incurred by the excessive number of grand dukes and duchesses by restricting the title to just children and the paternal grandchildren of the tsar.

as the matter was not mentioned to them again, for the next few years they continued to live much as they had before. But with Constantine now remarried, in the summer of 1823 Alexander drew up a manifesto confirming who would succeeed him, a document that was kept secret from all but a handful of people. Two years later in September the emperor and his wife left St Petersburg for the last time, and within weeks news of the tsar's illness began filtering back from Taganrog. Realising the possibility of an impending crisis, and wishing to ensure a smooth transition of power, Nicholas now announced that he would acknowledge the accession of Constantine, something which he then reaffirmed when shortly after on 27 November (OS) St Petersburg finally learnt of the tsar's death. With the rest of the court he swore his allegiance to his older brother in Poland, still insisting on abiding by this after the written manifesto had been discovered. But, to make things worse, even before Constantine's adamant refusal to accept the throne arrived from Warsaw, rumours had grown of a conspiracy to overthrow the whole Romanov dynasty. With the situation becoming steadily more serious, finally the ever-dutiful Nicholas felt obliged to take control. Renouncing his former oath to his brother, he reluctantly agreed to become emperor.

The nearly three weeks of indecision played into the hands of those plotting to change the constitution. During the last stages of the war against Napoleon, soldiers had come into contact with the new radical practices of the west. Pursuing the French emperor's army across Europe to the walls of Paris, they had discovered previously unknown ideas, customs and general standards of living, and many men had now returned to Russia determined to better their own lot. Consequently, after Constantine's abdication, certain officers who had preferred his less rigid ways to those of his younger brother felt the time had come for them to protest. On 14 December, the day after Nicholas was officially acknowledged as tsar, the oath was put before the troops, but soon trouble began to develop. Members of some of the Guards regiments marched to Peter's or Peter Square, where around 3,000 soldiers and other civilians were now gathered. While the imperial family cowered in the Winter Palace, terrified by the unfolding events, Nicholas sent the governor of the city to speak to the rebels, only for the man then to be shot and killed. At that point, the tsar turned to the Preobrazhensky Guards for their support, whereupon for the rest of the day the situation became a stand-off between the opposing sides. Finally, as darkness began to fall, Nicholas, wanting to resolve the crisis before it escalated further, ordered the loaded cannons to be fired into the crowd. With a stampede breaking out, people fled for safety to the frozen river, but here the ice gave way and many were drowned. Possibly 1,200 lost their lives during the day, and although Nicholas had not been responsible for the events leading up to the uprising, he would be blamed for its outcome, and his popularity was permanently damaged.

The next day the new tsar regretfully summed up the events when writing to his brother: 'My dear, dear Constantine! Your will has been done: I am the emperor, but, my God, at what a price! At the price of my subjects' blood.'[122] One hundred and twenty-one rebels, now called Decembrists, were later tried and sent to Siberia, some voluntarily accompanied by their dutiful wives. With Nicholas asking the judges to show a greater leniency, the lives of most of the Decembrists were spared, but the principal five were subjected to a particularly grim death by hanging. The public executions were fixed to be carried out on the night of 13 July 1826 (OS), but as those present would soon see, the proceedings were botched. First, there were delays because of the badly constructed scaffold, and then once the sentence began to be carried out, some of the ropes broke, requiring the whole process to be repeated on the now half-dead victims – a gruesome mishandling that only added to the negative way the emperor was fast becoming viewed. Among his detractors several mocked the administration as one that could not even execute its people successfully. But while in honour of the men that died, a century later Peter Square would be renamed Decembrist Square (a name kept until 2008 when it became Senate Square), in fact the rebels' reputation as martyrs of freedom did not reveal the full picture. Although using as their battle cry the 'Constitution and Constantine' – a slogan little understood by many of their followers – their objective was not so much an appeal to reform and a call for liberal values, as a desire to destroy the status quo and overthrow the Romanovs. Of more lasting significance, however, the rebellion, in spite of failing, would leave its mark on Nicholas, who never again trusted the nobility from whom many of the rebel officers had come. From this time, constantly aware of the dangers faced by the imperial family, he became determined to exert his iron grip. Just six months after his accession he introduced the Third Section of the Imperial Chancellery, and, with this secret service overseeing all elements of society, he set out to curb the growing radical thinking and revolutionary activities that he so feared. From now on, this would be the style of government, the tsar's guiding mantra being 'Orthodoxy, Autocracy, Nationality'.

These policies soon became apparent in both his domestic and foreign dealings. Unlike his brother Constantine, Nicholas felt no sympathy for the Poles, failing to understand their desire to gain independence. When in 1830 news reached him from Warsaw of the Polish uprising, during which the rebels had declared him to be deposed, Nicholas reacted with characteristic ruthlessness, dispatching his troops to put down the revolt. Having abolished the original autonomy of Congress Poland and demoted the whole region to a mere province of the Russian Empire, he then set out to advance religious Orthodoxy by repressing the Catholic faith. For the same reason, he also increased the restrictions already imposed on the Jewish people, in 1835 enlarging the region set up by Catherine II for their settlement. With most Jews now forbidden to live elsewhere, the area – from this time officially called the Pale – became increasingly crowded, its inhabitants reduced to conditions of ever-growing hardship. However, the tsar was more sensitive to the wrongs of serfdom. Changes had been in motion for some time to abolish the system in most other European countries, brought to an end in Prussia by Friedrich Wilhelm III in 1807, and in Austria in 1848.[123] Like his brother Alexander, Nicholas also wished to introduce reform, but remembering the disloyalty shown by the Decembrist officers he did not dare to question the nobles' rights to ownership. He therefore introduced moderate changes that only affected the lives of those serfs who belonged to the state.

Always preferring to wear uniform, like his father, Nicholas was a keen military man, who loved the army's precision and discipline.[124] Despite his lack of actual battle experience, he was thoroughly trained in parade ground skills, and had grown to have such faith in the generals and admirals that he often appointed them to governmental posts for which they were ill-qualified. While confident of such men, he was fearful of any who might harbour more radical thinking, and for that reason he put limits on the numbers allowed to enter university.

Nonetheless, during the early years of his reign, life for the aristocrats and the growing bourgeoisie continued to be good, with balls, banquets and other entertainments. In the just completed Bolshoi Theatre in Moscow they could now enjoy productions of the newly introduced French ballet, or Glinka's recent operas with their Russian themes that the tsar liked so much. And even while Nicholas' increasingly repressive regime imposed its own rules on cultural thinking, among the growing intelligentsia young talents were appearing, men such as Alexander Pushkin, Nikolai Gogol and Mikhail Lermontov.

Pushkin, who had been born in Moscow in 1799 to an aristocratic family, could trace his line back to Peter the Great's black godson Gannibal. He had gained recognition for his talent even before leaving school, and over his career he would go on to produce some of the first and greatest works of Russian literature. However, in May 1820, having joined a wild group of like-minded young men in St Petersburg, Pushkin attracted the attention of the authorities and was exiled from the city for his radical thoughts. While living in the south he took up the cause of the Greeks, who were seeking independence from the Ottoman Empire, and here too he mixed with Russians who were opposed to the Romanov rule. Thus, having now angered the authorities in Odessa, Pushkin was once more ordered to leave, and so he moved back to the region of Pskov in the north-west of the country. Here he settled at Mikhailovskoye, his mother's estate, which Empress Elizabeth had previously given to Gannibal. During the two years that he spent here, the Decembrist Revolt took place in the capital, and, although he was not in St Petersburg at the time, when his poems were found among the rebels' possessions he became implicated in their cause. In fact, Pushkin had wanted to return to the city during those days, but – according to his own story – he had, by a strange turn of fate, failed to do so, having superstitiously abandoned his journey when a hare had unexpectedly run across his path.[125] Eventually, with the tsar's permission the poet was able to move back to the capital, but even then he would remain under surveillance and be limited as to where he could go and what he could print.

On marrying Natalia Goncharova in early 1831, Pushkin moved into her apartment in St Petersburg, but within five years he was so seriously in debt that he again wanted to leave the capital. However, on this occasion he was refused permission by the authorities, who wished to keep him in their sights. Although his beautiful, flirtatious wife was popular with the tsar and other members of the court, those same people largely ignored Pushkin, and he received only minor recognition for his literary work. Already bitter, he was then further angered by his wife's apparent affair with the French-born Guardsman Georges-Charles d'Anthès, who mockingly declared Pushkin to be a cuckold. Although d'Anthès then chose to marry Natalia's sister in January 1837, he and Natalia continued to behave scandalously, and so just two weeks later Pushkin challenged his rival to a duel. This would leave the poet mortally wounded, and two days later he died in his apartment at No. 12 Moika Embankment. After his funeral, his body was returned for burial to the family estate. Although greatly mourned by the general public, he was little missed by the court. Lermontov condemned this treatment of Pushkin, and for this he too would earn the tsar's displeasure and be ordered into exile. Finally, in a strange twist, five years later Lermontov, like Pushkin, would also die following a duel.

The year that Pushkin died, Nicholas celebrated the arrival of the first train in Russia with a journey from Tsarskoe Selo to Pavlovsk. After that, other tracks were opened, in 1838 from Tsarskoe Selo to St Petersburg, and in 1851 from St Petersburg to Moscow. However, the development of a rail network around the empire was slow. By the end of Nicholas' reign there was still less than 600 miles of track, a figure that was paltry in comparison to the approximately 8,000 miles constructed in Britain at this time. In 1837, disaster struck in December when the Winter Palace caught fire, the blaze only finally being extinguished three days later, by which time the interior had been totally destroyed. While it had raged efforts had been made to save the treasures, but revealingly Nicholas showed the issues that really mattered to him, appearing at the time more concerned to save the private letters written to him by his adored wife. While Catherine the Great's Small Hermitage next door escaped the damage, the rest of the palace would then have to undergo major internal reconstruction. During this, Rastrelli's famous Jordan Staircase and Great Church (or Palace Cathedral) were restored as before, but in the rest of the building new rooms were created in the more recent decorative style. On their completion, in 1852 the galleries of the so-called New Hermitage were opened to the public for the first time as the Imperial Hermitage Museum.

While still grand duke, in 1817 Nicholas had visited England, and in 1844 he returned for a second time. Here he greatly impressed Queen Victoria, who, writing – with her usual emphasis – to her uncle Leopold on 4 June described him as 'a very *striking* man', 'still handsome', having a '*beautiful*' profile, and being 'full of attentions and *politenesses*'. She praised his civility and kindness to her children, particularly mentioning how during their meeting (conducted in French) he picked up and kissed her daughter Alice – years later the mother of the last unfortunate Empress Alexandra. But more revealingly, Victoria also spoke of the tsar's '*formidable*' eyes and how they conveyed a sense of how much he suffered under the weight of his enormous responsibilities. Although 'easy to get on with', he 'seldom' smiled and his expression was '*not* a happy one'.[126] These strains were also apparent to Nicholas' wife, who understood how much he needed the peace that he found in his private life. She wrote, 'We both were truly happy and content only when we found ourselves alone in our apartments, and he then was very tender and loving towards me.'[127]

While on the throne Nicholas would succeed in capturing more land from Persia in the Caucasus region, and he also extended the empire to the far east, where he took possession of new territories on the Pacific rim. But problems still continued to plague him. Just four years after his visit to England, cholera broke out in St Petersburg and a serious famine took hold in the countryside. That was not all, as now the stability of many of Europe's ruling houses had started to come under threat once more. In February 1848, a revolution in Paris had again toppled the French monarchy, forcing King Louis Philippe to flee his country, and shortly after at the beginning of March further rebellions had erupted in various German states and different regions of the Austrian Empire. At that point, Nicholas, concerned to see the possible overthrow of any sovereign government, declared himself ready to come to the defence of the embattled rulers. Believing Russia to be the major power on the continent, he offered his support, presenting himself as 'the gendarme of Europe'. He encouraged the Prussian king to stamp down on his revolutionaries, and played a minor role in helping the Austrian Emperor settle his affairs in Hungary. Ultimately, however, he would be left feeling undervalued and little appreciated by the various leaders, who had in their own time eventually succeeded in suppressing the opposition without his help.

During the year of revolutions Russia, under its autocratic regime, had been able to avoid the contagion of revolt that was sweeping Europe. But while Nicholas had been little more than a spectator, he would soon face problems in matters that related to his own foreign policy. Although he had hoped to keep the Ottoman Empire in its weakened condition, he now began to fear that Russian influence in the area was diminishing. Furthermore, in 1853, a dispute began to develop between him and the new French emperor, Napoleon III, over the question of who should be protector of the holy sites in Jerusalem – that is to say, Orthodox Russia or Catholic France.

Concerned for his empire's interests in the south, Nicholas sent troops into the region of the Danubian Principalities, and then turned his attention to ensuring Russia's free passage through the Dardanelles. Mistakenly believing he still had the support of the British, he ordered an attack on the Turkish fleet at the port of Sinope on the southern coast of the Black Sea. This would soon prove to be a disastrous decision, as the French and British immediately joined forces with the sultan and declared war. Shortly after, with Austria giving its diplomatic support to his enemies, and Prussia declaring itself to be neutral, the tsar found himself alone, abandoned even by the countries whom he had five years before tried to help.

Although Russia now had a large army, well drilled on the parade ground, it was in fact ill-prepared for the more modern warfare, and its weakness soon became apparent when its chief Black Sea port of Sebastopol came under siege. The Crimean War would develop into a bitter conflict, lasting two years and spreading beyond the immediate region, with other battles eventually being fought in places as far afield as Lisbon in the west, Kamchatka in the Far East, and Archangel in the north. So too, in the Baltic, while blockading Russian trade, the Anglo-French fleets had begun to carry out a series of raids and attacks on the coastal towns of Finland's southern shores, destroying the ships, goods, and even livelihoods of those in their path. Here, although sometimes they were met by local opposition and resistance, they became so ruthless that in time they were widely condemned, their actions causing questions to be raised in the House of Commons as to the morality of attacking 'defenceless villagers'. Meanwhile, the Russians had also to fend off other enemy assaults on their fortresses situated on the Åland Islands in the Gulf of Bothnia, Kronstadt in the Gulf of Finland, and Sveaborg at the entrance to Helsinki harbour. Despite a spirited defence in June that forced the British to retreat, in August 1854 a second attack on Bomarsund left the Åland fort destroyed.[128] Helped by Russia's newly created defence system of mines, the other two fortifications would manage to hold out until the end of the war, despite the heavy two-day bombardment, watched by the people of Helsinki, that took place on Sveaborg in August 1855.

In the meantime, the disasters were continuing in the main theatre in the south, with both sides having multiple casualties as a result of injury and disease. Then in November 1854 the Russians suffered one of their most serious defeats at Inkerman, and it was soon after receiving news of this that the tsar died on 18 February 1855 (OS). Still only fifty-eight, but worn down by overwork and ill health, Nicholas had caught a chill that had developed into pneumonia. He had been crushed by the recent tragic losses in the Crimea, and with deep regret he now informed his oldest son that in spite of his best efforts, he was bequeathing him a broken country. According to some witnesses, when told by the doctor of his terminal condition, the tsar faced his approaching death with the same controlled dignity that he had shown throughout his life, and having refused further food and treatment, said goodbye to his family. But with Nicholas' earlier despondency now well known, unfounded rumours would soon claim that he had committed suicide.

Nicholas had an untiring sense of duty, but throughout his reign he faced many problems, not the least being that his wife Alexandra was never strong. After a stillbirth in the early 1820s, she had spent a considerable time back in Berlin, only eventually returning to Russia in 1825, partly persuaded by Alexander I who had given the couple Peterhof. This would be their favourite place to stay, they having chosen to take up residence in the small Alexandrina Palace, which Nicholas had built on the estate to allow them to live more simply. And, having visited the Crimea, after the birth of their last child, he would later present his wife with another property at Oreanda near Yalta, where a new palace was finally completed a decade later. However, as Alexandra's health had seriously declined since 1832, she visited it just once, and thirty years later it would be destroyed in a fire. By then the area had become popular with younger generations of Romanovs, many of whom built their own palaces nearby. But Alexandra was now suffering from repeated heart attacks, and so in 1845, on her doctors' advice – and to her husband's deep regret – she was sent to Palermo to escape the harsh climate of St Petersburg. Nicholas still adored his wife, but left on his own, he took a mistress. On discovering this, Alexandra was heartbroken, but in time she came to accept the situation, later even befriending the young woman. Despite her poor health she outlived her husband by five years, choosing, when she was not abroad, to stay mainly in the Alexander Palace at Tsarskoe Selo.

With Nicholas' death in 1855, the oldest of his children now became Alexander II. For a time, the fighting continued, but on 24 August (9 September, NS), after a year under siege, Sebastopol finally fell, and so the following year the new tsar agreed to a peace treaty. The Crimean War had been a disaster for Russia, leaving the country impoverished and the Black Sea a demilitarised zone – off-limits to all Russian naval ships. Nonetheless, in St Petersburg in 1859 Alexander erected in his father's honour a remarkable equestrian statue that showed the emperor seated triumphantly on a rearing horse. This exceptional piece, where the whole structure rests solely on the two rear legs of the animal, was created by the Frenchman Auguste de Montferrand, an architect responsible for several other works that are found in St Petersburg, among them the Alexander Column, the golden Field Marshals' Hall in the Winter Palace, and St Isaac's Cathedral, in front of which the statue of Nicholas would be erected following the building's completion. After nearly forty years under construction, the cathedral, originally commissioned by Tsar Alexander I, now replaced the last of a series of churches dedicated to the saint. With its forty-eight massive, red-granite columns and a vast golden dome, this – the largest of all Orthodox cathedrals – remains a key landmark that still towers over the city skyline.

When he was twenty, the future Alexander II fell in love with the beautiful, intelligent, but shy, Marie of Hesse, a niece of his grandmother, the former Empress Elizabeth Alexeievna, wife of Tsar Alexander I. However, as Marie's legitimacy was questionable, before the grand duke could marry her in 1842 Alexander had to override his mother's objections. Called Maria Alexandrovna after her Orthodox conversion, she would become popular with the Russian public, much loved for her charity work and for her deep concern for the people's well-being. In later years as her husband's reputation declined, these qualities would also earn her a name for 'saintliness'. Over time Maria would add to the growing numbers of grand dukes and duchesses by giving birth to six sons and two daughters – the only surviving girl later becoming a daughter-in-law of Queen Victoria. But, as with previous empresses, the climate in St Petersburg proved physically detrimental to Maria and so, like her predecessor, she spent much time abroad, often returning to her former home. And – as in the case of her mother-in-law – her poor health and frequent absences soon encouraged her husband to look elsewhere. An attractive man, from his early teens Alexander had been passionately involved with various young women, and during a visit to England in 1839 he had also much impressed the new queen, Victoria. Although their relationship was not serious, she wrote in her diary that she had never enjoyed an evening more than the one spent with him, declaring, 'I really am quite in love with the Grand-duke; he is a dear, delightful young man.'[129] Alexander, unlike Nicholas I, was openly promiscuous, engaging in a series of love affairs until 1866, when he met his last and much-loved mistress, Catherine Dolgorukova, with whom he then began an even more shamelessly indiscreet relationship that would shock the court.

In August 1855 (OS) Alexander II's traditional coronation took place in Moscow. Despite the costs incurred by the war, no expense was spared, and to celebrate the occasion, the customary *cocaigne* of feasting was laid on for the public. Regardless of this extravagant and lavish display, the fact remained that the country had been crushed by its recent defeat, a disaster that had been caused by Russia's need for reform. Apart from its lack of more up-to-date equipment and strategy, one of the reasons for the military failure had been the lack of a well-trained conscripted army, a situation that had obliged the generals to make do with troops of mainly untrained serfs. Although, since the time of Catherine the Great, rulers had acknowledged the injustice of this form of slave labour, each in turn had realised the inherent difficulties of abolishing the system. However, in light of the catastrophe of the Crimean War, Alexander II now concluded that the situation could be shelved no longer, and so six years after his succession, on 19 February 1861 (OS) he finally abolished serfdom, in the process earning for himself the title of 'the Liberator'.

However, the problems faced by his predecessors had not gone away, and concerned by the probable opposition he could face from the nobility and lesser landowners, Alexander II introduced a new scheme offering the peasants the right to buy the lands that they had previously worked. After years of forced, unpaid servitude, this only reduced them to still greater poverty, and as a result, following the emancipation, many former serfs migrated to the cities in search of work. This new influx of disappointed and bitterly disenchanted people then gave rise to further unrest. Alexander's mistake was that his measures, through their very moderation, failed to satisfy either party, pleasing neither master nor servant. Indecision would influence all the tsar's dealings, with the result that his constant veering between liberal and reactionary policies would ultimately lead to his downfall. Having now gained a taste for freedom, the people would not be content until they had achieved all their aims, and after their first protests, having lost the fear of autocracy that had been felt by their fathers, they would be spurred on to ever more extreme action. As the threats grew, Alexander then tried to regain his authority, but his heavy-handed rearguard efforts only helped to escalate the situation further.

Before 1861 was even over, Alexander found himself not just forced to impose martial law in Poland to quell riots taking place in Warsaw, but also facing peasant uprisings and previously unseen student protests at home. In the meantime, within the growing bourgeoisie, among the newly named 'intelligentsia', radical groups had begun calling for revolution. Then the following May further fears were raised when fires broke out in St Petersburg in such numbers that they were suspected to be the work of arsonists. Nonetheless, for the time being the tsar still attempted to introduce reform, among other things creating a legal system that was fairer for all. Included in his changes was a reduction of the restrictions on some Jews, and the ending of brutal corporal punishment in the military. Furthermore, encouraged by his more liberal brother Constantine Nikolaevich, he tried to improve the situation for the Poles, but here his measures did not satisfy the people and again in 1863 rebellion broke out in the country. This uprising was ruthlessly put down by the tsar's representative, and now angered by the Poles' ingratitude, Alexander took away their last rights, thus ending all their hopes of independence. To the

Finns, however, he was more generous, rewarding their good behaviour by granting them permission to open their own parliament.

Despite these tensions, cultural life continued to flourish. In St Petersburg in 1860, in honour of the Empress Maria Alexandrovna, the Maryinsky Theatre was opened, and throughout the following years some of Russia's most famous musicians and writers continued to produce their works. Some of these, such as Peter Ilyich Tchaikovsky and Anton Rubenstein – the founder of the St Petersburg Conservatory – received the tsar's approval, but others like Leo Tolstoy and Feodor Dostoyevesky could at times find themselves in trouble with the authorities for their controversial, if not subversive, ideas. During the reign of Nicholas I, in 1849 Dostoyevesky had been arrested for being part of a suspect literary circle, and while imprisoned in the Peter and Paul Fortress had been put through the psychological trauma of a false execution. After being reprieved at the very last moment, he was then condemned to four years of hard labour, but, released in 1854, he later became a respected figure of the establishment, finally dying in St Petersburg less than a month before Alexander II.

Despite the difficulties faced by some intellectuals, and the continuing poverty of the majority of the Russian people, for the extended imperial family life continued much as before. The tsar and his wife loved the Crimean region and were fascinated by its culture, so in 1861 Alexander II bought another new property at Livadia near Yalta. Here, he then developed a park, where in time he added several other new palaces and buildings, most of which no longer survive.

In 1864 the emperor's oldest son, Nicholas, known to his relations as 'Nixa', became engaged to Dagmar, the second daughter of the new Danish king, Christian IX. He was slightly built, charming, intelligent, well-educated and cultured, a promising heir-apparent to the throne. Dagmar was delighted with her fiancé, but the following year, to her utter distress, while he was in Nice he became seriously ill. After stopping to see his mother on the French Riviera while he was on a tour of Europe, his health became progressively worse and, on 12 April (OS) he died from probable tuberculous meningitis. The imperial family, who had gathered at his bedside, were totally grief-struck and, although they returned his body to St Petersburg for burial, they built in Nice a chapel over the spot where he had died, later also erecting alongside a large traditional Slavonic-style Orthodox Cathedral.

From this time onwards Empress Maria became more pious and withdrawn, a situation that only helped to increase the distance now developing between her and her husband. And Dagmar, too, was shattered, but, according to some accounts, before dying Nixa indicated that she should marry his younger brother, Alexander, 'Sasha' – a practical solution that close on three decades later Dagmar's own nephew, the later British king George V, would similarly adopt when marrying the fiancée of the recently dead Prince Eddy. Other versions of this story are contradictory, claiming that the account rests on little more than a loose interpretation of the events, but whatever happened on Nixa's deathbed, the following year, after Dagmar's conversion, she married Sasha in St Petersburg. Having taken the same name as her predecessor (Tsar Paul's wife), she had become the new Grand Duchess Maria Feodorovna. Although her husband was very different from Nixa, he being large, bluff, and poorly educated, contrary to expectations the marriage would prove to be very happy.

Meanwhile, Russia was still feeling impoverished because of the recent war, and so in 1867 the tsar took up a scheme first mooted by Nicholas I, namely to sell Alaska to the United States. In addition to the financial reasons for doing this, Alexander had concerns regarding his Russian trading posts along the continent's western shores. These he felt could not be protected from either the Americans or the British – the latter in particular, should they wish some time later to extend their own interests from their neighbouring territory in Canada. Wishing to prevent a possible conflict breaking out, Alexander therefore decided to finalise the sale, agreeing to a price of $7,200,000. Although most Russians were against this plan, feeling disappointed by their loss of territory, the Americans too were unenthusiastic about the exchange. Still suffering from the after-effects of their Civil War, and with an understandable lack of foresight, they saw the process as a 'waste of money'. Their little interest in the area would remain until the discovery close on thirty years later of vast new fields of gold in the Yukon, and even then it would not be until the next century that they would come to appreciate fully Alaska's strategic and mineral importance. Alexander, now with money in his pocket, availed himself of some of the profits to pay for further gilding of St Isaac's dome.

Gradually the Russian situation abroad began to improve, and following the French defeat in the Franco-Prussian War, the tsar felt he could ignore the terms agreed in the earlier treaty that had ended the Crimean War. With the support of his uncle Wilhelm, the newly promoted German Emperor, he now regained Russia's right to free movement in the Black Sea. And with the relations between the countries being again strong, soon after in 1872 the Prussian Chancellor Otto Bismarck arranged a visit of Alexander and the Habsburg ruler Franz Joseph to Berlin. The purpose of this so-called Three Emperors' Meeting was to ensure the peace, in particular to prevent relations breaking down between Russia and Austria over the question of their common territorial interests in the Balkans.

All this time, Alexander was becoming increasingly anxious about the infiltration of new radical thought from the rest of Europe, and so he ordered Russians living abroad to return home. But this just brought the expatriate rebels with their foreign revolutionary ideas back into Russia, and accordingly around the country assassination attempts began to take place on officials, much as was happening in Italy, Spain and Germany. Having become more militant, the dissident groups no longer cared about innocent victims caught up in their activities, their focus mainly being on the total overthrow of the government and the killing of the tsar. Alexander was again uncertain how he should deal with these threats. While he still wanted to appease the opposing liberals and conservatives, his contradictory measures continued to waver between those that promised reform and others that were more reactionary, and thus he caused further discontent among all factions. But the situation was still more complicated. Among those most opposed to all revolutionary ideas, there were some who quite probably were content to use the extremism of the anarchists to promote their own right-wing agenda – a methodology still found in some quarters today. Believing that popular revulsion could serve to strengthen their own cause, in certain instances evidence suggests some police and other authorities may have been prepared to turn a blind eye towards the anarchists' activities, hoping that any atrocity on their part might cause a backlash in the reactions of the public. At this point, the tsar, who was genuinely concerned about the brutal repression being meted out in the Balkans on those rebelling against the Ottoman rule, saw a way to improve his popularity. Announcing his intention to protect the region's Orthodox populations, he declared war against the sultan in 1877, and after a year of heavy fighting he had managed to defeat the enemy and regain the love and trust of most Russians.[130] In addition to achieving the independence of Serbia, Romania and Montenegro, at the final peace treaty at San Stefano he received further highly beneficial terms that included the creation of a large Bulgarian state that would be under the protection of Russia. But the other European powers, encouraged particularly by the British, saw these conditions as too generous, and fearing the tsar's increased influence in the area, they gathered in Berlin to redraft the treaty and reduce his earlier gains. On learning of this, again the Russians grew critical of their emperor. They now condemned him for their country's heavy losses in the war and, giving him no credit for what he had achieved, reviled him for what he had surrendered. With the national mood having now turned against Alexander once more, his Minister of the Interior, Michael Loris Melikov, persuaded him to consider further reform. On having listened to and agreed with his adviser, the now visibly exhausted Alexander signed a new manifesto, one which he planned to present to his council at its next meeting on 4 March (OS).

These changes would never be put into practice. Following the first assassination attempt on the tsar by a gunman outside the Summer Gardens in April 1866, and a similar attack by a disgruntled Pole the next year in Paris, other episodes had followed. Although various offenders were executed, and censorship was introduced, the assaults had continued, becoming ever more ambitious as the perpetrators began using the newly invented dynamite. In 1879 conspirators tried to blow up the imperial train, a plot that failed only because of an unexpected change of plan. Although this attempt left no casualties, Alexander's confidence was further shaken, and security was therefore increased on all his future journeys from St Petersburg to Moscow, with troops guarding the whole length of the track. But the attacks continued and the following year an even more daring plot targeted the emperor in his own home, a bomb being placed below the dining room of the Winter Palace. This time there would be multiple casualties among the staff, but by chance Alexander survived because his brother-in-law had arrived late, delayed by the blizzard blowing at the time. However, on 1 March 1881 (OS), on their seventh attempt, the assassins finally achieved their aim.[m] First, when the tsar was driving back to his palace after his weekly Sunday visit to the Mikhailovsky *manège*, the riding academy, a bomb was thrown at his carriage by a member of the new revolutionary People's Will party. This failed to injure him, but after he had got out to see to the other victims, a second bomb was thrown, leaving him mortally wounded. With appalling injuries, and his blood literally staining the stairs, he was carried back to his rooms in the Winter Palace, where he was joined by the rest of the family, including his traumatised thirteen-year-old grandson, the future Nicholas II. At 3.30 in the afternoon Alexander finally died, just days before his new more liberal manifesto had been due to be presented. Horrified by his father's violent death, his son, the new Emperor Alexander III, now had the document destroyed, and with that he ordered the country to return to a rule of repressive autocracy, such as had been practised by his grandfather, Nicholas I.

Abroad there was equal horror at news of the tsar's death, with Queen Victoria being one of those to express her regret at the loss of 'a good ruler' who had sought to do 'the best for his country'. She summed up that 'in spite of his failings' he was 'a kind and amiable man' – a guarded compliment possibly meant to question his private life.[131] Less than a year before this on 22 May 1880 (OS), the extremely sickly Empress Maria Alexandrovna had finally died from tuberculosis at the Winter Palace while her husband was spending some time at Tsarskoe Selo with Catherine Dolgorukova, his adored long-term mistress. Earlier, to the disgust of the imperial family, and with incredible tactlessness, he had brought – probably for their safety – his beloved 'Katia' and their four surviving illegitimate children to the Winter Palace.

Although some past mistresses of the emperors had also lived here, Katia's less discreet arrival was seen as particularly insulting, and feeling against her was increased by the spread of false rumours that she was actually living in rooms directly above the dying empress, who could hear

---

m Reputedly, while in Paris in 1867, a palm reader had told Alexander that the seventh assassination attempt would be fatal, as then happened when the second bomb thrown during the sixth attack left him mortally wounded.

the children playing overhead. But Alexander was besotted, and he and Katia made no effort to conceal their affection, although many people considered that she dominated the infatuated tsar. Most of the court were outraged by this behaviour, none more so than Alexander's daughter-in-law, Maria Feodorovna, who in 1874 wrote to her mother in Denmark expressing her anger at the 'shamelessness' of the young woman.[n] Then, against advice, on 6 July (OS), little over a month after the Empress Maria Alexandrovna's death, the tsar – well aware of the continuing threats on his life – had secretly remarried. Wanting to acknowledge without delay the woman who had been with him for fourteen years, he had made her his morganatic wife, giving her the title Princess Yurievskaya. While his critics now feared that he had further ambitions for Katia, planning eventually to make her empress, after just eight months, the tsar was dead and all her hopes for the future were over. On the pronouncement of his death, she had become distraught, collapsing to the floor, covered in her husband's blood, and then in a last touching gesture had later cut off 'her magnificent hair and placed it in the hands of her deceased husband'.[132] While some would view Alexander's death as divine justice for his immoral behaviour, most of the imperial family now felt sympathy for the obviously grief-struck woman. Maria Feodorovna, again writing to her mother, declared,

> to see the unfortunate widow's despair was more than heartrending, so that in an instant, everything that we previously felt against her was gone and only the greatest, most sincere sympathy for her boundless pain remains. I cannot tell you how much I pity her; in such moments, one forgets and forgives everything.[133]

Later, finding herself without any particular position, and barely recognised by the Russians at large, Katia accepted the family's generous financial support and went abroad to France, where eventually in her seventies she would die in Nice in 1922.

Meanwhile, fifteen conspirators involved in the tsar's assassination were arrested and five of them, including one woman, the indomitable Sofia Perovskaya, were publicly hanged – she being the first such female political prisoner executed in Russia. Later, to commemorate Alexander II's death, where the attack had occurred on the embankment of the Catherine (today Griboedova) Canal, the family commissioned the building of a new church. Officially called the Church of Our Saviour on the Spilled Blood, it contains a shrine displaying exposed cobble stones, which poignantly mark the spot where the fatally wounded tsar fell. This church, paid for mostly by the imperial family and eventually completed in 1907, is particularly popular with tourists today, who see it as a typical example of Russian art or architecture. But in fact here there is a paradox. Its design marks the shift towards Slavophilism, a movement intended

n Katia was thirty-five years younger than Alexander II.

to reverse Western influence, which had grown in popularity over the century. This was now much favoured by the new emperor, Alexander III, who would increasingly draw away from the European ideas and liberal thinking that in his view were undermining the security of his country.

So, not just a memorial to his murdered father, this church also stands as a symbol of the new more separatist movement that was seeking to redefine the identity of Russia and its people by resurrecting and honouring the traditions of its past. At this time there were attempts to reinvent 'Russianness', as in the case of the famous matryoshka dolls that, although only first produced in 1890, are today seen by many as part of the country's long cultural history.

This all helps explain the appearance in St Petersburg at this time of the Church of the Spilled Blood, with its onion domes and ornate mosaics. It would be one of the first of its kind to appear in the city, its design marking a break from the past of its famous founder, Peter the Great. The church intentionally turns its back on the wishes of the city's creator, who had sought so determinedly to exclude such elements of old Russia from his much-loved capital, and as a result one can only imagine the horror with which he would have in fact viewed it.

17
Prussia's Path to Empire

Friedrich Wilhelm III of Prussia. (Courtesy of the Rijksmuseum)

When Frederick II died in 1786, Prussia was hit by a deep sense of loss. Over forty-six years the king had played a key role in European affairs, and many of his subjects could not remember life without him. Count Mirabeau, for one, considered that the country's days of greatness were over and the kingdom had now 'collapsed into smallness'.[134] The new monarch, Friedrich Wilhelm II, the former king's nephew, was a very different character: outward-going, dissolute, and extremely extravagant. Not lacking in intelligence and very musical, he was also a keen supporter of all the arts, but he left the running of affairs to his ministers, preferring to concentrate instead on erecting expensive, flamboyant buildings designed to proclaim Prussia's importance – among these the Marble Palace in Potsdam, and the imposing Brandenburg Gate that marks the beginning of Berlin's Unter den Linden. Such projects meant that by the end of his short reign Friedrich Wilhelm II had dissipated the wealth carefully accumulated by his uncle during his last years on the throne. Moreover, in place of Frederick II's ascetic and private existence, the new king's sybaritic lifestyle would be marked by loose morals and very public scandal. Even before coming to the throne, in 1769 his marriage to his close relation Elizabeth of Brunswick-Wölfenbuttel – the daughter of Frederick II's sister *and* his brother-in-law – ended in bitter divorce on the grounds of her obvious infidelity, little attention in the proceedings being given to the king's own multiple affairs. Elizabeth's latest lover was arrested and presumably beheaded, her unborn child aborted, and she condemned to lifelong confinement. After a period at Küstrin, the castle where years before the king himself had been imprisoned with his friend von Katte, Elizabeth would end her days in less austere surroundings in the region of Stettin, where she eventually died aged ninety-three. After her disgrace she never again saw her only living child – the girl being cared for by Frederick's rejected queen until finally married to George III's second son, the Duke of York.

Frederick II had always preferred Elizabeth to his nephew but, still anxious for the succession, just months after the divorce he ordered his heir to remarry. The bride now chosen was Friederike Luise of Hesse-Darmstadt, the sister of Tsar Paul's first wife. But without the exceptional intelligence of her mother, and the good looks of her predecessor, Friederike failed to please her husband. Even though she would give birth to eight surviving children, Friedrich Wilhelm would largely ignore her, fathering some twelve illegitimate offspring from his several other relationships, not to mention also contracting two bigamous marriages with his mistresses.

During the last decade of the century there began to be a re-questioning of the thinking of the Enlightenment, many people now considering its ideas to have gone too far. Accordingly, there was a return to formal spiritual belief, with religious adherence again being encouraged as a way to make society more cohesive. Just two years after his succession, the king issued an edict restricting press freedoms, and then in 1794 wrote angrily to Immanuel Kant in Könisberg, ordering him to stop intentionally 'distorting and disparaging several principal and fundamental doctrines of Holy Scripture and of Christianity'.[135] However, Berlin was becoming one of the great centres of culture and sophistication and, despite press censorship being tightened to confront the increasingly irreverent criticism of authority, there was a remarkable degree of free expression and open discussion of radical issues such as those raised by the French Revolution.

During his eleven-year reign, Friedrich Wilhelm would accumulate – at the expense of Poland – more new territory than any of his predecessors. Although he had initially congratulated the Polish king Stanislaw II on his recent constitution, the Prussian king had then become anxious, fearing that Poland's improving administration might eventually empower it to threaten the areas of Crown Prussia taken by Frederick II during the First Partition. Therefore, in 1793 in a treacherous turnaround Friedrich Wilhelm joined Catherine of Russia, taking part in a second land grab of Polish territory. With this he gained the important enclave surrounding the rich Baltic port Danzig (Gdańsk) and its neighbouring Thorn (Torún), areas that had been excluded from the First Partition. At the same time, he gained Posen, a most valuable and productive region lying just east of Silesia. But this was not enough for the king, so a second seizure followed soon after, namely the Third Partition of Poland that gave Prussia further swathes of land, including the capital Warsaw. In total these last two annexations carried out during Friedrich Wilhelm's reign would increase the size of his kingdom by about a third. But there was a negative side to this success.

In pursuit of his ambitions, the king had repeatedly made new alliances, only to break them soon after, and this behaviour had meant that he had ultimately lost the confidence and trust of others. Therefore, when Friedrich Wilhelm II's son succeeded four years later in 1797, he would find that his country was generally viewed with circumspection, and his neighbouring states were wary of entering into further agreements with Prussia. Another difficulty also threatened. With the demise of Poland, the country had lost the buffer state lying immediately to the east of Brandenburg, leaving it with a long, direct Russian border that would be virtually impossible to defend should the need arise.

The new king, Friedrich Wilhelm III, who was again a very different character, had detested his father's louche, extravagant behaviour. A private, devoted family man, he preferred to live away from the large Berlin City Palace, following instead a more bourgeois lifestyle in the small, much-loved country residence that he had bought from his childhood tutor at Paretz, some 12 miles from Potsdam. He saw his position as a burden, an unwanted role that he had been obliged to take on, and loathing war he announced that he only sought peace and tranquillity for his people. But Friedrich Wilhelm III would find himself a victim of his times, buffeted by the complicated political and ever-changing alliances that developed in the face of Napoleon's growing supremacy. Concerned for his country's vulnerable position in the centre of Europe between the great powers, the king attempted to avoid confrontation by maintaining the neutrality that in 1795 Prussia had promised France it would try and maintain among the northern German states. But after being put under considerable pressure by Tsar Paul and the other members of the League of Armed Neutrality, who wanted to defend their own interests, in April 1801 Friedrich Wilhelm III marched his troops into Hanover – the electorate that despite its union with the British crown still maintained its independent neutrality. By this action Friedrich Wilhelm showed the tsar his willingness to support his neighbours in their opposition to the British, whose aggressive activities were now harming trade in the Baltic. And for the king there were other reasons to support this move. Hanover had always held particular significance for him, as it separated the bulk of his lands from his scattered possessions to the west, and also acted as a buffer zone against any possible outside incursion of Prussian territory from France. Now with Napoleon having already indicated an intention to invade the electorate should Prussia fail to do so, Friedrich Wilhelm was eager to pre-empt a possible French presence being set up right on his doorstep. But the Prussian army remained in Hanover for just a few months, the king soon withdrawing his men after the international situation had changed and Europe began to enjoy a brief period of peace. But despite the ending of hostilities following Britain's naval assault on the Danes at Copenhagen, and the murder of the tsar in St Petersburg, in May 1803 the fighting started again and, before long, Napoleon was showing the real disregard in which he held the king. In spite of Friedrich Wilhelm's earlier attempts to appease the French emperor, the latter now marched his own troops into Hanover, and the following year appointed his marshal, Jean-Baptiste Bernadotte, governor of the region.

Regardless of these and other insults, Friedrich Wilhelm still continued to maintain his policy of neutrality, but finally things came to a head in 1805, when on 22 September, obeying Napoleon's orders, Bernadotte marched into Ansbach on his way to take on the Austrian army. This, a blatant violation of Friedrich Wilhelm's territory, proved a step too far for the Prussians, and the king was now put under further pressure by his family and advisers to take a more determined stand against France's overbearing behaviour. But others too had become concerned by Napoleon's obvious ambitions, and a month after the Austrians' defeat at Ulm, in November new tsar Alexander I came to Berlin with the intention of renewing the friendship that he had formed with the royal couple three years earlier. Here, during the private midnight excursion arranged by the queen to the Garrison Church in Potsdam, the two rulers stood before Frederick II's tomb and swore a secret oath. They promised their mutual support and co-operation, with the king also vowing to act as mediator in the tsar's future dealings with Napoleon. By now Friedrich Wilhelm had been persuaded at last to write in protest to the French emperor, and his minister Count von Haugwitz was already on his way. This letter, a virtual declaration of war, promised that Prussia would join the Third Coalition against Napoleon if he did not honour the terms of the treaty he had agreed with Emperor Franz II four years earlier – a treaty that had sought to protect the territories included within the still existent empire. But even before Napoleon had conceded to read the ultimatum, the situation had changed again with the Austrians and Russians suffering a crushing defeat at Austerlitz on 2 December. In the case of the Austrians, this disaster would hasten the end of their rule over the Holy Roman Empire, while for the Russians, it left them with little option other than to struggle back to Poland. Friedrich Wilhelm was now abandoned without the military support earlier promised by Alexander, but for him worse was to come when finally, after three days during which he had been intentionally kept waiting, the Prussian minister was able to see Napoleon. Count Haugwitz then congratulated the Frenchman on his great victory, and, ignoring Friedrich Wilhelm's earlier instructions, took it upon himself to agree to Napoleon's newest demands. These ordered the king to hand over some of his key territories, exchanging them for Hanover and a few other small areas. As Napoleon had intended, this deal excluded Friedrich Wilhelm from the Third Coalition, and – as the emperor had hoped – Britain soon retaliated by declaring war on Prussia.

With the collapse of the Holy Roman Empire, Napoleon now became the protector of the newly created Confederation of the Rhine, an association of various German states, whose numbers would increase over the next few years. Although it was eventually disbanded in 1813 after the French emperor's fortunes began to decline, while the confederation remained in existence, it further underlined the unreliability of all alliances, national, political, and also personal. Even the brother of Friedrich Wilhelm's much-loved queen would finally throw in his lot with Napoleon in early 1808. However, before that the Frenchman's double-dealing would at last prove too much for Friedrich Wilhelm, his patience having eventually run out when he discovered that the emperor had high-handedly offered to give his newly acquired Hanover back to George III. So after deciding to join the allies in the Fourth Coalition, in early October 1806 the king sent the emperor another ultimatum. In Berlin this change of policy was greeted enthusiastically by the people, who, still having faith in their past glory, were eager for their country to prove itself again in battle. But while cocky young officers blatantly sharpened their weapons outside the French embassy, others did not share their hubris, rightly fearing that the military was unprepared for conflict.

The king was among these doubters, realising that the army had remained essentially unreformed in recent years, and reportedly even the more militaristic queen would declare that it 'had fallen asleep on the laurels of Frederick the Great'.[136] The army was not just out of date and badly equipped, but also commanded by ageing generals, of whom more than half were now over sixty, some considerably older. But, as Friedrich Wilhelm lacked sufficient confidence in his own intelligence and common sense, he failed to assert his will, choosing instead to defer to the presumed wisdom of his older, but unimpressive, advisers. There was an additional problem. As many Prussian soldiers were deployed elsewhere, they, like the Russians, would not arrive in time to join the battle that would soon take place. When the fighting began some 150 miles to the south-west of Berlin at Jena-Auerstädt on 14 October 1806, the king's army was thus outnumbered. Having underestimated the speed of the French response, the Prussians, who were not yet prepared for a full-on attack, were taken by surprise when the enemy appeared out of the dense early morning mist. Within five hours at Jena the retreat had been called, only for it to turn into a rout soon after. A similar situation was now developing with the main force around 18 miles away at Auerstädt. Here, following the death of the commander, Karl Wilhelm Ferdinand, the Duke of Brunswick, the king took over from his cousin and decided to order the retreat. Again the initial good discipline of the men broke down as they soon became entangled with the panicking soldiers escaping the mayhem of Jena. Before long Friedrich Wilhelm found himself among those in flight, vast numbers choking the narrow roads in a desperate dash to escape their pursuers. With the Prussians having suffered some 20,000 or more casualties in these battles, and an almost equally large number taken prisoner, within just a few hours the catastrophe had destroyed Prussia's reputation as a major power. The country was left humiliated and its people dispirited.

Following some further small but equally unsuccessful engagements in the following days, all resistance disintegrated and Friedrich Wilhelm's only remaining option was to try and make peace with the French. However, Napoleon summarily turned down the request and demanded instead that the king agree to the further loss of territory. Finally, two weeks after the fiasco at Jena-Auerstädt the French troops marched into Berlin, parading the captured Prussian officers who had earlier displayed such anti-French bravado. Before joining his men, Napoleon chose to spend some time out at Potsdam where, underlining his triumph by staying in the Hohenzollern's royal palace, he (like Alexander before him) then visited Frederick II's tomb to pay his respects. While Napoleon admired Frederick as one of the greatest generals of all time, he also saw himself as his worthy successor, apparently – according to some witnesses – actually adopting a few of the old king's known mannerisms. However, even while acknowledging the importance of Frederick's role during the Seven Years' War, as revenge for the Prussian defeat of the French at Rossbach, he now took the king's sword and sash, sending these and other trophies back to Paris to be displayed in Les Invalides. Here they would remain until days before the fall of Paris in 1814, when they were intentionally burnt by the governor in order to prevent their recapture.[137]

After three days in Potsdam, Napoleon finally arrived in Berlin, entering the city in triumph through the recently constructed Brandenburg Gate. Before long this too was pillaged, the French emperor ordering the removal of the bronze quadriga on the top of the arch, although, unlike other booty, it would be returned to Berlin after the emperor's final defeat. But for now Prussia's collapse was total, made more evident by the royal family having abandoned their capital and fled north-east with the crown jewels and other treasure. After a long and difficult journey, they eventually arrived at Königsberg in the eastern part of their kingdom. Here they remained for a while, but in January, feeling threatened by the approaching French, they decided to move on still further, going closer to the Russian border, where they hoped to have more protection from Tsar Alexander. Despite the queen now being seriously unwell, for the next three days they struggled their way over the difficult terrain to Memel (today Klaipėda, Lithuania), the only town not to be occupied by Napoleon.

While Prussian morale had been seriously undermined by the recent disaster, things were made worse by the fact that the army was now made up of a majority of foreigners, men who did not feel the same loyalty to the country as those who were native-born. Therefore, although the soldiers still manned several fortresses, over the following days, as the enemy drew near, discipline began to fail. Having offered only minimal resistance – on occasion not even firing a shot – one after another the garrisons gave up the fight, and the strongholds fell into French hands. Greatly angered when he heard news of this, Friedrich Wilhelm threatened those responsible with the firing squad, and then promised a revolutionary new measure that would change Prussia's former elitist system of promotion. From this time, the officer class would be open to any soldier whose courage showed him worthy of the honour, a democratic recognition of merit that would later be reinforced by the king's creation of the Iron Cross, an order awarded to all ranks. Created out of the base metal normally used for weaponry, it would come – as intended – to epitomise Prussian strength of character and resistance in the face of austerity and adversity.

Gebhard Leberecht von Blücher would attempt a last stand against the French. Having been unable to escape east over the Oder, he had turned north-west, towards neutral Lübeck, and it was here on 6 November 1806 that his army suffered a final defeat. With some 6,000–8,000 Prussians lying dead or injured on the streets, the French then proceeded to sack the city and commit all manner of atrocities against the people. The next day, finding himself – in his own words – without bread or ammunition, Blücher finally surrendered. But one more positive result of this whole sorry affair would be Marshal Bernadotte's more humane treatment of the Swedish prisoners of war, who had been captured while attempting to escape back to their own country. The Frenchman's civilised behaviour towards them would four years later lead to his election as Sweden's new crown prince.

Although Friedrich Wilhelm now tried to reassert his authority by refusing to cede the lands earlier promised to Napoleon, in reality there was little that he could do except avoid further involvement in the ongoing war. So, concerned above all for the survival of Prussia, for the next few years he limited his ambitions to other domestic policies and reforms. During his three years in virtual exile, the king had the support of his wife, Luise of Mecklenburg-Strelitz, the niece of George III's wife, Charlotte. Luise's father Karl, Charlotte's favourite brother, later became duke of the small and comparatively backward duchy lying between Prussia and the neighbouring Mecklenburg-Schwerin, but during Luise's early childhood he was employed in the service of his brother-in-law, the British king. At this time the family lived in Hanover's more lavish surroundings, remaining there even after the premature death in childbirth of the children's mother, and the subsequent remarriage of their father to his sister-in-law. However, when Luise was eight her stepmother also died in childbirth, and so the family then moved from

Hanover to Hesse-Darmstadt, where she and two of her sisters were cared for by their widowed grandmother. Later, wanting to arrange good marriages for the girls, this woman made the most of her former husband's family connections. As he had been the uncle of Friedrich Wilhelm II's unfortunate second wife, during a visit to Frankfurt in 1793, the princess was able to arrange a 'chance' meeting between the two younger girls and the king.

By that time there had been various suggestions that the Prussian crown prince might marry one of the daughters of George III, but the latter's reluctance to part with them had persuaded Friedrich Wilhem II to find a bride for his son elsewhere. Although the status of the Mecklenburg-Strelitz princesses was less exalted than that of their British cousins, the beautiful seventeen-year-old Luise did not fail to impress the king when he met her. And having been similarly pleased with her sister, within weeks of the meeting Friedrich Wilhelm II had drawn up marriage contracts for both his sons. The following December, within two days of each other, Luise married the crown prince, and fifteen-year-old Friederike his younger brother Ludwig. After a short but unhappy marriage Friederike would be left a widow with three children, and then her life became more controversial. Following a broken engagement with her British cousin, Prince Adolphus (later Duke of Cambridge), she had an affair with the Prince of Solms-Braunfels that left her pregnant. A hurried marriage temporarily resolved the situation, but the couple's relationship ultimately failed and a threatened divorce was only avoided when unexpectedly (if not conveniently) her new husband died. Finally, Friederike married for the third time, again choosing a cousin, Prince Ernst Augustus, Duke of Cumberland – the brother of her earlier fiancé. Against the odds, this marriage proved successful, despite some doubts in certain quarters about the character of the duke himself. Immensely unpopular in England, Ernst August was rumoured to be guilty of a variety of heinous crimes, including murder and incest. However, he was more popular in Hanover, where he became king in 1837, succeeding to the throne in place of his niece, Queen Victoria, who – because of the former electorate's semi-Salic law – was barred from the accession. This finally separated Hanover from the British crown, and here Friederike, now the queen consort, would remain until her death just four years later.

The story of Friederike's older sister would be very different. From the start Luise had greatly endeared herself to the Prussian people, charming them with her naturalness and informality. On her arrival in Berlin, she had walked among the crowd, and unaware of the stiff Prussian protocol, had delighted the onlookers by picking up and kissing a child who had just welcomed her with a poem. Others, too, would fall under her spell. The young Alexander I – a close friend of the royal couple after their first meeting at Memel in 1802 – was one who became captivated by Luise, admiring her to such an extent that there were even ungrounded rumours of an affair, stories spread by her enemies who wished to undermine her reputation. Napoleon largely initiated this gossip after he had entered Berlin and discovered a portrait and correspondence from the tsar among her private possessions at Charlottenburg. While the French empress, Joséphine, disapproved of her husband's malicious attack on the queen's name, cartoons continued to make similar insinuations, not just suggesting Luise's intimate relationship with Alexander, but also her dominance over the king. But the queen's devotion to Friedrich Wilhelm and to her large family of nine surviving children could never be questioned. Although she acquired a high profile uncommon among all the Hohenzollern wives, she never sought to outshine her husband or achieve a position other than that of his consort. She loved and supported the king, and dedicated herself to building up his self-confidence. She insisted on going with him to Jena-Auerstädt, and, though finally persuaded to return to Berlin before the battle began, soon after the defeat rejoined him on the family's flight east.

Although private relations between the tsar and the Prussian royal family would continue to be good, in the public sphere the situation was different. Gradually Friedrich Wilhelm found himself faced by more and more impossible odds and, although he sought to form a new alliance with Alexander, two months later all his hopes were destroyed following the French defeat of the Russians at Friedland. With Königsberg having now fallen to the French, Napoleon had set up his headquarters at the nearby Tilsit, and here in early July 1807, just eleven days after the battle, the tsar agreed to start peace talks. Close to the town, the two emperors came together in an intentionally symbolic first meeting designed by Napoleon to take place on an elaborate raft in the middle of the River Niemen, the demarcation line between their two armies. Although this event was held on Prussian territory, Friedrich Wilhelm was excluded, reduced to watching the initial proceedings from the bank of the river. And over the next few days, as further meetings took place ashore, he was purposely sidelined by Napoleon, left as a mere observer while the two other men drew up their plans and dismantled his country. Alexander, remembering his friend, would be able to dissuade Napoleon from wiping Prussia totally from the map, but for Friedrich Wilhelm, who had been forced to cede almost 50 per cent of his lands, the final deal was a bitter humiliation. Some of the areas he had lost now became Napoleon's new Duchy of Warsaw, a region with its own constitution, but joined in personal union with the Elector of Saxony, who had joined the Frenchman's new Confederation of the Rhine. While Danzig was designated a Free City, some other former Prussian regions became a – short-lived – French vassal state, namely the Kingdom of Westphalia, where the emperor's own brother, Jérôme Bonaparte, ruled as king. As a result, besides his core possessions in Brandenburg, Friedrich William was now left with only Pomerania, Silesia and the Polish regions that had been gained in the First Partition.

Luise's dislike of Napoleon was intense, and she had always been determined to inspire her husband to stand up against him, regardless of the cost. Prepared to go to war, she had viewed death as a preferable option to the disgrace or destruction of Prussia. However, despite her loathing of the emperor – made worse by the slanderous stories he had spread about her – she agreed while at Tilsit to meet him, hoping that she might be able to persuade him to soften the harsh conditions he had imposed on her husband in the treaty. Using all her charm when begging for more generous terms, she was so persuasive that Napoleon later admitted to having been nearly swayed, adding that he considered the queen to be the king's 'best minister'. Following the meeting even Luise had become more optimistic, but nonetheless her hopes would soon be dashed as Napoleon remained resolute and implacable. With the situation therefore unchanged, Friedrich Wilhelm decided to remain with his family in East Prussia, refusing to come back to Berlin despite the pleas of the patriots. While this gave rise to rumours that he intended to abdicate, the king held fast, believing that his return would exacerbate Prussia's problems. However, in January 1808 he moved from Memel to Königsberg and spent the summer in his regional capital before making a winter visit to St Petersburg. Although Napoleon, when writing to the tsar, had commented that family ties counted 'for very little in political calculations', in fact the reverse was sometimes equally true, and Friedrich Wilhelm and Alexander still maintained their good personal relations despite the international tensions that were dividing their countries at this time.[138] Similarly, their wives now formed a friendship of their own, and they too would continue to correspond after the visit was over. During the six weeks of their stay the king and queen witnessed the opulence of the Russian court, with its ornate palaces, lavish banquets and sumptuous balls for thousands of guests. This all contrasted markedly with the more frugal life of the Prussians, but although the experience astounded Luise and her husband, it did not change things when they got home. Not just because of their financial difficulties, but also out of preference, the couple continued to follow their simpler lifestyle.

Finally, under pressure from Napoleon, on 23 December 1809 the royal family returned to Berlin. Although they were given a jubilant welcome, here they soon discovered the extent of the damage wreaked by the French, who by now had destroyed and looted much of the city. Luise, already worn out by her recent trials and past illnesses, was particularly distressed by the vandalism they had committed at Charlottenburg, and courtiers soon began to notice how her health was declining. Six months later on 19 July 1810, while on a visit to see her father in Mecklenburg-Strelitz, the queen died unexpectedly at the duke's summer palace in Hohenzieritz, around 80 miles north of Berlin. She was just thirty-four. Her husband was heartbroken, and although he later found companionship in a morganatic marriage, Luise had left an un-fillable void. Over the years memorials would be erected in her memory, and in 1814 Friedrich Wilhelm also created in her honour an award for women of courage. This, the Order of Luise, which continued to exist until the end of the dynasty, was equivalent in prestige to the Iron Cross that had recently been inaugurated by the king for his war heroes. When she died, it was not just the queen's family who grieved, she was equally mourned by the Prussian people. Having loved her for her warmth, modesty and many acts of charity, they now held her up as an example of ideal womanhood. In the early days of her marriage, Friedrich Wilhelm II had commissioned Johann Gottfried Schadow to create a statue of her with her sister. Although not appreciated by Luise's husband, who disliked his father's extravagance and immodest taste, this charmingly informal work would be much reproduced and today the marble version is displayed in Berlin's Alte Nationalgalerie, where it stands as a fitting memorial to Prussia's most beloved and eternally youthful queen.[139]

By this time Napoleon's alliance with Alexander had begun to falter, and soon he was making plans for his invasion of Russia. Although he had previously ordered Friedrich Wilhelm to stop building up his army, he now commanded the king to provide men to increase the size of his own force. In addition, when in March 1812 the *Grande Armée* began at last to make its way towards the Russian border, Napoleon instructed the king to provide it with any necessary supplies. But with the eastern regions already destitute after their recent poor harvests, the emperor's demands were increasingly difficult to fulfil. As a result, the soldiers grew more exacting, often taking matters into their own hands, plundering the last hidden supplies of the peasants, stealing their horses and livestock, and committing acts of dire savagery. Their brutality, even harsher than that of the earlier occupying troops, stirred up a vitriolic hatred of the French that grew in intensity over time. As a result, the local population would later be overjoyed when news began filtering back of the misfortunes being suffered by Napoleon's men in Russia. And then as the wretched frost-bitten and mutilated army started to reappear, the embittered Prussian people eagerly began to wreak their own savage revenge.

Friedrich Wilhelm remained undecided, however, still trapped between the two great powers. Eventually, to avoid capture by the French, he moved for a time to Silesia, and at that point, in his distant eastern territories his instructions began to be ignored. General Yorck now unilaterally disobeyed orders and, by agreeing with the Russians to remain neutral, in effect opened the country's borders to the tsar's advancing army. Just days before French troops left Berlin, on 28 February 1813 Friedrich Wilhelm decided to break his former agreement with Napoleon, and eight months later he joined the allies to crush the emperor at Leipzig – a brutal three-day battle during which his army would begin to repair his country's battered reputation. After that, for the next two years, the Prussians continued to play an important role in the so-called War of Liberation, gaining full international recognition at Waterloo, where General Blücher's arrival helped bring about the final defeat of Napoleon.

Descended from a family of the lesser nobility two years after Frederick the Great came to the throne, Blücher was born at Rostock in Mecklenburg, where today his statue stands in the University Square. Having spent his adolescence on the Swedish island of Rugen, near Stralsund, at the age of fifteen he joined the Swedish hussars, even though his brother was in service to the Prussian king. As a result, when the Seven Years' War began they were on opposing sides, but after Blücher's capture, he was enlisted in Frederick II's army. However, the brutality he displayed during the First Partition of Poland caused him to be dismissed and he would be unable to return to service until allowed to do so by Friedrich Wilhelm II. Having become a major general in 1794, this bluff, down-to-earth man would be seventy-two years old at the time of Waterloo, where despite his considerable age and recent serious injury, he fought on with determination. His significant role in helping sway the eventual outcome would ultimately help Prussia when the Congress of Vienna returned to business and finalised the new map of Europe. In the concluding agreement, the country was recognised for the part it had played in the French emperor's eventual overthrow and, besides regaining much of the land lost after Tilsit, Friedrich Wilhelm III was given new territories to compensate him for those that had now become part of the tsar's Kingdom or Congress Poland.

Friedrich Wilhelm III has received mixed press, loved and honoured by some, reviled by others, often depending on the period in which the judges were living. His contemporary Bishop Eylert praised his unostentatious modesty, honesty and inner strength, but F. Lorraine Petre and Field Marshal Earl Roberts, writing less than a decade before the outbreak of the First World War, condemned Friedrich Wilhelm III for his weakness, indecisiveness and even 'treachery', failings that they believed had only served Napoleon's ambitions. As the king's forefather the Great Elector had warned, neutrality in the face of danger was no guarantee of a country's security, and too often those pursuing it had earned the disrespect of others. A lover of peace, Friedrich Wilhelm was no doubt a weak ruler in a period that called for strong leadership, but from the moment of his accession he faced unequal odds. While the geographical positioning of his country made it vulnerable to foreign attack, he also faced an insatiable enemy at a time when Prussia's military force was in dire need of updating. Whoever had been the country's king at that time would have found himself to be in an exceptionally difficult situation, challenged by one of the most brilliant and ambitious military leaders of all time. His contemporaries would show equal uncertainty and indecisiveness in the face of this danger, the Habsburg emperor Franz alternately declaring war and making peace, and Tsar Paul switching allegiances on a whim. Paul's son Alexander, already more secure than the Prussian king – being further from France, and with a far larger army – would also repeatedly change his alliances. But for all there was deep uncertainty as to who would triumph in the end, and decisions are always easier to make in retrospect. In war, such choices rest on chance, and a snatched victory or unexpected defeat can decide whether or not an individual is held to be a hero or a failure. While Friedrich William has been blamed for his timidity, and criticised for following the bad advice of others, his overriding desire was to avoid bloodshed and preserve his country from Napoleon's imperialistic designs.

On the plus side, while he was on the throne, Friedrich Wilhelm sought to repair the damage caused by his father's extravagance and wasteful expenditure. In addition, he introduced certain much-needed reforms, among them the updating of the army and the ending of the stricter measures of corporal punishment, most notably the infamous 'running of the gauntlet'. He also made changes to the school education system and founded the Friedrich-Wilhelm's University that, later renamed the Humboldt, still occupies the palace of Frederick II's brother Heinrich near the Brandenburg Gate. Besides ordering the construction of the country's first railways, to increase trade with the neighbouring states he brought in the Customs Union – a measure of particular significance as it would later help Prussia rise to dominance in the region. Furthermore, having during his darkest days at Königsberg been inspired with a deeper spiritual conviction by Bishop Borowsky, he made changes to the country's religious system. Bringing together the two confessions, he joined the Lutheran and Calvinist faiths in the new Union of Churches, of which he was now the head. Most importantly for him, by the end of his reign he had achieved one of his earliest and greatest ambitions: soon after the disasters of 1806 he had begun to bring about the abolition of serfdom. Nevertheless, towards the end of his life, the king – like other rulers in this counter-revolutionary period – had grown more reactionary and conservative, and so his later reforms would be more limited, his chief concerns having by that time become the maintenance of the crown's authority.

When Friedrich Wilhelm III died on 14 June 1840, he was buried beside Luise at Charlottenburg in the mausoleum purposely built for her after her death thirty years earlier. Here, among others, he would be joined by his second wife, and eventually his son – the later Kaiser Wilhelm I. Now, however, the dead king was succeeded by his oldest middle-aged son, Friedrich Wilhelm IV, a traditionalist and supporter of the Counter-Enlightenment who was also a member of his father's Prussian United Church. Perhaps contrary to expectations, not only had he earlier married a Catholic Bavarian princess, but would also later display his religious tolerance in 1844 by attending the mass to celebrate the completion of Cologne Cathedral. Equally, on his succession he had shown his more liberal tendences by relaxing certain laws, although in the case of freedom of the press, these would later be reversed, censorship being partially reimposed in an effort to prevent the increasingly disrespectful cartoons that were mocking the king's growing obesity.

By that time more serious dangers were lurking, caused by the revolutionary movements that were sweeping across Prussia and much of the rest of Europe. Throughout his reign, Friedrich Wilhelm IV's authority would frequently come under attack. As towns and cities swelled in size, so the problems of urban poverty and hardship intensified, creating a situation that further stoked the brewing unrest. In this uncertain climate, a failed attempt was made on the king's life, and rioting and demonstrations broke out around the country. During the 'year of revolutions' the most serious disturbances occurred in Silesia, followed by others in Berlin, where in March 1848 some 400 people would lose their lives in the demonstrations. The king now showed his true mettle, personally preventing a more serious outcome by giving the order for his troops to withdraw. While this action for a time earned him his brother's scorn, the future Wilhelm I charging him with cowardice, in reality the king's actions helped calm the situation. Over the next few days he showed immense courage, first facing with equanimity the humiliation heaped on him by the angry mobs surrounding his balcony, and then silencing the opposition by riding out through the crowd unprotected. His obvious bravery and his subsequent promises of constitutional reform helped save the day, allowing Berlin, unlike many other cities around Europe, to return quickly to normal. However, the troubles of 1848 had left their mark on the king, and from that time he became increasingly reclusive, religious, and reactionary, later going back on his promises to grant new concessions.

The Danes had also suffered problems in 1848, brought to a head by Christian VIII's death in Copenhagen in January. With his successor, Frederik VII, not expected to produce an heir, tensions began to increase in Schleswig and Holstein, where the Salic laws of succession were different from those in Denmark. Now nationalist parties, inspired like others by the revolutionary ideas sweeping Europe, began openly taking sides, either giving their support to the Danish government, or to the demands of the pro-German population, who mainly lived in Holstein and the southern regions of Schleswig. The aims of this group were for the whole united region to be included in the German Confederation, the association of states that Holstein and Lauenburg had joined shortly after its formation by the Congress of Vienna some three decades before. The rebels, calling themselves Schleswig-Holsteiners, took up arms and, helped by the Prussians, defeated the Danes in April. But this victory was not total, and with foreign powers like Britain and Sweden backing Denmark, Friedrich Wilhelm was anxious about further involvement. Even his brother-in-law Tsar Nicholas I encouraged him to tread carefully, and before the year was over, the Prussian king had signed an armistice at Malmö. This was a humiliating climbdown, and Friedrich Wilhelm took the decision on his own without seeking approval from the newly opened federal parliament in Frankfurt. He realised not only that the German Confederation's actions had undermined his own position, but also that after several years of peace his army had lost its fighting edge. However, for another four years the war dragged on, not ending until a protocol was at last signed in London. With Prussia and Russia among the signatories,

A disrespectful cartoon of the two kings, Friedrich Wilhelm IV of Prussia [on the left] and Frederik VII of Denmark, at the time of their meeting in Malmo in 1848. Apart from mocking the kings' obesity, the image also indicates the Prussian view that the peace agreement was a humiliation.

this affirmed Schleswig as a Danish fief, and Holstein (and the neighbouring Lauenburg) as sovereign states within the German Confederation. The agreement brought the war to an end, but as all three duchies remained united in personal union with the Danish king, in reality the settlement just postponed the problem, making it all but inevitable that the fighting would be renewed when Frederik VII eventually died.

In 1848 the Frankfurt parliament proposed that Friedrich Wilhelm should become emperor over a united Germany that excluded Austria – a final demoting of the once great Habsburg empire that had for centuries dominated central Europe. However, being a traditionalist, the king turned this suggestion down, telling his sister, Empress Alexandra of Russia, that the parliament did not have the right to make such an offer. Rather, he wanted to see Germany's unification revived as a new Holy Roman Empire, ruled by a traditionally elected emperor – an unachievable ambition, as he soon realised. Change was still in the air and the following year the king agreed to the founding of a Prussian constitution and two-chamber parliament. While this left power still chiefly in the hands of the monarchy, aristocracy and military, it introduced a system of limited suffrage that continued until the end of the dynasty.

A follower of the Romantic movement, like other similar revivalists – including Queen Victoria and the later King Ludwig II of Bavaria – he was attracted to the Gothic style, and, just two years after coming to the throne, Friedrich Wilhelm IV decided to complete, with the addition of two spires, the unfinished work on Cologne's ancient cathedral. While this had been halted in 1560 shortly after the Reformation, for the king it now had the advantage of satisfying the many Catholic residents of the city, who, following a period under French rule, had on the fall of Napoleon become part of Prussia. And in the same Romantic-Gothic style, Friedrich Wilhelm IV would create the castles of Stolzenfels on the Rhine near Koblenz, and Burg Hohenzollern around 30 miles south of Stuttgart – the latter becoming the temporary resting place of Frederick II and his father in the 1950s. Meanwhile, in Berlin the king gave his support to many new building projects, among them the old National Gallery and the New Museum, both fully renovated today after their destruction in the Second World War. And finally, at Potsdam he was personally involved in the construction and design of the Orangery and the Church of Peace – the Friedenskirche. The latter was modelled on the basilica of San Clemente in Rome, its apse decorated with a Byzantine mosaic that Friedrich Wilhelm had bought from a church due for demolition on the Venetian island of Murano.

Having never had children, after he became seriously debilitated by a first stroke in 1857, his power began to pass to his brother, Prince Wilhelm, who became regent the following year. During the king's long illness, one marked by several more strokes, his wife continued to nurse him until he eventually died on 2 January 1861. His heart was then interred beside the graves of his parents in the mausoleum at Charlottenburg, but his body would be buried in his new Friedenskirche at Potsdam, where twelve years later it was joined by that of his wife.

When he succeeded his brother as Wilhelm I, the new king was already sixty-four, an imposing-looking man with his famous mutton chop sideburns, who despite his age would rule for the next seventeen years. He had taken part in the War of Liberation, but unlike his predecessor Friedrich Wilhelm, had done so with notable distinction, earning himself the Iron Cross for bravery and serving with courage under Blücher at the Battle of Waterloo. Proud of his military career, he liked to wear uniform, having since his youth always enjoyed the company of military men, and, after assuming power, he improved the army by increasing its size and extending the period of training. Although he was not such an intellectual as his brother, and had less of an interest in promoting the arts, Prussia was benefiting by this time from an international financial boom and as a result, there continued to be not just considerable growth in the country's industry and trade but also a rapid expansion of its rail network.

However, there was now a marked divide between the conservative and liberal elements in the country, the former supporting a Russian alliance and favouring its more autocratic form of government. In contrast, those who supported reform preferred the English model, as did the king's son Friedrich Wilhelm and his wife Vicky, Queen Victoria's oldest daughter. But the situation for this faction became more difficult only a year after Wilhelm's accession, when his minister, Otto von Bismarck, angered by the democratic demands of the parliament, was able with the king's support to become prime minister and remove the Prussian *Lantag*'s role in decision making. Now supremely powerful, the new chancellor began to impose his thinking on Wilhelm, directing him down a strongly reactionary path that left the crown prince excluded from all political discussion. As Bismarck knew, Wilhelm was the archetypal, brave Prussian officer, but while such a man was always ready to take orders, his fear of 'the condemnation of his superiors' prevented him from making decisions of his own.[140] Hating the liberal views of the crown prince and princess, for the next three decades Bismarck would plague the couple, reviling their ideas, undermining their reputation, and eventually creating a bitter gulf between them and their oldest son. Writing to her mother on 3 July 1863, Vicky declared, 'You cannot think how painful it is to be continually surrounded by people who consider your very existence a misfortune and your sentiments evidence of lunacy!'[141] After her son Wilhelm's difficult birth in 1859, which had left his arm permanently damaged, relations between him and his mother had not been close, the situation made worse as she tried to find increasingly drastic remedial treatments for the child. Unable to overcome her own feelings of guilt and responsibility, and her sense of failure for not having produced an heir that lived up to high Prussian expectations, Vicky's interactions with Wilhelm were ever more complex. While in his own different way the boy's feelings for his mother would on occasion appear equally confused, from his teen years on, he grew increasingly attached to his grandfather and, guided by Bismarck, began progressively to ignore the wishes of his parents. As he became closer to the ruler, his father was more and more bypassed, so that several years later in 1884 it would be young Wilhelm who was chosen to lead a state visit to St Petersburg. Although this infuriated the crown prince, in Russia his son's ideas fitted at the time with those of Alexander III, and this early visit was deemed a success. After the stay, the prince, already showing his belief in his self-importance, would begin to write directly to the tsar, instructing him to ignore his father's opinions.

In 1863, following Frederik VII's death without a legitimate male heir, as expected the tensions regarding the succession in Schleswig, Holstein and the smaller Lauenburg again came to the fore. Supporting those who opposed the new Danish king, troops from the German Confederation entered the country, only then to be given further backing by the independent forces from Prussia and Austria. However, rather than being concerned for the local populations, these two powers were in fact fighting for their own ends. Before long, Denmark suffered an embarrassing defeat and was forced to give up the whole disputed region, whereupon Prussia gained control of Schleswig, and Austria Holstein. However, this was a situation that was bound to cause further tension, as indeed happened in 1866 when war broke out between the two nations. Within seven weeks Prussia had defeated Austria, and in the aftermath the German Confederation was dissolved. It was then replaced with the North German Confederation, a federal regrouping of twenty-three states that included Hanover and the duchies of Schleswig and Holstein – these three areas having now been annexed by Prussia. With Austria excluded and no longer a major power, Prussia, with

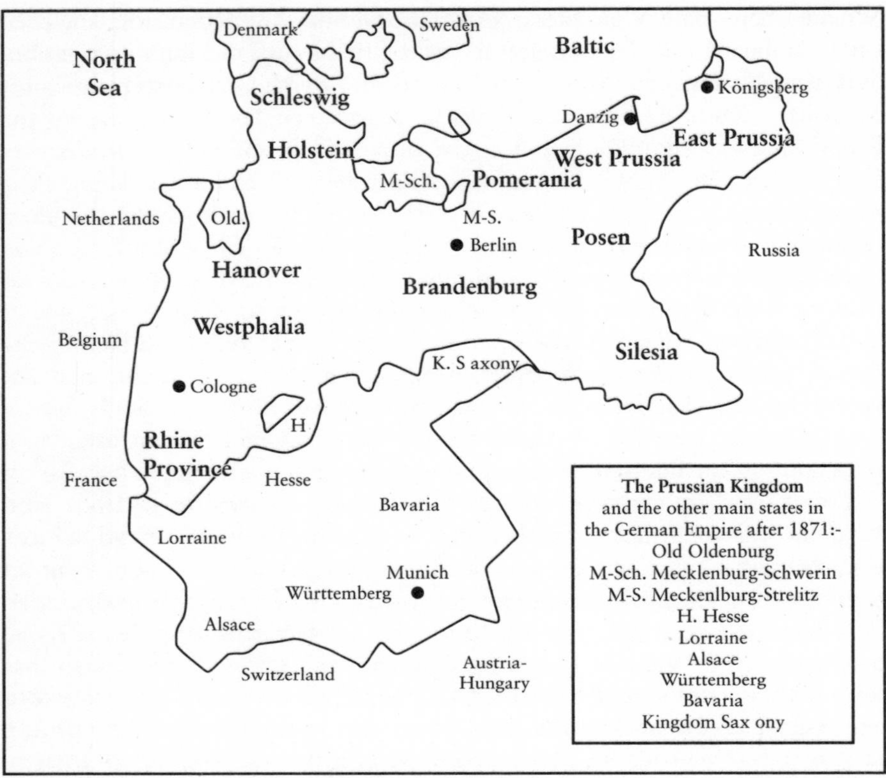

its vast territory and more than four-fifths of the confederation's overall population, became the dominant presence in the region.

As Wilhelm's own nephew Alexander II was among those who now began to fear the kingdom's growing dominance, in 1867 the tsar went to Paris, hoping by doing so that he might improve Russia's relations with the French. This objective, however, failed. Despite receiving a lavish welcome, eventually Alexander would leave the country in a fury. While out in his carriage with Emperor Napoleon III, he became the target of a second failed assassination attempt and, although the shot fired by a disgruntled Polish *emigré* missed its mark, the tsar was made angrier still on learning of the public's support for his attacker. With that, he lost all patience with France and soon after switched his favour back to Prussia.

Before long other new problems would further complicate the international situation. As Prussia became drawn into the dispute over the choice of Spain's new monarch, tensions began to mount on the country's western border with France. Eventually, after the French emperor had decided to mobilise his army, the situation escalated and full-scale war broke out. However, within weeks the French had been routed, Napoleon III taken captive, and France had suffered a humilating defeat, disasters that ultimately brought about the fall of the Second French Empire and the exile of its imperial couple. Following the victory, the southern states of Bavaria,

Württemberg, Baden and Hesse joined the German Confederation, and then on 1 January 1871, the anniversary of the first Prussian king's coronation, Wilhelm was acclaimed emperor of the Second *Reich*, now becoming Kaiser Wilhelm I. With the Hall of Mirrors in Versailles purposely chosen for the occasion, this ceremony did not just draw a line under Prussia's earlier defeats, but also emphasised how Germany – not France – was now the major power in western Europe. Nonetheless, despite his new status, even Wilhelm had to be satisfied with the lesser title of German Emperor, having been dissuaded by Bismarck to drop his preferred 'Emperor of Germany' so as not to offend the rulers of the other German states.

Throughout this time, the relations between the ruling party and the crown prince, Friedrich Wilhelm, remained fraught, the situation made worse by the machinations of Bismarck. While those wanting reform waited for the emperor to die, believing that his demise would usher in a better future for Prussia, fate would be against them. Despite expectations, Wilhelm lived on, even surviving two assassination attempts in 1878. And then the crown prince's health began to give concern. With the doctors disagreeing on the diagnosis and treatment, it was some time before throat cancer was confirmed, the public eventually told on 12 November 1887 that his condition was terminal. Although at last four months later on 9 March 1888 Wilhelm I died aged ninety, it was too late. Even those who had previously supported the new emperor – now called Kaiser Friedrich III – began to turn away from him, intent instead on currying favour with his heir. Just ninety-nine days after his succession, on 15 June Friedrich died, and with his death all hope was gone for the reforms that he and Vicky had favoured. The country was now in the hands of their unpredictable son, Kaiser Wilhelm II, and within two years he had made it evident that he was going to rule by himself. Disagreeing with Bismarck on how to resolve the strikes that were hitting the country, by the end of March 1890 he had forced the resignation of the septuagenerian chancellor who had played such a significant role in his upbringing. But Vicky had been treated with still greater insensitivity, her son having ordered the rooms that she had shared with her husband to be searched immediately after his death. No important papers were ever found, the couple having earlier taken the precaution of moving them to England for safety. The new emperor then forced his mother to leave Potsdam and she finally settled in Hesse, where, shortly after her own mother, Queen Victoria, she died in 1901. After being wrapped in a Union Jack as she had wished, she was buried beside her husband in the large sarcophagus in the Friedenskirche in Potsdam. All Vicky's hopes for her adopted country had been disappointed in her son, whose militaristic and antisemitic tendencies were so different from her own.[142] From the moment he came to the throne he, known to all future generations as 'the Kaiser', set out to exert his unfettered control, and to interfere in the affairs of others, not just annoying and antagonising his relations in England and elsewhere, but also ultimately leading Prussia down a path that would end with its own demise.

18

Maria Feodorovna: Russia's Danish Empress

Christian IX of Denmark, 'the Father-in-law of Europe', with three of his children [from left to right], Princess Dagmar (later Empress of Russia), Prince Vilhelm (later King of the Hellenes), and Princess Alexandra (later Princess of Wales and Queen of the United Kingdom).

Princess Marie Sophie Frederikke, better known by her last name, 'Dagmar', was born in Copenhagen in 1847, the second daughter of Louise of Hesse-Kassel and Christian of Schleswig-Holstein-Sonderburg-Glücksburg. Both her parents were descended from the Danish king Frederik V, her mother the king's great-granddaughter by his second marriage to Juliane Marie, and her father the great-nephew of his mentally unbalanced son, Christian VII. Being just a junior branch of the ruling Danish Oldenburg dynasty, and comparatively impoverished by the standards of other royalty, the family lived reasonably simply in the Yellow Palace near the Amalienborg, where Dagmar and her two sisters took part in some of the household duties, even mending and making their own clothes. Nonetheless, the six children enjoyed a happy, informal childhood, being visited from time to time by Hans Christian Andersen, who came and read them bedtime stories. Several years later, as she was about to leave Denmark for Russia, Dagmar spotted the writer in the crowd and made a point of going to say goodbye to him. This affectionate act of informal courtesy, typical of the Danish royal family, moved Andersen close to tears, but he was sure of her future happiness with her 'noble husband' and his 'excellent family'. Unable to foresee the many unexpected and bitter trials that she would later face, he declared her to be truly fortunate.[143]

By this time Andersen was famous, but his early life had been very different. Born in 1805 to an illiterate mother and a semi-educated father, after an impoverished childhood at Odense on the island of Fyn (Funen), he had moved when he was fourteen to Copenhagen, hoping that he might start a career on the stage. Instead, after being befriended by the theatre director, and having received some financial support from King Frederik himself, Andersen went on to a grammar school.[144] Here he would be deeply unhappy, but within ten years had begun to make a name for himself as a writer of poems, novels and other books – only later in the 1840s finally achieving recognition for his fairy tales. After some time spent travelling around Europe, two years before Dagmar was born he moved to No. 67 on the 'sunny' northern side of the Nyhavn, his home for nearly twenty years, and just one of three houses he would occupy in this harbour district that has now become such a popular area. By the time of his death in 1875, Andersen was an international figure, and twelve years later he would be honoured by a statue in the gardens of the Rosenborg Castle. However, it is Edvard Eriksen's work commissioned in 1909, depicting Andersen's fictional character 'The Little Mermaid' that is now the more famous. With its face modelled on that of the Danish ballet dancer Ellen Price, and the body on that of Eriksen's wife – Price having refused to pose for this – it was finally unveiled in 1913, and is today one of the most visited landmarks in the city.

When Dagmar was fifteen, the situation of her family began to change dramatically. In 1862 her second oldest brother, seventeen-year-old Vilhelm, was elected to the Greek throne, being officially acclaimed in Copenhagen as King George I of the Hellenes. Replacing the now ousted King Otto, two years later he moved to Athens and then in 1867 married sixteen-year-old Grand Duchess Olga Constantinovna, the niece of Tsar Alexander II. The couple became parents of eight children, having among their future eleven grandchildren Prince Philip, Duke of Edinburgh, who had the family name of Schleswig-Holstein-Sonderburg-Glücksburg up to the time of his engagement in 1947 to the future Queen Elizabeth. However, with anti-German feeling still evident in the immediate aftermath of the war, Prince Philip was made a British citizen and encouraged to adopt his mother's maiden name, Mountbatten, which had itself been anglicised from Battenburg by his maternal grandfather three decades before.

The year after George became the Greek king, on 10 March 1863, the status of Dagmar's family was further raised when her older, favourite sister, Alexandra, married Albert, Prince of Wales ('Bertie'), the later Edward VII. After a journey of nine days, Alexandra eventually arrived on the royal yacht, the *Victoria and Albert*, to a warm welcome at Gravesend, followed by three more days of public celebration in London. But with Albert, Prince Consort, having died a little over a year earlier, the wedding itself was low-key, the women ordered to wear the sombre colours of half-mourning, and the ceremony taking place in the small and more private St George's Chapel at Windsor, where the heavily shrouded Queen Victoria watched the proceedings from the balcony. Wallowing in her grief, she would even question her daughter on how anyone could consider it to be anything other than a sad occasion. But one person unconcerned by the solemnity of the event was the bridegroom's nephew, the four-year-old page – the future Kaiser Wilhelm II – who crawled around, scratching or biting the ankles of his uncles.

This marriage would not be the end of the Danish family's rising fortunes. Soon after Alexandra's wedding, in November the Glücksburgs' status was further increased when Dagmar's father became the new Danish king, Christian IX – his succession having been agreed eleven years earlier after it was accepted that Frederik VII would be unlikely to produce a legitimate heir. So now, following Frederik's death, Christian was declared king, his accession being affirmed by the public proclamation that had by this time replaced the previous coronation and anointing ceremonies, rituals abolished along with royal absolutism at the time of the new constitution in 1849.

However, shortly after he came to the throne, early the following year the Second Schleswig War broke out as a result of the complex ongoing relations between Denmark and the duchies of Schleswig, Holstein and Lauenburg – a political situation which was so complicated that Lord Palmerston was reported to have memorably declared that it had only really been understood by just three people: Prince Albert, now dead, a German professor, gone mad, and himself, who had 'forgotten all about it'.[145] And although the issues that had led to the First Schleswig War sixteen years earlier had been temporarily resolved, in reality the problems had only been suspended. Already seeing Christian as more pro-Danish than their preferred candidate – Duke Friedrich Christian August of Augustenburg – the German-speaking majority in the southern regions objected strongly to the new king's ratification of the November Constitution that introduced a joint parliament for Schleswig and Denmark. This, they believed, negated the terms of the former London Protocol that had guaranteed the duchies' coalition within the Danish federation. But while this had guarded against their separation, Holstein now upset the former agreement by refusing to accept Christian's accession through the female line. As a result, when he was presented with the November Constitution for signing, the king faced a dilemma; although realising the effect it would have on the secessionists, his refusal to ratify it would anger the very people who had brought him to the throne. With little choice, therefore, he finally decided his only option was to appease the Danes and accept their constitution. Then, with the tension already at its height, one further issue came into play. Prussia intended to construct a canal through Danish-controlled Holstein, one that would enable their fleets to enter the Baltic without having to make the long, often stormy, journey around northern Jutland. With all these issues having come to a head, on 1 February 1864 Prussia invaded and within five months the Danes were defeated and had been forced to surrender all the disputed lands. This, a massive knock to their self-esteem, would seriously damage the king's popularity for a considerable time. After the First World War, in 1920 a part of the former duchies, North Schleswig, was finally returned to Denmark, but Dagmar and her sister Alexandra never forgave the Prussians for what they had done.

During the summer of 1864 however, other events occurred to lighten the family's mood. By this time Slavophilism had taken hold in Russia as its followers turned their backs on European influences and determinedly promoted traditional Russian ideas. In line with this mood, Tsar Alexander II chose to break from the practice that had begun with Peter the Great, namely that of selecting a bride for his heir from the pool of eligible German-speaking, Lutheran princesses. With the German Confederation now becoming increasingly authoritative in central Europe, the imperial couple decided to look elsewhere for a suitable wife for their oldest son Nicholas – in the family better known as 'Nixa'. Having set his sights on the smaller, less dominant, Danish kingdom, the tsar originally considered Alexandra to be a fitting candidate, but on realising that she was no longer available, he issued a proposal to Christian IX suggesting a marriage for Nixa with the sixteen-year-old Dagmar. As the prestige of the Glücksburgs had been further promoted by their new connections to the British royal family, the match was now seen as highly suitable for a Romanov, and the whole scheme was made still more appealing by the fact that Dagmar was said to be attractive, lively and intelligent. Christian, however, insisted that the engagement would depend on the girl's approval, and so Nixa was therefore instructed to visit Copenhagen in June. Here his good looks and cultivated manners charmed everyone, most importantly Dagmar, who happily agreed to the engagement.

Nixa, however, had already started to show the first slight symptoms of an underlying illness, and over the next few months he began increasingly to suffer from back pain, most probably brought on by a form of tuberculosis. Various explanations as to the cause of his medical condition were later suggested, including an earlier fall from his horse, and an injury suffered to the spine when playfully wrestling with his cousins or brother, but the exact reasons for his physical decline in the following months remain uncertain. Nonetheless, he now set off on a cultural tour of Europe, breaking his journey in order to visit his sickly mother in the south of France, where she had gone to escape the Russian winter. But over the New Year Nixa's condition worsened considerably, and it continued to deteriorate throughout the spring. By Easter the prognosis was so bad that the tsar had been called from Russia, and Dagmar from Denmark, and finally, surrounded by his distraught family, the twenty-one-year-old *tsesarevich* died in Nice on 24 April 1865.

Despite the uncertainty over the truth of the story that on his deathbed Nixa proposed that his much-loved brother Alexander – 'Sasha' – should marry Dagmar in his place, undoubtedly he acknowledged Sasha as the heir to his position and responsibilities. But as his duties became obvious to him, the latter began to express his deep uncertainties. Already in love with another young woman, just a month after Nixa died Sasha voiced his concerns in his diary: 'I want to refuse Dagmar, whom I cannot love and don't want. [...] Perhaps it would be better if I relinquished my right to the throne. I feel incapable of ruling.'[146] But with dynastic marriages being little more than practical arrangements to confirm political and international alliances, his doubts soon had to be pragmatically put aside and by June the following year he and Dagmar were engaged. Five months later, having converted to Othodoxy and become Maria Feodorovna, she and Sasha were married at the Winter Palace on 28 October 1866 (OS). Among those who were absent were her parents, unable to afford the further expenses that they would now have to meet, and her sister, Alexandra, who was pregnant. But the Prince of Wales represented his wife and charmed his hosts, particularly enjoying the company of the younger grand dukes, who set about introducing him to St Petersburg's more risqué entertainments. After that, for the next fourteen and a half years, Maria and Sasha lived mainly in the Anichkov Palace on the Nevsky Prospekt, with summer visits to Gatchina, the Alexander Palace at Tsarskoe Selo, and the smaller Cottage Palace at Peterhof. And although Maria's husband was quite different from his cultured, delicately built brother, against the odds the marriage turned out be very successful. The couple were soon devoted to each other and, unlike his brother-in-law, Bertie – whose philandering he considered to be foolish and depraved – Sasha would remain ever faithful to his adored little 'Minnie'.

On the death of Nixa, preparations were immediately begun to remedy the new heir's obvious shortcomings. Unlike his intelligent, sophisticated brother, Sasha had received an education that was seriously lacking and, as the least promising of the emperor's children, he had been largely overlooked. A very tall, big, clumsy man, he was a poor linguist with little interest in intellectual matters. And because he was so untrained and unprepared for the role that lay before him, after Nixa died gossips soon began to suggest that the succession might pass directly to the two men's younger brother, Vladimir. Alexander II therefore set out immediately to rectify the situation, and, having arranged a hectic educational programme for his son, he then put an end to further uncertainty by officially acclaiming Sasha as his heir and ordering a public oath of allegiance.

Maria soon proved to be popular with the Russian people at large, earning their love and respect through her charity work. She was more intelligent than her sister Alexandra, and, although not such a remarkable beauty, she was pretty, vivacious and extremely gregarious – in Queen Victoria's view, 'very fit for the position in Russia' and 'a very nice girl'.[147] Unlike her husband, Maria enjoyed the social life of St Petersburg, with its balls and other entertainments, and she also loved the beautiful clothes and jewels she was expected to wear in her new role. At home she would often be joined by Sasha, who liked to sit with her while she painted, she being an accomplished artist – a talent she passed on to her daughters, the younger of whom would partially support herself in the years after the revolution by selling her pictures. Soon Maria became a devoted mother, the first of her children being born at Tsarskoe Selo on 6 May 1868 (OS); a little over three weeks later, he was christened Nicholas in the chapel of the Catherine Palace. Although, tragically, Maria's next child, Alexander, would die aged eleven months from meningitis, within a year of his death she had produced a third boy, George, who was then followed by Xenia in 1875, Michael in 1878, and finally Olga in 1882.

Although Maria supported the fashionably spartan upbringing that was favoured by English nannies, her children grew up in a happy environment, loved by both their parents. Their father always remained unsophisticated, and as a devotee of Slavophilism, chose when possible to follow traditional Russian customs, eating simple Russian food, dressing in plain Russian clothes, and eventually also speaking and writing to his wife in Russian. After his accession, he would carry this further, not just replacing the French still spoken at court but also making Russian the official language in Poland and the Baltic states. And, rather than the more European-sounding 'Emperor' that had been introduced by Peter the Great, he (and Nicholas II after him) preferred to be addressed as 'Tsar'. Moreover, both father and son – despite their predominantly German blood – would emphasise a presumed Slavic heritage by choosing to wear beards, the first Russian rulers to do so since Alexis I in the seventeenth century. The significance of this becomes particularly apparent when remembering that beards had first been outlawed by the modernising Peter the Great, and later again banned for the gentry in 1849 by Nicholas I, who saw them as symbolic of the period's growing radicalism.

For the time being life continued peacefully for Maria, and in 1873 she and Sasha went with their sons Nicholas and George to England, where they stayed with her sister, and also visited Queen Victoria at Windsor. The queen later recorded the meeting in her journal: 'At 2 Bertie and Alix arrived with the Césaréwitch and Minny [*sic*] (Dagmar) looking very dear & nice, quite unalterd [*sic*], & as simple as ever. He is very tall & big, good natured & unaffected.'[148] During their stay, Sasha was entertained in a variety of ways, with parades, naval reviews and visits to the Law Courts and Parliament, while Maria and her sister delighted the public by appearing dressed identically. But this was not the only opportunity for the families to get together. King Christian, soon dubbed the 'Father-in-law of Europe', would invite all his large family every summer to Denmark. At the palace of Fredensborg, around 25 miles north of Copenhagen, and occasionally in the smaller Bernstorff just outside the capital, the various relations would gather: Crown Prince Frederik with his wife Louise of Sweden; George, King of the Hellenes and Queen Olga; and later after 1885 Valdemar with his wife Princess Marie of Orléans, the great-granddaughter of Louis Philippe, the King of the French. Their youngest sister, Thyra, would also come with Ernst August, the son of the last King of Hanover, whom she had married in 1878, seven years after her earlier love affair had ended in tragedy. Having discreetly gone away to give birth to an illegitimate daughter, she had avoided further scandal by giving the baby up for adoption. Two months later, the child's father committed suicide after a particularly difficult meeting with King Christian.

For many years the Danish get-together continued as an annual event, the Russian relations arriving with around 100 servants, various pets, and quantities of luggage. On these occasions, when all political discussion was banned, the atmosphere was relaxed, and the family members were able to enjoy freedoms unknown to most of them at home. Here, where, for the benefit of the British relations, the common language spoken was English, several of the children would form lifelong friendships. But their cousin, Prince Wilhelm of Prussia (the later kaiser), would not be included in the party as most of the family did not like or trust him – he becoming still more unpopular after he had spoken unflatteringly to the tsar about his Uncle Bertie. Over the years Wilhelm would look on the Danish gatherings with a mixture of mistrust and envy, torn between his suspicion that his relations were plotting against him, and a desire to be included. Having actually invited himself to stay in 1903, there was considerable relief when he finally left. But for King Christian's children, these gatherings continued to be highly enjoyable, the Glücksburgs never losing their delight in silly games and practical jokes. Their childish sense of fun appealed also to Sasha, who had been brought up in the more formal world of the Romanov court, and he and his wife would be sad when the time came to go home to their 'Russian prison'. Alexandra's husband, on the other hand, was more relieved, he being only too happy to exchange the dull entertainment and lifestyle of the Danish court for other more sophisticated – if not worldly – pleasures, including better food and wine.

However, in 1881 the more carefree days of Maria's youth came to an end. Since the year of her marriage, repeated attempts had been made on the life of Alexander II, and now the anarchists were finally successful, mortally wounding the tsar with a bomb when he was out driving in St Petersburg. A few hours later he died from his injuries, and Sasha and Maria found themselves the new Emperor and Empress of Russia. She wrote to her mother three days later describing the horrors of her father-in-law's death, and how it had landed the 'heaviest blow' on her husband, adding, 'My peace and calm are gone, for now I can never again rest assured about Sacha [*sic*].'[149] On hearing the news, the Prince and Princess of Wales instantly decided, against the wishes of Queen Victoria, to travel to Russia for the funeral. Here they were soon aware of the changed mood in the capital and, although assured by the Minister of the Interior, Loris Melikov, that their own lives were not threatened, they witnessed the tight security surrounding the new imperial couple.

Following the assassination, Maria, Sasha and the children decided to spend more time out of St Petersburg at Gatchina, where they could be better protected from the risk of terrorist attack. This enormous palace that had once belonged to Catherine the Great's favourite, Count Orlov, and later become the country residence of Tsar Paul, was by this time in poor condition, and so the tsar began to update it, adding modern facilities such as a telephone, the latest plumbing, and electric lighting. Although now obliged to live permanently under tight security, Sasha loved the palace, choosing to live in a few small, low-ceilinged rooms on the mezzanine in one wing of the building. Maria felt quite differently about Gatchina, actively disliking it, but here the family's home life continued to be happy, the youngest child, Olga, being born the year after her father's accession.

As Sasha had been deeply shocked by Alexander II's violent death, he soon reversed the more liberal measures his predecessor had drawn up in his last days. Despite declaring that he would respect his father's wishes, influenced by his former tutor, the conservative Konstantin Pobedonostsev, he threw out Alexander II's proposed manifesto promising constitutional reforms. The new tsar reverted to the more reactionary measures of the past, and, with that, the manifesto's author, Loris Melikov, resigned and moved abroad. But as a consequence of the tighter restrictions now in force, the opposition went underground, becoming still more difficult to control. In this increasingly tense atmosphere, the Jews were made scapegoats for the former emperor's assassination, and so antisemitism began to rise with fresh pogroms breaking out around the country, to which the authorities paid scant attention. And as still more repressive laws were introduced and their rights became yet more limited, the Jews and other nonconformist groups started to leave the country and emigrate to Canada and the USA.

Having experienced the brutal realities of battle as a young man, Alexander III was determined to keep Russia out of all conflicts, with the result that during his thirteen years on the throne there would be no wars and he would be dubbed 'the Peacemaker'. Although previously opposed to the Germans, Sasha now wished to reunite with them, and in June shortly after his accession he attended a meeting with his great-uncle, the German Emperor Wilhelm I, at Danzig. With Bismarck on this occasion representing Austria, plans were made to renew the former League of Three Emperors, the alliance that, created a decade before, had broken down when Russia had gone to war against the Ottoman Empire. The meeting was presented as merely a get-together of family relations, but its real objectives were soon suspected, and analysts began theorising about the genuine reasons for the highly secret conference. *The Spectator*, for one, questioned whether the tsar was seeking agreement with Austria regarding the Balkans, where the situation 'could become serious', or if he was looking for support in his battle against the spread of nihilism and other such radical thinking. Finally, drawing attention to the difficulties and dangers that leaders everywhere now faced, the writer argued that greater repression would not be accepted in Germany, and Franz Joseph would be equally loath to take any action that might encourage the rise of revolutionary movements, since – he added significantly – the Austrian Emperor was 'the only sovereign left' able to walk about where he liked.[150] In America, too, these issues were being addressed, the debates having gained even more significance with the recent assassination of President Garfield. Two days after Garfield's funeral on 30 September 1881, the *Chicago Tribune* (again referring to the meeting at Danzig) declared that while the Balkan situation had been temporarily settled, Alexander III remained 'hedged in' on all sides by his problems at home:

> It is not likely that he would have been in such haste to arrange this meeting if he had not been anxious to crush out or place himself in a better position to crush out Nihilism, which is none the less dangerous because it is quiet at present. Besides, the Emperor of Germany and Bismarck, as well as the Czar, fear assasination [*sic*], and it is not likely that they could come together without arranging some mutual system for stamping out Nihilism on the one hand and Communistic Socialism on the other.

With a mistaken optimism, this particular article saw matters in the Balkans as of 'a less important nature', and, considering the problems first raised by the League as 'definitely settled', it predicted that 'Continental Socialism' would very possibly receive 'a hard blow from the three allied Powers'.[151] However, although the emperors met again at Skierniewiece in Poland in 1884, the disagreements over the Balkans would continue to develop, so that within three years of the renewed agreement the League had collapsed, and Italy had joined Germany and Austria in the new Triple Alliance.

Two years after Alexander II's assassination, in May 1883 Alexander III's coronation finally took place in Moscow. Witnesses spoke of the dignity that Maria showed on the occasion, although they commented as well on how she appeared gravely concerned for the safety of her husband. But for a period life returned more or less to normal, with the empress enthusiastically engaging in court functions when not at home with her beloved Sasha. On the domestic front, while life continued to be uncomplicated for the children, their parents were still able to engage in their simple pleasures, among them staying at their small lodge in Finland, where they both fished and Maria did the cooking. Nonetheless, Sasha understood his wife's love of beautiful things and so at Easter in 1885, twenty years after their engagement, he gave her the first of what would become the fabulous imperial collection of fifty Fabergé eggs – two of which were still awaiting delivery when the 1917 February revolution began. The first of these was considerably less ornate with its plain white enamel shell, but already it contained the surprise for which these eggs became famous: its golden interior enclosing a golden yolk, and within that a small golden hen that opened to reveal a tiny diamond imperial crown with a ruby pendant shaped like another egg. Seven of the collection are still missing, but this so-called 'Hen Egg' – minus its crown and pendant – has returned to Russia to be with eight others in the recently acquired Vekselberg Collection on display at the Fabergé Museum in St Petersburg.

Despite the peace the family experienced at home, in the country at large unrest was still brewing, and underground revolutionary movements were now on the rise. In 1887 after an assassination plot was uncovered, five of the conspirators were arrested and later hanged at Schlüsselburg, among them Alexander Ulyanov. Ulyanov's younger brother, Vladimir, better known by his pseudonym Lenin, never forgave the Romanovs for this execution. Then the next year the tsar and his family escaped when their train crashed at Borki on its way home from the Crimea, killing twenty-one people. While various stories were then spread of how Alexander, using his immense strength, had protected his family from the carriage roof that was about to crush them, whatever exactly happened, the event appeared to leave him permanently damaged in mind and body. Although the crash most probably was an accident caused by the poor state of the railways, the memory of the similar attack on his father convinced Sasha that he had been the target of a comparable assassination attempt. But it was not just the mental fears for the safety of himself and his family that now began to weigh on him. Having very possibly damaged himself physically during the rescue, from this time his general health began to decline seriously. The Princess of Wales would later be shocked by his changed appearance, the man who had previously demonstrated enough strength to rip apart a pack of cards, or bend a piece of metal, now looking sick and wasted. Prince Nicholas of Greece remarked, 'It was like seeing a magnificent building crumble.'[152]

With the fears of assassination constantly in mind, the family's sense of insecurity was not helped three years later when the heir to the throne, Nicholas, narrowly escaped death in 1891 while on a tour of the far east of the empire. Leaving in November with his brother George, he went to Greece where he was joined by his cousin, 'Greek George'. They travelled on to Egypt and India, and despite his younger brother having to leave the party because of the ill health that was already starting to plague him, Nicholas and his cousin continued on to Vladivostok. From here the *tsesarevich* embarked on an official visit to Japan, but this would be blighted when a fanatic attacked him with a knife, Nicholas only narrowly escaping death through his cousin's quick thinking. Although not seriously injured, the episode would have a profound long-term effect, leaving him with a lasting antipathy towards the Japanese people.

While on his tour, Nicholas would lay the foundations of the Trans-Siberian Railway, a track intended eventually to connect the capital with the Pacific, a hugely expensive project first approved by Alexander II, and now given the go-ahead by his successor, Alexander III. In this same period, other – more troubling – concerns were adding to the pressures on the tsar, the country suffering two disastrous periods of famine and another outbreak of cholera. Responsibility for these catastrophes, which according to a conservative estimate caused at least half a million deaths, was soon laid at the government's door. And to add to the misery, as the corpses mounted up, rumours were spread about the hurried burial of individuals who were still alive.

There was, however, one more positive development at this time. Alexander could now celebrate the improvement in Russia's relations with France, and, when the French fleet arrived to a warm reception at Kronstadt in July 1891, it was noted how he stood respectfully bareheaded as the previously banned revolutionary hymn the *Marseillaise* was played for the first time on Russian soil. This visit, welcomed by both parties, marked a significant change of policy, but it also added to the increasingly complex network of alliances that would end with the catastrophe of 1914, and the eventual overturning of the status quo in most of Europe. But, for the time being, the future seemed more promising for Russia, and the next year in Paris an official alliance was drawn up, celebrated by the commissioning of a new bridge over the Seine in the tsar's honour. Two years after Sasha died, the foundations of the Pont Alexandre III were finally laid in 1896 by Nicholas II, during a highly successful state visit remembered as 'the Russian week'.

A few months before his death, at Easter 1894 Alexander presented Maria with what would be the last Fabergé egg he would give her. This, poignantly, and perhaps intentionally, marked with the unfortunate date, sits today in the St Petersburg museum alongside the Hen Egg that the empress had received nine years earlier.[153] By this time the tsar's health was rapidly declining and so although in September the imperial couple were invited to stay in Corfu as guests of Maria's brother King George and his wife Queen Olga, his condition had deteriorated too much to undertake the journey. Having decided, therefore, to go no further than the Crimea, they remained at their Small Maily Palace on the Livadia estate. Alexander had now been told that his illness was terminal, and ten days before his death, his son's new fiancée, the twenty-two-year-old Alexandra ('Alix') of Hesse arrived to be with the family. Although the tsar was by this stage gravely ill, he was determined to receive his future daughter-in-law in the proper manner, and so, before meeting her, struggled into his uniform for one more time.

Alix – the child of Princess Alice, second daughter of Queen Victoria – had become very close to the British queen after her mother's early death in 1878. Similarly, on the other side of her family, her great-aunt Empress Maria, wife of Alexander II, had, during her frequent visits to her childhood home in Hesse, often cared for the recently bereaved children. Besides this, Alix had another connection to the Romanovs, her older sister Elizabeth ('Ella') being by this time married to Grand Duke Sergei, one of Sasha's younger brothers.[154] Dynastically, therefore, Alix had the right pedigree, but unfortunately she no longer had the cheerful disposition that in her childhood had earned her the nickname 'Sonny'. That trait had disappeared following the disastrous outbreak of diphtheria that had killed both her mother and sister when she was six years old. Now serious, inward-looking, stubborn and very shy, she little endeared herself to most people, and many would find her cold and distant. As a result, when Nicholas had told his parents of his wish to marry, they had opposed the engagement, having grave concerns as to Alix's suitability to be the future *tsaritsa*. And for a time, other obstacles also stood in the couple's way. A devout Lutheran, Alix at first refused to consider changing her faith, an essential requirement for any future Russian empress. However, Ella, who had herself converted to Orthodoxy just three years earlier, finally persuaded her sister that there was little difference between the two confessions. Although this resolved the religious problem, Queen Victoria, who by now had lost all confidence in Russia, still had serious concerns. Nonetheless, Alix was devoted to Nicholas, and she remained resolute, having already stood firm against her grandmother's earlier proposal that she should marry 'Eddy', the oldest son of the Prince and Princess of Wales. So, although the British queen could be equally immovable when dealing with the wishes of her own children, she finally gave in to her adored granddaughter, despite her not unreasonable fears for Alix's safety. Writing to her daughter Vicky, she declared, 'All my fears abt. her future marriage now show themselves so strongly & my blood runs cold when I think of her *so* young most likely placed on that vy. unsafe Throne, her dear life & above all her Husband's constantly threatened.'[155] Nonetheless, with the tsar's obviously failing health having already persuaded Alexander and Maria reluctantly to give their consent to Nicholas, the couple's official engagement at last went ahead.

On 20 October (OS) the forty-nine-year-old Alexander III finally died of kidney failure, leaving his wife devastated by her loss. The Prince and Princess of Wales now travelled to Russia to comfort Maria, Alexandra then staying with her sister throughout her ordeal, even sleeping in the same room to give her extra support. In the meantime, while in the Crimea, Bertie took care of most of the funeral arrangements, which included twice-daily visits to the local chapel. Eventually, after being shipped to Sebastopol, Alexander's body began the long journey of nearly 1,400 miles back to St Petersburg, travelling by train in order to allow thousands of Russians along the track to pay their last respects. Yet more people would join in the church masses that were periodically celebrated at the various stops along the route. Having arrived in Moscow, the cortège rested for two days, while crowds processed past the open coffin that lay in state in the Archangel Cathedral. Here there was a genuine display of grief, and everywhere the city was draped in mourning. After that Alexander's body was moved on again, finally reaching the capital, where there were more days of elaborate funeral ceremonies, during which members of the family again paid their respects and kissed the icon that the dead tsar held in his hands. Although the genuine expression of grief was less obvious in St Petersburg, Alexander's early death had taken the people by surprise, many having believed him divinely protected by God. Seeking to provide an explanation, the *Novoe Vremya* newspaper declared his health to have been undermined by 'his tireless devotion and extreme attention to his duties'.[156] Conscious of the underlying unrest, the authorities now wished his funeral to quieten the growing opposition to Romanov rule, and they sought to use it to emphasise the enduring nature of the dynasty's autocratic power. In pursuit of these aims, they virtually canonised the dead emperor, one of their first official announcements describing his legacy as leaving to his people 'the blessings of peace and the bright example of a noble life'.[157] The intentionally symbolic event they now devised was of a previously unheard-of splendour, *The Times* reporting that 'rarely or never, perhaps, in all history, had a more gorgeous open-air pageant been seen' – an event, it considered, on a par with Victoria's jubilee procession to Westminster Abbey.[158] Before a vast congregation, including royalty and dignitaries from all over Europe, and surrounded by elaborate trappings and 5,000 wreaths sent by the French alone, the burial took place in the Peter and Paul Cathedral on 7 November (OS). As the tomb was at last closed over the now obviously decaying body, an exhausted Maria broke down. For the rest of her life she would remain in mourning.

During the last weeks of his father's life, twenty-six-year-old Nicholas, a small, gentle man, found – to his fiancée's resentful vexation – that he was largely overlooked and ignored by the senior members of his family.

Many of the Romanov men, including his brothers George and Michael, were particularly tall, and at under 5 feet 6 inches he had inherited the small physique of his mother, so that he lacked the physical stature of his father and grandfather that many saw as virtually incumbent on the tsar. And despite some earlier efforts to introduce him to state administration, Nicholas still felt totally unprepared for the position that awaited him. Shocked by events, he said to his brother-in-law Grand Duke Alexander Mikhailovich, 'What is going to happen to me, to you, to Xenia, to Alix, to mother, to all of Russia? I am not prepared to be a Czar, I never wanted to become one. I know nothing of the business of ruling.' [159] Despite Sasha's earlier lack of preparation as second in line to the throne, and the way this had threatened the stability of the dynasty on the unexpected death of Nixa, Nicholas's parents had not avoided making some of the same mistakes. Although Sasha had clearly been in poor health for some time, the urgency of the situation had not been adequately recognised, with the result that both Nicholas and the grand dukes had grave misgivings as to his suitability to take up his responsibilities. Still more seriously, many suspected that his uncle Vladimir saw himself as a worthier successor, and had – possibly not for the first or last time – ambitions to take the throne.[o] This, some believed, lay behind the Prince of Wales' decision to extend his stay in Russia, Bertie possibly wanting to support the rights of his nephew at this moment of crisis.

The day after Alexander III's death, Alix converted to Orthodoxy and became Alexandra Feodorovna, thereby preparing herself for her marriage, which Nicholas – wanting her immediate support – proposed should now be celebrated quietly while they were still in the Crimea. However, he was overruled by the domineering grand dukes, who declared this unsuitable for the tsar, and consequently Nicholas agreed to its taking place at the Winter Palace in St Petersburg on 14 November (OS). Although, during the vast ceremony with its thousands of guests, Maria had the comfort of her father who had come to Russia for the funeral, the occasion was a trial for the dowager empress, whose forty-seventh birthday coincidently fell on the same day. More seriously, with the marriage occurring just a week after Alexander III's burial, many superstitious Russians believed the whole event to be highly inauspicious, seeing it as a bad omen that the wedding had followed 'behind a coffin'.

While no doubt the event had put considerable demands on the very diffident bride, after it was over she would have to contend with a still more difficult situation, as she was then expected to live with her husband's family in the Anichkov Palace. Unsurprisingly, before long tensions had begun to develop between her and her mother-in-law. Maria's own mother had earlier advised her that if she wanted to remain on good terms with

---

o Following the Borki train crash, Alexander III had wryly remarked, 'Imagine Vladimir's disappointment when he hears that we all escaped alive.' *See* John van de Kiste, *The Romanovs 1818-1959*, p.131.

her son, she should be loving to her daughter-in-law and treat her like her own child – advice that, in fact, the Danish queen herself had failed to follow. The characters of the two empresses were so markedly unalike that their relations had soon become strained. Finally, however, Nicholas and Alix would move out of the capital to the Alexander Palace at Tsarskoe Selo, and this, far from the court, would become their much-loved and very private home until the events of 1918 eventually forced them to leave.

A year and a half after Nicholas' accession the coronation took place in Moscow. Despite the time that had passed in the interim, Alix had still not come to terms with her role, and was unable to display Maria's natural openness that had so charmed the Russian people from the moment of her arrival in the country. Witnesses now remarked on the obvious difference in the public's affection for the two empresses, with the dowager outshining her daughter-in-law and receiving a far more enthusiastic welcome from the people. The popularity and self-assurance of Maria drew attention to the social inadequacy of the new *tsaritsa*, and throughout her time as empress, Alix's shy and awkward discomfort could not have been helped by her awareness of this, nor by the Romanov custom that expected her at public and court events to take second place to her glittering mother-in-law.

More seriously, a disastrous event occurred just four days after the coronation. The usual celebratory *cocaigne* was promised for the entertainment of the people of Moscow, but when the vast crowds arrived in Khodynka Field to share in the feasting, the arrangements made by Alix's brother-in-law – and Nicholas' uncle – Grand Duke Sergei, proved highly inadequate. With a badly chosen venue and insufficient forces to control the numbers, when a stampede broke out as people were eagerly pushing forward to get their coronation gifts, close on 1,400 of them died in the resulting crush, with around the same number left injured. The tsar and his wife were appalled when they heard the news, but again Nicholas listened to bad advice from the older grand dukes. Told by them that offence would be caused to the French ambassador if they did not attend his ball, he and Alix accepted the invitation, a shock to the grieving public, who incorrectly accused them of being unfeeling.

In November 1895, Olga, the first of the imperial couple's children, was born, and the next year after having visited Paris for the Exhibition, they took the child to Scotland to stay with Alix's grandmother, Queen Victoria. These were good times for Alix and over the next five years she would give birth to three more daughters. While she was a devoted wife and mother, and her home life was extremely happy, she had never overcome her reserve, and she was now only too aware that this had prevented her from becoming popular at court. However, Maria was also facing her own trials. Having just recently lost her mother, only five years after her husband's death she suffered another bitter loss when her beloved second son George died suddenly from tuberculosis far away in Georgia, where he had gone in search of a warmer climate. To his deep regret, his health had caused his separation from many of the family for some years, even keeping him from attending his father's funeral. Although sometimes visited by his mother, after his last trip with her to Denmark he had realised that his condition could no longer support the strain of travelling. And then, in August 1899, out alone in the countryside on his motorbike, he collapsed beside the road, to be discovered dying by a peasant woman. For Nicholas this was a terrible blow as he had been particularly close to this brother, who, popular, good-looking and intelligent, had been much loved by all the family. While his loss was keenly felt by everyone, the suddenness of his early death aged only twenty-eight, and the circumstances in which he had been found, added further to Maria's distress, leaving her barely able to support her grief at his funeral in the Peter and Paul Cathedral. As the ceremony ended, she hurried away declaring she could bear the situation no more.

Tragedies now began to mount up for the imperial family. Five years after George's death, the keenly awaited birth of a *tsesarevich* turned within weeks from joy to heartbreak when the realisation dawned that the child was suffering from a chronic illness. As Tsar Paul's manifesto had barred women for all intents and purposes from the succession, for a time in 1900, after being seriously ill, Nicholas had considered trying to overthrow the earlier constitution in favour of his oldest daughter Olga. Nonetheless, he and his wife still desperately longed for a son, and so with the arrival of Alexei their troubles at last seemed to be over, only then for them to discover that the child suffered from the incurable affliction of haemophilia. An illness passed through the female line, it had struck many of the descendants of Queen Victoria, and Alix, an emotionally vulnerable woman, was now overcome, not just with grief for her sick son, but also with an unmerited sense of guilt for what she saw as her responsibility for his condition. She had experienced the cruel effects of the disease in her relations, having had, among others, a brother and two nephews with the symptoms, one of whom, her sister's four-year-old son, Prince Heinrich of Prussia, had died from a brain haemorrhage just seven months before Alexei was born.[160] Horrified by what the *tsesarevich*'s illness meant to the succession, Nicholas and Alix decided to keep the truth hidden away, not making it public until an announcement was issued by the doctors eight years later.

In choosing to keep the news to themselves for so long, the imperial couple also concealed the reasons for Alix's increasingly strange behaviour, which grew more and more bizarre over time. The secrecy further undermined the *tsaritsa*'s popularity, with outsiders unable to understand her growing dependence on supposed healers, mystics and unconventional holy men such as Rasputin. Already impressed by the peasant *starets* after their first meeting in 1905, she had then begun to turn to him more and more. Finally, following Alexei's nearly fatal attack at the imperial hunting lodge at Spala in Poland in 1912, and the child's surprising recovery shortly after the arrival of Rasputin's telegram, she became fully dependent on the monk. From that time on, she turned to him for advice on all matters, including those of state; and her faith in him remained unquestioning. She refused to listen to any of the stories going around St Petersburg of his drunkenness, lewd behaviour, womanising, and other considerably worse crimes, which she dismissed as slanderous rumours.[p] While it is now generally accepted that such stories of his behaviour are essentially true, some Russians, who believe flaws to be a part of the character of holy men, still today consider Rasputin worthy of canonisation.

For the time being, the empire was more concerned with other issues, above all the outbreak of war against Japan in the east. Tensions had been building up in the area for some time, and then Nicholas helped light the final spark by treating the visiting ambassador with disdain. Since the assassination he had so narrowly avoided some years earlier, his attitude towards the Japanese had been at best dismissive, if not offensive, and his imperious lack of diplomacy on this occasion was ill considered. Infuriated by Russia's high-handedness and obvious territorial ambitions, in February 1904 Japan unexpectedly attacked the Russian fleet at Port Arthur in Manchuria. While Nicholas still believed in his country's superiority, his forces were, in reality, unprepared for the forthcoming conflict, and logistically they faced serious difficulties. First, the supporting Baltic fleet – initially forbidden by the British to use the Suez Canal – had the serious challenge of having to steam halfway around the world on a seven-month-long voyage to reach the combat area, and, second, the transport of troops and equipment was complicated by an incomplete central section of the Trans-Siberian Railway, a situation that required all military personnel and machinery to be unloaded and reloaded into alternative transport to cross the unfinished section of track.

Early the next year, Nicholas' problems escalated, as his country was soon caught up in the first revolution of his reign. Life had become increasing difficult for the city's poor, and as strikes began to break out, in January a peaceful demonstration led by the priest Father Gapon set out for the Winter Palace, hoping to present the workers' problems to their much-loved 'little father', the tsar. However, unknown to them, although earlier informed that this would take place, Nicholas had again listened to poor advice and decided to remain out at Tsarskoe Selo. With matters therefore left in the hands of the Guards, under the command of his uncle Vladimir, the decision was taken to fire on the unarmed marchers, who, carrying icons and singing hymns, had made their way to Palace Square. As a result of the Guards' disastrous action, scores of men, women and children were mown down, and with the senseless slaughter having left possibly 1,000 casualties in all, the events of what became known as

---

p Baptised Gregory Efimovitch, tellingly he was given his nickname when he was young, Rasputin meaning a profligate, rake or degenerate.

St Petersburg's 'Bloody Sunday' finally destroyed much of the remaining goodwill felt by the people towards their tsar.

Meanwhile, the war against the Japanese continued to go badly, eventually coming to a head in Russia's humiliating naval defeat at Tsushima in May 1905, where most of the combined Pacific and Baltic fleet was destroyed. Soon after this disaster, a mutiny broke out on the Black Sea battleship *Potemkin*, after which there were further riots in Odessa that left hundreds more dead. Nicholas now found himself facing anarchy and violent demonstrations throughout his empire. As the strikes continued in St Petersburg, in Warsaw thousands turned out to march under the red flag, and across the Baltic regions more than 4,000 officials came under attack. In this mood of rising chaos, pogroms broke out again, the Jews being accused not just of hindering the war efforts, but also being involved in the revolutionary activities now taking place. At the end of the year more than 400 would be murdered over four days in Odessa, and abroad Nicholas began to be personally charged with antisemitism. Discrimination against the Jews was far from new in Russia; more than a decade earlier the Governor General of Moscow, Grand Duke Sergei, had ruthlessly expelled around 20,000 of them from the city, a policy strongly criticised by his wife, who had remarked percipiently that God would punish them severely. She would have reason to remember her words when in February 1905, as feeling grew against all the Romanovs, her husband was blown to pieces when a bomb was thrown at his carriage. Proud and arrogant, he had become particularly unpopular after his failed preparations for the events at Khodynka Field. His loyal wife, the beautiful Ella, having rushed to the scene to gather up his grisly remains, later forgave his assassin and, having retired from society, renounced the luxuries of her former life to become a nun devoted to charity work.

Throughout 1905, the revolution continued with the authorities trying fruitlessly to regain control by carrying out many hundreds of courts martial and executions, and sending thousands more into exile. Finally, on the advice of his more moderate chief minister Sergei Witte, Nicholas agreed to consider introducing some reforms, and in October he issued a manifesto that promised a new constitution and the opening of an elected State Duma. While these concessions were viewed by the Romanovs as disastrous, the official opening of the parliament would also fail to please the people. When it took place in April 1906 in St George's Hall, the Throne Room of the Winter Palace, the atmosphere was tense, made still more so by the imperial family appearing dressed in their full finery. Later Maria recalled the 'terrible reception' given to her son, and the way those attending had looked at the family, appearing to see them as enemies for whom they had 'an incomprehensible hatred'.[161] But Nicholas still believed in the maintenance of autocracy, and although at this juncture he agreed to certain changes, he had little intention of keeping to his promises. Later, as with his earlier reforms, when he believed the danger had passed, he went back on his concessions and returned to the former status quo that he considered to be better for his country.

However, by now Maria had begun to concern herself more with political affairs, and was becoming increasingly anxious about the situation. Above all she was fearful of the detrimental influence Alix was apparently having on her weak and doting husband, and showing her true feelings for her daughter-in-law, Maria declared, 'If *she* was not there Nicky would be twice as popular. She is a regular German.'[162] She was not alone in thinking that it would be better if Alix were removed, she – like some others – feeling it would help matters if the *tsaritsa* were sent to a convent. Frustrated that when she tried to talk to her son he refused to listen to any criticism of his wife, in 1905 Maria was already anxious enough to declare to Grand Duke Paul, 'He can't see that he's leading Russia into disaster.'[163] While Maria was still devoted to Nicholas, and respected his position as tsar, she would often find it hard not to admonish him as she had done when he was a child. Her sister-in-law, Maria Pavlovna ('Miechen'), the wife of Grand Duke Vladimir, described the situation to the French ambassador:

> She's too outspoken and impetuous. The moment she begins to lecture her son, her feelings run away with her; she sometimes says the exact opposite of what she should; she annoys and humiliates. Then he stands on his dignity and reminds his mother that he is the Emperor. They leave each other in a rage.[164]

So when possible, Maria now chose to escape back to Denmark, and in 1907 she and Alexandra (by this time the British queen) bought Hvidore, a villa just outside Copenhagen, which, although visited only once by Edward VII, would prove to be a welcome retreat for the sisters. And there would also be other meetings between the various relations, family get-togethers that allowed them to talk over both political and private affairs. Like the Kaiser, in the summer months the tsar enjoyed sailing in the Baltic, and persuaded by his German cousin had secretly agreed to sign a peace agreement with him while on holiday at Björkö in the Gulf of Finland in 1905. In August 1907 the two had another reunion at Swinemünde, but on this occasion the event was marked by gun salutes and spectacular fireworks that were intended to publicise the good relations between the men. Then, having soon after signed a new Anglo-Russian Entente in St Petersburg, the following year Nicholas joined his Uncle Bertie for a similar, but more informal, meeting aboard their royal yachts at Reval (Tallinn). Here Maria would see her sister again, Alexandra having come to the Baltic – despite her deep reservations – via the new Kaiser Wilhelm Canal, where she had endeavoured to express her undying anti-German sentiments by refusing to open the blinds of her cabin. After that, over the next few years the two women would continue to meet regularly. And in 1909, Nicholas and his family also joined their British relations, seeing them for what would be the last time, during a visit to the Cowes regatta on the Isle of Wight. Many would remark on the similarity between the tsar and his cousin Prince George, but others were equally struck by the grandeur of the imperial family and the security that now surrounded them. By early the next year Edward VII was seriously ill, and on 6 May he died, deeply mourned by his wife, who, despite his very public affairs, had never stopped loving him. This time it was Maria who stayed and comforted her sister, and from now on the two widows would spend every autumn together at Hvidore until the outbreak of war made it impossible.

In May 1912, six years after their father's death, their oldest brother, Frederik VIII, died suddenly while out walking in Hamburg, and then the following March they suffered a still more shattering blow when their brother King George of the Hellenes was killed in Greece. After nearly fifty years on the throne, and just days after he had been hailed in Athens following the defeat of the Turks, a second attempt was made on his life and he was shot dead while he was out walking in Salonika.

Nonetheless, throughout 1913 the Romanovs celebrated their 300 years on the Russian throne. With a poignant lack of awareness of the approaching storm, the anniversary was marked with elaborate celebrations. Swept up by the enthusiasm of the moment, the people turned out in their thousands to share the occasion with their tsar, and for a time many were able to forget the tensions of the past. The affection shown to the imperial couple by the crowds deeply touched them and gave them the false impression that perhaps their previous pessimism had been misplaced, and the Romanovs' earlier difficulties were now over.

Yet, the international picture was becoming increasingly unstable, and although during early 1914 Nicholas and his cousin Kaiser Wilhelm continued to write regularly to each other, a communication known as the 'Nicky-Willy correspondence', neither of the men seemed fully to appreciate the seriousness of the situation that was now fast developing. Their generally good-natured telegrams would be exchanged until the very last moment before the hostilities began. In June the tensions had been further ratcheted up by the assassination at Sarajevo of the Austrian heir, Archduke Franz Ferdinand, and his wife – a double murder carried out by a Bosnian supporter of the militant Serbian separatist movement. While Russia had an age-old understanding with Serbia, having always promised to defend it, and Austria wanted to maintain the integrity of its empire, the alliances agreed over the previous half century had made things still more complex. None of the leaders now concerned were capable of dealing with the escalating situation, and, as Franz Joseph dithered over his response to the recent outrage, the uncertainty continued to grow. By the time the old emperor eventually declared war on Serbia on 28 July, the tsar had already, three days earlier, instructed military supplies be sent to the border. Soon this order had been followed by another calling for mobilization, which, although initially partial, became full-scale on 30 July. With Austria's ally Germany having been prompted by Nicholas' action to follow suit, on 1 August the Kaiser declared war on Russia. But that was not the end. With Wilhelm's generals concerned about a possible attack from France, three days later German troops marched into neutral Belgium, thus leaving Britain morally bound by a previous treaty to come to the Belgians' defence and join the fighting. The First World War had begun.

At the time Maria was staying with Alexandra in England, but she immediately decided to return to Russia, and the two sisters would not see each other again for nearly five years. While passing on her train through Berlin, Maria became trapped when a violent mob attacked her imperial coach in the station. But on the orders of Kaiser Wilhelm she was at last allowed to continue on to Denmark, and from there she eventually made her way home via Sweden and Finland. A week after leaving England, she finally reached the Russian capital – now called Petrograd so it might be rid of its Germanic-sounding name – and here she found the city buzzing with preparations for the conflict ahead.

Some quarter of a million people had gathered around the Winter Palace to hear Nicholas announce from the balcony that the country was again at war, and in the following days while things were still going well for the army, the Russians' love for their 'little father' remained strong. However, soon the dire shortage of supplies and equipment started to tell, and as news of the appalling losses and frequent disasters filtered home, his popularity began to decline. In 1915, against the advice of his mother and other relatives, Nicholas decided to dismiss his cousin from overall command, encouraged to do so by Alix, who begrudged the success of the impressive Grand Duke Nicholas Nikolaevich, whom she saw as a rival to her husband. Although the tsar believed it his duty to inspire his men at the front, in reality he lacked the necessary military experience, and his presence at the headquarters became little more than a formality. And even more seriously, just as he had been warned, when the situation started to deteriorate further, he began to be blamed personally for the mounting calamities.

With the outbreak of fighting, many of the royal residences, such as the Catherine and Anichkov palaces, were quickly turned into hospitals, and after the *tsaritsa* and her daughters had taken up nursing they all became very popular with their patients. Alix, who during her life was often a sickly woman, now found a new purpose, her readiness to take on the most basic and unattractive of tasks rapidly earning her the respect and love of all those immediately around her. But, the empress was also interfering in political affairs, sending messages of instruction to the tsar at the front. She would repeatedly encourage him to dismiss those ministers who, she considered, did not support him enough – her opinions being based on the advice of Rasputin, on whom she now totally depended.

Under Alix's direction, senior ministerial posts would be changed with an unfortunate regularity, some individuals being removed from office within weeks of their appointment.

In late 1916, Maria, having at last accepted that she was unable to influence her son, decided to leave Petrograd and go to Kiev. Here she moved into the Maryinski Palace, built for Empress Elizabeth by Rastrelli and today the residence of the Ukrainian president. But for the next two years, while she continued to carry out her charity work with the Red Cross, Maria still worried about the events unfolding elsewhere, writing repeatedly to her relations to tell them of her deep concerns. When, soon after her arrival in the city, Nicholas came with his son, Alexei, to visit her, she was struck by how tired and worried he appeared to be. As convinced as ever that her daughter-in-law needed to be stopped from interfering, she again tried to warn him against listening to Alix's mistaken advice, only to receive the reply, 'I believe no one but my wife.'[165] Ignoring his mother's pleas to get rid of Rasputin, he steadfastly refused to accept that the monk's lecherous reputation and political meddling was further damaging the Romanov name and the country's future.

However, in December of the same year the matter was taken in hand by other relatives of the family, who were equally concerned that Rasputin was destroying the tsar's reputation and threatening the dynasty. Felix Yusoupov, the immensely rich husband of Irina, Nicholas' niece, invited the monk to his sumptuous palace on the Moika River, where – according to Yusoupov's written account – the tsar's cousin, Grand Duke Dmitry Pavlovich, and three others joined him. While these men remained upstairs creating a diversion, Yusoupov attempted to murder Rasputin down in the cellar, plying the monk with previously prepared poisoned cakes and wine. But the whole affair was nearly bungled as the poison failed to take effect, and the plotters then had to resort to beating and ultimately shooting their now enraged victim. And even then, as the later autopsy report would show, he was not quite dead, apparently only finally succumbing to drowning after he had been thrown into the river.

Rasputin had always been a controversial figure in life, and arguments about the manner of his death are no less conflicting. Later the conspirators fell out among themselves, and so, while Yusoupov wrote his description of the events, more or less claiming sole responsibility for the murder, doubts would remain about what had exactly happened, particularly as Dmitry would refuse to speak again of that night. And among the alternative claims of what actually occurred, one theory proposes that the recently formed MI6 was behind the whole affair, its intention being to rid the tsar of Rasputin's anti-war influence that might lead to Russia's exit from the conflict. Evidence points to the British ambassador's prior knowledge of the plot, and the details of a later discussion among members of the diplomatic circle give support to the suggestion of his country's involvement. In line with this version, British spy Oswald Rayner, a friend of Yusoupov, who admitted that he was present in the palace that night – even though Yusoupov does not place him there – fired with his own gun the bullet that directly or indirectly led to Rasputin's death. Yet another twist to this tale has been put forward in Russia, where some have pointed to Prime Minister Lloyd George's supposed involvement in the crime. According to this argument, he wanted to bring about the fall of the Romanovs, believing that in the following upheaval Britain might be able to strengthen its presence in the Dardanelles.

Although some would claim that the tsar initially appeared relieved on hearing the news of the murder, he, the *tsaritsa* and their children were deeply shaken by the monk's death, their disillusion made still stronger because of the part their own relatives had played in the conspiracy. While Yusoupov had married into the Romanovs, Dmitry, the grandson of Alexander II, had been particularly close to the family, spending much of his adolescence in their household. Nonetheless, no one was prosecuted, the known conspirators just exiled from St Petersburg, Felix to his country estates, Dmitry to the Caucasus – sentences that, as it happened, would ultimately help them escape the bloodbath of the revolution. But although there was considerable satisfaction in certain quarters, with many among the nobility and the ordinary people glad to be rid at last of Rasputin, in the quickening pace of unfolding events his death would soon prove to have produced little long-term effect.[166]

Whatever the plotters had hoped to achieve, the changing situation in Russia had now taken on a life of its own. In early 1917 new demonstrations began to take place in Petrograd and within two months the February Revolution had broken out. But at the headquarters on the front, Nicholas, still receiving mistaken information from his wife at Tsarskoe Selo, did not seem to realise the gravity of the situation, and took no immediate steps to deal with the mounting problems. Finally, on 2 March (OS), while on his train travelling back to Petrograd, he was met by representatives of the new Provisional Government, who persuaded him that the situation had now become so grave that he should abdicate. Wishing to avoid further bloodshed, the tsar calmly accepted and signed the document, thereby passing the throne to his twelve-year-old son. But, within hours Nicholas had reconsidered and, believing that his sickly child would not survive a forced separation from his family, he abdicated in Alexei's name as well, passing the throne to his youngest brother, Michael. However, the following day the always more pragmatic and democratic Michael agreed, after discussion with government representatives, to his own abdication, adding the proviso that he would become tsar later if elected by the people. As this never happened, on 3 March 1917 (OS) the Romanov rule that had begun with Michael I quietly came to an end with the uncrowned Michael II. Nicholas was appalled when he heard of his brother's decision, writing in his diary, 'God knows what possessed him to sign such a vile thing!'[167] While Michael had understood the situation,

Nicholas still failed to appreciate its complexity and this demonstrates the difference between the two men. It also gives strength to the theory that Nicholas had retained a hope that the dynasty might be preserved, possibly visualising Michael acting almost as a temporary regent – if not caretaker – until his son Alexei was old enough to succeed.

The older brother's shock at Michael's decision was mirrored by that of Maria on hearing of Nicholas' own abdication, which she viewed as a personal humiliation. Shortly after this had taken place, the two met once more at Mogilev when she travelled up from Kiev in order to see him. In her memoirs she recalled how 'lonely and abandoned' her son appeared during those 'terrible' few days that they spent together, and the heartbreaking moment on 8 March (OS) when he had to leave her and return to Tsarskoe Selo. They would never see each other again. An initial plan, favoured by Alexander Kerensky – the head of the Provisional Government – for the family to take up exile in England never came about, first interrupted by the children catching measles, and then abandoned by George V after being advised against it by his private secretary. Although unfairly, and perhaps cravenly, suggesting it to be the decision of Lloyd George, it was in fact his own, having been persuaded that in light of the country's growing radical mood, if asylum were offered to the former autocratic tsar it might incur revolutionary unrest in Britain. Similar fears would lead the king in June to change his German-sounding family name to the more acceptable 'House of Windsor'.

For nearly five months the former tsar and his family would continue to live under light guard at the Alexander Palace, a period when Nicholas, despite the disrespectful and offensive treatment he sometimes received, appeared to be relieved to be rid of his earlier responsibilities. He now enjoyed the relatively simple life of a country gentleman, and was content to work, walk and play in the gardens with his children. Here Alexander Kerensky would come to see him, during his visit also meeting the empress, of whom he gives a more complimentary description, praising her courage, dignity, intelligence and beauty, and remarking on how good she appeared to be as a mother. In August Kerensky decided to move the family for better security east of the Ural Mountains to Tobolsk in Siberia – ironically the region of exile formerly chosen by the Romanovs for their enemies. Whether or not this played a part in his decision, Kerensky's reasons for selecting this remote spot some 1,750 miles from the capital are unclear. Even though he declared to the hardliners that he had no desire to be 'the Marat of the Russian Revolution', he still rejected the option of the more convenient Crimea from where it might have been easier to leave the country.[168] Now gradually the family's guards became more aggressive, and the next year in April, after the government had been overthrown by the Bolsheviks and civil war had started to take hold, the tsar, his wife and daughter Maria were transported to considerably harsher imprisonment back west at Ekaterinburg. As the *tsesarevich* was again seriously ill, his desperate parents had to leave him behind with his other sisters, and the family would not be reunited for another four weeks. Then two months later on 4/17 July 1918, the whole family were woken at two in the morning and told to get ready for another move, and having gone down to wait in the cellar, they, their doctor and three other faithful servants were summarily shot and bludgeoned to death. With that the butchery had really begun. The following day, Alexandra's sister, the nun Ella, suffered an equally brutal death when she and a group of others were pushed down a well before grenades were thrown on top of them. Despite their injuries, some of the victims survived long enough to tend to each other and suffer a cruel, lingering death; terrified peasants later reported having heard hymn singing coming from below ground.[169] And finally, a month before all these murders, the first Romanov victim of the Bolsheviks, Nicholas' brother Michael, and his loyal British secretary, Nicholas Johnson, were also shot at Perm. Although Maria did not know it, all her sons and five of her grandchildren were dead.

By this time the Bolsheviks had taken control under the leadership of Trotsky and Lenin, the latter having slipped back into the country in 1917, helped by the Germans who had given him free passage through their county in the hopes that his return might lead to Russia's early exit from the war. Following further mixed fortunes and a failed attempt to take control during the summer, the Bolsheviks had finally seized power in October. After the cruiser *Aurora* had fired a blank shot to give the signal for the start of the revolution, the Bolsheviks stormed the Winter Palace and expelled Kerensky and his Provisional Government. Having now taken full control, the new regime began to open peace negotiations with Germany, and in March the following year – four months before the imperial family's deaths at Ekaterinburg – the two countries signed the Treaty of Brest-Litovsk.

As this forced Russia to give up much of its European territory, and around one third of its population, Nicholas was deeply shocked when he heard the news, saying to his doctor that he should never have abdicated. And he was equally appalled that his 'cousin Willy' had made peace with the Bolsheviks, declaring, 'I should never have thought the Emperor William [*sic*] could stoop to shake hands with these miserable traitors.'[170] At this point a further line was drawn under the previous imperial past, the capital being transferred back to its ancient home in Moscow, where it still remains today.

Despite the peace with Germany, the situation at large had now become even more tense with the civil war having taken hold. The White Army, supported by the foreign powers, was seeking to overthrow the Reds and re-establish the Romanov dynasty and, although their efforts ultimately proved fruitless, the fighting would continue until 1921, the year before Russia became part of the newly created USSR that would exist for the next seven decades.

Just around six weeks after her last meeting with Nicholas, Maria realised that she was no longer welcome in Kiev, and regretfully on 23 March 1917 (OS) she said goodbye to her loyal Guards, who up to this time had protected her. She now moved south to the Crimea to join her relations who had taken refuge there. Since the area had first been made popular back in the time of Nicholas I, many members of the imperial family and court had continued to create their own buildings in the region. Nicholas and Alix as late as 1911 had constructed their new Livadia Palace, and although they enjoyed only four visits here before events had overtaken them, they had for a time after the abdication hoped to be able to make it their future home. However, now Maria moved to Ai-Todor to be with her daughters Xenia and Olga and their families, and it was from here that she wrote to her brother Valdemar on 4 May 1917. Bewailing the terrible situation in Russia, she spoke with frankness about how the family had for too long been playing with fire, refusing to open their eyes to what was happening in the country. Yet, for the time being, life was comfortable, though the next year on 10 March Maria was forced to move again to Dubler, the estate belonging to the brother of Grand Duke Nicholas Nikolaevich. In this more secure palace, where she was placed under the surveillance of the sailors of the Sebastopol Soviet, life became considerably harder, with the Guardss keeping their prisoners short of food and frequently insulting them. During this time, Maria continued to show her resilience, in the main refusing to be cowed by her captors, and defiantly standing up to their intentional efforts to humiliate her. But, unbeknownst to the elderly empress, as the situation became increasingly uncertain and her staff more concerned for her safety, plans were put in place to spirit her into hiding should the need arise. At the moment of greatest danger, the situation unexpectedly improved, as they came under the protection of the invading Germans. Nonetheless, to the surprise of the officer responsible for Maria's safety, she – true to her long-held dislike of the Prussians – still refused to accept the help offered by the Kaiser. Three months later, following the amnesty, British and French troops arrived at last to replace the Germans, and Maria once more became optimistic that she might be able to stay on in the Crimea and not leave her beloved Russia.

By the beginning of April 1919 the situation had changed again. By this time the Red Army were threatening the region, and with many Romanovs having been rounded up and killed by the Bolsheviks, Maria at last gave in to the pleading of her sister, who had persuaded her son George V to send HMS *Marlborough* to Yalta to rescue his aunt. But as news spread of the Romanovs' departure, thousands of would-be refugees flocked to the harbour, whereupon Maria stubbornly refused to leave until more ships had been sent to rescue them. Even the *Marlborough* would be obliged to accommodate far larger numbers than predicted, having to find space not just for the seventeen members of the imperial family but also for scores of attendants and other aristocrats. While dealing with the upheaval caused by this unexpected influx, the first lieutenant Francis Pridham was helped by the empress's older daughter Xenia, who would impress him with the practical way that she dealt with the problems. And besides noticing how very appreciative the family were for every small gesture of kindness they received, Pridham was also struck by their thoughtfulness towards their staff, behaviour that he declared contradicted starkly the popular accusations of the Romanovs being 'pitiless tyrants' who had held 'their people in bonds of cruel slavery'.[171]

Finally, on 11 April (NS) the *Marlborough* was ready to leave, but just before the ship cast off a boat sailed past carrying some Imperial Guards on their way to fight in the civil war. On seeing their former empress, the men then began to sing the imperial anthem in her honour, an episode recorded in a poignant photograph that was taken at the time. This shows Maria, dressed in her customary black, standing on the deck, a small dignified figure dwarfed by the Grand Duke Nicholas Nikolaevich who is behind her. According to Felix Yusoupov, who was among the *Marlborough*'s passengers, just moments before she left the country that had been her home for more than fifty years she listened with tears pouring down her face to the anthem being sung for the last time on Russian soil.

Having disembarked Grand Duke Nicholas and his family at Constantinople, the *Marlborough* took the remaining members of the party to Malta. Having made a brief stop, the empress continued on in another ship to Portsmouth, where she was personally greeted by her sister – the British government again feeling it wise to keep the occasion moderately low-key. Maria remained in England for some months, but before long began to feel uncomfortable as a royal guest. Here her status was ill defined, and after years presiding at the Russian court, she was uncomfortable taking a lesser position to her sister and others as protocol demanded. Unsuccessfully, she even tried to encourage the widowed Alexandra to take precedence over her daughter-in-law, as had been the custom in Russia. Finally, frustrated by her sibling's profound deafness and growing eccentricities, Maria decided to return to Denmark, where she would then pass the winters in the Amalienborg, but spend the rest of the year at Hvidore. After 1923 she received a pension from the British royal family, and was also given financial help by other organisations, but her relations became strained with her more frugal nephew Christian X, who objected to her continuing extravagance. As he was responsible for her daily bills, on one occasion he sent her a message asking for some of the lights to be turned off, only for his aunt to defy him by ordering the whole palace to be lit up.

As she had grown older, Maria had become more wilful, and now again in Denmark she found it hard to accept her new position, once more attempting to interfere in other people's affairs. Telling her nephew that he should act in a more autocratic manner, she encouraged Christian X to take a stronger stand in the 1920 negotiations involving the return of Schleswig to Denmark, a piece of advice that would bring the country to the brink of revolution, and for which she would never take the blame. Furthermore, she caused embarrassment to the king during an Italian state visit, making the excuse of ill-health so that she might refuse to receive the royal couple, who had been brought to visit her at Hvidore; she was furious that their country had recognised Russia's Soviet government.

In 1920 she would at least have her way regarding her younger daughter. Years before, Maria had arranged a disastrous first marriage for Olga to a relation who was considerably older and generally thought to be homosexual – a dynastically suitable match, but one that was doomed from the start. Having finally been allowed to divorce, in 1916 Olga had married commoner Nikolai Kulikovsky, with whom she had been in love for some years. The remarkably low-key ceremony had taken place in Kiev, where, to the bride's great delight, her mother had put aside her reservations and had joined the small number of guests. Olga later expressed her appreciation of this act of kindness on Maria's part. But although a year later the empress had described Kulikovsky to her brother Valdemar as being 'very nice', adding that he no longer appeared to feel 'a stranger' amongst them, people would always notice that she tended to treat him in a rather off-hand way, actually excluding him from the more official occasions. Despite her well-known qualities, there was a tough side to Maria, and even when she was a young woman her strictness had sometimes frightened her children. At times she could also be selfish, becoming, like her sister, more demanding as she aged. Although the two women were famously generous, after years of constant spoiling and attention, they had become matriarchs, both seeing it as their right to keep their younger daughters as companions, ever ready to tend to their needs. Consequently, just before leaving the Crimea, Maria had been furious that Olga had chosen to abandon her and follow her husband to the Caucasus, the empress even going so far as to declare that she would never forgive him for taking her daughter away. But because of Kulikovsky's non-aristocratic status, for some time he and his wife had chosen to remain in Russia, living in something akin to safety, protected by relatives of one of Maria's devoted Cossack Guards. However, as the situation became still more dangerous, the empress arranged for the whole family to be brought to Denmark, and from that time they all lived together.

For the rest of her life Maria would speak of her sadness at not seeing her sons and grandchildren again, but she refused to admit to the likelihood of their murders, even though Olga later wrote that she believed in her heart of hearts she knew this to be true. Maria was, nonetheless, shocked when in August 1924 Grand Duke Kirill, son of her brother-in-law Vladimir, declared that with the presumed deaths of Nicholas, Alexei and Michael, he was the rightful Tsar of all the Russias. His father and mother had always been suspected of having ambitions for the throne, and now he had taken up their claim. While his announcement caused distress to

Maria, it also led to divisions among the Romanovs in exile. Kirill had not only supported the Provisional Government during the early days of the revolution, actually marching under the red flag with his marines to swear allegiance to the Duma, but continued to favour some of their ideas. For that reason, many émigrés dubbed him 'Kirill Egalité' or 'the Soviet Tsar' and they chose instead to back the Grand Duke Nicholas Nikolaevich for the remaining five years of his life.

Although Maria joined Alexandra in 1923 for the marriage of her grandson, later George VI, after her return it was noticeable how she had aged and become weaker, so that two years later she was not well enough to attend the funeral of her sister. From then on her health began to decline rapidly, and, with all her remarkable resilience gone, after 1925 she remained at Hvidore, cared for by Olga and at times Xenia, who frequently visited her from her home in England. Olga described her mother as being 'tormented' at the end, and so her death was a relief when it came on 13 October 1928. The two daughters were left shaken by their loss, Xenia writing to Queen Mary,

> You know how much we loved our mother & how we clung to her always & how in these cruel years of exile more than ever. She was *all* that was left to us – everything was entered in her – our home, our country, all the dear past... The light of our life is gone.[172]

At first Maria's nephew Christian X refused the idea of giving her a state funeral in Denmark, but having come under pressure from her daughters and other members of the public, he was eventually persuaded to give in, and the occasion went ahead. Apart from the representatives coming from Britain, Sweden, and Norway, there were also members of the wider family, among them her sister Thyra's daughter-in-law, Viktoria Luise – the daughter of the Kaiser, whom Maria had so constantly reviled. After the ceremony in Copenhagen's Orthodox Cathedral that had earlier been built for Maria by her husband, her body was taken by train to Roskilde, where it was interred alongside the tombs of her parents. However, in 2006 her wishes finally came true, when President Putin and her great niece Margarethe, Queen of Denmark, reached an agreement, allowing her to be moved back to the old Russian capital, now renamed St Petersburg. On passing Kronstadt the Danish ship carrying her coffin was given a thirty-one-gun salute, and after another funeral in St Isaac's Cathedral that was attended by some of her descendants – among them Prince Michael of Kent representing Queen Elizabeth – she was laid to rest beside her much-loved Sasha in the Peter and Paul Cathedral.

Maria's life had been one of stark contrasts. A pretty daughter who had grown up in a happy, comfortable, unostentatious household surrounded by her loving parents and siblings, she had then moved into a world of incomparable splendour. Here, finding herself ideally suited to her new role, she had become immediately popular, not just at court, but also with the Russian people as a whole. Furthermore, being blessed with a happy marriage and a growing number of children, for a time she appeared to be someone destined for an unclouded future. But fate would prove otherwise. Besides the premature deaths of a fiancé, two sons and a husband, during her life she had to come to terms with the assassination of a father-in-law and brother, not forgetting the presumed murder of two more sons, five grandchildren and a daughter-in-law. As if this was not enough, by the time of her death she had lived through a disastrous war, savage revolution, house arrest, hardship, personal danger and exile, and then ultimately seen the total destruction of the world that she had loved.

Postscript

Into a New Era

Nicholas and his five children visiting Cossack troops in 1916. Just two years later, every Romanov in the photograph was murdered. (Courtesy of the Beinecke Rare Book and Manuscript Library, Yale University)

During the First World War, low-lying Denmark, aware of its vulnerable position without natural borders, had managed to maintain a policy of neutrality – initially one that according to the Foreign Minister Scavenius was 'favourable' to Germany. As a result, in 1918, following the latter's treaty with the Bolsheviks at Brest-Litovsk, Christian X directly approached the Kaiser to ask him to try and help secure the release of his embattled Romanov relations in Russia. In reply, Wilhelm II wrote to the king, 'I cannot deny the Imperial Family my compassion from the human point of view, and when it lies in my power, I will gladly do my part to ensure that the Russian Imperial Family has a safe and suitable situation.'[173] While, in the case of the tsar, *tsaritsa* and their children this soon proved to be impossible, Wilhelm ordered his troops to protect Maria Feodorovna from the Crimean

Soviets – an action for which the notoriously anti-Germanic dowager empress was remarkably ungrateful, and one that even her more down-to-earth daughter Olga would view as 'the ultimate degradation'.[174] But the Kaiser's statement again exposes the age-old tension running through the familial lines of international diplomacy, the call on the various heads of state to separate the political and the personal. As Nicholas II would write to Queen Victoria two years after coming to the throne, 'Politics alas! are not the same as private or domestic affairs and they are not guided by personal or relationship feelings.'[175] And in Wilhelm's case, there was yet another issue to exacerbate the situation. Despite his overconfidence in the role played by direct family interaction – its effective power to influence political and diplomatic affairs – from his early days his bombastic, brash behaviour had caused further strains to develop in his relations with his wider family. Over the years, most of the Kaiser's relatives would treat him with circumspection, many actively declaring their outright dislike, distrust or loathing of the man. Nonetheless, Wilhelm, whose own feelings towards them had often wavered – he alternately seeking their approval, or vilifying their actions – now appeared genuinely concerned for his cousins, and his daughter-in-law would later declare that he had spent 'sleepless nights in mourning over the Romanovs' fate'.[176]

Meanwhile, Denmark's neutrality would be to its advantage, enabling it after the Armistice to gain better terms at the Treaty of Versailles, when it was confirmed that there would be plebiscites to decide on the future of the long-disputed areas of Schleswig, lost to Prussia more than half a century earlier. When in February 1920 voting took place in Northern Schleswig, there was strong support for the region's reintegration into Denmark, but then – in total contrast – the following March the electorate in Central Schleswig chose four to one to stay as part of Germany. Despite the results of the second referendum, Christian X was determined to reincorporate both regions into his kingdom, and arbitrarily dismissed the government who opposed him, thus initiating the 'Easter Crisis' that threatened serious unrest and the overthrow of the monarchy. Eventually, the situation was resolved after the king at last conceded to popular demands and agreed that Central Schleswig should remain (with South Schleswig) as part of Germany – henceforth known as Schleswig-Holstein. By that time preparations for the Danish takeover of the northern region had begun, and Southern Jutland would be officially reunified with Denmark on 15 June 1920. The celebrations continued over the next month, and on 10 July the event was marked by the king riding his white horse across the old border at Kongeå, some 50 miles north of the new frontier. Although Christian had previously been unpopular for his efforts to impose his autocratic rule, this symbolic act drew attention to the more representational role he had now assumed, and his public image began to improve.

Over the years the Danish people would increasingly grow to respect their king, particularly after the German invasion of Denmark in 1940, when he openly took a stand against the Nazi presence in his country. During the two years that it was a virtual German protectorate, he demonstrated his quiet resistance every morning by riding out unguarded through the streets of Copenhagen, something that he continued to do until a fall eventually left him physically unfit to carry on. The situation changed again in 1943 when Hitler, angered by the king's dismissive response to his telegram, tightened his hold on Denmark and put it under direct military occupation. To the appreciation of the Danes, Christian and his wife, Alexandrine of Mecklenburg-Schwerin – described as the only German they wanted to keep – chose to stay on in the country, supporting their people until the end of the war. During this time, Christian also openly opposed the Nazis' persecution of the Jews, backing the escape programme that enabled the majority to flee across the Øresund to neutral Sweden. Before the war ended, in 1944 the people of Iceland elected to replace their independent kingdom with a republic, and so, having sent his congratulations, Christian abdicated. This marked the end of the island's short-lived independent monarchy that had been founded in 1918 in union with Denmark. Although no longer the Icelandic king, when Christian died three years later, after thirty-five years on the Danish throne, he had become one of the country's most popular monarchs. Further reforms would be brought in by his son, Frederik IX, who would also introduce a change to the constitution in 1953 that allowed his daughter to succeed him. On his death in 1972, she became Queen Margarethe II, Denmark's first female ruler since Margrete I, the *de facto* head of the Kalmar Union who died at the beginning of the fifteenth century.

Sweden, too, was not involved in the fighting of the First World War, having since 1814 turned its back on its former bellicose past and adopted a policy of neutrality. Four years later, when Napoleon's former marshal Jean-Baptiste Bernadotte became King Karl XIV Johan, he was also crowned Karl III Johan of Norway, the country having been recently taken from the defeated Danes as compensation – in the king's mind – for Sweden's loss of Finland to the Russians. During Karl Johan's reign, his maintenance of peace would enable the country to prosper, and its population to grow. In 1844, he was succeeded by his son Oscar I, who, having been born in France, after Bernadotte's election had moved with his mother Desideria to Sweden, where he had then learnt to speak good Swedish and Norwegian. His father in his later years had become increasingly autocratic, among other things introducing censorship of the press, measures that for a time had led to calls for his abdication, but Oscar proved to be considerably more liberal, a trait particularly noticeable in his dealings with Norway. Here, because of the bishop's qualms regarding the Catholicism of his queen, Josephine – the granddaughter of Napoleon's similarly named first wife – Oscar was never crowned, but he placed the country on a more equal footing to Sweden, an action that gained him much favour with the Norwegian people. On his death in 1859, Oscar I was succeeded by his son Karl XV, who in time would introduce further progressive reforms that ultimately made him one of the country's most popular kings. But this was a period of failed harvests and repeated outbreaks of famine, and so Scandinavians now began to seek a better life in the New

World, with Swedes emigrating in particularly large numbers. Between the 1860s and the First World War, one million people – around a quarter of the average overall population – would leave Sweden forever.

Meanwhile, on the domestic front, Karl XV was less understanding, virtually ignoring his wife and scandalising many at court by the way he indiscreetly conducted his affairs with his various mistresses. But he was much attached to his only surviving legitimate child, Lovisa, whose infant brother had died from pneumonia after contracting measles. Wishing to appoint her as his heir, for a time the king tried to change the Swedish constitution that since 1809 had banned women from the succession, but these plans were rejected, so instead he arranged her marriage with the Danish crown prince, the later Frederik VIII – the oldest brother of Empress Maria Feodorovna. Although his earlier suggestions of support for Denmark during the Second Schleswig War had come to nothing, nonetheless, Karl XV had remained on good terms with his neighbour, and now the marriage was greeted enthusiastically by all those who favoured closer ties between the Scandinavian countries. Although popular with the Danish people, the frank (and later profoundly religious) Lovisa got on less well at court, where she was never on good terms with her mother-in-law, who repeatedly criticised her taste and behaviour.

In 1872, aged forty-six, Karl XV died in Malmö, whereupon his younger brother succeeded to the Swedish and Norwegian thrones as Oscar II. In 1905, submitting to popular demand, the king finally granted Norway its full independence, thus, after nearly five centuries, ending forever the country's close union with its powerful neighbours and its rule by foreign monarchs. However, although Oscar had now given up this second crown, when two years later elections took place for a new Norwegian ruler, the country chose his great-nephew, Carl – the son of Lovisa (now the Danish Crown Princess Louise) and her husband Frederik. Having previously married his British cousin, Princess Maud, Carl then moved with his wife and son to Oslo, where, having adopted the old Norwegian name, he was acclaimed as King Haakon VII – grandfather of the present King Harald.

While Oscar II was seen as rather humourless by his Danish relations, whose childish pranks he did not appreciate – reputedly being furious when Empress Maria Feodorovna's husband, Tsar Alexander, turned the hose on him during one of the lively summer gatherings in Denmark – he was a keen supporter of the arts, commissioning, among other things, the new Stockholm Opera House. In 1907 he died and was succeeded by his son, Gustav V, who, by having no coronation, started a Swedish tradition that continues to this day. Like Christian X of Denmark, Gustav V would be on the throne throughout both world wars, but in his case – despite Sweden's continuing neutrality – doubts would be raised over his possible pro-German sympathies, questions being asked, in particular, about the nature of his relations with the Nazis. Nevertheless, he actively gave his approval to the plan to rescue the Danish Jews, agreeing to their being transported to his country for safety. Eventually, he was succeeded in 1950 by his sixty-seven-year-old son Gustav

VI Adolf, who in addition to his further popular reforms, introduced Sweden's present system of constitutional government, thereby reducing the king's remaining powers and establishing the new status quo that his son, the present king, Carl XVI Gustaf, inherited in 1973.

While Scandinavian countries were largely unaffected by the fallout of the First World War, elsewhere along the shores of the Baltic there was much greater upheaval as dynasties fell, territories changed hands, and states recovered their independence, or virtually disappeared. Following Tsar Nicholas II's abdication, Finland's claim to autonomy was rejected by the Russian Provisional Government, but within months this body was overthrown by the Bolsheviks, and after that the situation changed again. In accordance with the new administration's initial acknowledgement of the right of individual regions to self-determination, before December 1917 was over Finland had declared its independence.[q] However, by early the next year a brutal civil war had broken out in the country between the Whites (predominant in the north) and Reds (in the south), with atrocities committed on both sides. When, just over three months later, the butchery ended, thousands of Reds were dead, and although the Whites had emerged triumphant, the country had been left deeply divided, with some 35,000 Finns having died during the short period of fighting. After the conflict was over, the Germans, who had helped the Whites during the war, continued to exert their control over the region, even proposing for a time that it should take as its king the Kaiser's brother-in-law, Prince Friedrich Karl of Hesse, who was elected by the Finnish parliament on 9 October 1918. But the foreign presence would not last for long and within days of Germany's surrender, on 14 December the king abdicated and a new independent Finnish government came to power. After that the country began to heal its past divisions and start on its road to recovery. During the Second World War, Finland, like its southern neighbours, would again be drawn into the brutal mayhem, twice engaged against the Soviets, fighting off their invading forces in the Winter War of 1939–40, and joining the Germans as allies in the Continuation War of 1940–41 – the period of the Siege of Leningrad. For over twenty-eight months the old Russian imperial capital (now renamed after its former Soviet leader) found itself under attack, most of the time cut off from the outside. Although over the winter months more than a million people would escape via the Road of Life across the frozen Lake Ladoga, and some supplies reached the city by the same perilous route, dire starvation soon began to hit. As norms of society broke down, people were even forced to resort to cannibalism, so that by the time the city was relieved, possibly a further million to a million and a half of its civilian population

q Kirby explains the reason behind this Bolshevik policy: 'The very granting of Finnish independence by the new Soviet regime was an ideologically motivated act, very much in line with Lenin's belief that conceding the right of nations to self-determination would help intensify the class struggle in the newly independent states, which would in turn hasten the revolution and eventual reunification of the victorious socialist republics.' (See David Kirby, *A Concise History of Finland*, p.199) were dead; the exact number is still uncertain. The Germans had at last withdrawn – after wantonly wreaking untold damage on many of the great Romanov palaces in the surrounding area. Finland's exact role in the whole episode would remain unclear. Many would later claim that the army had not been actively engaged in Leningrad's bombardment, while others stressed that the Finns had helped keep open the Murmansk railway bringing supplies to Russia. Whatever the extent of the country's involvement, by this time it was ready to sign an armistice with the Russians. With that agreed, it then turned its attention elsewhere, going to war against the last of the retreating Germans. Like so much of the region, in order to maintain its autonomy, Finland had throughout these difficult years become entangled in the savage rivalry between its two neighbouring extremist powers, wavering when faced by the awful choice between Hitler's Germany or Stalin's Russia. Following the final peace agreement with the Soviet Union in 1948, Finland – although obliged to hand over more territory – was (unlike the less fortunate Baltic states) once more able to enjoy its sovereignty and rebuild its country.

Since the beginning of the century, other regional nationalist groups in the Baltic states had been calling for their independence, and the ruthlessness with which they pursued their demands had further escalated in the febrile atmosphere that had developed across the Russian Empire during the 1905 revolution. By the next year, still concerned about the growing unrest in Estonia, present-day Latvia and parts of Lithuania, the imperial government imposed martial law, an action that in turn led to more violence and further reprisals. However, just over a decade later, the area would be even more deeply embroiled in the affairs of its neighbours, when it found itself caught up in the chaotic and bloody events of the First World War and 1917 revolution. Although now freed from imperial rule, the following months were a time of dangerous uncertainty, with the Russian government and German Empire struggling to assert their control over the region. Repeatedly finding themselves torn between the two opposing sides, these states, just like Finland, were forced to decide which neighbour might best ensure the country's future. Despite Estonia declaring its independence on 24 February 1918, the next day the Germans marched into Tallinn just a week before the Bolsheviks at Brest-Litovsk officially ceded their Baltic possessions and Estonia was granted the right of self-determination. As events would soon prove, the treaty did not guarantee an end to foreign interference. The German occupiers stayed on in the country for eleven months, and then, within days of their final departure, were replaced on 28 November by the Russians. The latter's invasion initiated a new period of fighting between the Red Army and the Estonians, beginning a war that continued until early 1920. With peace finally agreed, for the next two decades Estonia would at last be able to maintain its hard-won independence.

Meanwhile, south of Estonia, the former Livonian capital of Riga had been growing over several decades, and in the last years before the First World War there was a particular flurry of construction work, resulting in the appearance of an exceptional number of buildings created in the Art Nouveau style. While this reflected the Latvian people's search for individuality, it also pointed to their growing desire to assert their own identity and, accordingly, like the Estonians, in 1917 they began to demand their autonomy. The next year, following the Russian-German peace agreement, the Bolsheviks surrendered most of the area and although for the remaining eight months of the war Courland and Semigallia would be part of Germany, the Livonian region was granted the right of self-determination. In November, within a week of the German armistice, the western powers officially recognised the new nation's declaration of independence. However, the situation was still not resolved. Soon the country was again experiencing unrest as rivalries developed between three different parties: the Provisional Government, the faction supported by the Red Army, and the German military units that were drawn from the local nobility. With each group determined to assume control, and the Russians temporarily taking over Riga, fighting would continue in Latvia until the end of 1919. Then at last an armistice was agreed, and the next year Russia gave up its hold in Latvia's eastern regions of Latgale.

Lithuania was equally eager to shake off Russian control, and, after its invasion by the Kaiser's army, in 1917 it considered declaring its statehood in union with Germany. But in February 1918, the country went further, claiming its full independence and also proposing to establish its own monarchy with the Count of Württemberg as king. Although Kaiser Wilhelm gave his backing to this, and to a similar plan for a new United Baltic Duchy – comprising Estonia and Latvia – both schemes were ultimately abandoned after Germany's defeat. Peace with the Soviets and the Poles took longer for Lithuania to achieve, the fighting not ending on the two fronts until 1920, by which time Poland had taken possession of the former Lithuanian capital of Vilnius. While it would keep this throughout the interwar years, the Lithuanians were more successful elsewhere, taking the Klaipėda (Memel) region that had been removed from Germany and put under French administration at the Treaty of Versailles.

Before long all the Baltic states would lose their recently won autonomy, when, shortly after the outbreak of the Second World War, in 1940 they came under the control of the Soviets. Although briefly recaptured by the Germans, who then incorporated the whole area into the Third Reich, the three countries were officially surrendered to the Russians in 1945, thereafter remaining part of the USSR until 1991, when, finally, they regained their independence.

Although Poland had been wiped from the map following the country's three Partitions at the end of the eighteenth century, the rise of Napoleon had changed the situation again. After defeating the Prussians in 1806, on 28 November the French had marched into Warsaw, the emperor himself arriving in triumph shortly afterwards. The next year, after coming under siege, Danzig would be captured, before being pronounced a Free City. Now, from territory taken from the defeated Prussia, Napoleon created – much to his own benefit – his new Duchy of Warsaw, a region that besides providing him with extra revenue through the sale of land to the Poles, gave him a useful source of manpower for his army. When two years later Polish troops under King Stanislaw II's nephew, Jozef Poniatowski, helped him defeat an Austrian invasion, he further increased the territory, adding Kraków to the duchy. For the Poles, this association with Napoleon would ultimately bring them further suffering. Three years later they and many Lithuanians were enlisted into his *Grande Armée* in preparation for the disastrous invasion of Russia.

After the eventual fall of Napoleon and the subsequent Congress of Vienna, further territorial changes were made to the region: the Frenchman's duchy was abolished, Prussia regained Danzig and acquired Posen, Kraków became a republic under the protection of the three powers, and Austria recovered some of its former lands. And despite the largest part of the earlier Duchy of Warsaw now becoming Congress or Kingdom Poland, a personal possession of the tsar, it was granted a more liberal constitution than that found in the rest of the Russian Empire. Here, enjoying their greater freedoms, the Poles would continue to live much as before, with Warsaw remaining a flourishing centre of learning, music and the arts. But as its people grew increasingly educated and demanded still more liberal reforms, the Russian rulers became more autocratic. Rebellion was already in the air, the Decembrist Plot in St Petersburg having threatened to overthrow the new tsar Nicholas I in 1825, and the Paris revolution succeeding in bringing down the Bourbon king Charles X in 1830. When in November that same year rebellion broke out in Warsaw, Grand Duke Constantine, Congress Poland's unofficial viceroy, was finally forced to flee and, as the rising began to take hold, the Poles declared their independence, renouncing Nicholas as their king. As a result, the tsar became even more determined to crush the growing revolt, telling his brother that he would 'never give way before force'. Instructing his Guards to be ready 'to punish these traitors, restore order, and avenge the now stained honour of Russia', he ordered his troops into the country, and with that a full-scale war began.[177] Within a year, despite their initial success and determined resistance against the larger Russian forces, the Poles had been defeated and all opposition ruthlessly quashed, whereupon Nicholas went further and fully integrated the kingdom into the Russian Empire. After that, 5,000–6,000 Poles left the country in 'the Great Migration', while those already abroad – like Chopin – never returned. The unsuccessful Polish risings would continue, trouble also breaking out in the Prussian-controlled border regions and in Kraków, which was then reannexed by Austria in 1846. Finally, in 1864, Tsar Alexander II put an end to the eighteen-month-long insurrection by removing all remaining Polish autonomy, and sending tens of thousands of Poles into exile.

After the Prussian king, Wilhelm, was acclaimed the first German Emperor, his Polish lands became part of the German *Reich*, and as a consequence during the First World War Danzig became one of three shipbuilding yards for the Imperial Navy. However, with the coming of peace, an independent Poland was at last revived, the new, Second Polish Republic being created out of lands taken from Prussia, Russia and the former Austrian-Hungarian Empire. Nonetheless, fresh hostilities soon broke out, and by 1919 Poland and Russia were again at war, with Warsaw for a time coming under real threat of capture by the Red Army. Peace was eventually agreed at Riga in 1921, and Poland then gained further territory on its eastern border. Meanwhile, following the Treaty of Versailles, Danzig had achieved its own status, becoming a Free City under the protection of the League of Nations. With its majority of German speakers, it now had its own parliament, government, constitution and even national anthem – a situation that caused increasing concern to the Poles, who, to safeguard their own interests, decided to create a new port around 15 miles up the coast at Gdynia.

In time, the strong German presence in Danzig would fuel Hitler's growing ambitions, driving his desire to reincorporate the whole region into his Third Reich. As a result, on 1 September 1939 his troops mounted an attack on a garrison situated on Danzig's Westerplatte peninsula at the entrance to the River Vistula. This, the first battle of the Second World War, would continue for a week until the 200 defenders were eventually defeated. On the day of the invasion, another attack was also made on the Polish Post Office. Here too, for several hours the workers put up a stiff resistance, but finally they were forced to surrender, and later most would be executed by the SS. In time, memorials would be created to honour the victims of these two assaults, one raised in the city remembering the postal workers, and another on the Westerplatte that honours 'the Coastal Defenders' – the latter, a landmark that, visible for miles, stands close to where the Teutonic Knights built their fortress many centuries before. After these initial battles, for the next six years Danzig would continue to suffer greatly, finding itself in the middle of the fighting for the whole duration of the conflict. Having already suffered major damage, in 1945 the city underwent further destruction at the hands of the advancing Russian army, who systematically reduced it to ruins.

Warsaw also suffered severely after the German invasion in 1939, being first besieged and then occupied. After that, the large Jewish population began to be persecuted, many being deported to the concentration camps that the Nazis now created on Polish soil. The remainder were herded into the overpopulated ghetto, until in 1943 Hitler ordered its annihilation. The occupants fought back for a month, holding out until almost all were dead. Then, the next year, the Russians began to approach, and a last attempt was made by the Poles to overthrow their German occupiers. This developed into the two-month-long Warsaw Uprising that finally ended with the Poles' defeat. Before abandoning the city, the retreating Germans carried out their orders to raze it to the ground, leaving it in ruins for the Russians, who arrived shortly after. Kraków, although occupied by the Germans, was more fortunate, and, despite further brutal persecution of the city's Jews, the city itself escaped virtually unscathed.

In 1945 Poland's borders were again changed with a shift towards the west. Russia now moved into areas that had belonged to Poland before the war, and in compensation the new Republic absorbed land that was earlier part of the Third Reich. Danzig reverted to its former name of Gdańsk, and with German speakers fleeing or being deported, Poles began to arrive from the east. From this moment communism started to take hold, and in 1952 the country became officially the Communist Polish People's Republic, just three years before joining the Warsaw Pact. At that point, in the capital itself a rebuilding programme began that would eventually include the reconstruction of Warsaw's historic areas. Hoping further to impress, if not appease, the Poles, the Russians started a similar, major restoration of Gdańsk, the city that they themselves had destroyed. Here, however, after years of growing financial and political problems, in 1970 anti-regime demonstrations broke out, which ended in bloodshed. Things began to improve after Karol Wojtyla became Pope John Paul II in 1978. His election at last gave a face to Poland in the West, and as it brought the world's attention to the situation in the country, the authorities, now under greater international scrutiny, began gradually to moderate their policies. Therefore, when ten years after the first outbreaks, new strikes – led by the Solidarity Movement – began to take place in the dockyards, the outcome was peaceful, and ushered in the end of communism in 1989 and the dissolution of the Warsaw Pact in 1991. More significantly for Poland, in the previous year, 1990, the Third Polish Republic was born, and with this nearly two centuries of struggle to attain and maintain its independent identity were finally over.

Following the outbreak of the First World War, significant political changes inevitably took place throughout Europe. Numbers of emperors or monarchs began to be deposed, among them the Orthodox heads of Russia, and the Catholic rulers of Austria (1918), Portugal (1910 and 1919) and – for a time – Spain, with the King of the Belgians alone holding onto his throne. Apart from the Romanovs in Russia, other Orthodox heads of state would later in the century be ousted in Yugoslavia (1941), Bulgaria (1946), Romania (1947), and finally, after repeated uncertainty, Greece (1973). However, most of the Protestant monarchies were more fortunate, their ability to survive perhaps being partly explained by their earlier acceptance of change. Unlike some of their peers, the rulers of these states had long renounced the idea of their divinely ordained authority, acknowledging that theirs was a right largely dependent on the will of the people. By the middle period of the nineteenth century the Protestant states had in the main rejected absolutism, and had adopted a more democratic form of constitution. However, an exception to this was found in Germany, where at his coronation in 1861 Prussian king Wilhelm I would proclaim his divine right. Although he would then allow himself to be largely overshadowed by Bismarck – he was later famously reported as saying that it was 'hard' being emperor under his chancellor – his grandson, Kaiser Wilhelm II, would deliberately project himself as the *Kaiserreich*'s all-powerful monarch, designated by God to be its sole ruler. In fact, by 1914 Wilhelm II wielded little real authority, but this mistaken sense of self-importance would in time hasten his fall and the end of his empire. The demise of the Hohenzollerns – like that of the Romanov dynasty in Russia – would bring about a seismic change, causing aftershocks that brought down the smaller allied sovereign powers whose territories lay within the imperial borders. With the new German Weimar Constitution forcing these heads of states to abdicate their thrones (as the Kaiser had already done), a total of some twenty kings, grand dukes, dukes and princes would also see their historic ruling houses abolished forever.

Although the Kaiser is no longer attacked with the biased vitriol of the First World War and the immediate post-war years, when charges of insanity, savagery, and psychopathic sadism were laid against him, to this day the debate continues as to his true state of mind, with questions still being asked as to his responsibility for the horrors of 1914–18. No doubt Wilhelm II's ostentatious bluster, diplomatic tactlessness, love of intrigue, and militaristic behaviour – not to mention vast expansion of the navy – did play a part in the build-up to the conflict, but that is not to say that he was lacking in intelligence or that he was a warmonger, intent on widespread murder and annihilation. Although he had stirred up trouble and encouraged differences between the other powers, often enthusing about local wars between his neighbours, he wished Germany to stand outside as a spectator. He was a man of changing moods and ideas, who rarely, if ever, committed to any policy for long, a trait that Chancellor Hohenlohe remarked on with some cynicism: 'It seems that His Majesty is recommending another new programme, but I don't take it too tragically; I have seen too many programmes come and go.'[178] And because of the Kaiser's maverick nature, over time his personal power would be further reduced by his ministers, who, despite continuing to pay lip service, often concealed important matters from him for fear of what he might do. Hating criticism, quick to take offence, and too often speaking spontaneously without carefully crafted notes, Wilhelm would respond to events with mistaken and unguarded comments that then caused a scandal or a serious crisis. Therefore, frequently left outside the final decision making on strategic matters, even by the military where he had greater authority, he would find his opinions and policies questioned or increasingly ignored. Yet, while the tensions escalated between the civilian and military factions, and between the German *Reichstag* and Prussian *Landtag* – a situation that had arisen because of the new German Empire's imprecise definition of responsibilities – Wilhelm would continue to declare his desire to maintain peace. Despite his former bravado, as the seriousness of the international situation became clearer to him, with the possibility of war becoming increasingly likely, so he appeared to call with growing urgency for a peaceful resolution, expressing even at the eleventh hour the hope that a major conflict might be avoided. But neither he nor his fellow emperors in Russia and Austria were up to dealing with the situation, and their late, uncertain changes of policy only served to exacerbate matters – both Wilhelm and Nicholas would later blame the other for starting the war. But even while the tsar declared that his cousin could have stopped it 'had he wanted to', he understood that Wilhelm had been largely driven by his advisers.[179]

As the war continued the Kaiser, like the tsar, faced rising opposition at home, where there were demands for the greater enfranchisement of his people. Consequently, he chose to remain mostly out of sight at the headquarters at Spa in Belgium, with the result that voices then began to question the ruler's role. Although Wilhelm still retained a certain amount of popular support, in October 1918 the imperial navy in Kiel mutinied, and in the following weeks other strikes and rebellions took place, events that finally at the end of the month persuaded him to leave Berlin and return to the headquarters. Following the public announcement on 9 November of his abdication, and the abolition of the monarchy and empire, Wilhelm was unable to return to Germany, and so on the 10th he crossed into the Netherlands, just a day before the war officially ended. After the Armistice, the Dutch queen, Wilhelmina – backed by King Albert of Belgium – insisted that he should not be extradited for trial as a war criminal, and through her protection he was then able to live out his days at Huis Doorn, where he eventually died, aged eighty-two, in June 1941.

The terms of the Treaty of Versailles were too stringent, leaving Germany so crushed that gradually through the 1930s growing numbers of dispirited people turned to the Nazis, hoping they might be able to redeem their country's situation and improve their own lives. The party began to take control, and in July 1932, at Altona in Schleswig-Holstein, a public demonstration by Hitler's stormtroopers led to an open confrontation with the local Communists, a clash that resulted in the deaths of some 100 people. Nonetheless, in certain places, such as the former Polish region of Masuria, Nazi support continued to be strong. At the end of the war, the former militarism of Prussia was accused of being largely responsible for encouraging the activities of the Third Reich, and as a result the state itself was finally demolished. Having disbanded Prussia, the Allies then redrew the state boundaries and divided up Germany into separate areas that were controlled by Britain, America, France and their Soviet allies, the same also being done to the city of Berlin itself. In addition, the area surrounding the former East Prussian capital, Königsberg, now renamed Kaliningrad, was given to the Soviet Union – still today a Russian possession, despite its separation from the rest of the country. At this point thousands of Germans, previously forbidden by Hitler to flee the Soviet advance, escaped the clutches of the Red Army by crossing the border into neighbouring Lithuania. Of those now seeking refuge in its woods, the majority were lone children, totalling some 5,000 of the vast numbers who during the war had lost their parents and homes and been left with nothing. The more fortunate of these so-called 'Wolfskinder' eventually found new families, where for their protection from the Soviets, they were given Lithuanian identities and prevented from speaking German. Others, however, even though adopted, were taken into households for less honourable reasons, from that time forced to engage in hard labour and endure unkindness, cruelty, and even physical abuse. Their story is only now starting to come out. At the same time, on the international scene the Cold War was beginning to take shape, causing new tensions to build up between the communist East and capitalist West – a situation that would leave Germany's case unresolved until reunification finally became possible four decades later.

Among those others who had joined the new *Reich* in 1871, had been three former important Hanseatic towns. After a period when Napoleon had incorporated Lübeck, Bremen and Hamburg into France, they had been established by the Congress of Vienna as Free Cities within the newly formed German Confederation of states that was later replaced by the North German Confederation. And while these had now lost most of their autonomy, the German emperors still liked to recall their important past. In 1895, Wilhelm II made reference to the Hansa when, after eight years construction work with some 9,000 labourers, he was finally able to open the 'Kaiser Wilhelm Kanal' (Kiel Canal).[180] During the First World War the three Hansa cities created their own medals, designed on the lines of the Iron Cross, but incorporating the red and white Hanseatic symbols of old. After 1918, during the period of

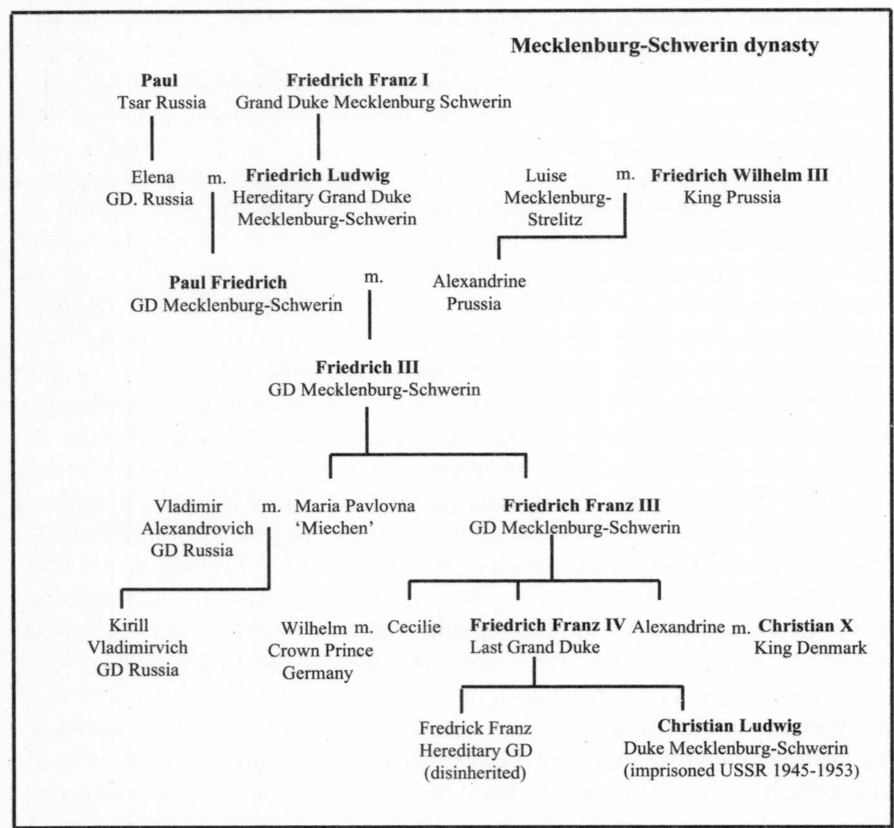

the Weimar Republic and until the rise of the Nazis, the three cities retained their self-rule, but when Hitler created the *Hansestadt* of Hamburg in 1937, he penalised Lübeck by incorporating it into Prussia, probably doing so to punish the city for its earlier refusal to grant him the right to hold a rally there. During the Second World War, Hamburg suffered major damage from allied bombing, but in the years since much has been reconstructed and today, as Hanseatic City Hamburg, it is a city state like Berlin. While Bremen was also made a Free Hanseatic City, becoming in combination with Bremerhaven the smallest state in Germany, Lübeck, in a less favourable position, just to the west of the country's inner border – the Iron Curtain – was instead incorporated into Schleswig-Holstein. However, in 1987, once again as the 'Queen of the Hansa', this was designated a World Heritage Site, just seven years after becoming the headquarters of a new cultural organisation that comprised several former members of the earlier association, including the Baltic ports of Visby, Tallinn, Riga, Gdańsk and Wismar.

Similarly, there were among those joining the German Empire in 1871 the two duchies of Mecklenburg, who, after repeated periods of union and separation, had by the time of the Congress of Vienna once more become separate independent states. The larger, Mecklenburg-Schwerin, in 1903 finally received Sweden's acknowledgement that it would give up all its rights to Wismar – the town that it had pawned to the duchy a hundred years before. Four years later, the duke at last brought the state's feudalism to an end, the system having lingered on despite the official ending of serfdom in the duchy nearly a century earlier. In 1918, after the suicide of his cousin the Duke of Mecklenburg-Strelitz, the last Duke of Mecklenburg-Schwerin briefly became regent of the neighbouring region as well. However, following Germany's surrender in November, he renounced both titles, whereupon Schwerin (rather than the larger Rostock) became the capital of the new Baltic state, Mecklenburg-Vorpommern. For a time, the duke was forbidden to return to his country, but besides being the husband of Christian IX's granddaughter, he was also the brother of the Danish queen, Alexandrine, and so he was now invited to Denmark. Although able to return to Germany the next year, to his fury, his oldest son Friedrich Franz joined Hitler's paramilitary SS, and then later, during the Second World War, served in the German Embassy in Copenhagen – a situation no doubt awkward for his uncle Christian X, who was now under Nazi occupation. As a result of his political leanings, Friedrich Franz's family cut him out of the succession, and with that his father's ducal title subsequently passed to his younger brother Christian Ludwig.

With the abdication of the last reigning duke in 1918, the family that had previously played an important role in the region lost its previously pre-eminent position. While in 1709, Peter the Great had arranged the marriage of his niece to the then duke – the pair ultimately becoming grandparents of the unfortunate Tsar Ivan VI – ninety years later another wedding had taken place between Tsar Paul's second daughter Elena Pavlovna and Friedrich Ludwig, a reportedly good, handsome man, even if, according to

Count Rostopchin, rather 'rustic and ignorant'. Later, often visiting Berlin, the young couple would become close to Friedrich Wilhelm III and Queen Luise, a friendship that encouraged the duchess to promote the king's first meeting with her brother, Tsar Alexander I. Although Elena's husband predeceased his father, and she too died young, their son Paul Friedrich would succeed, he having already reinforced good relations with the Prussian rulers by marrying their daughter. But Paul Friedrich is chiefly remembered for another reason, for choosing to return his capital to Schwerin, thereby abandoning his former capital around 25 miles to the south. After this move, the earlier Ludwigslust – dubbed the 'Northern Versailles' – the 'pleasure' palace of the earlier duke, Christian Ludwig II, became primarily the summer residence. However, following the abolition of the duchy, in 1921 Ludwigslust was again the family home, remaining as such until 1945, when to its west the boundary was established between the occupation zones of the Western allies and the Soviets. At that point the later Duke Christian Ludwig moved for a time to the Danish royal family's castle at Glücksburg in Schleswig-Holstein, but having then decided to return to his home, was arrested and imprisoned in Russia, only eventually being released in 1953 after serving some eight years of his twenty-five-year prison sentence. Meanwhile, Ludwigslust, like the rest of Mecklenburg-Vorpommern, would continue to remain as part of the DDR (Deutsche Demokratische Republik, or East Germany) until 1989.

In the nineteenth century, soon after Duke Paul's son Friedrich had adopted his father's plans for Schwerin, he began to have his own more ambitious projects, deciding at that point to carry out a complete rebuilding of his lakeside palace. This he replaced with a castle designed in the new romantic fairy-tale style that was now so fashionable, an extravagant undertaking that demonstrated the considerable wealth and high regard the duke enjoyed. And by the time of his death in 1883, his family's status had been raised still further by the marriage of his daughter Marie – 'Miechen' – to Tsar Alexander II's second son, Grand Duke Vladimir Alexandrovich of Russia.

Before she became Grand Duchess Maria Pavlovna, Miechen proved herself to be a strong woman, refusing at the time of her engagement to abandon her Lutheranism, she thus marking herself out as the first of the Romanov wives not to adopt Orthodoxy. Although years later in 1908 she would finally undergo conversion, many remained unconvinced of her religious sincerity, viewing her action with scepticism, believing that it was motivated by her desire to promote the dynastic claims to the throne of her son Kirill – a matter that had grown more relevant after the *tsesarevich*'s dubious state of health had become apparent. But it was not just the obvious ambitions of Miechen and her husband that earned them the displeasure of his brother Alexander III and Empress Maria Feodorovna. Until Grand Duke Vladimir's death in 1909, the couple dazzled St Petersburg with the unsurpassed opulence of their court, which rivalled – if not outshone – that of the tsar and his successor, Nicholas II. The grand duke and duchess were famous for their glittering balls and entertainments, as they were for

Miechen's fabulous jewels, including the tiara, later bought by Queen Mary, which is still part of the British royal collection.

Even after Vladimir's death, Miechen continued to entertain lavishly, but within a few years international events began to impact on her and many of her relations. While her niece, Alexandrine, married to Christian X of Denmark, largely escaped the horrors caused by the First World War, Alexandrine's sister was the wife of the German Crown Prince Wilhelm – the son of Kaiser Wilhelm II – who was fighting on the opposing side. After the Armistice, he, like his father and brother-in-law (the last Grand Duke of Mecklenburg-Schwerin), would be forced to abdicate and go abroad. But things would be still worse for those living in Russia, where all would ultimately suffer hardship, persecution and exile, if not a brutal death. Even though all Miechen's children escaped with their lives, among her wider Romanov family eighteen would be savagely murdered during the 1917–18 revolution. Nonetheless, Miechen was a woman of true grit, continuing to appear unbowed even after the horror had overturned her whole existence. Her remarkable resilience in the face of appalling adversity would impress even those who had never liked her; Nicholas II's sister Olga, for one, being struck by the bearing the grand duchess displayed until the very end. Although initially determined to remain in Russia, finally in February 1920 Miechen was persuaded by the White Army that the time had come when she must leave. So, after weeks living in a stinking compartment of a train, 'racked with illness, frozen with cold' and with only black bread and soup to eat, she was one of the last Romanovs to escape from Russia, finally leaving the country with her youngest son and his family from the Black Sea port of Novorossiysk.[181] Although she reached France in safety, the indomitable Miechen was now a sick woman and she would die just seven months later, aged sixty-six.

In time, among the refugees abroad, rival claimants would try to assert their rights to the throne, and still today different branches of the family dispute the succession, the primary claimant being one of Miechen's descendants, Maria Vladimirovna, who was born in 1953. The granddaughter of Grand Duke Kirill – who had so offended Empress Maria Feodorovna in 1924 when declaring himself the new Emperor of all the Russias – she has now pronounced herself head of the imperial house, and refers to her son, George, as the *tsesarevich*. However, Nicholas II's two sisters soon distanced themselves from these debates, quietly withdrawing into their own private worlds. Xenia, who had first escaped with her mother to England in 1919, chose to remain in the country and accepted the Grace and Favour residence offered to her by her cousin George V. Shortly before her father's death in 1894, she had married his cousin, Grand Duke Alexander Mikhailovich ('Sandro'), with whom she had been in love since she was fifteen, but by the end of their lives the couple were living apart and pursuing their own romantic affairs. Nonetheless, Xenia attended Sandro's funeral in 1933 at Roquebrune-Cap-Martin on the Côte d'Azur, where later she herself would also be buried. In contrast, Olga, who had arrived in Denmark in 1920, after her mother's death moved with her husband, Colonel Nicholas Kulikovsky, to a farm near Copenhagen, but with the outbreak of the Second World War she again found herself under threat, alternatively accused of having pro-Nazi or pro-Soviet sympathies. Although by 1945 the German occupiers had left the country, the couple still felt vulnerable, their situation being made still more difficult by their financial difficulties. Three years later they therefore decided to emigrate to Canada, where they bought another farm on which they worked until 1952, when it became too much for them to run. They then moved into a small house in Cooksville near Toronto, and here in 1960, two years after her husband, and just seven months after her sister Xenia in England, Olga finally died.

For most of the twentieth century rumours abounded about the fate of the children of Nicholas II and his wife Alexandra. Various theories were put forward, suggesting that one or more of the family might have escaped, and the claim that gained the most credence was that concerning the tsar's last daughter, Anastasia. In 1920 a young woman with mental problems, later called Anna Anderson, was fished out of a canal in Berlin, and soon she was said to be one of the missing grand duchesses, initially Tatiana, but later her youngest sister. In time certain members of the imperial family such as Olga and Felix Yusoupov would meet her, but opinions soon became divided with some declaring the pretender a fraud and others pronouncing her to be genuine. But after remains were discovered at Ekaterinburg in 1991, tissue previously taken from Anderson underwent DNA testing, and this confirmed that the latter was not who she had claimed to be. Final evidence found that she had been a Polish factory worker called Franziska Schanzkowska.

In 1922 a first-hand report of the murder at Ekaterinburg was written by the man in charge of the executions. Yakov Yurovsky confirmed that all the imperial family had died in a chaotic and frenzied slaughter, Tsar Nicholas being the first to be shot, followed soon after by his wife, son and faithful retainers. The event, however, was considerably worse for the poor daughters, who, partly protected by the jewels sewn into their bodices for safe keeping, survived the initial killing, only to be then dispatched by bayonet attacks and bullets to the head. Following their eventual discovery, the bones of most of the family were returned to St Petersburg, where in 1991 they were placed in the St Catherine's Chapel in the cathedral of the Peter and Paul Fortress, ten years after the Russian Orthodox Church Abroad had canonised them as 'martyrs'. The Church in Russia finally acclaimed them as 'passion bearers' in 2000. However, two sets of remains – badly damaged in the murderers' failed attempt to destroy the evidence – have not yet joined the rest. Generally presumed to belong to Maria and her brother Alexei, these were not discovered until 2007. Following their examination, they have remained in storage along with the archives.[182] Yet, despite the scientific evidence attained by DNA comparative analysis with material gathered from Prince Philip – Empress Alexandra's great-nephew and one of her closest living relations – there are still some in Russia who question the findings.[183] Their arguments rest on the fact that the blood found on a handkerchief used by Nicholas after the assassination attack he suffered in Japan in Otsu in 1891 does not match with the DNA of the remains found in the Urals. For sceptics these doubts remain, despite further analysis having shown a match with blood found on the shirt worn by Nicholas at the time of the earlier assault. President Putin, now siding with the Church authorities, is against further investigation, and has for the moment shelved the matter. So, until the last remains are released and all the members of the family are reunited, the story is not over.

Within the ruling classes, the First World War had of course caused bitter tensions, putting into stark relief the tangled nature of family ties. Dynastic alliances had always sought to stabilise diplomatic relations, but yet again the various royal houses found themselves fighting, not just a foreign enemy, or their rebellious subjects, but also their own close relatives. This was not a new problem, but in the savage, wide-ranging 1914–18 conflict relations became even more strained and complex, hatreds being stoked by the reactions of the public, who now were more personally engaged in the process of the war. Through the wider access to information, all – from the poorest worker to the noble – was brought face-to-face with the realities of the battlefield, truths revealed that in an earlier age would have been hidden from most people. This was not all. In addition to the heartache caused as contact broke down between children, siblings and cousins who were aligned on opposing sides, the personal loyalties of individuals were at times unfairly brought into question. And such attacks carried more weight as the whole propaganda machine began to roll into action. One such person to suffer particularly in this way was Russia's last *tsaritsa*, whose own brother and brother-in-law were serving German officers. Despite her devotion to her husband and his country, her close links to his British allies, and her loathing for her cousin the Kaiser and all things 'Prussian', she would be viewed with lasting suspicion, unfairly accused not only of supporting the much-hated enemy but also of intentionally betraying Russia and bringing about the disasters that were befalling it. Thus Empress Alexandra's experiences graphically epitomise the underlying trials, tensions and challenges that had for centuries marked the reality of dynastic temporal power and privilege.

The Great War would change the face of Europe. Although it ultimately promoted the cause of democracy, it altered the demographic in many countries, particularly those where the casualties were exceptionally high, or where civil war subsequently broke out. Society was now altered forever, and as veterans began to return, they and others, rejecting the previous status quo, began to demand new rights. Many saw no place for their earlier heads of state, most of whom they blamed personally for the recent catastrophe. Into the void left by the fallen dynasties stepped new extremist regimes, thus preparing the way for the next great conflict to break out a little over two decades later, a disaster that in turn lead to a further realignment of political boundaries, and the loss of many states' full autonomy or independence for most of the remaining years of the twentieth century.

While some modern social histories question the value of studies of past sovereigns and elite individuals, arguing that emphasis should be placed above all on the previously ignored majority of ordinary people, what they propound is made more difficult by the scarcity of relevant material that the poor or dispossessed have left behind them. And as it is the human story that can give us a greater, even if still limited, insight into the overall picture of what life was like at a particular period, evidence has to be taken from wherever it can be found – documents, paintings, monuments, whatever. We have to accept that it was those in power who not only created or commissioned these things, but also largely shaped the world as we see it. Even as we put aside the question of the artistic and practical heritage of past rulers, statesmen and the rest – the wealth of treasures, inventions and discoveries their patronage has left us – we should concede that people that are materially advantaged are no less deserving of our interest and understanding than everyone else. Besides sharing the same human qualities and failings, they, like the rest of mankind, were, or are, the victims of circumstance. However, when viewing their case, there is also another dimension. While their prosperity, authority and public standing may have allowed them to achieve vastly more than other people, it has also given them the wherewithal to create previously unimagined disasters. Accordingly, their actions may have made them either the objects of profound respect, possibly even adulation, or of bitter loathing and recrimination. And here an element of jealousy appears to play its part; even minor faults that could be forgiven or forgotten in others can become viewed as sins or crimes of a far greater magnitude, the judgement made purely on the grounds of the individual's perceived advantages and benefits. This apparent unmoderated desire to repay the unfairness of life by attacking the person who was previously revered or adored, society's 'fallen idol', is evident in today's celebrity culture. Perhaps historically, nowhere better illustrates this fall from grace than the Romanovs' story, where, despite their obvious mistakes and individual acts of selfishness or even cruelty, many of the family would become victims primarily – if not solely – because they had previously enjoyed the luxuries of wealth and privilege: some, like the tsar's children, were punished not for their failures, but as an act of vengeance against the position that they had acquired by an accident of birth. Even though Nicholas' sister, Grand Duchess Olga, would later remark that the family had for years been courting disaster by their self-centred hedonism, and earlier visitors to Russia had remarked on the nobility's blindness to the condition of the workers and peasants around them, the imperial family's behaviour did not deserve or justify the brutal treatment that they all received, nor does it exonerate the people that carried it out.

Those far from the nobility's privileged existence saw only the extravagant pleasure and opulence enjoyed by the members of the court and other aristocrats, many little appreciating the good that some achieved, and little realising the pressures experienced by those at the top. Again and again, Russia's emperors found themselves confronted by insurmountable challenges, which were not just beyond their personal capabilities, but also beyond the capabilities of the majority of people. Although cosseted by unsurpassed luxury and material advantages, these rulers were soon aware that the flip side of their unrestricted authority was the enormous responsibility that right entailed, and, on coming to power, most would see themselves as the victims of cruel fortune. Terrified by the role that had fallen to them, and openly telling those around them that they dreaded what lay ahead, they viewed their destiny with horror, declaring themselves unwilling, if not unfit, to take on the burden that had been thrust upon them. In the nineteenth century, the task facing the tsars became increasingly daunting as opposition grew alongside the improvement in both education and communication, a development that in turn helped make radicalism, violence and murder everyday realities. Although, in the main, the emperors were exceptionally fortunate in their marriages, most finding much support in their home lives, ultimately – if not killed by an assassin – all would die exhausted, worn out and demoralised.

Over the centuries this was not always the case, and throughout the Baltic region as a whole, there would be certain individuals who were eager to assume power, some actually going out of their way to attain it. And, while among them there would be despots and unworthy autocrats, caring little for the good of their people, others like Peter I would accomplish incredible feats of lasting value to their countries. Although the tsar achieved these things at great cost to his subjects, and was often brutally ruthless in pursuit of his aims, nonetheless, he worked incessantly throughout his reign to bring Russia into the modern age. Similar strides would be made elsewhere. Following the early achievements of the Danish queen Margrete and the Polish king Kazimierz III, the Swedish Gustavus Adolphus and Brandenburg Great Elector would equally set out to promote the development and public standing of their two growing nations. After them came Frederick II of Prussia and Catherine II of Russia, who, seeing themselves as 'servants' of the state, throughout their long reigns pursued their Enlightenment ideals and determinedly strove to improve the lot of their people. All these individuals were not without their share of human flaws, but they sincerely believed that they were qualified for the task before them. It would be their combination of ambition and dedication to service, more than their conquests or more extravagant actions, that still allows them to be remembered as among the 'Greats' of Europe and Russia.

Timeline

966 Mieszko I, the Piast ruler of Poland, converts to Christianity. Gdańsk founded
1025 Boleslaw I crowned first King of Poland
1035 Death of Canute (Cnut), the Danish King of England
1038 Kraków becomes capital of Poland
1157 Cologne becomes first official trader in London
1158 First merchants from Bremen arrive in Novgorod
1159 Henry the Lion founds Lübeck
1189 Start of Third Crusade. Frederick I 'Barbarossa' grants a charter to Hamburg, making it an Imperial Free City
1190 Founding of Teutonic Knights
1201 Bishop Albert establishes his castle in Riga, and next year founds the Livonian Brothers of the Sword
1205 The Hansa merchants establish themselves at Novgorod
1217 Pope calls for Northern Crusade
1219 Valdemar II of Denmark invades Estonia and captures Tallinn
1226 Konrad I, Duke of Masovia, appeals to Teutonic Knights for help. Lübeck becomes Imperial Free City
1236 Livonian Order becomes part of the Teutonic Order
1248 Danes recapture Tallinn from Teutonic Knights, ending their eleven years of rule
1266 German *hanse* becomes corporation in London
1282 Riga joins the Hansa
1284 Tallinn joins the Hansa
1308 'Gdańsk Slaughter'
1309 Teutonic Knights move to Marienburg (Malbork)
1333 Kazimierz III 'the Great' becomes the last Piast King of Poland
1340 Danish king Valdemar IV Atterdag sells Reval (Tallinn) to the Teutonic Knights
1343 St Georges' Night Uprising, 1343–45
1346 Start of Black Death
1347 Hansa divided into 'thirds'

1356 The Golden Bull: formal establishment of the Imperial electoral college
1359 Visby on Gotland joins the Hansa
1360 Bergen *kontor* officially opens
1361 Valdemar IV Atterdag attacks Visby and demands heavy ransom. Danzig attends a *hansetag* for the first time
1362 Magnus IV replaces his father as King of Norway
1363 Burgomaster Johann Wittenborg executed in Lübeck. Valdemar's 10-year-old daughter Margrete marries Haakon VI of Norway
1364 Albrecht of Mecklenburg takes Swedish crown
1370 Treaty of Stralsund: Hansa at peak of its power. Birth of Olaf, the son of Margrete and Haakon
1375 Death of Danish king, Valdemar IV Atterdag: succeeded by Olaf
1380 Death of Haakon VI of Norway: succeeded by Olaf
1384 Jadwiga crowned 'King of Poland'
1386 Marriage of Jadwiga and Jogaila establishes the Jagellion dynasty – personal union of Kingdom of Poland and Duchy of Lithuania
1387 Death of Olaf, the King of Norway and Denmark
1389 Albrecht, King of Sweden, deposed. Margrete appoints great-nephew Boguslaw as her heir, who, renamed Erik, is recognised as King of Norway
1390s Pirate attacks by the Victual Brothers
1396 Erik proclaimed king in Denmark, Norway and Sweden
1397 Margrete founds the Kalmar Union
1410 Battle of Grunwald (Tannenberg): Teutonic Knights suffer a serious defeat
1411 Sigismund of Luxembourg – brother-in-law of Jadwiga of Poland – elected King of the Romans
1412 Margrete dies
1415 The Hohenzollerns become margraves of Brandenburg
1429 Erik of Pomerania establishes the Sound Dues
1433 Jadwiga's brother-in-law, Sigismund, becomes Holy Roman Emperor
1443 Roskilde cathedral suffers a major fire. Copenhagen becomes the Danish capital
1448 Christian I becomes first of Denmark's Oldenburg kings
1453 Fall of Constantinople
1454 Start of Thirteen Years War between Poland and the Teutonic Knights
1466 Teutonic Knights surrender Royal Prussia and the eastern duchy becomes a vassal state of Poland: Teutonic Knights move to Königsberg
1469 Margaret, daughter of Christian I, marries James III of Scotland. England, already involved in War of the Roses, now at war with the Hanseatic League
1470 Edward IV of England forced to flee abroad: Denmark cedes Shetland and Orkney Isles to Scotland
1471 Hansa fleet help Edward IV regain his throne. October, Sweden's crushing defeat of Danes at Brunkeberg; Swedish independence under Sten Sture the Elder
1474 Treaty of Utrecht grants ownership of London Steelyard to Hansa merchants: other English trading posts established
1494 Ivan III closes the Novgorod *kontor*
1517 Luther's first public protest against the Catholic Church
1520 'Stockholm Bloodbath'

1521 Start of Sweden's War of Liberation: Christian II loses his Swedish crown
1522 Lübeck fleet helps Gustav Vasa return victorious to Sweden
1523 January, Christian forced to abdicate in Denmark and Norway: leaves Denmark. June, Gustav Vasa elected king of an independent Sweden
1525 Grand Master Albrecht converts to Lutheranism and order of Teutonic Knights secularised: Albrecht becomes Duke of Prussia. Men of Lübeck invade Visby
1527 Gustav Vasa crowned Gustav I of Sweden
1536 End of Denmark's 'Counts' War': Christian III becomes King of Denmark and Norway. Lübeck's former mayor, Jürgen Wullenwever, executed. Denmark pawns Bornholm to Lübeck
1544 Sweden's Vasa dynasty declared hereditary
1550 Gustav I Vasa founds Helsingfors (Helsinki)
1558 Start of Livonian War. Elizabeth I becomes Queen of England
1561 Swedes arrive to help Reval and take over Estonia: start of 'the good old Swedish times'. Disbanding of Teutonic Knights
1567 Erik XIV of Sweden's attack on the Sture family
1568 Marriage and coronation of Erik XIV's mistress: king deposed and imprisoned
1569 Union of Lublin unites Polish-Lithuanian Commonwealth: start of Poland's time of 'Golden Freedoms'. Swedish aristocracy becomes hereditary
1570 End of Northern Seven Years' War between Sweden and Denmark. Frederik II of Denmark accepts the end of the Kalmar Union
1570s Frederik II starts rebuilding of Kronborg Castle
1572 'St Bartholomew's Day Massacre' in France: Huguenots start leaving the country
1573 Poland's Great Election: Henri de Valois elected King of Poland
1574 February, Henri crowned in Kraków: June, Henri returns to France
1575 Anna and Stefan Batory (István Báthory) elected joint rulers of Poland
1576 Plague hits Berlin
1580s Creation of the Danish Order of the Elephant
1583 End of Livonian War
1586 Batory dies
1587 Johan III's son, Sigismund, elected Zygmunt III of Poland
1588 Death of Frederik II of Denmark: the next year his daughter Anne marries James VI of Scotland
1591 Ivan IV's son Dmitry dies in uncertain circumstances
1592 Johan III dies, his son Sigismund (Zygmunt III of Poland) becomes King of Sweden and within few years moves his court to Warsaw
1593 Bruges *kontor* closes
1594 Anna of Prussia marries Johann Sigismund, Elector of Brandenburg, uniting the two regions
1597 Elizabeth I expels Hansa from England
1598 Sigismund III defeated by his uncle Karl at Stångebro
1599 Sigismund III loses Swedish throne: separation of Sweden and Poland. Crushing of Finnish resistance in 'Åbo Bloodbath'
1600 'Linköping Bloodbath'
1603 Elizabeth I dies in England: Christian IV's brother-in-law James VI of Scotland succeeds as James I. Polish *Sejm* takes place for last time in Kraków
1604 Karl IX officially recognised as King of Sweden. First False Dmitry visits Poland and converts to Catholicism

1605 Tsar Boris Godunov dies: Godunov's son Feodor II murdered: First False Dmitry invades Russia and crowned tsar
1606 First False Dmitry murdered: Vasily Shuisky becomes tsar
1609 Sweden agrees an alliance with Tsar Vasily. Poland declares war on Russia: Poles begin siege of Smolensk
1610 July, Poles defeat Swedes and Russians at Klushino, and enter Moscow: Tsar Vasily deposed. Prince Wladyslaw of Poland declared Tsar of Russia. Start of Ingrian War between Sweden and Russia. Swedish capture of Oresek (Nöteborg – the later Schlüsselburg)
1611 Start of the two-year Kalmar War between Sweden and Denmark. June, Smolensk surrenders to Poles: Sigismund takes up permanent residence in Warsaw. July, Swedes capture Novgorod. October, death of Karl IX: succeeded by his son, Gustavus Adolphus
1612 Tsar Vasily dies in captivity in Poland: last Poles leave Russia
1613 End of Time of Troubles: Michael becomes first Romanov tsar
1617 Gustavus Adophus officially establishes the Swedish *Riksdag*. Peace of Stolbova ends Swedish war with Russia, which is now excluded from the Baltic
1618 May, the Thirty Years War breaks out. December, Russia cedes more territory to Polish-Lithuanian Commonwealth: Commonwealth at its maximum size
1620 Danish settlement founded at Tranquebar in India. 15 November, attempt on Sigismund (Zygmunt) III of Poland's life. 25 November, Gustavus Adolphus marries Maria Eleonora of Brandenburg
1621 Gustavus Adolphus captures Riga
1623 Gustavus Adolphus blockades Danzig
1624 Oslo burns down, Christian IV founds new city, Christiania
1625 Denmark joins the Thirty Years War
1626 May, Gustavus Adolphus invades his brother-in-law's Duchy of Prussia. December, birth of Queen Christina
1627 Swedes renew their fighting in the region of Danzig. August, Gustavus Adolphus badly wounded. November, Swedish fleet beaten by the Poles. Gustavus Adolphus gains *Riksdag*'s promise of allegiance to his young daughter
1628 August, the *Vasa* sinks on its maiden voyage. Imperial army occupies Jutland and takes Wismar. Swedes defend Stralsund against the Imperial army, and become protectors of the town
1629 Swedish truce with Poles, confirmation of Sweden's control of much of Livonia
1630 Gustavus Adolphus invades Pomerania and Swedes enter Thirty Years War
1631 Swedish victory over the Imperial army at Breitenfeld
1632 April, death of Sigismund (Zygmunt) III of Poland. November, Gustavus Adolphus killed in battle at Lützen: seven-year-old Christina becomes monarch
1634 May, Smolensk War between Russians and Poles ends: Russia cedes captured territory to the Commonwealth. Wladyslaw IV Poland renounces his claim to Russian throne
1635 Polish-Swedish truce
1640 Great Elector of Brandenburg succeeds his father

1642 Queen Christina becomes engaged to her cousin Karl Gustav. First Finnish translation of the Bible
1643 May, 4-year-old Louis XIV succeeds as King of France. Start of two-year Torstenson War between Sweden and Denmark
1644 Ending of the Swedish regency: Queen Christina starts to rule
1645 July, Alexis I becomes Tsar of Russia. August, end of Torstenson War between Denmark and Sweden: Denmark surrenders Gotland and other possessions. November, French astounded by the Polish retinue arriving for Marie Louise Gonzaga's wedding
1646 March, Marie Louise's marriage to Wladyslaw IV, and her coronation as Queen Ludwika
1648 Deaths of Christian IV of Denmark (February) and Wladyslaw IV of Poland (May). End of Thirty Years War: Bremen-Verden and western Pomerania become Swedish possessions
1649 Charles I executed in England. The *Riksdag* accept Queen Christina's naming of Karl Gustav as her heir. Jan Kazimierz, the newly elected Polish king marries his widowed sister-in-law
1650 René Descartes dies in Stockholm. Queen Christina gains the *Riksdag*'s approval of Karl Gustav's hereditary right to the throne. Queen Christina's coronation takes place in Stockholm
1654 Queen Christina abdicates: end of the Vasa dynasty: Karl of Palatinate-Zweibrücken succeeds. Queen Christina converts to Catholicism
1655 Start of Second Northern War. Karl X invades Poland: beginning of the 'Deluge': King and Queen of Poland flee to Silesia. Queen Christina arrives in Rome
1656 Combined Swedish-Brandenburg army captures Warsaw
1657 Frederik III of Denmark declares war on Sweden. Polish king acknowledges sovereignty of Hohenzollerns in Ducal Prussia
1658 Karl X of Sweden crosses the Belts: Treaty of Roskilde. Start of siege of Copenhagen: Battle of the Sound
1660 February, Karl X of Sweden dies: succeeded by five-year-old son. May, Treaty of Oliwa confirms the full sovereignty of the Brandenburg rulers in Duchy of Prussia. Polish Vasa king renounces claim to Swedish throne. 25 May, Charles II returns to England as king. 27 May, Treaty of Copenhagen ends Denmark's total control of the Sound. October, Denmark becomes an absolute monarchy
1661 Widowed Queen Hedvig Eleonora buys Drottningholm. Tessin the Elder commissioned to rebuild palace after it burns down
1668 Jan Kazimierz of Poland abdicates
1669 Last *Hansetag* takes place at Lübeck
1671 Christian V takes possession of St Thomas, the first of Denmark's Caribbean islands
1672 June (NS), birth of Peter the Great of Russia. 6 December, former Polish king Jan II Kazimierz dies in France. 18 December, Karl XI of Sweden reaches majority
1674 Jan Sobieski becomes King of Poland and Grand Duke of Lithuania
1675 June, official betrothal of Ulrikke, Princess of Denmark and Karl XI of Sweden. 28 June, Great Elector defeats Swedes at Fehrbellin. October, start of the Scanian War between Denmark, Brandenburg and allies, against Sweden and France

1676 January, death of Tsar Alexis of Russia. December, Karl XI defeats Danes at Battle of Lund
1677 July, Swedish victory at Battle of Landskrona
1679 Denmark cedes Gotland to Sweden
1682 May (NS), Feodor III dies: Streltsy uprising in Moscow: Sofia becomes regent for her brothers, Ivan V and Peter. June, birth of Karl XII of Sweden
1683 July, Prince George of Denmark marries Anne Stuart, future Queen of England. September, Jan Sobieski saves Vienna from falling to the 'Turks'
1685 February, Charles II dies in England, James II succeeds. 22 October, Revocation of Edict of Nantes in Edict of Fontainbleau. 29 October, Edict of Potsdam
1688 May, Great Elector of Brandenburg dies, succeeded by his son, Elector Friedrich III. November, William of Orange invades England and takes throne from James II
1689 15 April, Sophie Amalienborg palace in Copenhagen burns down. 19 April, Queen Christina dies in Rome. September, end of Sofia's regency in Russia
1691 Friedrich III, Elector of Brandenburg, founds new city of Berlin
1693 Tsar Peter visits Archangel. Swedish king, Karl XI, become absolute ruler
1694 Tsar Peter's mother dies: tsar revisits Archangel
1696 February, Ivan V dies: Peter becomes sole ruler of Russia. June, death of Polish king, Jan Sobieski. July, Tsar Peter takes Azov Fortress
1697 March, Peter's Grand Embassy sets off to Europe. April, Karl XI of Sweden dies, fifteen-year-old Karl XII becomes new absolute ruler. Tre Konor castle in Stockholm burns down. September, Elector of Saxony crowned King Augustus II of Poland
1698 Founding of Russian naval base at Taganrog. Peter visits Augustus on his way home from Vienna: massacre of Streltsy
1700 Outbreak of Great Northern War. August, Karl XII of Sweden lands in Denmark and forces Frederik IV to withdraw from war. 1 November, King Carlos II of Spain dies. 30 November (NS), Karl XII defeats Russians at Narva
1701 January, Elector of Brandenburg I crowns himself King Friedrich I in Prussia. 9 July, start of War of Spanish Succession. 19 July (NS), Karl XII crosses the Duna and defeats the Saxons
1702 February, Frederik IV abolishes serfdom in Denmark. May, Karl XII arrives in Warsaw. July, Swedish victory at Battle of Kliszów, death of 'Gottorp Fury'. October, Russians capture Nöteborg (Schlüsselburg)
1703 May, founding of St Petersburg
1704 July, Karl's protégé Stanislaw Leszczyński elected King of Poland. August, Russians capture Narva
1705 September, Leszczyński crowned Stanislaw I. November, Augustus II founds Order of the White Eagle
1706 August, Karl XII arrives in Altranstädt, Saxony. September, Augustus II officially abdicates Polish throne
1707 April, Karl XII meets John Churchill. September, Karl XII leaves Saxony at start of his Russian campaign
1708 Battles of Holowczyn and Lesnaya
1709 January, the Great Frost sets in. March, plague hits Danzig, soon spreading to other Baltic towns. 8 July (NS), Battle of Poltava: Karl XII flees to Bender. 11 July (NS), Lewenhaupt surrenders the remaining Swedish army at Perevolochna. Augustus II regains his throne. August, quarantine station set up on Saltholm to try and prevent arrival of plague

in Denmark. December, birth of Tsar Peter's daughter, the later Empress Elizabeth of Russia

1710 Besieged Riga surrenders to Russians in July, and Reval in October (NS). November (NS), Anna marries the Duke of Courland – the first Romanov officially to marry a foreigner. Plague reaches Zealand

1711 January, Duke of Courland dies: his widow, Anna, ordered to return to Courland. June, plague arrives in Copenhagen. July, Russians defeated at Battle of River Pruth. October, Peter's son Alexei marries Lutheran princess – the Romanov's first German bride

1712 January, birth of Frederick II of Prussia. February, Tsar Peter officially marries his former mistress Catherine. Danes' occupation of Bremen-Verden. St Petersburg declared the Russian capital

1713 1 February, Kalabalik at Bender. 25 February, Friedrich I of Prussia dies, succeeded by Friedrich William I: Prussian king takes Stettin from Swedes. Denmark occupies Duchy of Holstein-Gottorp, and Bremen-Verden

1714 Deaths of Sophie, Electress of Hanover (June) and Queen Anne of Great Britain (August). 1 August, the Prussian king's uncle becomes George I of Great Britain. 7 August (NS), Russian victory in naval Battle of Gangut: Start of Russian seven-year occupation of Finland, 'the Greater Wrath'. November, Karl races home from the Ottoman Empire to Stralsund

1715 June, Denmark agrees to sell Bremen-Verden to George I. September, Louis XIV dies, 5-year old Louis XV succeeds. December, Karl XII flees Stralsund before it falls to enemy, and returns to Sweden

1716 April, Wismar surrenders: Catherine Ivanovna marries Duke of Mecklenburg. July, Peter the Great visits Denmark. August, Peter the Great's son, Alexei flees abroad. October, Friedrich William I gives tsar the Amber Room. Russian troops enter Poland

1717 January, Carl Gyllenborg arrested in London. February, 'the Silent Sejm' opens with Russians acting as mediators. April, Peter begins two-month visit to France

1718 July, Peter the Great's son, Alexei, dies in Peter and Paul Fortress. November, Karl XII of Sweden killed: his sister Ulrika Eleonora becomes queen. December, the future Anna Leopoldovna born at Rostock

1720 March, Ulrika Eleonora abdicates and her husband become Fredrik I. July, Denmark makes peace with Sweden: Schleswig ceded to Denmark, Wismar returned to Sweden. South Sea Bubble crisis in England

1721 April, Lady Mary Wortley-Montagu brings the idea of inoculation to England. September, Treaty of Nystad agreed between Russia and Sweden brings end to the Great Northern War. Tsar Peter proclaims himself emperor

1724 May, Peter's wife crowned Empress Catherine. November, William Mons executed: Tsar Peter rescues drowning soldiers

1725 February (NS), Peter the Great dies, his widow becomes Catherine I. May, Peter's daughter Anna marries Duke of Holstein-Gottorp. August, Stanislaw Leszczyński's daughter's proxy marriage to Louis XV

1726 Fredensborg castle completed

1727 17 May, death of Catherine I: Peter II becomes tsar, the capital returns to Moscow: Menshikov sent into exile. 1 May, Karl August of Holstein-Gottorp, fiancé of future Empress Elizabeth dies before their marriage

1728 March, Anna Petrovna, Duchess of Holstein-Gottorp dies shortly after the birth of her son Karl Peter. October, Copenhagen fire
1729 Catherine the Great born at Stettin
1730 Peter II dies: Anna Ivanovna becomes Empress of Russia
1731 Empress Anna returns the capital to St Petersburg. Colin Campbell arrives in Göteborg (Gothenburg): founding of the Swedish East India Company
1733 1 February, death of Augustus II that leads to War of Polish Succession. 4 February, Christian VI of Denmark reintroduces a form of serfdom. June, marriage of Prussian Crown Prince Frederick (later 'the Great')
1734 Augustus III crowned King of Poland
1736 Stanislaw Leszczyński abdicates Polish throne for second time
1738 The Hats replace the Caps in Sweden
1740 May, death of Friedrich Wilhelm I of Prussia: Frederick II succeeds. August, birth of Ivan (VI). Deaths of Charles VI, Holy Roman Emperor (21 October) and Empress Anna of Russia (28 October NS). Anna Leopoldovna becomes regent for her son Ivan VI: Biron exiled to Siberia. December, Frederick II invades Silesia: start of War of Austrian Succession
1741 July, Swedish declaration of war on Russia ('Hats War'). November, Ulrika Eleonora of Sweden dies of smallpox. December (NS), Elizabeth takes throne of Russia: Ivan VI deposed and kept in captivity for the rest of his life
1742 Introduction of Swedish Celsius temperature scale. Russian occupation in Finland, 'the Lesser Wrath'
1743 Treaty of Åbo: Karl Peter renounces claim to Swedish throne: his cousin Adolf Friedrich made new heir: Karl Peter becomes Grand Duke Peter – Elizabeth's heir
1744 January, Sophie of Anhalt-Zerbst (Catherine II) sets off for Russia. June, Sophie converts to Orthodoxy, becomes known as Catherine and is officially betrothed to Grand Duke Peter. August, official marriage ceremony of Catherine's uncle, Adolf Friedrich of Holstein-Gottorp, and Luise Ulrike, sister of Frederick II
1745 Catherine (II) marries Grand Duke Peter. Foundations laid for Sans Souci
1746 Birth of Swedish crown prince, Gustav
1748 Oldenburgs celebrate 300 years on the Danish throne. Treaty of Aix-la-Chapelle ends the War of Austrian Succession
1750 Voltaire visits Potsdam
1751 Adolf Friedrich of Holstein-Gottorp becomes King of Sweden
1753 Sweden adopts the Gregorian calendar
1754 Birth of Catherine's son, Grand Duke Paul. Swedish royal family move back into rebuilt palace in Stockholm
1756 June, Luise Ulrike mounts failed coup in Sweden, her supporters executed. August, Frederick II invades Saxony: Seven Years War begins. Ivan VI taken to Schlüsselburg
1757 June, Prussian defeat at Battle of Kolin. Prussian victories at Battle of Rossbach (November) and Leuthen (December). December, birth of Catherine's daughter by Poniatowski
1758 June, death of Prussian heir, August Wilhelm. August, Poniatowski leaves St Petersburg. 25 August, Battle of Zorndorf
1760 Berlin occupied by Russians and Austrians
1761 (OS) Death of Empress Elizabeth: Russia retires from war
1762 Catherine II seizes power: Tsar Peter III murdered

1763 Death of Augustus III of Poland
1764 July, Tsar Ivan VI murdered. September, Stanislaw II Poniatowski elected King of Poland. Catherine buys her large collection of art works from a Berlin dealer and starts building of Small Hermitage
1765 Emperor Franz I dies, succeeded by Joseph II
1766 January, Frederik V of Denmark dies, succeeded by Christian VII. February, Stanislaw Leszczyński, Duke of Lorraine, dies after accident. 1 October/4 November, proxy and official marriages of Swedish Crown Prince Gustav to Danish Sofie Magdalene. 1 October/8 November, proxy and official marriages of Christian VII to British princess, Caroline Matilda
1767 Catherine II visits Kazan
1768 January, birth of Denmark's Crown Prince Frederik (VI). February, formation of the Bar Confederation in opposition to Stanislaw II and the Russian influence in Poland. April Christian VII meets his doctor, Struensee, at start of his European tour. October, Thomas Dimsdale inoculates Catherine and, a month later, her son Paul
1770 Beginning of Struensee affair with Caroline Matilde: rapid rise of Struensee. July, Russian naval victory at Çeşme during Catherine's first war with the Ottomans. October, Polish rebels in Hungary announce dethronement of Stanislaw II
1771 February, Adolf Frederik of Sweden dies: son Gustav III in Paris. July, birth of *la petite Struensee*: Struensee gains absolute power. August, statue of Frederik V unveiled in Amalienborg. September, plague and rebellion in Moscow. November, Stanislaw Poniatowski kidnapped in his carriage, but released the next day
1772 January, Danish coup, overthrows Struensee. April, Caroline Mathilde divorced, and death of Struensee: Christian VII declared unfit to rule. 3 May, Caroline Mathilde banished to Celle: Danish regency under Juliane Marie. 29 May, coronation of Gustav III in Sweden: mounts successful coup and introduces a new constitution. August, First Partition of Poland
1773 June, Grand Duke Paul exchanges his Holstein-Gottorp lands with Denmark. September, start of Pugachev Rebellion in Russia. October, Diderot visits St Petersburg
1774 Catherine II begins affair with Potemkin. July, Gustav III's brother Karl marries their cousin, Hedwig (Hedvig) Elizabeth Charlotte of Holstein-Gottorp. December, birth of Catherine's grandson Tsar Alexander I
1775 April, start of American Revolutionary War of Independence. May, death of Caroline Mathilde
1776 April, Tsar Paul's first wife dies. July, declaration of Independence by American colonies. September, Paul marries Sophie Dorothee of Württemberg
1778 July, start of War of Bavarian Succession ('the Potato War'). November, Gustav III's wife gives birth to son amid rumours regarding paternity
1779 Catherine buys Walpole collection
1780 Denmark in coalition with Sweden and Russia
1782 The *Bronze horseman* unveiled in St Petersburg. Dowager queen, Lovisa Ulrika of Sweden dies
1783 April, Catherine II annexes Crimea: June, meets her cousin Gustav III

1784 April, Caroline Mathilde's son, Crown Prince Frederik seizes the regency. July, Sweden buys St Barthelemy in the Caribbean
1786 Frederick II of Prussia dies. Swedish West India Company founded
1787 Catherine meets Stanislaw Poniatowski for first time after several years: empress visits the Crimea. Sultan declares war on Russia
1788 June, End of Danish serfdom. June, start of Russo-Swedish war: July, Battle of Hogland. August, during the Anjala Conspiracy the plotters approach Catherine II. October, opening of 'the Great Sejm'. December, siege of Ochakov
1789 February, Act of Union and Security introduces new Swedish constitution: Gustav III becomes virtually absolute. July, Storming of Bastille
1790 Swedish victory over Russians in Second Battle Svenskund: Russo-Swedish Peace
1791 February, Potemkin visits St Petersburg for last time. May, Polish first constitution introduced. June, Axel von Fersen attempts to rescue the French royal family. October, Potemkin dies
1792 January, end of Russo-Turkish war March, Gustav III dies days after assassination attempt in Stockholm: succeeded by Gustav IV Adolf. July, Duke Karl's 'Brunswick Manifesto'
1793 January, Second Partition of Poland: Louis XVI sent to guillotine. October, Marie Antoinette sent to guillotine. December, Luise of Mecklenburg-Strelitz marries Prussian crown prince
1794 February, Christiansborg castle burnt down in Copenhagen: Royal family move into the Amalienborg. March, start of Kosciuszko Uprising
1795 July, Copenhagen fire. October, Third Partition of Poland: Stanislaw II abdicates
1796 August, Gustav visits St Petersburg; insults Catherine by not appearing for betrothal to her granddaughter. 1 November, Gustav IV Adolf begins to rule for himself. 17 November (NS), Catherine II dies: Paul becomes Tsar of Russia
1797 Friedrich Wilhelm II dies and is succeeded by his son, Friedrich Wilhelm III
1798 February, Stanislaw II Augustus Poniatowski dies in St Petersburg. March, Louis XVIII accepts asylum from Tsar Paul, and settles at Mitau in Courland. July, Paul elected Grand Master of the Knights of Malta
1799 Marie-Antoinette's daughter, Madame Royale, arrives in Mitau
1800 The League of Armed Neutrality of Russia, Sweden, Denmark and Prussia. Georgia incorporated into Russian Empire
1801 January, orders Louis VIII to leave Mitau: king moves to Warsaw. March, Tsar Paul murdered. April, First Battle of Copenhagen
1802 Tsar Alexander I meets Prussian king and queen at Memel
1804 March, execution of Duke d'Enghien. December, Napoleon crowns himself emperor
1805 October, Tsar Alexander visits Berlin. December, Battle of Austerlitz
1806 July, end of the Holy Roman Empire, and Napoleon creates Confederation of the Rhine. 14 October, Battle of Jena-Auerstädt: Prussian royal family flee to Königsberg. 27 October, Napoleon enters Berlin. November, Battle of Lübeck. December, French arrive in Warsaw
1807 Prussian royal family move on to Memel. April, the last of Ivan VI's siblings dies in Denmark. June, Battle of Friedland. July, Treaty of Tilsit: Queen Luise pleads with Napoleon: Napoleon creates Duchy of Warsaw.

August, Second Battle of Copenhagen. September, Napoleon declares Danzig a Free City. November, ending of serfdom in Prussia

1808 February, Russians invade Finland, start of the Finnish War. March, Christian VII dies, Frederik VI finally king

1809 13 March, Gustav IV Adolf forced to abdicate: uncle becomes king Karl XIII of Sweden: Russians invade Sweden. March, start of Diet of Porvoo (Swedish: Borgå). June, new Swedish constitution bans women from the succession. July, Finland becomes new Grand Duchy in personal union with Russia. 15 July, Swedish *Riksdag* chooses Christian August of Augustenburg as its crown prince. December, Prussian royal family return to Berlin

1810 May, new crown prince of Sweden's sudden death. June, Fersen lynched during crown prince's funeral in Stockholm. July, Queen Luise of Prussia dies suddenly. August, Jean Bernadotte chosen as next crown prince

1812 Swedish alliance with tsar against Napoleon. September, Battle of Borodino: Fire in Moscow. October, start of Napoleon's retreat from Moscow. Helsinki becomes the Finnish capital

1813 March, Friedrich Wilhelm III joins Sixth Coalition against Napoleon: French leave Berlin October, Battle of Leipzig: Confederation of the Rhine disbanded

1814 January, Treaty of Kiel: Denmark cedes Norway to Sweden. 18 May, Assembly at Eidsvoll introduces new Norwegian constitution: Christian Frederik declared Norwegian king. 30 May, Napoleon begins exile on Elba. July, Swedes invade Norway: August, King Christian abdicates

1815 February, Napoleon escapes from Elba. June, Napoleon finally defeated at Waterloo: October, Napoleon sent to St Helena. Sweden cedes Stralsund to Prussia

1817 Future Nicholas I visits England

1818 Karl XIII dies: Jean Bernadotte becomes new Swedish king

1821 Napoleon dies on St Helena

1825 1 December (NS), Tsar Alexander dies in Taganrog: Grand Duke Constantine refuses to accept throne. 25 December (NS), Nicholas I becomes tsar: next day Decembrist Revolt in St Petersburg

1827 Fire in Turku, government buildings move to Helsinki

1830 November Uprising in Warsaw, start of Russian-Polish war

1834 Victory column raised in Palace Square, St Petersburg: opening of the Narva Gate, St Petersburg

1835 Enlargement of the Russian Pale

1837 7 February, Gustav IV Adolf dies in Switzerland. 10 February, Pushkin dies after a duel. June, Victoria becomes British queen: Ernst August, Duke of Cumberland, becomes King of Hanover. December, Winter Palace suffers major fire

1839 Future tsar Alexander II visits England. December, Frederik VI of Denmark dies, succeeded by his cousin Christian VIII

1844 Nicholas I visits England

1848 Year of Revolutions. January, death of Christian VIII: Frederik VII succeeds. March, First Schleswig War breaks out. June Constitution in Denmark marked ending of royal absolutism

1849 Dostoyevesky undergoes false execution. End of absolutism of Danish monarchy

1852 End of First Schleswig War: London Protocol

1853 Start of Crimean War
1854 British attack Finnish coastal towns. November, Russian defeat at Battle of Inkerman
1855 March (NS) Nicholas I dies: Alexander II succeeds. August, British-French fleet destroy Bomarsund fortress on the Åland islands, and bombard Sveaborg (Suomenlinna). September, fall of Sebastopol
1856 February, end of Crimean War
1857 Ending of the Sound Dues
1859 After a difficult labour, Crown Princess 'Vicky' gives birth to Wilhelm II
1860 Maryinsky Theatre opens in St Petersburg
1861 January, Friedrich Wilhelm IV of Prussia dies, and is succeeded by his brother Wilhelm I. March (NS), end of serfdom in Russia. Alexander II buys the Livadia estate in the Crimea. December, death of Prince Consort in England
1862 May, fires break out in St Petersburg. September, Otto von Bismarck becomes the Prussian prime minister
1863 January, manifesto issued by Polish rebels opposed to Russian rule. 10 March, Alexandra (daughter of Christian IX) marries Prince of Wales. 30 March, Vilhelm (son of Christian IX) elected King George of the Hellenes. September, Tsar Alexander II opens parliament in Finland. November, Frederik VII, last of Oldenburgs dies, Christian IX becomes king: start of Glücksburg dynasty
1864 February, Second Schleswig War: Denmark loses its duchies. June, Russian heir, 'Nixa', meets Christian IX's daughter, Dagmar, in preparation for their engagement. August, Polish 'January Rising' ends with execution of rebels: Alexander II removes last of Poland's autonomy. Alexander II first attracted to the sixteen-year-old Catherine Dolgorukova
1865 Nixa dies in Nice
1866 April, first assassination attempt on Alexander II. July, Alexander begins a passionate love affair with Catherine Dolgorukova. November (NS) Dagmar marries Grand Duke Alexander, the Russian heir
1867 March, Russia sells Alaska to the USA. June, second assassination attempt on the tsar in Paris. Famine in Finland
1870 July, start of Franco-Prussian War. September, surrender and capture of Emperor Napoleon III, fall of Second Empire in France
1871 January, King of Prussia becomes German Emperor Wilhelm I at Versailles. March, Napoleon III takes up exile in England
1872 Three Emperors' Meeting in Berlin
1877 Russia declares war on the sultan
1878 Treaties of San Stefano (March OS) and Berlin (July)
1879 Attempt to blow up tsar's train
1880s Finnish becomes Finland's official language
1880 Bomb explodes in the Winter Palace: tsar marries his mistress, Catherine Dolgorukova
1881 March, Alexander II prepares a more liberal manifesto with Loris Melikov: assassination of Tsar Alexander II. September, Alexander III meets Kaiser Wilhelm I at Danzig
1884 Meeting of emperors in Poland
1885 Fabergé makes the first of his Easter eggs
1887 Lenin's brother, Alexander Ulyanov executed for involvement in plot against the tsar

1888 March, Kaiser Wilhelm I dies. June, Kaiser Friedrich III dies: Kaiser Wilhelm II succeeds. October, Alexander III and his family survive a train crash at Borki

1891 11 May (NS) Grand Duke Nicholas (II) survives assassination in Japan; 31 May, Nicholas lays foundations of the Trans-Siberian Railway. July, French fleet greeted at Kronstadt

1894 Death of Alexander III. Nicholas II succeeds, marries Alexandra of Hesse in St Petersburg

1895 Opening of Kiel Canal

1896 May, coronation of Nicholas II in Moscow: disaster at Khodynka Field. October, Nicholas II and his wife visit Paris: he lays foundations of the Pont Alexandre III

1899 Nicholas II issues February manifesto in Finland, beginning a process of tightening Russian control and thus inspiring Sibelius to write his *Finlandia*

1903 Sweden officially gives up claims to Wismar

1904 February, start of Russo-Japanese war. August (NS), birth of the *tsesarevich*

1905 January, Bloody Sunday in St Petersburg: revolution in Russia: mutiny on the *Potemkin*. February, Grand Duke Sergei killed by a bomb in Moscow: Empress Alexandra first meets Rasputin. Violence breaks out in Baltic states. October, Norway gains full independence

1906 State opening of Russian Duma

1907 First European parliament elected by universal suffrage in Finland. Church of our Saviour on the Spilled Blood completed. Maria Feodorovna buys Hvidore with her sister Alexandra

1909 Last visit by Nicholas and his family to England

1912 May, Frederick VIII of Denmark dies suddenly. October, Alexis nearly dies at Spala: recovers after arrival of Rasputin's telegram

1913 March, King George of Hellenes assassinated. 300th anniversary of Romanov dynasty

1914 June, assassination of the Archduke Ferdinand and his wife in Sarajevo July, World War I begins. St Petersburg renamed Petrograd

1915 Nicholas takes over supreme command of his army

1916 October, Maria Feodorovna moves to Kiev, where she is visited by Nicholas and his son. December, Rasputin murdered

1917 March (NS), revolution breaks out in Russia; tsar abdicates: brother Michael abdicates. March, Nicholas' last meeting with his mother: Maria Feodorovna moves to Crimea. Nicholas and family under house arrest at Tsarskoe Selo. April, Lenin returns to Russia: second revolution in October. August, Nicholas and his family moved to Tobolsk. December, Finland declares its independence

1918 January, start of civil war in Finland. February, Lithuania and Estonia declare independence. 25 February, Germans enter Tallinn. March, Treaty of Brest-Litovsk. April, tsar moved to Ekaterinburg. July, tsar and his family murdered. October, establishment of Finnish monarchy. November, Kaiser Wilhelm II abdicates: Armistice signed; Latvians declare independence, Livonian region given self determination. 28 November, start of Estonian War of Independence. 1 December, Iceland becomes a monarchy in personal union with Denmark, and Soviet Russia invades Latvia. 14 December, Friedrich Karl rejects the Finnish crown

1919 February, war begins between Poland and Russia. April, George V sends ship to rescue Maria Feodorovna from Yalta. June, signing of the Treaty of Versailles

1920 2 February, end of Estonian War of Independence, Soviets acknowledge country's autonomy. February, the last of the Romanovs leave Russia. June, Denmark regains Southern Jutland. August, Russia gives up Latgale, and Latvia gains full independence: peace in Lithuania

1921 Poland and Russia make peace

1922 End of the Russian civil war

1924 Grand Duke Kirill declares himself the new tsar

1928 Maria Feodorovna dies

1939 August, the Molotov-Ribbentrop Pact agreed between Russia and Germany. September, Gdańsk attacked by Germans, Second World War begins. November, Finland's Winter War begins with Soviet invasion of Finland

1940 March, Finland signs peace with Soviets. April, German invasion of Denmark. June, Baltic states come under Soviet control

1941 4 June, death of Kaiser Wilhelm II. June, Hitler invades Russia, and Finland becomes involved in its Continuation War against the Soviets. September, start of Siege of Leningrad: beginning of three years of German occupation of Baltic states

1943 April, Hitler orders the wiping out of the Warsaw ghetto, leading to month-long Ghetto Uprising. August, Hitler tightens his grip on Denmark: Jews escape to Sweden

1944 June, Iceland becomes a republic. August, start of two-month Warsaw Uprising against the Germans who later destroy city before their withdrawal. September, Finland signs armistice with allies and withdraws from the fighting

1945 Baltic states become part of USSR: Polish borders are moved

1948 Finland makes peace with Soviet Union

1955 Poland joins the Warsaw Pact

1970 Demonstrations in Gdańsk end in bloodshed

1978 John Paul II becomes pope

1980 New demonstrations at Gdańsk

1989 Fall of the Berlin wall: end of Poland's Socialist People's Republic

1991 July, final dissolution of the Warsaw Pact. August, re-burial of Frederick II at Sans Souci. September, the independence of the Baltic states recognised by the Soviet Union. December, the collapse of the USSR

Notes

1. Lüneburg's important salt works would only finally close down in 1980.
2. This letter with its royal seal has today returned to Lübeck from Russia, where it had been taken with other archives by the Soviets at the end of the Second World War.
   Translation by Dr Alan Borthwick, National Records of Scotland, 2012.
3. The Sound Dues were only finally abolished in 1857.
4. Lübeck, Hamburg and Bremen continued to own the site long after the Hansa had disappeared. They eventually sold it in 1853, and their last building was finally demolished and replaced by Cannon Street station in 2005.
5. 'Turks' was a pejorative term used by Christian countries when referring to the Ottomans or Muslims.
6. Quoted from Julia Cartwright, Christina of Denmark – Duchess of Milan and Lorraine, p.318.
7. While Denmark was the first kingdom to convert to Lutheranism, the Duchy of Prussia had done so ten years earlier.
8. Paul Douglas Lockhart, Frederik II and the Protestant Cause, p.185.
9. Sophie Amalie was the aunt of the future British king George I.
10. Although not officially recognised as the capital until the early seventeenth century, Stockholm had by then been regarded as such for around 200 years. But even during Gustav Vasa's time, when the king was frequently on the move, there was no fixed court.
11. Jadwiga would go on to marry Joachim II Hector, Elector of Brandenburg, great-grandfather of Johann Sigismund, whose marriage united his electorate with the Duchy of Prussia.
12. With so many Queen Catherines in this period, here I have distinguished between them by keeping to the name they had before marriage.
13. Joseph Gonzalez points out that despite the lack of evidence, the message of the enduring 'body politique' is apparent in this display. Kabtorowicz explains this doctrine in more detail.
14. Walter Harte, The History of the Life of Gustavus Adolphus, King of Sweden vol. I, p.99.
15. Henrik Lunde, A Warrior Dynasty, p. 88.
16. The king and queen's daughter had from birth been destined to become a nun.
17. 'Il n'y a point ailleurs de noblesse plus magnifique, ni de pires citoyens.' Jacques-Henri-Bernadin de Saint-Pierre, Voyage en Pologne, p.15.
18. In the Truce of Altmark (1629) that ended Gustavus Adolphus' Polish War, the Swedes had gained control of certain Baltic ports, including Memel in Ducal Prussia and Elbing in Royal Prussia. In addition, they had received further

rights to a large share of the trading dues at Danzig. The Truce of Stuhmsdorf (1635) reversed all these concessions.

19. Anders Fryxell and Otto Sjögren Berättelser ur svenska historie, vol.19, [quoted from Wikipedia 'Ulrika Eleonora of Denmark'].
20. Until the twentieth century, in the West, Istanbul was usually referred to by its old name, Constantinople.
21. The numbering of tsars came in later.
22. J. N. Duggan, Sophia of Hanover: From Winter Princess to Heiress of Great Britain, 1630-1714, p.153-54.
23. Eugeni V. Ansisimov, Five Empresses, p.9. (I am particularly grateful to this author for much of this information on Martha's early life.)
24. R. Nisbet Bain, Charles XII and the Collapse of the Swedish Empire, p.74.
25. Later pontoon bridges would be put in place during the summer months, but even today parts of the city are cut off from each other throughout most of the night, when the bridges are left open to allow for the free movement of rivercraft.
26. Evgenii V. Anisimov, The Reforms of Peter the Great: Progress through violence in Russia, p.3.
27. Other claimants included Anna's younger sister later (Empress Elizabeth), Anna's son (later Peter III), Peter the Great's two nieces (Catherine and the later Empress Anna), and even Peter the Great's first wife.
28. Evgenii V. Anisimov, Five Empresses: Court Life in Eighteenth-Century Russia, p.182.
29. See Cecilia Nordenkull, Karl XII: Kungamord, pp.23-25.
30. R. Nisbet Bain, Charles XII, p.47.
31. Some of these events appear in the opera *Adriana Lecouvreur* by Francesco Cilea.
32. Boris Antonov, Russian Tsars, p.106.
33. Evgenii V. Anisimov, Five Empresses, p.219.
34. religiondocbox.com German History in Documents and Images (GHDI), From Absolutism to Napoleon, 1648-1815, vol.2, 'Edict of Potsdam', p.2.
35. Williams, Ernest Neville, The Ancien Régime in Europe: Government and Society in the Major States, 1648-1789, p.305.
36. Nancy Mitford, Frederick the Great, p.44.
37. Giles Macdonogh, Frederick the Great, p.89.
38. Thomas Carlyle, History of Friedrich II. of Prussia Called Frederick the Great, vol.3, p.130.
39. Nancy Mitford, Frederick the Great, p.68.
40. Giles Macdonogh, Frederick the Great, p.131.
41. Adam Zamoyski, Last King of Poland, p.30.
42. Nancy Mitford, Frederick the Great, p.167.
43. Voltaire, Memoirs of the Life of Voltaire, p.49.
44. David Fraser, Frederick the Great, p.192.
45. La Métrie had reported that the king had said, 'J'aurai besoin de lui (Voltaire) un an au plus; on presse l'orange et on jette l'écorce.' Voltaire to Madame Denis, 2 Sept 1751, D4564, XII, vol.96 (1971).
46. 'C'est l'affaire d'un fripon qui veut tromper un filou.' Frederick to Wilhelmine, 22 January 1751, D4358, XII, vol.96 (1971).
47. David Fraser, Frederick the Great, p.427.
48. Mark Cruse & Hilde Hoogenboom (translators), The Memoirs of Catherine the Great, p.214.
49. David Fraser, Frederick the Great, p.457.
50. David Fraser, Frederick the Great, p.479.
51. David Fraser, Frederick the Great, p.487.
52. Hajo Holborn, A History of Modern Germany, 1648-1840, p.218.
53. David Fraser, Frederick the Great, p.507.
54. Nancy Mitford, Frederick the Great, p.288.
55. Nancy Mitford, Frederick the Great, p.291.
56. Giles Macdonogh, Frederick the Great, p.30.

57. Giles Macdonogh, Frederick the Great, p.384.
58. Trans. by Mark Cruse and Hilde Hoogenboom, Memoirs of Catherine the Great, p.50.
59. Trans. by Mark Cruse and Hilde Hoogenboom, Memoirs of Catherine the Great, p.32.
60. Adam Zamoyski, The last King of Poland, p.54.
61. Simon Sebag Montefiore, Potemkin: Prince of Princes, p.40.
62. Miroslav Marek claims that Catherine had an earlier daughter by Orlov, Elizabeth Alexandrovna, born 1761, who later married Friedrich Maximilian von Klinger in 1790, and died in 1844.
63. 'The Letter of Catherine to Poniatowski', Appendix, in Mémoires of the Empress Catherine II: Written by Herself, preface by A. Hérzen, Kindle ebook loc.3706.
64. Giles Macdonogh, Frederick the Great, p.312.
65. 'The Letter of Catherine to Poniatowski', Appendix, in Mémoires of the Empress Catherine II: Written by Herself, preface by A. Hérzen, Kindle ebook loc.3706.
66. Elizabeth I did the same thing at the time of the Armada; in her speech at Tilbury before the battle she said, 'I know I have the body of a weak, feeble woman, but I have the heart and stomach of a king', and after the victory had herself represented as Gloriana, the triumphant ageless queen, whom God has chosen to save the nation.
67. Karen Bush Gibson, The Life and Times of Catherine the Great, p.22.
68. 'The Letter of Catherine to Poniatowsky', Appendix, in Memoirs of the Empress Catherine II: Written by Herself, preface by A. Hérzen, Kindle ebook, loc 3763.
69. William Monter, The Rise of Female Kings in Europe, 1300-1800, p.198.
70. 'on sait combien cette maladie est dangereuse en Russie'. Frederick the Great, Testament politique, in Full text of 'Die politicschen Testamente', p.221.
71. Maria Theresa of Austria would similarly seek to authorise her role within the male-dominated society by describing herself as 'the general and chief mother' of her country. See Justin C. Vovk, In Destiny's Hands: Five Tragic Rulers, Children of Maria Theresa, p.14.
72. Eugenii V. Anisimov, Five Empresses: Court Life in Eighteenth Century Russia, p.290.
73. Eugenii V. Anisimov, Five Empresses: Court Life in Eighteenth Century Russia, p.291.
74. Catherine would always seek to separate her personal interests from those of the state. After the Pugachev rebellion, she told Voltaire that, had the pretender acted against her alone, there could have been reason for her to pardon him, but, as his actions had been against the empire, she had had to respect its laws: 's'il n'avoit offensé que moi son raisonement pourroit être juste et je lui pardoneroit, mais cette cause est celle de l'Empire qui a ses Loix.' D19188, XLI, vol.125 (1774)
75. 'Me voilà en Asie ... Il y a dans cette Ville vingt peuple divers qui ne ce ressemblent point du tout, il faut pourtant leurs faire un habit qui leurs soit propre à tous.' D14219, XXXII, vol. 116 (1767).
76. Praising Dimsdale to Voltaire, Catherine reports that the doctor has lost just one three-year-old among the 6,000 people he has inoculated, and even that child had not shown any symtoms of smallpox. D15396, XXXIV, vol.118, (1768).
77. Catherine proudly describes her rostral column in her letter to Voltaire. D17340, XXXVIII, vol.122 (1771).
78. 'In truth, this famous eighteenth century has a lot to boast about, how very wise we have become.' 'En vérité ce fameux xviii siècle a bien là de quoi ce glorifier, nous voilà devenu bien sages.' D17407, XXXVIII vol.122 (1771).
79. Simon Sebag Montefiori, Potemkin: Prince of Princes, p.112.
80. The truth of what remained to be done was obvious to certain members of the party, although some evidence of this was intentionally hidden from Catherine herself. While it was clear to the Prince de Ligne that much work was needed on building streets and finishing houses, the empress was shown only those things that had been fully completed. Prince de Ligne, Lettres et Pensées,

Lettre VIII, De Toula, à madame la marquise de C. pendant l'année 1787, paragraph 86.

81. Robert K. Massie, Catherine the Great, p.516.
82. Robert K. Massie, Catherine the Great, p.306.
83. Memoirs of Madame Vigée le Brun, trans. Lionel Strachey, Chapter IX, pp.109-119.
84. 'Ce sont des gens faux et intéressés, pire encore que les Anglais.' Liselotte to Sophie of Hanover, 14 November 1697, in Correspondence de Madame, Duchesse d'Orléans, gallica.bnf.fr
85. Tony Sharp, Pleasure and Ambition, The Life, Loves and Wars of Augustus the Strong, p.77.
86. The Memoires of Charles Lewis Baron de Pollnitz, vol. I, Letter V, 1729, paragraph 97.
87. Tony Sharp, Pleasure and Ambition, The Life, Loves and Wars of Augustus the Strong, p.85.
88. Tony Sharp, Pleasure and Ambition, The Life, Loves and Wars of Augustus the Strong, p.293.
89. Adam Zamoyski, Poland: A History, p.180.
90. After her husband's death she stayed for the remaining two and a half years of her life in Saxony, while her orphaned daughter of her first marriage, Caroline, would later move to the care of Sophie Charlotte in Berlin, before marrying the later George II, and eventually becoming Queen of England.
91. The Memoires of Charles Lewis Baron de Pöllnitz, vol.1, Letter V, 1729, para. 97.
92. The London Magazine, or, Gentleman's Monthly Intelligencer, vol.2, 1733, February, p.100.
93. Earl of Ilchester, and Mrs Langford-Brooke, The Life of Sir Charles Hanbury Williams, p.149.
94. 'Je ne sens que trop les épines avec lesquelles ma couronne est semées. Je l'aurais déjà envoyée à les cinquante mille diables si je n'avais pas honte d'abandonner mon poste.' James Harris, 1st Earl of Malmesbury, Diaries and Correspondence, vol. I, p.20.
95. James Breck Perkins, 'The Partition of Poland', p.92.
96. Adam Zamoyski, The Last King of Poland, pp.198-199.
97. Julia Gelardi, In Triumph's Wake, p.194.
98. 'Ce dernier coup, je l'avoue, m'a percé le coeur parce qu'il attaque ma dignité et surtout parce qu'il me vient directement d'elle envers qui pourtant mon coeur n'eut jamais de torts.' Mémoires du roi Stanislas-Auguste Poniatowski, vol.2, p.242.
99. 'Le diner fut très-gai.' Prince de Ligne, Lettres et Pensées, Lettre III, de Cherson, à madame la marquise de C. pendant l'année 1787, p.44, paragraph 45.
100. Stanislaw to Kicinski II VI, 87, Bibliothèque Polonaise Paris, 38, p.209, quoted from Adam Zamoyski, The Last King of Poland, p.299.
101. Stanislaw to Badeni 7, V, 87, Korespondencja Krajowa, p.210, quoted from Adam Zamoyski, The Last King of Poland, p.299.
102. 'Né avec une vaste et ardente ambition, les idées de réformation, de gloire et d'utilité pour ma patrie sont devenues comme le canevas de toutes mes affaires et de toute ma vie.' Mémoires Secrets et Inédits de Stanislas-Auguste, p.2.
103. Stella Tillyard, A Royal Affair, p.86.
104. 'rien n'est assuré tant que le roi n'est pas assis dans sa voiture'. A. Friis, Bernstorffske Papirer (Les Papiers de Bernstorff) (Copenhagen, Gldendal, 1904), p.400, quoted from Ulrik Langen, 'Le roi et les philosophes: le séjour parisien de Christian VII de Danemark en 1768', note 9.
105. 'Le roi de Danemarck, que nous avons eu ici pendant six semaines, en est parti, il y a huit jours, excédé, ennuyé, harassé de fêtes dont on l'a écrasé, de soupers où il n'a ni mangé, ni causé, et les bals où il a dansé en bâillant à se tordre la bouche. Je ne doute point qu'à son arrivée à Copenhague il ne rende un édit pour défendre les soupers et les bals à perpétuité.' Jean le Rond d'Alembert, Œuvres completes IV (Slatkine, Geneva, 1967), p.281, quoted from Ulrik Langen, 'Le roi et les philosophes: le séjour parisien de Christian VII de Danemark en 1768', note 53.

106. Brandt had rejoined the king's circle after Struensee had become the favourite.
107. Balthasar Münter, A faithful narrative of the conversion and death of Count Struensee, p.305.
108. Johan Schioldann, 'Struensée's memoir on the situation of the King', page 247.
109. Sophie Dorothea had also been separated from her children, the later George II and his sister, Frederick II of Prussia's mother. The divorcée was then kept under house arrest for thirty years as punishment for her affair with Christoph of Königsmarck, the brother of Aurora, the former mistress of Augustus II of Poland. At the time of her arrest, Königsmarck disappeared, probably murdered on the orders of his brother-in-law, George I.
110. In the same period, there would be a second occupation of the Danish West Indies by the British, who had briefly occupied them in 1801-02.
111. The northern part of the region had been ceded to Denmark at the end of the Great Northern War in 1720, and the remaining area just over fifty years later by Catherine the Great and her son Paul – the titular Duke of Holstein-Gottorp – in exchange for the County of Oldenburg.
112. Marc Serge Rivière, '"Divine Ulrique": Voltaire and Louisa Ulrica, Princess of Prussia and Queen of Sweden (1751-1771)', p.50.
113. Virginia Rounding, Catherine the Great, p.935.
114. Today the assassin's weapons are displayed alongside the king's masquerade dress in the Royal Armoury beneath the Royal Palace.
115. The new Swedish crown prince, Christian August of Augustenburg, was the brother-in-law of Louise Auguste, *la petite Struensee*.
116. Michael Jenkins, Arakcheev: Grand-Vizier of the Russian Empire, p.40.
117. In a further twist, sixty-five years later Ludwig of Hesse-Darmstadt's own granddaughter would marry Alexander II.
118. Edmund Fitzmaurice, Charles Wilhelm Ferdinand, Duke of Brunswick: An Historical Study, 1735-1806, (Longmans, London, 1901), p.17, quoted from Henry L. Fulton, Dr. John Moore, 1729-1802: A Life in Medicine, Travel, and Revolution, p.306.
119. N. K. Shilder, Imperator Aleksandr I, ego zhizn' i Trsarstvovanie, II, 4 vols (St Petersburg, 1897), pp.312-3, quoted from Alan Palmer, Alexander I: Tsar of War and Peace, p.41.
120. Today called Auerstedt, in old texts the village is referred to as Auerstädt.
121. V. N. Lamsdorf, Dnevnik, 1894-1896 (Moscow, 1991), p.126, quoted from Tatiana Alexsandrovna Kapustina, 'Nicolas I', in Donald J. Raleigh (ed.) and A. A. Iskenderov (compiler), The Emperors and Empresses of Russia, p.258.
122. 'Pis'mo Nikolaia I k Konstantinu Pavlovichu', 14-16 December, 1925, in Schiemann, Die Ermordung Pauls und die Thronbesteigung Nikolaus I, p.103, quoted from W. Bruce Lincoln, Nicholas I: Emperor and Autocrat of All the Russias, p.47.
123. Although Joseph II had taken the first measures to end serfdom in 1781, a more limited form of forced servitude had continued.
124. Queen Victoria repeated how he had said how uncomfortable he was in tails, declaring that he was 'so "gauche" en frac'. Victoria to Leopold in The Letters of Queen Victoria, vol.2, ed. Bensen and Esher, loc. 364.
125. Hares were commonly seen as portents of bad luck, and when a similar incident occurred the day before Napoleon crossed the Niemen to start his invasion of Russia, some held it to be a bad omen. See Andrew Morton, Napoleon the Great, p.577.
126. Victoria to Leopold in The Letters of Queen Victoria, vol.2, ed. Bensen and Esher, loc. 351.
127. 'Imperatritsa Aleksandra Fedorovna v svoikh vospominaniiakh', p.25, quoted from W. Bruce Lincoln, Nicholas I: Emperor and Autocrat of All the Russias, p.68.
128. After the earlier battle the first Victoria Cross was awarded.
129. Queen Victoria's Journals, Monday 27 May 1839, p.268.
130. To care for the wounded Muslims, the Red Crescent was founded as an offshoot of the Red Cross organisation earlier set up at the Geneva Convention of 1864.

131. Queen Victoria's Journals, Sunday 13 March, 1881, p.112.
132. Novoe rustkoe solo, 25 December 1976, quoted from The Emperors and Empresses of Russia: Rediscovering the Romanovs, ed Donald J. Raleigh, p.329.
133. Julia P. Gelardi, From Splendor to Revolution: The Romanov Women, 1847-1928, p.100. [original emphasis]
134. Christopher Clark, Iron Kingdom, p.267.
135. Ian Hunter, 'Kant and the Prussian Religious Edict: Metaphysics with the Bounds of Political Reason'.
136. Tim Blanning, Frederick the Great: King of Prussia, p.307.
137. In his will Napoleon admitted to having kept the king's alarm clock, which he had 'removed from Potsdam'. See Andrew Roberts, Napoleon the Great, p.799.
138. Napoleon to Tsar Alexander, July 1808, quoted from Andrew Roberts, Napoleon the Great, p.527.
139. There are various copies of the work, among them the original gypsum version now in the Friedrichswerder Church, Berlin. That in the Old National Gallery is the second marble copy.
140. Edward Radzinsky, Alexander II, p.190.
141. Roger Fulford (ed.), Dearest Mama, pp.241-242.
142. As Christopher Clark has pointed out, Kaiser Wilhelm II's attitude towards the Jews was complex, and so alongside his various vile antisemitic comments there was his surprising reaction to a pogrom in November 1938. On that occasion he said, 'For the first time I am ashamed to be a German', and then added that 'all decent Germans' should speak out against the Nazis. See Christopher Clark, Kaiser Wilhelm II: Life in Power, p.355.
143. Hans Christian Andersen, The Story of My Life, p.542.
144. Frederik's patronage may have helped feed the unfounded rumour that Andersen was the illegitimate son of the king's father, Christian VIII.
145. Lytton Stracey, Queen Victoria, p.32.
146. May 15/27, 1865: Julia P. Gelardi, From Splendor to Revolution: The Romanov Women, 1847-1928, p.26.
147. To Vicky, Crown Princess of Prussia, 25 March, 1863, Roger Fulford (ed.), Dearest Mama, p.186.
148. Queen Victoria's journal, 21 June 1873.
149. Julia P. Gelardi, From Splendor to Revolution: The Romanov Women, 1847-1928, p.98. [original emphasis]
150. 10 September 1881, page 9, archive.spectator.co.uk
151. 30-Sep-1881, page 392, fold3.com
152. John van der Kiste, The Romanovs 1818-1959, p.150.
153. Maria would be given more eggs by her son who took up the custom, presenting them to both his mother and wife each Easter until 1916.
154. The future Kaiser Wilhelm II had been among the various people wanting to marry Ella.
155. 21 October 1894, in Hough Advice to My Grand-daughter, p.126, quoted from Julia P. Gelardi, From Splendor to Revolution, p.143.
156. Kathleen Marie Conti, 'Decay on Display: the funeral train journeys of Abraham Lincoln and Tsar Alexander III', p.29.
157. Charles Lowe, Alexander III of Russia, p.289. Interestingly, a similar extolling of Alexander's achievements appeared at two unveilings of statues of him in 2017: at Simferopol in August, the director of the Orthodox publishing house Rodnoye Slovo described him as 'one of the most brilliant and worthy representatives of the Romanov family'; and three months later outside Yalta at the site of Alexander's Small Maily Palace – destroyed in the war by the Nazis – President Putin declared that he had given 'Russia thirteen years of peace by not yielding but by a fair and unwavering firmness'. Alexander III, Royal Russia News, angelfire.com
158. Charles Lowe, Alexander III of Russia, p.66.
159. Julia P. Gelardi, From Splendor to Revolution: The Romanov Women, 1847-1928, p.145.

160. Heinrich was the grandson of Vicky, oldest daughter of Queen Victoria, and therefore a nephew of Kaiser Wilhelm II.
161. Julia P. Gelardi, From Splendor to Revolution: The Romanov Women, 1847-1928, p.204.
162. Julia P. Gelardi, From Splendor to Revolution, The Romanov Women, 1847-1928, p.191.
163. Julia P. Gelardi, From Splendor to Revolution: The Romanov Women, 1847-1928, p.190.
164. Julia P. Gelardi, From Splendor to Revolution: The Romanov Women, 1847-1928, p.295.
165. Julia P. Gelardi, From Splendor to Revolution: The Romanov Women, 1847-1928, p.309.
166. Some question this as Rasputin had claimed that if he should die at the hands of the tsar's relations, the dynasty would fall.
167. The Emperors and Empresses of Russia: Rediscovering the Romanovs, ed. by Donald J. Raleigh, compiled by A. A. Iskenderov, p.396.
168. Edmund Walsh, The Last Days of the Romanovs, from The Atlantic, March 1928, theatlantic.com
169. Ella's body, discovered by the White Army, eventually found its way to Jerusalem. Canonised by the Orthodox church, and officially rehabilitated by the Russian state in 2009, Ella is included among the twentieth-century martyrs depicted above Westminster Abbey's Great West Door.
170. Edmund Walsh, The Last Days of the Romanovs, from The Atlantic, March 1928, theatlantic.com
171. Julia P. Gelardi, From Splendor to Revolution: The Romanov Women, 1847-1928, p.352.
172. Justin C. Vovk, Imperial Requiem: Four Royal Women and the Fall of the Age of Empires, chapter 27, loc 10701, note 1280.
173. Greg King and Penny Wilson, The Fate of the Romanovs, p.212.
174. John Curtis Perry and Constantine Pleshakov, The Flight of the Romanovs: A Family Saga, chapter 9, loc.199.
175. Miranda Carter, The Three Emperors: Three Cousins, Three Empires and the Road to World War One, p.202.
176. Greg King and Penny Wilson, The Fate of the Romanovs, p.214.
177. W. Bruce Lincoln, Nicholas I: Emperor and Autocrat of All the Russias, p.140, p.141.
178. Christopher Clark, Kaiser Wilhelm II: A Life in Power, p.174.
179. Julia P. Gelardi, From Splendor to Revolution: The Romanov Women, 1847-1928, p.273.
180. This was first named in honour of his grandfather, but after 1918 renamed the Nord-Ostsee-Kanal (North Sea-Baltic Canal). However, English speakers know it better as the Kiel Canal.
181. Julia P. Gelardi, From Splendor to Revolution: The Romanov Women, 1847-1928, p.355. The party included Miechen's daughter-in-law, the former ballet dancer Mathilde Kschessinska, who had earlier been Nicholas II's mistress. That same month Nicholas II's sister, Olga, who had been sheltering for a time with the Danish Consul, also left Novorossisk with her husband and two sons.
182. Further identification was carried out by studying the shape of the skulls, comparing them with the photograph of the imperial children taken after they had had their heads shaved when recovering from measles.
183. Prince Philip was not just related through his father, first cousin of Nicholas II, but also through his mother, niece of 'Alix', Empress Alexandra Feodorovna.

Bibliography

Abbott, John, *A Short History of Prussia* (Didactic, 2013)

Ailes, Mary Elizabeth, *Courage and Grief: Women and Sweden's Thirty Years' War* (University of Nebraska, 2018)

Andersen, Hans Christian, *The Story of My Life* (New York: Hurd and Houghton, 1871)

Anderson, Perry, *Lineages of the Absolute State* (Verso, London, 1974)

Anisimov, Eugenii V., *Five Empresses: Court Life in Eighteenth Century Russia* (Praeger, Connecticut, 2004)

Anisimov, Eugenii, *The Reforms of Peter the Great: Progress through coercion in Russia* (M. E. Sharpe, New York, 1993)

Antonov, Boris, *Russian Tsars* (Ivan Fedorov, Russia, 2010)

Aronson, Theo, *A Family of Kings: The Descendants of Christian IX of Denmark* (Thistle, 3 December 2014)

Aselius, Gunnar, *Birth of the Russian Empire: Tenacious Retreat of Sweden as a Great Power*, 3 October 2011, balticworlds.com

ed. Trevor Aston, *Crisis in Europe 1560-1660* (Routledge Revivals, 2011)

Bain, R. Nisbet, *Gustavus III and His Contemporaries, 1746-1792*, vol.1, first published 1894 (Elibron, London 2005)

Bain, R. Nisbet, *Gustavus III and His Contemporaries, 1746-1792*, vol.2, first published 1894 (Elibron, London 2005)

Bain, R. Nisbet, *Gustavus III and His Contemporaries, 1746-1792*, vol.3, first published 1894 (Elibron, London 2005)

Bain, R. Nisbet, *Scandinavia: A Political History of Denmark, Norway and Sweden, 1513-1900*, first published 1905 (Cambridge University, UK, 1905)

Bain, R. Nisbet, *Charles XII and the Collapse of the Swedish Empire*, first published 1895 (Waxkeep, 21 June 2015)

Bak, János, 'The Late Medieval Period, 1382-1526' in *A History of Hungary*, ed. Peter F. Sugár (Indiana University, 1990)

Barnes, Hugh, *Gannibal: The Moor of Petersburg* (Profile Books, Great Britain, 2005)

Beerbühl, Margrit Schulte, *Networks of the Hanseatic League*, Original in German, in European History Online, published 2012-01-13, ieg-ego.eu

ed. Bensen and Esher, *The Letters of Queen Victoria*, II, first published 1908 (Kindle edition, Public domain, Amazon Media)

Berdichevsky, Norman, *The Abolition of Slavery in the Danish West Indies and the Governor's Mulatto Mistress* (May 2016) newenglishreview.org

Birstein, Dr Vadim, *Smersh: Stalin's Secret Weapon* (UK, Biteback, 2013)

Blanning, Tim, *The Pursuit of Glory: Europe 1648-1815* (Penguin, London, 2008)

Blanning, Tim, *Frederick the Great* (Penguin, London, 2016)

Breck Perkins, James, 'The Partition of Poland', p.92, Early Journal Content on JSTOR, archive.org

Bregnsbo, Michael, 'Danish Absolutism and Queenship: Louisa, Caroline Matilda, Juliana Maria' in *Queenship in Europe 1660-1815: The Role of the Consort*, ed. Clarissa Cambell Orr (Cambridge, UK, 2004)
Browning, Oscar, *Charles XII of Sweden* (Hurst and Blackett, London, 1899)
Buckley, Veronica, *Christina Queen of Sweden* (Harper, London, 2011)
Burckhardt, Jacob, *Italian Renaissance Painting According to Genres* (Getty, 2005)
Bush Gibson, Karen, *The Life and Times of Catherine the Great* (Mitchell Lane, USA, 2005)
ed. Clarissa Campbell Orr, *Queenship in Europe 1660-1815: The Role of the Consort* (Cambridge University, 2004)
Carlyle, Thomas, *History of Friedrich II. of Prussia Called Frederick the Great*, vol.3 (Books on Demand, 2012)
Carsten, F. L., *Essays in German History* (Hambledon, London, 1985)
Carter, F. W., *Trade and Urban Development in Poland: An Economic Geography of Cracow, from its Origins to 1795* (Cambridge University, 20 April 2006)
Carter, Miranda, *The Three Emperors: Three Cousins, Three Empires and the Road to World War One* (Penguin, London, 2009)
Cartwright, Julia, *Christina of Denmark: Duchess of Milan and Lorraine, 1522-1590* (Dutton, New York, 1913)
Cavendish, Richard, *Death of Christian V of Denmark*, Richard, vol. 49 Issue 8 August 1999, historytoday.com
ed Didier Chambaretaud, *Testament Politique de 1752 de Frédéric II de Prusse* (ACATL, 26 Jun. 2013)
Clark, Christopher, *Iron Kingdom: The Rise and Downfall of Prussia 1600-1947* (Penguin, London, 2007)
Clark, Christopher, *Kaiser Wilhelm II: Life in Power* (Penguin, London, 2009)
Conti, Kathleen Marie, 'Decay on Display: the funeral train journeys of Abraham Lincoln and Tsar Alexander III', thesis University of North Carolina (2013) cdr.lib.unc.edu
Coroban, Costel, 'Sweden and the Jacobite Movement (1715-1718)', in *Revista Română pentru Studii Baltice şi Nordice*, Vol. 2, Issue 2, 2010, pp. 131-152, academia.edu
Cracraft, James, *The Church Reform of Peter the Great* (Macmillan, London, 1971)
Crawford, Rosemary and Donald, *Michael and Natasha: The Life and Love of the Last Tsar of Russia* (Weinfeld & Nicolson, London, 1997)
Cronk, Nicholas, *Voltaire: A Very Short Introduction* (Oxford University, Oxford, 2017)
d'Alembert, Jean le Rond Œuv*res completes IV* (Slatkine, Geneva, 1967)
Dehn-Nielsen, Henning, *Kings and Queens of Denmark* (Rosenborg Castle, Copenhagen, 2007)
de Ligne, Prince Charles-Joseph, *Lettres et pensées du maréchal prince de Ligne* (Paschoud, Paris, 1809) fr.wikisource.org
De Madariaga, Isabel, *Catherine the Great: A Short History* (Yale, USA, 2002)
Denicke, H., *Rise Of The Hanseatic League*, trans. Joseph Sohn, history-world.org
de Saint-Pierre, Jacques-Henri-Bernadin, 'Il n'y a point ailleurs de noblesse plus magnifique, ni de pires citoyens', *Voyage en Pologne*, in Œuvres, vol.2 (Ledentu, Paris, 1840) [Google Books online]
Derry, T. K., *A History of Scandinavia: Norway, Sweden, Denmark, and Iceland* (University of Minnesota, USA, 1979)
Dixon, Simon, *Catherine the Great* (Profile, London, 2010)
Dollinger, Philippe, *The German Hansa* 2nd, Revised Edition, trans. by D. S. Ault and S. H. Steinberg (Stanford University, 1971)
Douglas Lockhart, Paul, *Denmark 1513-1660: The Rise and Decline of Renaissance Monarchy* (Oxford University, UK, 2007)
Duggan, J. N., *Sophia of Hanover: From Winter Princess of Great Britain, 1630-1714* (Peter Owen, London and Chicago, 2010)
Earl of Ilchester, and Mrs Langford-Brooke, *The Life of Sir Charles Hanbury Williams* (Thornton Butterworth, London, 1928)
Engel, Caroline, *The Notorious Infidelity of King Frederik VII of Denmark* (May 17, 2011) danishteakclassics.com

Englund, Peter, *The Battle that Shook Europe: Poltava and the Birth of the Russian Empire* (Tauris, London, 2003)

Enquist, Per Olov, *The Visit of the Royal Physician*, trans. by Tiina Nunnally (Maclehose, London, 2016)

Ferguson, Robert, *Scandinavians: In Search of the Soul of the North*, 2nd edition (Head of Zeus, UK, 2016)

Figes, Orlando, *Natasha's Dance: A Cultural History of Russia* (Penguin, London, 2002)

Fitzmaurice, Edmund, *Charles Wilhelm Ferdinand, Duke of Brunswick: An Historical Study, 1735-1806*, (Longmans, London, 1901)

Fraser, Antonia, *Warrior Queens: Boadicea's Chariot* (Phoenix, London, reprinted 2003)

Fraser, David, *Frederick the Great* (Alan Lane, London, 2000)

Frederick the Great, *Testament politique*, in Full text of 'Die politischen Testamente', ed. Dr Gustav Bertholdt Volz (Reimar Hobbin, Berlin, 1920), archive.org

Friis, A, *Bernstorffske Papirer* (*Les Papiers de Bernstorff*) (Copenhagen, Gldendal, 1904)

Frost, Robert I., *After the Deluge: Poland-Lithuania and the Second Northern War, 1655-1660* (Cambridge University, 2004)

ed. Roger Fulford, *Dearest Mama: Letters between Queen Victoria and the Crown Princess of Prussia 1861-1864* (Evans Brothers, London, 1968)

ed. Roger Fulford, *Your Dear Letter: Private Correspondence of Queen Victoria and the Crown Princess of Prussia 1855-1871* (Evans Brothers, London, 1971)

Fulton, Henry L., *Dr. John Moore, 1729-1802: A Life in Medicine, Travel, and Revolution*, by Henry L. Fulton (Rowman, 24 Dec 2014)

Garstein, Arnold, *Rome and the Counter-Reformation in Scandinavia: The Age of Gustavus Adolphus and Queen Christina of Sweden, 1622-1656* (Brill, 1992)

Garstein, Oskar, *Rome and the Counter-Reformation in Scandinavia: the Age of Gustavus Adolphus and Queen Christina of Sweden 1622-1656* (BRILL, 1992)

Geijer, Eric Gustave, *History of the Swedes*, trans. J. H. Turner (Whittaker & Co., London, 1845)

Gelardi, Julia P., *From Splendor to Revolution: The Romanov Women, 1847-1928* (St Martin's, New York, 2011)

Gelardi, Julia P., *In Triumph's Wake* (St. Martin's Griffin, New York, 2008)

Glenthøj, Rasmus, & Ottosen, Morten Nordhagen, *Experiences of War and Nationality in Denmark and Norway, 1807-1815* (Palgrave Macmillan, UK, 2014)

Gonzalez, Joseph M., 'Fashioning Death: Clothing, Memory and Identity in 16th Century Swedish Funerary Practice', in *The Archeology of Death in Post-medieval Europe*, ed. Sarah Tarlow (de Gruyter, Berlin, 2015)

Gonzalez, Joseph, 'Rassembling the king: transforming the tomb of Gustav Vasa, 1560-2014', in *Incomplete Archaeologies: Assembling Knowledge in the Past and Present*, eds Emily Miller-Bonney, Kathryn Franklin, James Johnson (Oxbow, USA, 31 March 2016)

Green, Vivian, *The Madness of Kings: Personal Trauma and the Fate of Nations* (Alan Sutton, UK, 1993)

Grey, Ian, *Boris Godunov: The Tragic Tsar* (Hodder and Stoughton, London, Sydney, Auckland, Toronto, 1973)

Grey, Ian, *Catherine the Great* (New World City, USA, 2016)

Hagen, Lorentz, and Patkul, Johann Reinhold, *Anecdotes Concerning the Famous John Reinhold Patkul: Or, and Authentic Relation of what Passed Betwixt Him and His Confessor, the Night Before and at His Execution, Translated from the Original Manuscript, Never Yet Printed*, 1761 (digitilised Oxford University, 6 April 2009)

Harris, James, 1st Earl of Malmesbury, *Diaries and Correspondence*, vol.1 (Bentley, London 1844) archive.org

Harreld, Donald, (Contributor) *A Companion to the Hanseatic League* (Brill, 2015)

Harte, Walter, *The History of the Life of Gustavus Adolphus, King of Sweden*, vol.1, (Hawkins, London, 1759)

Holborn, Hajo, *A History of Modern Germany, 1648-1840* (Princetown University, 1982)

Hughes, Lindsey, *Sophia, Regent of Russia, 1657-1704* (Yale University, New Haven and London, 1990)

Hughes, Lindsey, *Peter the Great: A Biography* (Yale University, 2002)

Hughes, Lindsey, *The Romanovs: Ruling Russia 1613-1917* (Continuum, UK, 2008)

Hunter, Ian, 'Kant and the Prussian Religious Edict: Metaphysics with the Bounds of Political Reason', A Paper for Presentation to the Institute for Philosophy and Religion, Boston University, 9 April 2003, citeseerx.ist.psu.edu

Iskenderov, A. A. (compiler), *The Emperors and Empresses of Russia: Rediscovering the Romanovs*, ed. Donald J. Raleigh (M. E. Sharp, 1996)

Ivleva, Victoria, 'Catherine as female ruler: the power of enlightened womanhood', in e-journal of eighteenth-century Russian studies, 3 (Durham University, 20 November 2015)

Jenkins, Michael, *Arakcheev: Grand-Vizier of the Russian Empire* (London, 1969)

Jespersen, Kund J. V., *A History of Denmark* (Palgrave Macmillan, 2011)

Kagan, Frederick W., *The End of the Old Order: Napoleon and Europe 1801-1805* (De Capo, USA, 2006)

Kalnins, Mara, *Latvia: A Short History* (Hurst & Co., London, 2015)

Kapustina, Tatiana Alexsandrovna, 'Nicholas I', in *The Emperors and Empresses of Russia: Reconsidering the Romanovs*, ed. Donald J, Raleigh and A. A. Iskenderov (Routledge, 24 Feb 2015)

Kasekamp, Andres, *A History of the Baltic States* (Palgrave Macmillan, UK, 2010)

Kauffmann, Jean-Paul, *A Journey to Nowhere: Detours and Riddles in the Lands and History of Courland*, trans. Euan Cameron (MacLehose, Quercus, London, 2012)

Kermina, Françoise, *Christine de Suède* (Perrin, Paris, 1995)

King, Greg and Wilson, Penny, *The Fate of the Romanovs* (Wiley, New Jersey, 2003)

Kirby, David, *A Concise History of Finland* (Cambridge, reprinted 2014)

Kluckhohn, August, *Louise, Queen of Prussia: A Memorial*, trans. by Elizabeth H. Denio, first published 1881(Leopold Classic, Poland, reprint)

Kolkey, Jonathan Martin, *Germany on the March: A Reinterpretation of War and Domestic Policies Over the Past Two Centuries* (University Press of America, New York & London, 1984)

Lancmanis, Imants, *Rundāle Palace*, 4th edition (Rundāle Palace Museum, 2016)

Langen, Ulrik, 'Le roi et les philosophes: le séjour parisien de Christian VII de Danemark en 1768', in *La France et la Scandinavie aux XVIIeme et XVIIIeme Siècle*, Histoire et Economie Société (Colin, 2010)

Larsen, James L., *Reforming the North: The Kingdoms and Churches of Scandinavia, 1520-1545* (USA, Cambridge University, 2010)

Latrobe, B. H., *Authentic Elucidation of the History of Counts Struensee and Brandt: and of the Revolution in Denmark in the Year 1772* (Privately published, London, 1789)

Leonard, Carol S., *Reform and Regicide: the Reign of Peter III of* Russia (Indiana University, USA, 1993)

Lieven, Dominic, *Russia against Napoleon: The Battle for Europe 1807 to 1814* (Allen Lane, London, 2009)

Lincoln, W. Bruce, *Nicholas I: Emperor and Autocrat of All the Russias*, (Northern Illinois, 1989)

Lindsay, Ivan, *The History of Loot and Stolen Art: from Antiquity until the Present Day* (Andrews, UK, 2014)

Lloyd, T. H., *England and the German Hanse, 1157-1611: A Study of their Trade and Commercial Diplomacy* (Cambridge University, UK, 2002)

Lockhart, Paul Douglas, *Frederik II and the Protestant Cause: Denmark's Role in the Wars of Religion, 1559-1596* (Brill, 2004)

Lockhart, Paul Douglas, *Denmark, 1513-1660: The Rise and Decline of a Renaissance Monarchy* (Oxford University, 23 Aug 2007)

Lowe, Charles, *Alexander III of Russia,* first pub. 1895 (reprinted Bibliolife, Amazon, UK)

Lukavski, Jerzy Tadeusz, *Liberty's Folly: The Polish-Lithuanian Commonwealth in the Eighteenth Century* (Routledge, IK, 1991)

Lunde, Henrik O., *A Warrior Dynasty: The Rise and Fall of Sweden as a Military Superpower, 1611-1721* (Casemate, USA, 2014)

Macdonogh, Giles, *Frederick the Great: A Life in Deed and Letters* (Phœnix, London, 2000)

MacGregor, Neil, *Germany: Memories of a Nation* (Allen Lane, Penguin, 13 Nov. 2014)

Mansel, Philip, 'From Exile to the Throne: The Europeanization of Louis XVIII', in *Monarchy and Exile: The Politics of Legitimacy from Marie de Médicis to Wilhelm II*, ed. Philip Mansel and Torsten Riot (Palgrave Macmillan, UK, 2011)

Massie, Robert K., *Nicholas and Alexandra* (Victor Gollancz, London, 1971)

Massie, Robert K., *Peter the Great: His Life and World* (Ballantine, USA, 1981)

Massie, Robert K., *Catherine the Great: Portrait of a Woman* (Head of Zeus, UK, 2012)

McGrigor, Mary, *The Tsar's Doctor: The Life and Times of Sir James Wylie* (Berlin, Edinburg, 2010)

Meinander, Henrik, *A History of Finland*, trans. Tom Geddes (Hurst, UK, 2011)

Memoirs:

Memoirs of Catherine the Great, trans. Katherine Anthony (Alfred Knopf, London, 1927)

The Memoirs of Catherine the Great, trans. Mark Cruse & Hilde Hoogenboom (Modern Library, New York, 2006)

Memoirs of the Empress Catherine II, written by herself, ed A. Hérzen, (Appleton, New York, 1859)

The Memoirs of Catherine the Great, ed. Dominique Maroger, introduction Dr. G. P. Gooch, CH., trans. Moura Budberg (Hamish Hamilton, London, 1955)

The Memoires of Charles Lewis Baron de Pollnitz, vol.1, 1729, gutenberg.org

Memoirs of Madame Vigée le Brun, trans. Lionel Strachey (Grant Richards, London 1904), gutenberg.org

Mémoires Secrets et Inédits de Stanislas Auguste (W. Gerhard, Leipzig, 1862) archive.org

Mémoires du roi Stanislas-Auguste Poniatowski, ed. S. Goriainov, vol.2, (Leningrad, 1924)

Merle D'Aubigne, J. H., *History of the Reformation: In the Time of Calvin, 1-16* (Delmarva, USA, 2013)

Mikhailovich, Grand Duke Alexander 'Sandro', *We the Romanovs* (re-ed. Kindle edition – formerly *Once a Grand Duke*, pub.1931, Winter Palace – 29 Aug. 2016)

Mitford, Nancy, *Frederick the Great* (Hamish Hamilton, London, 1970)

Monter, William, *The Rise of Female Kings in Europe, 1300-1800* (Yale, New Haven & London, 2012)

Morgan, Christopher & Orlova, Irina, *Saving the Tsars' Palaces* (Polperro, Great Britain, 2005)

Moss, Walter, *Russia in the Age of Alexander II, Tolstoy and Dostoevsky* (Anthem, Wimbledon, 2002)

Mühlbach, L. (Luise), *Louisa of Prussia and Her Times*, trans. by F. Jordan (Public Domain)

ed. Rainer A. Müller, Frederick William, Elector of Brandenburg (sole signatory); (29 October 1685). 'Edict of Potsdam', issued by Frederick William ("the Great Elector") (October 29, 1685)', in *Deutsche Geschichte in Quellen und Darstellung* (Deutschen Historischen Instituts, Washington, DC.) Retrieved 2 June 2016 [Wikipedia]

Münter, Dr Balthasar, *&* Hee, Jørgen Bishop, *A Faithful Narrative of the Conversion and Death of Count Struensee: Late Prime Minister of Denmark,* and *The History of Count Enevold Brandt*, (first published for U. Linde, London, 1773), uploaded January 13, 2011 archive.org

Nilsson, Victor, *Sweden* (Waxkeep, 2015)

Nolan, Cathal J., *Wars of the Age of Louis XIV, 1650-1715: An Encyclopaedia of Global Warfare and Civilization* (ABC-Clio, 2008)

Nordenkulls, Cecilia, *Karl XII: Kungamord* (ICONS OF EUROPE, Brussels, 5 Sept., 2018)

North, Michael, *The Baltic: A History*, trans. by Kenneth Kronenberg (Harvard, Massachusetts, 2015)

Nuse, Ingrid R., *The king who fought for the Norwegian constitution – and his son,* Ingrid R. Nuse, November 21, 2016, sciencenordic.com

Palmer, Alan, *Bernadotte: Napoleon's Marshal, Sweden's King*, first published 1990 (Endeavour, UK, 2015)

Palmer, Alan, *Alexander I: Tsar of War and Peace* (Phoenix, London,1997)

Palmer, Alan, *The Baltic: A New History of the Region and its People* (Duckworth, London, 2006)
Parkinson, Roger, *Clausewitz: A Biography* (Rowman & Littlefield, 1979)
Perry, John Curtis, & Pleshakov, Constantine, *The Flight of the Romanovs* (Perseus, USA, 1999)
Peterson, Gary Dean, *Warrior Kings of Sweden: The Time of an Empire in the Sixteenth and Seventeenth Centuries* (McFarland, 2007)
Petre OBE, Francis Loraine, *Napoleon's Conquest of Prussia – 1806*, first published 1904 (Pickle, 2011)
Pflaum, Rosalynd, *By Influence & Desire* (M. Evans, New York, Toronto, UK, 2014)
Radzinsky, Edward, *Alexander II: The Last Great Tsar*, trans. Antonina W. Bouis (Free Press, New York, 2005)
ed. Raeff, Marc, *Catherine the Great: A Profile* (Macmillan, 1972)
ed. Donald J. Raleigh, *The Emperors and Empresses of Russia: Rediscovering the Romanovs*, compiled by A. A. Iskenderov (Sharpe, New York, 1996)
ed. W. F. Reddaway, *Documents of Catherine the Great: The Correspondence with Voltaire and the Instruction of 1767 in the English Text of 1768* (Cambridge University, 29 March 2012)
Rivière, Marc Serge, "'The Pallas of Stockholm": Louisa Ulrica of Prussia and the Swedish Crown' in *Queenship in Europe 1660-1815: The Role of the Consort*, ed. Clarissa Cambell Orr (Cambridge, UK, 2004)
Roberts, Andrew, *Napoleon the Great* (Penguin, UK, 2015)
Roberts, Michael, *From Oxenstierna to Charles XII*, Four Studies (Cambridge University, UK, 1991)
Roberts, Michael, *The Age of Liberty: Sweden 1719-1772* (Cambridge University, UK, 1986)
Roberts, Michael, *The Early Vasas: A History of Sweden 1523-1611* (Cambridge University, UK, 1968)
Rounding, Virginia, *Catherine the Great* (Arrow, Great Britain, 2007)
Ruffles, Keith, *Baltic Lenin: A Journey into Estonia, Latvia, and Lithuania's Soviet Past* (Book Design Templates, UK, 2014)
Schimmer, Kark August, *The Two Sieges of Vienna by the Ottoman Turks: 1527-1683* (Didactic, 16 Dec 2014)
Schioldann, Johan, 'Struensée's memoir on the situation of the King' (1772: Christian VII of Denmark, Introduction and Translation, in *History of Psychiatry* (SAGE, Pennslyvania State University, May 9 2016, online)
Schorn-Schutte, Luise, *Königin Luise: Leben und Legende* (Verlag C. H. Beck, München, 2003)
Scott, Franklin Daniel, *Sweden: The Nation's History* (Southern Illinois University, 1989)
Sebag Montefiore, Simon, *Potemkin: Prince of Princes* (Phœnix, London, 2004)
Sharp, Tony, *Pleasure and Ambition: The Life, Loves and Wars of Augustus the Strong, 1670-1707* (I.B. Tauris, 2001)
Shubin, Daniel, *A History of Russian Christianity, The Patriarchal Age, Peter, the Synodal System*: vol.2 (Algora, 2004)
Singleton, Fred, *A Short History of Finland*, revised and updated by A.F. Upton (Cambridge University, 2010)
Sprague, Martina, *Sweden: An Illustrated History* (Hippocrene, New York, 2005)
Stone, Daniel, *The Polish-Lithuanian State, 1386-1795*: A History of East Central Europe, vol.4 (University of Washington, Seattle, 2001)
Strachey, Giles Lytton, *Queen Victoria* (Harcourt, Brace & World, New York, 1921)
Strickland, Lloyd, ed. and translator *Leibnitz and the Two Sophies: The Philosophical Correspondence* (Inter Inc Centre for Reformation and Renaissance Studies, Toronto, 2011)
Strindberg, August, *Queen Christina, Charles XII, Gustav III*, trans. Walter Johnson (University of Washington, Seattle, 1995)
Talbot Rice, Tamara, *Elizabeth Empress of Russia* (Weidenfeld & Nicolson, UK, 1970)

The Edinburgh Review, Or Critical Journal, vol.14, archive.org
The London Magazine, or, Gentleman's Monthly Intelligencer, vol.2 (C. Ackers, 1733; digitalised University of Michigan, 28 Jul 2006) babel.hathitrust.org
Thomas, Alistair H., *Historical Dictionary of Denmark*, Third Edition (Rowman & Littlefield, New York & London, 2016)
Thomson, *The Romanovs: Europe's Most Obsessive Dynasty* (Tempus, UK, 2007)
Tillyard, Stella, *A Royal Affair: George III and his Troublesome Siblings* (Vintage Random, UK, 2007)
Trigos, Ludmilla A., *The Decembrist Myth in Russian Culture* (Springer, 2009)
Van de Kiste, John, *The Romanovs 1818-1959* (Sutton, Stroud, revised 2003)
Van de Kiste, John, *Once a Grand Duchess: Xenia, Sister of Nicholas II* (History Press, Gloucestershire, 2013)
Varvounis, Miltiades, *Jan Sobieski: The King Who Saved Europe* (Xlibris Corporation, 2012)
Voltaire, Correspondence, ed. Theodore Besterman, in Œuvres complètes *de Voltaire* (Geneva Institut et Musée Voltaire, 1968-1971)
Voltaire, *Essai sur les mœurs et l'esprit des nations, ed. Bruno Bernard, John Renwick, Nicholas Cronk, Janet Godden,* in *Œuvres completes de Voltaire*, I-IX, vol.21-27 (Voltaire Foundation, Oxford, 2009-2018)
Voltaire, 'Epître au roi de Danemark, sur la liberté de la presse' (1770), ed. Simon Davies in *Œuvres complètes de Voltaire,* XIX, vol.73 (Voltaire Foundation, Oxford, 2004)
Voltaire, *L'histoire de Charles XII*, ed. Gunnar von Proschwitz, in *Œuvres complètes de Voltaire*, vol.4 (Voltaire Foundation, Oxford, 1996)
Voltaire, *Histoire de l'empire de Russie sous Pierre le grand*, ed. Michel Mervaud, in *Œuvres complètes de Voltaire,* vol. 46-47 (Voltaire Foundation, Oxford, 1999)
Voltaire, *Memoirs of the Life of Voltaire*, 1784 (Moncrieffe, 30 Jan 2007)
Vovk, Justin C., *In Destiny's Hands* (iUniverse, Bloomington, 1 July 2010)
Vovk, Justin C., *Imperial Requiem: Four Royal Women and the Fall of the Age of Empires* (iUniverse, Bloomington, 2012)
Walsh, Edmund, *The Last Days of the Romanovs*, from *The Atlantic*, March 1928, theatlantic.com
Ward, Sir Adolphus William, ed. *The Cambridge Modern History Atlas*, vol. 14 (Cambridge, UK, 1909)
Watanabe-O'Kelly, Helen, and Morton, Adam, *Queens Consort, Cultural Transfer and European Politics, c.1500-1800* (Routledge, 2016)
Watson, Paul, *Gustav Vasa* (Jovian, 2016)
Welch, Frances, *The Russian Court at Sea: The Last Days of a Great Dynasty: The Romanovs' Voyage into Exile* (Short Books, London, 2011)
Wilkins, William Henry, *A Queen of Tears: Caroline Matilda, Queen of Denmark and Princess of Great Britain and Ireland*, first pub. 2 vols, Longmans, London, 1904 (Library of Alexandria, 4 April 2016)
Williams, Ernest Neville, *The Ancien Régime in Europe: Government and Society in the Major States, 1648–1789* (Bodley Head, London, 1970)
Wilson, Peter H., *Lützen* (Oxford University, UK, 2018)
Wraxall, Sir C. F. Lascelles, *Life and Times of Her Majesty Caroline Matilda*, 3 vols (Allen, London, 1864) archive.org
Wubs-Mrozewicz, Justyna, *Traders, Ties and Tensions: The Interactions of Lübeckers, Overijssiers and Hollanders in Late Medieval Bergen* (Uitgeverij Verloren, Netherlands, 2008)
Youssoupoff, Prince Felix, *Lost Splendor: The Amazing Memoirs of the Man who Killed Rasputin*, trans by Ann Green and Nicholas Katkoff (Helen Marx, New York, 2003)
Zamoyski, Adam, *The Last King of Poland* (Jonathan Cape, London, 1992)
Zamoyski, Adam, *Poland: A History* (Collins, London, 2009)
Zimmern, Helen, *The Hanseatic League: A History of the Rise and Fall of the Hansa Towns* (Didactic, USA, 2015)

Websites

angelfire.com Alexander III, Royal Russia News
archives.chicagotribune.com *Chicago Tribune* Sept. 30, 1881
archive.spectator.co.uk *Frederick VII, The Republican King, 21* November 1863
archive.spectator.co.uk *The Meeting of the Emperors*, 10 September 1881
berliner-schloss.de 'The interior rooms of the Berlin Palace', Sources: *Günter Wermusch: Die Bernsteinzimmer – Saga; Goerd Peschken: Das Bernsteinzimmer, Prussian Palaces and Gardens Foundation* series, 2002
den-vestindiske-arv.dk*/en/ The West Indian Heritage*
erenow.com *Biographies and Memoirs*
fold3.com 30-Sep-1881
gallica.bnf.fr *Correspondence de Madame, Duchesse d'Orléans*
genealogy.euweb.cz Miroslav Marek
hansard.milbanksystems.com/commons/1848/apr/19/denmark-and-the-duchies Denmark and the Duchies (Hansard, 19 April 1848)
queenvictoriasjournals.org *Queen Victoria's Journal*
religiondocbox.com German History in Documents and Images (GHDI), *From Absolutism to Napoleon, 1648-1815*, vol.2, 'Edict of Potsdam'
rusartnet.com/biographies/russian-rulers
scottisharchivesforschools.org *The Lübeck letter, 1297*

Index